IMMIGRATION LAW

SECOND EDITION

Other books in the *Essentials of Canadian Law* Series

International Trade Law

Family Law

Copyright Law

The Law of Sentencing

Administrative Law

Securities Law

Computer Law 2/e

Maritime Law

International Human Rights Law

Franchise Law

Legal Ethics and Professional Responsibility 2/e

Refugee Law

Statutory Interpretation 2/e

National Security Law: Canadian Practice in International Perspective

Public International Law 2/e

Individual Employment Law 2/e

Bankruptcy and Insolvency Law

The Law of Partnerships and Corporations 3/e

Civil Litigation

Conflict of Laws

Legal Research and Writing 3/e

Religious Institutions and the Law in Canada 3/e

Detention and Arrest

Canadian Telecommunications Law

The Law of Torts 4/e

Intellectual Property Law 2/e

Animals and the Law

Income Tax Law 2/e

Fundamental Justice

Mergers, Acquisitions, and Other Changes of Corporate Control 2/e

Criminal Procedure 2/e

Criminal Law 5/e

Personal Property Security Law 2/e

The Law of Contracts 2/e

Youth Criminal Justice Law 3/e

Constitutional Law 4/e

Bank and Customer Law in Canada 2/e

The Law of Equitable Remedies 2/e

The Charter of Rights and Freedoms 5/e

Environmental Law 4/e

Pension Law 2/e

International and Transnational Criminal Law 2/e

Remedies: The Law of Damages 3/e

Freedom of Conscience and Religion

The Law of Trusts 3/e

The Law of Evidence 7/e

Ethics and Criminal Law 2/e

Insurance Law 2/e

IMMIGRATION LAW

SECOND EDITION

JAMIE CHAI YUN LIEW
Faculty of Law
University of Ottawa

DONALD GALLOWAY
Faculty of Law
University of Victoria

IRWIN
LAW

Immigration Law, second edition
© Irwin Law Inc., 2015

Published in 2015 by

Irwin Law Inc.
14 Duncan Street
Suite 206
Toronto, ON
M5H 3G8

www.irwinlaw.com

ISBN: 978-1-55221-392-6
e-book ISBN: 978-1-55221-393-3

Library and Archives Canada Cataloguing in Publication

Galloway, Donald
[Immigration law]
    Immigration law / Jamie Chai Yun Liew, Faculty of Law, University of Ottawa,
Donald Galloway, Faculty of Law, University of Victoria. — Second edition.

(Essentials of Canadian law)
Includes bibliographical references and index.
Issued in print and electronic formats.
ISBN 978-1-55221-392-6 (paperback).—ISBN 978-1-55221-393-3 (pdf)

    1. Emigration and immigration law—Canada. I. Liew, Jamie Chai Yun,
author II. Title. III. Series: Essentials of Canadian law

KE4454.G34 2015   342.7108'2   C2015-904030-2
KF4483.I5G34 2015   C2015-904031-0

Ontario Media Development
Corporation
Société de développement
de l'industrie des médias
de l'Ontario

Printed and bound in Canada.

1 2 3 4 5   19 18 17 16 15

SUMMARY
TABLE OF CONTENTS

PREFACE   *xxiii*

PART ONE: **Origins and Sources**   *1*

CHAPTER   1:   The Evolution of Canadian Immigration Law   *3*

CHAPTER   2:   Sources of Immigration Law   *32*

PART TWO: **Status in Canada**   *75*

CHAPTER   3:   Status in Canada   *77*

CHAPTER   4:   Temporary Status in Canada   *88*

CHAPTER   5:   Acquiring Permanent Resident Status: The Economic Classes   *132*

CHAPTER   6:   Acquiring Permanent Resident Status: The Family Class and Sponsorship   *177*

CHAPTER   7:   A Brief Introduction to Canadian Refugee Law   *223*

CHAPTER   8:   Acquiring Permanent Status: Refugee Resettlement   *227*

CHAPTER   9:   The Refugee Determination Process in Canada   *243*

CHAPTER   10:   Convention Refugees and Persons in Need of Protection   *298*

CHAPTER   11:   Pre-removal Risk Assessments and Refoulement   *360*

CHAPTER 12:   Applications Made on Humanitarian and Compassionate
Grounds *393*

CHAPTER 13:   Citizenship Status *436*

PART THREE: **Enforcement** *469*

CHAPTER 14:   Inadmissibility *471*

CHAPTER 15:   The Mechanics of Enforcement *532*

PART FOUR: **Judicial Supervision** *593*

CHAPTER 16:   Judicial Review *595*

CHAPTER 17:   Constitutional Challenges *636*

Appendix *673*

Table of Cases *677*

Index *723*

About the Authors *741*

DETAILED
TABLE OF CONTENTS

PREFACE *xxiii*

PART ONE: ORIGINS AND SOURCES *1*

CHAPTER 1:
THE EVOLUTION OF CANADIAN IMMIGRATION LAW *3*

A. Introduction *3*

B. Immigration and Colonialization *5*

C. Early Origins *6*

D. The Emergence of Restrictive Immigration Legislation, 1775–1872 *11*

E. The Racialization of Immigration Law, 1878–1914 *15*

F. The Modernization of Immigration Law, 1918–1976 *21*

G. Immigration Law in the Twenty-first Century *27*

CHAPTER 2:
SOURCES OF IMMIGRATION LAW *32*

A. The *Constitution Act, 1867* *32*
   1) Section 95: Concurrent Powers over Immigration *32*
   2) Section 91(25): Naturalization and Aliens *33*
   3) The *Canadian Charter of Rights and Freedoms* *37*

B. The *Immigration and Refugee Protection Act* (the *IRPA*)   38

   1) The General Structure of the Act   38
   2) The Objectives of the *IRPA*   42

C. The *Citizenship Act*   45

D. The *Department of Citizenship and Immigration Act*   46

E. The *Department of Public Safety and Emergency Preparedness Act*   47

F. The *Immigration and Refugee Protection Regulations*   47

G. *Immigration and Refugee Board Rules*   51

H. Ministerial Instructions   51

I. Ministerial Orders   53

J. Chairperson's Guidelines and Jurisprudential Guides   54

K. Program Delivery Instructions (Operational Manuals and Bulletins)   57

L. Federal–Provincial/Territorial Agreements   58

M. The *Canada-Québec Accord Relating to Immigration and Temporary Admission of Aliens*   60

N. International Law   63

   1) The *International Covenant on Civil and Political Rights* (*ICCPR*)   64
   2) The *Convention against Torture and Other Cruel, Inhuman or Degrading Treatment or Punishment*   66
   3) The *Convention on the Rights of the Child*   67
   4) The *American Declaration of the Rights and Duties of Man*   68
   5) The Domestic Significance of International Agreements   68
   6) Trade Agreements and Business Travel   70
   7) The Safe Third Country Agreement   71

O. Common Law Principles of Administrative Law   72

P. Previous Decisions and *Stare Decisis*   72

PART TWO: STATUS IN CANADA   75

CHAPTER 3:
STATUS IN CANADA   77

A. Introduction   77

B. Status and Open Borders   78

C. Conclusion   87

CHAPTER 4:
TEMPORARY STATUS IN CANADA 88

A. Introduction 88

B. Section 22.1 Declarations 89

C. An Overview of Temporary Residence 90

D. Temporary Resident Visas (TRVs) 91

   1) Types of Visa 91
   2) The "Super Visa" 92
   3) Exemptions 93
      a) Citizens of Listed Countries 94
      b) Particular Limited Purpose 95
      c) Re-entry 95
      d) Temporary Resident Permit (TRP) Holders 95
   4) Exemptions and Judicial Review 97
   5) Requirements for Acquiring a TRV 97

E. Electronic Travel Authorization (eTA) 103

F. Grant of Status 104

G. Applications for Extensions, Changed Conditions, and Restored Status 105

   1) Extensions and Implied Status 105
   2) Amendment of Conditions 105
   3) Restoration 106

H. Permits 107

   1) Students 107
   2) Workers 111
      a) The Legal Framework 112
         i) What Is Work? 112
         ii) Who Needs a Work Permit? 113
         iii) Criteria and Eligibility for a Work Permit 114
            a. Agricultural Workers 121
            b. Stream for Lower-Skilled Occupations 122
            c. Stream for Higher-Skilled Occupations 122
            d. Caregivers 123
      b) Reforming the Temporary Foreign Worker Program 128

I. Conclusion 130

CHAPTER 5:
ACQUIRING PERMANENT RESIDENT STATUS: THE ECONOMIC CLASSES 132

A. Introduction   132

B. The Economic Classes   132

   1) Skilled Workers   133
      a) The Federal Skilled Worker Class (*Regulations,* Sections 75–85)   134
         i) The Eligibility Requirements (*Regulations,* Section 75)   135
            a. National Occupational Classification (NOC)   136
            b. The Language Evaluation   137
            c. The Education Credential   138
            d. The Burden of Showing That the Requirements Have Been Met   138
         ii) The Points System (*Regulations,* Section 76)   140
            a. Education (*Regulations,* Section 78(1)) [25 Points]   141
            b. Language Proficiency in English and French (*Regulations,* Section 79) [28 Points]   143
            c. Work Experience (*Regulations,* Section 80) [15 Points]   144
            d. Age (*Regulations,* Section 81) [12 Points]   146
            e. Arranged Employment (*Regulations,* Section 82) [10 Points]   147
            f. Adaptability (*Regulations,* Section 83) [10 Points]   149
         iii) Self-Supporting upon Arrival (*Regulations,* Section 76(1)(b))   151
         iv) The Application Process   152
      b) The Quebec Skilled Worker Class (*Regulations,* Section 86)   155
      c) Provincial Nominee Class (*Regulations,* Section 87)   155
      d) Canadian Experience Class (*Regulations,* Section 87.1)   158
      e) Federal Skilled Trades Class (*Regulations,* Section 87.2)   159
      f) The Express Entry Program   160
   2) Business Immigrants   165
      a) The Self-Employed Person Class   165
         i) Selection Criteria for Self-Employed Persons   165
      b) Changes to the Investor and Entrepreneur Programs   168
      c) Entrepreneur Start-up Visa   168
      d) Provincial Nominee Business Programs   171
      e) Immigrant Investor Venture Capital Fund and Business Skills Programs   171
   3) Caregivers   172

C. Conclusion: Canada's Economic Immigration Scheme as an Uninspiring Approach to Building a Nation   174

CHAPTER 6:

ACQUIRING PERMANENT RESIDENT STATUS: THE FAMILY CLASS AND SPONSORSHIP 177

A. Introduction 177

B. Members of the Family Class versus Family Members 178

C. Members of the Family Class: Who Gets In? 181

   1) The Sponsor's Spouse, Common Law Partner, or Conjugal Partner 182
     a) Spouse 182
     b) Common Law Partner 190
     c) Conjugal Partner 193
     d) The Genuineness of the Relationship 194
     e) A Relationship Entered into for the Purpose of Acquiring a Benefit 195
     f) Pre-existing Undertaking 196
     g) Sponsored Partners in Canada: The Spouse or Common Law Partner in Canada Class 196
     h) Conditional Status 197
   2) Dependent Children 199
     a) Dependence 199
     b) Adoption Requirements 202
   3) Parents and Grandparents 205
   4) Other Relationships 207

D. Misrepresentation and Membership in the Family Class 208

E. Sponsorship Eligibility 212

F. The Undertaking 215

G. Sponsorship and the Immigration Appeal Division 217

H. Sponsorship and Judicial Review 219

I. Conclusion 220

CHAPTER 7:

A BRIEF INTRODUCTION TO CANADIAN REFUGEE LAW 223

A. Refugee Protection 223

B. Competing Accounts of the Underlying Principles 224

   1) The Discretionary-Humanitarian Approach 224
   2) The Rights-Based Approach 226

CHAPTER 8:

ACQUIRING PERMANENT STATUS: REFUGEE RESETTLEMENT 227

A. Introduction: Resettlement as a Durable Solution 227

B. Canada's Resettlement Program 228

1) Overview 228
2) Who May Be Resettled? 229
3) Exceptional Cases 231
4) Emergency Cases 232
5) Family Members 232
6) Settlement Assistance 234
    a) Resettlement Assistance Program (RAP) Available to Government-Assisted Refugees 234
    b) Private Sponsorship of Refugees 235
7) Eligibility to Sponsor 236
8) Sponsors 237
    a) Sponsorship Agreement Holders (SAH) 237
    b) Community Sponsors 238
    c) Groups of Five 238
    d) Joint Assistance Sponsorship (JAS) 238
    e) Blended Visa Office-Referred Program 239
9) Process: The Visa Officer's Decision 239

C. Conclusion: Canada's Diminishing Role in Overseas Refugee Protection 240

CHAPTER 9:

THE REFUGEE DETERMINATION PROCESS IN CANADA 243

A. The Refugee Hearing 243

1) Singh and the Right to an Oral Hearing 243
2) Reforming the Process 244
3) An Overview of Canada's Inland Refugee Determination System 244
    a) Making the Claim 245
        i) Port of Entry (POE) 245
        ii) Inland 245
    b) Interviewing and Obtaining Information from a Client 245
    c) Assessment of Eligibility 247
    d) Following a Finding of Eligibility 247
    e) Claimants from Safe Third Countries 248
        i) What Is a "Safe Third Country"? 248
        ii) The Process for Claimants from "Safe Third Countries" 250

iii) Implications for Claimants from "Safe Third Countries" 250

f) Claimants from a Designated Country of Origin (DCO) 252
   i) What Is a Designated Country of Origin? 252
   ii) The Process for DCO Claimants 255
   iii) Implications for DCO Refugee Claimants 255

g) Designated Foreign Nationals (DFNs) 257
   i) What Is a Designated Foreign National? 257
   ii) The Process for DFN Refugee Claimants 260
   iii) Implications for DFN Refugee Claimants 261

h) Other Refugee Claimants 261

i) Hearings at the Refugee Protection Division (RPD) of the Immigration and Refugee Board (IRB) 262
   i) Preliminaries 262
      a. Dates and Times of RPD Hearings 262
      b. Submitting Documentary Evidence 263
      c. Obtaining Medical Evidence and Vulnerable Persons Applications 264
      d. Notice of Constitutional Questions 267
   ii) Who May Participate in a Hearing? 267
      a. The Board Member 267
      b. The Minister or Ministerial Representatives 268
      c. Observers 268
      d. Interpreters 268
      e. Designated Representatives 269
      f. Claimants, Witnesses, and Their Representatives 270
   iii) Before the Hearing 272
   iv) During the Hearing 272
   v) A Note on Assessing Credibility 274

j) Withdrawing a Refugee Claim 277
   i) Abandoning a Refugee Claim 277

k) Cessation and the *IRPA*, Section 108 279

l) Vacation 285

m) Increases in Cessation and Vacation Applications 287

n) Reopening Refugee Claims 287

B. The Refugee Appeal Division (RAD) 288

1) Eligibility 289
2) Process 290
3) Submitting New Evidence 291
4) Paper-Based and Oral Hearings 293
5) Standard of Review or Intervention at the Refugee Appeal Division 294
6) Recourse from RAD Decisions 296

C. Applications for Permanent Resident Status 297

CHAPTER 10:
CONVENTION REFUGEES AND PERSONS IN NEED OF PROTECTION   298

A. Introduction   298

B. Section 96   298

    1) A Well-Founded Fear   299
    2) Persecution   302
        a) Prospectivity   303
        b) Discrimination and Harassment as Persecution   303
        c) Punishment or Prosecution as Persecution   304
        d) Economic Migrants versus Refugees   307
        e) Agents of Persecution   307
        f) Cumulative Grounds   308
        g) Individual versus Group Persecution   308
    3) The Five Enumerated Grounds   309
        a) Race   310
        b) Nationality   310
        c) Religion   311
        d) Political Opinion   314
        e) Membership in a "Particular Social Group"   319
            i)   Gender   322
            ii) Sexual Orientation   325
    4) State Protection   326
        a) The Canadian Conception of State Protection   326
        b) Multiple Nationalities   330
        c) The Adequacy of State Protection   333
        d) The Obligation to Seek State Protection   337
    5) Internal Flight Alternative (IFA)   341

C. Section 97   344

D. Section 98 and Exclusion   348

    1) *Refugee Convention*, Article 1E   349
    2) *Refugee Convention*, Article 1F   350
        a) Article 1F(a) and Crime against Peace, War Crime, or Crime against Humanity   352
        b) Article 1F(b) and Serious Non-political Crimes   355
        c) Article 1F(c) and Acts Contrary to Purposes of the United Nations   356
    3) After a Finding of Exclusion   357

E. *Sur Place* Claims   358

F. Conclusion   359

CHAPTER 11:
PRE-REMOVAL RISK ASSESSMENTS AND REFOULEMENT 360

A. **Introduction** 360

B. **General Eligibility for a Pre-removal Risk Assessment** 363

C. **Ineligibility for a Pre-removal Risk Assessment** 365
1) Refugees or Protected Persons 365
2) Persons Arriving via a Safe Third Country 366
3) Previously Rejected Refugee Claimants and PRRA Applicants 367
4) Persons Arriving from a Designated Country of Origin 368
5) Persons Subject to the *Extradition Act* 368

D. **Notification of Eligibility as a Prerequisite** 369

E. **Procedural Variations and Scope of Inquiry** 371
1) Persons at the Port of Entry 371
2) Refused Refugee Claimants and Repeat PRRA Applicants 371
   a) The Time Bar 371
   b) The New Evidence Rule 373
3) Persons Ineligible to Make a Refugee Claim 373
   a) Inadmissible Persons 373
   b) Persons Subject to Security Certificates 375
4) Non-refoulement Assessments (Section 115(1) Cases) 376
5) Regulatory Stay of Removal 376
6) Evidence and Submissions 379
   a) Applicant's Burden to Provide Evidence and Submissions 379
   b) PRRA Officer's Duty to Disclose Adverse Extrinsic Information 383
7) Assessment 385
   a) Oral Hearing 385
   b) Issues and Considerations 386
      i) Evaluations under the *IRPA*, Sections 96 and 97 386
      ii) Evaluations under Only Section 97 of the *IRPA* 387
      iii) Evaluating Exclusion under Section 98 of the *IRPA* 387
      iv) Best Interests of the Children 387
      v) Humanitarian and Compassionate Grounds 388
      vi) Country of Removal 388

F. **Decisions and Appeals** 389
1) Decision Final When Delivered 389
2) Positive PRRA Decisions 389
3) Deemed Rejected Decisions 390
   a) Vacation 390
   b) Abandonment 390

c) Withdrawal *391*

4) Judicial Review *391*

G. Conclusion: The Erosion of the Principle of Non-refoulement *391*

CHAPTER 12:

APPLICATIONS MADE ON HUMANITARIAN AND COMPASSIONATE GROUNDS *393*

A. The Humanitarian and Compassionate (H&C) Grounds Assessment *393*

B. Eligibility *395*

1) Foreign Nationals Who Do Not Meet the *IRPA* Requirements *395*
2) Inadmissible Persons *395*
3) Refugee Claimants and the Twelve-Month Bar *395*
4) Persons under a Removal Order with No Statutory Stay *397*
5) Designated Foreign Nationals and the Five-Year Bar *398*
6) Ministerial Instructions and H&C Applications *399*
7) Permanent Residents or Canadian Citizens *399*
8) Spouse or Common Law Partner of a Canadian or Permanent Resident *400*

C. Process *401*

1) Fees *401*
2) Paper Application *401*
3) Onus on Applicant *403*
4) Temporary Resident Permit (TRP) *404*
5) Assessing Officer *404*
6) Two-Step Assessment Process *404*
    a) Stage 1: Approval in Principle *405*
    b) Stage 2: Assessing Permanent Residence Eligibility *406*
7) Final Examination *407*

D. Evaluating the Application *407*

1) Balancing Flexibility and Consistency *407*
2) Standard of Proof *408*
3) Criteria *409*
    a) Hardship *409*
        i) Hardship in Country of Origin *411*
            a. Excluding Persecution or Torture *411*
            b. Discrimination *Not* Amounting to Persecution *412*
            c. Generalized Risk as Hardship *413*
            d. Other Adverse Country Conditions *414*
            e. Lack of Critical Health or Medical Care *414*

      ii) Hardship Caused by Denial of Entry or Removal from Canada 415

         a. *De Facto* Family Member 415

      iii) Hardship If Required to Apply from Outside Canada 416

         a. Establishment in Canada 417

   b) Best Interests of the Child 420

     i) *Baker* 420

     ii) Alert, Alive, and Sensitive 421

     iii) A Balancing of Factors 423

     iv) Test Is Not Unusual, Undeserved, or Disproportionate Hardship 424

     v) For Children within Canada 425

     vi) For Children outside Canada 425

   c) Undeclared Family Members 426

   d) Inadmissibility 428

     i) Criminal Charges Outstanding 429

     ii) Rehabilitation or Record Suspension? 430

     iii) Health Inadmissibility 431

     iv) Inadmissible Family Member 431

   e) Waiving of Other Criteria 432

E. Recourse after a Negative Decision 433

   1) Request for Reconsideration 433

   2) Judicial Review 434

F. H&C: An Alternate Remedy 434

CHAPTER 13:
CITIZENSHIP STATUS 436

A. Introduction 436

B. The Emergence of Canadian Citizenship 436

C. Obtaining Citizenship 439

   1) Birth in Canada 439

   2) Birth to a Canadian Parent outside Canada 440

   a) Special Circumstances: Adopted Children 443

   b) Special Circumstances: "Lost Canadians" 444

   3) Naturalization 445

   a) The Current Residency Requirement 445

   b) The New Physical Presence Test 447

   c) The New Requirement That Income Taxes Be Filed 447

   d) The New Requirement of an Intention to Reside in Canada 448

   e) Adequate Knowledge of an Official Language 448

   f) Adequate Knowledge of Canada and Citizenship Criteria 449

g) Waiving of the Language and Knowledge Requirements 451
h) Process 452
i) Oath or Affirmation of Citizenship 453
j) Barriers to Acquiring Citizenship 455

D. **Rights and Responsibilities** 456

1) In General 456
2) Passports 457

E. **Losing Citizenship** 460

1) Renunciation 460
2) Revocation 461
   a) The Current Law 461
   b) The New Amendments 463
3) Resumption of Citizenship 465

F. **Conclusion** 466

PART THREE: ENFORCEMENT 469

CHAPTER 14:
INADMISSIBILITY 471

A. **Introduction** 471

B. **Grounds of Inadmissibility** 473

1) Facts Arising from Omissions and Facts for Which There Are
   Reasonable Grounds to Believe They Have Occurred (Section 33) 474
2) Statutory Interpretation and Judicial Review 474
3) Security Risk (Section 34(1)) 476
   a) Espionage (Section 34(1)(a)) 476
   b) Subversion by Force of Any Government or Subversion
      against a Democratic Government, Institution, or Process
      (Sections 34(1)(b) and (b.1)) 478
   c) Terrorism (Section 34(1)(c)) 480
   d) Being a Danger to the Security of Canada (Section 34(1)(d)) and
      Engaging in Acts of Violence That Would or Might Endanger
      Persons in Canada (Section 34(1)(e)) 483
   e) Being a Member of an Organization (Section 34(1)(f)) 483
   f) Listed Terrorist Entities 487
   g) Alternative Remedies 489
4) Human or International Rights Violations (Section 35) 491
   a) Committing an Act outside Canada That Constitutes an Offence
      under the *Crimes against Humanity and War Crimes Act*
      (Section 35(1)(a)) 491

b) Being a Prescribed Senior Official in a Government That Has Engaged in Terrorism, Human Rights Violations, Genocide, War Crime, or Crime against Humanity (Section 35(1)(b)) *494*

c) Restricted by Sanctions (Section 35(1)(c)) *496*

5) Serious Criminality, Criminality, and Organized Criminality *497*

a) Serious Criminality (Section 36(1)) *497*

b) Criminality (Section 36(2)) *498*

   i) Equivalency of Foreign Offences *499*

   ii) Equivalency between Acts Committed outside Canada with Acts Committed inside Canada under Sections 36(1)(c) and 36(2)(c) *501*

   iii) "Term of Imprisonment" (Section 36(1)) *501*

   iv) Discharges, Record Suspensions, and Rehabilitation *502*

   v) "Having Been Convicted" (Sections 36(1)(a) and (b)) *503*

   vi) Rehabilitation (Section 36(3)(c)) *504*

      a. The Ten-Year Term of Imprisonment Bar on Rehabilitation *505*

   vii) Record Suspensions (Formerly Known as "Pardons") *505*

   viii) Young Offenders *506*

   ix) Multiple Permissible Entries in Canada after Conviction *506*

   x) No Automatic Obligation to Defer pending Criminal Proceedings *507*

c) Organized Criminality (Section 37(1)) *507*

   i) "Being a Member of an Organization" (Section 37(1)(a)) *508*

   ii) "Engaging, in the Context of Transnational Crime, in Activities" (Section 37(1)(b)) *509*

   iii) "People Smuggling" (Section 37(1)(b)) *510*

   iv) Precarious Distinction between Finding of Inadmissibility and Removal *511*

   v) Relying on a Conviction *512*

6) Health (Section 38) *513*

a) Medical Examination and Obtaining Evidence *514*

b) Danger to Public Health (Section 38(1)(a)) *515*

c) Danger to Public Safety (Section 38(1)(b)) *516*

d) Excessive Demand on Health or Social Services *516*

   i) Exceeding the Total Cost of an Average Canadian over Five Years *517*

   ii) Problematic Distinction between Social and Health Services *518*

   iii) Overcoming the Ground of Inadmissibility Based on Excessive Demand on Services *520*

   iv) Humanitarian and Compassionate Grounds *523*

   v) Change in Circumstances *524*

7) Financial Reasons (Section 39) *524*

8) Misrepresentation (Section 40) *525*
  a) Directly or Indirectly Misrepresenting or Withholding Material
     Facts *526*
9) Failure to Comply with the *IRPA* (Section 41) *528*
10) Inadmissible Family Member (Section 42) *529*

C. Inadmissibility and *Charter* Rights *529*

D. Conclusion: The Increase in Securitization of Our Borders *530*

CHAPTER 15:
THE MECHANICS OF ENFORCEMENT *532*

A. Introduction *532*

B. Removal from Canada *533*

1) Enforcing the *Immigration and Refugee Protection Act* and Its
   Regulations *533*
2) The Removal Order *533*
3) The Process of Removal *535*
  a) The Section 44 Report *535*
     i)   Issuing a Section 44 Report *535*
     ii) Section 44 Report against Family Members *536*
     iii) An Officer's Discretion in Issuing Section 44 Reports *537*
     iv) An Officer's Duty to Follow Principles of Procedural
          Fairness *541*
  b) Admissibility Hearings before the Immigration Division (ID) *543*
     i)   Public and Private Admissibility Hearings *543*
     ii) The Parties to an Admissibility Hearing *544*
     iii) Evidence in an Admissibility Hearing *545*
     iv) The Burden of Proof and Decisions from the Immigration
          Division *547*

C. Detention and Detention Review *548*

1) Detention *548*
  a) Shortcomings of Detention of Non-citizens in Canada *548*
  b) Decisions to Detain or Release an Individual *550*
     i)   The Standard Used *550*
     ii) Detention Reviews *551*
          a. Overview *551*
          b. Interpretation of Section 58 *554*
          c. Detention Where Identity Is in Question *556*
          d. Where Release May Not Be Immediately Granted *557*
          e. Detention of Children *559*
          f. Designated Foreign Nationals *560*

D. Appealing a Removal Order *562*

E. Statutory Stays   *564*

   1) Where Removal Orders Are Stayed Due to a Continuing Appeal or Application   *564*

   2) Where Removal Orders Are Stayed Independent of Further Appeal or Application   *565*

F. The Enforcement of a Removal Order   *569*

   1) Enforcing Removal   *569*
     a) "As Soon as Possible"   *569*
     b) Removal to Torture   *571*
     c) CBSA's Most Wanted List   *573*
     d) Sanctuary   *574*
   2) Security Certificates and Concealed Evidence   *576*
   3) Human Smuggling and Human Trafficking   *587*

G. Conclusion   *591*

PART FOUR: JUDICIAL SUPERVISION   *593*

CHAPTER 16:
JUDICIAL REVIEW   *595*

A. Introduction   *595*

B. The Federal Court   *596*

C. The Process of Judicial Review   *597*

   1) Commencing an Application for Judicial Review   *597*
   2) Serving and Filing a Notice of Application for Leave   *599*
   3) Perfecting an Application for Leave   *600*
   4) Obtaining Leave   *601*
   5) Hearings at the Federal Court   *604*
   6) Automatic or Statutory Stays of Removal   *605*

D. Grounds for Relief   *606*

E. Standards of Review   *607*

   1) Applying the Different Standards of Review   *608*
     a) Reviewing for Procedural Fairness   *608*
     b) Reviewing Substantive Aspects of a Decision   *613*
     c) Recent Pushback on the Deferential Approach   *616*

F. Remedies and Costs   *620*

   1) Prerogative Writs   *621*
     a) *Certiorari*   *621*
     b) Prohibition   *622*
     c) *Mandamus*   *623*

d) *Quo Warranto* 627
2) Ordinary Remedies 627
    a) Declarations 627
    b) Damages 628
    c) Injunctions 631
3) Costs 632

G. **Appealing to the Federal Court of Appeal** 633

H. **Appealing to the Supreme Court of Canada** 633

I. **Conclusion: Towards a Less Deferential Approach under the New System** 635

CHAPTER 17:

CONSTITUTIONAL CHALLENGES 636

A. **The *Charter* Rights of Non-citizens** 636

B. **The Ambit of the *Charter*** 636

C. **Standing to Make a *Charter* Challenge** 643

D. ***Charter* Rights** 645

1) Fundamental Freedoms 647
2) Democratic Rights 649
3) Mobility Rights 649
4) Legal Rights 650
    a) Section 7 Rights 650
        i)   Procedural Aspects of Fundamental Justice 651
        ii) The Rights to Life, Liberty, and Security of the Person 655
        iii) Fundamental Justice and Individualized Assessment 658
        iv) The Form of Law: Overbreadth, Vagueness, and Gross Disproportionality 660
    b) Rights Accompanying Detention 662
    c) Cruel and Unusual Treatment 664
    d) Right to an Interpreter 666
    e) Equality Rights 666

E. **The *Bill of Rights*** 667

F. **International Law Remedies** 668

G. **Conclusion** 671

APPENDIX 673

TABLE OF CASES 677

INDEX 723

ABOUT THE AUTHORS 741

PREFACE

This book builds upon the first edition as an introductory guide to immigration, refugee, and citizenship law. Its aim is to provide an overview, or a starting point, both for those who want to investigate the mechanics of Canada's immigration regime and for those who want to assess, critique, or question the aims and impacts of the law.

The book is divided into four parts and seventeen chapters. Part 1 provides context and delves into the sources and evolution of Canadian immigration law. Part 2 examines status in Canada, identifying how persons may obtain, keep, and lose temporary or permanent status. Part 3 discusses the devices that the Canadian government uses to enforce immigration law. Part 4 examines judicial supervision of government action under the immigration regime, and in particular judicial review and constitutional challenges.

Throughout the book, we aspire to provide some understanding of the rules and processes of the immigration system in Canada, as well as the effects the system has on migrants and Canadians, but we also hope that the text will plant a seed of skepticism about the policy rationales and justifications offered for various government decisions and actions. Over the last few years, the government has devolved power from the legislature and civil service to the hands of a few cabinet ministers, permitting them to micromanage through the exercise of discretion. Recent changes have resulted in revamped application and review processes that provide fewer checks and balances for many applicants. The government has also turned to "ministerial instructions" to make significant changes to immigration programs, leaving many to wonder whether thoughtful or informed decision making infused the new standards, rules, and criteria. Last, and perhaps most worrisome, are the government's persistent rhetorical references to migrants as liars, cheats, and queue jumpers, implying that many can be identified as criminals without the need for judicial inquiry, which provide support for a restrictive immigration regime. The consequences and long-term implications of these changes have not yet fully materialized, and we hope that in years to come, we will be writing a third edition of this book to document the successful challenges and changes to our immigration system.

We would like to acknowledge the Law Foundation of Ontario for providing financial support for the drafting of this publication. We also greatly appreciate the research assistance of Michelle Carlesimo, Fanni Csaba, Kassie Seaby, and Nhi Huynh. Jamie would like to thank John Currie and Nicole LaViolette for their encouragement and advice and Donald Galloway for his patient mentoring throughout the whole writing process. Jamie would also like to thank her partner, Roman Zakaluzny, for his support, and her children, Maxym and Vera Zakaluzny, for being so patient and for sharing their mother's time with this project. She would like to dedicate her work to her parents, James Liew and Bernadette Lim, who were stateless immigrants to Canada. Donald would like to thank the many students at the University of Victoria who participated actively in discussions about the issues raised in the text and who provided research assistance and critical appraisal. Thanks also to Sylvie and Hester for support, assistance, and being there. Donald would like to dedicate his work to his mother, Agnes Galloway.

PART ONE

ORIGINS
AND SOURCES

CHAPTER 1

THE EVOLUTION OF CANADIAN IMMIGRATION LAW

A. INTRODUCTION

Canadian immigration law in the early twenty-first century has been subject to frequent and seemingly frenzied revision and reformulation by the government of the day as it attempts to identify the country's social, economic, and demographic needs and to respond to perceived threats to its sovereign control over Canada's borders. In a period of about fifteen years, we have witnessed a series of substantial changes beginning in 2001 with the enactment of new legislation, the *Immigration and Refugee Protection Act (IRPA)*,[1] a statute which, according to the Supreme Court of Canada, reveals a set of priorities that differ significantly from those of its predecessors.[2] This statute has been modified extensively by a series of three other Acts: the *Balanced Refugee Reform*

---

1   SC 2001, c 27 [*IRPA*].

2   In *Medovarski v Canada (Minister of Citizenship and Immigration)*; *Esteban v Canada (Minister of Citizenship and Immigration)*, 2005 SCC 51 at para 10 [*Medovarski*], the Chief Justice made the following point:

> The objectives as expressed in the *IRPA* indicate an intent to prioritize security. This objective is given effect by preventing the entry of applicants with criminal records, by removing applicants with such records from Canada, and by emphasizing the obligation of permanent residents to behave lawfully while in Canada. This marks a change from the focus in the predecessor statute, which emphasized the successful integration of applicants more than security . . . .

Act,[3] the *Faster Removal of Foreign Criminals Act*,[4] and the *Protecting Canada's Immigration System Act*.[5] These Acts have radically reshaped the institutional framework established by the *IRPA*, facilitated the removal of individuals deemed inadmissible, and introduced severe measures aimed at deterring individuals from seeking Canada's protection. Numerous regulatory modifications have also been made, many of them seeking to shore up the system from the threat of possible fraud and abuse.

In addition, the *Citizenship Act*[6] has been modified in ways that have redefined the status and the processes of acquiring citizenship. We have also witnessed an increased devolution of power to the provinces and territories, most of which have developed their own programs to attract needed workers and business immigrants to meet local needs. We have seen an intensification of ministerial micromanagement, manifested in the issuance of specific instructions on how to fill gaps in the labour market; in seemingly endless tinkering with the rules governing the entry of temporary foreign workers, who are being admitted in unprecedented numbers; and in the redefinition of the opportunities for families to live together by setting quotas on the number of parents and grandparents who can be sponsored as permanent residents and by establishing more temporary possibilities for family cohabitation.

Both the scale and pace of this recent feverish hyperactivity are somewhat overwhelming and tend to suggest that we have experienced a revolutionary transformation. Nevertheless, they should not blind us to the fact that the general shape of the law and of the mechanisms created to administer it have evolved gradually and incrementally over many years. One can identify recurring patterns in the development of immigration law traceable to the ebb and flow of conflicting political values. A full appreciation of our current situation can be gained only through an understanding of the history and development of the political and legal traditions that continue to inform and influence legislative and judicial decision making. This chapter aims to place current law in a historical context — to provide a general overview of the path followed by the law and to identify some of the dominant factors and resilient beliefs that have guided policy making as it has evolved.

---

3   SC 2010, c 8.
4   SC 2013, c 16.
5   SC 2012, c 17.
6   RSC 1985, c C-29.

B. IMMIGRATION AND COLONIALIZATION

The evolution and mechanics of Canadian immigration policy need to be examined and studied through a lens that examines colonial, racist, and settler ideologies that have "ensured an enduring legacy of deeply rooted conflicts."[7] Acknowledging and understanding the role of immigration in colonizing Indigenous people in Canada is an essential preliminary to appraising policies regarding who is entitled to be here and who belongs. Daiva Stasiulis and Radha Jhappan remind us of the underlying myths:

> For the most part, Euro-Canadian historians have ignored the dynamism and diverse accomplishments of Aboriginal peoples prior to the European migration, preferring to support the socio-legal myth that North America was "a vacant territory, *terra nullius*, to which Europeans could freely take title". . . . The idea that indigenous peoples were only nomadic hunters lacking political or legal organization, and thus unencumbered by sovereignty over their territories, does not, however, hold up to anthropological scrutiny.[8]

Sherene Razack has teased out further details:

> A white settler society is one established by Europeans on non-European soil. Its origins lie in the dispossession and near extermination of Indigenous populations by the conquering Europeans. As it evolves, a white settler society continues to be structured by a racial hierarchy. In the national mythologies of such societies, it is believed that white people came first and that it is they who principally developed the land; Aboriginal peoples are presumed to be mostly dead or assimilated. European settlers thus *become* the original inhabitants and the group most entitled to the fruits of citizenship . . . . In North America, it is still the case that European conquest and colonization are often denied, largely through the fantasy that North America was peacefully settled and not colonized.

---

7   Daiva Stasiulis & Radha Jhappan, "The Fractious Politics of Settler Society: Canada" in Daiva Stasiulis & Nira Yuval-Davis, eds, *Unsettling Settler Societies: Articulations of Gender, Race, Ethnicity and Class* (London: Sage Publications, 1995) at 127. See also Valerie Knowles, *Canadian Immigration and Immigration Policy, 1540–2006*, rev ed (Toronto: Dundurn Press, 2007) at 11; Frances Abele & Daiva Stasiulis, "Canada as a 'White Settler Colony': What about Natives and Immigrants?" in Wallace Clement & Glen Williams, eds, *New Canadian Political Economy* (Kingston, ON: McGill-Queens University Press, 1989) 241.

8   Stasiulis & Jhappan, above note 7 at 99.

Mythologies or national stories are about a nation's origins and history. They enable citizens to think of themselves as part of a community, defining who belongs and who does not belong to the nation. The story of land as shared and as developed by enterprising settlers is manifestly a racial story . . . . If Aboriginal peoples are consigned forever to an earlier space and time, people of colour are scripted as late arrivals, coming to the shores of North America long after much of the development has occurred. In this way, slavery, indentureship, and labour exploitation — for example, the Chinese who built the railway or the Sikhs who worked in the lumber industry in the nineteenth-centry Canada — are all handily forgotten in an official national story of European enterprise.[9]

When reading any text on immigration and citizenship laws, it should be remembered that normative notions of citizenship in Canada and entitlement to be here have been shaped by perpetuating mythologies that continue to create "otherness" in immigration programs and laws by excluding identities and trivializing contributions to the development of our nation-state.[10]

C. EARLY ORIGINS

The origins of Canadian immigration law can be traced to England in the thirteenth century. The *Magna Carta* of 1215 includes clauses that regulate the comings and goings of both aliens and the king's subjects. For example, article 41 of that document states: "All merchants shall have safe conduct to go and come out of and into England, and to stay in and travel through England by land and water for purposes of buying and selling, free of illegal tolls, in accordance with ancient and just customs, except, in time of war, such merchants as are of a country at war with Us."[11]

Writing in the eighteenth century, Sir William Blackstone noted the anomalous nature of this clause, which aims at protecting the interests of foreigners. In his *Commentaries on the Laws of England*, he remarks that "it is somewhat extraordinary that it [article 41] should have found a place in *magna carta*, a mere interior treaty between the

---

9   Sherene Razack, *Race, Space, and the Law: Unmapping a White Settler Society* (Toronto: Between the Lines, 2002) at 1–3.

10   Stasiulis & Jhappan, above note 7 at 127.

11   See AE Dick Howard, *Magna Carta: Text and Commentary* (Charlottesville, VA: University Press of Virginia, 1964) at 44.

king and his natural-born subjects."[12] Blackstone goes on to resolve the anomaly by suggesting that the clause should not be understood as an altruistic effort to enhance the business interests of aliens, but should be regarded, instead, as an early indicator of a developing and self-interested English preoccupation with domestic commercial growth and economic wealth.[13] By granting rights of entry to foreign merchants, the monarch would thereby promote the wealth of the nation. The perceived linkage between unhindered cross-border movement and domestic economic prosperity has been a constant aspect of immigration regulation through the centuries to this day. One can find evidence of this continuity in section 3(c) of the *IRPA* which explicitly identifies economic development as a central determinant of current immigration policy.[14] Provisions facilitating the entry of business persons in the *North American Free Trade Agreement (NAFTA)* provide another obvious example of an effort to achieve the same goal.[15] More generally, one can discern a kernel of Blackstone's thought running through today's political manifestos that we should attend to the well-being of foreign nationals only if it is in our own self-interest to do so.

Blackstone's interpretation of the underlying rationale of article 41 of the *Magna Carta* is corroborated by the fact that, in subsequent years, English law began to develop a precise set of criteria of nationality in order to distinguish English subjects from aliens. At the same time, it began to define restrictively the rights of the latter. Those who were not English subjects would not enjoy the same privileges and entitlements, such as the right to own property or the right to bring an action in the courts.[16]

The fact that numerous significant restrictions were imposed on aliens from a very early time has sparked a recent debate about the existence of a common law right of aliens to enter England. Notwithstanding the clarity of the concession in article 41 of the *Magna Carta*, the dominant modern opinion seems to be that, at common law, no alien had such an unqualified right. This view has been articulated in

---

12   William Blackstone, *Commentaries on the Laws of England*, 17th ed (London: Tegg, 1830) vol 1 at 260.
13   *Ibid* at 261.
14   *IRPA*, above note 1.
15   *North American Free Trade Agreement*, 32 ILM 289 and 605 (1993).
16   Frederick Pollock & Frederic W Maitland, *The History of English Law: Before the Time of Edward I*, 2d ed (Cambridge: Cambridge University Press, 1968) vol 1 at 458–67.

a number of judgments by members of the Supreme Court of Canada.[17] It has been asserted most forcefully by Sopinka J in *Canada (Minister of Employment and Immigration) v Chiarelli*, where he stated: "The most fundamental principle of immigration law is that non-citizens do not have an unqualified right to enter or remain in the country. At common law an alien has no right to enter or remain in the country . . . ."[18] Each articulation of this view has relied directly or indirectly on the confidently stated, but nevertheless questionable claim of Lord Denning, in *R v Governor of Pentonville Prison*, that "[a]t common law no alien has any right to enter this country except by leave of the Crown . . . . If he comes by leave, the Crown can impose such conditions as it thinks fit."[19]

Although it may be accurate to say that statute law has never provided aliens with an unqualified right of entry, the account of the common law offered by Lord Denning and the various judges of the Supreme Court of Canada has not gone unchallenged. Richard Plender has given an alternative account, more consistent with the permissive provisions relating to merchants in the *Magna Carta*. Plender claims that the developing common law reflected two competing principles: that of sovereignty and that of freedom of movement. He explains their interplay as follows:

> [I]t was established at common law that an alien committed no offence if he entered England without the sovereign's permission, although he was liable to be denied admission if the King saw fit to exclude him. In this respect English common law reflected both the principle of sovereignty (whereby the King could exclude named individuals) and the principle of free movement (whereby aliens enjoyed *prima facie* the right to enter the kingdom).[20]

The historical record shows clear evidence of the operation of the first principle. As noted by Plender:

> Although for long periods successive English monarchs permitted alien merchants to "go and come with their merchandises after the manner of the Great Charter" the same sovereigns occasionally invoked an exceptional power to expel or exclude defined groups of

---

17   See, for example, the opinion of Martland J in *Prata v Canada (Minister of Manpower & Immigration)*, [1976] 1 SCR 376 at 380, and that of Wilson J in *Singh v Canada (Minister of Employment and Immigration)*, [1985] 1 SCR 177 at 189 [*Singh*].

18   [1992] 1 SCR 711 at para 24 [*Chiarelli*].

19   [1973] 2 All ER 741 at 747 (CA).

20   Richard Plender, *International Migration Law*, 2d ed (Dordrecht, Netherlands: Martinus Nijhoff, 1988) at 62–63.

aliens. That power was later invoked by the Tudors when the Flemish, Irish and Huguenot influxes prompted demands for a reduction in the overall rate of immigration.[21]

However, one can also find evidence of the competing influence of the second principle. In his authoritative *Commentaries*, Blackstone writes:

> Great tenderness is shown by our laws, not only to foreigners in distress . . . but with regard also to the admission of strangers who come spontaneously. For so long as their nation continues at peace with ours, and they themselves behave peacefully, they are under the king's protection; though liable to be sent home whenever the king sees occasion.[22]

The suggestion here is that by way of a default position the common law took a permissive stance towards the entry of aliens.[23]

The debate about the common law is not merely academic. In *Chiarelli*, Sopinka J's assessment of history and his ability to find corroborating authority for his opinions lend rhetorical force to his claim that there is a single fundamental principle of immigration law — namely, that "non-citizens do not have an unqualified right to enter or remain in the country."[24] As shall be seen, he then makes the important and influential claim that the absence of such a right should shape our understanding of how to interpret and apply the *Canadian Charter of Rights and Freedoms*.[25] If Plender is right, the idea that entry into national territory is purely a privilege may be a political idea of questionable pedigree. A re-evaluation of the historical record may provide a new lens through which such claims may be examined and reformulated, and may eventually diminish their legal force.

A second, very similar debate about sovereignty has focused on the related question of whether early international law recognized states to have an unqualified discretion to exclude and evict foreigners from their territory, with the historical record being used, once again, as a foundation on which to ground conclusions about current law. The dominant view is that a state's discretion to exclude and evict is an integral

---

21 *Ibid* at 62.
22 See Blackstone, above note 12 at 259–60.
23 For further discussion, without resolution, of the common law right of entry, see the opinion of Muldoon J in *Mannan v Canada (Minister of Employment & Immigration)* (1991), 48 FTR 259 (TD).
24 *Chiarelli*, above note 18 at para 24.
25 Part I of the *Constitution Act, 1982*, being Schedule B to the *Canada Act 1982* (UK), 1982, c 11.

aspect of its sovereignty and has always been absolute. In *Canada (AG) v Cain*,[26] the Privy Council, citing Emmerich de Vattel,[27] held that there was no international impediment to the exclusion of aliens by a state. It stated that "[o]ne of the rights possessed by the same supreme power in every State is the right to refuse to permit an alien to enter that State, to annex whatever conditions it pleases to the permission to enter it, and to expel or deport from the State, at pleasure, even a friendly alien . . ."[28]

However, a dissenting view has been propounded by, among others, James Nafziger,[29] who disputes the Privy Council's interpretation of the historical record. Nafziger refers to the Court's reliance on and misinterpretation of "highly selective snippets from the writings of Emmerich de Vattel,"[30] and notes that while the unfettered right to exclude aliens is now commonly identified as a crucial aspect of a state's sovereignty, the classical international law treatise writers — Grotius, De Vitoria, Pufendorf, and Vattel — did not recognize the existence of an unqualified right.[31] Nafziger concludes that there is a "firm basis for articulating a qualified duty of states to admit aliens."[32] This undercurrent of

---

26   [1906] AC 542 (PC) [*Cain*].

27   The citations are to Emmerich de Vattel, *The Law of Nations*, ed by Joseph Chitty (Philadelphia: T & JW Johnson, 1852), Book 1, s 23, and Book 2, s 125.

28   *Cain*, above note 26 at 546.

29   See James AR Nafziger, "The General Admission of Aliens under International Law" (1983) 77 *American Journal of International Law* 804.

30   *Ibid* at 807.

31   *Ibid* at 810–15.

32   *Ibid* at 845. See also Bas Schotel, *On the Right of Exclusion: Law, Ethics and Immigration Policy* (New York: Routledge, 2011). In a review of Schotel's book, Nafziger has written:

> A commonplace assumption of migration law is the concept, sometimes called a rule, of inherent sovereign power. Accordingly, a state is said to possess an unbridled power to exclude any or all foreigners from admission into its territory. This assumption is trumpeted as a hallmark of the nation-state system and a foundation of national communities. It is, however, highly questionable, and arguably discredited by general practice and the writings of qualified publicists since the 17th century. In fact, states normally admit limited numbers of foreigners, not only out of self-interest but also for reasons of international cooperation, solidarity, and other motivations premised in *opinio juris*. Still, the inherent sovereignty rule labours on against the evidence, not so much among policymakers and busy administrators, who ordinarily know better, but among academic writers, who should know better. Unfortunately, the concept is not just academic. Instead, it shapes public understanding and discourse about human migration and contributes to unnecessarily restrictive paradigms within which national and international regulation of migration is moulded.

thought is important since it strengthens the core legal arguments used to support the rights of migrants before international bodies.

D. THE EMERGENCE OF RESTRICTIVE IMMIGRATION LEGISLATION, 1775–1872

The late eighteenth century saw the enactment of legislation aimed specifically at the admission and exclusion of foreigners.[33] In what is now Canada, the earliest example of such legislation is an Act of the Legislature of Nova Scotia, entitled *An Act for the ready admission of His Majesty's Subjects in the Colonies on the Continent, who may be induced to take refuge in this Province, from the Anarchy and Confusion there, and for securing the Peace, and preserving the Loyalty and Obedience of the Inhabitants of this Province.*[34] Passed in 1775, the legislation was timely. It has been estimated that, from 1775 to 1784, between 40,000 and 50,000 United Empire Loyalists made their way to British North America, a large portion of whom settled in Nova Scotia.[35]

The French Revolution produced refugees in much the same way as the American Revolution did, and gave rise to similar concern for their welfare. The earliest statute in England dealing with immigration, the *Alien Act, 1793*, implemented a registration scheme for aliens. A response to the arrival of refugees from the French Revolution, it was shaped by the fear that the refugees might be importing seditious or incendiary ideas that could disturb the peace.[36]

Shortly after, in pre-Confederation Canada, similar concerns motivated colonial legislatures to regulate the movement of foreigners. In Lower Canada, in the same year, 1793, the legislature passed an Act described as "An Act for establishing regulations respecting Aliens and certain subjects of his Majesty, who have resided in France . . . ,"[37] which instituted a registry of information relating to aliens. A new arrival was required, under section 3 of the Act, to make a declaration as to his

---

James AR Nafziger, "Book Review of *On the Right of Exclusion: Law, Ethics and Immigration Policy* by Bas Schotel" (2013) 24 *European Journal of International Law* 235, online: http://ejil.oxfordjournals.org/content/24/2/735.full.pdf+html.

33 See Brian Coleman, "Immigration Legislation in Canada, 1775–1949" (1993) 18 *Immigration Law Reports* (2d) 177.

34 SNS 1775, c 6.

35 Valerie Knowles, *Strangers at Our Gates: Canadian Immigration and Immigration Policy, 1540–1990* (Toronto: Dundurn Press, 1992).

36 33 Geo III, c 4. See Plender, above note 20 at 65.

37 SQ 1793, c 5.

or her name, rank, occupation, and previous countries of residence.[38] Those neglecting or refusing to make such declaration were required to depart the province, and if found within the province, were liable to transportation for life. The perceived link between the presence of aliens and the possibility of public disorder is revealed by the inclusion of sections proscribing treason,[39] maliciously spreading false news and publishing "libellous or seditious papers . . . tending to excite discontent in the minds, or lessen the affections of his Majesty's subjects . . ."[40]

A similar Act was passed in Nova Scotia in 1798.[41] The preamble justified the subsequent regulations on the ground that they were "at present necessary, for the safety and tranquillity of the Province." Section 1 of the Act provided that "no alien . . . shall be permitted to be, and remain, within this Province, without a special permit, under the hand and seal of the Governor, Lieutenant-Governor, or Commander in Chief . . ."[42] Under section 3, those who failed to obtain a permit as well as those who engaged in seditious writing and speech were liable to "be transported beyond His Majesty's dominions in America, to such place as the Governor, Lieutenant-Governor, or Commander in Chief, may think proper to direct."[43]

Although the connection between foreigners and seditious or disruptive activity was the dominant theme of early pre-Confederation statutes, with a system requiring the documentation of identity being the preferred mode of coping, legislatures soon began to focus also on the health of the passengers being conveyed to Canada and on the need to secure funding for individuals who would otherwise become a burden on the public purse. Thus, in the first session of the Provincial Parliament of Canada in 1841, an Act was passed to "create a Fund for defraying the expense of enabling indigent Emigrants to proceed to their place of destination, and of supporting them until they can procure employment."[44] A levy was placed on emigrants to be collected by masters of vessels, the monies raised from which were to be applied "in defraying the expense of medical attendance and examination of des-

---

38 *Ibid*, s 3.
39 *Ibid*, s 29.
40 *Ibid*, s 31.
41 *An Act respecting Aliens coming into this Province, or residing therein*, SNS 1798, c 1.
42 *Ibid*, s 1.
43 *Ibid*, s 3.
44 SC 1841, c 13.

titute Emigrants."[45] The following year, a similar statute was passed in Prince Edward Island.[46]

By the time of Confederation, immigration had come to be identified as the most effective means by which land cultivation could be quickly achieved across the country. Hence, in the *Constitution Act, 1867* (formerly the *British North America Act*),[47] one finds the subject matters of Immigration and Agriculture located in the same section:

> In each Province the Legislature may make Laws in relation to Agriculture in the Province, and to Immigration into the Province; and it is hereby declared that the Parliament of Canada may from Time to Time make Laws in relation to Agriculture in all or any of the Provinces, and to Immigration into all or any of the Provinces; and any Law of the Legislature of a Province relative to Agriculture or to Immigration shall have effect in and for the Province so long and as far as it is not repugnant to any Act of the Parliament of Canada.[48]

In the early years after Confederation, it was agreed among the provincial and federal governments that the federal minister of agriculture would exercise control over immigration and that the provinces would be responsible for the settlement of immigrants. Evidence of this agreement is found in the 1869 *Immigration Act*[49] — the first passed after Confederation — where there is explicit reference to the principle of concurrent jurisdiction over immigration and to the idea that responsibility for the arrival and settlement of immigrants should be shared and negotiated between the federal and provincial authorities. The Act allowed for the government of Canada to establish and maintain immigration offices in the United Kingdom and Europe, and to maintain quarantine stations and immigration offices throughout Canada. It also permitted the provincial governments to "determine their policy concerning the settlement and colonization of uncultivated lands, as bearing on Immigration," and to appoint immigration agents in Europe and elsewhere as they thought proper.

Substantively, the Act of 1869 renewed, systematized, and updated the pre-Confederation legislation: it provided for the levying of a duty on all passengers[50] and also authorized the governor to prohibit "the landing of pauper or destitute Immigrants . . . until such sums of

---

45   *Ibid*, s 7.
46   SPEI 1842, c 5.
47   (UK), 30 & 31 Vict, c 3, s 91, reprinted in RSC 1985, Appendix II, No 5.
48   *Ibid*, s 95.
49   *An Act Respecting Immigration and Immigrants*, SC 1869, c 10.
50   *Ibid*, s 4.

money as may be found necessary are provided and paid into the hands of one of the Canadian Immigration Agents, by the master of the vessel carrying such Immigrants, for their temporary support . . . ."[51] Much of the rest of the Act specified the obligations and responsibilities of transportation companies and quarantine officers.

In section 91, the *Constitution Act* also allocated power over naturalization and aliens to the Dominion Parliament.[52] It exercised this power in 1868 by enacting the *Aliens and Naturalization Act*,[53] which permitted aliens to naturalize as local British subjects after three years of residence in Canada. At this time, the status of British subject, based on the notion of allegiance to the monarch, was the basic status shared by all individuals born in the British empire, although different countries within the empire were developing and implementing different rules of naturalization and immigration.

In 1872, Canadian immigration legislation began to impede access to the country by identifying classes of person who ought to be denied entry. Section 10 of the *Immigration Act* of that year[54] provided for the exclusion of any "criminal, or other vicious class of immigrants."[55] From this time onwards, the identification of prohibited classes — frequently defined in vague, value-laden, and vituperative terms — became a central element and defining characteristic of Canadian immigration law. As such, it has the potential for creating embarrassment within a legal system that commits itself to respecting principles of equality. As discussed below, the distinction between insiders and outsiders and the use of stereotype to exclude the latter on grounds of physical disability, wealth, or suspected criminality does not sit easily within a regime that regards governmental discrimination as suspect. The assertion of a principle of state's sovereignty over its borders provides a convenient defence for this distinction but ultimately begs the question. Within the Canadian context, this issue came to a head with the use of race as a ground of exclusion.

---

51   *Ibid*, s 16.
52   *Constitution Act, 1867*, above note 47, s 91(25).
53   SC 1868, c 66.
54   *An Act to Amend the Immigration Act of 1869*, SC 1872, c 28.
55   *Ibid*, s 6.

E. THE RACIALIZATION OF IMMIGRATION LAW, 1878–1914

Between 1878 and 1908, the legislature of British Columbia tried repeatedly to control the access of Asians to the province by enacting explicit prohibitions on their entry, by imposing entrance requirements that could not be met, or by imposing discriminatory burdens on those who had been admitted previously, for example, by disqualifying them from working in particular sectors and from participating in political decision making.[56] In doing so, it ignored previous constitutional arrangements and cited section 95 of the *Constitution Act, 1867*, as the source of its authority both to exclude immigrants and to use racial criteria in doing so. Thus, the nine immigration acts it passed during this period should be viewed as part of a larger package of legislation that discriminated in diverse ways against Asians.[57]

Initially, the Chinese were the primary targets of this legislation and suffered the greatest hardships as a result. The *Chinese Tax Act, 1878*, imposed a tax solely on Chinese residents.[58] In *Sing v Maguire*,[59] this discrimination was held to be unconstitutional. In the course of his judgment, Gray J made the following comment on the Act: "[I]t is plain it [the Act] was not intended to collect revenue, but to drive the Chinese from the country."[60]

The preamble of the *Chinese Regulation Act, 1884*,[61] gives a sense of the level of hostility aimed at the Chinese:

> Whereas the incoming of Chinese to British Columbia largely exceeds that of any other class of immigrant, and the population so introduced are fast becoming superior in number to our own race; are not disposed to be governed by our laws; are dissimilar in habits and occupation from our people; evade the payment of taxes justly due to the Government; are governed by pestilential habits; are useless in instances of emergency; habitually desecrate graveyards by the removal of bodies therefrom; and generally the laws governing

---

56   See Patricia E Roy, *A White Man's Province: British Columbia Politicians and Chinese and Japanese Immigrants, 1858–1914* (Vancouver: UBC Press, 1989).

57   See John PS McLaren, "The Burdens of Empire and the Legalization of White Supremacy in Canada, 1860–1910" in William M Gordon & TD Fergus, eds, *Legal History in the Making* (London: Hambledon Press, 1991) 187.

58   *An Act to provide for the better collection of Provincial Taxes from Chinese*, SBC 1878, c 35.

59   (1878), 1 BCR (Pt 1) 101 (SC).

60   *Ibid* at para 28.

61   SBC 1884, c 4.

the whites are found to be inapplicable to Chinese, and such Chinese are inclined to habits subversive of the comfort and well-being of the community.[62]

The *Act to prevent the Immigration of Chinese*[63] was disallowed by the governor general on the grounds that it infringed on federal powers.[64] Bruce Ryder has noted that "[a]ccording to federal cabinet interpretations of section 95, the provincial power to 'make laws in relation to immigration into the province' meant that the provinces had the authority to *promote* immigration into the province, but lacked the power to *prohibit* immigration."[65] Ryder argues that underlying such formalistic or legalistic distinctions was a strong political desire to ensure the continuation of a ready supply of Chinese labour for railway construction. The province, however, was not satisfied with this state of affairs. The 1884 Act was re-enacted in almost identical words the following year[66] and was again disallowed.[67]

In subsequent years, the British Columbia legislature also passed a series of laws that imposed literacy requirements on immigrants and demanded proficiency in a European language, thereby condemning most Asians to the ranks of the inadmissible.[68] In *Re Narain Singh*,[69] the British Columbia Supreme Court declared inoperative the last of these Acts, the British Columbia *Immigration Act, 1908*, on the ground that, even though it did not conflict with any provision of a federal act, it was repugnant to federal legislation.[70] During this same period, various other racist statutes of the British Columbia legislature were struck down by the courts on the ground that they encroached on the federal jurisdiction over "naturalization and aliens."[71]

---

62 *Ibid.*

63 SBC 1884, c 3.

64 On disallowance, see Peter W Hogg, *Constitutional Law of Canada*, 5th ed (Toronto: Carswell, 2012).

65 See Bruce Ryder, "Racism and the Constitution: The Constitutional Fate of British Columbia Anti-Asian Immigration Legislation, 1884–1909" (1991) 29 *Osgoode Hall Law Journal* 619 at 642–43.

66 *An Act to Prevent the Immigration of Chinese*, SBC 1885, c 13.

67 See Canada, House of Commons, "Telegram from Secretary of State JA Chapleau to the Lieutenant Governor" by JA Chapleau in *Sessional Papers*, No 21 (1888) at 288.

68 See, for example, *An Act to Regulate Immigration into British Columbia*, SBC 1900, c 11, which was disallowed in 1901.

69 SBC 1908, c 23. (1908), 13 BCR 477 (CA).

70 *Ibid* at para 11.

71 See Chapter 2.

Although the British Columbian anti-Asian policy met strong resistance from the federal government and also failed to meet judicially imposed criteria of legality, the province was eventually able to persuade the federal legislature to enact very restrictive legislation regulating Chinese immigration. Thus, while federal legislation in 1885 placed a head tax of $50 on Chinese immigrants,[72] this amount was increased to $100 in 1900[73] and to $500 in 1903.[74] Ultimately, in 1923, Parliament passed *The Chinese Immigration Act, 1923*,[75] which prohibited the entry of most Chinese into the country. This prohibition continued in force until 1947.[76] Today, critics have drawn a comparison between the overt discrimination of the head taxes of yesteryear and the recent imposition of higher fees. In both cases, there is a disproportional effect on immigrants from developing countries.[77]

Immigrants from other parts of Asia were not immune from federal regulation. Initially, the federal government felt constrained not to do anything that might disrupt the friendly relations between Japan and Great Britain. It was able to resist strong pressure from prominent and powerful political groups to enact restrictive measures against Japanese immigrants, aided in large part by the fact that, in 1900, the government of Japan undertook to prohibit emigration from Japan to Canada, an undertaking it maintained for about four years.[78] Gradually, however, the number of Japanese immigrants began to increase, including arrivals from Hawaii as well as directly from Japan, as did the number of immigrants from other parts of Asia. This influx provoked widespread hostility and antagonism. In 1907, a year during which 12,000 Asians arrived, the Asiatic Exclusion League in Vancouver organized

---

72   *The Chinese Immigration Act, 1885*, SC 1885, c 71.

73   *The Chinese Immigration Act, 1900*, SC 1900, c 32.

74   *The Chinese Immigration Act, 1903*, SC 1903, c 8.

75   SC 1923, c 38.

76   It was then repealed by *An Act to amend the Immigration Act and to repeal the Chinese Immigration Act*, SC 1947, c 19.

77   See, for example, Andrew Brouwer, "Protection with a Price Tax: The Head Tax on Refugees and Their Families Must Go" *Caledon Commentary* (June 1999), online: Caledon Institute of Social Policy http://maytree.com/PDF_Files/summaryheadtaxmustgo1999.pdf. See also Ethel Tungohan, "Is the Live-in Caregiver Program the Filipino-Canadian Community's Version of the Chinese Head Tax?" (30 July 2014), online: rabble.ca http://rabble.ca/blogs/bloggers/views-expressed/2014/07/live-caregiver-program-filipino-canadian-communitys-version-c.

78   See Terry Watada, "The Japanese Exclusion," online: www.collectionscanada.gc.ca/immigrants/021017-2421-e.html.

an "Anti-Asiatic" parade and protest meeting that quickly evolved into a spontaneous, violent, and destructive riot in the area known as China-town.[79] The reaction of the federal government was to impose more severe exclusionary measures, including restricting to 400 the number of Japanese immigrants admitted annually, a measure to which the Japanese government consented.[80] As Hawkins notes, Prime Minister William Lyon Mackenzie King came "to the firm conclusion that all Asian immigrants should be excluded for their own good and safety."[81] Sensitive to the delicacies of international relations, the government ensured that some of these restrictions were formulated in race-neutral language and concealed within a lengthy list of prohibited classes.

The most notorious example was the "continuous passage" rule. The *Immigration Act, 1906*,[82] relied heavily on a device that has remained a defining element of Canadian immigration law — the grant of broad discretionary powers of exclusion to the executive branch of government. To this day, the bulk of substantive changes to immigration law are the result of Cabinet or ministerial order rather than by legislation.[83] Thus, section 30 of the Act authorized the Governor in Council "by proclamation or order, whenever he considers it necessary or expedient, [to] prohibit the landing in Canada of any specified class of immigrants . . . ."[84] Citing the authority of this section, the federal Cabinet developed the "continuous passage" rule by passing an order in council prohibiting from landing immigrants who had not arrived on a continuous voyage from their countries of origin, an order that effectively barred all emigrants from Asia.[85] When this order was successfully challenged as not conforming with the power of the Cabinet, the legislation was amended in 1910 to allow explicitly for the making of such an order.[86] The Act provided that the government might prohibit

---

79   Freda Hawkins, *Critical Years in Immigration: Canada and Australia Compared*, 2d ed (Kingston, ON: McGill-Queen's University Press, 1991) at 18. See also Peter W Ward, *White Canada Forever: Popular Attitudes and Public Policy Toward Orientals in British Columbia*, 2d ed (Montreal: McGill-Queen's University Press, 1990) at 67–68.

80   Yoland Pottie-Sherman & Rima Wilkes, "Anti-immigrant Sentiment in Canada" in Mónica Verea, ed, *Anti-immigrant Sentiments, Actions, and Policies in North America and the European Union* (Mexico City: Centre for Research on North America, 2012) 275 at 277.

81   Hawkins, above note 79 at 18.

82   RSC 1906, c 93 [1906 Act].

83   See Chapter 2.

84   1906 Act, above note 82.

85   Order in Council, PC 1908-27 (1908) C Gaz II 4106.

86   *Immigration Act*, SC 1910, c 27 [1910 Act].

"any immigrant who has come to Canada otherwise than by continuous journey from the country of which he is a native or naturalized citizen and upon a through ticket purchased in that country or prepaid in Canada."[87] Although the provision is worded in abstract terms, it was clearly directed against arrivals from Asia.

One consequence of this latter legislation was the infamous treatment of 376 Indians who arrived in Vancouver from Hong Kong on the ship *Komagata Maru* in 1914. As British subjects, many Indians believed that they had a right of residence in all parts of the British empire. The arrival of such a large number was seen by many people in Canada as "a direct challenge to the policy of East Indian exclusion"[88] and it significantly increased racial tension in Vancouver. The ship remained for two months in the harbour with the passengers on board while the exclusion law was unsuccessfully challenged in court.[89] During this time, officials took steps to prevent the ship from getting supplies. Eventually, the ship was forced to return to Hong Kong, and it sailed on to India with all but twenty of its complement of passengers, the exceptions being Indians who had previously been admitted to Canada and who were, therefore, returning residents. In India, a riot broke out when the ship arrived, and police killed twenty-three of the passengers. This incident has become etched in Canadian history and has influenced many current debates about the treatment of immigrants and refugees.[90]

The 1910 Act[91] granted even wider powers to the Governor in Council "to prohibit . . . the landing in Canada . . . of immigrants belonging to any race deemed unsuited to the climate or requirements of Canada, or of immigrants of any specified class, occupation or character."[92] The subtext of this provision is quite transparent.[93]

The Acts of 1906 and 1910 included a greatly expanded list of the classes of person who could be excluded from Canada.[94] Thus, under section 26 of the 1906 Act, permission to land was denied to any person identified as "feeble-minded, an idiot, or an epileptic, or . . .

---

87   *Ibid*, s 38.
88   Ward, above note 79 at 88.
89   See Ninette Kelley & Michael Trebilcock, *The Making of the Mosaic*, 2d ed (Toronto: University of Toronto Press, 2010) at 152.
90   See, for example, Audrey Macklin, "A Shameful Parallel to the Sikh Ordeal" *The Globe and Mail* (17 September 1987) A7.
91   Above note 86.
92   *Ibid*, s 38.
93   See Hawkins, above note 79 at 17–20.
94   1906 Act, above note 82; 1910 Act, above note 86.

insane."[95] Those identified as "deaf and dumb" or as "dumb, blind or infirm" would be permitted to land only if their families were able to provide permanent support.[96] Furthermore, those afflicted with "a loathsome disease, or with a disease which is contagious or infectious," were also denied entry,[97] as was anyone identified as a "pauper, or destitute, a professional beggar, or vagrant, or who is likely to become a public charge."[98] Lastly, anyone "convicted of a crime involving moral turpitude, or who is a prostitute . . ." was also not permitted to land.[99]

The 1910 Act also introduced the term *citizen* into the Canadian legal lexicon.[100] However, it had a limited ambit and was not intended to supplant the status of British subject. At this point in history, a common code of naturalization was being developed, and was eventually implemented in 1914, to ensure that a uniform status of British subject existed throughout the British empire.[101] The concept of citizenship found in the *Immigration Act* was not regarded as a status that entitled its bearer to a broad range of civil and political rights. Instead, it was introduced merely to identify a category of individuals who had a right to enter the country. Nevertheless, use of the term can be seen as a significant step in Canada's evolution towards national sovereignty by revealing an intent to assert authority over its population without directly challenging or confronting imperial superiors.[102]

The 1910 Act is also significant in that it established boards of inquiry at ports of entry to determine the case of any immigrant seeking admission, thereby setting in motion the establishment of the modern administrative bureaucracy.[103] However, at this early stage, the legislature also enacted a privative clause in the legislation which aimed to restrain the courts from entering the field.[104] Section 23 of the Act deprived the courts of the jurisdiction to review and quash decisions

---

95 1906 Act, above note 82.

96 *Ibid*, s 26.

97 *Ibid*, s 27.

98 *Ibid*, s 28.

99 *Ibid*, s 29.

100 1910 Act, above note 86, art 2f.

101 See Donald Galloway, "The Dilemmas of Canadian Citizenship Law" in Douglas B Klusmeyer & Thomas Alexander Aleinikoff, eds, *From Migrants to Citizens: Membership in a Changing World* (Washington: Carnegie Endowment for International Peace, 2000) 82.

102 *Ibid* at 95.

103 1910 Act, above note 86, ss 13–24.

104 *Ibid*, s 39.

of a board of inquiry relating to detention or deportation unless it concerned a "citizen," as defined, or a person with Canadian domicile.[105]

F. THE MODERNIZATION OF IMMIGRATION LAW, 1918–1976

During the period between the wars, immigration policy continued to be shaped by the belief that it should be sensitive to immediate economic needs. At the same time, another aspect of modern immigration law — family sponsorship and the encouragement of family reunification — was developed. Section 3(t) of the 1919 Act[106] explicitly allowed for the admission of those who did not meet literacy requirements if they were related to people already in Canada.

Still, the most significant changes continued to be effected by executive regulation. An order in council in 1923[107] fundamentally altered the direction of immigration law by prohibiting the entry of all immigrants except for six narrowly defined classes. These were "agriculturalists" with sufficient means to begin farming; farm labourers with arranged employment; female domestic servants; wives and children under eighteen of those resident in Canada; citizens of the United States "whose labour is required"; and British subjects with sufficient means for self-maintenance.[108] Thus, Canadian immigration law was transformed from a generally permissive regime, with admittedly broad and undefined exceptions, to an exclusionary regime with narrow and well-defined exceptions.

Later, selection criteria that focused beyond agriculture to the need to attract skilled industrial workers were developed. However, during periods of labour surplus or during periods of economic decline such as the 1930s, the number of immigrants was severely restricted. Moreover, concern about labour strife led to the expansion of the criteria of exclusion and deportation to embrace anarchists, political radicals, and others who were identified as likely to be disruptive within and without the workplace. For example, section 41 of the 1919 Act provided that a person was liable to deportation

> who by common repute belongs to or is suspected of belonging to any secret society or organization which extorts money from or in

---

105 *Ibid.*
106 *An Act to amend The Immigration Act*, SC 1919, c 25.
107 PC 1923-183 (1923) C Gaz II 4106.
108 *Ibid.*

any way attempts to control any resident of Canada by force or by threat of bodily harm, or by blackmail, or who is a member of or affiliated with any organization entertaining or teaching disbelief in or opposition to organized government.[109]

Although these specific measures may now seem like heavy-handed attempts at social control, the legislation and the regulations passed before the Second World War had, in some respects, the same general focus as those of today, with emphasis on domestic economic growth, social stability, control over organized crime, and family reunification. Furthermore, recent amendments aimed at protecting the public from individuals deemed to be dangerous and at curtailing the penetration of international criminal organizations into Canada are framed in similarly broad strokes.[110]

There are, however, two major differences between modern provisions and those of this era. First, racial discrimination against all except northern Europeans continued to receive official sanction. Second, the law did not at this stage distinguish between refugees and immigrants of other types. As Dirks notes: "The reasons for people's departures from their homelands seldom interested officials responsible for processing those who wanted to settle in Canada. Instead, migrants from abroad were looked at for what they had to offer in terms of satisfying labour market needs, supplying capital and know-how for job-creating projects, or simply settling the land."[111]

One can attribute Canada's reluctance to assist Jews escaping from Nazi persecution to the combination of these two factors. Between 1933 and 1945, Canada admitted only 5,000 Jews and only 8,000 more in the three years after the end of the war.[112] Of the millions of people who had been displaced by the war, Canada admitted those who were

---

109 1910 Act, above note 86.

110 See, for example, *IRPA*, above note 1, s 37, which identifies as inadmissible any person who is a member of an organization that is believed on reasonable grounds to be or to have been engaged in activity that is part of a pattern of criminal activity planned and organized by a number of persons acting in concert in furtherance of the commission of an offence punishable under an Act of Parliament.

Section 33 expands the ambit of this section by providing "[t]he facts that constitute inadmissibility under sections 34 to 37 include facts arising from omissions and, unless otherwise provided, include facts for which there are reasonable grounds to believe that they have occurred, are occurring or may occur."

111 Gerald E Dirks, *Controversy and Complexity: Canadian Immigration Policy during the 1980s* (Montreal: McGill-Queen's University Press, 1995) at 61.

112 See Irving Abella & Harold Troper, *None Is Too Many: Canada and the Jews of Europe 1933–1948*, 3d ed (Toronto: Lester, 1991) at xxii.

regarded as easily assimilable. In the postwar years, Canada began to deal with refugee situations by initiating programs that proceeded on a case-by-case basis,[113] by suspending the application of normal immigration rules. But, as James Hathaway points out:

> All of these programs were of limited duration and scope, and as such did not signal a general openness to refugee resettlement. Most important, none of these refugee movements was inconsistent with the underlying economic determinants of Canadian immigration policy as the majority of the refugees were educated and skilled and were thus poised to make a positive contribution to Canada's economic prosperity.[114]

Initially, Canada was not a signatory to the 1951 United Nations *Convention Relating to the Status of Refugees*. As Hathaway documents, this was because "the Department of Citizenship and Immigration was of the view that the Convention was inconsistent with Canadian interests both because its definition [of *refugee*] was conceptually open-ended and because the duty to avoid the return of refugees might inhibit Canada's ability to turn away undesirable immigrants."[115] In 1969, however, Canada did sign the *Convention* as amended by the 1967 Protocol, although it failed to implement a systematic approach to fulfilling its assumed obligations until the enactment of the *Immigration Act, 1976*.[116] The signing of the *Convention* can be seen as the culmination of a series of major shifts in policy implemented in the aftermath of the Second World War. During this period, political leaders began to present Canada as a nation among equals in a global community, an image inconsistent with officially sanctioned racism and with a failure to endorse international moral norms.

In 1947, Canada had abandoned "the vestiges of colonial status"[117] by enacting the *Canadian Citizenship Act*. When introducing it in Parliament, Secretary of State Paul Martin stated, "It is a discreditable position in which we find ourselves as a nation among nations of the world

---

113 As is documented in Dirks, above note 111, 300,000 refugees, most of whom were Europeans, benefited as a result of these programs in the thirty years following the war.

114 James C Hathaway, "The Conundrum of Refugee Protection in Canada: From Control to Compliance to Collective Deterrence" in Gil Loescher, ed, *Refugees and the Asylum Dilemma in the West* (University Park, PA: Pennsylvania State University Press, 1992) 71.

115 *Ibid* at 73.

116 *Immigration Act, 1976*, SC 1976-77, c 52 [1976 Act].

117 Galloway, above note 101.

[today] not to be able clearly to address one another with the full sanction of the law and for all purposes as citizens of our own country."[118] He added, "Under this bill we are seeking to establish clearly a basic and definite Canadian citizenship which will be the fundamental status upon which the rights and privileges of Canadians will depend."[119]

However, the sincerity of these aspirations was somewhat diluted by the fact that simultaneously the Canadian government was engaged in a concerted effort it had initiated during the war to pressure Japanese Canadians — many of whom were born in Canada — to "repatriate" to Japan.[120] The government fought successfully against challenges to the legality of the orders in council that authorized this program, seemingly oblivious to the irony of doing so while promoting a conception of citizens as equal members in the political community.[121] It rescinded the measures imposed on Japanese Canadians only gradually and under overwhelming political opposition.[122] By revealing that the status of citizenship may not be able to meet the promises and aspirations associated with it, this episode is important to keep in mind particularly at a time when the value of citizenship is cited by the government as a reason for imposing a rigorous test on those who would obtain the status and as a reason for permitting it to revoke the status from some individuals.

In the postwar era, a period of liberalization ensued. In 1962, regulations that removed race as a criterion of selection, except in cases of family sponsorship, were enacted. Instead, the individual skills and education of the applicant were stressed. In 1967, immigration selection was greatly systematized through the development of the "points system," which aimed to add precision and definition to the process of assessing an applicant's desirability.[123] Only at this time were the discriminatory criteria for family sponsorship removed.[124] In the same

---

118 *House of Commons Debates*, 20th Parl, 2nd Sess, No 249 (2 April 1946) at 502 (Hon Paul Martin Senior).

119 *Ibid.*

120 Orders in Council PC 1945-7355, PC 1945-7356, and PC 1945-7357.

121 See *Co-operative Committee on Japanese Canadians v Attorney General of Canada*, [1946] UKPC 48.

122 See Patricia E Roy, *The Triumph of Citizenship: The Japanese and Chinese in Canada 1941–1967* (Vancouver: UBC Press, 2007) ch 5.

123 Citizenship and Immigration Canada, *Forging Our Legacy: Canadian Citizenship and Immigration, 1900–1977* (1 July 2006), Government of Canada, online: CIC www.cic.gc.ca/english/resources/publications/legacy/chap-6.asp#chap6-5 [CIC, *Forging Our Legacy*].

124 Although as documented by Wydrzynski, "the Assisted Passage Scheme, by which prospective immigrants could obtain interest-free loans from the Canadian government to assist them in financing their journey to Canada, was not

year, the Immigration Appeal Board was established in an effort to curtail abuses of discretionary power within the immigration bureaucracy.[125] During this period one also began to see the judicial development of principles of administrative law as a device to promote the rule of law, even in fields defined by broad discretionary powers.[126]

However, the 1967 *Immigration Regulations* created a process that did not operate smoothly. As Wydrzynski points out:

> Prospective immigrants, with little chance of acquiring the necessary points under the Norms for Assessment outside of Canada, would simply enter Canada as visitors and make such an application within the country, where a right of appeal from a rejection to the Immigration Appeal Board was virtually assured. In a matter of a few short years, the backlog of appeals to the Immigration Appeal Board was approaching the twenty thousand mark. Thus, even rejected applicants could not be forced to leave the country until their appeals had been finalized, a process which could take years.[127]

With larger numbers of people arriving in Canada, and with the development of this huge backlog of cases, there was created the impression that the government had lost control of the country's borders. In 1973, a review of immigration policy and practice was announced, a task force was established, and in the following year a green paper on immigration policy was published.[128] Subsequently, a Special Joint Committee of the Senate and the House of Commons on Immigration Policy reported to Parliament and recommended major changes in immigration law and policy, including the following:

1) Canada should continue to be a country of immigration for demographic, economic, family, and humanitarian reasons.

2) A new Immigration Act should contain a clear statement of principles and objectives including those pertaining to admission, non-discrimination, sponsorship of relatives, refugees, and the prohibition of certain classes of immigrants. Operational details and procedures should be specified in regulations.

3) The principle of non-discrimination in immigration on the basis of race, creed, nationality, ethnic origin, and sex should be

available to Asians until 1970." See CJ Wydrzynski, *Canadian Immigration Law and Procedure* (Aurora: Canada Law Book, 1983) at 56.

125 CIC, *Forging Our Legacy*, above note 123.

126 The classic case in Canada was *Roncarelli v Duplessis*, [1959] SCR 121.

127 Wydrzynski, above note 124 at 61.

128 Canada, Special Joint Committee of the Senate and the House of Commons, *Green Paper on Immigration Policy* (Ottawa: Queen's Printer, 1975).

continued and should be formally set out in the new Immigration Act.

4) A clear statement of Canada's refugee policy should now be made.[129]

In 1976 a new *Immigration Act*, which adopted many of the committee's recommendations, was introduced into Parliament. The first new statute since 1952,[130] it was proclaimed as law in 1978. Although it was significantly amended in later years, this Act endured until the *Immigration and Refugee Protection Act* (the *IRPA*) came into force in 2002.[131] Nevertheless, the problem of substantial backlogs has not been resolved. Many of the legislative and regulatory changes introduced by the government in recent years have been rationalized by reference to the need to gain control over the inventory of applications. The problem continues to infiltrate all aspects of immigration decision making as is witnessed by the inordinate delays experienced by refugee claimants, sponsored members of the family class, permanent residents seeking citizenship, live-in caregivers seeking residence, and members of the economic classes.

The shape of modern immigration law was solidified during the last quarter of the twentieth century. The positive economic and social benefits of immigration were touted by succeeding governments. New business immigration classes of immigrants were identified, members of whom gained status by investing money or establishing a business in Canada. The number of immigrants who acquired permanent residence wavered in the early 1980s, falling below 100,000 persons per annum, but then gradually increased. Since the 1990s well over 200,000 persons have been selected each year.[132] Asian Pacific countries became leading source countries, with China, Hong Kong, and India leading the way in the mid-1990s.[133] The *Immigration Act* established the Immigration and Refugee Board (IRB), a tribunal with three different divisions, each with its own function — determining inadmissibility, hearing appeals,

---

129 Cited in Hawkins, above note 79 at 60.
130 1976 Act, above note 116.
131 *IRPA*, above note 1.
132 Citizenship and Immigration Canada, "Immigration Overview: Permanent and Temporary Residents" (8 September 2011), online: CIC www.cic.gc.ca/English/resources/statistics/facts2010/permanent/index.asp.
133 AE Challinor, "Canada's Immigration Policy: A Focus on Human Capital" *Migration Information Source* (15 September 2011), online: Migration Policy Institute www.migrationpolicy.org/article/canadas-immigration-policy-focus-human-capital.

and deciding refugee claims.[134] With the entrenchment of the *Charter of Rights*, the judiciary began to play a central role in the immigration field, determining in an early case, *Singh*, that non-citizens were the bearers of some constitutional rights and, in particular, were entitled not to be deprived of their right to life, liberty, and security of the person except in accordance with the principles of fundamental justice.[135] In the case of a refugee claimant, this necessitated an oral hearing in which the credibility of the claim could be properly assessed.[136] Nevertheless, the courts also hesitated to apply the *Charter* expansively to address all the vulnerabilities experienced by non-citizens, preferring to give a free hand to the executive to determine who should be permitted to enter and remain in the country. In particular, it was determined that a deportation order by itself does not engage the rights to life, liberty, and security of the person.[137] At the same time, the judiciary expanded their scrutiny of administrative processes by identifying and delineating principles of procedural fairness that should be read into statutory grants of power and by applying them quite rigorously to immigration officers and members of the IRB.[138]

In sum, immigration law in Canada began to exhibit the influence of political values pulling in opposite directions. The liberalization tendency revealed itself in the increased numbers and the concern with fair and open procedures. However, the government also reacted in a more draconian fashion when faced with incidents that sparked public anxiety and anger, such as the arrival of boats carrying refugee claimants or the commission of violent crimes by individuals who had been ordered deported.

G. IMMIGRATION LAW IN THE TWENTY-FIRST CENTURY

Against this background, the list of innovations that we have witnessed in the last fifteen years begins to look less anomalous. Indeed, many of the justifications underlying the changes seem to have been borrowed from an earlier era.

---

134 1976 Act, above note 116, s 57.
135 *Singh*, above note 17.
136 *Ibid* at para 108.
137 *Ibid*; see also *Medovarski*, above note 2 at para 46.
138 *Singh*, above note 17 at paras 103–4.

Like its predecessor, the *Immigration and Refugee Protection Act* was introduced as "framework legislation" offering a skeleton of broad principles with the intention that the details would be specified in the accompanying regulations.[139] This was intended to allow for needed flexibility in times of economic volatility, but once again offered opportunity for discretionary decision making unconstrained by law.

When drafting the *IRPA*, the government resisted pressure to enact two statutes, one dealing with immigration and the other dealing with refugee protection. It did, however, incorporate two separate lists of objectives for each within the same Act.

The *IRPA* aimed initially to address the new economic realities by substantially modifying the points system, placing emphasis on educational credentials and adaptability rather than seeking to fill perceived gaps in the labour market.[140] The attempt was not successful as numerous highly educated immigrants discovered on arrival that they were overqualified for available work.[141] Within a few years the newly formed government began to alter the legislative blueprint and reshape the selection process.

The federal minister of Citizenship and Immigration has been authorized to issue ministerial instructions that focus on minutiae and has used the power to identify specific occupations where employment is scarce. Within a few years, the aspiration of the *IRPA* to select "the best and the brightest" as part of a nation-building model of immigration had been replaced by a model of immigration familiar to earlier generations in which immigration officials have taken on the task of filling employment gaps.[142] Looking forward, we see the promise of the government further privileging the economic objectives of immigration by offering private employers a more prominent role in the selection of immigrants and venture capitalists having the opportunity to greenlight the admission of entrepreneurs by supporting their businesses.

Alongside these developments in selection, we have witnessed other changes that can be attributed to the fact that the drafting and enactment of the *IRPA* coincided closely with the violent attacks of 11 September 2001 in the United States. These attacks prompted a series of

139 Canadian Bar Association, National Citizenship and Immigration Law Section, "Immigration and Refugee Protection Regulations: Issue Papers" (March 2002), online: www.cba.org/cba/submissions/pdf/02-03-2-eng.pdf at 1.

140 *Regulations Amending the Immigration and Refugee Protection Regulations*, PC 2012-1643 (2012) C Gaz II 2885.

141 See Li Xu, *Who Drives a Taxi in Canada?* (Ottawa: Citizenship and Immigration Canada, 2012), online: www.cic.gc.ca/English/resources/research/taxi/index.asp.

142 See Chapter 4.

new measures aimed at increasing security within Canada and North America generally. The Smart Border agreement with the United States introduced many joint efforts aimed at increasing the intensity of immigration screening.[143] It also afforded the Canadian government the opportunity to press for a measure that it had long sought to implement, a Safe Third Country agreement with the United States that would permit it to refuse to hear refugee claims from individuals who had arrived in the country directly from the United States, thereby reducing significantly the workload of the Immigration and Refugee Board.[144]

The administration of the law has also been modified. In 2003, the Canada Border Services Agency (CBSA) was established.[145] Until this point, Citizenship and Immigration Canada (CIC) was the administrative body that had full authority to administer immigration policy. The new agency was given full charge over all enforcement aspects of the regime, including port-of-entry decision making.[146] The reasons for division of functions were explained by the government as follows:

> The Government of Canada's decision to group similar activities under each of the two departments has been made with the best interests of Canadians in mind. It is based on the dual intent of facilitating the entry of people and goods to Canada, while ensuring stringent control of our borders and the safety and security of Canadians. Stakeholders agree that the way the immigration program is administered at ports of entry is more important than where responsibility for the program lies. The transfers allow CIC to focus on citizenship, selection, settlement and integration of immigrants while also offering Canada's protection to those in need. CIC will continue to issue visas and develop admissibility policies for immigrants, refugees and temporary residents.[147]

The division of functions has received extensive criticism. On the one hand, placing enforcement in the hands of decision makers who have no familiarity with the positive reasons for admitting individuals

---

143 A description of cooperative steps on border control taken by the US and Canada may be found in "Canada's Economic Action Plan," online: http://actionplan.gc.ca/en/page/bbg-tpf/canada-us-border-cooperation.

144 Canada Border Services Agency, "Canada-U.S. Safe Third Country Agreement" (23 July 2009), online: CBSA www.cbsa-asfc.gc.ca/agency-agence/stca-etps-eng.html.

145 Order in Council, PC 2003-2064 (2003) C Gaz II 3232.

146 Ibid.

147 Canada Border Services Agency, News Release, "Government of Canada Announces Transfer of Certain Functions between Citizenship and Immigration Canada and the Canada Border Services Agency" (12 October 2014).

has been regarded as a recipe for excessive emphasis on control. "Basic training of CBSA officers is nine weeks long but heavily focused on customs matters rather than immigration. In-depth investigation training — interview skills, document analysis, and intelligence debriefings — exists in short supply."[148] On the other hand, the CBSA has also been criticized for lack of experience with other security branches: "Immigration intelligence and enforcement is also undermined by a lack of training, equipment and exposure to the work of other security agencies."[149]

In addition, the Immigration and Refugee Board, the independent tribunal established under former legislation, was also altered by the *IRPA*. The Act has reshaped the refugee determination process in a number of ways but most significantly by authorizing single-member panels to determine refugee claims.[150] Recognizing that this could increase the potential for error, the Act also instituted a Refugee Appeal Division.[151] However, the sections of the Act creating this body were not brought into force until 2013, thereby ensuring that, for all intents and purposes, the fate of refugee claimants was for over a decade in the hands of a single individual. The eventual establishment of Refugee Appeal Division was not a particularly auspicious event. The statutory language defining the nature of the appeal was not noticeably clear, thus leading to a court challenge about the very basis of authority of the newly created body.[152]

As noted at the beginning of this chapter, the government has modified the operation of the *IRPA* in significant ways. Many of the liberal advances introduced during the previous decades have been reduced or halted. Enforcement measures have been entrenched and bolstered. Perhaps the most visible changes have related to refugee determination. The government has promoted strongly the idea that it is possible for the minister to determine whether a refugee claim is likely to be fraudulent prior to an individual claim being heard by the Immigration and Refugee Board. The need to attend to procedural niceties in cases where such a determination has been made is now identified as less pressing. As a consequence, a two-tier process of refugee determination has been established where those claims determined by the minister to be less likely to be genuine and well founded are dealt with

---

148 Arne Kislenko, "Guarding the Border: Intelligence and Law Enforcement in Canada's Immigration System" in Loch K Johnson, ed, *The Oxford Handbook of National Security Intelligence* (Toronto: Oxford University Press, 2010) 310 at 317.

149 *Ibid.*

150 *IRPA*, above note 1, s 163.

151 *Ibid*, s 110.

152 *Huruglica v Canada (Minister of Citizenship and Immigration)*, 2014 FC 799.

more expeditiously, with less opportunity being offered to the claimant to make a case. Whether such ministerial intervention is consistent with the principles of fundamental due process that the judiciary has developed and identified as being central to our constitutional law is highly controversial. In the near future, we are likely to witness a substantial number of challenges to executive action in the courts.[153] Should the liberalizing tendencies of the last decades of the twentieth century be interpreted as basic requirements of our legal system, and should they be identified as sufficiently resilient to resist the political aims of the executive branch of the government, we will see the spiral of history turn once more.

---

153 See *Canadian Doctors for Refugee Care v Canada (AG)*, 2014 FC 651.

CHAPTER 2

SOURCES OF IMMIGRATION LAW

This chapter identifies the legal sources that circumscribe the boundaries of authority of officials within the immigration system, empowering them to act in particular ways while constraining them from stepping in other directions.

A. THE *CONSTITUTION ACT, 1867*[1]

1) Section 95: Concurrent Powers over Immigration

As noted in Chapter 1, section 95 of the *Constitution Act, 1867*, gives concurrent powers over immigration to the Parliament of Canada and to the provincial legislatures. The section also provides that "any Law of the Legislature of a Province relative to . . . Immigration shall have effect in and for the Province as long and as far only as it is not repugnant to any Act of the Parliament of Canada." The task of determining whether there is repugnancy has proven to be difficult, and at different periods, the courts have adopted different approaches.

In an early case, *Re Nakane*,[2] Irving J offered this analysis: "It is not possible that there can be two legislative bodies having equal jurisdiction in this matter, and where the Dominion Parliament has entered

---

1 (UK), 30 & 31 Vict, c 3, reprinted in RSC 1985, Appendix II, No 5.
2 (1908), 13 BCR 370 (CA).

the field of legislation, they occupy it to the exclusion of Provincial legislation."[3] This approach, commonly called the "covering the field" test of repugnancy, was also developed in another British Columbia case of the same year, *Re Narain Singh*,[4] in which an attempt by the provincial legislature to impose a literacy test on immigrants was held to be of no effect, since Parliament had passed "a complete code as to what class or classes of immigrants shall be admitted or excluded."[5]

There is widespread agreement among authorities that this test is obsolete. In its most recent analysis, the Supreme Court of Canada has analyzed the idea of repugnancy in terms of "operational conflict" and "frustration of purpose." It has articulated the doctrine of federal paramountcy in the following terms:

> Paramountcy is engaged where there is a conflict between valid provincial and federal law. In such cases, the federal law prevails, and the provincial law is rendered inoperative to the extent of the conflict. Conflict can be established by impossibility of dual compliance or by frustration of a federal purpose: *Canadian Western Bank*, at para. 73.
>
> . . .
>
> Even where it is possible to simultaneously comply with both federal and provincial laws, situations will arise where requiring compliance with a provincial law will frustrate the purpose of a federal law.[6]

Thus, a provincial immigration law enacted under section 95 would be repugnant to a federal statute only where it is impossible to comply with both or where the aims of the latter are frustrated by it. Given the lengthy list of objectives found in the *Immigration and Refugee Protection Act* (the *IRPA*), many of which pull in different directions, it is difficult to frame a conception of what could count as frustration in this context.

2) Section 91(25): Naturalization and Aliens

The doctrine of paramountcy has also been discussed in relation to section 91(25) of the *Constitution Act* which vests jurisdiction over naturalization and aliens in the federal Parliament. The limits of this head of power are somewhat unclear, and caselaw has not provided

---

3   *Ibid* at 375.
4   (1908), 13 BCR 477 (CA).
5   *Ibid* at 480.
6   *Bank of Montreal v Marcotte*, 2014 SCC 55 at paras 70–71.

lucid direction. Without doubt, this is the source of Parliament's power to make laws that specify the processes by which non-citizens may become citizens; however, it is much less clear whether Parliament's authority over citizenship in general can be traced to this section.[7]

The most important cases that have analyzed this section have focused on the question whether provincial acts that place differential burdens on aliens are constitutional.[8] When determining whether legislation fits under a specific heading, such as "Naturalization and Aliens," courts first attempt to identify the pith and substance of the legislation.[9] Only the federal legislature has the authority to enact a statute that has, as its pith and substance, a subject matter identified in section 91.[10] Moreover, a provincial act which, in pith and substance, relates to a subject matter that the Constitution has assigned to the provincial legislatures may be valid, even if, as an incidental effect, it touches on a federal subject matter.[11]

The determination whether an act relates in pith and substance to naturalization and aliens has proven difficult. In *Cunningham v Homma*,[12] provincial legislation that prohibited Japanese residents of British Columbia from voting in provincial elections was held to be *intra vires*, on the ground that it related to race rather than alienage. In

---

7   In *Morgan v Prince Edward Island (AG)*, [1976] 2 SCR 349 at 355–56 [*Morgan*], Laskin CJ suggested that authority over citizenship may have its source in s 91(25) or in the Peace, Order, and Good Government clause in the Preamble to s 91.

8   See *Union Colliery Co of British Columbia Ltd v Bryden*, [1899] AC 580 (PC); *Cunningham v Homma*, [1903] AC 151 (PC) [*Homma*]; *Dickenson v Law Society (Alberta)* (1978), 10 AR 120 (SCTD) [*Dickenson*]; *Redlin v University of Alberta* (1980), 23 AR 31 (CA) [*Redlin*].

9   See Peter Hogg, *Constitutional Law of Canada*, 5th ed (Toronto: Carswell, 1997) (loose-leaf updated July 2014) at 15-7.

10   However, under the "double aspect" doctrine, a province may enact a statute that relates to these matters if it also relates to another subject matter within provincial jurisdiction. See *ibid* at 15-12.

11   See *ibid* at 15-9. The matter is somewhat more complex than this statement suggests since, in some cases, the courts will apply the doctrine of interjurisdictional immunity to create a realm of exclusive federal jurisdiction into which provincial legislation cannot encroach. According to this doctrine, a valid provincial law will be held to have a limited applicability — with those matters that fall within the area of federal jurisdiction lying beyond the limits. Thus, this is a doctrine about the *applicability* of a law rather than a doctrine about the *validity* of a law. It has not been applied in cases dealing with alienage or naturalization. See Hogg, *ibid* at 15-28.

12   *Homma*, above note 8.

many subsequent cases, provincial legislation that applied to aliens but also to others was held to be valid on the ground that it did not relate in pith and substance to alienage. For example, in *Morgan*,[13] legislation that prevented non-residents of a province from acquiring real property was held not to relate to alienage, since non-resident citizens were also covered.

In *Homma*, Lord Halsbury conceded that section 91(25) reserved the subject matters of alienage and naturalization for the exclusive jurisdiction of Parliament, but claimed that it did not aim "to deal with the consequences of either alienage or naturalization."[14] He identified it as an "absurdity" to suggest that the province could not exclude an alien from the franchise in that province.[15] The implication of this view is that section 91(25) merely empowers the federal Parliament to define the statuses and does not provide the authority to Parliament to attach burdens and privileges to them. Any consequences that are to attach to the status must be fitted under another head of legislation.

The major problem with this view is that one of the established ways of defining a status is by specifying the rights and obligations that attach to those who belong to it. If one accepts this objection, one will accept also that some rights and obligations are a necessary, defining aspect of the status while others are not. Extrapolating from this position, provinces would not be prevented from attaching or removing privileges from aliens or naturalized citizens, so long as such action is not seen as *redefining* the status. This alternative view would mean that the status of being naturalized, for example, carries with it a package of rights and that legislation which, in pith and substance, aims to alter these rights can be enacted only by the federal legislature. However, other non-essential privileges could be granted to or withdrawn from naturalized subjects by the provincial legislatures so long as the legislation does not aim to restrict the essential rights. This latter view is endorsed by the Supreme Court of Canada in *SMT (Eastern) Ltd v Winner*, where Rand J distinguished the "incidents of status" from "the attributes necessarily involved in [the] status itself."[16] In subsequent cases, where constitutional challenges were made on a provincial scheme that permitted only citizens and British subjects to be eligible for membership in the provincial law society, and on a provincial scheme that imposed higher fees on foreign students, both failed.[17] In each case, the

---

13   *Morgan*, above note 7.
14   *Homma*, above note 8 at 156.
15   *Ibid.*
16   [1951] SCR 887 at 919.
17   See *Dickenson*, above note 8, and *Redlin*, above note 8.

pith and substance test was applied, and it was held that the statutes did not fall under the heading "Naturalization and Aliens," because privileges essential to the relevant statutes were not at stake. The most problematic aspect of this approach is that of identifying which are the essential rights that adhere to the status and which are mere ancillary consequences. One cannot find in the caselaw precise criteria on which courts can rely to resolve this issue.

After the pith and substance hurdle has been overcome, the paramountcy issue must still be addressed to determine whether there is an operational conflict between provincial and federal laws or whether compliance with a provincial statute will frustrate the purpose of federal legislation. The Supreme Court of Canada considered such a situation in *Law Society of British Columbia v Mangat*.[18] In this case, the federal statute, the *Immigration Act, 1976*,[19] permitted immigration consultants who were not lawyers to represent individuals for a fee before the Immigration and Refugee Board. The aim of this measure was identified as the promotion of informal, accessible, and expeditious decision making. The relevant provincial statute, the *Legal Professions Act*, granted exclusive authority to practise law to members of the provincial law society. The Court found that the issue of representation of non-citizens before a tribunal had a "double aspect" and fell within both federal jurisdiction over naturalization and aliens, on the one hand, and provincial jurisdiction over property and civil rights on the other. Justice Gonthier addressed the issue of paramountcy and identified that the two statutory regimes were in conflict and that the provincial law frustrated the purpose of the federal legislation. He stated:

> In this case, there is an operational conflict as the provincial legislation prohibits non-lawyers to appear for a fee before a tribunal but the federal legislation authorizes non-lawyers to appear as counsel for a fee. At a superficial level, a person who seeks to comply with both enactments can succeed either by becoming a member in good standing of the Law Society of British Columbia or by not charging a fee. Complying with the stricter statute necessarily involves complying with the other statute. However, . . . dual compliance is impossible. To require "other counsel" to be a member in good standing of the bar of the province or to refuse the payment of a fee would go contrary to Parliament's purpose in enacting ss. 30 and 69(1) of the *Immigration Act*. In those provisions, Parliament provided that aliens could be represented by non-lawyers acting for a fee, and in

---

18   2001 SCC 67 [*Mangat*].
19   SC 1976-77, c 52.

this respect it was pursuing the legitimate objective of establishing an informal, accessible (in financial, cultural, and linguistic terms), and expeditious process, peculiar to administrative tribunals. Where there is an enabling federal law, the provincial law cannot be contrary to Parliament's purpose. Finally, it would be impossible for a judge or an official of the IRB to comply with both acts.[20]

3) The *Canadian Charter of Rights and Freedoms*[21]

In 1982, the Canadian Constitution was redesigned to include the *Canadian Charter of Rights and Freedoms*, which identifies and guarantees a set of fundamental rights. In one sense, the impact of the *Charter* on the practice of immigration law has been quite significant. There is now a legal requirement that every Act introduced in the House of Commons be examined for *Charter* compliance.[22] In addition, a

---

20   *Mangat*, above note 18 at para 72. Since the decision in *Mangat*, Parliament and the federal Cabinet have further regulated the ability of consultants to represent non-citizens before the Immigration and Refugee Board. In 2011, Parliament amended the *IRPA* by enacting the *Cracking Down on Crooked Consultants Act*, SC 2011, c 8, which created the offence, found in section 91(1) of the *IRPA*, of knowingly, directly or indirectly, representing or advising a person for consideration unless authorized. In addition, under regulations introduced in 2011, an immigration consultant is required to gain accreditation as a Regulated Canadian Immigration Consultant, subject to the authority of the Immigration Consultants of Canada Regulatory Council. The purpose of the regulations is "to better protect applicants to immigration processes and enhance public confidence in the immigration system by recognizing a regulator of immigration consultants that has demonstrated that it meets the necessary organizational competencies to effectively regulate immigration consultants."

    See *Regulations Designating a Body for the Purposes of Paragraph 91(2)(c) of the Immigration and Refugee Protection Act*, SOR/2011-142. The Regulatory Impact Analysis Statement is available, online: www.gazette.gc.ca/rp-pr/p2/2011/2011-07-20/html/sor-dors142-eng.html.

21   Part I of the *Constitution Act, 1982*, being Schedule B to the *Canada Act 1982* (UK), 1982, c 11 [*Charter*].

22   Section 3 of the *Canadian Charter of Rights and Freedoms Examination Regulations*, SOR/85-781, provides:

      3. In the case of every Bill introduced in or presented to the House of Commons by a Minister of the Crown, the Minister shall, forthwith on receipt of two copies of the Bill from the Clerk of the House of Commons,

         (a) examine the Bill in order to determine whether any of the provisions thereof are inconsistent with the purposes and provisions of the *Canadian Charter of Rights and Freedoms*, and

         (b) cause to be affixed to each of the copies thereof so received from the Clerk of the House of Commons a certificate, in a form approved by the Minister and signed by the Deputy Minister of Justice, stating that

number of legal challenges on behalf of those who have been subject to negative decisions from officials in the immigration system have been founded on *Charter* grounds.[23]

Immigration lawyers have come to recognize the *Charter* as an important source for argument. However, overall, in immigration law, unlike other areas of law such as criminal law, *Charter* challenges have not met with much success. With some notable exceptions, the courts have shown a marked reluctance to scrutinize, critique, and reshape the policies of the federal government in this area of decision making. After an early decision, *Singh v Canada (Minister of Employment and Immigration),*[24] that required the restructuring of the refugee determination process, the courts have, in general, settled into a pattern of decision making characterized by a rather narrow and restrictive approach to the rights of immigrants and refugee claimants. Leading cases and specific sections of the *Charter* are examined in Chapter 17.

B. THE *IMMIGRATION AND REFUGEE PROTECTION ACT* (THE *IRPA*)[25]

1) The General Structure of the Act

The *Immigration and Refugee Protection Act* (IRPA) is the primary source of immigration law in Canada, identifying the various decision makers and delimiting their powers. The body of the Act is divided into five parts, preceded by ten introductory sections.

The introductory sections address preliminary matters, providing the short title, definitions of terms found in the statute, and lists of the Act's objectives. They also identify which government ministers have authority to administer the Act. As a default, general administrative authority is vested in the minister of Citizenship and Immigration.[26] However, specific provision is made to place the minister of Public

---

the Bill has been examined as required by section 4.1 of the *Department of Justice Act,*

and one each of the copies thereof so certified shall thereupon be transmitted to the Clerk of the House of Commons and the Clerk of the Privy Council.

There is also a similar requirement for regulations.

23   See Chapter 17.
24   [1985] 1 SCR 177.
25   *Immigration and Refugee Protection Act,* SC 2001 c 27 [*IRPA*].
26   *Ibid,* s 4(1).

Safety and Emergency Preparedness in charge of enforcement and other matters.[27] Provision is also made for the minister of Employment and Social Development to be allocated powers by regulation.[28]

Section 6 allows for a delegation of powers from the minister of Citizenship and Immigration to designated officials. It also specifies that certain powers cannot be delegated. The powers that have been delegated by the current minister of Citizenship and Immigration are identified in an Instrument of Designation and Delegation, which is included in the published operational manuals.[29]

Sections 7 to 9 of the *IRPA* grant two other important powers to the minister: (1) the power to enter agreements with the governments of foreign states or with international organizations, and (2) the power to enter into an agreement with provincial governments. However, in each case, the minister is required to obtain the approval of the federal Cabinet. Section 10 requires the minister to consult with provincial governments on "the number of foreign nationals in each class who will become permanent residents each year, their distribution in Canada taking into account regional economic and demographic requirements, and the measures to be undertaken to facilitate their integration into Canadian society."

Parts 1 and 2 of the *IRPA*, each of which is organized into several divisions, contain the bulk of the statute's provisions. Titled "Immigration to Canada" and "Refugee Protection," these parts outline the administrative processes and controls to be followed by officials within the relevant government departments — Citizenship and Immigration Canada (CIC), under the direction of the minister of Citizenship and Immigration, and the Canada Border Services Agency (CBSA), under the direction of the minister of Public Safety and Emergency Preparedness. The powers granted to officials relate to such matters as issuing visas and permits, granting status, permitting entry into the country, determining eligibility to make a refugee claim, addressing detention and release, and determining inadmissibility and removal. Within each division of each of these parts, one finds a provision authorizing the Governor in Council (that is to say, the federal Cabinet) to make regulations governing the matters dealt with therein. What is more, sections 14.1 and 87.3 of the *IRPA* authorize the minister of Citizenship and Immigration to issue "instructions" establishing classes of economic immigrants and providing for the disposition of applications. Additional

27 *Ibid*, s 4(2).
28 *Ibid*, s 4(2.1).
29 See Citizenship and Immigration Canada, Operational Manuals — Legislation (IL), online: www.cic.gc.ca/english/resources/manuals/il/il03-menu.asp.

power is transferred to the minister of Citizenship and Immigration to issue orders, designating foreign nationals for special treatment as a result of their mode of arrival[30] and designating countries of origin as safe.[31] The powers to make regulations and to issue instructions and orders are outlined and discussed below.

Part 1 of the *IRPA* also establishes the role to be played by the Federal Court in reviewing any decision made under the Act but limits access to the court by providing that an individual does not have access as of right; one must seek leave from the court to apply for judicial review.[32] In addition, section 94 of the *IRPA* requires the minister of Citizenship and Immigration to submit an annual report to Parliament with required content.[33]

Part 3 of the *IRPA*, titled "Enforcement," contains provisions that define offences relating to immigration, including human smuggling, human trafficking, passport offences, misrepresentation, acceptance of a bribe when one is a government officer, and a general offence of "contravening a provision of this Act for which a penalty is not specifically provided."[34] Other sections in Part 3 outline the penalties available, specify the procedures for prosecution, and establish that enforcement

---

30   *IRPA*, above note 25, s 20.1.

31   *Ibid*, s 109.1.

32   See Chapter 16.

33   *IRPA*, above note 25, s 94 (2), which provides:

The report shall include a description of

(*a*) the instructions given under section 87.3 and other activities and initiatives taken concerning the selection of foreign nationals, including measures taken in cooperation with the provinces;

(*b*) in respect of Canada, the number of foreign nationals who became permanent residents, and the number projected to become permanent residents in the following year;

(*b.1*) in respect of Canada, the linguistic profile of foreign nationals who became permanent residents;

(*c*) in respect of each province that has entered into a federal-provincial agreement described in subsection 9(1), the number, for each class listed in the agreement, of persons that became permanent residents and that the province projects will become permanent residents there in the following year;

(*d*) the number of temporary resident permits issued under section 24, categorized according to grounds of inadmissibility, if any;

(*e*) the number of persons granted permanent resident status under each of subsections 25(1), 25.1(1) and 25.2(1);

(*e.1*) any instructions given under subsection 30(1.2), (1.41) or (1.43) during the year in question and the date of their publication; and

(*f*) a gender-based analysis of the impact of this Act.

34   *IRPA, ibid*, s 124(1)(a).

officers have the authority and powers of police officers, including those listed in the *Criminal Code*.[35] Section 139 is a particularly important provision since it provides officers with a broad power to search individuals coming into Canada.[36]

Part 4 of the *IRPA* establishes the Immigration and Refugee Board (IRB), an independent tribunal composed of four divisions:

1) the Immigration Division (ID) with the jurisdiction to conduct admissibility hearings, and reviews of detention;
2) the Immigration Appeal Division (IAD) with jurisdiction to hear appeals from sponsors of members of the family class from some individuals whose removal from Canada has been ordered and from the minister;
3) the Refugee Protection Division (RPD) with authority to determine whether an individual is entitled to Canada's protection under section 96 or section 97 of the *IRPA*, but is not excluded by section 98; and
4) the Refugee Appeal Division (RAD), which has the authority to consider appeals by some individuals whose claim for protection has been rejected by the Refugee Protection Division.

The duties and powers of the chairperson of the Immigration and Refugee Board are specified. They include the authority to make rules "respecting the activities, practice and procedure of each of the Divisions of the Board."[37] The exercise of this authority is subject to approval from the federal Cabinet. The minister of Citizenship and Immigration is required to lay rules before each House of Parliament after the Cabinet has given approval.

In addition, the chairperson may "issue guidelines in writing to members of the Board and identify decisions of the Board as jurisprudential guides, after consulting with the Deputy Chairpersons, to assist members in carrying out their duties."[38] Acting under this provision,

---

35 *Ibid*, s 138(1).
36 *Ibid*, s 139, which reads:

> 139(1) An officer may search any person seeking to come into Canada and may search their luggage and personal effects and the means of transportation that conveyed the person to Canada if the officer believes on reasonable grounds that the person
>
> (a) has not revealed their identity or has hidden on or about their person documents that are relevant to their admissibility; or
> (b) has committed, or possesses documents that may be used in the commission of, an offence referred to in section 117, (human smuggling) 118 (human trafficking) or 122 (passport offences).

37 *Ibid*, s 161(1)(a.2).
38 *Ibid*, s. 159(1)(h).

the chairperson has issued a number of guidelines, most prominent among which are the *Women Refugee Claimants Fearing Gender-Related Persecution*.[39] The legal status of these guidelines is discussed in Section J, below in this chapter.

Part 5 of the *IRPA* deals with provisions that were in effect during the transitional period as the *IRPA* came into force. It also identifies the amendments that were made to other statutes when the *IRPA* came into force to accommodate the new laws.

2) The Objectives of the *IRPA*

As identified above, the *IRPA* contains a section that specifies its objectives. In actuality, section 3 contains two lists: (1) the objectives relating to immigration and (2) the objectives with respect to refugees. It is noteworthy that within the list of objectives relating to immigration, one finds that it is an aim of the Act to "promote international justice and security by fostering respect for human rights and by denying access to Canadian territory to persons who are criminals or security risks." On the other hand, in relation to refugees, no mention is made of human rights. The equivalent provision identifies that it is an aim "to promote international justice and security by denying access to Canadian territory to persons, including refugee claimants, who are security risks or serious criminals." One may ask whether the omission of reference to human rights is an indicator that the legislature conceives that refugee law should not be a subset of international human rights law. As is outlined in Chapter 9, there is a tension between conflicting analyses of the basic principles of refugee law, and this omission may be used to build the case that the legislation has tried to resolve the conflict by adopting a decisive stance. However, the omission may also be an oversight. To justify this view one may turn to section 3 of the *IRPA*, which contains a subsection on the proper construction of the Act. Among the instructions included therein is the requirement that the Act be construed and applied in a manner that "complies with international human rights instruments to which Canada is signatory."

This requirement, found in section 3(3)(f), has proven to be difficult to interpret. In *de Guzman v Canada (Minister of Citizenship and Immigration)*, Evans JA made the point that the interpretive weight to be accorded to an international instrument should be dependent on whether or not it is binding and noted that some instruments to which

---

39   Immigration and Refugee Board of Canada, *Women Refugee Claimants Fearing Gender-Related Persecution: Guidelines issued by the Chairperson pursuant to Section 65(3) of the Immigration Act* (13 November 1996), online: IRB www.irb-cisr. gc.ca/Eng/BoaCom/references/pol/GuiDir/Pages/GuideDir04.aspx.

Canada is a signatory will not be binding (where, for example, they have not yet been ratified) whereas others will be.[40] He concluded:

> [I]t is my view that paragraph 3(3)(f) attaches more than mere ambiguity-resolving, contextual significance to "international human rights instruments to which Canada is signatory". If only available to resolve an ambiguity in the *IRPA*, an international human rights instrument might not be able to be used to expose a latent ambiguity in a statute . . . or to bring specificity to a vague statutory provision . . . .
>
> [A] legally binding international human rights instrument to which Canada is signatory is determinative of how the *IRPA* must be interpreted and applied, in the absence of a contrary legislative intention. However, paragraph 3(3)(f) also applies to non-binding instruments to which Canada is signatory . . . .
>
> [I]n view of the considerations outlined above regarding such instruments, I am inclined to think that Parliament intended them to be used as persuasive and contextual factors in the interpretation and application of the *IRPA*, and not as determinative. Moreover, of these non-binding instruments, not all will necessarily be equally persuasive.[41]

The lists of objectives and instructions on statutory construction have been used on many occasions to justify interpretations of particular provisions in the *IRPA* and its predecessors. In *Kha v Canada (Minister of Employment and Immigration)*, for example, Muldoon J offered a clear analysis of the operation of section 3 of the Act. In relation to the subsection identifying family reunification as a policy, he stated: "[It] directs visa officers and immigration officers not to be astutely technical, officious or petty when assessing the applications of [family members] of Canadian citizens. It should permeate the mental attitudes of all those who administer the *Act* and *Regulations*."[42] That said, however, he added some important caveats: "[T]he objectives stated in section 3 are enacted by Parliament in precatory expression, such that any duty which they impose amounts to an imperfect obligation, more structured and more precisely compelling than an extra-statutory moral duty, but not so detailed and specific as to compel compliance in disregard of the other detailed and specific provisions of the legislation."[43]

Another influential commentary on the objectives of the Act has been offered by the Supreme Court of Canada in *Medovarski v Canada*

---

40   2005 FCA 436.
41   *Ibid* at paras 82, 87, and 89.
42   (1986), 5 FTR 150 at 158 (TD).
43   *Ibid*.

(*Minister of Citizenship and Immigration*); *Esteban v Canada* (*Minister of Citizenship and Immigration*).[44] One of the most problematic aspects of section 3 is that it does not identify any ranking among the various listed aims that would point the way to a resolution when they conflict. Decision makers have been left to decide for themselves the relative importance of the various needs, which leads to inconsistency in application of the laws. Most obvious is the section's failure to identify whether the facilitative aims of the Act should be given greater weight than its exclusionary aims. The section fails to assist decision makers in determining whether they are primarily gatekeepers, or whether their chief role is to assist immigrants and others in gaining entry and remaining within Canada. The Supreme Court has sought to remedy this failure by offering an interpretion of the the legislature's priorities. In *Medovarski*, the Chief Justice stated:

> The *IRPA* enacted a series of provisions intended to facilitate the removal of permanent residents who have engaged in serious criminality. This intent is reflected in the objectives of the *IRPA*, the provisions of the *IRPA* governing permanent residents and the legislative hearings preceding the enactment of the *IRPA*.
>
> The objectives as expressed in the *IRPA* indicate an intent to prioritize security. This objective is given effect by preventing the entry of applicants with criminal records, by removing applicants with such records from Canada, and by emphasizing the obligation of permanent residents to behave lawfully while in Canada. This marks a change from the focus in the predecessor statute, which emphasized the successful integration of applicants more than security: e.g., see s. 3(1) (*i*) of the *IRPA* versus s. 3(*j*) of the former Act; s. 3(1)(*e*) of the *IRPA* versus s. 3(*d*) of the former Act; s. 3(1) (*h*) of the *IRPA* versus s. 3(*i*) of the former Act. Viewed collectively, the objectives of the *IRPA* and its provisions concerning permanent residents, communicate a strong desire to treat criminals and security threats less leniently than under the former Act.[45]

This view can be contrasted with the view expressed by Jerome ACJ in relation to the former Act. In *Ho v Canada* (*Minister of Employment and Immigration*), he stated: "It is important to bear in mind that Parliament's intention in enacting the *Immigration Act* is to define Canada's immigration policy both to Canadians and to those who wish to come here from abroad . . . . The purpose of the statute is to permit immigration,

---

44   2005 SCC 51 [*Medovarski*].
45   *Ibid* at paras 9–10.

not prevent it."[46] Justice Jerome relied on this view to justify imposing a rigorous duty of fairness on immigration officers.

Although section 3 of the Act has proven to be of some use to judges and members of the Immigration and Refugee Board, one should not overemphasize its role. The section is of little value to those who are authorized to implement matters of general policy. It does not assist those who have the authority to determine levels of immigration or the relative priority to be given to the different types of applicants received. The government is not prevented from increasing or decreasing the number of individuals admitted under the various immigrant classes that are recognized, nor from instructing visa officers to give priority to applicants of some types over others. In other words, the failure to specify how the various needs should be met ensures that immigration policy making will continue to be largely a matter of discretion rather than something guided by law.

In addition, section 3 of the *IRPA* should not be regarded as the sole source of interpretive assistance. Legislative debates, reports of parliamentary committees, and other documents that can be characterized as part of the statute's "legislative history" will also be used as interpretive aids.

C. THE *CITIZENSHIP ACT*[47]

There are many references in the *IRPA* to the status of citizenship. The *Charter* also refers to the status (and that of permanent resident), recognizing the right of citizens to enter, remain in, and leave Canada, as well as the right to vote in elections.[48] The constitutional provisions do not explicitly preclude the legislative grant of a similar package of rights to non-citizens, nor do they reserve these rights exclusively for citizens. They merely guarantee the enumerated rights to those with citizenship. Moreover, there is no constitutionally entrenched definition of citizenship, nor are there any characteristic qualities or criteria identified in the Constitution that are prerequisites for acquiring or losing the status. These matters are addressed in the *Citizenship Act* and the *Citizenship Regulations*.[49] As a consequence of its being subject to legislative amendment, the legal concept in Canadian citizenship of

---

46   (1989), 8 Imm LR (2d) 38 at 40–41 (Fed TD).
47   RSC 1985, c C-29.
48   *Charter*, above note 21.
49   *Citizenship Regulations*, SOR/93-246.

"citizenship" has a level of fluidity not found in jurisdictions where the prerequisites for citizenship are defined in the Constitution. Moreover, a difficult legal conundrum is created by the paradox that the government acts on behalf of and in the name of the citizenry but may also identify the criteria for belonging to this group. The relevant provisions of the *Citizenship Act* and its regulations are discussed in Chapter 13.

D. THE *DEPARTMENT OF CITIZENSHIP AND IMMIGRATION ACT*[50]

This third frequently overlooked statute establishes Citizenship and Immigration Canada (CIC) and provides that the minister's powers, duties, and functions "extend to and include all matters over which Parliament has jurisdiction relating to citizenship and immigration and that are not by law assigned to any other department, board or agency of the Government of Canada." The Act also explicitly grants some significant powers to the minister. Section 5.1, added to the Act in 2012, provides:

> 5.1 (1) The Minister, with the approval of the Governor in Council, may enter into an agreement with any foreign government for the provision of services in relation to the collection, use and disclosure of biometric information and for the provision of immigration application services and other related services on that government's behalf for purposes related to the administration and enforcement of their immigration laws.
>
> (2) The Minister may enter into an arrangement with any foreign government for the provision of services in relation to the collection, use and disclosure of biometric information and for the provision of immigration application services and other related services on that government's behalf for purposes related to the administration and enforcement of their immigration laws.

The Act also confirms the authority found in the *IRPA* to enter into federal–provincial agreements and international agreements relating to immigration.[51]

---

50   SC 1994, c 31.

51   The wording of the grant of authority is different from that found in the *IRPA*, s 5(1), which provides:

> The Minister, with the approval of the Governor in Council, may enter into agreements with any province or group of provinces or with any foreign

E. THE *DEPARTMENT OF PUBLIC SAFETY AND EMERGENCY PREPAREDNESS ACT*[52]

This statute establishes the Department of Public Safety and Emergency Preparedness and authorizes (in section 5) the minister of Public Safety and Emergency Preparedness to

> coordinate the activities of the entities for which the Minister is responsible, including the Royal Canadian Mounted Police, the Canadian Security Intelligence Service, the Canada Border Services Agency, the Canadian Firearms Centre, the Correctional Service of Canada and the Parole Board of Canada, and establish strategic priorities for those entities relating to public safety and emergency preparedness.

F. THE *IMMIGRATION AND REFUGEE PROTECTION REGULATIONS*[53]

As noted, various sections in the *IRPA* give authority to the Governor in Council to approve of regulations on specified topics.[54] Any regulatory measure taken by the Governor in Council which cannot be traced to a legislative source will be held to be beyond its powers (*ultra vires*) and may be quashed for that reason.[55]

The *Immigration and Refugee Protection Regulations* (*Regulations*) are divided into twenty parts covering a wide range of issues. The most significant parts provide a detailed description of the criteria for selection of the various classes of application for permanent residence, the criteria that must be met by individuals seeking to sponsor a person's application, a description of the process of application for those seeking temporary and permanent residence and for those seeking to work and study in Canada, and a description of the various removal orders that may be enforced against an individual and the consequences of

---

> government or international organization, for the purpose of facilitating the formulation, coordination and implementation — including the collection, use and disclosure of information — of policies and programs for which the Minister is responsible.

52 SC 2005, c 10.
53 SOR/2002-227 [*Regulations*].
54 See *IRPA*, above note 25, ss 14, 17, 32, 53, 61, 87.2, 102, 111.1, 116, 150, and 150.1.
55 *Canadian Society of Immigration Consultants v Canada (Citizenship and Immigration)*, 2011 FC 1435. The exceptional case is a regulation made under the authority of the royal prerogative. See the discussion on the *Passport Order* in Chapter 13.

imposing them. While many of the regulations are formulated as precise rules with terms defined to a high level of exactitude, others give the relevant minister and other government officials broad discretion. Contrast, for example, section 72(1) with section 74(3). The former is highly specific, with most of the general terms being defined in other sections. It reads:

> A foreign national in Canada becomes a permanent resident if, following an examination, it is established that
>
> (a) they have applied to remain in Canada as a permanent resident as a member of a class referred to in subsection (2);
> (b) they are in Canada to establish permanent residence;
> (c) they are a member of that class;
> (d) they meet the selection criteria and other requirements applicable to that class;
> (e) except in the case of a foreign national who has submitted a document accepted under subsection 178(2) or of a member of the protected temporary residents class,
>   (i) they and their family members, whether accompanying or not, are not inadmissible,
>   (ii) they hold a document described in any of paragraphs 50(1) (a) to (h), and
>   (iii) they hold a medical certificate — based on the most recent medical examination to which they were required to submit under paragraph 16(2)(b) of the Act and which took place within the previous 12 months — that indicates that their health condition is not likely to be a danger to public health or public safety and, unless subsection 38(2) of the Act applies, is not reasonably expected to cause excessive demand; and
> (f) in the case of a member of the protected temporary residents class, they are not inadmissible.

The latter, on the other hand, is content to leave matters in the hands of the minister. It provides:

> The Minister may designate, for any period specified by the Minister, any organization or institution to be responsible for evaluating language proficiency if the organization or institution has expertise in evaluating language proficiency and if the organization or institution has provided a correlation of its evaluation results to the benchmarks set out in the *Canadian Language Benchmarks* and the *Niveaux de compétence linguistique canadiens*.

The result of the varying levels of specificity is that, in some circumstances, individuals who are covered by the detailed rules have a clear idea of what to expect. It is also possible to advise them precisely on how to achieve their goals most advantageously. In other contexts, the individual's future may be in the hands of a government official with few indicators available on which factors will determine an outcome.

The process of making regulations is governed both by law, the *Statutory Instruments Act*[56] and the *Statutory Instruments Regulations*,[57] and by established government policies such as the Cabinet Directive on Regulatory Management.[58]

Section 2 of the *Statutory Instruments Act* defines a *regulation* as

a statutory instrument

(a) made in the exercise of a legislative power conferred by or under an Act of Parliament, or

(b) for the contravention of which a penalty, fine or imprisonment is prescribed by or under an Act of Parliament, and includes a rule, order or regulation governing the practice or procedure in any proceedings before a judicial or quasi-judicial body established by or under an Act of Parliament, and any instrument described as a regulation in any other Act of Parliament[59]

The broader term *statutory Instrument* is defined (with some exclusions) to mean

(a) . . . any rule, order, regulation, ordinance, direction, form, tariff of costs or fees, letters patent, commission, warrant, proclamation, by-law, resolution or other instrument issued, made or established

(i) in the execution of a power conferred by or under an Act of Parliament, by or under which that instrument is expressly authorized to be issued, made or established otherwise than by the conferring on any person or body of powers or functions in relation to a matter to which that instrument relates, or

---

56   RSC 1985, c s-22.

57   CRC, c 1509.

58   Treasury Board of Canada Secretariat, *Cabinet Directive on Regulatory Management*, online: www.tbs-sct.gc.ca/rtrap-parfa/cdrm-dcgr/cdrm-dcgrtb-eng.asp; see also Privy Council Office, *Guide to Making Federal Acts and Regulations*, 2d ed (2002), online: www.pco.gc.ca/index.asp?lang=eng&page=information&sub =publications&doc=legislation/table-eng.htm [Privy Council Office Guide].

59   *Statutory Instruments Act*, above note 56, s 2.

(ii) by or under the authority of the Governor in Council, otherwise than in the execution of a power conferred by or under
an Act of Parliament,[60]

Thus, for the purposes of the *IRPA*, the rules of the four divisions of
the Immigration and Refugee Board count as regulations.

The *Statutory Instruments Act* requires that a proposed regulation
be forwarded to the Clerk of the Privy Council for examination to ensure that it is authorized by the statute and that it is consistent with the
Charter of Rights and the *Canadian Bill of Rights*.[61] In addition, section 5 of
the *IRPA* requires that proposed regulations be laid before each House
of Parliament for examination in committee. It reads:

> (2) The Minister shall cause a copy of each proposed regulation made
> under sections 17, 32, 53, 61, 87.2, 102, 116, 150 and 150.1 to be laid
> before each House of Parliament, and each House shall refer the pro-
> posed regulation to the appropriate Committee of that House.[62]

The *Statutory Instruments Act* also requires registration of a regulation after it has been made and its publication in the *Canada Gazette*.[63]
The *Statutory Instruments Regulations* provide for exemptions from examination, registration, and publication in exceptional circumstances.[64]

When published in the *Canada Gazette*, regulations are usually accompanied by an impact analysis statement that identifies their aim and
the various alternatives considered. These statements provide useful
interpretive assistance. As described in the *Guide to Making Federal Acts
and Regulations*,[65] the Regulatory Impact Analysis Statement (RIAS) is
intended to explain

- the elements of the regulatory proposal, including what problems
  or situations it addresses and what it is meant to achieve;
- what alternatives to regulation have been considered;
- what are the anticipated costs and benefits of the regulations;
- what consultations have been carried out and what opportunities
  Canadians have had to be heard;
- what is the response of the department or agency to the concerns
  voiced or suggestions made;

---

60 *Ibid.*
61 SC 1960, c 44.
62 *IRPA*, above note 25, s 5(2).
63 *Statutory Instruments Act*, above note 56, s 6.
64 *Statutory Instruments Regulations*, above note 57.
65 Privy Council Office Guide, above note 58.

- what mechanisms are built in to ensure compliance with the regulations once they are in force;
- how the effectiveness of the regulations will be measured.[66]

G. *IMMIGRATION AND REFUGEE BOARD RULES*

Section 161(1) of the *IRPA* provides statutory authority for the creation of rules establishing procedures within each of the four divisions of the Immigration and Refugee Board. As described in the Regulatory Impact Analysis Statement:

> Rules are necessary for the proper functioning of the IRB, as they provide clear and transparent direction on the practices and procedures of the IRB to parties and their counsel appearing before the IRB, the members who render decisions on cases and the IRB staff who support the decision-making process. This direction ensures that parties appear and present their cases before the IRB's Divisions in a consistent manner, thereby facilitating the fair and efficient administrative processing of cases. It also provides guidance to the Divisions to ensure that all cases are processed in a consistent manner that respects the principles of fairness and natural justice.[67]

H. MINISTERIAL INSTRUCTIONS

As noted above, sections 14.1 and 87.3 of the *IRPA* authorize the minister to issue "instructions."[68] Section 14.1 provides:

> For the purpose of supporting the attainment of economic goals established by the Government of Canada, the Minister may give instructions establishing a class of permanent residents as part of the economic class referred to in subsection 12(2) and, in respect of the

---

66 *Ibid*, Part 3.
67 Immigration and Refugee Board of Canada, *Regulatory Impact Analysis Statement*, online: IRB www.irb-cisr.gc.ca/Eng/BoaCom/references/ActRegLoi/Pages/RiasReir.aspx.
68 *IRPA*, above note 25, ss 14.1 and 87.3.

class that is established, governing any matter referred to in paragraphs 14(2)(a) to (g), 26(a), (b), (d) and (e) and 32(d) . . . .[69]

Section 87.3(3) provides:

(3) For the purposes of subsection (2), the Minister may give instructions with respect to the processing of applications and requests, including instructions

(a) establishing categories of applications or requests to which the instructions apply;

(a.1) establishing conditions, by category or otherwise, that must be met before or during the processing of an application or request;

(b) establishing an order, by category or otherwise, for the processing of applications or requests;

(c) setting the number of applications or requests, by category or otherwise, to be processed in any year; and

(d) providing for the disposition of applications and requests, including those made subsequent to the first application or request.[70]

Where the minister issues instructions under these sections, the requirements of the *Statutory Instruments Act* will not apply since the grant of the authority in the *IRPA* specifically provides that it should not. Section 93 provides:

Instructions given by the Minister or the Minister of Employment and Social Development under this Act . . . are not statutory instruments for the purposes of the *Statutory Instruments Act*.[71]

Thus, there will be no requirement for pre-examination to ensure their legality although the *IRPA* does require that they be published in the *Canada Gazette*. Moreover, there will be no requirement for proposed instructions to be laid before Parliament for review by committee as is required for regulations.

The minister has issued several sets of instructions under the authority provided in the *IRPA*.[72] They direct officials to take into account specific considerations when selecting individuals under various cat-

---

69 *Ibid*, s 14.1: The paragraphs identified are paragraphs that list subject matters on which regulations are authorized.

70 *Ibid*, s 87.3(3).

71 *Ibid*, s 93.

72 See Citizenship and Immigration Canada, Ministerial Instructions, online: CIC www.cic.gc.ca/english/department/mi/.

egories and impose limits on the intake of applicants in relation to specified categories of application. In a paper for the Canadian Bar Association, Mario Bellissimo has reviewed the impact of issuing ministerial instructions:

> As can be gleaned from the above outline, Ministerial Instructions have led to major changes in the Canadian immigration regime. Various immigration categories have been paused, reformulated, capped, and fundamentally transformed. What is particularly concerning about this form of innovative law-making is the extreme power granted to the Minister to unilaterally decide how, when, and to what degree applications are to be processed — if at all. This amounts to an extreme accrual of power within the Ministry, which is, of course, not subjected to the same degree of democratic scrutiny . . . Primarily, there is no opportunity for Parliament to review and amend these instructions . . . .[73]

Although it is undeniable that a high level of flexibility has been obtained by vesting in the minister the power to micromanage the standards and processes of selection, it has been gained at the cost of diminishing the accountability of the minister, allowing him to evade a prerequisite of defending the changes to be introduced. Where the minister has attempted to meet conflicting aims, such as where he has tried to make a pool of temporary foreign workers readily available to employers while seeking to ensure that there is incentive for employers to fill employment positions with Canadian workers, the grant of the power to issue instructions with little prior debate on options has led to high levels of dissatisfaction from all parties involved.[74]

I. MINISTERIAL ORDERS

The authority to make ministerial orders is similar to the authority to give or issue ministerial instructions in that the *IRPA* explicitly states that certain orders issued by the minister are not statutory instruments.[75] Under section 20.1 of the *IRPA*, the minister may, by order, designate a foreign national for special treatment as a result of her

---

73   Mario Bellissimo, "Law-Making Innovation in the Canadian and International Immigration Context: International Comparisons and Cautions for Canadians" (2013), online: Canadian Bar Association www.cba.org/CBA/cle/PDF/IMM13_paper_bellissimo.pdf.
74   See Chapter 4.
75   *IRPA*, above note 25, ss 20.1(3) and 109.1(4).

mode of arrival and under section 109.1, may designate a country of origin as safe.[76] The designations must be published in the *Canada Gazette* but are not otherwise subject to the internal controls of the legal process for making regulations. The orders create special processes that will apply to individuals so designated and limit access to various procedures and appeals that would otherwise be available.

J. CHAIRPERSON'S GUIDELINES AND JURISPRUDENTIAL GUIDES

Guidelines issued by the chairperson of the Immigration and Refugee Board are classified in section 93 of the *IRPA* alongside ministerial instructions, and as such, are not statutory instruments.[77] The guidelines, however, have a different legal status. In *Thamotharem v Canada (Minister of Citizenship and Immigration)*,[78] the Federal Court of Appeal considered whether the guidelines should be regarded as a form of "delegated legislation" binding on the members of the Immigration and Refugee Board and concluded that they should not. Justice Evans offered the following analysis:

> An initial question is whether guidelines issued under *IRPA*, paragraph 159(1)(h) constitute delegated legislation, having the full force of law ("hard law") . . . .
>
> In my view, despite the express statutory authority of the Chairperson to issue guidelines, they do not have the same legal effects that statutory rules can have. In particular, guidelines cannot lay down a mandatory rule from which members have no meaningful degree of discretion to deviate, regardless of the facts of the particular case before them. The word "guideline" itself normally suggests some operating principle or general norm, which does not necessarily determine the result of every dispute.
>
> However, the meaning of "guideline" in a statute may depend on context. For example, in *Society of the Friends of Oldman River v. Canada (Minister of the Environment)*, [1992] 1 S.C.R. 3 at 33–37, La Forest J upheld the validity of mandatory environmental assessment guidelines issued under section 6 of the *Department of the Environment Act*,

---

76   *Ibid.* See Chapter 9 for more information regarding these provisions.

77   *Ibid*, s 93: The full text of s 93 of the *IRPA* provides: "Instructions given by the Minister or the Minister of Employment and Social Development under this Act and guidelines issued by the Chairperson under paragraph 159(1)(h) are not statutory instruments for the purposes of the *Statutory Instruments Act*."

78   2007 FCA 198.

R.S.C. 1985, c. E-10, which, he held, constituted delegated legislation and, as such, were legally binding.

In my view, *Oldman River* is distinguishable from the case before us. Section 6 of the *Department of the Environment Act* provided that guidelines were to be issued by an "order" . . . of the Minister and approved by the Cabinet. In contrast, only rules issued by the Chairperson require Cabinet approval, guidelines . . . do not. It would make little sense for *IRPA* to have conferred powers on the Chairperson to issue two types of legislative instrument, guidelines and rules, specified that rules must have Cabinet approval, and yet given both the same legal effect . . . .

In my opinion, the scheme of *IRPA* is different, particularly the inclusion of a potentially overlapping rule-making power and the absence of a provision that guidelines are binding on adjudicators. In addition, the word *"directives"* in the French text of paragraph 159(1)(*h*) suggests a less legally authoritative instrument than *"ordonnance"*.

I conclude, therefore, that, even though issued under an express statutory grant of power, guidelines issued under *IRPA*, paragraph 159(1)(*h*) cannot have the same legally binding effect on members as statutory rules may.[79]

Although guidelines, unlike instructions or orders, are not legally binding, a failure to take them into account may lead to a decision being quashed. The basis for such a conclusion would be that a decision that fails to take into account factors mentioned in guidelines as relevant factors to be considered is substantively unreasonable. In *Evans v Canada (Minister of Citizenship and Immigration)*,[80] Mosley J explains this clearly as follows:

The reasonableness standard applies to credibility findings made by the Board: *Aguirre v. Canada (Minister of Citizenship and Immigration)*, 2008 FC 571. Because deference is owed to the trier of fact, the Court must not intervene unless the Board's determination does not fall within the range of possible, acceptable outcomes which are defensible in respect of the facts and law . . . .

In cases where a refugee claimant has alleged various forms of physical, sexual and psychological abuse, this Court must review the Board's decision with an eye to the *Guidelines issued by the Chairperson Pursuant to Section 65(3) of the Immigration Act: Women Refugee Claimants Fearing Gender-Related Persecution* ("*Gender Guidelines*").

---

79   *Ibid* at paras 65–68 and 71–72.
80   2011 FC 444.

In such instances the *Gender Guidelines* "become subsumed in the standard of review of reasonableness as applied to credibility findings" . . . .

> [W]hile the Board did state that the *Gender Guidelines* were considered, the analysis given in this decision with respect to the applicant's financial dependence and the personal letter suggests they were not applied in a meaningful way. This Court has held that it is not sufficient for a Board to simply say that the *Gender Guidelines* were applied and then fail to demonstrate how they were applied . . . .[81]

The Immigration and Refugee Board has also issued a policy on the use of Chairperson's Guidelines which provides:

> The issuance of a set of guidelines will be communicated to the public. Parties and their counsel will therefore be expected to know that a set of guidelines have been issued on a particular subject.
>
> Although not binding, members are *expected to follow guidelines*, unless compelling or exceptional reasons exist to depart from them.
>
> A member must *explain in his or her reasoning* why he or she is not following a set of guidelines when, based on the facts or circumstances of the case, they would otherwise be expected to follow them.[82]

The chairperson has issued eight sets of guidelines on a wide range of subjects, including these titles: *Civilian Non-combatants Fearing Persecution in Civil War Situations, Detention, Child Refugee Claimants: Procedures and Evidentiary Issues, Women Refugee Claimants Fearing Gender-Related Persecution, Scheduling and Changing the Date or Time of a Proceeding, Preparation and Conduct of a Hearing in the Refugee Protection Division,* and *Procedures with Respect to Vulnerable Persons Appearing before the Immigration and Refugee Board of Canada.*

The chairperson has also been granted statutory authority to identify decisions of the Immigration and Refugee Board as jurisprudential guides.[83] The purpose of this power is to promote consistent decision making. Only two cases have ever been identified as jurisprudential guides, both in 2003. As a result of changed conditions, their status as guides was revoked in 2011.[84]

---

81 *Ibid* at paras 7, 8, and 15.

82 Immigration and Refugee Board of Canada, *Policy on the Use of Chairperson's Guidelines* (27 October 2003), online: IRB www.irb-cisr.gc.ca/Eng/BoaCom/references/pol/pol/Pages/PolGuideDir.aspx [emphasis in original].

83 *IRPA,* above note 25, s 159.

84 Immigration and Refugee Board of Canada, *Policy Note: Notice of Revocation of Two Jurisprudential Guides — Costa Rica,* online: IRB www.irb-cisr.gc.ca/Eng/BoaCom/references/pol/notes/Pages/NoteTA015870_TA214980Rev.aspx.

K. PROGRAM DELIVERY INSTRUCTIONS (OPERATIONAL MANUALS AND BULLETINS)

Citizenship and Immigration Canada (CIC) also publishes operational manuals and bulletins that are intended as guides to immigration officials. It is in the process of changing the format of these guides under a new name – Program Delivery Instructions.[85] Like the chairperson's guidelines, these manuals and bulletins do not have the force of law.

In *Kanthasamy v Canada (Minister of Citizenship and Immigration)*,[86] a case that hinged on the factors to be taken into account when interpreting section 25(1) of the *IRPA*, Stratas JA offered the following clear analysis of the status of operational guidelines, the use to which they may be put, and their limitations:

> In my view, the decided cases show that the factors set out in section 5.11 of the processing manual, above, are a reasonable enumeration of the types of matters that an Officer must consider when assessing an application for humanitarian and compassionate relief under subsection 25(1) of the Act. They encompass the sorts of consequences that, depending on the particular facts of particular cases, might meet the high standard of hardship associated with leaving Canada, associated with arriving and staying in the foreign country, or both.
>
> That being said, I wish to caution against Officers applying the processing manual and, in particular, the factors listed in section 5.11 of the processing manual as if they describe a closed list of circumstances.
>
> The processing manual is an administrative guideline, nothing more. Administrative guidelines are desirable when dealing with a provision such as this, as they promote consistency in decision-making . . . . This manual goes some way toward shedding light on the meaning of "unusual and undeserved, or disproportionate hardship." Indeed, the Federal Court regularly upholds Officers' determinations that are based on a sensitive consideration of these factors that are live on the facts before them.
>
> However, the processing manual is not law: administrative policy statements are only a source of guidance and in no way amend the provisions of the Act or the Regulations (see *Maple Lodge Farms Ltd. v. Government of Canada*, [1982] 2 S.C.R. 2). It would be reviewable

---

85   Citizenship and Immigration Canada, Operational Bulletins and Manuals, online: CIC www.cic.gc.ca/English/resources/manuals/index.asp.

86   2014 FCA 113.

error for an Officer to see the processing manual as presenting a closed list of factors to consider and, in that way, to regard the processing manual, and not subsection 25(1), as the law. That would constitute an impermissible fettering of discretion . . . .[87]

These comments should be read alongside the observations of L'Heureux-Dubé J in *Baker v Canada (Minister of Citizenship and Immigration)*[88] where, once again, the relevance of the contents of a manual to the interpretation of section 25 was considered:

As described above, immigration officers are expected to make the decision that a reasonable person would make, with special consideration of humanitarian values such as keeping connections between family members and avoiding hardship by sending people to places where they no longer have connections. The guidelines show what the Minister considers a humanitarian and compassionate decision, and they are of great assistance to the Court in determining whether the reasons of Officer Lorenz are supportable. They emphasize that the decision-maker should be alert to possible humanitarian grounds, should consider the hardship that a negative decision would impose upon the claimant or close family members, and should consider as an important factor the connections between family members. The guidelines are a useful indicator of what constitutes a reasonable interpretation of the power conferred by the section, and the fact that this decision was contrary to their directives is of great help in assessing whether the decision was an unreasonable exercise of the H & C power.[89]

Thus, it would seem that where an official either appears to consider guidelines in a manual to be binding or where he fails to pay any heed to them, the decision may be quashed, in the first instance for improperly fettering one's discretion, and in the second for failing unreasonably to take account of relevant considerations.

L. FEDERAL–PROVINCIAL/TERRITORIAL AGREEMENTS

Acting under the authority granted by the *IRPA* and the *Department of Citizenship and Immigration Act*, the minister has negotiated agreements

---

87   *Ibid* at paras 50–53.
88   [1999] 2 SCR 817 [*Baker*].
89   *Ibid* at para 72.

on immigration with all provinces, the Northwest Territories, and the Yukon.[90] The most significant aspect of these agreements is that they permit the province or territory to participate in the selection of immigrants. With the exception of Quebec, the involvement is defined in separate agreements establishing provincial nominee programs. The class of provincial nominees is defined in section 87(2) of the *Regulations* which provides:

> A foreign national is a member of the provincial nominee class if
>
> (a) . . . they are named in a nomination certificate issued by the government of a province under a provincial nomination agreement between that province and the Minister; and
> (b) they intend to reside in the province that has nominated them.[91]

The agreements give the province (or territory) the responsibility to assess potential immigrants and nominate them to Citizenship and Immigration Canada for selection. For example, the agreement with British Columbia contains the following provisions:

> 3.1 British Columbia has the sole and non-transferable responsibility to assess and nominate candidates who, based on British Columbia's determination: will be of significant benefit to the economic development of British Columbia; and have a strong likelihood of becoming economically established in British Columbia.
>
> 3.2 British Columbia will nominate foreign nationals on the basis of economic benefit to British Columbia. The nomination criteria of the Provincial Nominee Program categories shall demonstrate the economic benefit to the Province. Provincial Nominees may be nominated for purposes that include, but are not limited to, meeting critical skill shortages in British Columbia, the immigration of key individuals of businesses that wish to locate in British Columbia and the establishment or enhancement of new and existing businesses.
>
> 3.3 Non-economic factors shall not provide the primary basis upon which a nomination is made.
>
> 3.4 In exercising its nomination authority under this Agreement, British Columbia will follow the procedures and criteria for nomination established by British Columbia, as amended from time to time, insofar as those procedures and criteria are consistent

90 See Appendix.
91 *Regulations*, above note 53, s 16.

with the IRPA, the IRPR or any successor legislation and regulations and the terms of this Agreement and this Annex. British
Columbia will respect the purpose and objectives of this Annex
in developing and implementing these procedures and criteria.
British Columbia will share its criteria with Canada prior to implementation and keep written records of its assessments of its
nominees against those criteria.

3.5 Canada will consider foreign nationals who are nominated by
British Columbia as applicants in the Provincial Nominee Class.

3.6 Canada agrees to process economic class applicants nominated
for permanent resident status by British Columbia on a priority
basis and as expeditiously as possible with a view to achieving
Canada's annual levels plan.[92]

Most provincial nominee programs are employer driven. Thus the
Opportunities Ontario website explains:

Ontario employers can nominate key individuals with critical skills
and expertise for work permits and permanent residence in Canada
through Opportunities Ontario. This is helpful for employers who
are having difficulty finding the skilled workers they need.

Please note that Opportunities Ontario is employer-driven. This
means that you can only apply if your employer is pre-screened, the
position is approved, and your employer provides you with a nominee application package from Opportunities Ontario.[93]

M. THE CANADA-QUÉBEC ACCORD RELATING TO IMMIGRATION AND TEMPORARY ADMISSION OF ALIENS[94]

The *Canada-Québec Accord Relating to Immigration and Temporary Admission of Aliens*, which came into force on 1 April 1991 and supplanted

---

92 Citizenship and Immigration Canada, *Canada-British Columbia Immigration
Agreement*, online: CIC www.cic.gc.ca/English/department/laws-policy/
agreements/bc/bc-2010.asp.
93 www.ontarioimmigration.ca/OI/en/before/OI_BEFORE_HOWTO.html.
94 Citizenship and Immigration Canada, *Canada-Québec Accord relating to Immigration and Temporary Admission of Aliens*, online: CIC www.cic.gc.ca/english/
department/laws-policy/agreements/quebec/can-que.asp [*Canada-Québec Accord*].

previous accords between the two governments,[95] is the most comprehensive agreement between the federal government and the provinces and territories. The preamble to the Accord states that its purpose is to "provide Québec with new means to preserve its demographic importance in Canada, and to ensure the integration of immigrants . . . in a manner that respects the distinct identity of Québec."[96]

The Accord distinguishes between the selection of immigrants and their admission. Thus, section 3 provides that "Canada shall determine national standards and objectives relating to immigration and shall be responsible for the *admission* of all immigrants and the *admission* and control of aliens."[97] Section 12 underlines this division of powers, granting to Quebec, subject to sections 13 to 20, "the sole responsibility for the selection of immigrants destined to that province" while retaining for Canada "sole responsibility for the admission of immigrants to that province."[98] However, it also provides that "Canada shall admit any immigrant destined to Québec who meets Québec's selection criteria, if the immigrant is not in an inadmissible class under the law of Canada."[99]

Section 7 of the Accord provides that "Québec undertakes to pursue an immigration policy that has as an objective the reception by Québec of a percentage of the total number of immigrants received in Canada equal to the percentage of Québec's population compared with the population of Canada."[100] Similarly, section 8 provides that Quebec undertakes to receive a proportional percentage of refugees.[101] It states: "In order to assume its full responsibility for the reception of immigrants based on humanitarian considerations, Québec undertakes to receive, out of the total number of refugees and persons in similar situations received by Canada, a percentage at least equal to the percentage of immigrants that it undertakes to accept."[102]

Under section 28 of the Accord, Canada retains responsibility for services relating to citizenship.[103] Annex A of the Accord establishes a joint committee to "promote the harmonization of the economic,

---

95 The *Lang-Cloutier Agreement*, 1971, was replaced by the *Andras-Bienvenue Agreement* in 1975. In turn, it was supplanted by the *Cullen-Couture Agreement* in 1978.
96 *Canada-Québec Accord*, above note 94, Preamble.
97 *Ibid*, s 3 [emphasis added].
98 *Ibid*, s 12.
99 *Ibid*.
100 *Ibid*, s 7.
101 *Ibid*, s 8.
102 *Ibid*.
103 *Ibid*, s 28.

demographic and socio-cultural objectives of the two parties in the area of immigration and integration" and an implementation committee whose mandate is to "coordinate implementation of the Accord and develop the necessary terms and conditions of operation."[104] Annex B establishes a complex formula for calculating the financial compensation payable to Quebec.[105] Annex C provides arrangements governing the presence of Quebec agents abroad.[106]

As a result of the accords between the two governments, Quebec has developed an immigration process that, in significant ways, is autonomous and distinct from the Canadian one. The legislation that deals with the Quebec process is *An Act Respecting Immigration to Quebec* (Quebec Act).[107] Like the Canadian Act, it authorizes the making of detailed regulations on a wide variety of subject matters. The Quebec Act identifies seven main purposes that govern the selection of those who wish to settle permanently or temporarily in Quebec:

1) contribution to the socio-cultural heritage of Quebec;
2) stimulation of Quebec's economic development;
3) pursuit of Quebec's demographic objectives;
4) reuniting in Quebec Canadian citizens and permanent residents with their close relatives from abroad;
5) enabling Quebec to assume its share of responsibilities regarding refugees;
6) favouring the coming of persons who will be able to successfully establish themselves in Quebec; and
7) facilitating the conditions of stay of temporary arrivals.[108]

Regulations relating to the selection of foreign nationals that identify a set of admission criteria for those seeking admission to Quebec have also been passed.[109]

The constitutionality of the Quebec legislation under section 95 of the *Constitution Act, 1867*[110] has never been tested and, given the level of cooperation between the governments, is unlikely to be so by either government.

---

104 *Ibid*, Annex A.
105 *Ibid*, Annex B.
106 *Ibid*, Annex C.
107 RSQ c I-0.2.
108 *Ibid*.
109 CQLR c I-0.2, r 4. See also the *Regulation respecting the weighting applicable to the selection of foreign nationals*, CQLR c I-0.2, r 2.
110 Above note 1.

N. INTERNATIONAL LAW

Canada is a party to various international agreements that have both direct and indirect impact on decision making on immigration matters. Most notable are the agreements relating to refugees. For example, the United Nations *Convention Relating to the Status of Refugees*[111] and the *Protocol Relating to the Status of Refugees*[112] contain basic definitions and principles that shape the core of Canadian refugee law. Chapters 7 to 10 provide more detail on refugee protection in Canada.

The importance of other agreements should not be undervalued, however, since they may offer the grounds for both political and legal challenges in domestic and international forums,[113] including the United Nations Human Rights Committee, the United Nations Committee on Torture, and the Inter-American Commission on Human Rights. Among the most significant documents are the *International Covenant on Civil and Political Rights*,[114] the *Convention against Torture and Other Cruel, Inhuman or Degrading Treatment or Punishment*,[115] the *Convention on the Rights of the Child*,[116] and the *American Declaration of the Rights and Duties of Man*.[117]

Nevertheless, research by Stephen Meili[118] has revealed that references in Canadian jurisprudence to international human rights treaties have steadily declined over a period of fifteen years. He suggests that "invoking human rights treaties indiscriminately may hurt refugees, as it can create the impression that the refugee's lawyer is desperate" and advocates a strategic use of these sources.[119]

---

111 28 July 1951, 189 UNTS 150 (22 April 1954).

112 21 January 1967, 606 UNTS 267 (4 October 1967).

113 See Sharryn Aiken & Tom Clark, "International Procedures for Protecting the Human Rights of Non-citizens" (1994) 10 *Journal of Law & Social Policy* 182.

114 19 December 1966, 999 UNTS 171 [*ICCPR*].

115 10 December 1984, Can TS 1987 No 36, 23 ILM 1027 [*Convention against Torture*].

116 20 November 1989, 28 ILM 1448.

117 2 May 1948, 43 AJIL (Supp) 133 [*American Declaration*].

118 Stephen Meili, "When Do Human Rights Treaties Help Asylum Seekers? A Study of Theory and Practice in Canadian Jurisprudence since 1990" (2014) 51 *Osgoode Hall Law Journal* 627.

119 *Ibid* at 670.

1) The *International Covenant on Civil and Political Rights* (*ICCPR*)[120]

Canada acceded to the *ICCPR* and its Optional Protocol[121] in 1976. The Protocol is a particularly important document since, in article 1, it binds signatory states to recognize "the competence of the [Human Rights] Committee [established in the Convention] to receive and consider communications from individuals subject to its jurisdiction who claim to be victims of a violation by that State Party of any of the rights set forth in the Covenant."[122] However, article 2 of the Protocol requires individuals to exhaust all available domestic remedies before submitting a written communication for consideration.[123] The rights and freedoms identified in the *ICCPR* itself are far ranging, often appearing to be broader in ambit than those contained in the *Charter*.[124] In addition, under the *ICCPR*, each state party is required to report on the implemetation of the *ICCPR* to the committee on a regular basis (usually every four years).[125] The committee responds with a set of "concluding observations,"[126] commenting on the standards achieved and making recommendations for change.

The following articles of the *ICCPR* are the most important in the immigration context:

1) article 7, which proscribes "cruel, inhuman or degrading treatment or punishment";
2) article 9, which grants everyone the right to liberty and security of the person, proscribes arbitrary arrest or detention, and entitles those deprived of liberty by detention to take proceedings before a court, in order that the court may decide without delay on the lawfulness of the detention;

---

120 *ICCPR*, above note 114.
121 *Optional Protocol to the International Covenant on Civil and Political Rights*, 19 December 1966, 999 UNTS 302 [*ICCPR Protocol*].
122 *Ibid*, art 1.
123 *Ibid*, art 2. The jurisprudence of the committee is available online. Decisions on complaints made against Canada may be found at United Nations Human Rights, Communications, online: UN OHCHR http://tbinternet.ohchr.org/_layouts/treatybodyexternal/TBSearch.aspx?Lang=en&TreatyID=8&DocTypeID=17.
124 See Chapter 3.
125 *ICCPR*, above note 114, art 40.
126 The most recent concluding observations from 2006: United Nations, *Consideration of Reports Submitted by State Parties Under Article 40 of the Covenant: Concluding Observations of the Human Rights Committee – Canada* (20 April 2006), online: Refworld www.refworld.org/pdfid/453777a50.pdf.

3) article 12, which grants to everyone lawfully within the territory of a state the right to liberty of movement and "freedom to choose his residence," qualified by the following clause: "The above-mentioned rights shall not be subject to any restrictions except those which are provided by law, are necessary to protect national security, public order (*ordre public*), public health or morals or the rights and freedoms of others, and are consistent with the other rights recognized in the present Covenant"; article 12 also grants everyone the freedom to leave any country, including "his own" — it can readily be seen that the mobility rights contained in this article are articulated in terms that appear to be broader than those found in the *Charter*, and the restrictions are narrower than those found in section 1 of that document;

4) article 13, which establishes that

[a]n alien lawfully in the territory of a State Party to the present Covenant may be expelled therefrom only in pursuance of a decision reached in accordance with law and shall, except where compelling reasons of national security otherwise require, be allowed to submit the reasons against his expulsion and to have his case reviewed by, and be represented for the purpose before, the competent authority or a person or persons especially designated by the competent authority;

5) article 18, which grants everyone the right to freedom of thought, conscience, and religion;

6) article 19, which grants the right to freedom of expression;

7) article 22, which grants the right to freedom of association (with restrictions placed on this right similar to those placed on the rights contained in article 12);

8) article 23, which identifies the family as "the natural and fundamental group unit of society" and entitles it to protection (possibly having bearing on the regulations applying to the sponsorship of family members); and

9) article 24, which recognizes that children have the right to such measures of protection as are required by their status as minors.

2) The *Convention against Torture and Other Cruel, Inhuman or Degrading Treatment or Punishment*[127]

Canada is a party to the *United Nations Convention against Torture and Other Cruel, Inhuman or Degrading Treatment or Punishment*. Torture is defined very broadly in this agreement to include the intentional infliction of severe pain or suffering, whether physical or mental. The states that are party to the *Convention against Torture* are obliged not only to take effective measures to prevent acts of torture in any territory within their jurisdiction but, by article 3, not to "expel, return ('refouler') or extradite a person to another State where there are substantial grounds for believing that he would be in danger of being subjected to torture."[128] The same article also specifies how the determination of whether there are substantial grounds should be made:

> For the purpose of determining whether there are such grounds, the competent authorities shall take into account all relevant considerations including, where applicable, the existence in the State concerned of a consistent pattern of gross, flagrant or mass violations of human rights.[129]

The *Convention against Torture* also establishes a committee on torture, which will receive and consider, in closed meeting, communications from individuals who claim to be victims of a violation of the *Convention* and who have exhausted all available domestic remedies.[130] A number of communications[131] from individuals concerning treatment by Canada have been forwarded to the committee. State parties are also required to report on the implementation of the *Convention* to the committee on a regular basis, and concluding observations are published in response.[132]

---

127 *Convention against Torture*, above note 115.

128 *Ibid*, art 3.

129 *Ibid*.

130 *Ibid*, art 17.

131 For example, *RSM v Canada*, Communication No 392/2009 CAT/ C/50/D/392/2009; for committee decisions, see United Nations Office of the High Commissioner for Human Rights, Committee against Torture Jurisprudence, online: UN Human Rights www.ohchr.org/EN/HRBodies/CAT/Pages/ Jurisprudence.aspx.

132 For concluding observations, see United Nations Office of the High Commissioner for Human Rights, Communications, online: United Nations Human Rights http://tbinternet.ohchr.org/_layouts/treatybodyexternal/TBSearch.aspx? Lang=en&TreatyID=8&DocTypeID=17.

3) The *Convention on the Rights of the Child*[133]

One of the most important aspects of the *Convention on the Rights of the Child*, which Canada ratified in 1991, is article 3, which stipulates:

> In all actions concerning children, whether undertaken by public or private social welfare institutions, courts of law, administrative authorities or legislative bodies, the best interests of the child shall be a primary consideration.[134]

The principle of the "best interests of the child" has received criticism because of its vagueness and indeterminacy. However, its continued use was defended by McLachlin J of the Supreme Court of Canada in *Gordon v Goertz* where she stated:

> The best interests of the child test has been characterized as "indeterminate" and "more useful as legal aspiration than as legal analysis". . . . The multitude of factors that may impinge on the child's best interest make a measure of indeterminacy inevitable. A more precise test would risk sacrificing the child's best interests to expediency and certainty.[135]

The principle has been incorporated into the *IRPA* in the following ways:

1) Section 25(1) requires the minister to take into account "the best interests of a child directly affected" when determining whether humanitarian and compassionate considerations justify exceptional treatment.

2) Section 28(2)(c) allows a permanent resident to retain permanent residence, despite failing to meet the physical residency requirement, where an immigration officer determines that this is justified by humanitarian and compassionate considerations "taking into account the best interests of a child directly affected by the determination."

3) Section 60 affirms as a principle that a minor child is to be detained only as a measure of last resort, "taking into account the other applicable criteria including the best interests of the child."

4) Section 67(1)(c) empowers the Immigration Appeal Division to allow an appeal where sufficient humanitarian and compassionate

---

133 *Convention on the Rights of the Child*, above note 116.
134 *Ibid*, art 3.
135 [1996] 2 SCR 27 at para 20.

considerations warrant special relief "taking into account the best interests of a child directly affected by the decision."[136]

The *Convention on the Rights of the Child* also established a committee on the Rights of the Child, for the purpose of "examining the progress made by States Parties in achieving the realization of the obligations undertaken."[137]

4) The *American Declaration of the Rights and Duties of Man*[138]

In 1990, Canada became a member of the Organization of American States. By so doing, it committed itself to abiding by the terms of the *American Declaration of the Rights and Duties of Man*. It also came under the jurisdiction of the Inter-American Commission on Human Rights, which is empowered to entertain petitions from individuals alleging violations of human rights, provided that similar complaints have not been raised before other international bodies.[139] In a memorandum from the Legal Bureau of the Department of External Affairs, it is noted that "Canadian compliance with the human rights provisions of the OAS Charter and the 1948 American Declaration should not pose any major difficulties since these provisions largely correspond to rights enshrined in the *Canadian Charter of Rights and Freedoms* and to Canada's existing international obligations."[140]

In 2011 the Inter-American Commission on Human Rights ruled that Canada had breached its obligations by returning three refugee claimants to the United States in 2003 under its "direct back policy."[141]

5) The Domestic Significance of International Agreements

The status of international law as a legal source for decision makers in the immigration system has been addressed in a number of judicial

---

136 *IRPA*, above note 25.
137 *Convention on the Rights of the Child*, above note 116, art 43.
138 *American Declaration*, above note 117.
139 *Ibid*, art XXIV.
140 As quoted in EG Lee, "At the Department of External Affairs in 1989–90" (1990) 28 *Canadian Yearbook of International Law* 471 at 497.
141 See *John Doe v Canada*, Case P-554-04, Report No 121/06 Inter-Am CHR OEA/Ser.L/V/II.127 Doc 4 rev 1 (2007), online: www1.umn.edu/humanrts/cases/121-06.html.

decisions. The reference to international law in the *IRPA*, section 3(3)(f), has already been noted.[142]

In addition, for the Supreme Court of Canada, Lebel J in *R v Hape*[143] has outlined the general principle of statutory interpretation that requires conformity with international law:

> It is a well-established principle of statutory interpretation that legislation will be presumed to conform to international law. The presumption of conformity is based on the rule of judicial policy that, as a matter of law, courts will strive to avoid constructions of domestic law pursuant to which the state would be in violation of its international obligations, unless the wording of the statute clearly compels that result. R. Sullivan, *Sullivan and Driedger on the Construction of Statutes* (4th ed. 2002), at p. 422, explains that the presumption has two aspects. First, the legislature is presumed to act in compliance with Canada's obligations as a signatory of international treaties and as a member of the international community. In deciding between possible interpretations, courts will avoid a construction that would place Canada in breach of those obligations. The second aspect is that the legislature is presumed to comply with the values and principles of customary and conventional international law. Those values and principles form part of the context in which statutes are enacted, and courts will therefore prefer a construction that reflects them. The presumption is rebuttable, however. Parliamentary sovereignty requires courts to give effect to a statute that demonstrates an unequivocal legislative intent to default on an international obligation.[144]

This principle has also been acknowledged in *Baker*,[145] and there it is stated that an international agreement is not a part of Canadian law unless it has been formally incorporated therein. Justice L'Heureux-Dubé writes:

> International treaties and conventions are not part of Canadian law unless they have been implemented by statute: *Francis v. The Queen*, [1956] S.C.R. 618, at p. 621; *Capital Cities Communications Inc. v. Canadian Radio-Television Commission*, [1978] 2 S.C.R. 141, at pp. 172–73. I agree with the respondent and the Court of Appeal that the Convention has not been implemented by Parliament. Its provisions therefore have no direct application within Canadian law . . . .

---

142 See Section B(2), above in this chapter.
143 2007 SCC 26.
144 *Ibid* at para 53.
145 Above note 88.

> Nevertheless, the values reflected in international human rights law may help inform the contextual approach to statutory interpretation and judicial review.[146]

Where two international conventions have been incorporated into domestic law there may be potential conflict between them. This situation was considered by the Ontario Court of Appeal in *AMRI v KER*.[147] The case concerned a twelve-year-old girl from Mexico who made a refugee claim in Canada. Her claim was that she faced a threat of persecution from her mother, who had legal custody of her. Canada's obligations under the *Convention Relating to the Status of Refugees*, incorporated into section 115 of the *IRPA*, required that a refugee not be returned to her country to face such a risk. However, under article 12 of the Hague *Convention on the Civil Aspects of International Child Abduction*, which had been incorporated into an Ontario statute, the *Children's Law Reform Act*, there is a mandatory requirement for the return "forthwith" of wrongfully removed or retained children. The Ontario Court of Appeal resolved the potential conflict by recognizing that the *Hague Convention* contained an exception where "the return would expose the child to a grave risk of physical or psychological harm or otherwise place the child in an intolerable situation."[148] It concluded:

> Nothing in the *IRPA* purports to exempt child refugees from the application of s. 115 in a Hague Convention case. Nor does the Hague Convention purport to elevate its mandatory return policy above the principle of *non-refoulement*.[149]

6) Trade Agreements and Business Travel

Canada is a party to various free trade agreements such as The *North American Free Trade Agreement*[150] and the *General Agreement on Trade in Services*,[151] which have had a major impact on the admission of temporary

---

146 *Ibid* at paras 69–70; confirmed in *Suresh v Canada (Minister of Citizenship and Immigration)*, 2002 SCC 1.

147 2011 ONCA 417.

148 *Ibid* at para 52.

149 *Ibid* at para 67.

150 *North American Free Trade Agreement*, 32 ILM 289 and 605 (1993) [*NAFTA*].

151 *General Agreement on Trade in Services*, 15 April 1994, Marrakesh Agreement Establishing the World Trade Organization, Annex 1B, The Legal Texts: The Results of the Uruguay Round of the Multilateral Trade Negotiations 284 (1999), 1869 UNTS 183, 33 ILM 1167 (1994) [*GATS*].

workers into Canada.[152] In December 1992, Canada, the United States, and Mexico signed the *North American Free Trade Agreement (NAFTA)*. Subsequently, Parliament passed *An Act to Implement the North American Free Trade Agreement*, which came into force in 1994. The agreement aims to remove trade barriers and to facilitate the movement of goods and services among the three countries. In order to achieve this aim, *NAFTA* chapter 16 establishes criteria and procedures for the temporary entry of business persons from each country into the other countries. The agreement has no effect on permanent residence, because *temporary entry* is defined as entry without the intent to establish permanent residence. Some of the details of the agreement are outlined below in Chapter 4.

On 1 January 1995, the *Agreement Establishing the World Trade Organization* came into force. Annex 1B of this agreement is the *General Agreement on Trade in Services (GATS)*.[153] Under this agreement, Canada has committed itself to allowing temporary entry of business persons from member nations who work in particular service sectors and has developed detailed policies to regulate their entry.[154]

7) The Safe Third Country Agreement[155]

As well as the general agreements above, the minister is authorized by section 7 of the *IRPA*, with the approval of the Governor in Council, to enter into agreements with other countries for the purpose of facilitating the coordination and implementation of immigration policies and programs.[156] Under the authority of this section, an agreement relating to responsibility for examining refugee claims has been signed with the United States.[157]

---

152 A full list of Canada's free trade agreements is found at Foreign Affairs, Trade and Development Canada, "Canada's Free Trade Agreements," online: Government of Canada www.international.gc.ca/trade-agreements-accords-commerciaux/agr-acc/fta-ale.aspx?lang=eng.

153 *GATS*, above note 151.

154 See, for example, Citizenship and Immigration Canada, Operational Bulletin 575: *Expanded Guidelines for Officers Assessing Work Permit Applications for Intra-Company Transferees with Specialized Knowledge* (9 June 2014), online: CIC www.cic.gc.ca/english/resources/manuals/bulletins/2014/ob575.asp.

155 US Department of State, *US-Canada Agreement Covering Third-Country Asylum Claims at the Border* (5 December 2002), online: United States Government www.state.gov/s/l/38616.htm [*Safe Third-Country Agreement*].

156 *IRPA*, above note 25, s 7.

157 *Safe Third-Country Agreement*, above note 155.

O. COMMON LAW PRINCIPLES OF ADMINISTRATIVE LAW

As discussed below in Chapter 16, decisions made by immigration officials may be reviewed by the Federal Court and quashed on a number of grounds enumerated in section 18.1 of the *Federal Courts Act*.[158] The court has developed standards that limit the exercise of discretion and also impose safeguards to ensure that a person affected by a decision has adequate participatory rights and to ensure that process is untainted by a reasonable apprehension of bias.

P. PREVIOUS DECISIONS AND *STARE DECISIS*

Immigration decisions are made by officials and adjudicators working within a complex institutional framework built upon a hierarchical structure in which decisions reached at one level may be appealed or reviewed by decision makers operating at a higher level. Thus, many decisions made by members of the Immigration Division of the Immigration and Refugee Board may be appealed to the Immigration Appeal Division; decisions of the IRB's Refugee Protection Division may be appealed to the the Refugee Appeal Division. Decisions reached by the appeal bodies may be reviewed by the Federal Court, whose decisions may be appealed to the Federal Court of Appeal and then to the Supreme Court of Canada.

Within this hierarchical framework, judicial decision makers adhere to a doctrine of precedent according to which they are bound by decisions on questions of law made at a higher level within the hierarchy. This principle is known as *stare decisis*. Thus, the Federal Court of Appeal is bound by decisions of the Supreme Court of Canada; the Federal Court is bound by decisions of both the Federal Court of Appeal and the Supreme Court of Canada. The lower position of tribunals within the hierarchy has led to decisions that they too are bound by the principle of *stare decisis*:

Thus, in *Canada (Minister of Citizenship and Immigration)* v *Stephenson*,[159] Dawson J of the Federal Court stated:

> First, the IAD [Immigration Appeal Division] is bound to follow decisions of this Court . . . . This Court has held in the context of conditional orders made under the Act that the condition to "be of good

---

158 RSC 1985, c F-7.
159 2008 FC 82 at para 41.

behaviour" requires that one abide by federal, provincial, and municipal statutes and regulations. The doctrine of *stare decisis* precludes the IAD from reaching a contrary conclusion, even where the IAD believes that the Federal Court has reached its decision in error . . . .

Three complexities relating to the principle of *stare decisis* are worthy of note.

First, recent Supreme Court decisions focusing on the relationship between courts and tribunals have indicated that courts when reviewing decisions by administrative tribunals and agencies should show deference to their interpretation of their home statute, unless the question is of "central importance to the legal system as a whole and outside the adjudicator's expertise."[160] To the extent that courts are now required to apply a standard of reasonableness rather than correctness when reviewing decisions on questions of law not of central importance and outside the adjudicator's expertise, the principle of *stare decisis* has lost much of its sway.

Second, the principle does not apply in relation to decisions made by a tribunal at the same level in the hierarchy.[161] Thus, members of each of the divisions of the Immigration and Refugee Board are not bound by decisions of their colleagues,[162] and judges in the Federal Court are not bound by their colleagues' decisions. Where judges in the Federal Court reach contradictory decisions, it is possible for a lower tribunal to follow the principle of *stare decisis* by selecting and applying one of the rulings.[163]

Third, the position of the Refugee Appeal Division is somewhat unusual. The *IRPA* provides that

---

160 *Canada (Canadian Human Rights Commission) v Canada (AG)*, 2011 SCC 53. For further discussion, see Chapters 14 and 16.

161 In *Miller v Canada (AG)*, 2002 FCA 370 at paras 9–10, the Federal Court of Appeal made the following remarks about abiding by its own decisions:

> To summarize, the jurisprudence cited by Urie JA holds that, in the interests of certainty and consistency, sound judicial administration requires that, save in exceptional circumstances, a Court of intermediate appellate jurisdiction should follow its prior decisions. The Court is responsible for the stability, consistency and predictability of the law.
>
> The test used for overruling a decision of another panel of this Court is that the previous decision is manifestly wrong, in the sense that the Court overlooked a relevant statutory provision, or a case that ought to have been followed.

162 See, for example, *Espinoza v Canada (Citizenship and Immigration)*, 2012 FC 502 in relation to the Refugee Protection Division.

163 See *Canada (Citizenship and Immigration) v Zhou*, 2008 FC 939.

a decision of a panel of three members of the Refugee Appeal Division has, for the Refugee Protection Division and for a panel of one member of the Refugee Appeal Division, the same precedential value as a decision of an appeal court has for a trial court.[164]

The implication is that most decisions rendered by the Refugee Appeal Division, being made by single member panels, have no precedential value for the Refugee Protection Division.[165]

---

164 *IRPA*, above note 25, s 171(c).
165 See Chapter 9 for further analysis of the Refugee Appeal Division.

PART TWO

STATUS IN CANADA

CHAPTER 3

STATUS IN CANADA

A. INTRODUCTION

Canadian immigration law determines who may enter, remain in, work in, or study in Canada. It has a geographical focus in that it is concerned primarily with *place*. Immigration law has little to say about individuals who live, work, or study outside Canada, even if they are employed by a Canadian company or enrolled in a distance education program run by a Canadian university.[1] Immigration law becomes relevant only when an individual seeks to enter, work, or study within the territory over which Canada claims sovereignty.

As a body of law, Canadian immigration law rests on an uncomplicated foundational pillar by attributing a status to every living person in the world and by citing this status as a crucial factor to be used in determining whether a person should be permitted to enter Canada

---

1   In some circumstances, the law does disregard geography. For example, Canadian citizens who are born outside the country and who are working outside the country can pass on their status to their child born outside the country if working for a Canadian government. They are thus placed in the same position as Canadian citizens located in Canada. Because of their employment, their geographical location is treated as irrelevant. Similarly, permanent residents are usually under a residency obligation. To retain their status they must spend a proportion of each five-year period in Canada. However, they too may fulfill their residence obligation by working outside the country in some exceptional circumstances. See *Immigration and Refugee Protection Act*, SC 2001, c 27, s 28 [*IRPA*].

and, if so, under what conditions. At the most basic level, only three distinct statuses are recognized: foreign national, permanent resident, and citizen.[2] However, as one examines in detail the edifice supported by this pillar, one finds that various categories of foreign nationals are recognized, including visitors, students, temporary workers, refugee claimants, protected persons, and others, each carrying its own opportunities and constraints. A person registered as an "Indian" under the *Indian Act* is also given special recognition, even if that person would otherwise count as a foreign national.[3] In addition, if one looks at the ways in which the law has developed and matured, one sees different conceptions of citizenship and permanent residence emerging and declining over time. In sum, one finds that the structure constructed on the simple pillar of status is both elaborate and complex.

This introductory chapter reveals the basic architecture of Canadian immigration law by considering some of the legal and theoretical problems created by the ascription of status and by examining in general terms the basic statuses attributed to non-citizens.

B. STATUS AND OPEN BORDERS

The idea that one's status should determine one's entitlement to enter Canada, or to work or study within the country, appears to have widespread popular support. When immigration policy emerges as an issue in election campaigns, it is rare that one comes across a political platform based on the idea that foreign nationals should be entitled to enjoy the same social, economic, or political benefits as citizens. Nevertheless, the idea that our borders should be open, or more open, continues to percolate and flourish both within academic circles and beyond. Various influential moral, political, and economic arguments

---

2   See *IRPA, ibid*, ss 2 and 19: Section 2 defines *foreign national* and *permanent resident*. Section 19 makes reference to a citizen "within the meaning of the *Citizenship Act*."

3   *IRPA, ibid*, s 19. In *Sandy Bay Ojibway First Nation v Canada (Minister of Citizenship and Immigration)*, 2006 FC 903, the Sandy Bay First Nation had adopted a Nigerian woman who was under a removal order as a band member and sought judicial review of the decision that she should be removed and a stay of the removal. Justice Harrington, at para 11, held that the First Nation had no standing to seek judicial review and did not address the claim that "each and every band (and there are more than 600) has the power to usurp the discretion of the Minister of Citizenship and Immigration by accepting non-residents as band members and thereby granting them permanent resident status."

have begun to challenge the dominant perspective and have gained recognition.

As we entered the twenty-first century, it became commonplace to hear references to "the forces of globalization." The world appeared to shrink as it became easier and cheaper to travel far from one's country of origin. The fact that hundreds of thousands of people are taking the opportunity to visit, work, and study in different countries has encouraged theorists to re-examine with closer scrutiny some of the legal institutions that developed in an earlier, more stable era when mobility was enjoyed by only a small elite. As barriers impeding cross-border movement of commodities and services disappear, one hears more often the question whether the same should happen to the barriers impeding the movement of people.[4]

For example, in a number of articles, the developmental economist Michael Clemens has made the case that there are large economic gains to be made by removing barriers to migration from poorer to richer countries. He concludes one article, "Economics and Emigration: Trillion-Dollar Bills on the Sidewalk," by stating:

> The available evidence suggests that the gains to lowering barriers to emigration appear much larger than gains from further reductions in barriers to goods trade or capital flows — and may be much larger than those available through any other shift in a single class of global economic policy.[5]

In similar fashion, John Kennan has defended the following conclusions:

> Liberal immigration policies are politically unpopular. To a large extent, this is because the beneficiaries of these policies are not allowed to vote. It is also true, however, that the enormous benefits associated with open borders have not received much attention in the economics literature. Economists are generally enthusiastic about free trade. But if free movement of goods is important, then surely free movement of people is even more important. One conclusion of this paper is that open borders could yield huge welfare gains: more than $10,000 a year for a randomly selected worker from a less-developed country

---

4   Nandita Sharma, "Global Apartheid and Nation-Statehood: Instituting Border Regimes" in James Goodman & Paul James, eds, *Nationalism and Global Solidarities* (New York: Routledge, 2007) 71; Joseph H Carens, "Aliens and Citizens: The Case for Open Borders" (1987) 49 *Review of Politics* 251 [Carens, "Aliens and Citizens"].

5   (2011) 25 *Journal of Economic Perspectives* 83 at 101.

(including non-migrants). Another is that these gains are associated with a relatively small reduction in the real wage in developed countries, and even this effect disappears as the capital–labor ratio adjusts over time; indeed if immigration restrictions are relaxed gradually, allowing time for investment in physical capital to keep pace, there is no implied reduction in real wages.[6]

Others have based their challenge to closed borders on considerations of justice rather than on an increase in economic welfare. The ideal of open borders is now presented more frequently as a basic precept of justice rather than as a utopian chimera. The fluidity of the modern world challenges the very idea that justice may be realized only within a multiplicity of distinct societies each with its own rigid rules of membership.[7]

Despite increased mobility, we still inhabit a world where economic and cultural opportunities are distributed unevenly in different regions of the globe, where people are frequently condemned to a life of destitution predominantly as a result of their place of birth or kinship. The very practice of allocating different statuses according to location or pedigree may be critiqued as arbitrary, irrational, and unjust. For some, the dominant mode of allocating citizenship by place of birth and/or by descent, coupled with the imposition of a lesser status on others, is blatantly unjust because this distribution of status grants unequal access to the world's limited but concentrated sources of wealth and opportunities according to an arbitrary criterion. Thus, Ayelet Schachar observes:

> [I]n our world, the global disparities are so great that under the present regimes of birthright citizenship, "some are born to sweet delight" as William Blake memorably put it in the *Auguries of Innocence*, while others (through no fault or responsibility of their own) are "born to an endless night." The reality of our world is that the endless night is more prevalent tha[n] the sweet delight. More than a billion people live on less than a dollar a day; about 2.7 billion live without access to adequate sanitation and more than 800 million are seriously malnourished.[8]

6   John Kennan, "Open Borders" (2013) 16 *Review of Economics Dynamics* L1 at L-11.
7   *Ibid.*
8   Ayelet Shachar, *The Birthright Lottery: Citizenship and Global Inequality* (Cambridge, MA: Harvard University Press, 2009) at 11–12.

Within this context, theorists in many disciplines have begun to explore different ways of understanding or conceptualizing the status of citizenship. For example, Thomas Simon views citizenship as a weapon against outsiders, against the economically disadvantaged, and even against insiders,[9] while others such as Rupaleem Bhuyan and Tracy Smith-Carrier characterize citizenship as a market or economic concept that may be applied to refer to individuals within their local communities and transnationally as well as at the state level.[10]

Others have focused on the injustice of denying permanent resident status to or deporting individuals who have resided for lengthy periods of time in a country because of their failure to regularize their status. Joseph Carens has made such an argument, proposing that

> [t]he moral right of states to apprehend and deport irregular migrants erodes with the passage of time. As irregular migrants become more and more settled, their membership in society grows in moral importance, and the fact that they settled without authorization becomes correspondingly less relevant. At some point, a threshold is crossed, and they acquire a moral claim to have their actual social membership legally recognized.[11]

Carens is also renowned for defending a broader position, namely, that a system of closed borders cannot be supported on grounds of justice. He argues that there can be strong reasons for wanting to migrate that support recognition of a basic liberty of movement between states:

> [P]eople might have powerful reasons to want to migrate *from* one state to another. Economic opportunities for particular individuals might vary greatly from one state to another even if economic inequalities among states were reduced by an international difference principle. One might fall in love with a citizen from another land, one might belong to a religion which has few followers in one's native land and many in another, one might seek cultural opportunities that are only available in another society. More generally, one has only to ask whether the right to migrate freely *within* a given society is an important liberty. The same sorts of considerations make migration across state boundaries important.[12]

---

9   Thomas Simon, "Citizenship as a Weapon" (2013) 17 *Citizenship Studies* 505.

10 Rupaleem Bhuyan & Tracy Smith-Carrier, "Constructions of Migrant Rights in Canada: Is Subnational Citizenship Possible?" (2012) 16 *Citizenship Studies* 203.

11 Joseph H Carens, *The Ethics of Immigration* (Oxford, UK: Oxford University Press, 2013) at 150.

12 Carens, "Aliens and Citizens," above note 4 at 258.

These arguments and perspectives have not gone unanswered. Indeed, they have generated sophisticated and thorough responses. Many scholars see some merit in the idea that there is "heft" in the concept of citizenship that has been adopted by our legislature as it provides protection, recognizable identity,[13] and formal legal status. For example, Ryan Pevnick has proposed that a system of closed borders can be defended and founded on the idea that members of a political society have a right to self-determination based on an idea of "associative ownership." He argues that

> citizens have no good reason to exclude those who seek mere territorial access (such as hikers eager to see the Grand Canyon . . .), but they do have reason to block those immigrants (the vast majority) who seek territorial access as a way to gain access to a set of public goods to which they are not entitled.[14]

The absence of entitlement, he explains, follows from the fact that the public goods in question exist only as a result of the efforts of the citizenry.

Despite the intellectual excitement generated by the concept of citizenship and the wide variety of critical views, the dominant framework has endured, a framework in which the nation-state is presented as having sovereignty to identify its own members and to operate as a closed system with closed borders.[15]

Policy statements from the legislature have, for the most part, ignored the subtleties of the academic debates, tended to assume the naturalness of the dominant modes of recognizing, and allocated citizenship by place of birth or by descent. They have proceeded on the assumption that regulatory measures concerning human movement from other states should be shaped by a judgment of what is in the best interest of current Canadians. Thus, the decision to increase the number of permanent residents admitted in 2015 to 285,000, the highest number in recent years, was defended by the minister of Citizenship and Immigration on the grounds that those being admitted are "a higher calibre of economic immigrant."[16] For the purposes of immigration law,

---

13   Audrey Macklin, "Who Is the Citizen's Other? Considering the Heft of Citizenship" (2007) 8 *Theoretical Inquiries in Law* 333.

14   Ryan Pevnick, *Immigration and the Constraints of Justice* (Cambridge: Cambridge University Press, 2011) at 59–60.

15   Catherine Dauvergne, "Amorality and Humanitarianism in Immigration Law" (1999) 37 *Osgoode Hall Law Journal* 597.

16   Joe Friesen, "Canada to Open the Door Wider to 'Higher Calibre' Immigrants" *The Globe and Mail* (31 October 2014), online: www.theglobeandmail.com/news/politics/canada-to-open-the-door-wider-to-higher-calibre-immigrants/article21417126/.

it appears that the government regards immigrants as primarily a form of human capital. Such philistinism has produced some serious causes for embarrassment and some legal paradoxes worthy of note.

A major paradox can be traced to the failure to acknowledge Carens's insight that individuals who have lived within a community for lengthy periods of time should have a claim to social membership: a claim that increases in strength as time passes. Underlying this insight is the idea that the state has a moral and political obligation to base criteria of membership on factors that reflect the actual experiences of individuals who live within the community, on their legitimate expectations, and on principles of fair treatment and on their vulnerability to exploitation. Instead of one's status determining one's rights, the inverse should be the case: an appreciation of a person's well-being and the pre-existing links with a community should determine one's status. Yet, Canadian courts have been unwilling to embrace this position, preferring instead to regard the legislature's determination of the strength of a person's entitlements to membership as authoritative, despite the fact that those whose claims are not recognized and are not represented within the legislature. The *Citizenship Act*[17] and the *Immigration and Refugee Protection Act*[18] are regarded as being the basic source of status and consequent rights. Although the *Canadian Charter of Rights and Freedoms (Charter)* includes reference to citizenship and permanent residence, in section 6, these concepts are not regarded by the courts as having a constitutional meaning.[19] This was established in *Solis v Canada (Minister of Citizenship and Immigration)*, where the appellant had argued that, notwithstanding the fact that he was not a citizen under the *Citizenship Act*, he had an independent *Charter*-based right to be considered a citizen because of his family ties and roots in Canada. Justice Rothstein, then sitting on the Federal Court of Appeal, rejected the argument, stating:

> We agree with Professor Hogg that the concept of citizenship has no meaning apart from statute. Citizenship is a creature of federal statute law. The *Citizenship Act* is subject to the overriding provisions of the *Charter* such that if some provision of the *Citizenship Act* is found by a court to violate the *Charter*, a *Charter* remedy is available. However, the appellant here does not challenge the *Citizenship Act* as such. He only says there is an additional *Charter*-based notion of

17   RSC 1985, c C-29.
18   *IRPA*, above note 1.
19   *Charter of Rights and Freedoms*, s 3, Part I of the *Constitution Act, 1982*, being Schedule B to the *Canada Act 1982* (UK), 1982, c 11 [*Charter*].

citizenship. For the reasons we have given we cannot agree with this submission.[20]

The same paradoxical relationship between rights and status is visible in the tension between the constitutional commitment to equality and the assignment of rights according to status. In *Andrews v Law Society of British Columbia*,[21] the first case in which the Supreme Court of Canada analyzed and applied the equality rights guaranteed by section 15 of the *Charter*, the Court held that a provincial law that reserved membership in the law society for citizens and denied access to permanent residents discriminated on a ground analogous to those enumerated in section 15.[22] The Court based its decision on recognition of the vulnerability of permanent residents as a consequence of their lack of capacity to vote. The decision magnifies the need to justify differential treatment between permanent residents and citizens. One may ask, Why is it not discriminatory to deport permanent residents when citizens are not subject to the same sanction? The answer that the Court has provided is not wholly satisfactory. In *Charkaoui v Canada (Citizenship and Immigration)*,[23] it noted that the *Charter* itself distinguishes between citizens and permanent residents, explicitly identifying only the former as having the right to enter and remain in the country. It then concludes that it must be constitutional to distinguish between citizens and permanent residents for the purposes of immigration but not for ulterior purposes. The primary difficulty with this resolution is that immigration is not a purpose in itself and is governed by ulterior considerations by a range of other purposes. The distinction between legitimate and unconstitutional differentiation becomes very difficult to discern.[24]

---

20   2000 CanLII 15121 at para 4 (FCA) [footnote omitted]; see also *Lee v Canada (Minister of Citizenship and Immigration)*, 2008 FC 614.

21   [1989] 1 SCR 143 [*Andrews*].

22   *Charter*, above note 19, s 15: Section 15 provides:

   15. (1) Every individual is equal before and under the law and has the right to the equal protection and equal benefit of the law without discrimination and, in particular, without discrimination based on race, national or ethnic origin, colour, religion, sex, age or mental or physical disability.

   (2) Subsection (1) does not preclude any law, program or activity that has as its object the amelioration of conditions of disadvantaged individuals or groups including those that are disadvantaged because of race, national or ethnic origin, colour, religion, sex, age or mental or physical disability.

23   2007 SCC 9.

24   *Ibid*: Charkaoui had argued that it was discriminatory to detain permanent residents while deportation proceedings were proceeding. The Court responded at para 130:

Further complications are revealed by a second decision. In *Lavoie v Canada*, a differentiation between citizens and permanent residents was held to be discriminatory,[25] but nevertheless it was held that the differentiation was justifiable under section 1 of the *Charter*, on the ground that there were good reasons to privilege citizens and to thereby create incentives to individuals to become citizens. The questionable premise on which the Court based this view was that, in a multicultural society, citizenship is the glue that keeps society together, and therefore it is defensible to attach privileges to it. It would seem that the legality of differential treatment between citizens and non-citizens may hinge on untheorized intuitions about the strength of the bonds that prevent or delay social entropy.

In a more recent decision, *Toussaint v Canada (AG)*,[26] the Federal Court of Appeal addressed the question whether immigration status qualifies as a ground of discrimination under section 15 and concluded that it does not. Toussaint had remained in Canada for several years without authorization. She claimed that an order in council that made available emergency health care to some foreign nationals who had been admitted into Canada discriminated against her by not providing assistance to persons in her situation. In his analysis, Stratas JA relied heavily on an earlier decision of the Supreme Court, *Corbière v Canada (Minister of Indian and Northern Affairs)*,[27] which focused on the grounds of discrimination that could be regarded as analogous to those enumerated in section 15 of the *Charter*. The relevant passage of this case states:

> What then are the criteria by which we identify a ground of distinction as analogous? The obvious answer is that we look for grounds of distinction that are analogous or like the grounds enumerated in s. 15 — race, national or ethnic origin, colour, religion, sex, age, or

---

[T]here are two ways in which the IRPA could, in some circumstances, result in discrimination. First, detention may become indefinite as deportation is put off or becomes impossible, for example because there is no country to which the person can be deported. Second, the government could conceivably use the IRPA not for the purpose of deportation, but to detain the person on security grounds. In both situations, the source of the problem is that the detention is no longer related, in effect or purpose, to the goal of deportation. In *Re A*, the legislation considered by the House of Lords expressly provided for indefinite detention; this was an important factor leading to the majority's holding that the legislation went beyond the concerns of immigration legislation and thus wrongfully discriminated between nationals and non-nationals . . . .

25   2002 SCC 23.
26   2011 FCA 213 [*Toussaint*].
27   [1999] 2 SCR 203.

mental or physical disability. It seems to us that what these grounds have in common is the fact that they often serve as the basis for stereotypical decisions made not on the basis of merit but on the basis of a personal characteristic that is immutable or changeable only at unacceptable cost to personal identity . . . . To put it another way, s. 15 targets the denial of equal treatment on grounds that are actually immutable, like race, or constructively immutable, like religion. Other factors identified in the cases as associated with the enumerated and analogous grounds, like the fact that the decision adversely impacts on a discrete and insular minority or a group that has been historically discriminated against, may be seen to flow from the central concept of immutable or constructively immutable personal characteristics, which too often have served as illegitimate and demeaning proxies for merit-based decision making.[28]

Justice Stratas applied this analysis to conclude:

"Immigration status" is not a "[characteristic] that we cannot change." It is not "immutable or changeable only at unacceptable cost to personal identity." Finally "immigration status" — in this case, presence in Canada illegally — is a characteristic that the government has a "legitimate interest in expecting [the person] to change." Indeed, the government has a real, valid and justified interest in expecting those present in Canada to have a legal right to be in Canada . . . .[29]

This passage is strange and problematic, insofar as it is odd to state that individuals can change their immigration status — this decision is usually in the hands of the government. The idea that seven billion individuals on this planet have chosen not to be Canadian does not accurately explain why people have the status that they have. Moreover, although he accepts the analysis of "discrimination" offered in the case of *Andrews*,[30] Stratas JA does not try to reconcile his conclusion that

---

28   *Ibid* at para 13.
29   *Toussaint*, above note 26 at para 99.
30   *Andrews*, above note 21 at 174–75: In *Andrews*, discrimination is analyzed as

   . . . a distinction, whether intentional or not but based on grounds relating to personal characteristics of the individual or group, which has the effect of imposing burdens, obligations, or disadvantages on such individual or group not imposed upon others, or which withholds or limits access to opportunities, benefits, and advantages available to other members of society. Distinctions based on personal characteristics attributed to an individual solely on the basis of association with a group will rarely escape the charge of discrimination, while those based on an individual's merits and capacities will rarely be so classed.

immigration status is not an analogous ground with the decision in that case. Nevertheless, in *Canadian Doctors for Refugee Care v Canada (AG)*, MacTavish J considered herself to be bound by this decision and held that "'immigration status' does not qualify as an analogous ground under section 15 of the *Charter*."[31]

C. CONCLUSION

The chapters that follow examine the details of a legal regime that accepts the existence of multiple statuses, each carrying its own package of rights and privileges. Within that regime it is all too easy to assume without question that this is a natural or self-evidently legitimate state of affairs. However, occasionally, cracks appear in the system as its tectonic plates collide or grind against each other. The commitment to universal ideals of equality and human dignity cannot be easily reconciled with a set of principles of inclusion and exclusion that distinguish members from outsiders. This chapter has aimed to bring these fundamental tensions to central stage in an effort to counterbalance the tendency of the regulatory system to represent itself as doctrinally consistent and incontrovertibly defensible.

---

31   2014 FC 651 at para 14.

CHAPTER 4

TEMPORARY STATUS IN CANADA

A. INTRODUCTION

Foreign nationals may seek to enter Canada temporarily for a variety of reasons. They may come to visit family or to be tourists, students, business visitors, or workers.[1] As discussed in Chapter 5, some apply for temporary status because, in specified cases, Canadian law offers the inducement of future permanent status but only after the applicants have endured the insecurity of living as temporary residents for an extended period. This chapter examines the legal framework that supports the established regimes of temporary residence, focusing on the legal rules that define the process of obtaining and retaining temporary status. Underpinning the technical details, one finds, are controversial assumptions about the reasons for imposing conditions and limits on the time foreign nationals, particularly workers and students, may remain in Canada. Research and public discussion have drawn attention to the hardships and unintended consequences that such restrictions

---

1 See Citizenship and Immigration Canada, *Facts and Figures 2013 – Immigration Overview: Permanent and Temporary Residents*, online: www.cic.gc.ca/english/resources/statistics/menu-fact.asp [*Facts and Figures 2013*], listing that in 2000 there were 122,700 foreign students and in 2013 there were more than double that figure of 304,876. Although the personal and institutional experiences are somewhat different, the increase in the number of international students who normally pay large sums for a Canadian education has had a major impact on post-secondary education.

can cause.[2] Statistics reveal a substantial increase in the number of foreign nationals who have been admitted into Canada as temporary workers,[3] yet many of these have been denied a safe working environment or the benefits that Canadian workers would expect.[4] The emergence of a large, temporary population unrepresented in our political institutions and excluded from social benefits has raised deep questions about the integrity of our community and about the social and economic impacts of our reliance on their labour.

B. SECTION 22.1 DECLARATIONS

Before examining the routes that a foreign national may take to acquire temporary resident status, it is illuminating to look first at a section of the *Immigration and Refugee Protection Act*[5] that came into force in 2013. Section 22.1 provides:

(1) The Minister may, on the Minister's own initiative, declare that a foreign national may not become a temporary resident if the Minister is of the opinion that it is justified by public policy considerations.

(2) A declaration has effect for the period specified by the Minister, which is not to exceed 36 months.

(3) The Minister may, at any time, revoke a declaration or shorten its effective period.

(4) The [Annual Report to Parliament] must include the number of declarations made under subsection (1) and set out the public policy considerations that led to the making of the declarations.

---

2   For example, Luin Goldring, Carolina Berinstein, & Judith Bernhard, "Institutionalizing Precarious Migratory Status in Canada" in (2009) 13 *Citizenship Studies* 239; Nandita Rani Sharma, "Race, Class, Gender, and the Making of Difference: The Social Organization of 'Migrant Workers' in Canada" (2000) 24 *Atlantis* 5.

3   *Facts and Figures 2013*, above note 1: In 2000, Canada admitted 67,345 temporary foreign workers who hold work permits, while in 2013, Canada admitted 176,613 temporary foreign workers. Also note that the 2013 statistics distinguish between temporary foreign workers and those in the International Mobility Program (work permits granted where no LMIA is needed). In 2013, there were 284,050 that were in Canada under this program.

4   See Canadian Labour Congress, *Canada's Temporary Foreign Worker Program (TFWP): Model Program – or Mistake?* (April 2011), online: www.canadianlabour.ca/sites/default/files/pdfs/model-program-or-mistake-2011-en.pdf.

5   *Immigration and Refugee Protection Act*, SC 2001, c 27 [*IRPA*].

The breadth of discretion delegated to the minister by this section is quite remarkable. Although the minister must report the reasons for the exercise of this power to Parliament annually, the section appears to give the minister a *carte blanche* to prohibit any particular individual from entering Canada. The ability of Canadians to associate with nationals from other countries has been substantially curtailed and is now dependent not on a framework of legal rules but on the government's assessment that such association is not contrary to public policy. While it is technically possible that, on judicial review, the Federal Court might hold that a declaration made on this ground is unreasonable, it is difficult to conceive of cases where a judicial body would consider itself competent to render such a decision. On the other hand, there is scope for a constitutional challenge to this provision based on grounds of vagueness and overbreadth; again, though, the likelihood of success of such a challenge may be somewhat tenuous.[6] In any event, the section reveals the government's willingness, if not eagerness, to dispense with the legal rules that define the acquisition of temporary resident status in order to achieve results that it wants to achieve.

C. AN OVERVIEW OF TEMPORARY RESIDENCE

When applying for temporary resident status, a foreign national may apply as a member of one of three classes: the visitor class,[7] the student class,[8] or the worker class.[9] While all three classes are subject to a visa regime, which is qualified by a wide range of exemptions, students and workers are also required to obtain a permit, subject to a narrower range of exemptions. In most circumstances, a person will apply for the needed visa and permit from outside the country. Beginning in 2015, a person who is exempted from the visa requirement and who is travelling to Canada by air will also be required to obtain an Electronic Travel Authorization before boarding. On arrival at a port of entry, foreign nationals are examined and only then may be granted temporary status. The status expires at the end of the authorized period but, in

---

6   *Canadian Charter of Rights and Freedoms,* s 7, Part I of the *Constitution Act, 1982,* being Schedule B to the *Canada Act 1982* (UK), 1982, c 11 [*Charter*].

7   *Immigration and Refugee Protection Regulations,* 2002 SOR/2002-227, ss 191–92 [*Regulations*].

8   *Ibid,* ss 210–11.

9   *Ibid,* ss 194–95.

some cases, the temporary resident may apply for an extension during that period. After expiry, or in some circumstances where status is lost, the individual may apply for restoration of status.

D. TEMPORARY RESIDENT VISAS (TRVs)

A temporary resident visa (TRV) is "an official counterfoil document issued by a visa office that is placed in a person's passport to show that he or she has met the requirements for admission to Canada as a temporary resident."[10] Section 7(1) of the *Immigration and Refugee Protection Regulations* provides, "A foreign national may not enter Canada to remain on a temporary basis without first obtaining a temporary resident visa."[11] However, this is a default position and is subject to exemptions that significantly limit its ambit.[12]

1) Types of Visa

There are three types of visitor visas: the single-entry visa, the multiple-entry visa, and the transit visa. The single-entry visa allows foreign nationals to enter Canada only once during the validity of the TRV.[13] This TRV can be issued up to six months before the expected date of travel and expires at least one month after the expected date of arrival in Canada.[14] Despite its name, foreign nationals with a single-entry visa may re-enter Canada following a visit to the United States or to St. Pierre and Miquelon within the authorized period of stay.[15] A multiple-entry visa allows the foreign national to seek entry into Canada from any country as often as necessary during the validity of the visa.[16] A transit visa allows foreign nationals to travel through Canada without stopping or visiting. A transit visa may be issued to a foreign national who is in Canada for less than 48 hours.[17] Two programs — the "Transit without

---

10 Citizenship and Immigration Canada, *What Is a Temporary Resident Visa (TRV)?*, online: www.cic.gc.ca/english/resources/tools/temp/visa/what.asp.

11 *Regulations*, above note 7, s 11.

12 *Ibid.*

13 Citizenship and Immigration Canada, *Temporary Residents: Three Types of Temporary Resident Visas*, online: www.cic.gc.ca/english/resources/tools/temp/visa/types/three.asp [*Temporary Residents*].

14 *Ibid.*

15 *Regulations*, above note 7, s 190(3)(f).

16 *Temporary Residents*, above note 13.

17 *Ibid.*

Visa Program" (TWOV), available to citizens of Indonesia, Thailand, Taiwan, and the Philippines, and the "China Transit Program" (CTP), available to Chinese citizens — allow transit through Canada to and from the United States without a Canadian transit visa where specified conditions are met.[18]

2) The "Super Visa"

As noted in Chapter 6, the most recent addition to the visitor visa program is the parent and grandparent super visa.[19] In November 2011, the Canadian government imposed a temporary pause on the acceptance of applications for sponsoring parents and grandparents as permanent residents and instead introduced the parent and grandparent super visa.[20] The stated policy rationale for this new TRV was to

- facilitate multiple entry and longer term stays for Temporary Resident Visas (TRVs) issued to applicants who require a TRV to visit their child or grandchild who is a citizen or permanent resident of Canada; and
- facilitate authorized stays of longer duration for those coming from visa-exempt countries.[21]

Multiple-entry TRVs under this category are valid for up to ten years. Each period of residence may extend to up to two years.[22] In order to be granted a "super visa," parents or grandparents of Canadian citizens or permanent residents must undergo a medical examination and be admissible on health grounds.[23] They must provide evidence of private medical insurance and evidence of financial support from their child or grandchild for the duration of the requested stay.[24] The government

---

18   *Ibid.* See Citizenship and Immigration Canada, *Determine Your Eligibility – Transit without a Visa*, online: www.cic.gc.ca/english/department/twov/travellers.asp; Citizenship and Immigration Canada, *Temporary Residents: China Transit Program (CTP)*, online: www.cic.gc.ca/english/resources/tools/temp/visa/china.asp.

19   This visa program came into force on 1 December 2011.

20   Minister of Citizenship and Immigration Canada, *Ministerial Instruction regarding the Parent and Grandparent Super Visa* (1 December 2011), online: www.cic.gc.ca/english/department/mi/supervisa.asp [*Ministerial Instruction Super Visa*].

21   *Ibid.*

22   *Ibid.*

23   Citizenship and Immigration Canada, *Parent and Grandparent Super Visa* (17 January 2014), online: www.cic.gc.ca/english/visit/supervisa.asp [*Super Visa*].

24   *Ibid.* Applicants must provide proof of the relationship to the child or grandchild. Proof of financial support can include an invitation letter outlining the living arrangements, care, and support of the parent or grandparent during the

advocates that even those who are exempt from obtaining a temporary visa may benefit from acquiring a visa of this type since it authorizes a two-year stay, which is longer than would normally be granted to a visa-exempt applicant for temporary status.[25]

This new program is premised on the assumption that it will facilitate faster family reunification, albeit through temporary sojourns rather than through a permanent residence program. Although lengthy processing of permanent resident applications of family members was problematic, the solution presented through this temporary residence program may not provide an adequate alternative: it permits only an insecure form of impermanent and provisional reunification of family in two ways. First, this scheme does not allow for the benefits of support that can be offered to parents and grandparents by family members who are fully integrated in Canadian society. Some parents and grandparents who are most in need of support may be unable to obtain medical insurance. This lack may necessitate travel and absences from Canada by the children or grandchildren. In the case of permanent residents, their status may be jeopardized since they are required to be physically present in Canada for at least two years in every five year period.[26] As noted in Chapter 6, it is now once again possible to sponsor parents and grandparents as permanent residents, but an annual quota has been instituted. In 2014, the number was capped at 5,000.[27] Second, this scheme assumes that parents and grandparents cannot themselves offer support. Such persons can provide childcare and other support for family members in Canada, allowing them to integrate more fully into Canadian society through full-time work or other activities.

3) Exemptions

There are four classes of exemptions to the general rule that a TRV must be acquired. The first exempts persons of particular nationality.[28] The second exempts persons because of the limited purpose behind their

---

duration of the stay. Similar to entering into an undertaking in the sponsorship process for permanent resident applications, applicants should establish that they meet the minimum income threshold according to the low-income cut off (LICO) for their household. See Chapter 5 for more information on LICO. Private medical insurance must provide a minimum coverage of $100,000.

25 *Super Visa*, above note 23.
26 *IRPA*, above note 5, s 28.
27 See Citizenship and Immigration Canada, *Sponsoring Your Family* (24 December 2012), online: CIC Help Centre www.cic.gc.ca/ENGLISH/helpcentre/questions-anwsers-by-topic.asp?t=14&wbdisable=true.
28 *Regulations*, above note 7, ss 7(2)(a) and 190(1)–(2.1).

need to enter Canada.[29] The third includes persons who have previously obtained authorization and who are re-entering Canada.[30] Finally, the fourth covers those who have obtained a temporary resident permit (TRP) to overcome requirements surrounding inadmissibility under the IRPA.[31] The existence of this fourth category emphasizes the important difference between a visa (the TRV) and a permit (the TRP).

a) Citizens of Listed Countries

The first class of exemptions is described in the *Regulations*. Section 190(1), which provides that citizens from listed countries do not need to apply or obtain a TRV to enter Canada.[32] Special provision is also made for diplomats and individuals in possession of particular types of passports.[33] The list of countries subject to the nationality exemption has been modified frequently. The imposition of a visa on the citizens of another country has proven to be a sensitive issue in international relations. It may interfere with free trade relations between countries or may be interpreted as an unfriendly slight.[34] The presence or absence of countries on the list may depend on the number of citizens from that country who have overstayed their period of authorization in Canada. The imposition of a visa provides a prophylactic measure that aims to filter out such cases. It has also been used as a barrier to prevent the arrival of refugee claimants. In some circumstances where the number

---

29 *Ibid*, ss 7(2)(a) and 190(3)–(4).

30 *Ibid*, s 7(2)(c).

31 *IRPA*, above note 5, s 24(1); *Regulations,* above note 7, s 7(2)(b).

32 *Regulations, ibid*, s 190(1). Currently, the exemption applies to citizens from the following countries: Andorra, Antigua and Barbuda, Australia, Austria, Bahamas, Barbados, Belgium, Brunei Darussalam, Croatia, Cyprus, Denmark, Estonia, Finland, France, Federal Republic of Germany, Greece, Hungary, Iceland, Ireland, Italy, Japan, Republic of Korea, Latvia, Liechtenstein, Luxembourg, Malta, Monaco, Netherlands, New Zealand, Norway, Papua New Guinea, Portugal, St Kitts and Nevis, Samoa, San Marino, Singapore, Slovakia, Slovenia, Solomon Islands, Spain, Sweden, or Switzerland. Further, the following are also exempt: British citizens, a British overseas citizen who is readmissible to the United Kingdom, or a citizen of a British overseas territory who derives that citizenship through birth, descent, naturalization, or registration in one of the British overseas territories, a national of the United States, or a person lawfully admitted to the United States for permanent residence.

33 *Regulations, ibid*, ss 190(2)–(2.1). This section provides detailed requirements for passports issued in specific countries.

34 For example, see Colin Robertson, "Canada Needs to Lift Visa Requirements for Mexicans" *The Globe and Mail* (28 October 2014), online: www.theglobeandmail. com/news/world/world-insider/why-canada-needs-to-lift-visa-requirement-for-mexicans/article21334644/#dashboard/follows/.

of "overstays" or refugee claimants has been volatile, a country's inclusion or exclusion in the list has changed within a short time span.[35] It is always important to consult the most current version of the *Regulations* to determine whether a visa is required.[36]

b) Particular Limited Purpose

The second class of persons exempted from obtaining a TRV embraces persons who have a particular limited purpose for entering Canada. This class includes members of a transportation crew,[37] passengers on transiting flights stopping over in Canada to refuel,[38] persons coming to Canada to carry out official duties as members of armed forces of a country,[39] persons entering from the United States for an interview with a US consular officer concerning their immigration visa for the United States,[40] persons conducting inspections on flights,[41] and persons who are accredited representatives or advisers to an aviation accident or incident investigation.[42]

c) Re-entry

Those who have previously obtained authorization whether through an existing TRV or by other means may be exempt from obtaining a visa if they leave the country and re-enter.[43]

d) Temporary Resident Permit (TRP) Holders

A temporary resident permit (TRP) is an exceptional document issued by an immigration officer to a foreign national, who is either inadmissible or who does not meet the requirements of the *IRPA,* where the

---

35 For example, in April 1996, Canada lifted the visa requirement on nationals of the Czech Republic but reimposed it in October 1997 to prevent persons of Roma descent from entering Canada. In October 2007, Canada removed the visa requirement in response to political pressure from the European Commission when the Czech Republic joined the European Union. See Citizenship and Immigration Canada, *Backgrounder – The Visa Requirement for the Czech Republic,* online: CIC www.cic.gc.ca/english/department/media/ backgrounders/2009/2009-07-13a.asp.

36 Proposed amendments to s 190 of the *Regulations* have already been announced as part of the package of amendments establishing the Electronic Travel Authorization, due to come into force in 2015. See Section E, below in this chapter.

37 *Regulations,* above note 7, ss 190(3)(a) and 190(3.1).

38 *Ibid,* ss 190(3)(b)–(c).

39 *Ibid,* s 190(3)(d).

40 *Ibid,* s 190(3)(e).

41 *Ibid,* s 190(3)(g).

42 *Ibid,* s 190(3)(h).

43 *Ibid,* s 7(2)(c). This exemption will apply to those with multiple-entry visas.

officer is of the opinion that its issuance is justified under the circumstances.[44] As explained in the Operational Manual, a TRP should be issued only for "compelling" reasons. The manual states:

> Normally, persons who do not meet the requirements of the Immigration and Refugee Protection Act are refused permanent resident or temporary resident visas abroad, denied admission at a port of entry, or refused processing within Canada. In some cases, however, there may be compelling reasons for an officer to issue a temporary resident permit to allow a person who does not meet the requirements of the Act to enter or remain in Canada.[45]

An officer may weigh the seriousness of the ground of inadmissibility or the seriousness of the failure to comply with the Act or *Regulations* or the risk that an inadmissible person would present in Canada against the contributions the applicant may make to the community[46] or any humanitarian and compassionate grounds.[47] Relevant factors include the existence of family ties or the best interests of children.[48] Where an application for a TRP has been made, an officer has an obligation to consider the request and a failure to do so is a reviewable error.[49] The onus, however, is on the applicant to justify why a TRP should be granted.[50]

Although the grant of a TRP is a discretionary decision,[51] there are restrictions on those to whom it may be issued. Foreign nationals whose refugee claims have been rejected, withdrawn, or abandoned are barred from requesting a TRP for twelve months after their claim

---

44   IRPA, above note 5, ss 24(1)–(2): Where the TRP has been issued outside Canada, the holder cannot become a temporary resident in Canada until that person has been examined upon arrival in Canada. See, generally, Citizenship and Immigration Canada, Operational Manual OP 20: *Temporary Resident Permits*, online at www.cic.gc.ca/english/resources/manuals/op/op20-eng.pdf [Operational Manual OP 20].

45   *Ibid* at 5.1.

46   See, for example, *Alvarez v Canada (Minister of Citizenship and Immigration)*, 2011 FC 667.

47   See, for example, *Ferraro v Canada (Minister of Citizenship and Immigration)*, 2011 FC 801.

48   *Ali v Canada (Minister of Citizenship and Immigration)*, 2008 FC 784.

49   See, for example, *Shah v Canada (Minister of Citizenship and Immigration)*, 2011 FC 1269; *Lee v Canada (Minister of Citizenship and Immigration)*, 2006 FC 1461.

50   *Farhat v Canada (Minister of Citizenship and Immigration)*, 2006 FC 1275.

51   See, for example, *Rodgers v Canada (Minister of Citizenship and Immigration)*, 2006 FC 1093.

has been rejected, withdrawn, or abandoned.[52] Designated foreign nationals[53] are barred from requesting a TRP for a period of five years.[54]

A TRP may be issued for a period of up to three years, and the period of validity may be extended.[55] It may also be cancelled at any time.[56] It is deemed to be cancelled when the foreign national leaves without obtaining prior authorization to re-enter Canada.[57] A TRP holder who has been granted temporary status is eligible, after a passage of time, to apply for permanent residence as a member of the permit-holder class.[58]

4) Exemptions and Judicial Review

Where an officer errs in failing to apply an exemption to a person trying to enter Canada without a TRV, the person may have recourse to judicial review at the Federal Court. While this solution may not be efficient, the court has, in the past, quashed such errors.[59]

5) Requirements for Acquiring a TRV

A foreign national who is not exempt from obtaining a TRV must submit a paper application to a visa office before arriving at a port of entry. An application for a TRV may be made to a visa office in a country other than the applicant's country of nationality as long as she has valid immigration status within that country. Thus, a person who has valid status in Canada may apply for a new visa from within Canada.[60] This would allow re-entry should the person leave the country.

The onus is on the applicant to show that he has met the requirements for a TRV. In *Obeng v Canada (Minister of Citizenship and Immigration)*, Lagacé J states:

---

52 *Regulations*, above note 7, s 24(4); *Dhandal v Canada (Minister of Citizenship and Immigration)*, 2009 FC 865. See Chapter 14 for more information on inadmissibility.

53 The laws defining designated foreign nationals are examined in Chapter 9.

54 *Regulations*, above note 7, s 24(5): For designated foreign nationals (DFNs) that have made a refugee claim or application for protection, the five-year period commences the day after which a final determination has been made. For other DFNs, the five-year period commences the day after they are deemed a DFN.

55 Operational Manual OP 20, above note 44 at 5.4.

56 *IRPA*, above note 5, s 24(1).

57 Operational Manual OP 20, above note 44 at 5.17.

58 *Regulations*, above note 7, ss 64–65.

59 See, for example, *De Brito v Canada (Minister of Citizenship and Immigration)*, 2003 FC 1379. See Chapter 16 for more information on judicial review.

60 See Citizenship and Immigration Canada, *Apply for a New Temporary Resident Visa from within Canada*, online: www.cic.gc.ca/english/visit/cpp-o-apply.asp.

A foreign national seeking to enter Canada is presumed to be an immigrant, and it is up to him to rebut this presumption. It was therefore up to the applicant, in the present instance, to prove to the visa officer that he is not an immigrant and that he would leave Canada at the end of the authorized period that he requested.[61]

If an applicant is denied a TRV, there is no right of appeal. The applicant may apply for leave to seek judicial review at the Federal Court.[62] In *Thomas v Canada (Minister of Citizenship and Immigration)*, the court held that the principles of procedural fairness do not require the officer to provide the applicant with an interview to address questions that arise from the materials submitted.[63] The officer is entitled to make a determination based on the application as it was presented. In *Toor v Canada (Minister of Citizenship and Immigration)*, however, the court held that an officer has an obligation to confront the applicant with adverse conclusions when the officer relies on material *not known* to the applicant.[64] In some cases, the court has insisted that the officer should offer an opportunity for response from the applicant when basing the decision on "stereotypes and generalizations."[65] Where an officer is required to draw concerns to the attention of the applicant and seek a response, the officer may send a "fairness" letter instead of having an interview.

---

61 2008 FC 754; see *Regulations*, above note 7, s 11(2). See also *da Silva v Canada (Minister of Citizenship and Immigration)*, 2007 FC 1138, where the court held that the applicant has no legal right to obtain a visa and bears the burden of establishing the merits of his claim.

62 *IRPA*, above note 5, s 72(1). See Chapter 16 on judicial review and, for example, *Kuewor v Canada (Minister of Citizenship and Immigration)*, 2010 FC 707, where the court held that the conclusion must be connected to the evidence presented in the application; *Groohi v Canada (Minister of Citizenship and Immigration)*, 2009 FC 837, where the court held that an officer must provide reasons and an analysis of evidence provided; *Rudder v Canada (Minister of Citizenship and Immigration)*, 2009 FC 689; *Villagonzalo v Canada (Minister of Citizenship and Immigration)*, 2008 FC 1127, where the court held that the officer should consider the applicant's explanations.

63 2009 FC 1038.

64 2006 FC 573.

65 For example, in *Bonilla v Canada (Minister of Citizenship and Immigration)*, 2007 FC 20 [*Bonilla*], the court held that the applicant should be given an opportunity to respond to concerns an officer had about her not returning home after the authorized period because she would have lost ties to her home country as a result of the length of her stay in Canada.

In general, the requirements to be met are that the applicant

1) has applied for a TRV as a member of one of the three classes of applicant (visitor, worker, or student) and has met and continues to meet the requirements for that class;[66]
2) will leave Canada by the end of the period authorized for stay;[67]
3) is not inadmissible;[68]
4) is not subject to a section 22.1 determination by the minister that the applicant should not be allowed entry into Canada on public policy considerations;[69]
5) holds a passport or other document that may be used to enter the country that issued it or another country;[70] and
6) has passed a medical examination in the rare circumstances where one is required.[71]

Of these requirements, the intention to leave Canada at the end of the authorized period is scrutinized most carefully both by decision makers and in judicial review. Officers will look at various factors to determine whether an applicant intends to remain in Canada after the authorized period: these include whether the applicant has family or economic ties to the country of origin;[72] whether the applicant has

---

66 *IRPA*, above note 5, s 11; *Regulations*, above note 7, ss 179(a), 179(d), and 180. A number of documents must be submitted along with an application for one of the TRV classes. For a complete list, consult Citizenship and Immigration Canada. See *Regulations*, above note 7, s 11(2), for information about where to submit applications. Applicants outside Canada submit their applications to a visa office either in the country in which the applicant was lawfully admitted or in the applicant's country of nationality or habitual residence. Applicants already in Canada can submit their applications to a case-processing centre identified by Citizenship and Immigration Canada.

67 *IRPA*, above note 5, ss 20(1)(b) and 22(1); *Regulations*, above note 7, s 179(b).

68 *IRPA*, above note 5, s 22(1); *Regulations*, above note 7, s 179(e).

69 *IRPA*, above note 5, ss 22(1) and 22.1.

70 *Regulations*, above note 7, s 179(c).

71 *IRPA*, above note 5, s 16(2)(b); *Regulations,* above note 7, ss 30(2)–(3) and 179(f).

72 An officer may review whether the applicant will be accompanied by family or whether the family will stay in the country of origin. An officer may view the absence of family ties as a reason why the applicant may not leave Canada after the authorized period has ended. An officer may also examine the applicant's employment in the home country and also the person's financial situation. If an applicant does not have a job to return to or any property or investments to return to, an officer may see this as an indication that the applicant will not leave after the authorized period has ended. See, for example, *Calma v Canada (Minister of Citizenship and Immigration)*, 2009 FC 742; and *Li v Canada (Minister of Citizenship and Immigration)*, 2008 FC 1284. In this latter case the court held that an interview would have been appropriate for the applicant to explain the

enough financial resources for a stay in Canada;[73] the economic and political situation in the country of origin;[74] any personal obligations or responsibilities the applicant may have in the country of origin;[75] the purpose of the foreign national's visit to Canada;[76] and whether the applicant has permanent status or citizenship in the country of origin or the country in which she applied for the TRV. Where an application has been made outside the country of habitual residence/nationality and the applicant's status in that country has expired, officers may regard this contravention of immigration rules as an indication that the applicant may not leave Canada after the authorized period of temporary residence has expired.

---

extent of his family ties in China; see also *Ogbonnaya v Canada (Minister of Citizenship and Immigration)*, 2008 FC 317; *Murai v Canada (Minister of Citizenship and Immigration)*, 2006 FC 186 [*Murai*]; and *Paramasivam v Canada (Minister of Citizenship and Immigration)*, 2010 FC 811.

73   An officer may review whether the applicant has sufficient funds for her stay in Canada, including the return trip at the end of the authorized period. An officer may rely on information such as bank statements, letters of employment, and documentation showing evidence of various kinds of assets. An officer may also accept proof of adequate support by a host or family member in Canada, which can be provided through letters of invitation along with documentation of the host's income and number of members in the host's family.

74   For example, instability in the country of origin may cause a decision maker to consider whether an applicant has a true intention to return to that country. See, for example, *Baylon v Canada (Minister of Citizenship and Immigration)*, 2009 FC 938, where the court stated that local conditions in the applicant's home country can be part of the broader picture which the visa officer can consider, but oversimplified generalizations cannot and should not form the basis of what must be an individualized assessment based on the circumstances of the individual. See also *Obot v Canada (Minister of Citizenship and Immigration)*, 2012 FC 208, in which the court held that an officer's knowledge of the conditions in a country does not constitute a form of judicial notice as there could be a difference of opinion as to the conditions in a particular country. *Bahr v Canada (Minister of Citizenship and Immigration)*, 2012 FC 527, decided that the onus is on the applicant to ensure that the application is comprehensive and contains all that is needed to make a convincing case and that an officer can rely on general experience and knowledge of local conditions to draw inferences and reach conclusions on the basis of what is provided by the applicant.

75   Factors such as an elderly parent, business obligations, or other responsibilities may convince an officer that the applicant will leave within the authorized period on the TRV. See, for example, *Calaunan v Canada (Minister of Citizenship and Immigration)*, 2011 FC 1494 [*Calaunan*].

76   See, for example, *Radics v Canada (Minister of Citizenship and Immigration)*, 2004 FC 1590 [*Radics*]; and *Stanislavsky v Canada (Minister of Citizenship and Immigration)*, 2003 FC 835.

On judicial review, it is well established that a decision to deny a TRV based on an unreasonable assessment that the person will overstay should be quashed. It has been held that officers have some discretion to "rely on their common sense and rationality"[77] to consider factors such as an applicant's language abilities,[78] failure to communicate with her future employer,[79] possession of sufficient funds to stay in Canada,[80] or long-term objectives.[81] However, an officer must be careful not to speculate or take into consideration factors that are irrelevant or unreasonable. A wide range of factors has prompted the Federal Court to characterize an assessment as unreasonable.[82] In *Cao v Canada (Minister of Citizenship and Immigration)*, where the officer decided that a person who had applied to work temporarily in Canada would be unlikely to return to China because the financial benefits of staying would be a strong incentive to stay, the Federal Court stated:

> The impugned decision is unreasonable not simply because it is stereotypical, but also because it relies on the very factor which would induce someone to come here temporarily in the first place as the main reason for keeping that person out.[83]

While it has been held that it is quite appropriate to take into account a person's travel history as a positive factor showing that the person is likely to return (having done so in the past), the applicant's lack of travel cannot be used as the principal reason for refusing an

---

77   *Calaunan*, above note 75.

78   *Li v Canada (Minister of Citizenship and Immigration)*, 2012 FC 484, where the court held that the applicant's English capability might not be high but was adequate for the work sought. Further, the applicant should have been given an opportunity to respond to this concern held by the officer; *Minhas v Canada (Minister of Citizenship and Immigration)*, 2009 FC 696 [*Minhas*].

79   *Vairea v Canada (Minister of Citizenship and Immigration)*, 2006 FC 1238.

80   *Onyeka v Canada (Minister of Citizenship and Immigration)*, 2009 FC 336 [*Onyeka*].

81   *Boni v Canada (Minister of citizenship and Immigration)*, 2005 FC 31.

82   See, for example, *Momi v Canada (Minister of Citizenship and Immigration)*, 2013 FC 162, where the court found the officer's inferences or considerations regarding whether the applicant would leave Canada during the authorized period were irrelevant or unreasonable. Among the considerations were that the applicant's status in Australia was expiring. See also *Sempertegui v Canada (Minister of Citizenship and Immigration)*, 2009 FC 1176; and *Dhillon v Canada (Minister of Citizenship and Immigration)*, 2009 FC 614.

83   2010 FC 941 at para 11. See also *Minhas*, above note 78; and *Kindie v Canada (Minister of Citizenship and Immigration)*, 2011 FC 850 [*Kindie*], where the court held that there must be an objective reason to question the motivation of the applicant and that TRVs are premised on the notion that people may come to Canada in order to better their economic situation.

application.[84] Other improper considerations that have led to a successful judicial review are the number of previous applications the person has made and any modifications made in applications,[85] the fact that an applicant is single and has no dependants,[86] the idea that long-term separation from family due to a study program would inevitably lead the applicant to stay in Canada,[87] the awareness that there are less costly education programs elsewhere,[88] the length of time taken by the applicant to learn English, [89] and the immigration history of a relative.[90]

An applicant for a TRV who wishes to become a permanent resident at some point may be considered as having a "dual intent." Such an applicant should not be denied a TRV where the officer is satisfied that the applicant will nevertheless leave at the end of the authorized period if the application for permanent residence has not been submitted, is unsuccessful, or has not yet been granted or denied.[91]

---

84   See, for example, *Dhanoa v Canada (Minister of Citizenship and Immigration)*, 2009 FC 729, where it is stated at para 12: "Lack of previous travel can only at most be a neutral factor. If one had travelled and always returned, the visa officer's concerns might be lessened."

85   See, for example, *Singh v Canada (Minister of Citizenship and Immigration)*, 2009 FC 621. In *Singh v Canada (Minister of Citizenship and Immigration)*, 2008 FC 15, the court held that the applicant is entitled to have his visa application reviewed fully and fairly — to address allegations relating to previous application processes; *Dhillon v Canada (Minister of Citizenship and Immigration)*, 2003 FC 1446: An officer needs to consider new evidence provided in subsequent applications.

86   *Onyeka*, above note 80.

87   *Bonilla*, above note 65.

88   *Zuo v Canada (Minister of Citizenship and Immigration)*, 2007 FC 88: Here, the court said that cost is only one factor to be considered in assessing an applicant's motives for applying for a study permit and that the choice in educational program is based on more than one reason, of which cost may be one. On the other hand, see *Tran v Canada (Minister of Citizenship and Immigration)*, 2006 FC 1377, where the court held that it was reasonable for the officer to review whether there were alternatives in the applicant's home country of Vietnam, especially given the applicant's level of English.

89   *Dang v Canada (Minister of Citizenship and Immigration)*, 2007 FC 15. The court held that the student need only establish that she is in good standing with her educational institution.

90   *Khatoon v Canada (Minister of Citizenship and Immigration)*, 2008 FC 276: The court held that people are to be judged on their own behaviour. However, see *Kindie*, above note 83, where the fact that the applicant's mother had come as a visitor and then promptly claimed refugee protection was held to be a reason to deny the applicant a TRV.

91   IRPA, above note 5, s 22(2); see *Ogunfowora v Canada (Minister of Citizenship and Immigration)*, 2007 FC 471; *Murai*, above note 72; *Patel v Canada (Minister of Citizenship and Immigration)*, 2006 FC 224; *Rebmann v Canada (Solicitor General)*,

E. ELECTRONIC TRAVEL AUTHORIZATION (ETA)

The electronic travel authorization (eTA), scheduled to be in operation by March 2016, is a requirement that will be imposed on foreign nationals who are visa-exempt. Citizens of the United States will be exempt from the requirement, a fact that can be explained by its history. The initiative was prompted by the signing of the *Beyond the Border* agreement between Canada and the United States in which the federal government committed itself to introducing an electronic travel authorization that would mirror one already developed in the United States.[92] The aim was to create a safer North American perimeter. The proposed regulation reads:

> 7.1 (1) A foreign national referred to in paragraph 7(2)(a) who is exempt from the requirement to obtain a temporary resident visa under subsection 7(1) and is seeking to enter Canada by air to remain on a temporary basis is, nevertheless, required to obtain an electronic travel authorization before entering Canada, unless they are exempted by subsection (3) from the requirement to obtain one.
>
> . . .
>
> 12.01 (4) The application must contain the following information:
>
> (a) the applicant's name;
> (b) the applicant's date and place of birth;
> (c) the applicant's gender;
> (d) the applicant's marital status;

2005 FC 310; *Moghaddam v Canada (Minister of Citizenship and Immigration)*, 2004 FC 680; and *Odewole v Canada (Minister of Citizenship and Immigration)*, 2008 FC 697, where the court held that the fact that the applicant also submitted a permanent resident application should not be held against her when considering a TRV. However, see also *Loveridge v Canada (Minister of Citizenship and Immigration)*, 2011 FC 694, where the court regarded the applicant's statement of her plans as contradictory. At para 18 the court stated that she

> indicates both an intention to stay in Canada as well as an intention to leave Canada and return to the UK. This is different from indicating a "dual intent" within the meaning of subsection 22(2) of the *IRPA*, because that type of a "dual intent" is actually an intention to remain permanently in Canada, coupled with an intention to abide by immigration laws as required — i.e. a willingness to leave Canada if required to do so.

92   The White House, News Release, "Beyond the Border: A Shared Vision for Perimeter Security and Economic Competitiveness" (4 February 2011), online: www.whitehouse.gov/the-press-office/2011/02/04/declaration-president-obama-and-prime-minister-harper-canada-beyond-bord.

(e)   the applicant's address;

(f)   the applicant's nationality;

(g)   the number of the applicant's passport or other travel document, together with its date of issue and its expiry date and the country or the authority that issued it;

(h)   the purpose and duration of the applicant's temporary visit to Canada;

(i)   if the applicant is an applicant referred to in any of paragraphs 10(2)(c.1) to (c.4), the information required by that paragraph; and

(j)   a declaration that the information provided in the application is complete and accurate.[93]

The rationale for the new measure is offered in the Regulatory Impact Analysis Statement accompanying the published rules:

> Currently, visa-exempt foreign nationals are not examined until they arrive at the border, where assessing admissibility is more challenging due to time pressure and the limited access to information that could support the determination. This creates a small but significant program integrity pressure given the potential gravity of admissibility concerns. Such concerns include war crimes, crimes against humanity, international human rights violations, security or criminality. The eTA requirement would also act as a deterrent to inadmissible travellers, as they would be required to undergo screening prior to travel and it would be unlawful to travel to Canada by air without an eTA. For example, foreign nationals seeking to enter Canada using lost or stolen travel documents may be deterred from applying because the system would electronically check against lost and stolen document databases prior to issuing an eTA electronically.[94]

F. GRANT OF STATUS

An applicant who has been issued a TRV outside Canada must appear at a port of entry for examination. Only after the officer at this examination is satisfied that the individual meets the requirements will he be granted temporary resident status [95]

---

93   *Regulations Amending the Immigration and Refugee Protection Regulations*, (2014) C Gaz I 1542, ss 2–3, online: www.gazette.gc.ca/rp-pr/p1/2014/2014-06-21/html/reg1-eng.php [*Regulations Amending IRP Regulations*].

94   *Ibid.* It is comforting to note that Her Majesty the Queen and members of the royal family are exempted from this requirement.

95   *Regulations*, above note 7, s 180.

G. APPLICATIONS FOR EXTENSIONS, CHANGED CONDITIONS, AND RESTORED STATUS

1) Extensions and Implied Status

Foreign nationals may apply for an extension of the time that they are authorized to remain in Canada but must do so before the end of the period authorized when they were granted status.[96] The onus is on the applicant to show that she has complied with all conditions originally imposed,[97] including the requirements needed to obtain the TRV.[98] An applicant who applies for an extension in a timely manner but who has not received a response before the expiry of status is granted implied status.[99]

2) Amendment of Conditions

When originally granted status, the person is authorized to reside temporarily in Canada under specified conditions.[100] Thus, a person admitted as a visitor cannot work or study without first applying to have the conditions amended. For example, a person who is issued a work permit must work for a named employer, and a student must study in

---

96 *Ibid*, s 181(1)(a).

97 *Ibid*, ss 181(1)(b) and 183: Conditions normally imposed include these: the foreign national must leave Canada by the end of the authorized period for the stay and not work unless authorized to.

98 *Ibid*, ss 179 and 181(2); see, for example, *Patel v Canada (Minister of Citizenship and Immigration)*, 2009 FC 602: The court here found the officer's reasons to deny an extension — that obtaining another degree or further studies was redundant — unreasonable; see also *Kaur v Canada (Minister of Citizenship and Immigration)*, 2011 FC 219 [*Kaur*]: An officer is not obliged to inform the applicant about any concerns regarding the application which arise directly from the requirements of the legislation or regulations, but an officer is obliged to inform the applicant if, for example, there are concerns regarding the veracity of documentation provided.

99 See Citizenship and Immigration Canada, *Temporary Resident: Implied Status (Extending a Stay)*, online: CIC www.cic.gc.ca/english/resources/tools/temp/visa/validity/implied.asp.

100 *Regulations*, above note 7, ss 186–89; see, for example, *Brar v Canada (Minister of Citizenship and Immigration)*, 2006 FC 1502, where the applicant's work permit was cancelled because the Immigration and Refugee Board deemed the applicant to have contravened the permit's conditions. The applicant was granted leave in a judicial review of the decision and the Federal Court found that the applicant did not breach the terms of the work permit.

a designated institution. In order to amend the conditions, an application must be made at least thirty days prior to the status expiring.[101]

3) Restoration

Where a foreign national has lost temporary resident status as a result of failing to comply with a condition by overstaying or by working or studying in an unauthorized way, that person may apply to have the TRV restored or reinstated within ninety days after losing his status.[102] An applicant may seek a restoration when an extension is no longer available. For example, a restoration can be sought when the authorized period has elapsed, but ninety days following the expiry date has not yet passed,[103] where the foreign national has changed the type of studies or an aspect of study without first requesting a change of conditions,[104] and where the foreign national changed employment or an aspect of employment without first requesting a change of conditions.[105] As the onus is on the applicant to justify a restoration, requests for restoration should be accompanied with submissions and supporting documentation indicating an explanation for the failure to comply with a condition.[106] It is important to note that no restoration is available for foreign nationals who did not comply with a condition for which a six-month ban may be imposed, such as engaging in unauthorized work

---

101 *Regulations*, above note 7, s 183(5): The applicant should provide all of the application forms required for the request for changing the conditions of status along with an explanation of why she wants to stay in Canada longer, proof of identity, proof of the current status, evidence of how she will support herself and any dependants in Canada, and proof of intention to leave Canada, such as a purchased ticket.

102 *Ibid*, above note 7, s 182.

103 See *Radics*, above note 76.

104 See *Zhang v Canada (Minister of Citizenship and Immigration)*, 2006 FC 1381.

105 See *Lim v Canada (Minister of Citizenship and Immigration)*, 2005 FC 657, where the court discusses the point of the ninety-day grace period and the approach that officers should take in reviewing restoration applications when it comes to temporary workers. In particular, the court spoke of being mindful of the drastic effects of a denial when temporary workers, such as live-in caregivers, have obtained status and worked in Canada already, accumulating time towards building a permanent residence application.

106 See, for example, *Kaur*, above note 98, where the court held that the onus is on the applicant to satisfy the officer on all parts of her application and that the officer was under no obligation to ask for more information where the application was insufficient. An officer, however, is obligated under procedural fairness to notify an applicant where there are concerns related to the veracity of documentary evidence and should allow an applicant to respond to such concerns.

or study.[107] Restoration of status is granted only in cases where the applicant has complied with all other conditions of the status.[108] Once ninety days has elapsed, the foreign national is required to leave Canada, and a restoration cannot be granted.[109]

H. PERMITS

The *Regulations* provide that a foreign national may not study or work in Canada without first obtaining a permit, although several exemptions from this requirement are listed. The nature of these permits and the processes for acquiring them are outlined in the following two sections.

1) Students

The executive summary of a report prepared for the Department of Foreign Affairs and International Affairs by Roslyn Kunin and Associates in December 2013 provides some impressive statistics. It reads:

> We estimate that in 2010, international students in Canada spent in excess of $7.7 billion on tuition, accommodation and discretionary spending; created over 81,000 jobs; and generated more than $445 million in government revenue.
>
> Altogether there were more than 218,200 long-term (staying for at least six months) international students in Canada in 2010, generating more than $6.9 billion to the Canadian economy. It is estimated that nearly 37 percent of that revenue came from two countries — China and South Korea. As of December 2010 there were 56,900 Chinese and 24,600 South Korean citizens in Canada undertaking a formal education program. Ontario and BC hosted nearly two thirds of the international students in Canada (85,300 and 60,500 respectively) while Quebec was a distant third.
>
> Short term students who pursued language training also contributed an estimated $788 million to the Canadian economy.
>
> Overall, the total amount that international students spend in Canada ($8.0 billion) is greater than our export of unwrought alum-

---

107 *Regulations*, above note 7, ss 200(3)(e) and 221.

108 *Ibid*, s 182.

109 *Ibid*; see, for example, *Adroh v Canada (Minister of Citizenship and Immigration)*, 2012 FC 393, where the court held that the language in s 182 is not discretionary and that if the application for restoration is brought outside the ninety-day period, the officer must refuse the application.

inum ($6 billion), and even greater than our export of helicopters, airplanes and spacecraft ($6.9 billion) to all other countries.[110]

Clearly, the international student program makes an important contribution to the Canadian economy. The presence of international students on university campuses also adds to the vibrancy and diversity of the campuses.

Under the *Regulations*, section 213, a foreign national must apply for a study permit from outside Canada, although some individuals, most prominently citizens and permanent residents of the United States, may apply for one at a port of entry.[111] Others may apply from inside Canada. This latter group includes individuals who have a work permit, those who already have a study permit, those who are subject to an unenforceable removal order, and those who hold a temporary resident permit (TRP) that is valid for more than six months.[112] Yet others are fully exempt from the requirement of acquiring a permit: these include students enrolled in a program of studies that is to last six months or less.[113] The same section was amended in 2014 to exempt "Indians," presumably a reference to persons registered under the *Indian Act*, who have special status under section 19 of the *IRPA*.[114]

Recent changes to the student permit regime reveal the Canadian government's overall distrust of both foreign nationals and educational institutions. As with amendments dealing with other aspects of the immigration system, fraudulent conduct has become a prominent target, in this case, as perpetrated both by those who feign to be genuine students and by institutions pretending to offer educational programs. The Regulatory Impact Assessment Statement (RIAS) accompanying the new amending regulations articulated the policy rationale for the amendments as follows:

> International student-related fraud poses risks to the immigration system and to public safety. Some foreign nationals use study permits as a means to enter Canada for purposes other than study, including conducting illegal activities. Some educational institutions take advantage of international students by promising programs of study

---

110 Department of Foreign Affairs and International Affairs, *Economic Impact of International Education in Canada — An Update* by Roslyn Kunin and Associates (December 2013), online: www.international.gc.ca/education/report-rapport/economic-impact-economique/index.aspx?lang=eng.
111 *Regulations*, above note 7, s 214.
112 *Ibid*, s 215.
113 *Ibid*, s 188.
114 *Ibid*, s 188 (1)(d).

they are unauthorized or unequipped to deliver, while others operate as visa mills with the sole purpose of facilitating the entry of foreign nationals into Canada . . . .

The regulatory amendments limit the issuance of study permits to international students attending designated learning institutions . . . .[115]

Thus, one of the main changes to the regime has been to restrict the issuance of student permits to those accepted and enrolled in a "designated learning institution" (DLI). As of 16 June 2014, applicants and study permit holders must indicate the institution at which they will be studying. The *Regulations* provide that a designated learning institution includes

(a) a learning institution administered by a federal department or agency;
(b) a post-secondary institution that hosts international students designated by a province in an agreement with the Minister of Citizenship and Immigration; and
(c) a primary or secondary learning institution that hosts international students.[116]

Where an institution loses its designation, the student is permitted to continue study there for the duration of the validity period of the student's permit.[117]

A study permit will "not be issued to a foreign national unless they have written documentation from a DLI where they intend to study that states that they have been accepted to study there,"[118] and unless the student has sufficient financial resources to pay tuition fees, maintain himself, and pay for travel.[119] Further, the *Regulations* also provide that a permit will not be issued to a foreign national who has engaged in unauthorized work or study in Canada or who has failed to comply with a condition of a permit unless (a) six months have elapsed since the unauthorized work or study, (b) the condition in question is minor,

---

115 *Regulations Amending IRP Regulations*, above note 93.
116 *Regulations*, above note 7, ss 211.1–211.2: Note that there are separate regulations under s 211.1(b) that define "designated learning institution" in Quebec. The minister will publish a list of provinces with which the minister has entered into an agreement or arrangement in respect of a learning institution that hosts international students.
117 *Ibid*, s 220.1(2).
118 *Ibid*, s 219.
119 *Ibid*, s 220.

or (c) the foreign national was subsequently issued a temporary resident permit (TRP).[120]

A fee is charged for the study permit, although the *Regulations* include a list of those who are exempt from paying: these include refugee claimants and those who have been provided refugee protection.[121]

Not surprisingly, people who have been issued study permits are subject to two continuing conditions. First, they must be enrolled at a designated learning institution and remain enrolled until the completion of their studies,[122] and second, they shall "actively pursue their course of program of study."[123] The student may be asked to produce evidence of compliance with these two conditions as part of a random assessment or because there may be reasons for the officer to believe that the study permit holder is not complying with the conditions.[124] What counts as "active pursuit of a program of studies" has yet to be determined, but it would appear that the new regime has a disciplinary aspect that authorizes government officers to assess the student's devotion to the studies. Failing to comply with these conditions could result in loss of status and a removal order being issued on the foreign national.[125] Interestingly, neither of the two conditions applies to those who were exempted from paying the fees for the student permit or to those who can apply for a permit from within Canada.[126]

Holders of permits may work off campus within Canada.[127] Thus, international students no longer need to seek a separate work permit if they obtain work off campus related to a research program or employment that is an essential part of a post-secondary academic, vocational, or professional training program offered by the learning institution.[128]

Study permits become invalid in a number of circumstances:

1) ninety days after the completion of the studies;[129]

---

120 *Ibid*, s 221; see also s 185 on the kinds of conditions that can be imposed.
121 To see all the applicable persons, see *Regulations, ibid*, ss 300(2)(a)–(i).
122 *Ibid*, s 220.1(1)(a).
123 *Ibid*, s 220.1(1)(b).
124 *Ibid*, s 220.1(4).
125 *Ibid*, s 228(1)(c)(v).
126 *Ibid*, ss 222(1)–(2). Exceptions are listed under s 222(2) and comprised of persons described in ss 300(2)(a)–(i) or in ss 215(2)(a)–(i).
127 *Ibid*, s 205(c)(i).
128 *Ibid*.
129 *Ibid*, ss 222(1)(a), 222(2), 300(2)(a)–(i), and 215(2)(a)–(f). Note that persons listed in ss 300(2) and 215(2) are exempted from the expiration of a study permit under s 222(2).

2) the day on which a removal order of the foreign national becomes enforceable;[130] or

3) the day on which the permit expires.[131]

A student may apply for a renewal of a permit if the application is made before the expiry of the permit and the student has met with all the conditions imposed on entry.[132]

2) Workers

For more than forty years the Canadian immigration system has included a program that has permitted foreign nationals to work in Canada on a temporary basis in order to fulfill short-term needs, but it has also regulated strictly their ability to do so by placing severe restrictions on the modes of acquiring authorization. An early precursor of today's Temporary Foreign Worker (TFW) program was the Non-Immigrant Employment Authorization Program (NIEAP) established in 1973. It required workers to obtain permits before entering the country and also to depart the country in order to change any aspect of their employment.[133] While the details of the program may have changed, although not dramatically so, the aims of the program and its underlying tensions have not. In a paper prepared for the CD Howe Institute, Dominique Gross has articulated with great clarity the dilemmas underpinning the current TFW program. She writes:

> Between 2002 and 2013, Canada eased the hiring conditions of TFWs several times, supposedly because of a reported labour shortage in some occupations, especially in western Canada. By 2012, the number of employed TFWs was 338,000, up from 101,000 in 2002, yet the unemployment rate remained the same at 7.2 percent. Furthermore, these policy changes occurred even though there was little empirical evidence of shortages in many occupations. When controlling for differences across provinces, I find that changes to the TFWP that

---

130 *Ibid*, s 222(1)(b).

131 *Ibid*, s 222(1)(c).

132 *Ibid*, s 181.

133 For an analysis of the NIEAP and a clear general introduction to the TFW program, see Judy Fudge & Fiona MacPhail, *The Temporary Foreign Worker Program In Canada: Low Skilled Workers as an Extreme Form of Flexible Labour* (2009), online: Social Science Research Network http://papers.ssrn.com/sol3/papers.cfm?abstract_id=1552054.

eased hiring conditions accelerated the rise in unemployment rates in Alberta and British Columbia.[134]

The TFW program has become the most controversial branch of the immigration regime, principally because of factors such as those identified by Gross: a substantial increase in the number of temporary foreign workers, increased unemployment, unclear evidence of the real need for the workers, skepticism about the controls placed on employers who seek to reduce labour costs to a minimum and their willingness to meet the legal requirements imposed to maintain the integrity of the system, and concern that the program is being used to fill chronic gaps in the labour market rather than to meet short-term needs. This critique has been bolstered by another stance that focuses on the conditions experienced by workers and also on the realization that the exploitation of individuals who will do work that Canadians will not, produces a level of social and political inequality quite inconsistent with basic values that underpin out legal system. Cumulatively, these factors have led to concerted public opposition to the program and to the initiation of a program overhaul to be implemented over the next few years.

a)   The Legal Framework
i)   What Is Work?
Work is defined in the Regulations as "an activity for which wages are paid or commission is earned, or that is in direct competition with the activities of Canadian citizens or permanent residents in the Canadian labour market."[135] In general, foreign nationals wanting to work in Canada must obtain a work permit, which is defined as "a written authorization to work in Canada issued by an officer to a foreign national."[136] Foreign nationals are prohibited from working in certain jobs. For example, the Regulations provide, "A foreign national must not enter into an employment agreement, or extend the term of an employment agreement, with an employer . . . who, on a regular basis, offers

---

134   Dominique Gross, Temporary Foreign Workers in Canada: Are They Really Filling Labour Shortages? (April 2014), online: CD Howe Institute www.cdhowe.org/pdf/commentary_407.pdf [Gross, Temporary Foreign Workers].

135   Regulations, above note 7, s 2. See Duroseau v Canada (Minister of Citizenship and Immigration), 2008 FC 72, where the court held that the definition of work set forth in the Regulations does not require compensation to have been received in order for an activity to be considered work. The activity merely has to be "in direct competition with activities of Canadian citizens or permanent residents in the Canadian labour market." Childcare meets this definition of work.

136   Regulations, ibid.

striptease, erotic dance, escort services or erotic massages."[137] Likewise, they are prohibited from working for employers who have not complied with conditions regarding the foreign worker program.[138]

ii) Who Needs a Work Permit?

The *Regulations* provide that a foreign national may not work in Canada without first obtaining a work permit.[139] Exemptions are granted to people in various categories.[140] Most prominent is the exemption extended to the business visitor, a category defined carefully in the *Regulations* to include (a) people who are engaged in international business activities without entering the Canadian labour market (which will be the case only if the primary source of remuneration for the business activities is outside Canada and the principal place of business and actual place of accrual of profits remain predominately outside Canada); and (b) foreign nationals acting in specified ways on behalf of a foreign business.[141]

Included, as well, are a motley group of others: performing artists, athletes and team members, news reporters and media crew, public speakers, convention organizers, clergy,[142] judges, referees, examiners, evaluators, expert witnesses, investigators, health-care students, civil aviation inspectors, aviation accident or incident inspectors, transportation crew, and emergency service providers among them.[143]

In general, those who need a work permit must apply from outside Canada.[144] The *Regulations*, however, do identify situations where a work permit may be obtained at the port of entry or within Canada.[145] For example, international students with valid student permits may apply for a work permit from within Canada.[146]

---

137 *Ibid*, s 196.1.
138 *Ibid*, s 196.1(b).
139 *Ibid*, ss 8(1) and 195–96.
140 *Ibid*, s 8(2); see also s 186.
141 *Ibid*, s 187.
142 See *Duraisami v Canada (Minister of Citizenship and Immigration)*, 2005 FC 1008, where the court held that not every person who assists in a place of worship (ushers, singers, teachers of children's religious studies) falls under this exemption.
143 See *Regulations*, above note 7, ss 186–87, for the full list. Persons who hold valid student permits and persons who are awaiting the renewal of their expired work permits are exempt from holding a valid work permit while working in Canada.
144 *Ibid*, s 198.
145 *Ibid*, ss 198–99. For example, these situations include where the foreign national is a permanent resident of the United States or is a resident of Greenland or St Pierre and Miquelon, or the foreign national is a participant in an international youth exchange program.
146 *Ibid*, s 199(c). See s 199 for the full list of exemptions.

It is important to note that a work permit becomes invalid when it expires but also when a removal order has been made against the holder of the work permit and becomes enforceable.[147]

iii) Criteria and Eligibility for a Work Permit

The archetypical application is made by a person who is outside Canada and who has received a job offer. The *Regulations* present as the norm the following requirements:

1) The applicant must submit a proper application.[148]
2) The applicant must satisfy the officer that he or she will leave the country after the period of authorization has lapsed.[149]
3) The applicant has received a job offer and the officer has made the required positive determination about the offer.[150]
4) The applicant must be capable and qualified to perform the duties of the work, and have the intention to work in the job indicated in the offer.[151]

The third of these requirements is complex. The required determination must be based on an opinion known as a labour market impact assessment (LMIA), which is supplied by Employment and Social Development Canada (ESDC) and confirms a number of matters: (a) the job offer is genuine;[152] (b) the employment of a foreign national in the particular position is likely to have a neutral or positive effect on the labour

---

147 *Ibid*, s 209.
148 *Ibid*, s 200(1)(a).
149 *Ibid*, s 200(1)(b).
150 *Ibid*, s 200(1)(c).
151 *Ibid*, ss 200(1)(c) and 200(3)(a). See, for example, *Singh v Canada (Minister of Citizenship and Immigration)*, 2010 FC 1306, where the officer found that the applicant did not meet the requirements of the job offer due to concerns on the part of the officer about the veracity of past experience letters. The court held that the officer should have given the applicant notice of the concern and a chance to respond; *Randhawa v Canada (Minister of Citizenship and Immigration)*, 2006 FC 1294, where the court held that the officer must consider the on-the-job training the applicant would receive and cannot grill an applicant on standard of hygiene and sanitation when the officer is not an expert in the area.
152 *Regulations*, above note 7, ss 200(1)(c)(ii.1)(A), 203(1)(a), and 200(5): The following factors may be examined to determine whether an offer of employment is genuine: (a) whether the employer is actively engaged in the business in respect of which the offer is made unless the offer is for a caregiver; (b) whether the offer is consistent with the reasonable employment needs of the employer; (c) whether the terms of the offer are ones that the employer is reasonably able to fulfill; and (d) the past compliance of the employer.

market in Canada;[153] (c) the issuance of a work permit to the applicant would not be inconsistent with a federal–provincial agreement;[154] and (d) the employer has not for a period of six years underpaid any foreign national who has been made a similar offer.[155]

The determination that the impact will likely have a neutral or positive effect on the labour market is to be based on several factors:

1) whether the hiring of a foreign national will result in job creation or retention for Canadians;
2) whether there are benefits such as the development or transfer of skills[156] and knowledge to domestic workers;
3) whether the employment is likely to fill a labour shortage;
4) whether the wages offered are consistent with the prevailing wage rate;
5) whether the employer is taking steps to train domestic workers for future positions;
6) whether the hiring of a foreign national will affect a labour dispute; and
7) whether the work permit would be inconsistent with the terms of a federal–provincial agreement that applies to the employment of foreign nationals.[157]

The labour market impact assessment must be based on information provided by the potential employer. Thus, employers seeking foreign workers must apply through Employment and Social Development Canada to obtain the assessment.[158] Because an opinion is needed, a work permit requires the co-operation of not only the applicant but

---

153 *Ibid*, ss 203(1)(b), 203(1.01), and 203(2)–(3.1); Citizenship and Immigration Canada, "What Is a Labour Market Impact Assessment?" (23 March 2015), online: CIC Help Centre www.cic.gc.ca/english/helpcentre/answer. asp?q=163&t=17; *Construction and Specialized Workers' Union, Local 1611 v Canada (Minister of Citizenship and Immigration)*, 2013 FC 512 [*CSWU*], where the court held that the officer was entitled to use his discretion when examining the advertising an applicant made both in terms of timing and accuracy.

154 *Regulations*, above note 7, s 203(1)(c).

155 *Ibid*, s 203(1)(e).

156 See, for example, *CSWU*, above note 153: The court held that the officer's assessment of whether the employment of foreign nationals would likely result in the creation or transfer of skills or knowledge for the benefit of those in Canada was reasonable.

157 *Regulations*, above note 7, s 203(3). An employer may also provide documentary evidence that they have tried to recruit domestic workers showing they complied with minimum advertising requirements.

158 *Ibid*, ss 203(1)(e) and 203(2)–(5).

also an employer in Canada.[159] The employer not only has to engage with Employment and Social Development Canada but must also comply with requirements under the *IRPA* and the *Regulations*. Thus, the ministry will both review whether or not there is a need for a foreign worker to fill a vacancy and examine the employer's history as an employer.[160] For example, an employer must be actively engaged in the business in respect of which the offer of employment was made unless it was made for a caregiver, must comply with employment laws, and must provide working conditions and wages set out in the offer of employment while ensuring that the workplace is free of abuse.[161]

The *Regulations* give power to Employment and Social Development Canada to examine and investigate whether or not the employer is complying with requirements in the *IRPA* or its regulations, including entering employment premises,[162] and also the power to list an employer on a public ineligible employer list that indicates the employer has not complied with the *Regulations*, denying them access to the TFW program.[163]

The *Regulations* also provide that work permits will *not* be issued to foreign nationals who

1) have not complied with conditions of previous authorizations or permits to enter or remain in Canada;[164]
2) have engaged in unauthorized study or work in Canada;[165]
3) have worked in Canada for one or more periods totaling four years unless four years have elapsed or they fall under an exception, such as being covered by a seasonal agricultural agreement;[166]
4) intend to work for an employer that offers striptease, erotic dance, escort services, or erotic massages;[167] or
5) have an offer of employment from an employer who is listed as contravening the *IRPA* or its *Regulations*.[168]

---

159 See *Koo v 5220459 Manitoba Inc*, 2010 MBQB 132, where the court held that an employer may disregard the salary stated in an LMIA and pay the applicant less where there is an agreed-upon contract. This raises questions as to whether officers consider the LMIA or the contract as indicative of the salary to be paid to workers and what kind of protection is afforded to workers within the TFW program.

160 *Regulations*, above note 7, ss 209.1–209.91.

161 *Ibid*, ss 209.2(1)(a) and 209.3(1)(a).

162 *Ibid*, ss 209.4–209.9.

163 *Ibid*, s 209.91.

164 *Ibid*, s 200(3)(e).

165 *Ibid*.

166 *Ibid*, ss 200(3)(g) and 200(4).

167 *Ibid*, s 196.1.

168 *Ibid*, s 200(3)(h).

In some very limited circumstances, an applicant may be required to pass a medical examination.[169] Finally, foreign workers must still meet the requirements that every foreign national has to meet when entering Canada, inadmissibility being one.[170]

The third of the requirements listed above reveals the commitment to temporariness: the norm is that temporary workers may not extend their sojourn in Canada and may not have a permit renewed beyond four years.

The above is an outline of what is regarded as a normal application; however, statistics do not confirm its normalcy. In 2013, this category of LMIA-based application comprised only 37.8 percent of the total.[171] Herein lies one of the sources of controversy: Why is it so easy to evade the LMIA requirement?

An answer may be found by examining the range of less "normal" but statistically more prevalent circumstances that may lead to the issuance of a work permit without a labour market impact assessment. The first category deals with indigent or deserving applicants:

1) a refugee claimant in Canada or a person subject to an unenforceable removal order if they cannot support themselves,[172]

2) a spouse or common law partner of a Canadian citizen or permanent resident,[173]

3) a protected person,[174]

4) a person who has applied for permanent residence on humanitarian and compassionate grounds,[175]

5) and a family member of person who is one of the above,[176]

6) a student permit-holder,[177] or

7) a person who holds a valid TRP.[178]

---

169 *IRPA*, above note 5, s 16(2)(b); see *Regulations*, above note 7, s 30(1), to see who is exempt from medical examinations.

170 For more on inadmissibility, see Chapter 14.

171 Employment and Social Development Canada, *Improving Clarity, Transparency and Accountability of the Temporary Foreign Worker Program*, online: www.esdc. gc.ca/eng/jobs/foreign_workers/reform/index.shtml.

172 *Regulations*, above note 7, s 206(1).

173 *Ibid*, ss 199(e) and 207(b).

174 *Ibid*, s 207(c).

175 *Ibid*, s 207(d).

176 *Ibid*, ss 199(e) and 207(e).

177 *Ibid*, s 208(a).

178 *Ibid*, s 208(b).

The mere issuance of a work permit to refugee claimants, persons subject to an unenforceable removal order, protected persons under section 95(2) of the *IRPA*, and persons who have applied for permanent residence under humanitarian and compassionate grounds does *not* make these foreign nationals temporary residents.[179] None of these applicants need first obtain a job offer or a labour market impact assessment. Individuals who fall within these categories are issued an open work permit that does not tie them to a particular position with a particular employer.[180]

There is another category of persons who may be granted a permit without first obtaining an assessment. The *Regulations* provide that a work permit may be issued to a foreign national who intends to perform work of importance to Canada, including

1) work pursuant to an international agreement between Canada and one or more countries, other than an agreement concerning seasonal agricultural workers;[181]
2) work pursuant to an agreement entered into by one or more countries and by or on behalf of one or more provinces;[182]
3) work pursuant to a federal–provincial agreement;[183]
4) work that would create or maintain significant social, cultural, or economic benefits or opportunities for Canadian citizens or permanent residents;[184]
5) work that would create or maintain reciprocal employment of Canadian citizens or permanent residents of Canada in other countries;[185]
6) work that is designated by the minister as being work that can be performed by a foreign national on the basis of being related to a research program or essential to an educational or professional training program, or work of a religious or charitable nature.[186]

Individuals who fall within this general category need not have a job offer nor do they require a labour market impact assessment, although if they do have a job offer its genuineness will be assessed. Thus, work pursuant to an agreement between Canada and one or more

---

179 *Ibid*, s 202.
180 Citizenship and Immigration Canada, "Work Permits" (9 February 2015), online: CIC Help Centre www.cic.gc.ca/english/helpcentre/answer.asp?q=177&t=17.
181 *Regulations*, above note 7, s 204(a).
182 *Ibid*, s 204(b).
183 *Ibid*, s 204(c).
184 *Ibid*, s 205(a).
185 *Ibid*, s 205(b).
186 *Ibid*, s 205(c).

countries or with a province,[187] such as companies hiring through intra-firm transfers[188] or from a country that has an international agreement with Canada, such as the United States or Mexico under the *North American Free Trade Agreement*, does not require a labour market impact assessment.[189]

Employment and Social Development Canada (ESDC) refers to these examples of LMIA-exempt work as the "International Mobility Programs" and describes them as follows:

> The International Mobility Programs (IMP) includes all streams of work permit applications that are LMIA-exempt under one umbrella. By exempting some foreign nationals from needing a labour market

187 *Ibid*, s 204.

188 See, for example, *Arora v Canada (Minister of Citizenship and Immigration)*, 2011 FC 241, where the officer examined whether the applicant met the requirements of an intra-company transferee. While an officer can assess whether the applicant has the qualities of a manager as outlined in the operational manual, an officer cannot make the assessment with irrelevant factors such as the age of the applicant and the level of salary the applicant was making.

189 *Ibid*; *North American Free Trade Agreement*, 32 ILM 289 and 605 (1993) [*NAFTA*]: NAFTA was created to facilitate trade and the movement of people between Canada, United States, and Mexico. NAFTA covers four categories of foreign workers: (1) business visitors, (2) professionals, (3) intra-company transferees, and (4) traders or investors. Business visitors under NAFTA refers to citizens of Mexico or the United States who seek to engage in international business activities. They do not require a work permit. A professional under NAFTA refers to a citizen of the United States or Mexico who has pre-arranged employment with a Canadian employer and whose occupation is listed in NAFTA. An intra-company transferee is a citizen of Mexico or the United States who is sent to Canada to work on a short-term basis for the same company for which he has worked on an ongoing basis for at least one of the previous three years. A trader or investor is an executive involved in planning a substantial trade in goods or services or a large investment in Canada. See "Business People," online: www.cic.gc.ca/english/work/special-business.asp.

    The *IRPA* also can apply to the *General Agreement on Trade in Services (GATS)*. *General Agreement on Trade in Services*, Apr. 15, 1994, Marrakesh Agreement Establishing the World Trade Organization, Annex 1B, The Legal Tests: The Results of the Uruguay Round of the Multilateral Trade Negotiations 284 (1999), 1869 UNTS 183, 33 ILM 1167 (1994). Under the *GATS*, a professional refers to a person who seeks to engage in an activity at a professional level in a designated profession and who meets listed criteria in the Agreement. *GATS* professionals are not permitted to work in certain service sectors and visas are restricted to a particular duration. It is best to consult the agreements and the *Regulations* to determine the exact criteria and application process. See, for example, *Garro v Canada (Minister of Citizenship and Immigration)*, 2007 FC 670, where the court held that the officer's finding that the applicant failed to meet the conditions required to obtain investor status under NAFTA was unreasonable.

impact assessment before being able to work in Canada, the IMP aims to provide competitive advantages to Canada and reciprocal benefits to Canadians.

For example, labour mobility is a key part of the *North American Free Trade Agreement (NAFTA)*. *NAFTA* provides reciprocal benefits, allowing foreign nationals in certain occupations from partner countries to work in Canada without the requirement of a labour market test like the Labour Market Impact Assessment (LMIA), but also allow Canadians to work abroad with similar privileges. While about 12,000 Americans worked in Canada through the *NAFTA* professional occupation provision in 2011, the number of Canadians working in the United States through the same provision more than tripled that, with about 39,000 in all.[190]

Primarily because the criteria for issuing work permits are so vague and create the opportunity for abuse, the ministry has identified the need to re-evaluate and overhaul these programs.

The federal government has also announced a general overhaul of other parts of the TFW program. It now charges employers $1000 to apply for a labour market impact assessment, a sum that is non-refundable if the application is denied.[191] It has imposed a cap on low-wage positions[192] and is requiring employers seeking temporary workers in high-wage positions to submit transition plans with their LMIA application to ensure that they are taking steps to reduce their reliance on temporary foreign workers.[193] A complete timeline for other projected changes has been published on the ESDC website.[194]

The following section will give a brief overview of the current programs, but it is advisable for applicants to review the most up-to-date information provided in changes to the *Regulations*, through ministerial instructions and via Citizenship and Immigration Canada.

---

190 Employment and Social Development Canada, *Reforming the International Mobility Programs* (29 September 2014), online: ESDC www.esdc.gc.ca/eng/jobs/foreign_workers/reform/imp.shtml.

191 Employment and Social Development Canada, *Restricting Access* (12 November 2014), online: ESDC www.esdc.gc.ca/eng/jobs/foreign_workers/reform/restrict.shtml [ESDC, *Restricting Access*].

192 *Ibid.*

193 *Ibid.*

194 Employment and Social Development Canada, "Timeline of Measures Coming into Force" (27 August 2014), online: ESDC www.esdc.gc.ca/eng/jobs/foreign_workers/reform/timeline.shtml.

a.   Agricultural Workers

Agricultural workers may be hired under two unique streams. The first stream, the seasonal agricultural worker (SAW) program, is a temporary foreign worker program that allows the agriculture sector[195] to recruit temporary foreign workers for short periods to fill labour shortages. Workers are brought into Canada on a seasonal basis to pick fruits, flowers, and vegetables, and do other specified kinds of work, such as harvesting tobacco, collecting honey, or laying sod. The SAW program allows employers in Canada to hire temporary foreign workers from participating countries[196] for a maximum duration of eight months provided they offer the workers a minimum of 240 hours of work within a period of six weeks or less.[197] Employers must meet a number of requirements, such as arranging and paying for transportation of the temporary foreign worker, providing suitable housing, registering the worker for health insurance, arranging and paying for workplace safety insurance coverage, providing protective equipment, training and supervision, providing an employment contract specifying each party's rights and obligations, paying for the work permit fee, and abiding by conditions outlined in the work permit and the IRPA

---

195 *Regulations*, above note 7, ss 315.2(4)–(5), define agriculture sector.

196 Employment and Social Development Canada, *Hiring Seasonal Agricultural Workers*, online: ESDC www.esdc.gc.ca/eng/jobs/foreign_workers/agriculture/seasonal//index.shtml [ESDC, *Hiring SAW*]: The SAW program operates according to bilateral agreements between Canada and participating countries. The participating countries include Mexico and the Caribbean countries of Anguilla, Antigua and Barbuda, Barbados, Dominica, Grenada, Jamaica, Montserrat, St Kitts-Nevis, St Lucia, St Vincent and the Grenadines, and Trinidad and Tobago. See Elizabeth Ruddick, "Managing the Movement of Peoples: What Can Be Learned from Mode 4 of the *GATS*?" (Presentation delivered on behalf of Citizenship and Immigration Canada at the IOM-WTO-World Bank Seminar on Managing Trade and Migration, 4–5 October 2004), online: www.wto.org/english/tratop_e/serv_e/sem_oct04_e/canada_e.pdf at 2:

> The program was first implemented in 1966 following negotiations between Canada and Jamaica. Trinidad-Tobago and Barbados became participants in 1967, and in 1974 an agreement was signed with Mexico. In 1976 the program was extended to include Organization of East Caribbean States. In other words, the program is a series of bilateral agreements which operate under the umbrella or framework of the SAWP.

See, for example, *Agreement for the Employment in Canada of Seasonal Agricultural Workers from Mexico – 2013*, online: www.esdc.gc.ca/eng/jobs/foreign_workers/agriculture/seasonal/sawpmc2013.shtml [SAW Agreement].

197 ESDC, *Hiring SAW*, above note 196; see, for example, SAW Agreement, above note 196, which specifies the requirements.

and its *Regulations*.[198] In order to obtain a temporary foreign worker in the SAW program, an employer must also obtain a labour market impact assessment.

The second stream is the agricultural worker program, which offers similar opportunities to workers from other countries. However, the regulations provide some privileges and restrictions to those who are covered by international agreements.[199] Thus, this stream permits the employer to hire a foreign worker for a maximum of twenty-four months.[200]

b.   Stream for Lower-Skilled Occupations

In 2002, the government introduced a pilot project that would allow employers to recruit workers for jobs that require only a high-school diploma or on-the-job training, with the jobs lasting a maximum of twenty-four months.[201] No longer a pilot project, employers now must obtain a labour market impact assessment, agree to engage in activities to help reduce their reliance on temporary foreign workers and transition to using a Canadian workforce, pay for round trip transportation costs for the foreign worker, provide affordable housing, ensure that the worker is covered by private or provincial health insurance, provide an employment contract, provide proof of a business licence or documentation, demonstrate that the applicable union has been consulted, and provide appropriate wages and safe working conditions.[202] It is important to note that there may be provincial or territorial variations to the application process, and thus applicants are advised to consult provincial legislation or regulations regarding any requirements or documentation needed specifically for jobs located in a specific province.[203]

c.   Stream for Higher-Skilled Occupations

As noted on the website of Employment and Social Development Canada:

> Under the Stream for Higher-skilled Occupations, employers can hire foreign workers in higher-skilled positions such as: management,

---

198   *Ibid.*

199   See, for example, *Regulations*, above note 7, s 200(3)(g).

200   ESDC, *Restricting Access*, above note 191.

201   Naomi Alboim, "Abolish the Low-Skilled Temporary Foreign Worker Program" (December 2009) Issue 10 *Maytree Policy in Focus*, online: Maytree Foundation http://maytree.com/PDF_Files/MaytreePolicyInFocusIssue10.pdf at 3; Employment and Social Development Canada, *Stream for Lower-Skilled Occupations* (9 January 2015), online: ESDC www.esdc.gc.ca/eng/jobs/foreign_workers/lower_skilled/index.shtml. Note that the jobs in this stream are coded at the C or D skill level of the National Occupational Classification.

202   *Ibid.*

203   *Ibid.*

professional, scientific, technical or trade occupations. These occupations can be found throughout many sectors of the economy, and as a result often have very diverse recruitment practices and regulatory requirements.[204]

The requirements for hiring a person under this stream are identified in detail on the website.[205] One of the important variations imposed on employers relates to advertising the position. As noted on the ESDC website:

> as a minimum, employers must choose one method [of recruitment] that is national in scope, since people in higher-skilled positions are often mobile and willing to re-locate for work.[206]

d. Caregivers

For a number of years, the Canadian government has permitted caregivers to work temporarily in Canada, with the added inducement of being able to apply for permanent resident status after a period of at least two years. Until 2014, the program required that the caregiver undertake to live in the private residence in which she would be working.[207] This requirement was imposed because the demand for live-in caregivers was believed to be greater than the local supply. Failure to maintain residence could lead to cancellation of the work permit.

---

204 Employment and Social Development Canada, *Hiring Foreign Workers for Higher-Skilled Occupations* (31 December 2014), online: www.esdc.gc.ca/eng/jobs/foreign_workers/higher_skilled/index.shtml.

205 *Ibid.*

206 *Ibid.*

207 The requirement that the caregiver live in the residence has now been removed through the issuance of ministerial instructions, which provide that

> [n]o new permanent resident application under the Live-in Caregiver Class . . . will be accepted for processing unless it is supported, at the time of application receipt by CIC, by evidence that the underlying work permit associated with the foreign national's initial entry as a live-in caregiver under the Live-in Caregiver Program (LCP) was based on a Labour Market Impact Assessment (LMIA) that was requested from Service Canada on or before November 30, 2014.

See Canada, Department of Citizenship and Immigration, *Government Notices: New Ministerial Instructions*, online: Canada Gazette www.gazette.gc.ca/rp-pr/p1/2014/2014-11-29/html/notice-avis-eng.php.

Specific regulations governed the eligibility for a work permit under this program.[208]

The live-in caregiver program was bedevilled by serious unintended consequences. Being required to live in the private residence of their employer exposed caregivers to exploitation, sexual harassment, and assault. Moreover, a large backlog of applications for permanent resident status developed. Although the government has halted processing of applications under this program, there are still many individuals currently in Canada who arrived as live-in caregivers and are still subject to the former requirements. The government has introduced some detailed measures to control the problems that they face. Thus, the terms of the contract of employment have been carefully controlled.[209] The live-in caregiver contract is required to be consistent with provincial/territorial employment standards and labour laws.[210] In addition, it is required to include a description of the following:

1) employer-paid benefits, including transportation from the applicant's home country, medical insurance, workplace safety insurance coverage, and recruitment fees;
2) job duties;[211]

---

208 *Regulations*, above note 7, s 112. Section 112 provides:

> A work permit shall not be issued to a foreign national who seeks to enter Canada as a live-in caregiver unless they
> (a) applied for a work permit as a live-in caregiver before entering Canada;
> (b) have successfully completed a course of study that is equivalent to the successful completion of secondary school in Canada;
> (c) have the following training or experience, in a field or occupation related to the employment for which the work permit is sought, namely,
> (i) successful completion of six months of full-time training in a classroom setting, or
> (ii) completion of one year of full-time paid employment, including at least six months of continuous employment with one employer, in such a field or occupation within the three years immediately before the day on which they submit an application for a work permit;
> (d) have the ability to speak, read and listen to English or French at a level sufficient to communicate effectively in an unsupervised setting; and
> (e) have an employment contract with their future employer.

209 A template for the employer–live-in caregiver contract is available online: CIC www.cic.gc.ca/english/pdf/pub/LCP-sample_contract.pdf.

210 Citizenship and Immigration Canada, Operational Manual OP 14: *Processing Applicants for the Live-in Caregiver Program*, s 2, online: CIC www.cic.gc.ca/english/resources/manuals/op/op14-eng.pdf.

211 *Ibid*, s 5.7: Housework, cleaning, or other similar domestic duties such as food preparation may be allowable as a small part of the overall job duties outlined in the contract when clearly related to the duties of caring for the individual(s),

3) hours of work that are full time or a minimum of thirty hours per week;
4) current acceptable wages;
5) accommodation arrangements in a private unit or room with a lock;
6) holiday and sick leave entitlements;
7) termination and resignation terms.[212]

In addition, options have been made available to caregivers who have experienced abuse.[213] For example, live-in caregivers who have been forced to leave their current place of employment due to a situation of abuse[214] can ask for an emergency processing of both labour market impact assessment and their work permit application to facilitate a fast transition from one employer to another.[215] To be eligible for emergency processing, a live-in caregiver must present documentation to Citizenship and Immigration Canada from a medical practitioner, police officer, shelter worker, psychiatrist, psychologist, or social worker indicating abuse by the employer or someone in the employer's home.[216] While this exception is a laudable tool to protect abused live-in caregivers, the process under which a live-in caregiver can access this exception does not provide as much protection as needed. First, many

---

but such domestic duties cannot be the primary duty of the prospective live-in caregiver.

212 *Ibid.*
213 Thus the operational manual allows for the issuance of an "emergency" work permit for the victims of abuse. It provides:

> Abusive situations, for the purposes of emergency work permit processing under the LCP, would include any intentional physical contact that causes harm, physical violence such as assault or sexual assault, and psychological abuse such as threats or intimidation.

See Citizenship and Immigration Canada, Operational Manual IP 4: *Processing Live-in Caregivers in Canada*, s 8.6, online: www.cic.gc.ca/english/resources/manuals/ip/ip04-eng.pdf.
214 *Ibid.* Situations of abuse are defined by ESDC as including "physical violence or any intentional physical contact that causes injury, such as physical or sexual assault or psychological abuse (e.g. threats or intimidation)." Abuse is also defined in *Regulations*, above note 7, s 72.1(7)(a): (i) physical abuse, including assault and forcible confinement, (ii) sexual abuse, including sexual contact without consent, (iii) psychological abuse, including threats and intimidation, and (iv) financial abuse, including fraud and extortion. See also provincial legislation such as Ontario's *Employment Protection for Foreign Nationals Act (Live-in Caregivers and Others)*, SO 2009, c 32.
215 *Regulations*, above note 7, s 209.3, which lays out the conditions that employers of live-in caregivers must comply with. (See also *ibid*, ss 209.5–209.7 and 209.9–209.91.)
216 *Ibid.*

live-in caregivers may be isolated and may not know about this exception. Second, the onus is put on live-in caregivers to find another employer before they can leave the abusive situation and continue living in Canada. Third, live-in caregivers in abusive situations often have to continue living in the abusive situation until Citizenship and Immigration Canada or Employment and Social Development Canada allows a transition to the new employer. Recognition of these shortcomings was a major reason for the program being fundamentally altered. However, it is still possible for a prospective employer and caregiver to agree that the latter should reside in the residence as part of the employment contract. On housing, Employment and Social Development Canada now offers the following instructions:

> Employers cannot under any circumstance require a caregiver (either lower-skilled or higher-skilled) to live in their home. However, if an employer and foreign caregiver decide that a live-in arrangement is the most suitable, for the needs of the person requiring care or to assist the TFW, there are certain criteria that must be met. Specifically, employers must ensure the
>
> - accommodation is being provided in the home of the person receiving care;
> - accommodation is private and furnished bedroom;
> - bedroom door has a lock and safety bolt on the inside;
> - bedroom meets the municipal building requirements and the provincial/territorial health standards; and
> - foreign caregiver is NOT charged room and board for the accommodations, as per the policy, under the TFW program.
>
> Employers must submit the completed in-home Employer Supplied Bedroom Description form (EMP5599) with the application.
>
> Employers of lower-skilled in-home caregivers who are not providing live-in accommodations must ensure that suitable and affordable accommodation is available to the TFW [temporary foreign worker]. In addition, these employers should be prepared to provide proof (e.g., newspaper ads) that affordable housing is available in the community where the TFW will be employed. Meanwhile, employers of higher-skilled in-home caregivers do not have to meet this requirement.[217]

---

217 Employment and Social Development Canada, *Families Hiring In-home Caregivers* (4 March 2015), online www.esdc.gc.ca/eng/jobs/foreign_workers/caregiver/index.shtml#Housing [ESDC, *Families Hiring*].

It is interesting that the government has recognized the short-comings of the live-in requirement but has nevertheless permitted its continuance where the parties agree. It appears that the government assumes that there is an equality of bargaining power between potential employers and potential caregivers or that any inequality may be remedied by regulating the contract.

> Under the new regime caregivers must have the education level required for the position they are seeking and must have a level of language fluency that, at the least, enables them to communicate effectively and independently in an unsupervised setting [218]

As a prerequisite for obtaining a labour market impact assessment, employers are required to advertise the job adequately within Canada, and the level of advertising will depend on whether the position is classified as high-skilled or low-skilled. Employers must submit proof that a dependant is in need of care, which may include a certificate from a doctor. They must show that they have the financial ability to pay the required wages by submitting copies of their Notice of Assessments from the Canada Revenue Agency.[219] Copies of pay stubs, bank statements, personal work contracts, or other documentation to show proof of income are helpful.[220] Employers must obtain a business number from the Canada Revenue Agency so that they are able to register and advertise on the national job bank, to pay a worker's wages, make deductions prescribed by law from the worker's wages, and issue pay stubs, statements, T4s, or Records of Employment.[221]

A caregiver may still apply for permanent residence from within Canada after working in Canada for two years out of the previous four. The government has undertaken to process such applications speedily.[222]

The new program recognizes two new classes of individuals who may be admitted into Canada in this program:[223] (1) caregivers for children under the age of eighteen, which are classified as lower skilled; and (2) caregivers for people with high medical needs such as registered nurses, registered psychiatric nurses, or licensed practical nurses,

---

218 *Ibid.*
219 *Ibid.*
220 *Ibid.*
221 *Ibid.* A business number is a nine-digit identifier mainly used for tax purposes and obtained from Canada Revenue Agency. See Canada Revenue Agency, *Register Now* (10 March 2015), online: www.cra-arc.gc.ca/tx/bsnss/tpcs/bn-ne/bro-ide/rstrctns/menu-eng.html.
222 The process of applying for permanent resident status is examined in Chapter 5.
223 *Ibid.*

all of which are higher skilled occupations; or nurse aides or home support workers, which are classified as lower skilled.[224]

b) Reforming the Temporary Foreign Worker Program

In the past few years, the TFW program has undergone increased public scrutiny.[225] For example, in 2012, the BC Federation of Labour brought a legal challenge against HD Mining International in northern British Columbia when it obtained permits to hire more than 200 temporary foreign workers.[226] In April 2013, the Royal Bank of Canada apologized for its use of inter-company transfers to outsource IT workers, leading to Canadians being displaced by temporary foreign workers.[227] Further, allegations arose in April 2014 of temporary foreign workers displacing Canadian workers at fast food restaurants.[228] Finally, there have been ongoing reports of mistreatment, abuse, or discrimination of temporary foreign workers once they are in Canada.[229]

---

224 ESDC, *Families Hiring*, above note 217, online: www.esdc.gc.ca/eng/jobs/foreign_ workers/caregiver/index.shtml#Language-Proficiency.

225 See, for example, Delphine Nakache & Paula J Kinoshita, "The Canadian Temporary Foreign Worker Program: Do Short-Term Economic Needs Prevail over Human Rights Concerns?" *IRPP Study No 5* (May 2010), online: Institute for Research on Public Policy http://irpp.org/research-studies/study-no5/ at 1; Abigail B Bakan & Daiva K Stasiulis, "Foreign Domestic Worker Policy in Canada and the Social Boundaries of Modern Citizenship" (1994) 58 *Science and Society* 7. See also Chapter 5.

226 CBC, "BC Mine to Hire Only Chinese Temporary Workers for Years" (12 December 2012), online: www.cbc.ca/news/canada/british-columbia/story/2012/12/12/bc-chinese-miners-documents.html.

227 Grant Robertson & Bill Curry, "Royal Bank Apologizes to Employees over Outsourcing Move" *The Globe and Mail* (11 April 2013), online: www.theglobe andmail.com/report-on-business/economy/jobs/royal-bank-apologizes-to-employees-over-outsourcing-move/article11061489/; Sunny Freeman, "RBC Foreign Workers Controversy: A Sign of an Increasingly Anxious Middle Class" *Huffington Post* (12 April 2013), online: www.huffingtonpost.ca/2013/04/12/rbc-foreign-workers-middle-class_n_3065554.html.

228 See, for example, Bill Curry, "Pizza Place Faces Federal Grilling over Temporary Foreign Workers" *The Globe and Mail* (21 April 2014), online: www.theglobe andmail.com/report-on-business/economy/jobs/pizza-place-faces-federal-grilling-over-temporary-foreign-workers/article18088550/; Bill Curry & Justine Hunter, "B.C. McDonald's Franchise at Centre of Latest Foreign Worker Case" *The Globe and Mail* (7 April 2014), online: www.theglobeandmail.com/news/politics/mcdonalds-moves-swiftly-to-review-hiring-of-temporary-foreign-workers/article17855627/.

229 Canadian Council for Refugees, *Migrant Workers: Provincial and Federal Report Cards*, online: CCR http://ccrweb.ca/sites/ccrweb.ca/files/migrant-worker-report-cards.pdf: The report lists a number of factors that open the door to abuse of migrant workers' rights including: (a) the lack of permanent status leads

Underlying this scrutiny one finds deep skepticism about the continued existence of the TFW program. Does the TFW program deal efficiently with regional or occupational labour market shortages as it intends to? As noted, Dominique Gross's report for the CD Howe Institute indicates that easier access to temporary foreign workers did not always equate to efficient filling of shortages but may have adversely affected the employment of permanent residents and Canadians.[230]

As a result of the media-publicized attention to the TFW program, the government has embarked on a large-scale reform and is developing the International Mobility Program, designed to help alleviate short-term needs of Canadian employers without unduly contributing to the unemployment of those residing in Canada, and to deter and prevent abuse of foreign workers.[231] Applicants should consult Citizenship and Immigration Canada, the *IRPA* and its *Regulations,* and ministerial instructions to ensure that they have the most up-to-date information on the TFW program.

---

migrant workers to fear being fired or deported for complaining about perceived abuses or trying to negotiate conditions; (b) closed work permits are tied to specific employers and thus workers have limited options if an employer is mistreating them; (c) migrant workers are socially isolated by their lack of knowledge of English or French, unfamiliarity with Canada, and limited information about their rights, not to mention physical isolation as many have no means of transportation; (d) even if workers want to complain, the complaints system is inaccessible, and the processing of complaints means that resolutions may occur after a worker has left Canada; (e) the gap between federal and provincial jurisdictions means that while the TFW program is federally regulated, labour standards are provincially regulated; (f) there is little monitoring of workplaces or conditions of employment, and employers rarely face serious consequences where breaches are identified.

230 Gross, *Temporary Foreign Workers*, above note 134 at 4.
231 See Susana Mas, "Temporary Foreign Worker Overhaul Imposes Limits, Hikes Inspections" *CBC News* (20 June 2014), online: www.cbc.ca/news/politics/ temporary-foreign-worker-overhaul-imposes-limits-hikes-inspections-1.2682209: Reforms of the program include barring employers from hiring low-wage temporary foreign workers in regions where the unemployment rate is above 6 percent, a cap of 10 percent on the number of low-wage temporary foreign workers that employers can hire per work site by 2016, the gradual phasing in of the cap, an increase in the number of inspections and the hiring of more inspectors, an increase of the application fee for employers, fines of up to $100,000 for employers who contravene the *IRPA* or the *Regulations*, and additional funding for Canada Border Services Agency so it can pursue more criminal investigations.

I. CONCLUSION

Recent reform of the immigration system in Canada has revealed a greater tendency of the Canadian government to rely on temporary status in Canada to manage its immigration programs. The "occurrence and persistence of temporariness in Canada," however, contributes to the "systematic exclusion of a growing number of non-citizens, who live and work on the territory, from a wide range of rights."[232] Temporariness in Canada "implies limited rights based on temporality (often limiting period of stay) and conditionality (rights conditional upon their behaviour, e.g. they must satisfy a specific employer to remain in the country)."[233] As demonstrated in this chapter, foreign nationals can hold temporary status through a multitude of forms or programs.

Historically, those with temporary status are "predominantly portrayed in a negative light" with "[p]opular representations project[ing] the image of criminal, selfish, degenerate, diseased and dangerous" or "incapable of autonomy, self-representation."[234] Further, the "temporary-permanent divide" has been conceptualized as a "permeable paper border for the transnational elite that is less permeable for the majority of temporary migrants" thus providing "privileged forms of temporariness and inclusive membership to those categorized as highly skilled whilst reserving restrictive and restricting forms of temporariness for those categorized as 'low skilled'" coding such exclusion within economic or labour discourse.[235]

The result is that gaining access to more permanent status in Canada has become lengthier, more complicated, and more onerous despite the government's claims that they have reformed the system to create

---

232 Amrita Hari, "Temporariness, Rights and Citizenship: The Latest Chapter in Canada's Exclusionary Migration and Refugee History" (2014) 30 *Refuge* 35 at 37; see also Cecilia Menjivar, "Liminal Legality: Salvadoran and Guatemalan Immigrants' Lives in the United States" (2006) 111 *American Journal of Sociology* 999; Judith Bernhard et al, "Living with Precarious Legal Status in Canada: Implications for the Wellbeing of Children and Families" (2007) 24 *Refuge* 101.

233 Hari, *ibid* at 1; Amrita Hari, Susan McGrath, & Valerie Preston, *Temporariness in Canada: Establishing a Research Agenda* (CERIS Working Paper No 99) (2013), online: www.ceris.metropolis.net/wp-content/uploads/2013/04/CWP_99_Hari_McGrath_Preston.pdf.

234 *Ibid* at 7.

235 *Ibid* at 1; Deepa Rajkumar et al, "At the Temporary-Permanent Divide: How Canada Produces Temporariness and Makes Citizens through Its Security, Work, and Settlement Policies" (2012) 16 *Citizenship Studies* 483; see also Yessy Byl & Jason Foster, "Opinion: Creating an Underclass of Disposable Workers" *Edmonton Sun* (1 December 2013), online: http://ccrweb.ca/en/node/20382.

greater efficiencies and methods to ensure *bona fide* applicants are accepted. As scholars have noted, the new system gives us reason to consider temporariness not as its own category of immigration programming in Canada, but as something that should be studied as a lens on the system as a whole. In this way, we can critically examine Canada's exclusionary approach to immigration and question whether temporariness does provide better policy design in meeting the objectives of the immigration program in Canada.[236]

---

236 *Ibid.*

CHAPTER 5

ACQUIRING PERMANENT RESIDENT STATUS: THE ECONOMIC CLASSES

A. INTRODUCTION

Generally speaking, foreign nationals may select one of three routes to obtain permanent resident status. They may apply under one of the economic classes, under the family class, or under the refugee or humanitarian class.[1] In this chapter, applications of the first type are examined.

B. THE ECONOMIC CLASSES

Members of the economic classes made up 62 percent of the total number of permanent residents admitted into Canada in 2012.[2] Thus, this category represents a significant part of our immigration program.

---

1   There are also other exceptional routes that may be taken. For example, a person who is admitted into Canada under a temporary resident permit (TRP) may, in some circumstances, later apply for permanent resident status. The permit holders class is described in the *Immigration and Refugee Protection Regulations*, 2002 SOR/2002-227, ss 64–65.1 [*Regulations*]. In addition, and again exceptionally, the minister may grant permanent resident status for public policy reasons under the *Immigration and Refugee Protection Act*, SC 2001, c 27, s. 25.2 [*IRPA*].

2   Citizenship and Immigration Canada, *Annual Report to Parliament on Immigration 2013*, online: CIC www.cic.gc.ca/english/pdf/pub/annual-report-2013.pdf at 14 [*Annual Report, 2013*].

However, the statistic is somewhat deceptive. It should be noted that a large percentage of this total includes dependants of principal applicants who may be included within an application.[3] While principal applicants may have skills and experience that will allow them to contribute to the economy, the same may not be true of dependants.

This immigration stream was designed to achieve the goal of permitting Canada "to pursue the maximum social, cultural and economic benefits of immigration."[4] With this objective in mind, policies, programs, and bureaucratic structures have been developed to fill labour market shortages and develop the Canadian economy with a boost of specific skills, expertise, and other resources.

The *Immigration and Refugee Protection Act* (IRPA) currently specifies that "a foreign national may be selected as a member of the economic class on the basis of their ability to become economically established in Canada."[5] Program details are framed in the *Immigration and Refugee Protection Regulations*[6] and other instruments, thus affording the government the opportunity to respond to immediate shortages and the needs of the day. It is an opportunity that the current government has grasped with alacrity. There has been an explosion of regulatory adjustment and micromanagement in this branch of immigration. While flexibility, open-ended legislation, and enthusiastic, hyperactive governmental administration may enhance the achievement of objectives, it presents applicants and practitioners with the daunting challenge of remaining well informed about ever-changing criteria, processes, and quotas.

A foreign national may be selected as a member of the economic classes by applying as one of following: (a) a skilled worker, (b) a business immigrant, or (c) a caregiver. Under each of these headings, one finds different subcategories. Each subcategory and program is explored below.

1) Skilled Workers

Several objectives in the *IRPA* are related to the admission of skilled workers: (a) to permit Canada to pursue the maximum social, cultural, and economic benefits of immigration; (b) to support the development

---

3   Citizenship and Immigration Canada, *Facts and Figures 2013*, online: CIC www.cic.gc.ca/english/resources/statistics/facts2013/permanent/02.asp [*Facts and Figures 2013*].

4   *IRPA*, above note 1, s 3(1)(a).

5   *Ibid*, s 12(2).

6   *Regulations*, above note 1.

of a strong and prosperous Canadian economy, in which the benefits of immigration are shared across all regions of Canada; (c) to support, by means of consistent standards and prompt processing, the attainment of immigration goals established by the Canadian government in consultation with the provinces; and (d) to enrich and strengthen the cultural and social fabric of Canadian society, while respecting the federal, bilingual, and multicultural character of Canada.[7]

a)   The Federal Skilled Worker Class (*Regulations*, Sections 75–85)

The *Regulations* characterize the federal skilled worker class as "a class of persons who are skilled workers and who may become permanent residents on the basis of their ability to become economically established in Canada and who intend to reside in a province other than the Province of Quebec."[8]

A successful application by an individual in this category will lead to an issuance of a permanent resident visa.[9] Where the individual is applying from outside Canada, permanent resident status will be granted after examination at a port of entry.[10] For those applying from within Canada, the status will be granted with the visa.[11]

The *Regulations* provide that an officer assessing an application must first determine whether the principal applicant is eligible to be assessed in this category.[12] The applicant must meet the definition of a skilled worker, which stipulates a set of minimum requirements focusing on work experience.[13] In addition, the applicant must supply education credentials and evidence of language skills in English or French.[14] If these requirements are not met, the assessment will terminate, and the application will be rejected.

These requirements have been supplemented by instructions from the minister of Citizenship and Immigration, which further restrict the processing of applications.[15] Initially, the instructions identified a list of occupations in which applicants who did not have arranged employment in Canada were required to have experience.[16] Recently, the min-

---

7   *IRPA*, above note 1, s 3.
8   *Regulations*, above note 1, s 75(1).
9   *Ibid*, ss 70(1) and 70(2)(b).
10   *Ibid*, s 71.1(1).
11   *Ibid*, s 71.1(2).
12   *Ibid*, ss 70(1) and 72(1).
13   *Ibid*, ss 75–76 and 80.
14   *Ibid*, ss 78–79.
15   The most recent ministerial instructions have been published on the CIC website at www.cic.gc.ca/english/department/mi/.
16   See Minister of Citizenship and Immigration Canada, Ministerial Instructions 2 (MI 2) (2010), C Gaz I, 1669, online: http://gazette.gc.ca/rp-pr/p1/2010/2010-06-

ister has introduced a set of instructions that substantially alter the process of selection by replacing a system of "first come, first served" with the "express entry" system.

Under the former (described in Sections B(1)(a)(ii), (iii), and (iv), below in this chapter), an applicant who met the eligibility requirements would be evaluated on the basis of six factors (education, proficiency in the official languages of Canada, work experience, age, arranged employment, and adaptability) and be awarded points for each.[17] The applicant was required to achieve a minimum number of points set by the minister.[18] Where the applicant did not have arranged employment she was required to have sufficient funds to support herself and her dependants for a period of six months.[19] Under the express entry system (described in Section B(1)(f), below in this chapter), which applies beyond the skilled worker program to include applicants under other classes, eligible applicants are invited to apply after having been assessed according to a comprehensive ranking system that awards points on different grounds in which arranged employment is more heavily weighted.

The eligibility requirements for the skilled worker program have been retained under the express entry system. In addition, officers continue to assess applicants and family members according to criteria of inadmissibility.[20] In the text that follows, the eligibility criteria for the skilled worker class are first outlined followed by a detailed account of the former processing system that is still in force for applications received before 1 January 2015. The new express entry system that covers applications received from 1 January 2015 is discussed after the eligibility criteria for other classes are outlined. While the "points system" may not be currently active *per se*, the criteria and how they are assessed may inform how decisions are being made under the "express entry" system.

i)   The Eligibility Requirements (Regulations, Section 75)

The *Regulations* provide that a foreign national is a skilled worker if the following criteria are met:

(a)   Within the last ten years, the person has accumulated at least one year of continuous full-time work experience, or the equivalent part-time amount, in his or her primary occupation listed in

---

26/html/notice-avis-eng.html, listing experience using the National Occupational Classification (NOC) codes.

17   *Regulations*, above note 1, s 76(1)(a).
18   *Ibid*, s 76(2).
19   *IRPA*, above note 1, s 3; *Regulations*, above note 1, s 76(1)(b).
20   *Regulations*, *ibid*, s 72(1)(f); see Chapter 15 for more information.

Skill Type 0 management occupations or Skill Level A or B of the National Occupational Classification (NOC).[21]

(b) During the employment period, the person performed the actions described in the NOC lead statement.[22]

(c) During the employment period, the person performed a *substantial number of the main duties* and *all of the essential duties* listed in the NOC.[23]

(d) The foreign national has submitted a language evaluation showing a level of skill in either English or French that meets a designated threshold.[24]

(e) The foreign national has submitted a Canadian educational credential or foreign diploma, certificate, or credential, and the equivalency assessment.[25]

Full-time work is defined as thirty hours per week, and *work* is defined as "an activity for which wages are paid or commission is earned."[26]

a.   National Occupational Classification (NOC)

Employment and Social Development Canada (ESDC), previously known as Human Resources and Skills Development Canada (HRSDC), describes the National Occupational Classification (NOC) as

> . . . the nationally accepted reference on occupations in Canada. It organizes over 40,000 job titles into 500 occupational group descriptions. It is used daily by thousands of people to compile, analyze and communicate information about occupations, and to understand the jobs found throughout Canada's labour market . . . . It is used to manage the collection and reporting of occupational statistics and to provide understandable labour market information.[27]

---

21   *Regulations*, above note 1, s 75(2)(a).
22   *Ibid*, s 75(2)(b).
23   *Ibid*, s 75(2)(c) [emphasis added].
24   *Ibid*, s 75(2)(d).
25   *Ibid*, s 75(2)(e). Further, the principal applicant's occupation must *not* be considered a restricted occupation. Section 73(1) of the *Regulations* defines *restricted occupation* as "an occupation designated as a restricted occupation by the Minister, taking into account labour market activity on both an area and a national basis, following consultation with Employment and Social Development Canada (ESDC), provincial governments and any other relevant organizations or institutions." Currently, there are no occupations listed as restricted.
26   *Ibid*, s 73.
27   Human Resources and Skills Development Canada, *About the NOC 2011*, online: www5.hrsdc.gc.ca/NOC/English/NOC/2011/AboutNOC.aspx.

The NOC is updated every five years and is available online.[28] It classifies occupations according to skill type and skill level.[29] The first digit of a NOC code identifies the skill type of an occupation, which indicates a broad area of work.[30] NOC skill types range from 0 to 9. For example, management occupations start with the digit 0. NOC skill levels are classified under four levels using A through D.[31] For example, management occupations, which span all skill types, are included in Skill Level A. Employment and Skills Development Canada describes the four different skill levels thus:

> Skill Level A represents occupations usually requiring university education. Skill Level B refers to occupations usually requiring college education or apprenticeship training. Skill Level C occupations generally require completion of secondary school and some job-specific training or completion of courses directly related to the work. Skill Level D occupations usually require some secondary school, on-the-job training, short demonstration sessions or instruction that takes place in the work environment.[32]

b.   The Language Evaluation

An applicant must also submit the results of a language test conducted by a recognized body[33] to show that the applicant's language skills meet a pre-published minimum threshold fixed by the minister.[34] This relatively expensive requirement applies even to applicants from an English- or French-speaking country.

The purpose of this requirement[35] is to ensure that applicants "meet or exceed the threshold set by the Minister for proficiency in either

---

28 Human Resources and Skills Development Canada, *Welcome to the National Occupational Classification 2011*, online: www5.hrsdc.gc.ca/NOC/English/ NOC/2011/Welcome.aspx: "The 2011 National Occupational Classification (NOC) is currently being updated. The updated NOC will be available in 2016."

29 Human Resources and Skills Development Canada, *National Occupational Classification Matrix 2011*, online: www5.hrsdc.gc.ca/NOC/English/NOC/2011/pdf/ Matrix.pdf.

30 Human Resources and Skills Development Canada, *Frequently Asked Questions*, online: www5.hrsdc.gc.ca/NOC/English/NOC/2011/FAQ.aspx.

31 *Ibid.*

32 *Ibid.*

33 Designated language testing agencies are listed in Government of Canada, *Designated Language Testing Agencies*, online: www.cic.gc.ca/english/resources/ tools/language/agencies.asp.

34 *Regulations*, above note 1, s 75(2)(d).

35 *Ibid*, s 74.

English or French for each of the four language skill areas: reading, writing, speaking and listening."[36]

The minister fixes the minimum language proficiency threshold on the basis of three factors: (1) the number of applications by skilled workers being processed; (2) the number of skilled workers projected to become permanent residents; and (3) the potential for the establishment of skilled workers in Canada.[37] The *Regulations* also mandate the minister to establish the language proficiency threshold in reference to the benchmarks described in the *Canadian Language Benchmarks* and the *Niveaux de compétence linguistique canadiens.*[38]

c.   The Education Credential

An applicant must also submit a Canadian education credential[39] or an Educational Credential Assessment (ECA), defined as "a determination, issued by an organization or institution designated [by the minister] that a completed foreign diploma, certificate or credential is equivalent to a completed Canadian educational credential as defined above."[40] In order to remedy previous difficulties faced by those with foreign professional or trade credentials, the minister has been authorized by the *Regulations* to designate assessment institutions.[41] Currently, four agencies have been designated.[42]

d.   The Burden of Showing That the Requirements Have Been Met

The onus is on the principal applicant to satisfy a visa officer that she meets the minimum requirements.[43] Nevertheless, the Federal Court has held that where an application is adequate, but the officer entertains doubts, there is a duty on the part of the officer to seek clarification of

---

36   Citizenship and Immigration Canada, *Language Requirements – Federal Skilled Workers*, online: CIC www.cic.gc.ca/english/resources/tools/language/work.asp [*Language Requirements*].

37   *Regulations*, above note 1, s 74(1).

38   *Ibid*, s 74(2). More information on *Canadian Language Benchmarks* can be found online: www.cic.gc.ca/english/pdf/pub/language-benchmarks.pdf.

39   *Regulations*, above note 1, s 73(1): The *Canadian education credential* is defined as "any diploma, certificate or credential, issued on the completion of a Canadian program of study or training at an educational or training institution that is recognized by the provincial authorities responsible for registering, accrediting, supervising and regulating such institutions."

40   *Ibid.*

41   *Ibid*, s 75(4). See www.cic.gc.ca/english/immigrate/skilled/language-testing.asp.

42   *Regulations*, above note 1, s 75; see also Citizenship and Immigration Canada, News Release, "Backgrounder – Information for Applicants to the New Federal Skilled Worker Program" (2 February 2015), online: www.cic.gc.ca/english/department/media/backgrounders/2013/2013-04-18.asp.

43   *Shangguan v Canada (Minister of Citizenship and Immigration)*, 2007 FC 75 [*Shangguan*].

the information from the applicant.[44] Thus, where a visa officer has a doubt based on extrinsic evidence, the officer must seek clarification to either substantiate or eliminate the doubt.[45]

When evaluating whether an applicant performs the duties required, an officer may not import extraneous criteria into the occupation's duties listed in the NOC to find that an applicant does not meet the minimum requirements.[46] Further, the *Regulations* require that only a "substantial" number of the main duties, not all of the main duties, be performed.[47] It also requires that all the "essential" duties be performed, but the NOC does not specify which duties are essential, thus leaving the issue within the discretion of the officer. It is well established that the Federal Court will show deference to the assessments of officers and will review them using a standard of reasonableness. The Federal Court has emphasized that an officer cannot fixate on one or two duties and deny an application on the lack of performance of those duties, without examining whether most other duties listed in the NOC are performed.[48] Further, where an applicant obtains an arranged employment opinion or assessment from Employment and Skills Development Canada, such opinion cannot be ignored, especially if the duties listed are relevant in assessing the applicant's past work experience.[49] Finally, an officer cannot reason that an applicant's duties fit with another NOC category rather than the one selected to deny an application; the officer has a duty to determine whether the applicant satisfies the requirements of the category in question.[50]

It is important for an applicant to realize that, at this stage of the assessment, an officer is only obligated to look at employment experience within the ten years preceding the date of the application as specifically set out in the *Regulations*.[51] A principal applicant cannot rely on experience accumulated after the application has been submitted to meet the definitional requirement of experience. Where the experience is insufficient, an applicant should evaluate whether she should delay in submitting an application.

---

44   *Sandhu v Canada (Minister of Citizenship and Immigration)*, 2010 FC 759 [*Sandhu*].
45   *Ibid.*
46   *Shangguan*, above note 43.
47   *Regulations*, above note 1, s 75(2)(c); see also *Benoit v Canada (Minister of Citizenship and Immigration)*, 2013 FC 185 [*Benoit*].
48   *Benoit, ibid.*
49   *Gulati v Canada (Minister of Citizenship and Immigration)*, 2010 FC 451. For more information on labour market impact assessments, see below.
50   *Hussain v Canada (Minister of Citizenship and Immigration)*, 2013 FC 636.
51   *Regulations*, above note 1, s 77; *Dash v Canada (Minister of Citizenship and Immigration)*, 2010 FC 1255.

ii) The Points System (Regulations, Section 76)[52]

The points system is a mechanism created to help officers determine whether an applicant is likely to become economically established. Officers are required to assign points up to a fixed maximum under six headings. As one author has noted, "The point system was designed to improve consistency and fairness by reducing discretion and the potential for discrimination in selecting immigrants."[53] Thus, in addition to meeting the definitional eligibility requirements discussed above, a principal applicant must also achieve a passing score under the points system.[54] Currently, applicants must be awarded a minimum of 67 out of 100 points.[55] The minister fixes the minimum number of points based on (a) the number of applications by skilled workers being processed; (b) the number of skilled workers projected to become permanent residents; and (c) the potential for the establishment of skilled workers in Canada.[56] While an applicant may supplement an application with information and documentation up until the date a decision is made, it is important to note that an officer will evaluate whether there are enough points accumulated and whether the criteria were met the day the application was made and issued.[57]

In May 2013, the federal government implemented a revamped points system.[58] The changes were prompted by research findings that showed that language proficiency and youth are two important factors in the economic success of immigrants.[59] Accordingly, the recent chan-

---

52   It should be emphasized that since 1 January 2015, the points system has been superseded by the express entry system, a model of selecting skilled workers authorized by ministerial instruction. For more information on express entry, see Section B(1)(f), below in this chapter. The following description of the points system describes the mode of selecting skilled workers that was in force until 31 December 2014. Although it is no longer in force, its legal status has endured since the regulations by which it was established remain valid.

53   Lynn Fournier-Ruggles, *Canadian Immigration and Refugee Law for Legal Professionals*, 2d ed (Toronto: Emond Montgomery, 2013) at 196.

54   *Regulations*, above note 1, s 76.

55   *Ibid*, s 76(2); Citizenship and Immigration Canada, *Six Selection Factors – Federal Skilled Workers*, online: CIC www.cic.gc.ca/english/immigrate/skilled/apply-factors.asp.

56   *Regulations, ibid*, s 76(2).

57   *Ibid*, s 77.

58   Citizenship and Immigration Canada, News Release: "New Federal Skilled Worker Program to accept applications beginning May 4, 2013" online: http://news.gc.ca/web/article-en.do?nid=712839: "The improvements to the FSWP points grid are based on a large body of research which has consistently shown that language proficiency and youth are two of the most important factors in the economic success of immigrants."

59   *Ibid*.

ges have favoured younger applicants who are more proficient in one of Canada's official languages.[60]

The six selection factors for which points may be awarded will be examined in turn.

a.   Education (*Regulations*, Section 78(1)) [25 Points]

A visa officer may award up to twenty-five points to an applicant under this heading. The credentials that were submitted to meet the eligibility requirements, discussed above, will be assessed to determine how many points should be awarded. The onus is on the applicant to provide clear evidence of the education credential, including the level achieved.[61] It is important to note that proof of the credential or equivalency assessment is sufficient. An applicant need not prove how many hours of classes she attended, or whether classes were attended full time.[62] The chart below illustrates the permissible points allocation:

Table 5.1   Education: Permissible Points Allocation[63]

Credential and Number of Years of Education	Points
Secondary school credential	5
One-year post-secondary program credential	15
Two-year post-secondary program credential	19
Post-secondary program credential of three years or longer	21
Two or more post-secondary program credentials (one of which must be issued on completion of a post-secondary program of three years or longer)	22
University-level credential at the master's level or at the level of an entry-to-practice professional degree for an occupation listed in the NOC at skill level A for which licensing by a provincial regulatory body is required	23
University-level credential at the doctoral level	25

The *Regulations* define an education credential as "the completion" of a program of study; therefore, an officer will not award any points for partial completion of a program.[64] Further, if an applicant has com-

---

60   *Ibid.*

61   *Rabiee v Canada (Minister of Citizenship and Immigration)*, 2011 FC 824: In this case, the Federal Court found it reasonable that the officer used discretion to award only twenty-two points of education because it was not clear that the specialty that the applicant completed was at a master's or doctoral level.

62   *Hameed v Canada (Minister of Citizenship and Immigration)*, 2009 FC 527.

63   *Regulations*, above note 1, s 78(1).

64   *Ibid*, s 73(1); see also *Tiwana v Canada (Minister of Citizenship and Immigration)*, 2008 FC 100.

pleted two or more post-secondary credentials, cumulative points are not awarded; rather, an applicant will receive the highest number of points on the basis of the highest level credential obtained.[65]

Applicants are entitled to an explanation of the evaluation made by the officer. Although the Supreme Court has held that a failure to provide full reasons should not be regarded as a breach of the principles of procedural fairness, it is possible to attack the reasonableness of a decision based on the lack of transparency.[66]

A provision formerly in force gave the officer discretion to award points for achieving an educational credential, even if the number of years studied to achieve that credential fell short of the requirements. In 2013, the government repealed this measure.[67] In so doing it has transferred from the visa officer to an assessment institution the authority to determine whether the credential is the equivalent of a Canadian education credential. Thus, officers no longer have discretion to recognize the attainment of an education credential.[68] Less litigation may arise from the new procedure, but only because it may be more difficult to persuade a reviewing court that the decision of a designated institution is unreasonable in the circumstances. Since more than one institution

---

65   *Regulations*, above note 1, ss 78(1)(e) and (2); see also *Bhuiya v Canada (Minister of Citizenship and Immigration)*, 2008 FC 878, where the applicant had sixteen years of full-time education leading up to a master's degree to which the officer awarded twenty-two points. The applicant disputed that the officer did not take into account a one-year personnel management diploma taken after the sixteen years of education. The Federal Court held that the highest education credential held by the applicant was her master's degree and that she was entitled only to the number of points set out in s 78(1)(e); *Rabeya v Canada (Minister of Citizenship and Immigration)*, 2011 FC 370; *Khan v Canada (Minister of Citizenship and Immigration)*, 2011 FCA 339.

66   *Newfoundland and Labrador Nurses Union v Newfoundland and Labrador (Treasury Board)*, 2011 SCC 62; *Alberta (Information and Privacy Commissioner) v Alberta Teachers' Association*, 2011 SCC 61; *Healey v Canada (Minister of Citizenship and Immigration)*, 2009 FC 355; *Lak v Canada (Minister of Citizenship and Immigration)*, 2007 FC 350.

67   See SOR/2012-274 (2012) C Gaz II, 2885, online: www.gazette.gc.ca/rp-pr/p2/2012/2012-12-19/pdf/g2-14626.pdf (*Regulations Amending the Immigration and Refugee Protection Regulations*). Section 78(4) was not officially repealed until the 4 May 2013 to 30 July 2013 version of the *Regulations* (online: http://laws-lois.justice.gc.ca/eng/regulations/SOR-2002-227/20130504/P1TT3xt3.html). The amendment to repeal s 78(4) was published in the 19 December 2012 version (SOR/2012-274) of the Official Regulations in Part II of the *Canada Gazette*, online: www.gazette.gc.ca/rp-pr/p2/2012/2012-12-19/html/sor-dors274-eng.html. The relevant section of these amendments (s 7) came into force on 4 May 2013.

68   See cases to which the previous law applied: *McLachlan v Canada (Minister of Citizenship and Immigration)*, 2009 FC 975; *Marr v Canada (Minister of Citizenship and Immigration)*, 2011 FC 367.

has been designated to make the determination of equivalency, an applicant who has received a negative determination from one source may be able to look elsewhere for a positive one.[69]

b. Language Proficiency in English and French (*Regulations*, Section 79) [28 Points]

Points are awarded for language proficiency in recognition of the fact that "[b]eing able to communicate and work in one or both of Canada's official languages . . . helps you in the Canadian job market."[70] The language assessment evaluated in the eligibility stage is examined again for the purposes of determining how many points should be awarded to the applicant. A principal applicant must indicate in his application which language, English or French, is to be considered his first official language in Canada.[71] This determination is important because more points are awarded for proficiency in the first official language. A visa officer can award anywhere up to twenty-eight points under this selection factor: up to twenty-four points for the applicant's first official language and a maximum of four points for the applicant's second official language.[72] The following chart explains how officers should award points for each of the four language skills of reading, writing, speaking, and listening in the applicant's first official language:

Table 5.2   **Language Skills: Permissible Points Application**[73]

Proficiency of Language Skill	Points
If the applicant meets the threshold fixed by the minister	4
If the applicant exceeds the threshold fixed by the minister by one benchmark level	5
If the applicant exceeds the threshold fixed by the minister by two benchmark levels	6

For the second official language, an applicant can receive four points if her proficiency in that language meets or exceeds a specified benchmark in each of the four language skill areas.[74] For proficiency

---

69 For example, the cases of *Bano v Canada* (*Minister of Citizenship and Immigration*), 2011 FC 401, and *Shahid v Canada* (*Minister of Citizenship and Immigration*), 2011 FCA 40, may have been dealt with differently if an educational assessor was involved in the process.

70 Citizenship and Immigration Canada, *Six Selection Factors — Federal Skilled Workers*, online: CIC www.cic.gc.ca/english/immigrate/skilled/apply-factors.asp.

71 *Regulations*, above note 1, s 79(1).

72 *Ibid*, s 79(3).

73 *Ibid*, s 79(3)(a).

74 *Ibid*, s 79(3)(b).

in a second official language, the results of an evaluation must not be more than two years old from the date on which the application is made.[75] No other written evidence will be considered.[76] Further, all original evaluations of language proficiency must be submitted with the application, as applicants will not be afforded an opportunity to provide official language test results at a later stage in the process.[77]

Formerly, officers had discretion to look at other written evidence of language proficiency. Recent changes in the *Regulations* removed this option, something that may create more certainty and standardization in the evaluation of language and result in fewer judicial reviews.[78] However, the requirement that officers consider only the assessments from designated organizations and only evidence provided at the date of the application severely restricts their power to meaningfully inquire into the true proficiency of the applicant in any official language by requesting more information or looking at alternative sources of language ability.[79]

Further, streamlining the mode of evaluation signals Canada's normative regard for a certain kind of immigrant. Preference is being shown for ready-to-work immigrants who do not need any further language training.

c.   Work Experience (*Regulations*, Section 80) [15 Points]

The third factor — work experience — like the first two, operates both at the preliminary stage of determining eligibility and also at the stage of assessment. An applicant may receive up to fifteen points for full-time work experience or the equivalent in part-time work, within the ten years before the date the application was made.[80] The experience must be of the same type as is required for eligibility. First, the work has to be full-time or the equivalent in part-time work.[81] Second, the work

---

75   *Ibid*, s 79(2).

76   *Language Requirements*, above note 36.

77   *Ibid*.

78   For decisions made under the former law, see *Al-Kassous v Canada (Minister of Citizenship and Immigration)*, 2007 FC 541; *Aramouni v Canada (Minister of Citizenship and Immigration)*, 2011 FC 430. See also *Islam v Canada (Minister of Citizenship and Immigration)*, 2006 FC 424, in which the Federal Court held it was a reviewable error that the officer conducted his own test in lieu of the prescribed test.

79   See, for example, *Grewal v Canada (Minister of Citizenship and Immigration)*, 2011 FC 167.

80   *Regulations*, above note 1, s 80(1).

81   *Ibid*, s 73(1): As noted above, the *Regulations* define *full-time work* as "at least 30 hours of work over a period of one week" and *work* as "an activity for which wages are paid or commission is earned."

experience must have been obtained during the ten years preceding the date of application.[82] Third, the work experience must have been acquired in occupations listed at Skill Type 0 (managerial occupations), Skill Level A (professional occupations), or Skill level B (technical occupations and skilled trades) of NOC 2011.[83]

Table 5.3   Work Experience: Permissible Points Application[84]

Work Experience	Points
One year	9
Three years	11
Five years	13
Six or more years	15

As with the assessment of experience for the purpose of determining eligibility, officers have considerable discretion in determining whether an applicant satisfies the requirements of a given occupation and in interpreting the NOC.[85] They are required to give the NOC categories a liberal interpretation and must assess the requirements of the job in question with flexibility.[86] Job requirements have to be assessed in the operational context in which the individual actually worked.[87] The officer must determine the pith and substance of the work performed by the applicant; tangential performance of one or more functions under one or more job categories does not convert the job or functions from one NOC category to another.[88] In assessing whether the applicant has the requisite work experience, the applicant is not required to perform all the main duties in an NOC job category, but is required to perform a substantial number, that is, more than one.[89]

---

82   *Ibid*, s 80(1).

83   *Ibid*, s 80(2): A fourth qualification is also included — the occupation for which work experience was acquired must not have been designated by the minister as a restricted occupation. *Restricted occupation* is defined as "an occupation designated as a restricted occupation by the Minister, taking into account labour market activity on both an area and a national basis, following consultation with the ESDC, provincial governments and any other relevant organizations or institutions." At the date of writing, no occupations are listed as restricted.

84   *Ibid*, s 80(1).

85   *McHugh v Canada (Minister of Citizenship and Immigration)*, 2006 FC 1181.

86   *Ibid*.

87   *Ibid*.

88   *Rodrigues v Canada (Minister of Citizenship and Immigration)*, 2009 FC 111 [*Rodrigues*].

89   *Norman v Canada (Minister of Citizenship and Immigration)* 2002 FCT 1169 at para 31; *Rodrigues*, above note 88 at para 9.

As with the other factors, the onus is on the applicant to supply the pertinent information to demonstrate the requisite work experience.[90] An officer will have a duty to inform applicants about any concerns based on extrinsic evidence about the information put forth to demonstrate work experience and must give applicants a chance to clarify.[91]

The requirement that applicants have experience in managerial, professional, and technical occupations is a clear indicator of the government's preferences in economic migrants or the gaps in the labour market that the government is seeking to fill. The grant of permanent residence, rather than temporary status, is an indicator either of the government's belief that it is improper or ineffective to offer such work on a temporary basis or, more likely, that the offer of temporary work in these areas would not attract many applicants.

d. Age (*Regulations*, Section 81) [12 Points]

Up to twelve points may be awarded based on the age of the applicant. The *Regulations* specify that the applicant's age on the date of the application is what should determine the number of points according to the following table:

Table 5.4   Age: Permissible Points Application[92]

Age	Points
18 years old and above until 36 years old	12
36 years old	11
37 years old	10
38 years old	9
39 years old	8
40 years old	7
41 years old	6
42 years old	5
43 years old	4
44 years old	3
45 years old	2
46 years old	1
Less than 18 years old or 47 years old and older	0

90 *Kaur v Canada (Minister of Citizenship and Immigration)*, 2010 FC 442.
91 *Kniazeva v Canada (Minister of Citizenship and Immigration)*, 2006 FC 268.
92 *Regulations*, above note 1, s 81.

The recent changes in the mode of allocating points on this basis have clearly benefited younger persons, although those under eighteen are *de facto* rendered ineligible. The principal reason for the change is that statistics reveal that those who arrive at a younger age are more likely to integrate better and earn more and perform better financially than those who arrive at a later age.[93] Moreover, concern about an aging population and the increasing number of retirees has prompted a focus on younger arrivals.

e.   Arranged Employment (*Regulations*, Section 82) [10 Points]

Under this heading, ten points shall be awarded to an applicant for having arranged employment[94] in Canada. *Arranged employment* is defined to embrace the following components:

- There is an offer of employment in an occupation listed in Skill Type 0 management occupations or Skill Level A or B of the National Occupational Classification matrix.
- The offer is made by an employer other than an embassy, high commission, or consulate in Canada or a blacklisted employer (unless two years have elapsed since the blacklisting).
- The offer is for full-time work in Canada, that is, work that is non-seasonal and indeterminate.[95]

Essentially, four groups of individuals may benefit from the award of points under this heading:

a) The applicant is currently working on a work permit for which a labour market impact assessment (LMIA) was issued by Employment and Social Development Canada (ESDC)[96] where the work is of the required skill type or level. For such an individual, the permit must be valid at the time of application, the applicant must be employed, and the current employer must have made an indeterminate offer of full-time employment for a position of the required skill type or level.[97]

b) The applicant is currently working in Canada on a work permit that was LMIA exempt under an international agreement such as the *North American Free Trade Agreement* or the *General Agreement on Trade in Services*, or under a Canada–provincial/territorial

---

93   See note 58.
94   *Regulations*, above note 1, s 82(2).
95   *Ibid*, s 82(1).
96   See Chapter 4 for more information about LMIAs.
97   *Regulations*, above note 1, s 82(2)(a).

agreement.[98] Such an individual must be currently employed, and the current employer must have made an indeterminate offer of full-time employment for a position of the required skill type or level.[99]

c) The applicant does not hold a valid work permit and is not authorized to work in Canada on the date of the application for permanent residence. For such an individual, the employer must make an offer for the appropriate type of position and obtain a labour market impact assessment from ESDC.[100]

d) The applicant holds a work permit or is authorized to work in Canada but does not fit into category (a) or (b). For such an individual, the employer must make an offer for the appropriate type of position and obtain a labour market impact assessment from ESDC.[101]

Although a labour market impact assessment from ESDC is now required, in most circumstances, for arranged employment, it is not conclusive proof of arranged employment; an officer must still assess whether the applicant is able to perform the job described in the validation[102] and whether the employment offer was genuine.[103]

Finally, foreign nationals may have a temporary work permit that is due to expire and therefore may require facilitation to enable them to maintain their status and continue working in Canada while they await a final decision on their application. These individuals may apply for a bridging open work permit. To be eligible, an applicant must

- currently be in Canada
- have valid status on a work permit that is due to expire within four months
- have received a positive determination of eligibility on their application
- have made an application for an open work permit[104]

---

98 See Chapter 4 for more information about LMIAs and international trade agreements.

99 *Regulations*, above note 1, s 82(2)(b).

100 *Ibid*, s 82(2)(c).

101 *Ibid*, s 82(2)(d).

102 *Bellido v Canada (Minister of Citizenship and Immigration)*, 2005 FC 452.

103 *Zhong v Canada (Minister of Citizenship and Immigration)*, 2011 FC 980; *Profirio v Canada (Minister of Citizenship and Immigration)*, 2011 FC 794; *Osorio v Canada (Minister of Citizenship and Immigration)*, 2012 FC 882.

104 Citizenship and Immigration Canada, "Extend Your Work Permit – Economic Class Applicants" (2 May 2013), online: CIC www.cic.gc.ca/english/work/permit/extend/permanent.asp; Citizenship and Immigration Canada, "Temporary Foreign Worker Program: Provincial Nominees or Permanent Residence Applications – Bridging Open Work Permits for Certain Federal Economic Class Applicants,"

f.   Adaptability (*Regulations*, Section 83) [10 Points]
Under this heading, points are awarded for a variety of factors that are believed to increase a principal applicant's chance of successful integration into Canadian society. A total of ten points can be awarded for this selection factor. The following chart explains how an applicant can earn the maximum ten points:

Table 5.5   Adaptability: Permissible Points Application

Adaptability Criteria	Proof	Points
Language Proficiency Accompanying spouse or common law partner, other than a permanent resident residing in Canada or a Canadian citizen, has a level of proficiency in either official language at benchmark level four for each of the four language skill areas (speaking, listening, reading and writing) as set out in the *Canadian Language Benchmarks*.[a]	The principal applicant must provide original language test results that are not more than two years old at the time of the application, for their accompanying spouse or common-law partner from a designated testing agency.[b]	5
Previous Study in Canada Principal applicant completed at least two academic years of full-time study[c] of a program of at least two years in duration at a secondary or post-secondary institution in Canada.	The principal applicant must show proof of good academic standing during the period of full-time study in Canada, but does not need to show he/she obtained an educational credential.	5
Previous Study in Canada Accompanying spouse of common-law partner, other than a permanent resident residing in Canada or a Canadian citizen, completed at least two academic years of full-time study[d] of a program of at least two years in duration at a secondary or post-secondary institution in Canada.	The principal applicant must show that his/her spouse or common-law partner had good academic standing during the period of full-time study in Canada, but does not need to show he/she obtained an educational credential.	5

online: CIC www.cic.gc.ca/english/resources/tools/temp/work/prov/bridging.asp: Open work permits are issued under *Regulations*, above note 1, s 205(a).

Adaptability Criteria	Proof	Points
Work Experience in Canada Principal applicant completed at least one year of full-time work in Canada authorized under a work permit or as permitted without a work permit under the *Regulations*.[e]	Proof that the applicant completed one year of full-time work equivalent to Skill type 0, Skill level A or B of the NOC.[f]	10
Work Experience in Canada Accompanying spouse or common-law partner, other than a permanent resident residing in Canada or a Canadian citizen, completed at least one year of full-time work in Canada authorized under a work permit or permitted without a work permit under the *Regulations*.[g]	Proof that the spouse or common-law partner completed one year of full-time work.	5
Family Relationships If the principal applicant or accompanying spouse or common-law partner has a relative (parent, grandparent, child, grandchild, aunt/uncle, or niece/nephew)[h] who is 18 years of age or older as of the date of application and who is a Canadian citizen or permanent resident residing in Canada.[i]	Points for relatives in Canada may be awarded only once either to the principal applicant or the accompanying spouse or common-law partner but not to both.[j]	5
Arranged Employment If the principal applicant has been awarded points for arranged employment.[k]		5

a   For more on language proficiency, see Section B(1)(a)(ii)(b), above in this chapter.
b   See *Regulations,* above note 1, s 74(3): A list of designated organizations can be found at Government of Canada, *Designated Language Testing Agencies*, above note 33.
c   *Regulations,* above note 1, s 83(2): *Full-time study* is defined as at least fifteen hours of instruction per week during the academic year, authorized under a study permit or under s 188 (where no permit is required), at a secondary or post-secondary institution in Canada that is recognized by the provincial authorities responsible for registering, accrediting, supervising, and regulating such institutions, including any period of training in the workplace that forms part of the course of instruction. See *McLachlan v Canada (Minister of Citizenship and Immigration)*, 2009 FC 975.
d   *Regulations*, above note 1, s 83(2).
e   *Ibid*, s 186, which describes where a foreign national may work in Canada without a work permit.

f   See Section B(1)(a)(i)(a), above in this chapter, regarding National Occupation Classifi-
    cation (NOC).

g   *Regulations*, above note 1, s 186, which describes where a foreign national may work in
    Canada without a work permit.

h   *Ibid*, s 83(5), lists the family relationships recognized under the selection factor of
    adaptability.

i   See *Wang v Canada (Minister of Citizenship and Immigration)*, 2008 FC 798, where an
    officer did not award points for relatives in Canada because the applicant's brother had
    prolonged absences in Canada, casting doubt as to the residence of the relative. In *Gill
    v Canada (Minister of Citizenship and Immigration)*, 2010 FC 466, the applicant provided
    evidence of a relative who was a permanent resident but the officer was not satisfied
    with the evidence. The court held that the officer should have asked for more evidence
    if he wanted more. See also *Hadwani v Canada (Minister of Citizenship and Immigra-
    tion)*, 2011 FC 888, where the officer was not satisfied that the applicant supplied a
    government-issued birth certificate in support of otherwise satisfactory proof that the
    applicant had a nephew residing in Canada. The court held that government-issued
    birth certificates are not a requirement and that the officer should not have dismissed
    hospital records.

j   Government of Canada, "Six selection factors—Federal skilled workers," online:
    www.cic.gc.ca/english/immigrate/skilled/apply-factors.asp.

k   *Regulations*, above note 1, s 82(2).

Formerly, points were awarded for a spouse or common law partner's education credentials acquired outside Canada, but under the
current selection matrix, no points are awarded for this. The current
matrix places more emphasis on Canadian experience.

iii) *Self-Supporting upon Arrival* (Regulations, *Section 76(1)(b)*)

In order to be considered able to become economically established in
Canada, a principal applicant must also do one of two things: she must
either obtain points for arranged employment[105] or show she has sufficient settlement funds to support herself and any dependants (accompanying or not accompanying) upon arrival in Canada.[106]

For those who need to show sufficient settlement funds, the funds
must be available and transferrable and also unencumbered by debts or
other obligations.[107] Citizenship and Immigration Canada relies upon
the current low income cut-offs (LICO) from Statistics Canada to determine the appropriate amount of settlement funds needed for a particular family.[108]

---

105 *Ibid*, s 76(1)(b)(ii).
106 *Ibid*, s 76(1)(b)(i).
107 *Ibid*.
108 See Citizenship and Immigration Canada, *Sponsorship of Adopted Children and
     Other Relatives — The Sponsor's Guide*, online: CIC www.cic.gc.ca/english/
     information/applications/guides/5196ETOC.asp#table3, Table 3, to see LICO
     figures; see Statistics Canada, *Low Income Cut-offs*, online: www.statcan.gc.ca/
     pub/75f0002m/2009002/s2-eng.htm, for an explanation of LICO; *Regulations*,
     above note 1, s 2: see the definition for *minimum necessary income*.

The current amounts needed are set out in the table below:[109]

Table 5.6   Determination of Settlement Funds

Number of Family Members	Funds Required in Canadian Dollars
1	$11,931
2	$14,853
3	$18,260
4	$22,170
5	$25,145
6	$28,359
7 or more	$31,574

The onus of providing proof of the appropriate amount of settlement funds is on the principal applicant. Despite this, an applicant should know that an officer has a duty to give an applicant the opportunity to supply missing documentation concerning settlement funds.[110] An officer also must evaluate all the evidence submitted regarding settlement funds.[111]

iv) The Application Process

Generally, an applicant must fill out the requisite documents, submit pertinent documents, and pay the application fees. The onus is on the applicant to supply evidence and information that would help an officer determine whether the requirements set out in the *Regulations* are met.[112] The application documents are published online.[113]

In general, officers can make a decision by reviewing the paper application and supporting documentation. There are, however, circumstances in which an officer may need to contact the applicant or conduct an interview. Where an officer has concerns about the accuracy or authenticity of information or documentation, the officer has a duty to raise these concerns with the applicant.[114] Further, an officer may conduct an interview to help garner information in assessing whether the

---

109 Citizenship and Immigration Canada, *Proof of Funds – Skilled Immigrants (Express Entry)* (28 January 2015), online: www.cic.gc.ca/english/immigrate/skilled/funds.asp.

110 *Hernandez v Canada (Minister of Citizenship and Immigration)*, 2004 FC 1398.

111 *Gay v Canada (Minister of Citizenship and Immigration)*, 2007 FC 1280.

112 *Wang v Canada (Minister of Citizenship and Immigration)*, 2008 FC 798.

113 Citizenship and Immigration Canada, *Apply – Skilled immigrants (Express Entry)* (25 March 2015), online: www.cic.gc.ca/english/immigrate/skilled/apply-how.asp.

114 *Shangguan*, above note 43; *Sandhu*, above note 44.

content of the application is truthful and complete, to clarify aspects of the application, and conduct quality control.[115] Officers may not conduct interviews to assess language abilities as recent changes in legislation have removed their former discretionary power to evaluate these aspects.[116] Finally, officers may engage in random verification checks as part of Citizenship and Immigration Canada's efforts to detect and deter fraud. Thus, in some cases, although an application may not warrant it, an officer may still contact an applicant to identify whether the applicant is engaging in fraud or misrepresentation, which would render the applicant inadmissible.[117]

While a cap on the number of applications accepted has applied to the federal skilled worker program in the past, the advent of the Express Entry program has done away with annual caps for certain skilled workers.[118] Applicants would be wise to consult the ministry and its website regularly to determine whether there is a cap, and whether the cap has been met before filing an application. There is no obligation on the part of Citizenship and Immigration Canada to process an application once the annual cap has been reached.[119]

Processing times vary depending on the visa office to which the applicant submits the application. In the last quarterly update of 10 March 2014, processing times ranged from three to sixty-eight months depending on the location.[120]

Section 76(3) of the *Regulations* provides that an officer (with the concurrence of another officer) has discretion to substitute the requirements under the points system where an applicant does not have the requisite number of points if, in their evaluation, there is a likelihood of the applicant becoming economically established in Canada.[121] In cases where an applicant may not reach the requisite number of points, a request must be made to the officer to exercise positive discretion

---

115 See "Conducting Interviews," online: www.cic.gc.ca/english/resources/tools/ interview/applicant/conduct.asp and "Assessing for Misrepresentation," online: cic.gc.ca/english/resources/tools/perm/express/refuse.asp.

116 *Ibid.*

117 *Ibid*, s 12.4; see Chapter 14 for more information regarding inadmissibility on the basis of fraud and misrepresentation.

118 Minister of Citizenship and Immigration Canada, Updated Ministerial Instructions (26 April 2014), online: http://gazette.gc.ca/rp-pr/p1/2014/2014-04-26/ html/notice-avis-eng.php.

119 *Agama v Canada (Minister of Citizenship and Immigration)*, 2013 FC 135.

120 Citizenship and Immigration Canada, *Processing Times for Federal Skilled Worker Applications* (3 February 2015), online: www.cic.gc.ca/english/information/ times/perm/skilled-fed.asp.

121 *Regulations*, above note 1, s 76(3) and (4).

to engage in a "substituted evaluation." Absent a request, there is no obligation for the officer to consider an alternative evaluation.[122] Accompanying such a request, it is advised, although not required, that the applicant provide a rationale to satisfy the officer that a positive discretion or substituted evaluation is justified.[123] The Federal Court has held that consideration under an alternative evaluation is not limited to the assessment of points but open to all factors in the *Regulations*.[124] Although an officer must consider exercising discretion under section 76(3) after a request has been made, the officer does not need to give reasons for refusing to exercise the discretion.[125] Further, the fact that a different person may have exercised discretion in a different matter is not a sufficient ground to have the application returned for a redetermination.[126]

Section 76(3) can also be used to exercise discretion where, despite meeting the points requirements, an officer considers that the applicant would not be able to become economically established in Canada. For example, in the case of *Philbean v Canada (Minister of Citizenship and Immigration)*, the Federal Court accepted the officer's evaluation, which was based on a concern that the applicant would not only be unable to find employment in Canada, but would also be unwilling. The officer considered her particular circumstances, including the fact that she had retired in her home country and that she had not taken steps towards certification in her field of work or finding employment in Canada.[127]

Where an application has been denied, an individual can apply to seek leave for judicial review to the Federal Court. Although the court has shown deference towards officers' decisions, it will step in to quash the decision and refer the application to another officer for redetermination where it has found that an officer's decision was unreasonable or where the officer failed to respect the principles of procedural fairness.[128] Under the former, the consideration of irrelevant or extraneous factors has been a reason to send the application back to another officer.[129] Under the latter, a failure to ask for clarification of an obvious

---

122 *Nayyar v Canada (Minister of Citizenship and Immigration)*, 2007 FC 199; *Tathgur v Canada (Minister of Citizenship and Immigration)*, 2007 FC 1293; *Eslamieh v Canada (Minister of Citizenship and Immigration)*, 2008 FC 722.

123 *Ibid.*

124 *Choi v Canada (Minister of Citizenship and Immigration)*, 2008 FC 577 at para 21.

125 *Fernandez v Canada (Minister of Citizenship and Immigration)*, 2008 FC 243.

126 *Esguerra v Canada (Minister of Citizenship and Immigration)*, 2008 FC 413.

127 2011 FC 487; see also *Sharma v Canada (Minister of Citizenship and Immigration)*, 2011 FC 337.

128 See, for example, *Turizo v Canada (Minister of Citizenship and Immigration)*, 2013 FC 721; *Bazaid v Canada (Minister of Citizenship and Immigration)*, 2013 FC 17. See Chapter 16 for more information on judicial review.

129 *Hussain v Canada (Minister of Citizenship and Immigration)*, 2009 FC 209; *Tan v Canada (Minister of Citizenship and Immigration)*, 2012 FC 1079; *Nathoo v*

error has been sufficient reason and lack of reasons associated with the awarding of points.[130]

b) The Quebec Skilled Worker Class (*Regulations*, Section 86)

The *Canada–Québec Accord* gives Quebec sole responsibility for determining the selection criteria for skilled workers intending to reside in Quebec.[131] As a result, separate rules for skilled workers in Quebec have been created. While Quebec may govern the selection criteria and eventual integration of skilled workers in Quebec, the federal government still determines whether a person is admissible or inadmissible, and also issues the permanent resident visa to Quebec skilled workers.[132]

A foreign national is a member of the Quebec skilled worker class if the applicant intends to reside in the province of Quebec and is named in a *Certificat de sélection du Québec* issued by the province.[133]

c) Provincial Nominee Class (*Regulations*, Section 87)[134]

The *IRPA* allows the minister of Citizenship and Immigration, with the approval of the Governor in Council, to enter into agreements with the government of any province in Canada for the purposes of the *IRPA*.[135] Further, the minister may consult with the governments of the provinces on immigration and refugee policies and programs in order to facilitate co-operation and implementation of the *IRPA*.[136]

The provincial nominee program (PNP), the product of agreements between the federal and provincial governments, is a vehicle by which the provinces can select or target foreign nationals to fill local labour markets and economic needs of that province.[137] In addition, the PNP

Canada (Minister of Citizenship and Immigration), 2007 FC 818.

130 *Kumar v Canada (Minister of Citizenship and Immigration)*, 2011 FC 770; *Zheng v Canada (Minister of Citizenship and Immigration)*, 2008 FC 430.

131 *Canada–Québec Accord relating to Immigration and Temporary Admission of Aliens* (5 February 1991), online: www.cic.gc.ca/english/department/laws-policy/agreements/quebec/can-que.asp. See Chapter 4 for more information.

132 *IRPA*, above note 1, s 8(2). See Chapter 14 for more information on inadmissibility.

133 *Regulations*, above note 1, s 86(2).

134 As with the selection of skilled workers, the express entry mode of selection now applies to this class of applicant. See Section B(1)(f), below in this chapter, for more information on express entry.

135 *IRPA*, above note 1, s 8(1).

136 *Ibid*, s 10(1).

137 See *Annual Report, 2013*, above note 2 at 20; for example: Ontario, *Opportunities Ontario: About the Program* (12 March 2014), online: www.ontarioimmigration.ca/OI/en/pnp/OI_PNPABOUT.html: "If you are an Ontario employer having difficulty finding the workers you need, Opportunities Ontario may be the program for you . . . . The Government of Ontario established Opportunities Ontario

"was designed to spread the benefits of immigration across Canada by promoting immigration to areas that are not traditional immigrant destinations."[138] After the federal skilled worker program, this program attracts the largest number of economic immigrants to Canada.[139]

Like the federal skilled worker program, applicants under this category "may become permanent residents on the basis of their ability to become economically established in Canada."[140] Unlike the federal skilled worker program, semi- and low-skilled applicants may apply.

Applicants are not assessed on the criteria used in the federal skilled worker program.[141] To be a member of the provincial nominee class, a foreign national must first be named in a nomination certificate issued by the government of the province under a provincial nominee agreement, and second, the foreign national must intend to reside in the province that nominated them.[142] In most circumstances it is the potential employer who drives the process by applying to the province.[143]

to help employers succeed in the global competition for talent. Opportunities Ontario has a target of 2,500 nominations in 2014." Another example: Alberta, *Alberta Immigrant Nominee Program* (7 July 2014), online: www.albertacanada. com/opportunity/immigrating/ainp.aspx: "The AINP is an economic immigration program operated by the Government of Alberta with the Government of Canada's department of Citizenship and Immigration Canada (CIC). It supports Alberta's economic growth by attracting and retaining work-ready immigrants to the province."

138 *Annual Report, 2013*, above note 2 at 20.
139 *Ibid:* In 2012, Canada admitted a record number of nominees under the PNP with 40,899 persons.
140 *Regulations*, above note 1, s 87(1).
141 *Annual Report, 2013*, above note 2; for example: *Alberta Immigrant Nominee Program,* above note 137: "The AINP offers options for both skilled and semi-skilled workers."
142 *Regulations,* above note 1, s 87(2).
143 See, for example, British Columbia, *Skills Immigration*, online: www.welcomebc. ca/Immigrate/About-the-BC-PNP/Skills-Immigration.aspx: The British Columbia instructions on how to apply for the PNP state:

You accept an offer of indeterminate full-time employment from a B.C. employer who is willing to support your application for permanent residence through the PNP. If you are currently working in B.C. on a temporary work permit, your employer will need to offer you an indeterminate position without an end date.

If you and your current or prospective employer meet the program criteria, you will submit a joint application to the PNP office.

We assess your application against program criteria, and if we approve your application, we will nominate you for permanent residence. If necessary, we will provide you with a work permit support letter so you can apply

Because provinces conduct their own recruiting and selection of foreign nationals, often obtaining permanent residence through a PNP is quicker than if applying through the federal program. Despite the ability of provinces to recruit and select foreign nationals through the PNP, the federal government retains jurisdiction to assess whether the foreign nationals and their family members are inadmissible.[144]

Thus, applying to be a permanent resident under the PNP is a two-step process. First, an applicant applies to the province to be nominated; and second, the applicant applies to a federal visa officer for permanent residence.[145] During the second step, federal visa officers review applications to ensure that the applicant has the ability to become economically established and also assesses inadmissibility.[146]

Although, in normal circumstances, deference is shown once a nomination certificate has been issued by a province, it is clear that the *Regulations* allow a federal visa officer to substitute her own evaluation on the likelihood of economic establishment as Canada has the ultimate responsibility for immigration matters.[147] Federal visa officers may also refuse to allow an application, after consultation with a provincial counterpart, if they are not satisfied that the applicant intends to reside in the province that nominated her.[148] While a federal visa officer has some discretion, he may not evaluate the ability to become economically established on criteria in the federal skilled worker program, but must consider criteria and factors that persuaded the province that the applicant will become economically established.[149]

Since each province has its own agreement with the federal government (see the Appendix), and its own local needs and policies, criteria

---

to Citizenship and Immigration Canada (CIC) to obtain or renew a work permit to start or continue working in B.C. for your employer.

After the PNP nominates you for permanent residence, you (and your spouse and dependent children if applicable) will submit a separate application for a permanent resident visa to CIC in the Provincial Nominee Class. You will have six months from the date of your nomination to apply to CIC.

If CIC approves your application, you will be issued a permanent resident visa to live in Canada.

144 See step 2 as outlined by Citizenship and Immigration Canada, *Apply, Provincial Nominees* (1 January 2015), online: www.cic.gc.ca/english/immigrate/provincial/apply-how.asp. For more information about inadmissibility, see Chapter 14.

145 *Regulations*, above note 1, ss 87(2)–(3).

146 *Ibid*, s 87(3).

147 *Ibid*, s 87(2)(b); *Wai v Canada (Minister of Citizenship and Immigration)*, 2009 FC 780. Note that s 87(3) of the *Regulations* requires the concurrence of a second officer for this decision to be made.

148 *Kikeshian v Canada (Minister of Citizenship and Immigration)*, 2011 FC 658.

149 *Sran v Canada (Minister of Citizenship and Immigration)*, 2012 FC 791.

upon which to be nominated by the province vary. Each province has its own application package, requirements, and process.

d) Canadian Experience Class (*Regulations*, Section 87.1)[150]

The Canadian experience class is a relatively new program that offers permanent resident status to individuals who have acquired skilled work experience in Canada while holding temporary resident status. This economic stream aims to recruit foreign students[151] or foreign workers who have already demonstrated a level of integration and establishment in Canada.[152] Through this program, Canada is, in a sense, recruiting from within, aiming to attract those who have spent time in Canada and who have already contributed significantly in the workplace.

A foreign national is eligible under the Canadian experience class if he

1) plans to live outside the province of Quebec;[153]
2) has at least twelve months of full-time[154] skilled work experience,[155] or part-time equivalent, in Canada in the three years before the application is submitted;[156]
3) has gained the work experience while retaining valid immigration status;[157] and
4) meets the required language proficiency needed for the applicant's job for each skill (speaking, reading, writing, and listening).[158]

---

150 As with the selection of skilled workers, the express entry mode of selection now applies to this class of applicant. See Section B(1)(f), below in this chapter, for more information on express entry.

151 Foreign students may apply to be permanent residents, not only under the Canadian Experience Class, but also the federal skilled worker program and the provincial nominee program. Those who want to work in Canada after graduating from studies in Canada must apply for a work permit under the post-graduation work permit program.

152 *Regulations*, above note 1, s 87.1(1).

153 *Ibid.*

154 *Ibid*, ss 73(1)–(2): *full-time work* means at least thirty hours of work over a period of one week.

155 *Ibid*, ss 87.1(2)(a)–(c): Skilled work experience must be one or more occupations listed in Skill Type 0 (management occupations) or Skill Level A or B of the NOC, and not be a restricted occupation. The work experience must have included actions described in the lead statement for the occupation as set out in the NOC, and the applicant must have performed a substantial number of occupational duties as set out in the NOC, including all essential duties.

156 *Ibid.*

157 *Ibid*, s 87.1(3)(c).

158 *Ibid*, ss 87.1(d)–(e): The proficiency of English or French must be evaluated by an organization or institution designated under the *Regulations*, s 74(3), and

Skilled work experience refers to experience in occupations listed in the NOC under Skill Type 0 or Skill Level A or B.[159] The work experience need not be continuous, but employment during full-time study and any period of self-employment is not included in the period of work experience.[160] As with the test for work experience used for eligibility under the skilled worker program, the applicant must show that he has performed the actions described in the lead statement for the occupation(s), as set out in the occupational description of the NOC,[161] and performed a substantial number of the main duties, including all the essential duties, of the occupation(s), as set out in the NOC's occupational description.[162] It is important to note that eligible applicants are still subject to being scrutinized as to whether they are inadmissible to Canada.[163]

e)   Federal Skilled Trades Class (*Regulations*, Section 87.2)[164]

This economic stream aims to bring more persons with experience in needed skilled trades to Canada. The program was developed to fill gaps in the labour market identified by both the provinces and the federal government.

Currently, only those trained in specified skilled trades are eligible. These trades include the following:

(a) industrial, electrical, and construction trades;[165]

(b) maintenance and equipment operation trades;[166]

(c) supervisors and technical jobs in natural resources, agriculture, and related production;[167]

(d) processing, manufacturing, and utilities supervisors and central control operators;[168]

---

have met the applicable threshold fixed by the minister under s 74(1) for each of the four language skill areas. The language proficiency must also meet the threshold fixed by the minister under s 74(1) for the occupation in which the applicant acquired the work experience.

159 *Ibid*, ss 87.1(2)(a)–(c).
160 *Ibid*, ss 87.1(3)(a)–(b).
161 *Ibid*, s 87.1(2)(b).
162 *Ibid*, s 87.1(2)(c).
163 See Chapter 14 for more information on inadmissibility.
164 As with the selection of skilled workers, the express entry mode of selection now applies to this class of applicant. See Section B(1)(f), below in this chapter, for more information on express entry.
165 *Regulations*, above note 1, s 87.2(a).
166 *Ibid*, s 87.2(b).
167 *Ibid*, s 87.2(c).
168 *Ibid*, s 87.2(d).

(e)   chefs and cooks;[169] and

(f)   butchers and bakers.[170]

All listed skilled trades are from the NOC skill level B group. Applicants are advised to check with Citizenship and Immigration Canada to see which applications they are currently accepting.

An officer reviewing a skilled trade application will assess whether an applicant will become economically established in Canada.[171] It is also important to note that applicants, while being eligible, are still subject to being scrutinized as to whether they are inadmissible to Canada.

f)   The Express Entry Program

From 1 January 2015,[172] a new electronic system, Express Entry, has been used to manage applications for permanent residence in certain economic programs that have been received after that date.[173] The program is described as follows:

> Express Entry will actively target highly skilled immigrants under key economic immigration programs while providing new recruitment possibilities for employers.
>
> Express Entry is an application management system that facilitates the active recruitment, assessment and selection of skilled immigrants. Candidates complete an online submission to "express interest" in coming to Canada and provide information about their skills and experience, which determines their eligibility for entry into the EE pool. Provinces and territories as well as Canadian employers will have the option to consider Express Entry candidates to meet their immigration and labour market needs.[174]

Applicants in the following economic streams can submit an application through Express Entry: (a) federal skilled workers program;

---

169   *Ibid*, s 87.2(e). It is odd that cooks are excluded from the Canadian experience class but included within the skilled trades class. One is tempted to infer that this reveals a prejudice against Canadian cuisine.

170   *Ibid*, s 87.2(f).

171   *Regulations*, above note 1, s 87.2(2).

172   Minister of Citizenship and Immigration Canada, *Ministerial Instructions Respecting the Express Entry System* (28 November 2014), online: www.cic.gc.ca/english/department/mi/express-entry.asp, s 35 [*Ministerial Instructions Express Entry*].

173   An overview of the Express Entry Program is now available, online: www.gic.gc.ca/english/resources/tools/perm/econ/fsw/index.asp.

174   Canada's Economic Action Plan, *Express Entry*, online: http://actionplan.gc.ca/en/initiative/express-entry [Backgrounder: *Express Entry*].

(b) federal skilled trades program; and (c) Canadian experience class.[175] Applicants must submit an "expression of interest" through an online electronic system which details information that would convince the minister of Citizenship and Immigration and/or the minister's delegates that they deserve to have their applications expedited through this program.[176]

In general, applicants must

1) meet the requirements of the immigration economic program they are applying under, whether it be the federal skilled worker program, the federal skilled trades program, or the Canadian experience class.[177]

2) have one of the following:

   a) arranged employment, as defined in section 82 of the *Regulations*, and a valid labour market impact assessment, as specified under section 82(2)(c)(ii);[178]

   b) employment in Canada as a skilled worker under a valid work permit as per section 82(2)(b) of the *Regulations*;[179]

   c) a certificate of qualification issued by a provincial authority in a skilled trade occupation under section 87.1(3)(d)(i) of the *Regulations*;[180]

   d) employment in Canada under a valid work permit in a skilled trade occupation, as per section 87.1(3)(d)(ii) of the *Regulations*.[181]

3) have one of the following:

   a) a "qualifying offer of arranged employment," which includes the requirement to have a labour market impact assessment;[182]

---

175 *Ministerial Instructions Express Entry*, above note 172, s 2.
176 *Ibid*, ss 3(2) and 5(2).
177 *Ibid*, s 5(1)(a).
178 *Ibid*, s 5(1)(b)(i).
179 *Ibid*.
180 *Ibid*, s 5(1)(b)(ii).
181 *Ibid*.
182 *Ibid*, s 5(1)(c); see s 1, which defines qualifying offer of arranged employment. In general, it pertains to the following:

   (a) a job offer for an occupation listed in Skill Type 0 (management) or Skill Level A or B of the NOC made to a foreign national

   (b) a job offer for an occupation listed in Skill Level B of the NOC listed in categories under s 87.2(1) of the *Regulations* for continuous full-time work in Canada for at least one year

   (c) a job offer for an occupation listed in Skill Type 0 (management) or Skill Level A or B of the NOC made by an employer listed on an applicant's work permit

b) a nomination certificate issued by a province;[183]
c) registration with the job bank of Employment and Social Development Canada within thirty days of submitting an expression of interest with the Express Entry program if the applicant does not have a qualifying offer of employment or is not named in a provincial nomination certificate.[184]

Applicants who meet these requirements are eligible for the Express Entry program and entered into a pool of candidates, from which they can be selected to apply for permanent residence status in an expedited fashion.[185]

Applicants in the pool will be assessed according to a skills-based ranking system, called a "Comprehensive Ranking System," that awards points for, among other things, language proficiency, education, and Canadian work experience.[186] The Comprehensive Ranking System also ranks foreign nationals relative to other applicants in the pool. Periodically throughout the year the minister will issue instructions indicating that a given number of candidates will be accepted from the pool and identifying the minimum number of points from the Comprehensive Ranking System that must be obtained for an invitation to apply for permanent residence to be extended to a person in the pool. Applicants ranked highest will be issued an invitation to submit their permanent residence application within sixty days to be processed with priority.[187]

Section 8 of the ministerial instructions outlining the Express Entry program provides that the total amount of points that can be assigned under the Comprehensive Ranking System is 1,200 and that they can be allocated as follows:

1) for a foreign national who has no accompanying spouse or common-law partner

---

(d) a job offer for an occupation listed in Skill Level B of the NOC listed in categories set out in s 87.2(1) of the *Regulations* made by an employer identified on an applicant's work permit

Job offers must not come from the following: embassies, high commissions, or consulates in Canada, employers listed under s 209.91(3) of the *Regulations*, or employers in seasonal work. Further, each job offer must have an LMIA in support of it.

183 See Section B(2)(d), below in this chapter.

184 See *Ministerial Instructions Express Entry*, above note 172, s 5(2), which exempts persons who have physical or mental disabilities from registering with a job bank or an electronic system.

185 *Ibid*, s 6. Candidates will be placed in the pool for approximately one year.

186 Backgrounder: *Express Entry*, above note 174; *Ministerial Instructions Express Entry*, above note 172, s 3. For point allocations, see ss 8–30.

187 *Ibid*, ss 3(2) and 8.

a) a maximum of 500 points for the core human capital factors,[188]
b) a maximum of 100 points for skill transferability factors,[189] and
c) a maximum of 600 points for either a provincial nomination[190] or a qualifying offer of arranged employment;[191] and

2) for a foreign national who has an accompanying spouse or common law partner

a) a maximum of 460 points for the core human capital factors,
b) a maximum of 40 points for accompanying spouse or common law partner factors,[192]
c) a maximum of 100 points for skill transferability factors,[193] and
d) a maximum of 600 points for either a provincial nomination or a qualifying offer of arranged employment.[194]

Applicants can add or update any information to the Express Entry system at any time up until an invitation is issued.[195] Points assigned

---

188 *Ibid*, ss 8(1)(a) and 9–15. Section 9 defines core human capital factors as including age, level of education, official language proficiency, and Canadian work experience. Section 10 outlines how many points are to be allocated for the age factor. Section 11 outlines how many points are to be assigned for the level of education factor. Sections 12–14 outline how many points are to be assigned for official language proficiency. Section 15 outlines how many points are to be assigned for Canadian work experience.

189 *Ibid*, ss 8(1)(c) and 20–26. Section 20 provides that the skill transferability factors include the level of education, foreign work experience, and certificate of qualification in a trade occupation. Section 21 outlines how points are to be assigned for the combination of level of education and official language proficiency. Section 22 outlines how many points are to be assigned for the combination of level of education and Canadian work experience. Section 23 outlines how points are to be outlined for the combination of foreign work experience and official language proficiency. Section 24 outlines how many points are to be assigned for a combination of Canadian work experience and foreign work experience. Section 25 outlines how many points are to be assigned for foreign work experience. Section 26 outlines how many points are to be assigned for a combination of certificate of qualification and official language proficiency.

190 *Ibid*, s 28, outlines how many points can be assigned for provincial nomination.

191 *Ibid*, s 29, outlines how many points can be assigned for an offer of arranged employment.

192 *Ibid*, s 8(1)(b), states that the accompanying spouse or common law partner factors are the level of education, official language proficiency, and Canadian work experience of the spouse or partner. See also ss 17–19: Section 17 outlines the points that could be assigned for the level of education. Section 18 outlines how many points are to be assigned for official language proficiency. Section 19 outlines how points are to be assigned for Canadian work experience.

193 *Ibid*. See *Ministerial Instructions Express Entry*, above note 172, ss 3(2) and 8.

194 See notes 188–89.

195 *Ibid*, s 31(a).

will be recalculated as information is changed or added, and eligibility for an invitation will be redetermined.[196]

Applicants can improve their chances of being selected from the pool by "promoting themselves" and matching themselves with employers through Employment and Social Development Canada's job bank or private-sector job boards.[197] Provinces may also nominate persons in the pool to allow for an applicant to apply for permanent residence more quickly.[198] Express Entry does not do away with the requirement of a labour market impact assessment, and thus, employers may still need to obtain one. Citizenship and Immigration Canada promises that persons pulled from an Express Entry pool will have an application for permanent residence processed within six months.[199]

The Express Entry program essentially allows persons to circumvent the normal course of processing where first in line is first processed. While the federal government strongly condemns and is combatting alleged "queue jumping" on the part of those seeking refugee status in Canada, the government seems to be encouraging, promoting, and facilitating queue jumping in the skilled worker program.[200] Not only does this build hypocrisy into Canada's immigration policy, the Express Entry program also shows a bias towards those whom the current government views as ideal or suitable immigrants, shaping our normative discourse of legitimate immigrants.

Further, the Express Entry program is not accessible to many applicants experiencing processing delays in other immigration programs, including those seeking family reunification in Canada through sponsorship applications, leaving many persons in limbo. Only applicants

---

196 *Ibid*, s 31(b).

197 Backgrounder: *Express Entry*, above note 174. See also *Ministerial Instructions Express Entry*, above note 172, s 7, which allows the federal government to share the applicant's information with ESDC and the provinces to facilitate registration of applicants with the job bank or match an applicant to a provincial nominee program.

198 *Ministerial Instructions Express Entry*, *ibid*, s 2; see also s 7.

199 Backgrounder: *Express Entry*, above note 174; see *Ministerial Instructions Express Entry*, above note 172, s 32, where an invitation to make an application for permanent residence must be accepted by submitting an application for permanent residence within sixty days.

200 See, for example, CBC News, "Mexicans Trying to Immigrate 'Through the Back Door,' Says Kenney" (15 April 2009), online: www.cbc.ca/m/touch/canada/calgary/story/1.792456. Kenney stated, "That would indicate to me that the vast majority – something like 90 per cent of these claimants – are actually trying to immigrate to Canada through the back door of the refugee system and I think that's unacceptable. That's basically queue jumping."

in specified categories of the economic immigration program can obtain faster processing of their applications.

Finally, the program's creation through ministerial instructions means that there has been little debate or consultation on this program. The creation of the Express Entry program demonstrates that the federal government has no coherent vision in its immigration policy, preferring to prioritize or privilege certain kinds of applicants in a piecemeal fashion through *ad hoc* programs.

2) Business Immigrants

a) The Self-Employed Person Class[201]

The self-employed class attracts a small number of applicants. In 2013, only ninety-four principal applicants became permanent residents as members of this class.[202]

A self-employed person must have the "relevant experience" and the intention and ability to be self-employed in Canada.[203] Relevant experience for this class of persons is a minimum of two years of experience within the five years preceding the date the application was submitted.[204] Experience depends on the type of business activity and is more specifically set out in the *Regulations*.[205] Currently, the government is targeting those with relevant experience in cultural activities or athletics, or experience in farm management.[206] Those that would qualify as having experience in cultural activities or athletics include music teachers, painters, illustrators, film makers, freelance journalists, choreographers, theatrical or musical directors, set designers, coaches, and trainers.

i)   Selection Criteria for Self-Employed Persons

Foreign nationals applying for permanent residence status in Canada under the self-employed persons class are assessed on the basis of age, education, proficiency in the official languages of Canada, experience, and adaptability.[207] A modified points system governs how the selection

---

201 *Regulations*, above note 1, s 100(1). See also s 88(a), which states that a self-employed person selected by the province has the meaning provided by the laws of the province.

202 *Facts and Figures 2013*, above note 3.

203 *Regulations*, above note 1, s 88(1).

204 *Ibid.*

205 *Ibid.*

206 *Ibid.*

207 *Ibid*, s 102(1).

criteria are to be assessed.[208] As with the federal skilled worker class, where an officer deems a foreign national who has not obtained the required number of points but is likely to become economically established in Canada, the application may be approved if another officer concurs with that opinion.[209] Similarly, where an applicant has the requisite number of points, a negative decision may be made on the ground that a person is unlikely to become economically established where there is concurrence from a second officer.[210]

The following is a brief synopsis of the current points system for this class of applicants. It is best to consult the *Regulations* to determine in more detail what may be required of each selection criterion. Note that age, education, and language proficiency are measured in the same manner as for skilled workers, but experience and adaptability are not. The applicant must attain a minimum of thirty-five points.

Table 5.7   Summary of Points System for Applicants Who Are Self-Employed

Selection Criteria	Maximum Number of Points	How Points Are Allocated
Age[a]	10	• 21 to 50 years of age = 10 • 20 or 50 years of age = 8 • 19 or 51 years of age = 6 • 18 or 52 years of age = 4 • 17 or 53 years of age = 2 • <17 or 54 years of age or older = 0
Education[b]	25	For each credential: • Secondary school = 5 • One-year post-secondary (not university) and 12 years of full-time or equivalent studies = 12 • One-year post-secondary (not university) and 13 years of full-time or equivalent studies = 15 • One-year university at bachelor's level and total of 13 years of full-time or equivalent studies = 15 • Two-year post-secondary (not university) and 14 years of full-time or equivalent studies = 20 • Two-year university at bachelor's level and 14 years of full-time or equivalent studies = 20

208 *Ibid*, ss 108(2)–(4).
209 *Ibid*, s 109.
210 *Ibid*, s 76(3).

Selection Criteria	Maximum Number of Points	How Points Are Allocated
Education[b] (continued)	25	• Three-year post-secondary (not university) and 15 years of full-time or equivalent studies = 22 • Three-year university at bachelor's level and 15 years of full-time or equivalent studies = 22 • Master's or doctorate with total of at least 17 years of full-time or equivalent studies = 25 Note that an applicant can be awarded only one educational credential and therefore cannot be awarded cumulatively on the basis of more than one.[c]
Language[d]	24	First official language and for each of the four skill areas: • 4 points for a benchmark of 8 or higher • 2 points for a benchmark of 7 or higher • 1 point (with maximum of 2 points) with a benchmark of 4 or 5 Second official language and for each of the four skill areas • 2 points for a benchmark of 8 or higher • 2 points for a benchmark of 6 or 7 • 1 point (with maximum of 2 points) with a benchmark of 4 or 5
Experience for Self-Employed Persons[e]	35	• Two one-year periods of experience = 20 • Three one-year periods of experience = 25 • Four one-year periods of experience = 30 • Five one-year periods of experience = 35
Adaptability[f]	6	• 3–5 points for educational credentials of accompanying spouse or common-law partner • 5 points for any previous period of study in Canada by applicant or accompanying spouse or common-law partner • 5 points for being related to a person living in Canada

a *Ibid*, s 102.1.
b *Ibid*, s 102.2(2).
c *Ibid*, s 102.2(3).
d *Ibid*, ss 102.3(1)–(3).
e *Ibid*, s 103(3).
f *Ibid*, ss 104–5.

b) Changes to the Investor and Entrepreneur Programs

In June 2014, Citizenship and Immigration Canada announced that it had terminated two federal programs: the Immigrant Investor Program and the Entrepreneur Program.[211] New pilot programs will replace these programs. The following was offered as the rationale:

> The current [Immigrant Investor Program] provides limited economic benefit to Canada. Research shows that immigrant investors pay less in taxes than other economic immigrants, are less likely to stay in Canada over the medium- to long-term and often lack the skills, including official language proficiency, to integrate as well as other immigrants from the same countries.
>
> Eliminating the [Immigrant Investor Program] and the [Entrepreneur Program] — and the associated backlog of applications — will allow the government to focus on attracting experienced business people and raising investment capital that is of maximum benefit to Canada's economy.
>
> The government will replace these programs with more focused and effective pilot programs that will ensure that immigrants who come to Canada deliver meaningful benefits to our economy.[212]

c) Entrepreneur Start-up Visa

Citizenship and Immigration Canada has developed the new "Start-up Business Class" pilot program to attract "innovative entrepreneurs."[213] This program endeavours to link immigrant entrepreneurs with experienced private-sector organizations that are identified as experts in working with start-ups.[214] The stated objectives of this pilot program are to

- test the potential for increased economic benefit to Canada by linking foreign entrepreneurs with Canadian private-sector partners (venture capital funds, angel investor groups and business incu-

---

211 Minister of Citizenship and Immigration Canada, Updated Ministerial Instructions, above note 118; Government of Canada, News Release, "Building a Fast and Flexible Immigration System" (11 February 2014), online: http://news.gc.ca/web/article-en.do?nid=814939.

212 *Ibid.*

213 Citizenship and Immigration Canada, Operational Manual IP 13/OP 27: *Start-up Business Class*, online: CIC www.cic.gc.ca/english/resources/manuals/ip/ip13-eng.pdf, s 1 [OP 27].

214 Government of Canada, *Start-up Visa* (20 May 2014), online: www.cic.gc.ca/english/immigrate/business/start-up/index.asp?utm_source=slash-startup&utm_medium=short-url&utm_campaign=generic.

bators) that have experience and expertise dealing with start-up businesses;

- enable immigrant entrepreneurs to create jobs in Canada and build innovative companies that can compete on a global scale; and

- provide private-sector firms with access to a broader range of entrepreneurs, including the best and brightest minds from around the world.[215]

As with other economic immigration streams, foreign nationals can become members of the start-up business class if they show they have the ability to become economically established in Canada,[216] while meeting the other class requirements through written evidence or documentation that they[217]

a) have obtained a commitment[218] from one, two, or more designated angel investor groups[219] confirming that they are investing at least $75,000 in a qualifying business[220]; or have obtained a commitment from one, two, or more designated venture capital funds[221]

---

215 *Ibid.*
216 Minister of Citizenship and Immigration Canada, *Ministerial Instructions Respecting the Start-up Business Class* (15 March 2013), online: http://gazette.gc.ca/rp-pr/p1/2013/2013-03-30/html/notice-avis-eng.html, s 2(1). See also s 12, where an officer has the discretion, with the concurrence of another officer, as with other economic classes, to substitute his evaluation of the applicant's ability to become economically established if the stated requirements in the ministerial instructions are not a sufficient indicator whether the applicant will become economically established in Canada.
217 *Ibid,* ss 8 and 10.
218 *Ibid,* s 6: Section 6 of the ministerial instructions specifies what form the commitment must take and what information must be included. Section 11 provides that an officer may ask that a commitment be independently assessed by a peer review panel.
219 *Ibid,* s 4(a): Schedule 1 lists entities that are designated as angel investor groups.
220 *Ibid,* s 7: Section 7 of the ministerial instructions defines *qualifying business* as

> a corporation that is incorporated in and carrying on business in Canada, if at the time the commitment is made, (a) the applicant holds 10% or more of the voting rights attached to all shares of the corporation outstanding at the time; and (b) no persons or entities, other than qualified participants, hold 50% or more of the total amount of the voting rights attached to all shares of the corporation outstanding at that time.

> Further, "[a] business that is not incorporated at the time the commitment is made is still considered to be a qualifying business if its incorporation is conditional on the issuance of a permanent resident visa to one or more of the applicants in respect of that business."

221 *Ibid,* s 4(b): Schedule 2 lists entities that are designated as venture capital funds.

confirming that they are investing a total of at least $200,000 in a qualifying business;[222]

b) have attained language proficiency of at least benchmark level 5 in either official language for the four language skill areas;[223]

c) have completed at least one year of post-secondary education;[224]

d) have settlement funds in the amount equal to one half of the low income cut-offs; and[225]

e) have paid the requisite application fees.[226]

No more than five foreign nationals can form a group and be considered members of the start-up business class in respect of the same business.[227] If there is more than one applicant in respect of the same business, and one applicant is refused a permanent resident visa for any reason, the other applicants are considered not to have met the requirements and their applications are also refused.[228]

Citizenship and Immigration Canada is currently accepting no more than 2,750 applications per year.[229] Applicants would be wise to include as much information as possible either in the application or directly in the commitment letter. Information that should be provided includes bio-data of any persons related to the business, business information such as the nature of business operations, the structure of the business, the applicant's role in the business, terms and conditions applicable to the investment or commitment, and names of persons who

---

222 *Ibid*, s 2(2)(a).

223 *Ibid*, s 2(2)(b): The evaluation must be conducted by an organization or institution designated by the minister for the purpose of evaluating language proficiency under s 74(3) of the *Regulations* and set against the benchmarks in the *Canadian Language Benchmarks*.

224 *Ibid*, s 2(2)(c): The applicant must have been in good standing at the educational institution, and the completion of one year does not need to have resulted in obtaining an educational credential.

225 *Ibid*, s 2(2)(d): The funds must be unencumbered by debts or other obligations, and the low income cut-offs are identified by looking at the most recent information published by Statistics Canada for urban areas of residence of 500,000 persons or more as the minimum amount of before-tax annual income necessary to support a group of persons equal in number to the total number of the applicant and his family members.

226 *Ibid*, s 13: The principal applicant's fee is $1,050; the fee for a family member who is twenty-two years or older or is less than twenty-two years of age and is a spouse or common law partner is $550; the fee for a family member who is less than twenty-two years of age and is not a spouse or common law partner is $150.

227 *Ibid*, s 2(4).

228 *Ibid*, s 9(2).

229 Minister of Citizenship and Immigration Canada, *Ministerial Instructions Respecting the Start-up Business Class*, above note 216.

have functions or interests in the business.[230] Documents to submit include those related to business plans; corporate documents; customers and suppliers; material contracts; intellectual property; financial information; corporate financing; employees and benefit plans; management team, and others.[231]

Membership in the start-up business class is based on a pass/fail system where applicants must meet the minimum qualifying requirements for all criteria for the application to be approved.[232] As with other economic classes, meeting the criteria is not enough; applicants must also not be inadmissible.[233]

d) Provincial Nominee Business Programs

In addition to the skilled worker programs that have been developed by provinces, some business programs have also been made available provincially. For example, in British Columbia, five categories have been established: the Entrepreneur Category, the Regional Entrepreneur Category, the Strategic Projects Category, the Regional Business Succession Option, and the Farming Business Option.[234] Details of the various programs established by different provinces are available online.[235]

e) Immigrant Investor Venture Capital Fund and Business Skills Programs

At time of writing, these pilot programs were not yet operational. It is anticipated that they will replace the Immigrant Investor Program in 2015.[236]

---

230 OP 27, above note 213, s 9.1.
231 *Ibid*, s 11.6.
232 *Ibid*, s 10.1.
233 *Ibid*, s 12. See Chapter 14 for more information about inadmissibility.
234 See British Columbia, *Business Immigration*, online: www.welcomebc.ca/ Immigrate/About-the-BC-PNP/Investing-in-B-C.aspx. On its website the BC government describes access to these programs as follows:

> If you are an entrepreneur ready to invest in and actively manage a business in the province, you may be eligible for the BC Provincial Nominee Program's (PNP) Business Immigration stream. This stream accelerates the permanent residence application process for individuals who can establish themselves in B.C. and develop a business that will provide significant economic benefits to the province. To qualify, you must meet specific personal net worth thresholds, make a minimum investment in an eligible business, be actively involved in the daily management of the business, and create one or more new jobs for Canadian citizens or permanent residents. Please note that meeting the minimum eligibility requirements does not guarantee approval.

235 For more information, see Appendix.
236 Canada's Economic Action Plan, *Immigrant Investor Program*, online: http://actionplan.gc.ca/en/initiative/immigrant-investor-program. See also Ben

3) Caregivers

In October 2014, the government announced radical changes to what was formerly known as the live-in caregiver program,[237] now to be known as the "Caregiver Program."

The live-in caregiver program was created to respond to a labour market shortage of live-in caregivers in Canada, specifically, in the areas of in-home childcare, senior home support care, and care of people with disabilities.[238] The program allowed caregivers to come to Canada on a temporary work permit and permitted an application for permanent residence from within Canada after having been employed full time as a live-in caregiver for at least twenty-four months or a total of 3,900 hours in a minimum of twenty-two months within the four years following entry to Canada.[239]

Similar to the Canadian experience class, this program aimed to reward those who spent time working as live-in caregivers, contributing to society and the economy with permanent residence status. By having spent two years in Canada, it was intended that those applicants would become economically established into Canadian society, with the transition from temporary to permanent status being made after the applicants got a chance to experience life in Canada.

As noted in Chapter 4, significant unintended consequences plagued the live-in caregiver program. Reports of widespread exploitation prompted the government to develop rigorous guidelines to be followed by employers and to provide various options to workers who had been subject to abuse. There also developed a large backlog of applications for permanent residence by caregivers who had fulfilled the work experience for permanent residence, which, in turn, produced lengthy waiting periods. Since caregivers could not, in most circumstances, bring their families with them while working on a permit, the program

---

Dummett & Alistair MacDonald, "Canada Set to Announce New Immigrant Investor Plan" *The Wall Street Journal* (27 November 2014), online: http://online.wsj.com/articles/canada-set-to-announce-new-immigrant-investor-plan-1417110338: "Ottawa will create [a] new immigrant class for individuals who could place C$1 million to C$2 million in a [venture capital] fund that would in turn invest in startups, according to a person familiar with the matter."

237 Government of Canada, News Release, "Backgrounder, Improving Canada's Caregiver Program" (31 October 2014), online: http://news.gc.ca/web/article-en.do?nid=898719.

238 Citizenship and Immigration Canada, Operational Manual OP 14: *Processing Applicants for the Live-in Caregiver Program*, online: www.cic.gc.ca/english/resources/manuals/op/op14-eng.pdf, s 2 [OP 14]. See Chapter 4.

239 *Regulations*, above note 1, s 113; OP 14, above note 238.

contributed to lengthy separations between the caregivers and their own families.

The most significant change introduced in 2014 is the abandonment of the requirement that a caregiver must live in the home of the person for whom she is caring, hence the change in name of the program. Individuals may still work temporarily in Canada and then apply for permanent status, but the program has been opened up to individuals who live outside a private residence. In addition, the proposed changes provide two distinct routes to permanent resident status. One route focuses on child-care providers, while another provides opportunities for those giving care to people with "high medical needs." In ministerial instructions published in November 2014, the minister established the criteria for participation in each stream and has imposed a quota on each.[240] An applicant is eligible for the caring for children class if, at the date of her application for permanent residence,

- she is a foreign national who intends to reside in a province other than Quebec;
- she has acquired two years of full-time work experience in Canada within the previous four years as a homecare provider as set out in unit group 4411 of the NOC;
- she has met the employment requirements listed in the NOC;
- she has achieved a level of language proficiency of benchmark 5 in an official language for each of the four language skill areas; and
- she has obtained either a Canadian credential of one year of post-secondary studies or a foreign diploma along with an equivalency assessment.[241]

An applicant in the caring for people with high medical needs class must meet the same education and language criteria. In addition, she must have two years of full-time work experience in Canada within the previous four years as one of the following:

- a registered nurse or registered psychiatric nurse (unit group 3012 of the NOC);
- a licensed practical nurse (unit group 3233 of the NOC);
- a nurse aide (unit group 3413 of the NOC); and

---

240 See Minister of Citizenship and Immigration Canada, *Ministerial Instructions Establishing the Caring for Children Class* and *Ministerial Instructions Establishing the Caring for People with High Medical Needs Class* (24 November 2014), online: http://gazette.gc.ca/rp-pr/p1/2014/2014-11-29/html/notice-avis-eng.php.
241 *Ibid.*

- a home-support worker or someone in a related occupation but not a housekeeper (unit group 4412 of the NOC).[242]

The government has undertaken to accept 2,750 applicants and family members each year under each of these streams. It has also undertaken to process applications within a six-month period.[243]

C. CONCLUSION: CANADA'S ECONOMIC IMMIGRATION SCHEME AS AN UNINSPIRING APPROACH TO BUILDING A NATION

This chapter has examined the pathways to permanent residence in Canada that have been developed to attract those who will likely contribute to the Canadian economy. It should not be assumed that our economic immigration programs are benign or that they produce the intended results. Many practitioners and authors have identified significant problems associated with these programs.

For some, the government's approach to crafting the economic immigration streams leaves little room for public debate, evaluation, and planning and is an approach that favours temporary entrants, provincial nominees, and the Canadian experience Class.[244] This is manifested by the fact that many changes have been introduced by changing the *Regulations* or providing ministerial instructions. From 2008 to the present,

---

242 *Ibid.*

243 See Susana Mas, "Express Entry System Floated as Government's Fix to Live-in Caregiver Woes" *CBC News* (9 October 2014), online: www.cbc.ca/news/politics/express-entry-system-floated-as-government-s-fix-to-live-in-caregiver-woes-1.2782850. For information about Express Entry, see Section B(1)(f), above in this chapter. The article states, "Live-in caregiver groups are concerned the move will make it harder for new caregivers to come to Canada while making it more difficult for those already here to obtain permanent residency. They are also concerned the move to express entry would fail to address a large backlog of caregivers still waiting to come to Canada or awaiting residency."

244 Naomi Alboim, *Adjusting the Balance: Fixing Canada's Economic Immigration Policies* (Toronto: Maytree Foundation, 2009) at 45; Mario Bellissimo, "Law-Making Innovation in the Canadian and International Immigration Context: International Comparisons and Cautions for Canadians" (2013) 16 Imm LR (4th) 151; Mario Bellissimo & Sindura Dar, "The Federal Skilled Worker Program: Reset, Reshaped and Reintroduced Law Making & Litigation Implications" (2014) 20 Imm LR (4th) 175.

several sets of ministerial instructions have been issued.[245] Publishing sweeping changes to programs via this mechanism leaves no room for public debate or input. As one author writes, the tactics used to change our immigration policy have "enormous personal and societal implications at play" and avoid "scrutiny of our democratic functions," destabilizing the rule of law and fundamental values and principles associated with proper procedure.[246]

Second, those examining these policy shifts argue that the government's focus on short-term, two-step immigration and the devolution of the federal government's role in economic immigration are both problematic.[247] Focusing on short-term economic immigration means that no investment is made in the infrastructure through economic immigration recruitment.[248] In addition, a "two-step process reduces Canada's competitive edge for attracting immigrants and delays services and supports that improve their prospects for successful integration to Canadian life."[249]

Third, in giving the provinces a greater role in economic immigration selection, the federal government is playing less of a role in selecting future citizens and maintaining a narrow focus that our immigration policy is simply recruiting workers, not people who can help build the nation.[250] As well, allowing temporary foreign workers to fill in our labour gaps has led to increased exploitation, abuse, and concern about working conditions for such workers.[251]

Fourth, it has been noted that the effectiveness of the government's efforts to recruit the highly skilled has been diminished by the fact that Canadian employers discount foreign-earned skills or experience and engage in discrimination and that credential recognition practices are expensive and onerous.[252] They argue that such persons come to

---

245 Minister of Citizenship and Immigration Canada, Ministerial Instructions (1 May 2014), online: CIC www.cic.gc.ca/english/department/mi.

246 Bellissimo, above note 244 at 9.

247 Alboim, above note 244 at 45.

248 *Ibid.* Chapter 4 discusses temporary foreign workers in more detail.

249 Alboim, above note 244 at 49.

250 *Ibid* at 50.

251 Sarah Marsden, "Assessing the Regulation of Temporary Foreign Workers in Canada" (2011) 49 *Osgoode Hall Law Journal* 39 at 40; Judy Fudge & Fiona MacPhail, "Canada: The Temporary Foreign Worker Program in Canada: Low-Skilled Workers as an Extreme Form of Flexible Labour" (2009) 31 *Comparative Labour Law & Policy Journal* 5 at 43–44.

252 Kara Somerville & Scott Walsworth, "Vulnerabilities of Highly Skilled Immigrants in Canada and the United States" (2009) 39 *American Review of Canadian Studies* 147 at 148; see also Bryan Schwartz & Mark Melchers, "Improving For-

Canada with high expectations only to find themselves employed in low-skilled, low-paying jobs, given little support to work in the fields for which they are selected and aspire to work.[253] Although Canada is engaging in more economic immigration programs that require an employer to "sponsor" an applicant, some argue this approach should be used more often.[254] Further, some also argue that the government should take a more active role in developing foreign credential recognition processes to assist in economic integration into Canada's labour force.[255]

Finally, Canada's immigration policy lacks economic and social coherence across the categories. For example, the family class should be characterized as more than a "non-economic category."[256] The discourse and view that only economic stream immigrants are contributing members to our society is not only false, but reveals that perhaps we can be harnessing other immigration categories to better meet our labour or market needs.

Thus far, Canada's economic immigration policy presents itself to be purely functional. It does not inspire nation building or reflect a visionary approach to immigration policy, where economic concerns are integrated into the general fabric of our wider immigration scheme.

---

eign Credential Recognition through Reform in Immigration Law and Policy" in Bryan Schwartz, ed, *Admitted but Excluded – Enhancing Access to Regulated Occupations for Newcomers to Canada*, FCPP Policy Series No 138 (Winnipeg: Frontier Centre for Public Policy, 2012) 127 at 128; Canada, Parliamentary Information and Research Service, Social Affairs Division, *Recognition of the Foreign Qualifications of Immigrants* by Sandra Elgersma, Library of Parliament Background Paper No 2004-29-E (Ottawa: Library of Parliament, 2012).

253 Somerville & Walsworth, above note 252.
254 *Ibid.*
255 Schwartz & Melchers, above note 252; Elgersma, above note 252.
256 Bellissimo, above note 244 at 11.

CHAPTER 6

ACQUIRING PERMANENT RESIDENT STATUS: THE FAMILY CLASS AND SPONSORSHIP

A. INTRODUCTION

A primary objective of immigration law, identified in the *Immigration and Refugee Protection Act*, section 3(1)(d), is "to see that families are reunited in Canada."[1] To achieve this objective, Canadian law permits Canadian citizens and permanent residents to sponsor applications for permanent residence by close relatives who meet the criteria for membership of the family class. An essential aspect of this program is that the sponsor must sign an undertaking to reimburse the federal or provincial government within a specified time "for every benefit provided as social assistance to or on behalf of the sponsored foreign national and their family members."[2]

Section 12 of the *IRPA* provides the underlying principle. It states:

> A foreign national may be selected as a member of the family class on the basis of their relationship as the spouse, common-law partner, child, parent or other prescribed family member of a Canadian citizen or permanent resident.[3]

---

1   SC 2001, c 27 [*IRPA*].
2   *Immigration and Refugee Protection Regulations*, SOR/2002-227, s 132(1) [*Regulations*].
3   *IRPA*, above note 1, s 12(1).

Apart from showing that they are in one of the specified relationships with their sponsor, family class immigrants are not required
to meet any other selection criteria, such as those imposed on immigrants in the economic classes. They are, however, subject to criteria
of inadmissibility[4] and, as discussed below, in some circumstances the
status they receive may be conditional. In addition, their sponsor must
meet a number of onerous eligibility conditions. This chapter examines
each of the components of the family class program. First, it outlines
the criteria used to determine membership in the family class, including the standards devised to adjudge whether a relationship is genuine.
Next, it focuses on the rules defining eligibility to sponsor and the nature of the undertaking that a sponsor must make. Finally, it outlines
the appeal rights of a sponsor whose application has been rejected and
introduces the process of applying for judicial review.

B. MEMBERS OF THE FAMILY CLASS VERSUS FAMILY MEMBERS

As a preliminary matter, it is important to recognize that the program
that permits sponsorship of family class members is only one of the
ways in which our laws pay heed to the importance of familial relations.
Most important, this program should be distinguished from the program that allows individuals who are applying to immigrate to Canada
to seek admission simultaneously on behalf of their spouses, common
law partners, and dependent children. Section 1(3) of the *Regulations*
tries to draw this distinction, but does so in a somewhat hamfisted
way by referring to the latter group as *family members*.[5] The attempt is
clumsy because the *IRPA* also uses the term *family member* less technically in a number of sections, including section 12, quoted above. By
adopting this confusing terminology, the *Regulations* become unwieldy
and prolix.[6]

---

4   It should be noted that under the *IRPA*, s 38, and the *Regulations*, s 24, the crite-
    ria of inadmissibility are reduced for intimate partners and dependent children.
5   *Regulations*, above note 2.
6   *Ibid*, s 1(2): Section 1(3) of the *Regulations* provides the following definition for
    family member:

    For the purposes of the Act, other than section 12 and paragraph 38(2)(*d*),
    and for the purposes of these Regulations, other than sections 159.1 and
    159.5, "family member" in respect of a person means:
        (*a*) the spouse or common-law partner of the person;

The law defining membership in the family class (those who may be sponsored) overlaps with the law defining family members (those who may be included as dependants in an application for a permanent resident visa) in three distinct ways. First, some relationships that fit under both categories (spouse, common law partner, and dependent child) are defined or analyzed identicially in both contexts.[7] It should, however, be noted that the family class includes many more relationships than does the law defining *family member*.[8] Second, a person who is sponsored as a member of the family class may include family members in an application.[9] A sponsor's spouse, for example, may include dependent children in the application for permanent resident status. This opportunity can lead to an apparent anomaly. Although, in most circumstances, a person cannot sponsor a sibling as a member of the family class, a person can sponsor a parent who is able to attach a dependent child (the sponsor's sibling) to the application. Third, and discussed in greater detail below, a person applying to immigrate to Canada as a permanent resident must identify all family members who are not accompanying her.[10] Should the applicant fail to do so, any individual who should have been so identified is ineligible to be sponsored as a member of the family class by the applicant at a later time, after the applicant has been granted status.[11]

The distinction between membership in the family class and family members is partially reflected in how the government reports immigration statistics. In its preliminary tables, *Facts and Figures 2013: Immigration Overview: Permanent Residents*,[12] Citizenship and Immigration Canada (CIC) reports that, in 2013, the Canadian government accepted 148,181 individuals as economic immigrants; however, a subgroup of these newcomers includes a large number of individuals (79,684 in total) who are identified as spouses and dependants of "principal

---

    (b) a dependent child of the person or of the person's spouse or common-law partner; and

    (c) a dependent child of a dependent child referred to in paragraph (b).

7   *Ibid*, ss 116–22: Sections 116 to 122 of the *Regulations* refer to "family class"; s 70 refers to "family member" in the context of permanent resident visa applications.

8   *Ibid*, s 117(1): Section 117(1) of the *Regulations* lists these relationships. See Section C, below in this chapter, for the list.

9   *Ibid*, ss 121–22.

10 *Ibid*, s 10(2).

11 *Ibid*, s 117(9)(d).

12 Citizenship and Immigration Canada, *Facts and Figures 2013: Immigration Overview: Permanent Residents, Canada – Permanent Residents By Category*, online: www.cic.gc.ca/english/resources/statistics/facts2013/permanent/02.asp.

applicants."[13] The table labeled as "Permanent Residents by Category" shows that the government of Canada selected 60,778 individuals as members of the family class—39,165 of these were spouses and partners, and 2,727 were sons and daughters.[14] These family class members have been sponsored by individuals who already have citizenship or permanent resident status in Canada. The government has seen no need to separately identify dependants of a sponsored member of the family class.

Although the commitment to family reunification is frequently cited as the single goal underlying the laws permitting sponsorship of members of the family class, a cursory examination of the criteria reveals that such an explanation of the program's goals is insufficient. The idea of reunification implies that a family has been previously split apart. Yet not only people who have been separated from their family may apply to sponsor relatives. A large percentage of sponsorships concern newly formed relationships rather than pre-existing ones. Most obviously, the *IRPA* recognizes that a citizen or permanent resident is entitled to form an intimate relationship with a non-Canadian and has the additional right to live in Canada with the partner. Reference to "reunification" in such cases is misleading.

Moreover, the commitment to reunification is clearly tempered and qualified by other values. For example, only a person who has reached the age of eighteen may sponsor a person as a member of the family class. Our immigration laws bar children below that age from sponsoring their parents and thus operate as a barrier to family reunification in cases where the Canadian citizen or permanent resident is a minor.

To obtain a full appreciation of the range of values and concerns that inform family class immigration, one must look beyond the generalities found in the *IRPA*, section 3, and examine the legal details.

---

13   *Ibid.* The importance of family ties is also recognized in less prominent provisions of Canadian immigration law. For example, refugee claimants who arrive in Canada at a land border with the United States are not eligible to make a claim before the Immigration and Refugee Board unless they have a family member in Canada. See the *Regulations*, above note 2, s 159.5. Interestingly, the *Regulations* give an extended definition of *family member* that qualifies this section: see s 159.1. These regulations are discussed in greater detail in Chapter 9.

14   Citizenship and Immigration, *Facts and Figures 2013, Immigration Overview: Permanent Residents, Canada – Permanent Residents by Category (Principal Applicants)*, online: www.cic.gc.ca/english/resources/statistics/facts2013/permanent/03. asp.

C. MEMBERS OF THE FAMILY CLASS: WHO GETS IN?

The full list of the relationships with a Canadian citizen or permanent resident that qualify a person as a member of the family class is found in the *Regulations*, section 117. The section reads as follows:

117. (1) A foreign national is a member of the family class if, with respect to a sponsor, the foreign national is

(*a*) the sponsor's spouse, common-law partner or conjugal partner;

(*b*) a dependent child of the sponsor;

(*c*) the sponsor's mother or father;

(*d*) the mother or father of the sponsor's mother or father;

(*e*) [Repealed]

(*f*) a person whose parents are deceased, who is under 18 years of age, who is not a spouse or common-law partner and who is

(i)   a child of the sponsor's mother or father,

(ii) a child of a child of the sponsor's mother or father, or

(iii) a child of the sponsor's child;

(*g*) a person under 18 years of age whom the sponsor intends to adopt in Canada if

(i)   the adoption is not being entered into primarily for the purpose of acquiring any status or privilege under the Act,

(ii) where the adoption is an international adoption and the country in which the person resides and their province of intended destination are parties to the *Hague Convention on Adoption*, the competent authority of the country and of the province have approved the adoption in writing as conforming to that Convention, and

(iii) where the adoption is an international adoption and either the country in which the person resides or the person's province of intended destination is not a party to the *Hague Convention on Adoption*

(A) the person has been placed for adoption in the country in which they reside or is otherwise legally available in that country for adoption and there is no evidence that the intended adoption is for the purpose of child trafficking or undue gain within the meaning of the *Hague Convention on Adoption*, and

(B) the competent authority of the person's province of intended destination has stated in writing that it does not object to the adoption; or

(h) a relative of the sponsor, regardless of age, if the sponsor does not have a spouse, a common-law partner, a conjugal partner, a child, a mother or father, a relative who is a child of that mother or father, a relative who is a child of a child of that mother or father, a mother or father of that mother or father or a relative who is a child of the mother or father of that mother or father

   (i)   who is a Canadian citizen, Indian or permanent resident, or

   (ii) whose application to enter and remain in Canada as a permanent resident the sponsor may otherwise sponsor.[15]

The determination that an applicant and a sponsor are in the required relationship can be complex and may hinge on definitions found elsewhere in the *Regulations*, principles of family law, and principles of private international law. Adding to the complexity is the fact that some individuals who fit within one of the listed relationships may be determined not to be members of the family class for a variety of countervailing reasons, including the suspicion that their relationship is not genuine or is simply a means to obtain a benefit under the *IRPA*.[16] In addition, the law may exclude an applicant from the family class because his sponsor has already made an undertaking incompatible with a later undertaking on behalf of the applicant,[17] or because the sponsor has failed to identify the individual as a family member when previously required to do so.[18] The following sections examine these issues and focus on each of the prescribed relationships in turn.

1) The Sponsor's Spouse, Common Law Partner, or Conjugal Partner

The *Regulations* recognize three distinct categories of intimate partner: spouse, common law partner, and conjugal partner.

a) Spouse

Neither the *IRPA* nor the *Regulations* defines the spousal relationship.[19] However, one can infer from various sections that the term *spouse* is

---

15 *Regulations*, above note 2.

16 *Ibid*, s 4(1).

17 *Ibid*, s 117(9)(b).

18 *Ibid*, s 10(1)(e).

19 Regulations made under the *Immigration Regulations, 1978*, SOR/78-172, which were in force immediately prior to the enactment of the *IRPA*, had provided that "spouse, with respect to any person, means the party of the opposite sex to whom the person is joined in marriage" (s 2(1)). Although this definition has been deleted from the current *Regulations*, a substitute has not been included;

used narrowly to refer to individuals who are married to each other.[20] A gloss on the term *marriage* can be found in the *Regulations*, section 2:

> "marriage", in respect of a marriage that took place outside Canada, means a marriage that is valid both under the laws of the jurisdiction where it took place and under Canadian law.[21]

It is uncontested that this conception of marriage should be used to determine whether a person is a member of the family class by reason of being a sponsor's spouse. Thus, in *Igbinigie v Canada (Minister of Citizenship and Immigration)*, a sponsorship appeal, the Immigration Appeal Division (IAD) of the Immigration and Refugee Board (IRB) held that the parties must show that they are married and that the marriage meets the definitional requirements found in the *Regulations*:

> The first matter to be addressed in this case is whether the appellant and applicant are legally married, i.e., whether the applicant is a spouse who may be sponsored for permanent residence in Canada . . . . The definition of marriage is met when the marriage is legally valid, which is established by demonstrating that both formal and essential requirements of marriage have been respected. The definition of marriage anticipates that there may be differences between Canadian and other jurisdictions as to what constitutes a legally valid marriage. It must be established that the marriage is valid in the jurisdiction in which it took place. Furthermore, notwithstanding that a marriage may be considered legally valid in the foreign jurisdiction, it will only be considered legally valid for the purposes of the *Act* if it meets Canadian requirements for recognition of the marriage as well.[22]

Where a marriage has taken place in Canada, there will usually be little difficulty in assessing that the individuals in question are spouses. Section 91(26) of the *Constitution Act, 1867* gives authority over marriage

---

however, as explained below, it is clear that the law no longer understands the spousal relationship as one that excludes same-sex couples.

20 This is confirmed by the operational manual. It offers a definition of a spouse as "a married person": Citizenship and Immigration Canada, Operational Manual OP 2: *Processing Members of the Family Class*, online: www.cic.gc.ca/english/resources/manuals/op/op02-eng.pdf, s 6 [OP 2].

21 *Regulations*, above note 2.

22 [2009] IADD No 2800. See also *Rahman v Canada (Minister of Citizenship and Immigration)*, 2006 FC 1321 at para 17: "Pursuant to sections 2 and 4 of the *IRPR* [*Regulations*] a foreign national spouse who wants to immigrate to Canada as a member of the family class must satisfy the officer that his or her marriage: is genuine; was not entered into primarily for the purpose of acquiring a privilege under the Act; and is legally valid in both Canada and where it took place."

and divorce to the Parliament of Canada.[23] Under section 92(12), provincial legislatures have authority over "the solemnization of marriage in the province."[24] Parliament has exercised its constitutional powers by enacting legislation that specifies the factors that determine the *essential* validity of a marriage, that is, the factors that determine whether the individuals have the capacity to marry. For example, the *Marriage (Prohibited Degrees) Act*[25] identifies relationships of consanguinity and kinship that bar the possibility of marriage. In addition, the *Civil Marriage Act* has expanded the pool of individuals who may marry by including the following provisions:

2.   Marriage, for civil purposes, is the lawful union of two persons to the exclusion of all others . . . .

4.   For greater certainty, a marriage is not void or voidable by reason only that the spouses are of the same sex.[26]

Provincial laws determine the *formal* criteria of validity, which cover the processes of solemnization. However, each province has also enacted measures that determine the minimum age at which one may marry with and without the consent of a parent or a recognized authority.[27]

Individuals who have married outside Canada may have more difficulty persuading Canadian immigration officers that they are spouses and that accordingly, one of them is a member of the family class. Immigration officers may have reason to look behind the record of the putative marriage to determine whether the legal requirements in the relevant jurisdiction have been met. Establishing this will entail some familiarity with, or access to expert opinion about, the requirements of the foreign law. In some jurisdictions, it may also require an inquiry into the existence of customary practices. For example, in India, custom can override statutory requirements. The *Hindu Marriage Act, 1955* lists prohibited degrees of relations that prevent marriage, but it also permits marriages where "custom or usage governing each of [the parties] permits a marriage."[28] The Act further specifies what *custom* and *usage* mean:

---

23   (UK), 30 & 31 Vict, c 3, reprinted in RSC 1985, App II, No 5.
24   *Ibid.*
25   SC 1990, c 46.
26   *Civil Marriage Act*, SC 2005, c 33.
27   In British Columbia, an individual under the age of sixteen may marry with the consent of the British Columbia Supreme Court.
28   Act 25 of 1955, s 5(iv) (India).

[T]he expression "custom" and "usage" signify any rule which, having been continuously and uniformly observed for a long time, has obtained the force of law among Hindus in any local area, tribe, community, group or family.[29]

In various cases, applicants have argued that a regional custom permits marriage that would otherwise be prohibited.[30] In these cases, the onus has been placed on the applicant to introduce evidence and prove the existence of custom.[31]

Foreign law determinations are questions of fact that must be proved to the satisfaction of the court. In *Magtibay v Canada (Minister of Citizenship and Immigration)*, the Federal Court held that "it was well settled that this Court will only interfere with a finding of fact, including a finding of fact with regard to expert evidence, if there has been a palpable and overriding error."[32]

The additional requirement in the *Regulations* that a marriage be valid under Canadian law permits the assessment that a marriage, although valid in the country where it took place, is nevertheless insufficient for immigration purposes.[33] Where the Canadian criteria of essential validity have not been met, the marriage will not be recognized. It is unclear whether a marriage that fails to meet the formal criteria recognized in Canadian provinces will be found to be invalid under Canadian law. Little would be gained by adopting such an interpretation.[34]

The requirement that a foreign marriage must be valid according to Canadian criteria is supplemented by more specific provisions that specify when a spousal relationship will be insufficient to render a person a member of the family class, even though that person has a valid marriage in the country of origin. Section 5 of the *Regulations* provides:

29　*Ibid*, s 3(a).

30　See, for example, *Sahota v Canada (Citizenship and Immigration)*, 2008 CanLII 45193 (CA IRB).

31　*Canada (Minister of Employment and Immigration) v Taggar*, [1989] 3 FC 576 at para 3: Pratte J stated that "a person who relies on custom must prove it by clear and unambiguous evidence since custom is a departure from ordinary law."

32　2005 FC 397 at para 15; see also *Canada (Minister of Citizenship and Immigration) v Saini*, 2001 FCA 311.

33　*Constitution Act, 1867*, above note 23.

34　See Immigration and Refugee Board of Canada, "Chapter 5: Spouses, Common-Law Partners and Conjugal Partners," *Sponsorship Appeals* (1 January 2008), online: www.irb-cisr.gc.ca/Eng/BoaCom/references/LegJur/Documents/SpoPar05_e.pdf.

For the purposes of these Regulations, a foreign national shall not be considered

(a) the spouse . . . of a person if the foreign national is under the age of 16 years; or

(b) the spouse of a person if

(i) the foreign national or the person was, at the time of their marriage, the spouse of another person, or

(ii) the person has lived separate and apart from the foreign national for at least one year and is the common-law partner of another person.[35]

Section 117(9) of the *Regulations* confirms and adds to these provisions:

(9) A foreign national shall not be considered a member of the family class by virtue of their relationship to a sponsor if

. . .

(c) the foreign national is the sponsor's spouse and

(i) the sponsor or the foreign national was, at the time of their marriage, the spouse of another person, or

(ii) the sponsor has lived separate and apart from the foreign national for at least one year and

(A) the sponsor is the common-law partner of another person or the sponsor has a conjugal partner, or

(B) the foreign national is the common-law partner of another person or the conjugal partner of another sponsor.[36]

These provisions indicate that polygamous marriages will not be recognized as valid. However, the operational manual allows for the possibility that a polygamist's first marriage may be recognized. It states:

R117(9)(c)(i) . . . prohibits a second (or third, etc.) wife from being recognized as a spouse within the family class and provides that only the first marriage may potentially be recognized for immigration purposes.[37]

In order for the first marriage to be recognized as legally valid under Canadian law, the couple must live together in a monogamous

---

35 *Regulations*, above note 2.

36 *Ibid.* These sections seem to offer inconsistent messages: Section 5 identifies that the individual in question shall not be considered a spouse, whereas s 117(9) appears to state that the individual is the spouse, but not a member of the family class.

37 OP 2, above note 20.

marriage in Canada. Common law imparts that a polygamous marriage can be converted into a monogamous marriage provided that the couple live together in a monogamous relationship from the time of arrival in Canada. This conversion is effected by the stated intention of the parties to so convert their marriage, followed by some factual evidence that they have complied — usually by divorcing the other spouses and/or by a remarriage in a form valid in Canada.[38]

Additional complexities can arise when one of the spouses has been divorced previously and has remarried. Where the divorce is not recognized in the jurisdiction where the later marriage takes place, the second marriage will be invalid according to that jurisdiction's law or Canadian law by falling foul of the prohibition against being married to more than one person. For example, in *Uriol v Canada (Minister of Citizenship and Immigration)*,[39] the court determined that since Peruvian law does not recognize foreign divorces, but requires a married person to obtain a Peruvian divorce before remarrying in Peru, an individual who had obtained a foreign divorce was ineligible to marry a second time. The later marriage was found to be invalid and the "spouse" was determined not to be a member of the family class.[40]

Where Canadian law does not recognize a foreign divorce, a later marriage, although valid in the country where it took place, may be insufficient to meet the immigration requirements. Two provisions in the Canadian *Divorce Act* deal with the recognition of foreign divorces.[41] Section 22(1) provides:

> A divorce granted, on or after the coming into force of this Act, pursuant to a law of a country or subdivision of a country other than Canada by a tribunal or other authority having jurisdiction to do so shall be recognized for all purposes of determining the marital status in Canada of any person, if either former spouse was ordinarily resident in that country or subdivision for at least one year immediately preceding the commencement of proceedings for the divorce.[42]

---

38 *Regulations*, above note 2, s 13.2. See Bill S-7, *Zero Tolerance for Barbaric Cultural Practices Act*, 2nd Sess, 41st Parl, 2014 (Second Reading and Referral to Committee in the House of Commons 23 March 2015). This contentiously titled bill, introduced in the Senate in November 2014, will, if enacted, amend the IRPA to specify that a permanent resident or foreign national is inadmissible on grounds of practising polygamy in Canada.

39 [2009] IADD No 210.

40 *Ibid* at paras 6–7.

41 RSC 1985, c 3 (2nd Supp).

42 *Ibid*.

Section 22(3) qualifies the requirements that the divorce be grant-ed "by a tribunal or other authority" and that one of the spouses be ordinarily resident in the country granting the divorce.[43] Section 22(3) provides for the continuation of common law rules governing the recog-nition of foreign divorces: "Nothing in this section abrogates or dero-gates from any other rule of law respecting the recognition of divorces granted otherwise than under this Act."[44]

These provisions have received close scrutiny in a number of spon-sorship cases. Some cases deal with a party whose marriage has been dissolved by religious rather than legal authorities. A leading case is *Amin v Canada (Minister of Citizenship and Immigration)*, which focuses on the validity of a religious *talaq* divorce.[45] In this case, Barnes J ana-lyzes the issue as follows:

> As far as I can tell from the record before me and from relevant legal authorities, the pronouncement of *talaq* is nothing more than a uni-lateral declaration of divorce made by the husband, usually in the presence of witnesses, and sometimes recorded in a private divorce deed. Such a process is clearly insufficient to fulfill the requirements of section 22(1) of the *Divorce Act* and, to the extent that the *Bhatti* decision suggests otherwise, it is, with respect, wrong . . .
>
> I would add that, for the purpose of applying domestic law, I have serious reservations about the appropriateness of recognizing extrajudicial divorces of the sort in issue here. The obvious intent of section 22(1) of the *Divorce Act* was to require that some form of adjudicative or official oversight be present before Canada will recog-nize a foreign divorce. Many of those concerns were identified in the following passage from *Chaudhary* . . . :
>
>> The essentials of the bare *talaq* are, as I understand it, merely the private recital of verbal formula in front of witnesses who may or may not have been specially assembled by the husband for the purpose and whose only qualification is that, presumably, they can see and hear. It may be, as it was in this case, pronounced in the temple. It may be, as it was here, reinforced by a written docu-ment containing such information, accurate or inaccurate, as the husband cares to insert in it. But what brings about the divorce is the pronouncement before witnesses and that alone. Thus in its essential elements it lacks any formality other than ritual per-

---

43   *Ibid.*
44   *Ibid.*
45   2008 FC 168 [*Amin*].

formance; it lacks any necessary element of publicity; it lacks the invocation of the assistance or involvement of any organ of, or recognised by, the state in any capacity at all, even if merely that of registering or recording what has been done.[46]

A more complex set of facts was considered in *Canada (Citizenship and Immigration) v Hazimeh*.[47] The respondent and H had married in Lebanon. H sponsored Hazimeh in her application for permanent resident status in Canada. One month after arrival, she applied for and was granted a religious *talaq* divorce in Ontario from a representative of the Supreme Shiite Islamic Council. She was not eligible to obtain a legal divorce in Ontario then because she had been a resident for such a short time. Six years later, she registered the *talaq* certificate of divorce with a religious court in Lebanon. She then married F in Lebanon and applied to sponsor him. Her application was refused. She reapplied three years later, and again her application was refused on the basis that, while the divorce was purported to have taken place in Lebanon, neither the respondent nor H was resident there for a year as section 22(1) of the Canadian *Divorce Act* requires.[48]

On appeal, the Immigration Appeal Division, citing *Amin*, concluded that the *talaq* ceremony does not grant a divorce.[49] However, the IAD held that the divorce occurred in Lebanon, and that section 22(3) of the *Divorce Act* recognized the common law rule that where a party had a real and substantial connection with a jurisdiction, a divorce granted there should be recognized.[50] The Division determined that the respondent had such a connection with Lebanon.[51] The Federal Court quashed this decision, determining that

[t]he recognition and registration of a talaq divorce that took place in Canada cannot, in my view, produce a divorce granted pursuant to a law other than Canadian law. If simple registration in Lebanon would suffice, then it would turn a talaq divorce that Canada does not recognize into a divorce that Canada must recognize.[52]

The full scope of the common law rules recognized in section 22(3) of the *Divorce Act* has been outlined in *Zhang v Lin*, where the court states:

---

46   *Ibid* at paras 19–20.
47   2009 FC 380 [*Hazimeh*].
48   *Ibid*.
49   *Ibid* at para 8; see *Amin*, above note 45 at para 20.
50   *Hazimeh*, above note 47 at para 9.
51   *Ibid* at para 10.
52   *Ibid* at para 67.

Subsection (3) merely emphasizes that all of the rules of the common law relating to the recognition of foreign divorces, which rules of law are found in the area known as "conflicts of laws" but have not been codified in any statute, continue to apply in Canada. What are those rules? . . . In *Orabi*, the Nova Scotia Court of Appeal summarized the common law of conflicts in divorce in this way:

> Section 22(3) recognizes common law principles governing the recognition of foreign divorce decrees. Domicile was the traditional common law test. Following the decision of the House of Lords in *Indyka v. Indyka*, [1967] 2 All E.R. 689, Canadian courts added "real and substantial connection" as a basis for recognition . . . . Later cases have stated subcategories to these two basic tests for recognition of a foreign divorce.[53]

Included within these subcategories are cases where the divorce is recognized by a foreign jurisdiction to which either of the parties has a real and substantial connection. The court in *Zhang* also cites with approval the following excerpt:

> Although the foreign court that granted the decree may be jurisdictionally competent in the eyes of Canadian law, recognition will be refused if the respondent did not receive notice of the proceeding, especially if fraud was present. The jurisdiction of the foreign court must not be established "through any flimsy residential means" and the petitioner must not have resorted to the foreign court for any fraudulent and improper reasons such as solely "for the purpose of obtaining a divorce." The foreign decree must not be contrary to Canadian public policy. Denial of natural justice may also be a reason for refusing recognition, as was the case when a divorce was granted in Jordan ex parte and there was evidence that the respondent wife, who was notified after the fact and who had no connection to Jordan, would have had no role to play in the proceedings. In sum, there must be no injustice in granting recognition, but lack of consent is not itself a ground for refusing recognition . . . .[54]

b) Common Law Partner
The *Regulations* expanded the family class by introducing two relationships that supplement spousal relationships. The first relationship is common law partnership. A common law partner is defined, in relation

---

53   2010 ABQB 420 at paras 46–47 [*Zhang*].
54   Jean-Gabriel Castel & Janet Walker, *Canadian Conflict of Laws*, 6th ed (Markham: LexisNexis Canada, 2005), s 17(2)(c).

to a person, as an individual who is *cohabiting* with the person in a *conjugal relationship, having so cohabited for a period of at least one year.*[55] This definition is supplemented by an interpretive gloss that states:

> For the purposes of the Act and these Regulations, an individual who has been in a conjugal relationship with a person for at least one year but is unable to cohabit with the person, due to persecution or any form of penal control, shall be considered a common-law partner of the person.[56]

Thus, the components of a common law partnership are that the parties are in a conjugal relationship, that they have been in the relationship for at least a year, and that they have cohabited and continue to do so, unless the reason for not doing so is (the threat of) persecution or punishment. Cumulatively, the definition and gloss reveal a concern that individuals who have lived in a place where cohabitation is punitively sanctioned should still be considered to be in a conjugal relationship.

The *Regulations* do not specify the indicia of a conjugal relationship; however, the Supreme Court of Canada has filled the gap in *M v H*, where it offered the following analysis:

> *Molodowich v. Penttinen* (1980), 17 R.F.L. (2d) 376 (Ont. Dist. Ct.), sets out the generally accepted characteristics of a conjugal relationship. They include shared shelter, sexual and personal behaviour, services, social activities, economic support and children, as well as the societal perception of the couple. However, it was recognized that these elements may be present in varying degrees and not all are necessary for the relationship to be found to be conjugal. While it is true that there may not be any consensus as to the societal perception of same-sex couples, there is agreement that same-sex couples share many other "conjugal" characteristics. In order to come within the definition, neither opposite-sex couples nor same-sex couples are required to fit precisely the traditional marital model to demonstrate that the relationship is "conjugal."[57]

The requirement that a common law partner be in a conjugal relationship for at least a year is regarded as a surrogate or alternative way of demonstrating commitment, rather than engaging in a legal ceremony and exchanging marriage vows. This may be an overly onerous require-

---

55   *Regulations*, above note 2, s 1(1).
56   *Ibid*, s 1(2).
57   [1999] 2 SCR 3 at para 59.

ment where it is impossible for a couple, such as a same-sex couple in many jurisdictions, to get married. Thus, while the recognition of common law relationships may be regarded as a step towards the equal treatment of same-sex couples, it may nevertheless be insufficient to realize equality before the law.

Individuals in common law relationships who are applying as members of the family class are subject to many of the eligibility criteria that apply to spouses. Thus, under section 5(a) of the *Regulations*, a foreign national who is under the age of sixteen shall not be considered the common law partner of a person.[58] In addition, this is reiterated under section 117(9)(a) of the *Regulations* where the foreign national is identified as a common law partner but not as a member of the family class.[59]

In *Canada (Minister of Citizenship and Immigration) v Kimbatsa*, the court determined that cohabitation can be compatible with periods of physical separation.[60] The court cites the operational manual,[61] which states:

> Despite the break in cohabitation, a commonlaw relationship exists if the couple has cohabited continuously in a conjugal relationship in the past for at least one year and intend to do so again as soon as possible. There should be evidence demonstrating that both parties are continuing the relationship, such as visits, correspondence, and telephone calls.
>
> This situation is similar to a marriage where the parties are temporarily separated or not cohabiting for a variety of reasons, but still considers themselves to be married and living in a conjugal relationship with their spouse with the intention of living together as soon as possible.[62]

In *Lindao v Canada (Minister of Citizenship and Immigration)*, the board member considered the question of whether a person who was married could be in a common law relationship:

> The fact that the appellant was married to another person up to 1999 in the panel's opinion is not relevant in the circumstances of this case. There is nothing in the *Immigration and Refugee Protection Act* or in any case the panel is aware of that would say that you could

---

58　*Regulations*, above note 2.
59　*Ibid*.
60　2010 FC 346 [*Kimbatsa*].
61　OP 2, above note 20.
62　*Kimbatsa*, above note 60 at paras 43–44. The court noted that while it was not bound by the manual when interpreting the *Regulations*, it considered this statement to be an accurate representation of the applicable law.

not have a conjugal relationship with a person while being legally married to another provided that it can be established that the *indicia* of a conjugal relationship are present. Thus we have evidence of financial support, communication, sexual relations and a marriage-like relationship; all supporting a conjugal relationship. Based on the evidence this relationship has been in existence for many years. Therefore, there is ample evidence presented to the panel, to find on a balance of probabilities, the definition of conjugal partner has been satisfied in this appeal.[63]

One can infer from this analysis that a relationship of more than two parties will not be held to be conjugal. This understanding is confirmed in the operational manual, which states:

> A common-law or conjugal partner relationship cannot be established with more than one person at the same time. The term "conjugal" by its very nature implies exclusivity and a high degree of commitment; a conjugal relationship cannot exist among more than two people simultaneously. Polygamous-like relationships cannot be considered conjugal and do not qualify as common-law or conjugal partner relationships.[64]

c) Conjugal Partner

Section 2 of the *Regulations* defines a *conjugal partner* in the following terms:

> "conjugal partner" means, in relation to a sponsor, a foreign national residing outside Canada who is in a conjugal relationship with the sponsor and has been in that relationship for a period of at least one year.[65]

The reference to a sponsor in this definition indicates that it has application only to *members of the family class*. Thus, it is unlike the definition of a common law partner, which also includes eligible *family members* of individuals applying to immigrate.[66] The conjugal partner definition differs substantively from the common law partner definition in that the former does not refer to the need for cohabitation. It recognizes that Canadian citizens and permanent residents may be unable to cohabit with persons with whom they are in a conjugal relationship

---

63   [2008] IADD No 1108 at para 15.
64   OP 2, above note 20, s 5.42.
65   *Regulations*, above note 2.
66   *Ibid.*

because of immigration laws and recognizes that this factor should not bar their sponsorship of such a partner.

The absence of any hard-and-fast criteria to identify a relationship as conjugal has raised some difficulties in applying the definition. Conjugal relationships should be distinguished from "pre-conjugal" relationships, where the parties are, for example, merely dating. In *Leroux v Canada (Citizenship and Immigration)*,[67] Tremblay-Lamer J made this point by stating that "a conjugal relationship is more than a precursor, or plan, to share a conjugal relationship in future."[68] However, this does not clarify how the line should be drawn between the two.

Conjugal partners are subject to the exclusions found in the *Regulations*, section 117(9), relating to individuals who are below the age of sixteen. In addition, as noted previously, the operational manual denies that "polygamous-like" relations are conjugal.[69] It is noteworthy that the exclusionary provisions found in section 5 of the *Regulations* dealing with age and polygamous-like relations do not apply to conjugal partners.[70]

d)   The Genuineness of the Relationship

Some recent amendments to the *Regulations* have been motivated by a preoccupation with the possibility of fraud and relationships of convenience. Section 4 of the *Regulations* specifies two factors that spouses, common law partners, and conjugal partners must meet. It reads:

> 4. (1) For the purposes of these Regulations, a foreign national shall not be considered a spouse, a common-law partner or a conjugal partner of a person if the marriage, common-law partnership or conjugal partnership
>
> (a) was entered into primarily for the purpose of acquiring any status or privilege under the Act; or
> (b) is not genuine.[71]

The two factors are alternative routes to disqualify a relationship. A previous version of this section had contained a conjunctive *and* rather than a disjunctive *or*, thereby requiring an officer to be satisfied of both

---

67   2007 FC 403.
68   *Ibid* at para 24. See *Porteous v Canada (Minister of Citizenship and Immigration)*, [2004] IADD No 560.
69   OP 2, above note 20, s 5.42.
70   *Regulations*, above note 2, s 5.
71   *Ibid*, s 4.

factors before disqualifying the relationship. The current law disqualifies the relationship as ineligible if either factor is found to exist.[72]

In relation to the genuineness requirement, courts have held that a number of factors should be considered when the genuineness of a marriage is in question. In the frequently cited case of *Chavez v Canada (Minister of Citizenship and Immigration)*, the Immigration Appeal Division stated:

> The genuineness of the marriage is based on a number of factors. These are not identical in every appeal as the genuineness can be affected by any number of different factors in each appeal. They can include, but are not limited to, such factors as the intent of the parties to the marriage, the length of the relationship, the amount of time spent together, conduct at the time of meeting, at the time of an engagement and/or the wedding, behaviour subsequent to a wedding, the level of knowledge of each other's relationship histories, level of continuing contact and communication, the provision of financial support, the knowledge of and sharing of responsibility for the care of children brought into the marriage, the knowledge of and contact with extended families of the parties, as well as the level of knowledge of each other's daily lives.[73]

e) A Relationship Entered into for the Purpose of Acquiring a Benefit

Section 4 of the *Regulations* requires that individuals not enter a marriage, common law partnership, or conjugal partnership primarily for the purpose of acquiring a benefit under the *IRPA*.[74] If they act contrary to this section, this factor alone will sufficiently disqualify a relationship. When this regulatory change was proposed, the Canadian Bar Association submitted a brief arguing that the measure discriminated against arranged marriage.[75] These marriages are frequently based on the economic prospects and, accordingly, the immigration status of the parties involved. In the Regulatory Impact Analysis Statement (RIAS) accompanying the published changes, the government responded to this objection by stating:

---

72 *Ibid.*
73 [2005] IADD No 353 at para 3.
74 *Regulations*, above note 2.
75 Letter from Alex Stojicevic on behalf of the Canadian Bar Association to Brenna MacNeil (17 July 2008), online: www.cba.org/cba/submissions/pdf/10-28-eng.pdf.

The changes are not intended to target arranged marriages, the majority of which are genuine relationships, and not undertaken for the primary purpose of obtaining benefits related to permanent residency . . . . Canada's immigration officers base their decisions on the information made available to them at the time they consider an application. They are trained to take into account cultural practices, including arranged marriages, in reaching a decision on the bona fides of a relationship. Guidelines will be developed to ensure the proper application of the amended regulation, and officers will receive training in order to ensure that the amended "bad faith" regulation is interpreted and applied as intended, taking into account sensitivities with cultural practices, such as arranged marriages.[76]

The Regulatory Impact Analysis Statement also justifies the change by stating, "Clarification of the bad faith rule will enable more consistent assessment and identification of relationships entered into for immigration purposes."[77] However, it is now possible that an intimate and loving relationship may be disqualified for the sole reason that the individuals began their relationship for improper reasons.

f) Pre-existing Undertaking

Section 117(9)(b) of the *Regulations* includes an anomalous provision that states that a spouse, common law partner, or conjugal partner is not a member of the family class if the sponsor has an existing sponsorship undertaking in respect of a spouse, common law partner, or conjugal partner, and the period referred to in section 132(1) in respect of that undertaking has not ended.[78] It is odd that this factor affects the status of the applicant instead of affecting the eligibility of the sponsor.

g) Sponsored Partners in Canada: The Spouse or Common Law Partner in Canada Class

Applications for permanent resident status as a member of the family class are usually made by individuals who do not reside in Canada. A special class of immigration has been established for spouses and common law partners — not conjugal partners — who are already in Canada so that a spouse or common law partner may apply to become a permanent resident without leaving the country. The class, known as the "spouse or common-law partner in Canada class," excludes conju-

---

76   *Regulations Amending the Immigration and Refugee Protection Regulations (Bad Faith)*, SOR/2010-208.

77   *Ibid.*

78   *Regulations*, above note 2.

gal partners because these individuals are unable to cohabit according to immigration rules, a condition that does not apply where both parties are in Canada.

Section 124 of the *Regulations* identifies the conditions that must be met by an individual applying as a member of this class: The individual must be "the spouse or common-law partner of a sponsor and cohabit with that sponsor in Canada,"[79] "have temporary resident status in Canada,"[80] and be "the subject of a sponsorship application."[81] The government, acting under the authorization of the *IRPA*, section 25(1),[82] has also introduced public policy allowing for individuals who lack temporary resident status to apply as members of this class.[83] The policy is outlined in the Inland Processing manual as follows:

> CIC is committed to family reunification and facilitating processing in cases of genuine spouses and common-law partners already living together in Canada. CIC is also committed to preventing the hardship resulting from the separation of spouses and common-law partners together in Canada, where possible. This means that spouses or common-law partners in Canada, regardless of their immigration status, are now able to apply for permanent residence from within Canada in accordance with the same criteria as members of the Spouse or Common-law Partner in Canada class. This facilitative policy applies only to relationships in which undertakings of support have been submitted. The effect of the policy is to exempt applicants from the requirement under R124(b) to be in status and the requirements under A21(1) and R72(1)(e)(i) to not be inadmissible due to a lack of status; however, all other requirements of the class apply.[84]

h) Conditional Status

Section 72.1 of the *Regulations*, which came into force in October 2012, provides that some spouses, common law partners, and conjugal partners will be granted only conditional permanent resident status. It earmarks

---

79   *Ibid*, s 124(a).

80   *Ibid*, s 124(b).

81   *Ibid*, s 124(c). After being approved in principle, the spouse or common law partner may be issued an open work permit. See Citizenship and Immigration Canada, *One Year Pilot*, online: www.cic.gc.ca/english/resources/tools/updates/2014/2014-12-22.asp.

82   *IRPA*, above note 1.

83   Citizenship and Immigration Canada, IP 8: *Spouse or Common-Law Partner in Canada Class* (16 October 2006), online: www.cic.gc.ca/english/resources/manuals/ip/ip08-eng.pdf at 60.

84   *Ibid*.

those who have been in a relationship with the sponsor for less than two years and who have no children in common with the sponsor. An individual who fails to meet the cohabitation requirement may be inadmissible, lose status, and be removed from Canada.

The section contains some exceptions that aspire to cope with the real risk that coerced cohabitation will impose hardship or will lead to physical, sexual, or mental abuse by the other partner.[85] The adequacy of the exceptions and the processes identified for their implementation may be challenged, as the relevant operational bulletin notes:

> Spouses and partners who are or were subject to the condition and who are or were unable to meet it as a result of the death of the sponsor, or as a result of abuse or neglect during the two-year period of conditional permanent residence, may request an exception from the application of the condition at any time during the two-year conditional period or at the time of an investigation.[86]

The operational bulletin instructs officers where relationships involve abuse and neglect:

> Evidence must clearly show the abuse or neglect was the reason for the breakdown of the marriage.[87]

CIC officers must be satisfied that the sponsored spouse or partner continued to *cohabit* in a *conjugal* relationship with the sponsor until the cohabitation ceased as a result of abuse or neglect.[88]

Conditional permanent residence raises several significant concerns for persons subject to abuse or neglect. The Canadian Council for Refugees has exposed the most serious problems raised by these measures:

1) Making permanent residence conditional on staying in the marriage for two years traps abused partners (mainly women) into staying in abusive relationships for fear of losing their status.

2) Abused partners, especially women, will not be able to take advantage of the exemption because of barriers to access information on the exemption (e.g., language, isolation), the burden of proving their own abuse, and the cost of providing evidence of abuse.

---

85 *Regulations*, above note 2, ss 72.1(6)–72.1(7).

86 Citizenship and Immigration Canada, Operational Bulletin 480: *(Modified) Conditional Permanent Residence Measure for Spouses and Partners in Relationships of Two Years or Less and Who Have No Children in Common* (11 June 2014), s 3.1.

87 *Ibid*, s 3.4.1(a).

88 *Ibid*, s 3.4.2.

3) Children will also be hurt, for example, when they remain with their parent in an abusive home, or if they face being separated from one parent if the sponsored parent is removed from Canada.

4) Making permanent residence for the sponsored partner/spouse conditional puts all the power into the hands of the sponsor, who can use the precarity of his partner's status as a tool for manipulation — at any time, he can declare the spouse fraudulent and have her deported. This can be a constant threat and source of fear for the sponsored person.

5) This power imbalance affects all sponsored partners, regardless of "genuineness" of relationship, and reinforces unequal gendered power dynamics.

6) There is no evidence that this measure is necessary and that marriage fraud is a significant problem in Canada.

7) There is no evidence presented to indicate that a two-year conditional period will deter sponsored partners entering relationships with the objective of obtaining legal status in Canada, who may simply wait out the conditional period. However, this period will have significant impact on those in genuine relationships that break down, whether due to abuse or not.[89]

8) The instructions leave open the possibility that an officer may look for other reasons for the breakdown, and identify any abuse as merely an ancillary factor.[90]

2) Dependent Children

a) Dependence

Prior to 2014, the *Regulations* contained a definition of *dependent child* which heeded the fact that, in many situations, particularly where they are enrolled in post-secondary education, children may be economically dependent on their parent or parents after reaching the age of majority. However, the most recent iteration of the definition has used the age of majority as the dominant indicator of dependence, with a minor qualification that applies only where a physical or mental condition

---

89 Canadian Council for Refugees, Media Release, "Conditional Permanent Residence for Sponsored Spouses," online: CCR ccrweb.ca/en/conditional-permanent-residence.

90 Canadian Council for Refugees, Media Release, "Conditional Permanent Residence: Towards Vulnerability and Violence," online: CCR ccrweb.ca/sites/ccrweb.ca/files/cprstoriesen.pdf.

hinders financial independence.[91] Thus, while in the past, this category allowed dependent children to be defined in a more flexible and fluid manner, today, the strict requirement of the age of nineteen determines who belongs in this category.[92]

The reasons proffered for this change were purely economic. The Regulatory Impact Analysis Statement accompanying the published new regulations states:

> Government and academic research has demonstrated that older immigrants have a more challenging time fully integrating into the Canadian labour market; this is more evident for immigrants who are not selected based on their own merits (e.g. dependent children) . . . .
>
> While Citizenship and Immigration Canada (CIC) has tightened the selection criteria of economic migrants over the years, little consideration has been given to the role of younger dependent children, who have better social and economic integration outcomes.
>
> In sum, the current definition of a dependent child for immigration purposes is out of step with the Government of Canada's objective of selecting migrants who contribute best to Canada's economic growth and sustainability.[93]

The use of purely economic indicators to justify the change in the definition of dependence indicates a deep lack of concern for the values that underlie the family class program. Again, it is important to distinguish between members of the family class and family members of immigrants. Where a migrant is selected on the basis of the projected economic impact he will make, it may make sense to consider the economic impact of the migrant's family members. On the other hand, it is anomalous to apply the same considerations to the family class program or to the dependants of individuals who are selected as members of the family class program, given that the *raison d'etre* of this is to ensure that citizens and permanent residents are able to live with their families and are not separated from those who depend on them. One needs to justify why economic concerns should trump the interests of family members in this particular case. So far, there have been no real attempts to offer such a justification. None is found in the Regulatory Impact Analysis Statement.

In any event, the definition of *dependent child* that applies to the family class program now reads as follows:

---

91   See *Regulations Amending the Immigration and Refugee Protection Regulations*, SOR/2014-133.

92   *Ibid.*

93   *Ibid.*

"dependent child", in respect of a parent, means a child who

(a) has one of the following relationships with the parent, namely,

    (i) is the biological child of the parent, if the child has not been adopted by a person other than the spouse or common-law partner of the parent, or

    (ii) is the adopted child of the parent; and

(b) is in one of the following situations of dependency, namely,

    (i) is less than 19 years of age and is not a spouse or common-law partner, or

    (ii) is 19 years of age or older and has depended substantially on the financial support of the parent since before the age of 19 and is unable to be financially self-supporting due to a physical or mental condition.[94]

The definition reveals that both biological children (unless adopted by a third party) and adopted children may be considered dependent children and, therefore, may apply for permanent resident status as members of the family class. In 2008, amendments to the *Citizenship Act* introduced a complication to this framework by permitting a child adopted by a Canadian citizen to obtain citizenship at the moment of adoption.[95] This change eliminated the requirement to sponsor the child as a permanent resident. However, this option is offered only in restricted circumstances. First, it is not available to sponsors who are only permanent residents.[96] A permanent resident must still sponsor her adopted child's application to immigrate. Second, the option is available only to some Canadian citizens: those who obtained citizenship by being born in Canada or having naturalized.[97] The option is not available to a parent who obtained citizenship by descent, in other words, was born outside Canada to a Canadian parent. Third, negative consequences attach to selecting the option of obtaining citizenship at the moment of adoption.[98] A child who is first sponsored as a permanent resident and who later obtains citizenship through naturalization will later be able to pass on citizenship to his own child born or adopted outside the country. On the other hand, a child who acquires citizenship at the moment of adoption will be regarded as having obtained

---

94   *Regulations*, above note 2, s 2.

95   Bill C-14, *An Act to amend the Citizenship Act (adoption)*, 1st Sess, 39th Parl, 2006 (assented to 22 June 2007), SC 2007, c 24. For more information, see Chapter 13.

96   *Citizenship Act*, RSC 1985, c C-29, s 5.1.

97   See Citizenship and Immigration Canada, "Citizenship Act and Adoption," online: CIC www.cic.gc.ca/english/citizenship/rules_2009/adoption.asp.

98   *Citizenship Act*, above note 96, s 5.1(4).

citizenship by descent and will be unable to pass citizenship on later to a child born or adopted outside the country.[99]

b) Adoption Requirements

Section 3(2) of the *Regulations* offers a broad gloss on adoptions:

> For the purposes of these Regulations, "adoption", for greater certainty, means an adoption that creates a legal parent–child relationship and severs the pre-existing legal parent–child relationship.[100]

Interestingly, the rules governing adopted children who are sponsored as members of the family class differ from the rules governing adopted children who apply as family members. Section 4(2) states that a foreign national shall not be considered an adopted child *either* where the adoption was entered into to obtain a benefit under the *IRPA or* where it did not create a genuine parent–child relationship.[101] However, section 4(3) then states that section 4(2) does not apply to adopted children who are sponsored as members of the family class.[102] Sections 117(2) to 117(4) place a more detailed overlapping set of restrictions on the latter category. Section 117(2) reads:

> (2) A foreign national who is the adopted child of a sponsor and whose adoption took place when the child was under the age of 18 shall not be considered a member of the family class by virtue of the adoption unless
>
> (a) the adoption was in the best interests of the child within the meaning of the *Hague Convention on Adoption*; and
>
> (b) the adoption was not entered into primarily for the purpose of acquiring any status or privilege under the Act.[103]

Section 117(3) lists a set of factors to be taken into account when determining whether the child's best interests are served by the adoption:

> (3) The adoption referred to in subsection (2) is considered to be in the best interests of a child if it took place under the following circumstances:

---

99 See Citizenship and Immigration Canada, "Choose a Process — Intercountry Adoption," CIC, online: www.cic.gc.ca/english/immigrate/adoption/differences.asp.

100 *Regulations*, above note 2.

101 *Ibid.*

102 *Ibid.*

103 *Ibid.*

(a)   a competent authority has conducted or approved a home study of the adoptive parents;

(b)   before the adoption, the child's parents gave their free and informed consent to the child's adoption;

(c)   the adoption created a genuine parent–child relationship;

(d)   the adoption was in accordance with the laws of the place where the adoption took place;

(e)   the adoption was in accordance with the laws of the sponsor's place of residence and, if the sponsor resided in Canada at the time the adoption took place, the competent authority of the child's province of intended destination has stated in writing that it does not object to the adoption;

(f)   if the adoption is an international adoption and the country in which the adoption took place and the child's province of intended destination are parties to the *Hague Convention on Adoption*, the competent authority of the country and of the province have stated in writing that they approve the adoption as conforming to that Convention; and

(g)   if the adoption is an international adoption and either the country in which the adoption took place or the child's province of intended destination is not a party to the *Hague Convention on Adoption*, there is no evidence that the adoption is for the purpose of child trafficking or undue gain within the meaning of that Convention.[104]

The recognition of provincial governments as the competent authorities to administer the processes ensures that the immigration process operates alongside and intersects with provincial laws governing adoption. It also ensures that the province coordinates its decision making with that of the authorities in the country of adoption. By way of example, British Columbia has imposed a moratorium on adoptions from various countries. It has placed a moratorium on adoptions from Guatemala because of concerns about child-trafficking.[105] In 2013, it ceased taking new applications from Pakistan for the following reasons:

> In Pakistan, Islamic Shari'a law (Kafala) does not allow for adoptions. Kafala neither terminates the birth parent–child relationship, nor grants full parental rights to the person (guardian) under whose care the child is entrusted. The concept of Kafala is recognized as distinct

---

104   *Ibid.*

105   British Columbia, Ministry of Children and Family Development, "Intercountry Adoption Alerts: China, Cambodia, Guatemala" (September 2013), online: www.mcf.gov.bc.ca/adoption/alerts_fact_sheets/china_cambodia_guatemala.pdf.

from the Western legal concept of adoption, which severs birth ties between birth parent(s) and the child and in its stead, creates a permanent child relationship between the adoptive parents.[106]

Although section 117(2) restricts adoptions to children under eighteen (which is anomalous because dependent children are defined as being under nineteen), section 117(4) allows for exceptions in relation to some children who were adopted after the age of eighteen.[107] Again, by way of example, these provisions could apply to adoptions in British Columbia, where the *Adoption Act* defines a child as an unmarried person under nineteen years of age and also permits the adoption of an adult where the court issuing the order "considers the reason for the adoption to be acceptable."[108]

The following passage from *De Guzman v Canada (Minister of Citizenship and Immigration)* has been cited frequently when the issue is whether a genuine parent–child relationship has been created:

[T]he panel identified some of the factors that may assist in assessing a relationship of parent and child. These are:

(a) motivation of the adopting parent(s) and;

(b) to a lesser extent, the motivation and conditions of the natural parent(s);

(c) authority and suasion of the adopting parent(s) over the adopted child;

(d) supplanting of the authority of the natural parent(s) by that of the adoptive parent(s);

---

106 British Columbia, Ministry of Children and Family Development, "Intercountry Adoption Alerts: Russia, Pakistan, Nepal, Liberia" (December 2013), online: www.mcf.gov.bc.ca/adoption/alerts_fact_sheets/russia_pakistan_nepal_liberia.pdf.

107 *Regulations*, above note 2, s 117(4). Section 117(4) reads as follows:

A foreign national who is the adopted child of a sponsor and whose adoption took place when the child was 18 years of age or older shall not be considered a member of the family class by virtue of that adoption unless it took place under the following circumstances:

(*a*) the adoption was in accordance with the laws of the place where the adoption took place and, if the sponsor resided in Canada at the time of the adoption, the adoption was in accordance with the laws of the province where the sponsor then resided, if any, that applied in respect of the adoption of a child 18 years of age or older;

(*b*) a genuine parent-child relationship existed at the time of the adoption and existed before the child reached the age of 18; and

(*c*) the adoption was not entered into primarily for the purpose of acquiring any status or privilege under the Act.

108 RSBC 1996, c 5, s 44.

(e) relationship of the adopted child with the natural parent(s) after adoption;

(f) treatment of the adopted child versus natural children by the adopting parent(s);

(g) relationship between the adopted child and adopting parent(s) before the adoption;

(h) changes flowing from the new status of the adopted child such as records, entitlements, etc., including documentary acknowledgment that the [child] is the son or daughter of the adoptive parents; and

(i) arrangements and actions taken by the adoptive parent(s) as it relates to caring, providing and planning for the adopted child.

This list of factors is not exhaustive. Some factors may not be applicable to facts of a particular case, while others not included in this list may be relevant.[109]

3) Parents and Grandparents

Although one may still apply for permanent residence as a parent or grandparent of a Canadian citizen or permanent resident, changes introduced in ministerial instructions have placed severe restrictions on this category.[110] At the same time, as discussed below, new onerous restrictions have been placed on those who wish to sponsor their parents and grandparents.

As of January 2014, the government placed a cap of 5,000 on the number of applications that it will process in this category each year.[111] These instructions replaced earlier instructions, (MI4),[112] which, in 2011, had placed temporary pause on processing applications in this category. The pause was justified as being part of a broader strategy to address the large backlog and wait times in the parents and grandparents category, supporting the attainment of immigration goals set by the federal government.[113]

---

109 [1995] IADD No 1248.

110 Minister of Citizenship and Immigration Canada, Ministerial Instructions 9 (MI9): *Parents and Grandparents* (15 June 2013), online: www.cic.gc.ca/english/department/mi/#mi9.

111 *Ibid.*

112 Minister of Citizenship and Immigration Canada, Ministerial Instructions (MI4): *Parents and Grandparents, Federal Skilled Workers* (5 November 2011), online: www.cic.gc.ca/english/department/mi/#mi4.

113 Department of Citizenship and Immigration, *Updated Ministerial Instructions* (2011) C Gaz I, 3385. A broad discussion of the strategy may be found in House

It does not appear that this broader strategy involved hiring additional officers to process the large backlog of applications that existed. Instead, the central plank of the strategy was to divert grandparents and parents from applying under this program by offering an alternative program — the super visa program — that could be processed faster.[114] However, the super visa made available to parents and grandparents is not a permanent resident visa. Super visa holders have access neither to permanent resident status nor to citizenship. Further, unlike a visitor visa holder, the super visa holder may stay in Canada for two years initially (rather than six months) and be eligible for multiple entries (for six-month periods) within a ten-year period.

As described in a CIC operational bulletin, a person is eligible for a super visa if that person meets four conditions. The person must

1) provide proof of the parent or grandparent relationship to the Canadian citizen or permanent resident;

2) undergo a medical examination and be admissible on health grounds;

3) provide satisfactory evidence of private medical insurance from a Canadian insurance company, valid for a minimum period of one year from the date of entry which (a) covers the applicant for health care, hospitalization and repatriation; (b) provides a minimum of $100,000 coverage; and (c) is valid for each entry to Canada and available for review by the examining officer upon request; and

4) provide a written and signed promise of financial support (e.g., a letter of invitation, from the host child or grandchild for the entire duration the applicant intends to stay in Canada.[115]

Difficulties in obtaining insurance coverage ensure that this option will be unavailable to some parents and grandparents.

To a large extent, the new strategy is shaped by economic factors: access to permanent resident status gives rise to public health care, and health costs can be expected to increase as an individual ages. However, nowhere in the government's explanations for introducing the changes is there a detailed accounting of projected costs that citizens and

---

of Commons, Standing Committee on Citizenship and Immigration, *2nd Report of the Standing Committee on Citizenship and Immigration, "Cutting the Queue: Reducing Canada's Immigration Backlogs and Wait Times"* (9 February 2012).

114 *Ibid*, s 3. See Chapter 5 for more information on super visas.

115 Citizenship and Immigration Canada, OB 357: *Parents and Grandparents Extended Stay Temporary Resident Visa (Super Visa) and Authorized Period of Extended Stay* (1 December 2011), online: www.cic.gc.ca/english/resources/manuals/bulletins/2011/ob357.asp.

permanent residents will incur by paying for the care of their parents who live abroad. Nor does the government account for the impact on the Canadian economy of monies being paid by Canadian parents to foreign agencies for the care of their relatives. In addition, one may infer that the government is now disinclined to recognize any obligation on its part to offer meaningful options or incentives for citizens not to return to their country of origin when familial bonds require personal care for their parents. The government seems willing to rupture its connection with current permanent residents by failing to recognize that parental needs may require filial presence and that the immediate consequence may be the inability to continue to remain in Canada.

Further, there is no acknowledgment of the economic contribution of the parents and grandparents. The presence of some parents and grandparents may mean that they can provide childcare and other assistance in family homes, allowing more permanent residents and Canadians to enter the formal workforce or engage in business opportunities. Just as feminists try to gain recognition for the value of work in the home, there is no recognition of the value that immigrants in this category may bring to Canada.

4) Other Relationships

Section 117 of the *Regulations* recognizes other exceptional relationships that render a person eligible for membership in the family class.[116] Although in most circumstances an individual cannot sponsor a sibling, nephew, niece, or grandchild within the program, section 117(f) creates an exception where the individual in question is orphaned, is under eighteen, is unmarried, and is not in a common law relationship.[117]

Section 117(g) allows an individual to sponsor a child under eighteen as a member of the family class where the sponsor intends to adopt the child in Canada.[118] In such cases, the child is not applying as a dependent child.

Finally, section 117(h) recognizes a wide-ranging category by providing that a relative of any age may be a member of the family class. Elsewhere, a *relative* is defined as "a person who is related to another person by blood or adoption."[119] However, this provision applies only if two conditions relating to the sponsor are met: (1) The sponsor must not have a relative in one of the other categories who could be

---

116 *Regulations*, above note 2.
117 *Ibid.*
118 *Ibid.*
119 *Ibid*, s 2.

sponsored;[120] and (2) the sponsor must not have a listed relative who already has permanent status in Canada (as a permanent resident, registered Indian, or citizen).[121] The list identifies the following relatives:

> [A] spouse, a common-law partner, a conjugal partner, a child, a mother or father, a relative who is a child of that mother or father, a relative who is a child of a child of that mother or father, a mother or father of that mother or father or a relative who is a child of the mother or father of that mother or father.[122]

This provision seems to provide some flexibility for a permanent resident or citizen who is otherwise alone in Canada to be reunited with one person in the family.

D. MISREPRESENTATION AND MEMBERSHIP IN THE FAMILY CLASS

As noted above, the *Regulations* deny membership in the family class to a person whose would-be sponsor had earlier immigrated to Canada and had failed to identify the person as a dependant as part of the application.[123] Section 117(9)(d) reads as though the reason for the denial is because there was no examination, rather than because the sponsor failed to meet the obligation to identify all dependants:

> (9) A foreign national shall not be considered a member of the family class by virtue of their relationship to a sponsor if . . .

> (d) subject to subsection (10), the sponsor previously made an application for permanent residence and became a permanent resident and, at the time of that application, the foreign national was a non-accompanying family member of the sponsor and was not examined.[124]

However, section 117(10) reveals that it is not the mere fact that the accompanying family member was not examined that later excludes the individual.[125] Where the applicant has declared the individual as a family member but the officer decides not to examine the person, the

---

120 *Ibid*, s 117(1)(h)(ii).
121 *Ibid*, s 117(1)(h)(i).
122 *Ibid*, s 117(1)(h).
123 *Ibid*, s 117(9)(d).
124 *Ibid*.
125 *Ibid*.

person will not be excluded later.[126] Nevertheless, section 117(11) provides that the individual described in section 117(10) will be excluded where

(a) the sponsor was informed that the foreign national could be examined and the sponsor was able to make the foreign national available for examination but did not do so or the foreign national did not appear for examination; or

(b) the foreign national was the sponsor's spouse, was living separate and apart from the sponsor and was not examined.[127]

The opacity of these provisions has provoked a voluminous catalogue of caselaw. In many cases, the failure to identify a dependant cannot be traced to a fraudulent intent.[128] A wide range of more innocent explanations has been considered. The applicant may have received bad legal advice,[129] may not have been aware of the consequences of failing to declare the individual as a dependant,[130] may have believed the dependant to be dead,[131] or may not have realized that Canadian law would recognize their relationship to count as a common law relationship (where, for example, they have cohabited for a year).[132]

In a number of cases, the court has identified the underlying aim of the provision as preserving the integrity of immigration law by penalizing those who have tried to benefit by misrepresenting relevant facts.

Thus, in *De Guzman v Canada (Minister of Citizenship and Immigration)*, Kelen J states:

---

126 *Ibid,* s 117(10): Section 117(10) of the *Regulations* reads: "Subject to subsection (11), paragraph (9)(d) does not apply in respect of a foreign national referred to in that paragraph who was not examined because an officer determined that they were not required by the Act or the former Act, as applicable, to be examined."

127 *Ibid.*

128 See, for example, *Chen v Canada (Minister of Citizenship and Immigration)*, 2005 FC 678 [*Chen*]; see Jamie Liew, "Violence and the Form: The Ultrahazardous Activity of Excluding Children in Canada's Immigration Family Class" *Gender and Sexuality Law Online* (14 February 2011), online: http://blogs.law.columbia.edu/genderandsexualitylawblog/2011/02/14/new-from-gsl-online-violence-and-the-form-the-ultrahazardous-activity-of-excluding-children-in-canada%E2%80%99s-immigration-family-class/.

129 *Chen*, above note 128; *Vandy v Canada (Minister of Citizenship and Immigration)*, 2011 CanLII 89877 (CA IRB).

130 *Du v Canada (Minister of Citizenship and Immigration)*, 2012 FC 1094 [*Du*]; *Jankovic v Canada (Minister of Citizenship and Immigration)*, 2003 FC 1482.

131 *Munganza v Canada (Minister of Citizenship and Immigration)*, 2008 FC 1250.

132 *Trokhanovskyy v Canada (Minister of Citizenship and Immigration)*, 2007 CanLII 68155 (CA IRB); *Mafwala v Canada (Minister of Citizenship and Immigration)*, 2009 CanLII 77783 (CA IRB).

I am satisfied that the purpose of subsection 117(9)(d) of the *Regulations* is for the proper administration of Canada's immigration law. It is reasonable that the immigration law would require an applicant for permanent residence disclose, on his or her application, all members of his or her family. Otherwise, the application for permanent residence could not be assessed properly for the purposes of the immigration law. Accordingly, subsection 117(9)(d) of the *Regulations* is for a relevant purpose, i.e. to prevent the fraudulent concealment of material circumstances which might prevent the applicant from being admitted to Canada.[133]

However, other judges have indicated that fraud is not a prerequisite for the section to come into operation. For example, O'Keefe J in *Du* offers the following explanation:

Paragraph 117(9)(d) of the *Regulations* excludes foreign nationals as members of the family class if at the time of their sponsor's permanent residence application, the foreign national was a non-accompanying family member of that sponsor and was not examined. The often cited purpose of this provision is to "ensure that foreign nationals seeking permanent residence do not omit non-accompanying dependent members from their applications thereby avoiding their examination for admissibility at that time, and then, once having obtained their own permanent residence status, seek to sponsor their dependants and benefit from the preferential processing as well as admission treatment given to members of the 'family class'" (see *Natt v Canada (Minister of Citizenship and Immigration)*, 2004 FC 810, [2004] FCJ No 997 at paragraph 14).[134]

Justice O'Keefe also notes, "It has been well recognized that the effects of subsection 117(9)(d) of the *Regulations* can be harsh."[135] This is confirmed in *Kimbatsa*:

The case law is unanimous. An incorrect statement resulting in a foreign national not being examined prevents that foreign national from being considered under the family class for sponsorship purposes, regardless of the reasons for the incorrect statement. Therefore, whether or not the incorrect statement was made in good faith, the foreign national will be excluded from the sponsor's family class.[136]

---

133 2004 FC 1276 at para 35.

134 *Du*, above note 130 at para 49.

135 *Ibid* at para 60.

136 *Kimbatsa*, above note 60 at para 51.

This view is confirmed in *Desalegn v Canada (Minister of Citizenship and Immigration)*, where a sponsor had failed to reveal his marriage to the applicant at the earlier time of his own application.[137] Justice Rennie states:

> The essence of the applicant's argument is that her sponsor was unaware of the requirement that he disclose his marriage and that he did not intend to break the law. This consideration was weighed by the First Secretary and rejected. Failure to know the law or a lack of intention to break it have never been considered compelling arguments in Anglo-Canadian jurisprudence.[138]

In *Adjani v Canada (Minister of Citizenship and Immigration)*, the court goes further by holding that the mistake in question may be a mistake of fact:

> Here, however, the Applicant did not know of his son's existence at the time of his application for permanent residence. He cannot, therefore, be said to have concealed this information or to have misrepresented his circumstances. In my view, it matters not whether non-disclosure is deliberate or not. The regulation is clear, paragraph 117(9)(d) makes no distinction as to the reason for which [a] non-accompanying family member of the sponsor was not disclosed in his application for permanent residence. What matters, is the absence of examination by an officer that necessarily flows from the non-disclosure. This interpretation is consistent with the findings of my Colleague, Justice Mosley in *Hong Mei Chen v. M.C.I.*, [2005] F.C.J. No. 852, 2005 FC 678, where the scope and effect of the impugned regulation were found not to be limited to cases of fraudulent non-disclosure.[139]

On the other hand, a glimmer of generosity is perceivable in *Woldeselassie v Canada (Minister of Citizenship and Immigration)*, where the court held it was unreasonable for the visa officer to ignore the fact that the sponsored child was born almost eight months after the IMM8 form was completed, and thus, could not have been included as a dependant.[140]

---

137 2011 FC 268.

138 *Ibid* at para 10.

139 2008 FC 32 at para 24.

140 2006 FC 1540 at para 25. This is true, but the matter was sent back to a different IAD panel for appeal. On appeal, the judge interprets s 117(9)(d) strictly and does consider the daughter to be a member of the family class because she was

The sole remedy available to the applicant is to make an application for permanent residence on humanitarian and compassionate grounds under the *IRPA*, section 25(1).[141] Unfortunately, this alternative is rarely successful as applicants are seen as asking to be exempt from the regular rules while seemingly contravening the rules through non-disclosure. In *Kimbatsa*, the court attempted to justify the hardline approach by referring to the availability of this option:

> Parliament's intention could not be more clearly expressed. The generous immigration regime applicable to the family class is subject to the express condition that the sponsor make truthful statements in his or her application for permanent residence, enabling the Canadian authorities to examine in advance all of the individuals potentially belonging to the family class in the event that the sponsor is granted permanent resident status. Foreign nationals who are not examined are therefore excluded from the family class of the sponsor, regardless of the reasons for the sponsor's incorrect statement. However, the Minister may overlook incorrect statements in circumstances justified by humanitarian and compassionate considerations, pursuant to subsection 25(1) of the Act. This approach ensures the integrity of the immigration system.
>
> Canada's immigration system is not open to manipulation by sponsors who adjust their family situations to suit their purposes. The system is primarily based on the principle of true and complete disclosure of information by the applicants. Deviations from this principle cannot be tolerated by the courts. It is for the Minister, not the courts, to decide under subsection 25(1) which exceptional cases involve humanitarian and compassionate considerations justifying a departure from this principle.[142]

E. SPONSORSHIP ELIGIBILITY

Two separate sections of the *Regulations* delineate the conditions that must be met before a sponsorship of a member of the family class will be approved. Section 130 offers a definition of the conditions that must be met for a person to be a sponsor.[143] Section 133 provides a checklist of requirements that must be met before the sponsor's application will

---

not examined by immigration authorities (*Woldeselassie v Canada (Minister of Citizenship and Immigration)*, [2007] IADD No 1187).

141 *IRPA*, above note 1. See also Chapter 12 on permanent resident applications on humanitarian and compassionate grounds.

142 Above note 60 at paras 53–54.

143 Above note 2.

be approved.[144] There is an obvious overlap between the two sections: the first requirement noted in section 133(1)(a) is that the sponsor "is a sponsor as described in section 130."[145]

Nevertheless, it is important to distinguish between the two sections. As discussed below, when an appeal is made to the Immigration Appeal Division of the Immigration and Refugee Board, the tribunal has an option available in cases where it finds that the appellant actually meets the definition of a sponsor.[146] In such cases, the tribunal may allow an appeal on the ground that, "sufficient humanitarian and compassionate considerations warrant special relief in light of all the circumstances of the case."[147] Thus, although the Division may not permit individuals who do not meet the definitional criteria to sponsor a member of the family class (section 130), they may allow sponsors who otherwise do not meet the *other criteria required for approval* (section 133). In this latter case, overriding humanitarian and compassionate reasons may justify the decision.[148]

Unfortunately, the *Regulations* do not clearly distinguish between definitional criteria (which identify who is a sponsor) and eligibility criteria (which identify the criteria that a sponsor must meet). Section 130(1) provides:

> (1) Subject to subsections (2) and (3), a sponsor, for the purpose of sponsoring a foreign national who makes an application for a permanent resident visa as a member of the family class or an application to remain in Canada as a member of the spouse or common-law partner in Canada class under subsection 13(1) of the Act, must be a Canadian citizen or permanent resident who
>
> (a) is at least 18 years of age;
>
> (b) resides in Canada; and
>
> (c) has filed a sponsorship application in respect of a member of the family class . . .[149]

---

144 *Ibid.*

145 *Ibid.*

146 *IRPA*, above note 1, s 65, provides: "In an appeal under s 63(1) or (2) respecting an application based on membership in the family class, the Immigration Appeal Division may not consider humanitarian and compassionate considerations unless it has decided that the foreign national is a member of the family class and that their sponsor is a sponsor within the meaning of the regulations."

147 *IRPA, ibid,* s 67(1)(c).

148 See Section G, below in this chapter.

149 Above note 2.

From these words, there can be no doubt that *citizenship or permanent resident status, age, place of residence*, and *completion of an application* are definitional requirements. However, the residence requirement is qualified by subsection (2), but only in relation to Canadian citizens. It reads:

> A sponsor who is a Canadian citizen and does not reside in Canada may sponsor a foreign national who makes an application referred to in subsection (1) and is the sponsor's spouse, common-law partner, conjugal partner or dependent child who has no dependent children, if the sponsor will reside in Canada when the foreign national becomes a permanent resident.[150]

By referring to a person who resides outside Canada as a "sponsor," this provision implies that residence in Canada is not a definitional requirement. This leaves open the question whether the Immigration Appeal Division may hear appeals from citizens who are not resident and who do not intend to reside in Canada at the time when the member of the family class would get permanent resident status.

Even more problematic is section 130(3), an amendment to the *Regulations* made in 2012, which aims to disqualify citizens and permanent residents from sponsoring a spouse, common law partner, or conjugal partner for a period of five years if they themselves had been sponsored to come to Canada as a spouse, common law partner, or conjugal partner.[151] It reads:

> A sponsor who became a permanent resident after being sponsored as a spouse, common-law partner or conjugal partner under subsection 13(1) of the Act may not sponsor a foreign national referred to in subsection (1) as a spouse, common-law partner or conjugal partner, unless the sponsor
>
> (a) has been a permanent resident for a period of at least five years immediately preceding the day on which a sponsorship application referred to in paragraph 130(1)(c) is filed by the sponsor in respect of the foreign national; or
>
> (b) has become a Canadian citizen during the period of five years immediately preceding the day referred to in paragraph (a) and had been a permanent resident from at least the beginning of that period until the day on which the sponsor became a Canadian citizen.[152]

---

150 *Ibid*, s 130(2).
151 *Ibid*.
152 *Ibid*, s 130(3).

The words of the subsection imply that, although the person described may not succeed in sponsoring an intimate partner, that individual is nevertheless a "sponsor." On this reading, the potential sponsor will be able to make an appeal to the Immigration Appeal Division and may succeed where there are overriding humanitarian and compassionate reasons. On the other hand, the location of the provision within section 130 implies that it is a definitional requirement for a person to be a sponsor. It is, after all, one of the factors qualifying the definition found in section 130(1). If this is the proper reading, then the individual in question will not be a sponsor and will not have access to the Division. This issue remains open.

The criteria found in section 133 that specify the characteristics or conduct that will prevent the approval of a sponsor's application can be classified under general headings: *poverty* (receipt of social assistance or undischarged bankrupt income deemed insufficient to support);[153] *criminality* (detained in prison, or convicted of sexual offence, or of causing bodily harm to a relative);[154] *breaches of immigration law* (being under a removal order);[155] *financial mismanagement* (defaulting on previous undertaking or support payment or debt to the government of Canada);[156] and where there is evidence that the sponsor *does not intend to fulfill his undertaking.*[157]

F. THE UNDERTAKING

Audrey Macklin has noted the anomalous nature of the undertaking required from sponsors. She writes:

> One unsolved mystery of the family sponsorship regime is the rationale behind imposing sponsorship undertakings on immigrant families whose members arrive at different times, whereas families who arrive together as principal applicant and accompanying [family members] are not similarly encumbered. The putative justification for sponsorship undertakings is that immigrants are beholden to Canada for receiving them. The state extends to them the privilege of entry, but only on condition that they do not exploit Canada's beneficence by drawing on public services. As a pragmatic matter, the

---

153 *Ibid*, 133(1)(k).
154 *Ibid*, 133(1)(e)(f).
155 *Ibid*, 133(1)(c).
156 *Ibid*, 133(1)(h)(i).
157 *Ibid*, 133(1)(b).

fact that non-citizens are disenfranchised means that the government can impose burdens on them at low political cost. Yet these factors cannot explain the disparity in treatment of accompanying dependants versus members of the family class. Nor is it apparent why immigrant families (especially nuclear families) warrant greater surveillance of their mutual support obligations than do Canadian families. Do policy makers suspect that, absent the sponsorship undertaking, immigrants are more likely to wilfully abandon family members? Do they consider the family support provisions under the *Criminal Code* and family law legislation singularly inadequate with respect to immigrant families?[158]

As part of the application, the sponsor is required to sign a formal statement, which includes the following:

> I undertake to provide for the basic requirements of the sponsored person and his or her family members who accompany him or her to Canada, if they are not self-supporting. I promise to provide food, clothing, shelter, fuel, utilities, household supplies, personal requirements, and other goods and services, including dental care, eye care, and other health needs not provided by public health care . . . .
>
> I understand that all social assistance paid to the sponsored person or his family members becomes a debt owed by me to Her Majesty in right of Canada and her Majesty in right of the province concerned. As a result, the Minister and the province concerned have a right to take enforcement action against me . . . .[159]

The undertaking takes effect on the day the sponsored person enters Canada, and its duration depends on the relationship involved. Where the sponsored person is a spouse, common law partner, conjugal partner, or a dependent child over the age of nineteen, it lasts for three years.[160] Where the sponsored person is a dependent child under the age of nineteen, it lasts for ten years or until the child reaches the age of twenty-two.[161] For parents and grandparents, it lasts for twenty

---

158   Audrey Macklin, "Public Entrance/Private Member" in Judy Fudge & Brenda Cossman, eds, *Privatization, Feminism and Law* (Toronto: University of Toronto Press, 2002) 218.

159   Citizenship and Immigration Canada, "Application to Sponsor and Undertaking," online: CIC immigrationcanadaservices.com/wp-content/themes/immigration/pdfs/sponsor-and-undertaking.pdf.

160   *Regulations*, above note 2, s 132(1)(b)(i).

161   *Ibid*, s 132(1)(b)(ii).

years.[162] For all individuals who fit within other categories, it lasts for ten years.[163]

In *Canada (AG) v Mavi*, the Supreme Court of Canada considered the appeals of eight sponsors who were required to pay back social assistance received by sponsored family members.[164] In some cases, the assistance had been received after the relationship had dissolved or had soured. The appellants argued that since the government had discretion to forgive or reduce the debt when the sponsor experienced hardship, it also owed the sponsor a duty to act fairly when exercising this discretion.[165] However, the Supreme Court held that the government had no discretion to forgive the debt and had only limited discretion to delay enforcement.[166] The Court concluded that principles of procedural fairness imposed limited obligations on the government, requiring it "to afford the sponsor an opportunity within limited time to explain in writing his or her relevant personal and financial circumstances that are said to militate against immediate collection."[167]

G. SPONSORSHIP AND THE IMMIGRATION APPEAL DIVISION

As outlined above, the decision not to approve a sponsorship may be based on a number of factors. It may be determined that the individual seeking permanent residence is not a member of the family class; that the person is inadmissible; that the person seeking to sponsor the individual does not meet the definition of a sponsor; or that the conditions that must be met for approval have not been met. Where a negative decision has been made, only the sponsor has a right to appeal to the Immigration Appeal Division of the Immigration and Refugee Board.[168] No appeal may be made to the Division by a sponsor or by a permanent resident if the member of the family class has been found to be inadmissible on grounds of security, violation of human or international rights, serious criminality, or organized criminality.[169]

---

162 *Ibid*, s 132(1)(b)(iv).

163 *Ibid*, s 132(1)(b)(v).

164 2011 SCC 30.

165 *Ibid* at para 6.

166 *Ibid* at para 4.

167 *Ibid* at para 79.

168 IRPA, above note 1, s 63(1): "A person who has filed in the prescribed manner an application to sponsor a foreign national as a member of the family class may appeal to the Immigration Appeal Division against a decision not to issue the foreign national a permanent resident visa."

169 *Ibid*, s 64(1).

A sponsorship appeal is a hearing *de novo* where issues not raised before the officer making the original decision may be raised and considered.[170] A notice of appeal must be submitted by the sponsor to the Immigration Appeal Division within thirty days after receiving the written reasons for the refusal.[171] The Division is required to provide the notice of appeal and the reasons for refusal to the minister of Citizenship and Immigration who must draw up an appeal record, containing a table of contents; the application for a permanent resident visa that was refused; the application for sponsorship and the sponsor's undertaking; any document that the minister has that is relevant to the applications, to the reasons for the refusal, or to any issue in the appeal; and the written reasons for the refusal.[172]

The *IRPA* identifies three circumstances in which the Immigration Appeal Division may allow an appeal, namely, where it is satisfied that

(a)   the decision appealed is wrong in law or fact or mixed law and fact;

(b)   a principle of natural justice has not been observed; or

(c)   other than in the case of an appeal by the Minister, taking into account the best interests of a child directly affected by the decision, sufficient humanitarian and compassionate considerations warrant special relief in light of all the circumstances of the case.[173]

However, the *IRPA* also makes clear that the third of these options is *not* available unless the Division has decided that the foreign national is a member of the family class and that the foreign national's sponsor is a sponsor within the meaning of the *Regulations*.[174] Thus, it is not possible for the Division to consider humanitarian and compassionate factors where, for example, it determines that the applicant falls under section 117(9)(d) of the *Regulations*.[175] As a consequence, where a person has been rejected because the applicant is inadmissible, the applicant, if found to be a member of the family class, may be able to persuade the Division that humanitarian reasons outweigh the

---

170   See Immigration and Refugee Board of Canada, "Sponsorship Appeals" (1 January 2008), online: IRB www.irb-cisr.gc.ca/Eng/BoaCom/references/LegJur/Documents/SpoParIntro_e.pdf, Introduction.

171   *Immigration Appeal Division Rules*, SOR/2002-230, s 3.

172   *Ibid*, s 4.

173   *Ibid*, s 67(1).

174   *Ibid*, s 65. See Section E, above in this chapter.

175   Above note 2.

countervailing reasons for denying entry.[176] On the other hand, where an applicant has been found not to be a member of the family class because of the sponsor's earlier failure to disclose her existence, such an argument may not be raised.[177]

H. SPONSORSHIP AND JUDICIAL REVIEW[178]

Under the *IRPA*, section 72, an application to the Federal Court seeking judicial review may not be made until any right of appeal that may be provided by the *IRPA* is exhausted. In *Somodi v Canada (Minister of Citizenship and Immigration)*, the appellant argued that he should be able to seek judicial review of a visa denial because only his sponsor had the right to appeal to the Immigration Appeal Division.[179] The Federal Court of Appeal nevertheless concluded that it should not entertain the application for judicial review until the sponsor's appeal had been decided.[180] The appeal court reasoned as follows:

> It should be remembered that, on a family sponsorship application, the interests of the parties are congruent. Both the sponsor and the foreign national seek a reunification of the family. It would be illogical and detrimental to the objectives of the scheme to allow a multiplicity of proceedings on the same issue, in different forums, to parties pursuing the same interests. It would also be detrimental to the administration of justice as it would open the door to conflicting decisions and fuel more litigation. This is precisely what Parliament intended to avoid.

> In addition, the appellant is not deprived of all remedies. He has other avenues such as an application to the Minister based on humanitarian and compassionate considerations pursuant to section 25 of the IRPA. We were told that such an application is pending. He has also unsuccessfully prevailed himself of the right to apply for refugee status as well as the right to apply for a pre-removal risk assessment.[181]

By way of contrast, in *Habtenkiel v Canada (Minister of Citizenship and Immigration)*, the appellant applied as a member of the family

---

176 *IRPA*, above note 1, s 65.
177 *Ibid*.
178 See Chapter 16 for more information on judicial review.
179 2009 FCA 288 [*Somodi*].
180 *Ibid* at para 32.
181 *Ibid* at paras 29–30.

class sponsored by her father.[182] She was excluded as a member of the family class because her father had not disclosed her when he himself applied.[183] She applied for humanitarian and compassionate consideration, but this was denied. She sought judicial review of this latter decision. The Federal Court denied the judicial review on the ground that she should wait for the Immigration Appeal Division to hear an appeal by her father.[184] The Federal Court of Appeal distinguished this case from *Somodi* and reasoned as follows:

> The question that arises in cases where the applicant is excluded from the family class is whether subsection 63(1) and paragraph 72(2)(*a*) of the Act abrogate the applicant's right to apply for judicial review of the Minister's exercise of his discretion pursuant to section 25 of the Act. In my opinion, they do not.
>
> . . .
>
> The result in *Somodi* is premised on the existence of a real right of appeal to the IAD. The sponsor's right to bring that appeal abrogates the foreign national's right to bring an application for judicial review. Section 65's exclusion of humanitarian and compassionate considerations from the scope of the appeal that may be brought by the sponsor means that, in effect, no right of appeal has been granted with respect to those considerations. If there is no right of appeal, there is no adequate alternate remedy which impedes the foreign national's right to bring an application for judicial review. As a result, paragraph 72(2)(*a*) of the Act is not a bar to Ms. Habtenkiel's right to bring an application for judicial review, but only with respect to the Minister's exercise of his discretion under section 25.[185]

Nevertheless, the appellant lost her appeal because the Federal Court of Appeal determined that the visa officer's original decision met the required standards of reasonableness.[186]

I. CONCLUSION

Canada's immigration system is moving its focus away from family reunification and is concentrating instead on filling labour shortages

---

182   2014 FCA 180.
183   *Ibid* at para 1.
184   *Ibid* at para 2.
185   *Ibid* at paras 34 and 36.
186   *Ibid* at para 48.

and protecting Canada from alleged security and criminal threats and those "abusing the system." In doing so, Canada may be neglecting its obligations under international law. For example, article 16(3) of the *Universal Declaration of Human Rights*[187] and article 23(1) of the *International Covenant on Civil and Political Rights*[188] state: "The family is the natural and fundamental group unit of society and is entitled to protection by society and the State."[189]

Despite such provisions, the current government is modifying the family class program in ways that permit it to develop and shape a narrative of distrust towards foreign nationals. In justifying certain changes to the legislation, for example, Jason Kenney, then minister of Citizenship and Immigration, transported the parlance of fraudulent foreign nationals from the discourse surrounding refugee protection into discussions on how foreign nationals are using the family reunification system in Canada:

> Canada's doors are open to the vast majority of newcomers who are hard-working and follow the rules, but Canadians have no tolerance for anyone who tries to jump the immigration line to gain entry to Canada or acquire permanent residency or citizenship through fraudulent means.[190]

The result is that more permanent residents and citizens are separated from loved ones, for longer periods of time, while the legitimacy of their relationships is scrutinized more closely; what is more, they are required to accept temporary instead of permanent solutions. This situation speaks to a deep mistrust not only of foreign nationals, but

---

187 *Universal Declaration of Human Rights*, GA Res 217(III), UNGAOR, 3d Sess, Supp No 13, UN Doc A/810, (1948) 71.

188 *International Covenant on Civil and Political Rights*, 19 December 1966, 999 UNTS 171, arts 9–14, Can TS 1976 No 47, 6 ILM 368 (entered into force 23 March 1976, accession by Canada 19 May 1976).

189 See also Conference of Plenipotentiaries, which, when it adopted the United Nations *Refugee Convention*, recognized the significance of this principle for refugees in its Final Act: "*Considering* that the unity of the family, the natural and fundamental group unit of society, is an essential right of the refugee . . . ."

190 Diana Mehta, "'Sometimes Marriage Is a Scam': Ottawa Launches Fresh Ad Campaign Targeting Immigration Fraud" *National Post* (20 March 2013), online: http://news.nationalpost.com/2013/03/20/sometimes-marriage-is-a-scam-ottawa-launches-fresh-ad-campaign-targeting-immigration-fraud/; Nicholas Keung, "Marriage Fraud Crackdown: Spouses Sponsored by Canadians Now Face Two-Year Probation" *Toronto Star* (26 October 2012), online: www.thestar.com/news/canada/2012/10/26/marriage_fraud_crackdown_spouses_sponsored_by_canadians_now_face_twoyear_probation.html.

also of Canadian permanent residents and citizens, as it is their selection of family members that is being questioned.

CHAPTER 7

A BRIEF INTRODUCTION TO CANADIAN REFUGEE LAW

A. REFUGEE PROTECTION

Canadian law permits foreign nationals to acquire permanent resident status by first establishing that they are in need of protection as a result of conditions in their country or countries of nationality. In general terms, where the foreign national is outside Canada, the individual may apply through a visa office for a permanent resident visa. The person's need for protection will be examined, and he will also be assessed on other criteria. Where the visa is granted, the individual will be examined on arrival in Canada and at that moment will acquire permanent status. Where a foreign national has made her own way to Canada, she may seek protection on arrival or, if she has been granted temporary status, she may do so at a later time. It will be determined whether such individuals are eligible to make a claim before the Refugee Protection Division (RPD) of the Immigration and Refugee Board (IRB). If they are eligible and they make a successful claim, they then have the opportunity to make an application for permanent resident status from within Canada. If they are found ineligible to make a claim or if their claim is unsuccessful, they may apply to the minister of Citizenship and Immigration for an assessment of their need for protection prior to any measures taken to remove them from Canada. Some individuals, whose applications are successful, may be granted temporary status that would prevent removal from Canada, or they may be found to be protected persons and may subsequently apply for permanent resident status.

B. COMPETING ACCOUNTS OF THE UNDERLYING PRINCIPLES

In current political and legal discourse, one can find two competing accounts of the principles and values that lie at the core of Canadian refugee law. The sharp contrast between these two positions has become more evident in recent years as the government has developed and implemented wide-ranging policies that are clearly antithetical to the central tenets of one of these models, and in response, social groups have engaged in push-back by challenging the legitimacy of the new measures in both the courtroom and the media. The two approaches may be labelled the "discretionary-humanitarian account" and the "obligatory rights-based account." The first view is the one that has been articulated by the government in defence of many of the legal amendments that it has introduced; one may find the second approach articulated in the views of most refugee scholars and in the legal and constitutional arguments that have been developed by leading legal and social organizations.

1) The Discretionary-Humanitarian Approach

The discretionary-humanitarian approach identifies generosity and humanitarian goodwill as the fundamental factors that have defined and should continue to define Canada's response to the plight of the millions of people in this world who experience the need to flee from their home state to escape persecution and who must live elsewhere for lengthy periods as aliens. On several occasions in the past, Canada has shown exceptional altruism by offering resettlement to large numbers of individuals who have been in this desperate predicament — for example, those who were expelled from Uganda by President Idi Amin, those who fled Chile during the Pinochet regime, those who fled Vietnam in the aftermath of the war, and Eastern Europeans and Salvadorans in the 1980s. Canada continues to demonstrate a willingness to address the needs of this vulnerable population — and the government has not been hesitant to engage in self-congratulations for doing so — by selecting overseas refugees as candidates for permanent residence. Using the definition of refugee found in the *Convention relating to the Status of Refugees* and the *Protocol relating to the Status of Refugees*[1] as the primary standard for selection, but expanding it further to embrace

---

1   *Convention relating to the Status of Refugees*, 28 July 1951, 189 UNTS 137 (entered into force 22 April 1954) [*Refugee Convention*]; *Protocol relating to the*

deserving individuals who fall outside its ambit (again creating an opportunity for self-congratulations for the broad compass of its generous spirit), Canada has developed legal processes to facilitate the admission and settlement of these individuals. These normative structures are presented by the adherents of this approach as defining the core of refugee law.

Advocates of the discretionary model are careful to emphasize its limitations. Generosity has its bounds: supererogatory demands — that is, those that exist beyond the call of duty or obligation — are defeasible and may be reduced by factors such as the lack of available resources. Where one extends generosity to many different groups, each facing its own extreme predicament, or where one's resources are insufficient to cope with one's own needs, the amount that one can offer to each group will by necessity be reduced. In addition, although the approach is identified as essentially humanitarian, its practitioners have not necessarily met a high level of generosity. Instead, the approach signifies that practitioners understand the practice of welcoming refugees as an exercise in generosity and expect political debate to focus on a single question: whether the government's level of generosity, which may be quite low, is nevertheless defensible in the circumstances. Where there is an assessment that it is not in the country's best interest to extend generosity to particular groups or individuals, the humanitarian urge will likely be outweighed by other discretionary factors.

Where discretionary benevolence or munificence is identified as driving our legal policies, a distinction may also be drawn between those in need who show respect for our sovereignty by remaining outside our territory while they wait for our largesse and those who force the issue by arriving at our borders unannounced and uninvited to seek our assistance. Although it may be proper that we not expel any such individuals to face persecution or risk to life, as required by the *Refugee Convention*, we may legitimately create hurdles to impede their arrival, or be miserly in the benefits that we make available while we determine the merits of their plea for our protection. In particular, we should not be regarded as having a special relationship to individuals who have arrived uninvited to our territory that could be regarded as giving rise to the duty to accord better treatment than is made available to those who remain outside the country. From this perspective, the rules that we have developed to cope with unanticipated arrivals should be regarded as marginal aspects of our refugee law. In those

---

Status of Refugees, 31 January 1967, 606 UNTS 267 (entered into force 4 October 1967).

spheres, where our commitment to generosity is legitimately restricted by our commitment to other values, particularly our desire to maintain sovereign control of our borders, we will not find the core values that inform refugee law.

2) The Rights-Based Approach

By way of contrast, proponents of the second view, the obligatory rights-based approach, emphasize that Canada, by acceding to the *Refugee Convention*, has bound itself to certain undertakings towards individuals who have a well-founded fear of persecution on one of the grounds listed therein. It has also bound itself to giving a liberal and expansive interpretation of its obligations under the *Refugee Convention*. From this point of view, refugees do not appeal for largesse when seeking protection: they claim to have an entitlement to protection, a claim that they can make against whichever state party to the *Refugee Convention* they may choose. If it is simpler or more sensible or more profitable for a claimant to escape his country by plane and touch down in Canada, then Canada must live up to its responsibilities: first, by determining whether the claimant is indeed a refugee; and if so, by then offering protection. There is no requirement that, as rights-holders, refugees wait until selected by Canada; they may come seeking the undertaking to be fulfilled.

From this perspective, there is something deeply problematic about a country creating impediments that will prevent a person from asserting her rights against a state party to the *Refugee Convention*. There is also something deeply problematic about a state party devising policies that are intended to deter claimants from seeking protection. Hence, from this perspective, it is quite improper to place the processes of status determination in Canada at the margins of refugee law — they reflect its very essence. Adherents of this view tend not to devalue the processes of resettlement that have been developed to select refugees outside Canada, although they do recognize that they are not demanded by the *Refugee Convention* and amount, in any event, to so little that they should not be conceived as our primary tool in addressing one of the most compelling global issues of the twenty-first century.

Against the background of these two opposing perspectives, the following chapters of this book examine the legal structures that have been developed to regulate, first, the selection of refugees outside Canada; and second, the determination of claims by individuals who have succeeded at arriving in the country.

CHAPTER 8

ACQUIRING PERMANENT STATUS: REFUGEE RESETTLEMENT

A. INTRODUCTION: RESETTLEMENT AS A DURABLE SOLUTION

In 2013, according to the United Nations High Commissioner for Refugees, or the UNHCR:

> 51.2 million individuals were forcibly displaced worldwide as a result of persecution, conflict, generalized violence, or human rights violations. Some 16.7 million persons were refugees: 11.7 million under UNHCR's mandate and 5.0 million Palestinian refugees registered by UNRWA [United Nations Relief and Works Agency]. The global figure included 33.3 million internally displaced persons (IDPs) and close to 1.2 million asylum-seekers. If these 51.2 million persons were a nation, they would make up the 26th largest nation in the world.[1]

In framing its response to a situation of such staggering proportions, the UNHCR has developed three "durable solutions" to address the plight of populations that have fled across borders en masse: (1) voluntary repatriation; (2) local integration in the country of first asylum;

---

1 UN High Commissioner for Refugees, "UNHCR Global Trends 2013: War's Human Cost" (20 June 2014), online: UNHCR www.unhcr.org/5399a14f9.html at 2.

and (3) resettlement.[2] Resettlement occurs when "refugees are selected and transferred from the country of refuge to a third State which has agreed to admit them as refugees with permanent residence status"[3] with the possibility of obtaining citizenship.[4] It is proposed not only as a durable solution but also as "a mechanism for refugee protection . . . and an element of responsibility sharing with refugee-hosting countries."[5] This chapter focuses on Canada's policies and practices of resettlement.[6]

B. CANADA'S RESETTLEMENT PROGRAM

1) Overview

Canada's resettlement program, initiated in 1978, is administered by the Department of Citizenship and Immigration Canada (CIC).[7] Its main objectives are "to save lives, offer protection to the displaced and persecuted, meet Canada's international legal obligations with respect to refugees, and respond to international crises by providing assistance to those in need of resettlement."[8]

The number of persons who are annually resettled in Canada and who acquire permanent resident status is not large. In 2013, only 5,756 government-assisted refugees (GARs) were admitted, a figure 15 percent below target. In addition, 6,277 privately sponsored refugees were admitted.[9] Although the federal government hoped to increase the number of resettled refugees to as many as 13,900 in 2014, it is as yet unclear whether the target was reached.[10] Nevertheless, the Canadian

---

2   UN High Commissioner for Refugees, *UNHCR Resettlement Handbook: Division of International Protection*, revised ed (Geneva: United Nations High Commissioner for Refugees, 2011) at 11.

3   *Ibid* at 28.

4   *Ibid* at 36.

5   *Ibid*.

6   *Immigration and Refugee Protection Act*, SC 2001, c 27, s 12(3) [*IRPA*].

7   Government of Canada, *UNHCR Resettlement Handbook, Country Chapters – Canada*, revised ed (Ottawa: Government of Canada, 2014) at 2–3 [*UNHCR Resettlement Handbook, Canada Chapter*]; see also *IRPA*, above note 6, s 12(3).

8   *UNHCR Resettlement Handbook, Canada Chapter*, above note 7 at 3.

9   Citizenship and Immigration Canada, *Annual Report to Parliament on Immigration 2013* (Ottawa: Citizenship and Immigration Canada, 2013) at 17.

10 *Ibid* at 17–18. See also *UNHCR Resettlement Handbook, Canada Chapter*, above note 7 at 6: The range for refugee resettlement admissions in 2014 was 11,800 to 14,200.

government has repeatedly indicated that it intends to focus more on its resettlement program. As one of twenty-three states participating in the UNHCR resettlement program, it currently ranks as the eighth highest for receiving refugees.[11]

2) Who May Be Resettled?

Driven by a set of overarching humanitarian ideals, Canada's resettlement program applies only to individuals outside Canada who must meet specified criteria.[12] Section 139 of the *Regulations* provides eight general selection criteria for individuals who are not intending to settle in Quebec.[13] An officer is required to issue a permanent resident visa where

1)   The foreign national is outside Canada.

---

11   UN High Commissioner for Refugees, *UNHCR Statistical Yearbook 2012*, 12th ed (Geneva: UNHCR, 2013) at 45; UN High Commissioner for Refugees, *UNHCR Statistical Yearbook 2011: Trends in Displacement, Protection and Solutions: Eleven Years of Statistics*, 11th ed (Geneva: UNHCR, 2012) at 39: Canada ranked ninth in 2010–11; UN High Commissioner for Refugees, *UNHCR Statistical Yearbook 2010: Trends in Displacement, Protection and Solutions: Ten Years of Statistics*, 10th ed (Geneva: UNHCR, 2011) at 42: Canada ranked eighth in 2009–10; UN High Commissioner for Refugees, *UNHCR Statistical Yearbook 2009: Trends in Displacement, Protection and Solutions*, 9th ed (Geneva: UNHCR, 2010) at 36: Canada ranked sixth in 2008–09; UN High Commissioner for Refugees, *UNHCR Statistical Yearbook 2008: Trends in Displacement, Protection and Solutions*, 8th ed (Geneva: UNHCR, 2009) at 52: Canada ranked fifth in 2007–08; UN High Commissioner for Refugees, *UNHCR Statistical Yearbook 2007: Trends in Displacement, Protection and Solutions*, 7th ed (Geneva: UNHCR, 2008) at 47: Canada ranked sixth in 2006–07; UN High Commissioner for Refugees, *UNHCR Statistical Yearbook 2006: Trends in Displacement, Protection and Solutions*, 6th ed (Geneva: UNHCR, 2007) at 46: Canada ranked seventh in 2005–06; *UNHCR Statistical Yearbook 2005: Trends in Displacement, Protection and Solutions*, 5th ed (Geneva: UNHCR, 2007) at 51: from 1996 to 2005, Canada ranked fifth in the world for total admissions per 1000 inhabitants.

12   *Immigration and Refugee Protection Regulations*, SOR/2002-227, s 139 [*Regulations*] provides among other criteria: (a) the foreign national is outside Canada; (b) the foreign national submitted an application for permanent residence; (c) the foreign national has no reasonable prospect of a durable solution in a country other than Canada; and (d) the foreign national is eligible under one of the classes listed in the *Regulations*. For an outline of who can be sponsored, see also Section B(2), below in this chapter.

13   *Regulations*, above note 12, s 158. The Quebec regulations are described on the Government of Quebec's website, online: www.immigration-quebec.gouv.qc.ca/en/immigrate-settle/refugees-other/index.html.

2)   The foreign national has submitted an application for a perma-
     nent resident visa.

3)   The foreign national is seeking to come to Canada to establish
     permanent residence.

4)   The foreign national is a person in respect of whom there is no
     reasonable prospect, within a reasonable period, of a durable
     solution in a country other than Canada, namely,

     a)   voluntary repatriation or resettlement in the country of na-
          tionality or habitual residence, or

     b)   resettlement or an offer of resettlement in another country.

5)   The foreign national is a member of one of the classes prescribed.

6)   One of the following is the case:

     a)   A sponsor has been approved.

     b)   Financial assistance in the form of funds from a governmental
          resettlement assistance program is available in Canada.[14]

     c)   The foreign national has sufficient financial resources to
          provide for the lodging, care, and maintenance.

7)   The foreign national (and family members included in the appli-
     cation) for protection will be able to become successfully estab-
     lished in Canada, taking into account

     a)   their resourcefulness and other similar qualities that assist
          in integration in a new society,

     b)   the presence of their relatives, including the relatives of a
          spouse or a common law partner, or their sponsor in the
          expected community of resettlement,

     c)   their potential for employment in Canada, given their edu-
          cation, work experience, and skills, and

     d)   their ability to learn to communicate in one of the official
          languages of Canada.

8)   The foreign national and family members included in the appli-
     cation for protection are not inadmissible.[15]

The rules of inadmissibility are relaxed somewhat for applicants
in this stream.[16] For example, section 22 of the *Regulations* provides
an exemption from the misrepresentation provisions of the *IRPA*.[17] As
well, an applicant will not be excluded on the ground that he might reasonably be expected to cause excessive demand on health or social ser-

---

14   The option of government assistance is available only to one class of applicant:
     the Convention refugee class. See note 19, below in this chapter.

15   *Regulations*, above note 12, s 158.

16   For more information on inadmissibility, see Chapter 14.

17   *Regulations*, above note 12, s 22.

vices.[18] Since other grounds of inadmissibility do apply, applicants are subjected to medical examinations and criminal and security checks.

The *Regulations* also provide that a person may apply as a member of one of two classes: (1) the Convention refugees abroad class;[19] and (2) the country of asylum class. This latter class is a subclass of the more general humanitarian-protected persons abroad class. It is, however, the only subclass that has endured.[20]

A foreign national is a member of the Convention refugees abroad class if she has been determined, outside Canada, by an officer, to be a Convention refugee.[21] The country of asylum class includes persons who have been determined to be in need of resettlement because they are

1) outside their country or countries of citizenship or habitual residence;[22] and
2) have been and continue to be seriously and personally affected by civil war or armed conflict or massive violations of human rights in these countries.[23]

A person will be considered under either class only if she has been referred by the UNHCR or another designated organization, or has a private sponsor. The minister of Citizenship and Immigration may dispense with a referral where circumstances demand in particular geographical areas.[24] Officers at a Canadian visa office assess whether a person is a member of one of the two classes and meets the criteria by conducting interviews; reviewing supporting documentation; reviewing medical, security, and admissibility examinations; and determining whether the refugee has the ability to establish himself successfully in Canada.[25]

3) Exceptional Cases

The *Regulations* specify that where applicants are identified as "vulnerable" or "in urgent need of protection," the likelihood that they will establish themselves will not be used as a criterion of assessment.

---

18   *IRPA*, above note 6, s 38(1)(c).
19   *Ibid*, ss 144–45: This class must meet the requirements under the *IRPA*, s 96.
20   *Ibid*, s 146.
21   See *Regulations*, above note 12, s 145. The definition of Convention refugee will be discussed in Chapter 9.
22   *Ibid*, s 147(a).
23   *Ibid*, s 147(b).
24   *Ibid*, ss 140.3(2)–(3)
25   *IRPA*, above note 6, s 15; *Regulations*, above note 12, s 139.

Vulnerable is defined to mean a "person [who] has a greater need of protection than other applicants for protection abroad because of the person's particular circumstances that give rise to a heightened risk to their physical safety."[26] *Urgent need of protection* is defined to mean that the person's "life, liberty or physical safety is under immediate threat and, if not protected, the person is likely to be killed; subjected to violence, torture, sexual assault or arbitrary imprisonment; or returned to their country of nationality or of their former habitual residence."[27]

In addition, some individuals will be earmarked for special assistance when they arrive in Canada: these include survivors of torture who may be processed under the joint assistance sponsorship program,[28] children,[29] the elderly[30] and women covered by the women at risk program established to benefit "women who do not have the normal protection of a family unit and who find themselves in precarious situations where the local authorities cannot ensure their safety."[31]

4) Emergency Cases

Where the UNHCR has identified a case as urgent, the regulations allow for the normal processing to be bypassed. The individual in question may be issued a temporary resident permit (TRP) and may travel to Canada immediately.[32] As a member of the protected temporary resident class, the individual may then apply for permanent status from within Canada.

5) Family Members

As with other immigration streams, applicants in this stream may include family members in their application. However, a special provision applies: the one-year window. As explained by Citizenship and Immigration Canada:

> Under the one-year window of opportunity provision (OYW), non-accompanying family members (following family members) may be

---

26   *Ibid*, s 138.

27   *Ibid*.

28   See Section B(8)(d), below in this chapter.

29   *UNHCR Resettlement Handbook, Canada Chapter*, above note 7, s 8.4.

30   *Ibid*, s 8.5.

31   Citizenship and Immigration Canada, "Guide to Private Sponsorship of Refugees Program" (7 January 2015), online: CIC www.cic.gc.ca/english/pdf/pub/ref-sponsor.pdf at 28 [CIC, "Private Sponsorship"].

32   *Regulations*, above note 12, s 151.1. For more information on TRPs, see Chapter 4.

eligible to be processed in the same class as the principal applicant for a period of one year following the confirmation of permanent residence of the principal applicant in Canada. All family members must be identified on the principal applicant's application form to be eligible for OYW processing.[33]

In other words, where an applicant has identified dependants on the application form, those persons who may have been separated from the applicant by turmoil have one year to apply under the same category, even though they are not accompanying the applicant.[34] In addition it seems that there is a certain laxity about who counts as a dependant. Under the heading "De facto dependants," the operational manual provides:

> *De facto* dependants (who may or may not be blood relatives) do not meet the definition of family members. The officer must be satisfied that these persons are dependent on the family unit in which membership is claimed and cannot apply as a family member. The dependency may be emotional or economic and will often be a combination of these factors. Such persons would normally, but not exclusively, reside with the Principal Applicant (PA) as members of the same household. They must be the dependants of a PA who has been determined to be a member of one of the three refugee classes. The *de facto* dependant must also meet the definition of refugee in his own right even when a dependency relationship is established. Persons who form part of the family unit should be examined sympathetically. This is consistent with efforts to keep family units together if at all possible. If the de facto relationship cannot be established, then the refugee must be assessed in his/her own right as a refugee and, failing that, could be considered under H&C grounds.[35]

33 Citizenship and Immigration Canada, "Procedure: One-Year Window of Opportunity Provision (OYW)" (18 August 2014), online: CIC www.cic.gc.ca/english/resources/tools/refugees/resettlement/processing/OYW.asp.

34 Citizenship and Immigration Canada, "Procedure: One-Year Window of Opportunity Provision" (18 August 2014), online: CIC www.cic.gc.ca/english/resources/tools/refugees/resettlement/processing/OYW.asp.

35 Citizenship and Immigration Canada, Operational Manual IP 3: *In Canada Processing of Convention Refugees Abroad and Members of the Humanitarian Protected Person Abroad Classes*, online: CIC www.cic.gc.ca/english/resources/manuals/ip/ip03-part1-eng.pdf.

6) Settlement Assistance

The resettlement program has two main streams: (1) the government-assisted refugees (GAR) program; and (2) private sponsorship of refugees.[36] The second of these provides for a number of types of partnerships of private and state resources and efforts.[37] Two distinct assessments are required before an individual may be admitted under the private sponsorship stream: (1) in-Canada processing of the sponsor(s); and (2) overseas screening and selecting of the sponsored refugees. For those being resettled in Quebec, different rules and regulations apply.[38]

a) Resettlement Assistance Program (RAP) Available to Government-Assisted Refugees

Under the Refugee Assistance Program (RAP), government-assisted refugees, or GARs, are supported financially at social assistance levels for a period of up to twelve months.[39] Government-assisted refugees are members of the Convention refugees abroad class who have been referred by the UNHCR or a foreign state.[40] The minister of Citizenship and Immigration sets an annual target for individuals who are eligible to receive financial aid.[41] In 2013, 5,756 refugees were government assisted. This number was below the targeted range of 6,800 to 7,100.[42]

Temporary accommodation is provided as is help in finding permanent accommodation.[43] The federal government administers an immigration loans program to help government-assisted refugees to cover the costs of medical examinations abroad, travel documents, and transportation to Canada.[44] Loans are also made available for covering the costs of housing, telephone deposits, and work tools.[45]

---

36   *IRPA*, above note 6, s 13(1).
37   *Ibid.*
38   *Regulations*, above note 12, s 158.
39   *UNHCR Resettlement Handbook, Canada Chapter*, above note 7.
40   Citizenship and Immigration Canada, *Assistance Available for Refugees* (25 February 2013), online: CIC www.cic.gc.ca/english/resources/tools/refugees/support/index.asp.
41   *UNHCR Resettlement Handbook, Canada Chapter*, above note 7 at 6: "The target refers to individuals and not cases, and operates on a calendar year."
42   Citizenship and Immigration Canada, *Annual Report to Parliament on Immigration 2014*, online: CIC www.cic.gc.ca/english/resources/publications/annual-report-2014/index.asp#sec-2-1.
43   Citizenship and Immigration Canada, "Financial Assistance – Refugees: Resettlement Assistance Program," online: CIC www.cic.gc.ca/english/refugees/outside/resettle-assist.asp [CIC, "Financial Assistance"].
44   *Ibid.*
45   *Ibid.*

b) Private Sponsorship of Refugees

The private sponsorship of refugees program enables organizations and private individuals to facilitate the resettlement of Convention refugees and members of the country of asylum class to Canada.[46] Organizations and private individuals enter into sponsorship agreements with the federal government[47] and submit an undertaking[48] that they will be responsible for providing financial assistance and other integration assistance to the sponsored refugee for a period of twelve months or until the refugee becomes self-sufficient, whichever comes first.[49] In some cases, the period may last up to thirty-six months.[50] Sponsors agree to support the sponsored refugees by giving support in various ways, including providing cost of food, rent, utilities, and other day-to-day living expenses; providing clothing, furniture, and other household goods; locating interpreters; selecting a family physician and dentist; assisting with applying for provincial health-care coverage; enrolling children in school and adults in language training; introducing the refugees to people with similar personal interests; providing orientation with regard to banking, transportation, and so on; and helping in the search for employment.[51] It is expected that sponsors provide the equivalent of social assistance.[52] Sponsorship kits include a table to allow potential sponsors to make an estimate of the costs.[53] A sponsor's responsibility extends to an entire refugee family; it is not restricted to the principal applicant, regardless of when the principal applicant's family arrives in Canada.[54]

The federal government also provides an immigration loans program to assist privately sponsored refugees to cover the costs of medical examinations abroad, travel documents, and transportation to Canada.[55] Loans

---

46 *IRPA*, above note 6, s 13(1); *Regulations*, above note 12, ss 144–47; *UNHCR Resettlement Handbook, Canada Chapter*, above note 7 at 3.

47 *Regulations*, above note 12, s 152.

48 *Ibid*, s 138: "*undertaking* means an undertaking in writing to the minister to provide resettlement assistance, lodging, and other basic necessities in Canada for a member of a class prescribed by this Division, the member's accompanying family members, and any of the member's non-accompanying family members who meet the requirements of s 141, for the period determined in accordance with ss 154(2) and (3)."

49 *IRPA*, above note 6, ss 13.1–13.2; *Regulations*, above note 12, ss 153–54; *UNHCR Resettlement Handbook, Canada Chapter*, above note 7 at 6.

50 *Regulations*, above note 12, ss 153–54.

51 *Ibid*, ss 152–54; CIC, "Private Sponsorship," above note 31, s 2.6.

52 *Ibid*.

53 *Ibid*, s 2.7.

54 *Regulations*, above note 12, s 140.

55 CIC, "Financial Assistance," above note 43.

are also available for covering the costs of rental housing, telephone deposits, and work tools.[56] In 2013, the target for privately sponsored refugees was between 4,500 and 6,500.[57] Citizenship and Immigration Canada claims that 6,277 were admitted.

7) Eligibility to Sponsor

According to the *Regulations*, *sponsor* means (a) a group, a corporation, or an unincorporated organization or association referred to in section 13(2) of the Act, or any combination of them, that is acting for the purpose of sponsoring a Convention refugee or a person in similar circumstances; or (b) for the purposes of section 158, a sponsor within the meaning of the regulations made under *An Act respecting immigration to Québec*.[58] Section 153 of the *Regulations* imposes the requirements that a sponsor

(a)   must reside or have representatives in the expected community of settlement;

(b)   must make a sponsorship application that includes a settlement plan, an undertaking, and, if the sponsor has not entered into a sponsorship agreement with the Minister, a document issued by the UNHCR or a foreign state certifying the status of the foreign national as a refugee; and

(c)   must not be — or include — an individual, a corporation, or an unincorporated organization or association that was a party to a sponsorship in which they defaulted on an undertaking and remain in default.[59]

Those that are ineligible include

1)   persons convicted in Canada of the offence of murder or other listed offences, and a period of five years has not elapsed since the completion of the sentence imposed under the *Criminal Code of Canada*;[60]

2)   persons convicted of an offence outside of Canada that, if committed in Canada, would constitute an offence in (1);[61]

3)   persons subject to a removal order;[62]

---

56   *Ibid*.
57   *UNHCR Resettlement Handbook, Canada Chapter*, above note 7 at 6.
58   *IRPA*, above note 6, s 13(2); *Regulations*, above note 12, s 138.
59   *Ibid*, s 153(1).
60   *Ibid*, ss 156(1)(a)–(b) and (2).
61   *Ibid*, s 156(1)(b).
62   *Ibid*, s 156(1)(d).

4) persons subject to revocation proceedings under the *Citizenship Act*;[63]

5) persons detained in any penitentiary, jail, reformatory, or prison;[64] and

6) persons in default of any court-ordered support payments.[65]

8) Sponsors

Five types of private sponsorship are recognized: (a) sponsorship by sponsorship agreement holders (SAH); (b) community sponsorship; (c) sponsorship by a group of five Canadian citizens or permanent residents (Group of Five); (d) the joint assistance sponsorship program; and (e) the blended visa office-referred program.

a) Sponsorship Agreement Holders (SAH)

Sponsorship agreement holders (SAH) are incorporated organizations that have signed general sponsorship agreements with the government of Canada to help support refugees from abroad resettle in Canada.[66] Such an organization may work independently or may enter into partnerships with other community groups to sponsor refugees.[67] It assumes full responsibility for administration and management, and although it may be a national organization, it must be located in the community where the refugee and his family are expected to resettle.[68] An SAH may sponsor individuals that other groups may not. For example, other sponsors are limited to sponsoring individuals who have been identified as refugees by the UNHCR or a foreign state. Since an SAH is not so restricted, it can nominate an individual who may fit within the country of asylum class.

---

63   *Ibid*, s 156(1)(e).

64   *Ibid*, s 156(1)(f).

65   *Ibid*, s 156(1)(c).

66   *Ibid*, s 152; Citizenship and Immigration Canada, "Sponsorship Agreement Holders – Sponsoring Refugees" (11 February 2014), online: CIC www.cic.gc.ca/english/refugees/sponsor/sah.asp: "Most sponsorship agreement holders are religious, ethnic, community or service organizations" and are incorporated entities that are local, regional, or national organizations.

67   Citizenship and Immigration Canada, "Determine Your Eligibility – Sponsorship Agreement Holders" (11 October 2012), online: CIC www.cic.gc.ca/english/refugees/sponsor/sah-who.asp: "A SAH can authorize other groups in the community to sponsor refugees under its agreement. These groups are known as 'constituent groups' . . . . A SAH can also form a partnership with an individual or other organization. These are known as co-sponsors. The co-sponsor must agree to help deliver settlement assistance and share the responsibility for supporting the sponsored refugees."

68   *Ibid*; *Regulations*, above note 12, s 153(1)(a).

b) Community Sponsors

A community sponsor[69] is an organization or association that need not be incorporated. It must be located in the community where the refugees are expected to settle.[70] It can form partnerships with individuals or other organizations to help deliver settlement assistance and share responsibility for supporting a sponsored refugee.[71] Since the community sponsor must select an individual identified as a refugee by the UNHCR or a foreign state, its power to nominate an individual refugee will be limited. Moreover, unless the UNHCR refers an individual who falls outside the Convention refugee definition, the community sponsor will be unable to nominate a member of the asylum class (which is not recognized outside Canada).

c) Groups of Five

Group of Five sponsorship involves five or more Canadian citizens or permanent residents who have arranged to sponsor a refugee living abroad to come to Canada.[72] All group members must be eighteen years of age or older and live in the representative area where the refugee will settle. As with community sponsorship, the Group of Five must agree to give emotional and financial support to the refugee and her family for the full sponsorship period.[73] Like the community sponsor, a Group of Five can sponsor only refugees who are recognized as refugees by either the UNHCR or a foreign state.[74]

d) Joint Assistance Sponsorship (JAS)

Citizenship and Immigration Canada sometimes partners with organizations to resettle refugees with special needs under a program called "Joint Assistance Sponsorship."[75] JAS aims to provide assistance to refugees who may need more support due to trauma from violence or

---

69 Citizenship and Immigration Canada, "Determine Your Eligibility – Community Sponsors" (20 May 2014), online: CIC www.cic.gc.ca/english/refugees/ sponsor/community-who.asp [CIC, "Community Sponsors"]: "The organization, association or corporation does not have to be incorporated under federal or provincial law."

70 *Regulations*, above note 12, s 153(1)(a).

71 CIC, "Community Sponsors," above note 69: Individuals or other organizations who partner with a community sponsor are known as co-sponsors.

72 Citizenship and Immigration Canada, "Groups of Five – Sponsoring Refugees" (20 May 2014), online: CIC www.cic.gc.ca/english/refugees/sponsor/groups.asp.

73 *Ibid.*

74 *Ibid.*

75 Citizenship and Immigration Canada, "Joint Assistance Program — Sponsoring Refugees with Special Needs" (20 May 2014), online: CIC www.cic.gc.ca/ english/refugees/sponsor/jas.asp. For example, recently, the government has allocated funds and extended a pilot project involving Rainbow Refugee Canada

torture, medical disabilities, the effects of systemic discrimination, or having many family members.[76] Under this program, refugees receive support for between twenty-four and thirty-six months depending on needs.

e) Blended Visa Office-Referred Program

Finally, the federal government, in 2013, launched the blended visa office-referred program.[77] This program is designed to match refugees identified by the UNHCR with private sponsors in Canada. In this program, the federal government provides six months of income support through the resettlement assistance program, with private sponsors providing another six months of financial support and one year of social and emotional support.[78]

9) Process: The Visa Officer's Decision

Visa officers are tasked with interviewing and assessing whether persons are eligible for a permanent resident visa.[79] If a visa officer deems that an applicant is not eligible for resettlement in Canada, this decision may be judicially reviewed at the Federal Court of Canada.[80] Among other things, the applicant can ask the court to review whether an officer properly considered documentary evidence, whether the officer considered relevant or irrelevant considerations (including the fact that the applicant has status as a UNHCR refugee),[81] whether the officer properly considered all grounds/classes that the applicant could be subject to, whether there were any breaches in procedural fairness during the interview or decision-making process, or whether findings of credibility were unreasonable.[82] Further, a visa officer's decision may

---

to assist with the sponsorship of LGBT asylum seekers outside of Canada. See Rainbow Refugee Canada, online: www.rainbowrefugee.ca.

76   *Ibid*; *Regulations*, above note 12, s 157.

77   Citizenship and Immigration Canada, "Blended Visa Office-Referred Program – Sponsoring Refugees" (30 April 2014), online: CIC www.cic.gc.ca/english/ refugees/sponsor/vor.asp: The government pledged to match 200 Iraqi, Iranian, Burmese, Eritrean, and Bhutanese refugees with interested sponsors in 2013.

78   *Ibid*.

79   *Regulations*, above note 12, s 139.

80   *IRPA*, above note 6, s 72(1). See Chapter 16 for more information on judicial review.

81   *Ghirmatsion v Canada (Minister of Citizenship and Immigration)*, 2011 FC 519 [*Ghirmatsion*]; *Kidane v Canada (Minister of Citizenship and Immigration)*, 2011 FC 520 [*Kidane*]; *Weldesillassie v Canada (Minister of Citizenship and Immigration)*, 2011 FC 521 [*Weldesillassie*].

82   *Ghirmatsion*, above note 81; *Kidane*, above note 81; *Weldesillassie*, above note 81; *Muhazi v Canada (Minister of Citizenship and Immigration)*, 2004 FC 1392

be judicially reviewed on the basis that the officer did not consider the proper class into which the applicant falls. As the Federal Court has stated:

> Refugee protection for persons abroad is however wider than that set out in section 96 of the Act. Indeed, the humanitarian-protected persons abroad classes include the country of asylum class . . . . [F]oreign nationals who are not Convention refugees may nevertheless be extended protection if they meet the criteria for membership in the country of asylum class . . . .
>
> Members of the country of asylum class . . . need not demonstrate a well-founded fear of persecution for reasons of race, religion, nationality, membership in a particular social group or political opinion. Rather, they must demonstrate that they are displaced outside of their country of nationality and habitual residence and have been and continue to be seriously affected by civil war, armed conflict or massive violations of civil rights, and that there is no reasonable prospect within a reasonable period of a durable solution elsewhere for them.[83]

C. CONCLUSION: CANADA'S DIMINISHING ROLE IN OVERSEAS REFUGEE PROTECTION

The recent conflict in Syria provides an illustration of the shift in Canada's approach to responding to the plight of refugees overseas. Millions of people from Syria have been displaced both within Syria and in neighbouring countries. The UNHCR reports that almost one-third of Syria's pre-conflict population is uprooted.[84] Canada's response has been min-

---

at para 21: Among the procedural fairness issues, the court identified the consideration of extrinsic evidence without giving the applicant an opportunity to respond to the evidence; see also the following examples: *Mushimiyimana v Canada (Minister of Citizenship and Immigration)*, 2010 FC 1124; *Rudi v Canada (Minister of Citizenship and Immigration)*, 2003 FC 957; *Mezbani v Canada (Minister of Citizenship and Immigration)*, 2012 FC 1115, where the court found that the findings of credibility were not reasonable; *Asl v Canada (Minister of Citizenship and Immigration)*, 2007 FC 459, where the court held that the visa officer ignored evidence.

83 *Saifee v Canada (Minister of Citizenship and Immigration)*, 2010 FC 589 at paras 38–39; see also *Faizy v Canada (Minister of Citizenship and Immigration)*, 2012 FC 961.

84 UN High Commissioner for Refugees, "Countries Hosting Syrian Refugees: Solidarity and Burden-Sharing" (September 2013), online: UNHCR www.unhcr. org/525fe3e59.pdf at 2.

imal. It has done extremely little to assist the three million registered Syrian refugees, half of which are children, to find a safe haven.[85] While Canada has promised significant financial contributions for international humanitarian assistance efforts in Syria and neighbouring countries,[86] the immigration response has been both unexpected and shocking given Canada's capacity to supply the needed help and also its long history of providing a safe haven to those most in need. In July 2013, the government announced a commitment to resettle only 1,300 refugees from Syria by the end of 2014. Of this total, 200 places are made through the GAR program while the remaining 1,100 are to be processed through private sponsorship. Organizations that frequently privately sponsor refugees were not consulted before the Canadian government announced their official response to the Syrian refugee crisis.[87] Following the first eight months of 2013, only nine Syrians were resettled by the government to Canada.[88] As of July 2014, only 177 Syrian refugees had come to Canada under the GAR program, and 108 had arrived through private sponsorship.[89] Further, processing times at visa offices in proximity to Syria range from twenty-one to forty months.[90] Despite efforts to speed up the processing of refugee applications, the government has not acceded to calls to increase the commitment to allow greater numbers of refugees to be resettled in Canada.[91]

Canada's response to the Syrian refugee crisis is indicative of two things. First, Canada is placing more emphasis on providing overseas support for refugees rather than resettlement or inland protection to those who have been able to make their way to Canada. Former minister of Citizenship and Immigration Canada Jason Kenney has stated: "You cannot solve a refugee crisis involving millions of people by just

---

85 OXFAM Canada, "Syrian Refugee Crisis" (September 2014), online: OXFAM Canada www.oxfam.ca/our-work/emergencies/syrian-refugee-crisis.

86 Canadian Council for Refugees, "Canadian Immigration Responses to the Syrian Crisis – Backgrounder" (October 2013), online: CCR ccrweb.ca/en/syrian-crisis-backgrounder: Canada has promised $203.5 million since January 2012 for international humanitarian assistance efforts in Syria and neighbouring countries and $110 million to support development projects in Jordan and Lebanon.

87 Ibid.

88 Ibid.

89 Steven Chase, "Canada to Boost Efforts to Help Syrian Refugees" The Globe and Mail (4 July 2014), online: www.theglobeandmail.com.

90 Ibid; Laura Lynch, "Syrian Refugee Applications Quietly Sped Up by Ottawa" CBC News (27 June 2014), online: www.cbc.ca. Following media scrutiny, processing of Syrian refugee applications was quietly sped up.

91 Ibid.

seeking to airlift them to a handful of developed countries. That is completely unrealistic and, in fact, is not a long-term solution."[92] The new Canadian approach is an arm's length approach whereby money is sent to strengthen the UN's global resettlement capacity and to provide aid to the surrounding region.[93]

Second, it is clear that the government has abandoned the deeply entrenched humanitarianism of past decades. The current response is significantly different from Canada's responses to past refugee crises when, for example, it accepted 60,000 Vietnamese, Cambodian, and Laotian refugees, 18,000 Iraqis, or 3,300 Haitians.[94]

History will be the judge of Canada's refugee protection record. The current approach will challenge Canada's reputation as a country built not only on immigration, but also upon a humanitarian approach to refugees.

---

92   Dean Bennett, "Jason Kenney: Canada to Resettle 1,300 Syrian Refugees by End of 2014" *Canadian Press* (3 July 2013), online: www.huffingtonpost.ca.
93   *Ibid.*
94   *Ibid.* "Canada Must Give More Syrian Refugees Safe Haven: Editorial" *Toronto Star* (23 September 2014), online: www.thestar.com.

CHAPTER 9

THE REFUGEE DETERMINATION PROCESS IN CANADA

A. THE REFUGEE HEARING

1) *Singh* and the Right to an Oral Hearing

Canada has held oral refugee hearings since the seminal case of *Singh v Canada (Minister of Employment and Immigration)* in 1985. In *Singh*, the Supreme Court of Canada held that "where a serious issue of credibility is involved, fundamental justice requires that credibility be determined on the basis of an oral hearing" and that it would be difficult to "conceive of a situation in which compliance with fundamental justice could be achieved by a tribunal making significant findings of credibility solely on the basis of written submissions."[1] The *Singh* case prompted the Canadian government to pass legislation in 1985 and 1987, providing oral hearings, among other procedural safeguards, to refugee claimants.[2] Shortly after, in 1989, the independent Convention Refugee Determination Division (CRDD) of the Immigration and Refugee Board (IRB) was established. Its sole function was to determine whether a claimant was a Convention refugee,[3] a decision made after an oral hearing.

---

1   [1985] 1 SCR 177 at para 59 [*Singh*].
2   Ninette Kelley & Michael Trebilcock, *The Making of the Mosaic: A History of Canadian Immigration Policy*, 2d ed (Toronto: University of Toronto Press, 2010) at 403.
3   See Chapter 10 on what it means to be a Convention refugee.

2) Reforming the Process

In 2001, the newly renamed Refugee Protection Division (RPD) of the IRB was given a broader mandate. Not only was it authorized to determine whether a claimant was a Convention refugee under section 96 of the *Immigration and Refugee Protection Act* (*IRPA*), it was also authorized to determine whether the claimant was in need of protection on other consolidated grounds identified in section 97 of the *IRPA*.[4]

As of 15 December 2012, the refugee determination process was again modified dramatically. The Canadian government's reform of the refugee determination system has taken inspiration from a policy paper published by the Fraser Institute[5] which identified a number of "dysfunctional" aspects of the system then in operation and proposed remedies, many of which have now been adopted.

The following section reviews how the process now operates, discusses the various categories under which refugee claimants may fall, and describes the associated procedures they must follow.

3) An Overview of Canada's Inland Refugee Determination System

Figure 9.1   The Process of Refugee Determination

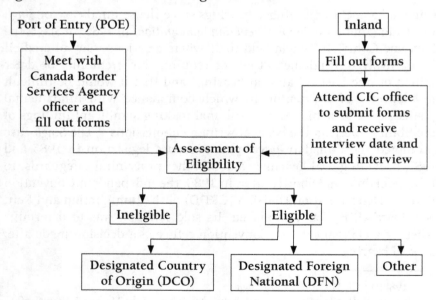

---

4   *Immigration and Refugee Protection Act*, SC 2001, c 27 [*IRPA*].
5   Stephen Gallagher, "Canada's Dysfunctional Refugee Determination System: Canadian Asylum Policy from a Comparative Perspective" (2003) 78 *Public Policy Sources* (A Fraser Institute Occasional Paper).

a) Making the Claim

As Figure 9.1 illustrates, the initial steps in the process of assessing a refugee claim differ slightly depending on whether the person making the claim has appeared at a port of entry (airport, land border, or seaport), or has initiated the claim after having been admitted into Canada.

i) Port of Entry (POE)

Where a claimant has arrived at a port of entry, a Canada Border Services Agency (CBSA) officer will conduct an assessment to determine whether the claimant is eligible to present a claim to the IRB's Refugee Protection Division.[6] A claimant will be asked to provide information for the assessment and, if found eligible, will be asked to submit further forms within a set time limit.[7] For example, those who wish to pursue a claim are required to submit a Basis of Claim (BOC) form within fifteen days of receiving the forms.[8]

ii) Inland

A person may have entered Canada without making a claim for protection[9] but may subsequently decide to do so. In such cases, a person needs to obtain the requisite forms from an office of Citizenship and Immigration Canada and return the completed forms to the CIC office, which will then schedule a date for the eligibility interview and assessment.[10]

b) Interviewing and Obtaining Information from a Client

Refugee claimants may approach their first meeting with a lawyer with some trepidation. Many have never interacted with a lawyer in their own country, let alone in Canada. Claimants may have recently arrived in Canada and may be dealing with culture shock or the stress of finding shelter and other amenities for their family. Some may have survived arrest, detention, separation from family, loss of a job and

---

6   IRPA, above note 4, ss 99(1)(3) and 100.

7   The forms the person will be asked to complete are IMM 0008, Schedule A (Background/Declaration), and Schedule 12 (Additional Information – Refugee Claimants inside Canada).

8   *Immigration and Refugee Protection Regulations*, SOR/2002-227, s 159.8(2) [*Regulations*].

9   IRPA, above note 4, s 99(1)(3.1).

10   IRPA, *ibid*, ss 100–101; *Regulations*, above note 8, s 159.8(1); *Refugee Protection Division Rules made under the Immigration and Refugee Protection Act*, SOR/2012-256, s 7 [*RPD Rules*]: The forms the person will be required to fill out include IMM 0008, Schedule A, Schedule 12 (Additional Information – Refugee Claimants inside Canada), and the Basis of Claim (BOC).

status, torture, and other trauma. For these reasons, in spite of the limited time claimants have to complete and submit the BOC form, if circumstances allow, counsel may decide to approach the task slowly. At a first meeting with a claimant, it may be advisable to go over easy background information, such as the claimant's date of birth, place of birth, citizenship, the date on which the claimant left her country and entered Canada, and the names of family members in Canada and abroad. As well, counsel may ask for a very general account of the reasons the claimant left her country or why she is afraid to return. At this point, details need not be specifically requested. During this first meeting, it may be apt to explain the refugee determination process and to ask the claimant if she has any questions. At the end of the meeting, the lawyer will want to confirm the due date for the BOC form, and some may want to verify this with Citizenship and Immigration Canada.

During a second meeting, counsel may begin filling in the BOC form, including the background information. While this may seem mundane, it is recommended that counsel go over every question in the form to ensure that the answer is accurate. Sometimes, claimants may have already completed the background portion of the BOC with the assistance of an interpreter, settlement worker, family member, or friend. In such cases, it is imperative that every answer is reviewed with the claimant.

Counsel will then need to obtain information required for the narrative part of the BOC form. While a claimant may have previously prepared a written narrative, it is beneficial to obtain the information through a question-and-answer interview to ensure that only information from the claimant is being provided rather than information supplied by someone helping to author or contribute to the narrative's content. If the claimant has difficulty answering questions, it may be an early sign of vulnerability or of other problems that the claimant is facing and these may need to be addressed before the hearing at the Refugee Protection Division.

It is beneficial to revisit as early as possible the claimant's personal history and to work chronologically to the present. It is important to ask about the claimant's mode of arrival in Canada and the measures that the claimant had to take to succeed. While being sensitive to the claimant's cultural background and the difficulty she may have in recounting certain parts of her story, it is valuable to obtain as much detail as possible. Although a sensitive and supportive approach is appropriate, pointing out any apparent contradictions, discrepancies, or factors that do not make sense or that sound incredible or difficult to believe is also important. Counsel has the opportunity to clarify the claimant's narrative, but also to identify issues that a board member may raise at the hearing. In some cases, where the story appears inconsistent, unclear, or improbable, there may be a perfectly logical explanation or a claimant may simply be exaggerating.

While opinions may differ, it can be beneficial for the claimant to disclose as much detail as possible about traumatic events such as rape and torture. Such detail enhances the narrative and also, in some cases, the board member will not require the claimant to repeat such information at the hearing if the narrative adequately describes a particularly sensitive subject.

Counsel can be creative in their approach to filling out the BOC. Sometimes, a claimant may find it comforting to have a friend or family member or counsellor present during the preparation. Sometimes, a claimant will want to prepare his narrative in advance and then it can be used as a stepping-stone for questioning. Whatever the process, counsel should draft the narrative, which is the most important part of the BOC. A well-written, persuasive account of what led the claimant to seek refugee status in Canada will create a positive impression.

c) Assessment of Eligibility

Claimants are ineligible to pursue a claim in a number of circumstances:[11]

1) where they have made a previous claim in Canada;[12]
2) where they already have been granted refugee status in Canada or another country;[13]
3) where they have arrived in Canada directly from a country designated as safe;[14]
4) where they are inadmissible on security or certain criminality grounds.[15]

d) Following a Finding of Eligibility

If found eligible to make a claim, the claimant will be provided an identity document, a date for a hearing at the RPD,[16] and a removal order (in most circumstances, a departure order), which will come

---

11   *IRPA*, above note 4, ss 100–101. Note that a claim's eligibility has to be determined within three days of receiving the claim unless there are reasons to suspend the consideration of eligibility.
12   *Ibid*, ss 101(1)(b) & (c).
13   *Ibid*, s 101(1)(a)
14   *Ibid*, s 101(1)(e). To this point only the United States has been so designated.
15   *Ibid*, s 101(1)(f).
16   *Ibid*, s 100(4.1).

into effect should the claim not be accepted and can be converted to a deportation order should the claimant fail to leave Canada by the end of the period authorized.[17]

Where a POE claimant fails to submit a BOC within fifteen days, an abandonment hearing will be scheduled five days after the date the BOC form was due to be submitted.[18]

The refugee determination process differs significantly for claimants who belong in different categories. Each category is discussed below.

e)   Claimants from Safe Third Countries

i)   What Is a "Safe Third Country"?

As explained in Chapter 2, the minister of Citizenship and Immigration, with the approval of the Governor in Council, may enter into an agreement with another state to facilitate and implement programs pursuant to the *IRPA*.[19] Section 102(2) of the *IRPA* provides a list of factors that may be considered in designating a country as a "safe third country":

(a)   whether the country is a party to the Refugee Convention and to the Convention Against Torture;

(b)   its policies and practices with respect to claims under the *Refugee Convention* and with respect to obligations under the *Convention Against Torture*;

(c)   its human rights record; and

---

17   *Regulations*, above note 8, ss 228(1)(c) and (3). See Citizenship and Immigration Canada, Operational Bulletin 440-G: *Processing of Refugee Claims by CIC under the New Legislation* (17 April 2013), online: CIC www.cic.gc.ca/english/resources/manuals/bulletins/2013/ob440G.asp.

18   See *IRPA*, above note 4, s 168; *RPD Rules*, above note 10, s 65(2). For more information on abandonment hearings, see Section A(3)(j)(i), below in this chapter.

19   *IRPA*, above note 4, ss 7 and 102. Section 102(2)(e) specifies the need for an agreement in designating a country as a safe third country. See *Regulations*, above note 8, s 159.3, which designates the United States as a "country that complies with Article 33 of the *Refugee Convention* and Article 3 of the *Convention against Torture*, and is a designated country" under the safe third country regime.

See the *Convention relating to the Status of Refugees*, 28 July 1951, 189 UNTS 137 (entered into force 22 April 1954) [*Refugee Convention*]; and *Convention against Torture and Other Cruel, Inhuman or Degrading Treatment or Punishment*, 10 December 1984, Can TS 1987 No 36, 23 ILM 1027 [*Convention against Torture*].

(d) whether it is party to an agreement with the Government of Canada for the purpose of sharing responsibility with respect to claims for refugee protection.

On 5 December 2002, Canada entered into an agreement with the United States known as the *Canada-US Safe Third Country Agreement*.[20] The agreement came into effect on 24 December 2009.[21]

The essence of the agreement is that Canada recognizes the United States as "safe," and the United States recognizes Canada as "safe" for refugee claimants. This recognition of a "safe" country raises the expectation that refugee claimants should make their claim in the first "safe" country they reach. Thus, those that may have either transited or sojourned in the United States, for example, are expected to make a refugee claim in the United States first, rather than come to Canada at a later date to make a refugee claim. The agreement renders those who have spent time in the "safe" country (i.e. the United States) ineligible to make a refugee claim in the other "safe" country (i.e. Canada).[22]

There are exceptions to the general rule that a claim be made in the first safe country provided in the *Regulations*. First, the agreement generally applies only to those entering at a land port of entry.[23] Thus, those coming by air or sea are not subject to the *Safe Third Country Agreement*. Second, the agreement does not apply to those without a family member[24] in Canada.[25] Third, unaccompanied minors whose parents are not in the United States or Canada are not subject to this

---

20   US Department of State, *US-Canada Agreement Covering Third-Country Asylum Claims at the Border* (5 December 2002), online: United States Government www.state.gov/s/l/38616.htm [*Safe Third Country Agreement*].

21   Citizenship and Immigration Canada, "Canada-US Safe Third Country Agreement" (25 February 2015), online: CIC www.cic.gc.ca/english/department/laws-policy/menu-safethird.asp.

22   *IRPA*, above note 4, s 101(1)(e).

23   *Regulations*, above note 8, s 159.4(1). See, however, s 159.4(2), which provides that the agreement does apply to those coming by air if the person seeking refugee protection in Canada is a person who was determined not to be a refugee in the United States, has been ordered deported from the United States, and is in transit through Canada for removal from the United States.

24   *Ibid*, s 159.1. *Family member*, "in respect of a claimant, means their spouse or common-law partner, their legal guardian, and any of the following persons, namely, their child, father, mother, brother, sister, grandfather, grandmother, grandchild, uncle, aunt, nephew or niece."

25   *Ibid*, s 159.5. The family member must be a Canadian citizen (s 159.5(a)), a protected person under s 95(2) of the *IRPA* (s 159.5(b)(i)), a permanent resident (s 159.5(b)(ii)), a person subject to a removal order but that removal order has been stayed (s 159.5(b)(iii)), a person eighteen years or older who has made a refugee claim that has not been withdrawn, abandoned, rejected, or terminated

agreement.[26] Fourth, refugee claimants who hold a valid visa other than a transit visa, work permit, or study permit, or are otherwise not required to obtain admission documents to enter Canada are exempted.[27]

ii)   The Process for Claimants from "Safe Third Countries"

Claimants from safe third countries who have been able to enter Canada either by coming through a port of entry that is not a land border, or through one of the exceptions provided in the *Regulations*, are not treated as other refugee claimants in Canada.

Although claimants under this category are subject to the same timelines as other refugee claimants, they will not be able to appeal a refugee decision from the RPD to the Refugee Appeal Division (RAD) and can apply for leave to judicially review the decision only at the Federal Court.[28] While waiting for the Federal Court to make its decision, the claimants in this category also will not enjoy a statutory stay of removal.[29]

iii)   Implications for Claimants from "Safe Third Countries"

The agreement basically allows Canada to transfer its obligations under the *Refugee Convention* and other international legal instruments, such as the *Convention against Torture*, by delegating them to another state that, at the very least, does not conduct refugee determinations in the same manner that Canada would, and as asserted by many, may be contravening international and human rights law.[30] In doing so, Canada not only loses quality control over such assessments, but also seemingly passes off responsibility over cases that do not penetrate our

---

(s 159.5(c)), or a person eighteen years or older who holds a valid work or study permit (s 159.5(d)).

26   *Ibid*, s 159.5(e). A minor is a person who has not attained the age of eighteen years and has neither a spouse nor common law partner.

27   *Ibid*, s 159(f).

28   *IRPA*, above note 4, s 110(2). See Chapter 16 for more information on judicial review.

29   *Regulations*, above note 8, s 231. For more information on stays of removal, see Chapter 15 on enforcement and Chapter 16 on judicial review.

30   Sonia Akibo-Betts, "The *Canada-US Safe Third Country Agreement*: Why the US Is Not a Safe Haven for Refugee Women Asserting Gender-Based Asylum Claims" (2005) 19 *Windsor Review of Legal and Social Issues* 105; Andrew Moore, "Unsafe in America: A Review of the *US-Canada Safe Third Country Agreement*" (2007) 47 *Santa Clara Law Review* 201. The *Convention Relating to the Status of Refugees*, adopted July 28, 1951, entered into force Apr 22, 1954, 189 UNTS 150 (*Refugee Convention*); *Protocol relating to the Status of Refugees*, adopted Jan 31, 1967, entered into force Oct 4 1967, 606 UNTS 267 (*Protocol*); *The Convention against Torture and Other Cruel, Inhuman, or Degrading Treatment or Punishment*, 10 December 1984, Can TS 1987, No. 36, 23 ILM 1027 [*Convention against Torture*].

border: such cases are simply turned away. The discourse surrounding the need for such an agreement has allowed for the "blurring of asylum seekers and 'illegals.'"[31] As well, while there are exceptions for those who have family in Canada, the requirement to prove this at the port of entry can be problematic. Refugee claimants must be able to contact the family member. Officers have ultimate discretion to determine whether a family connection exists as well and may deny persons entry where they do not believe that such a connection is *bona fide*.

The agreement has been reviewed by different stakeholders. The main criticism has been that the United States is not always a safe country for refugees given their processes and standards for determining who is a refugee. Thus, there is abundant concern that the agreement has led to the decrease in protection to persons who may otherwise have obtained protection in Canada. For example, the Canadian Council for Refugees published a report showing that, in the first year of the agreement alone, some 922 Colombians who would have received protection in Canada faced either detention or removal from the United States, and that women fleeing gender-based persecution are disadvantaged, as the United States assesses gender-based refugee claims differently.[32] As well, the United Nations High Commissioner for Refugees (UNHCR) has reported concerns about the "direct back policy" which "has been especially problematic for asylum-seekers directed back from Canada to the United States, as a number were detained in the United States and unable to attend their scheduled interviews."[33] Further, the

---

31 Audrey Macklin, "Disappearing Refugees: Reflections on the *Canada-US Safe Third Country Agreement*" (2005) 36 *Columbia Human Rights Law Review* 365.

32 Canadian Council of Refugees, *Closing the Front Door on Refugees: Report on the First Year of the Safe Third Country Agreement* (December 2005), online: CCR http://ccrweb.ca/sites/ccrweb.ca/files/static-files/closingdoordec05.pdf. See also Amy Arnett, "One Step Forward, Two Steps Back: Women Asylum-Seekers in the United States and Canada Stand to Lose Human Rights under the *Safe Third Country Agreement*" (2005) 9 *Lewis & Clark Law Review* 951; Lynn Hodgens, "Domestic Silence: How the *US-Canada Safe Third Country Agreement* Brings New Urgency to the Need for Gender-Based-Asylum Regulations" (2006) 30 *Vermont Law Review* 1045. Note that the United States recently has recognized gender-based asylum claims under the refugee definition under the ground of particular social group, but it remains to be seen how widely this will be applied and what kinds of claims will be recognized on this ground. See *Cece v Holder*, No 11-1989 (7th Cir August 9, 2013).

33 UN High Commissioner for Refugees, *Monitoring Report: Canada-United States 'Safe Third Country' Agreement* (June 2006), online: UNHCR www.unhcr. org/455b2cca4.html at 6: "The UNHCR is aware of six asylum seekers who were directed back to the U.S. and subsequently removed to their country of origin without having their claims processed by the Canadian Government under the Agreement." In *John Doe et al v Canada*, Report No 78/11, 21 July 2011, the Inter-

UNHCR, among others, had concerns about the lack of communication between the two governments on cases of concern, the lack of training of staff in both countries, the adequacy of reconsideration procedures, and the detention conditions in the United States.[34]

The *Safe Third Country Agreement* was challenged in the Federal Court. Although Phelan J of the Federal Court held that the regulations implementing the agreement contravened sections 7 and 15 of the *Canadian Charter of Rights and Freedoms*,[35] the Federal Court of Appeal allowed the appeal on other grounds.[36] The Court of Appeal declined to assess whether sections 7 and 15 were violated and instead focused on the fact that the challenge was not brought by a refugee who had been denied entry to Canada[37] and that the *IRPA* gives the Governor in Council broad grant of authority to designate safe third countries, not requiring actual compliance with the conditions laid out in the *IRPA*, section 102(2).[38]

A future challenge to the *Regulations* implementing the *Safe Third Country Agreement* is likely forthcoming as the exclusion of this category of claimants from the Refugee Appeal Division, and the lack of an automatic stay of removal, raises questions as to whether sections 7 and 15 of the *Charter* are violated.

f) Claimants from a Designated Country of Origin (DCO)

i) What Is a Designated Country of Origin?

The minister of Citizenship and Immigration may designate countries of origin so that persons from those countries will have their refugee claims assessed under more stringent rules and processes.[39] According to Citizenship and Immigration Canada, the policy rationale for creat-

---

American Commission on Human Rights held that the practice of directing back claimants to the United States to wait for a scheduled hearing in Canada violated rights under arts 17 and 18 of the *American Declaration of the Rights and Duties of Man* by failing to conduct individualized risk assessments before returning them to the United States. The Commission did not address the legality of the *Safe Third Country Agreement*. It did recommend that Canada make full reparation, including monetary damages, to individuals who had been directed back to the United States. Canada declined to accept this and other recommendations made by the Commission.

34   *Ibid* at 7.
35   *Canadian Council for Refugees v Canada*, 2007 FC 1262.
36   *Canadian Council for Refugees v Canada*, 2008 FCA 229.
37   *Ibid* at paras 102–3: "There is, in this case, no factual basis upon which to assess the alleged *Charter* breaches."
38   *Ibid* at paras 72–82.
39   *IRPA*, above note 4, s 109.1.

ing such a category includes the recognition that there are "places in the world where it is less likely for a person to be persecuted compared to other areas" or "countries that do not normally produce refugees, but do respect human rights and offer state protection" and "too much time and resources are spent reviewing these unfounded claims."[40]

The designated country of origin (DCO) scheme gives sole discretion to the minister to designate a country as "safe." Legislation provides that the minister may consider either quantitative or qualitative factors before designating a country under this scheme.[41] The minister is given the power to determine by order when the different criteria should apply.[42] Quantitative triggers currently apply to countries having at least thirty finalized claims in the Refugee Protection Division in a twelve-month period in the three years preceding designation.[43] Combined rejection, withdrawal, and abandonment rates of refugee claims from a particular country of at least 75 percent or higher, or combined withdrawal and abandonment rates of refugee claims of 60 percent or higher may lead to a country being designated.[44] Where fewer than thirty decisions have been made, the qualitative criteria will apply.[45] In this context, the *IRPA* requires that the minister consider three factors:

- whether there is an independent judicial system;
- whether the country recognizes and has mechanisms for redress if basic democratic rights and freedoms are infringed; and
- whether any civil society organizations exist.[46]

Once a country has been identified as meeting the quantitative or qualitative triggers, the minister may conduct a review in consultation with other governmental departments. According to the CIC Backgrounder:

---

40 Citizenship and Immigration Canada, "Designated Countries of Origin," online: CIC www.cic.gc.ca/english/refugees/reform-safe.asp [CIC, "DCO"].
41 *IRPA*, above note 4, ss 109.1(2)–(3).
42 *Ibid.*
43 Citizenship and Immigration Canada, *Order Establishing Quantitative Threshold for the Designation of Countries of Origin* (15 December 2012), online: Canada Gazette www.gazette.gc.ca/rp-pr/p1/2012/2012-12-15/html/notice-avis-eng. html; see also Citizenship and Immigration Canada, Backgrounder: *Designated Countries of Origin* (16 February 2012), online: CIC www.cic.gc.ca/english/ department/media/backgrounders/2012/2012-02-16i.asp [CIC Backgrounder: DCO].
44 *Ibid.*
45 *Ibid.*
46 *IRPA*, above note 4, s 109.1(2)(b).

Countries that meet either quantitative or qualitative triggers then undergo a review in consultation with other Canadian federal government departments. The review examines a select set of criteria, specifically

- democratic governance;
- protection of right to liberty and security of the person;
- freedom of opinion and expression;
- freedom of religion and association;
- freedom from discrimination and protection of rights for groups at risk;
- protection from non-state actors (which could include measures such as state protection from human trafficking);
- access to impartial investigations;
- access to an independent judiciary system; and
- access to redress (which could include constitutional and legal provisions).

The Minister of Citizenship, Immigration and Multiculturalism makes the final decision on whether to designate a country.[47]

No other experts from non-governmental organizations (NGOs) or other organizations need be consulted. The final decision to designate rests with the minister. In designating a country under this scheme, the minister may do so simply by issuing a ministerial order, and no changes in legislation need be made.[48]

The list of countries is subject to amendment. It is best to consult CIC and ministerial orders for the most up-to-date list. A current list is found online:[49]

---

47   CIC Backgrounder: *DCO*, above note 43.

48   *IRPA*, above note 4, ss 109.1(3)–(4).

49   See CIC, "DCO," above note 40; see also Minister of Citizenship and Immigration Canada, *Ministerial Order Amending the Order Designating Countries of Origin* (29 May 2013), online: Canada Gazette www.gazette.gc.ca/rp-pr/ p1/2013/2013-06-15/html/notice-avis-eng.html#d111; *Ministerial Order Amending the Order Designating Countries of Origin* (14 February 2013), online: Canada Gazette www.gazette.gc.ca/rp-pr/p1/2013/2013-02-23/html/notice-avis-eng. html#d105; *Ministerial Order Designating Countries of Origin* (15 December 2012), online: Canada Gazette www.gazette.gc.ca/rp-pr/p1/2012/2012-12-15/ html/notice-avis-eng.html#d114; *Ministerial Order Amending the Order Designating Countries of Origin* (10 October 2014), online: Canada Gazette www.gazette. gc.ca/rp-pr/p1/2014/2014-10-25/html/notice-avis-eng.php.

ii) The Process for DCO Claimants

The *IRPA* specifies that refugee claimants who are nationals of a designated country of origin may be subject to regulations that provide for time limits that differ from those that apply to other claimants.[50] The *Regulations* made under this authority provide that a hearing before the IRB's Refugee Protection Division for persons from a designated country of origin, who make a claim from within Canada, must be scheduled no later than thirty days after the finding of eligibility.[51] For claimants from a designated country of origin who made a claim at a port of entry, a date for their hearing may be set forty-five days after they have been found to be eligible.[52] These timelines differ from those that apply to claimants not from a designated country of origin: their hearing date is set no later than sixty days after eligibility is determined.[53]

A further implication for refugee claimants from a designated country of origin is that they do not have access to the IRB's Refugee Appeal Division (RAD).[54] Where their initial claim is denied, the only recourse for such claimants is to seek leave to apply for judicial review at the Federal Court of Canada.[55]

Claimants from designated countries of origin also face other restrictions designed to facilitate their faster removal:

1) They are barred for thirty-six months from applying for a pre-removal risk assessment following a negative decision on their refugee claim.[56]
2) They have no access to an automatic stay of removal upon application for judicial review at the Federal Court.[57]

iii) Implications for DCO Refugee Claimants

Criticism of the DCO scheme has focused on the premise upon which its policy rationale rests. The current government prejudges that individuals from designated countries can be painted with one wide brush as likely "bogus refugees" because their country is "safe." While undoubtedly there is a need to streamline the determination process and

---

50 *IRPA*, above note 4, s 111.1(2).
51 *Regulations*, above note 8, s 159.9(1)(a)(i).
52 *Ibid*, s 159.9(1)(a)(ii).
53 *Ibid*, s 159.9(1)(b).
54 *IRPA*, above note 4, s 110(2)(d.1).
55 *Ibid*, s 72(1). See Chapter 16 for more information on judicial review.
56 *Ibid*, s 112(2)(c); see also *IRPA*, *ibid*, s 25: This is compounded by the fact that all refugee claimants are barred from making a humanitarian and compassionate grounds application for twelve months following a negative refugee determination. See Chapter 11 for more information on pre-removal risk assessments.
57 *Regulations*, above note 8, s 231(2).

provide efficient means of making decisions, measures taken should not undermine the integrity of the process. As it stands, the DCO scheme presupposes that it is highly unlikely that a refugee can come from a certain country simply because the rejection rate from that country is high or because the country has a democratic political system. However, the fact that a particular country has produced a given number of rejections should not create suspicion about any particular case. The designation encourages the decision maker to approach a claim with a preset opinion rather than with an open mind. Moreover, as many scholars have noted, the fact that a country is democratic has no bearing on whether there could be legitimate refugees coming from that country.[58] For example, while a country may have democratic institutions, a subset of the population, such as gays and lesbians[59] or Roma in Hungary,[60] may be subject to persecution despite the existence of the institutions. In sum, the main problem with the DCO scheme is that it encourages prejudgment and presumption about the good faith of a claimant labelled as coming from a "safe country." Instead of encouraging decision makers to apply greater scrutiny to the claims of such individuals, it promotes an attitude of cavalier laxity.

The shortened time limits for refugee claimants coming from a designated country of origin also present severe obstacles. First, since DCO claimants have only thirty to forty-five days before appearing at the IRB's Refugee Protection Division, they may have greater difficulty finding legal representation or information prior to their hearing. Second, DCO claimants may have difficulty obtaining or preparing evidence for the hearing. For example, documentary evidence that may be needed from an expert or medical professional takes time and may not be available within the thirty to forty-five day window before a hearing. As well, vulnerable or traumatized claimants will not have the luxury of developing a trusting or comfortable relationship with settlement workers or legal representatives in order to divulge all of the pertinent

---

58 See, for example, Jamie Liew, "Beyond Country of Origin: *Smith v Canada* and Refugees from Unexpected Places" (2011) 23 *Canadian Journal of Women and the Law* 686; Jamie Liew, "Creating Higher Burdens: The Presumption of State Protection in Democratic Countries" (2009) 26 *Refuge* 207; Marina Stefanova, "The 'Safe' Need Not Apply: The Effects of the Canadian and EU 'Safe Country of Origin' Mechanisms on Roma Asylum Claims" (2014) 49 *Texas International Law Journal* 121; Petra Molnar Diop, "The 'Bogus' Refugee: Roma Asylum Claimants and Discourses of Fraud in Canada's Bill C-31" (2014) 30 *Refuge* 67.

59 See, for example, *Smith v Canada (Minister of Citizenship and Immigration)*, 2009 FC 1194.

60 See, for example, *Kotai v Canada (Minister of Citizenship and Immigration)*, 2013 FC 412.

information that may be helpful or useful in a refugee determination. Thus, *viva voce* evidence is also jeopardized through the hurried time-lines instituted by the legislation.

Finally, as outlined above, the difference in access to appeal bodies or alternative processes or remedies with disadvantages to refugee claimants from a designated country of origin. They are barred from appealing to the Refugee Appeal Division;[61] disqualified, as are all refugee claimants, from making an application for permanent residence on humanitarian and compassionate grounds for twelve months after a negative determination;[62] ineligible to apply for a pre-removal risk assessment for thirty-six months;[63] and denied a stay of removal while a negative refugee decision is being judicially reviewed.[64] In sum, DCO claimants may be removed from Canada before a full and complete resolution of their claim and a full review of whether they face persecution, torture, and cruel and unusual punishment or other forms of hardship. Anecdotally, counsel have reported that removal orders are being enforced despite the fact that a judicial review is pending at the Federal Court. Given the potential risks to DCO claimants in their country of origin, it is anticipated that counsel will raise *Charter* challenges to test the validity of the restrictions placed on access to alternative remedies or processes.

g) Designated Foreign Nationals (DFNs)

i) What Is a Designated Foreign National?

The minister of Public Safety and Emergency Preparedness has the exclusive power to designate the arrival of a group of persons in Canada as an irregular arrival by simply issuing a ministerial order.[65] The legislation provides that such a designation may be made if the minister is of the opinion that the group cannot be examined in a timely manner with regard to establishing identity or determining inadmissibility;[66] or if the minister has reasonable grounds to suspect that the group may be involved in human smuggling or working in association with a criminal

---

61 *IRPA*, above note 4, s 110(2)(d.1).

62 *Ibid*, s 25. See Chapter 12 for more information on permanent resident applications on humanitarian and compassionate grounds.

63 *Ibid*, s 112(2)(c). See Chapter 11 for more information on pre-removal risk assessments.

64 *Regulations*, above note 8, s 231(2).

65 *IRPA*, above note 4, s 20.1(1); see *IRPA*, *ibid*, s 6(3), which specifies that the minister may not delegate the power conferred by s 21.1(1).

66 *Ibid*, s 20.1(1)(a).

organization or terrorist group.[67] Where a group has been designated, a foreign national who is found to be a member becomes a designated foreign national.[68] In December 2012, five groups of eighty-five claimants, including thirty-five children, from Romania who entered at the US–Quebec border were designated by the minister.[69]

The development of this designation policy may be attributed to the arrival of two boats, the MV *Sun Sea* and the *Ocean Lady*, on the west coast of Canada carrying migrants from Sri Lanka.[70] The government suspected passengers of engaging in and facilitating human smuggling and concluded that mechanisms should be created to combat this criminal activity and to provide a strong deterrent for those organizing such operations.[71] One news report stated:

> Just hours after the arrival of the second ship, the MV Sun Sea, in August of 2010, Public Safety Minister Vic Toews stood in front of almost two dozen reporters in an auditorium at CFB Esquimalt and said the federal government "must ensure that our refugee system is not hijacked by criminals or terrorists."[72]

Then-minister of Citizenship and Immigration, Jason Kenney, provided another justification for the DFN scheme, stating: "But for too

---

67   *Ibid*, s 20.1(1)(b).

68   *Ibid*, s 20.2(2); see also s 19.

69   Public Safety Canada, "*Immigration and Refugee Protection Act*, Designation as Irregular Arrival" (5 December 2012), online: www.publicsafety.gc.ca/cnt/nws/ nws-rlss/2012/20121205-eng.aspx; "Romanian Human Smuggling Ring Busted in Ontario" *CBC News* (6 December 2012), online: CBC www.cbc.ca/news/politics/ romanian-human-smuggling-ring-busted-in-ontario-1.1292783.

70   See, for example, "Tamil Migrants in Good Shape: RCMP" *CBC News* (14 August 2010), online: CBC www.cbc.ca/news/canada/tamil-migrants-in-good-shape- rcmp-1.898419.

71   *House of Commons Debates*, 41st Parl, 1st Sess, No 12 (21 June 2011) at 17:25 (Hon Vic Toews): The Minister of Public Safety and Emergency Preparedness stated:

> The truth is that human smugglers are not at all interested in helping individuals in need. They do not care about individuals. They do not care about families. They make victims of their passengers, who must pay dearly, and risk their lives to undertake perilous journeys. Human smugglers only care about money and are working every day to increase the profits from their illegal activities.

72   Katie De Rosa, "A Sea of Troubles: Canada's Plan to Confront Human-Smuggling by Following Australia's Lead Worries Refugee Advocates" (17 November 2012), online: Canada.com http://o.canada.com/news/national/a-sea-of-troubles-can- adas-plan-to-confront-human-smuggling-by-following-australias-lead-worries- refugee-advocates.

many years, our generous asylum system has been abused by too many people making bogus refugee claims."[73] Such remarks reveal a willingness to approach the refugee claims of people arriving irregularly with preset ideas about the likelihood that they are illegitimate. A primary problem with the DFN scheme is that the legislation targets and imposes sanctions on persons who may indeed be legitimate claimants. Indeed, as the UNHCR has stated:

> This designation is also problematic from a non-discrimination point of view. UNHCR does not believe that the stated grounds for the designation as irregular arrival provide for a legitimate justification for a substantially differentiated treatment of refugees and asylum-seekers with respect to detention, access to an appeal or access to permanent residency in conjunction with the right to a travel document for refugees. The legislation may therefore be at variance with human rights based non-discrimination guarantees (e.g. Articles 2 and 26 of the *International Covenant on Civil and Political Rights* (*ICPR*) and potentially also Article 3 of the 1951 Convention).[74]

It is expected that legal practitioners will challenge this scheme on the ground that it is not *Charter*-compliant.[75] Designated individuals may suffer sanctions even if they have had no contact with a human smuggler. This could occur because the bill authorizes the minister to designate a group arrival as irregular *either* where he is of the opinion that the examination of members of the group cannot be conducted "in a timely manner" *or* where he has reasonable grounds to suspect that the arrival contravened the human smuggling provision in the *IRPA*. In other words, undefined bureaucratic convenience rather than any connection to smuggling may justify ministerial action. In addition, even successful refugee claimants may be designated long after arrival and despite statutory provisions that exempt refugees from prosecution for entry without the requisite documents.

---

73   Government of Canada, "Speaking Notes for the Honourable Jason Kenney, PC, MP Minister of Citizenship, Immigration and Multiculturalism" (16 February 2012), online: CIC www.cic.gc.ca/english/department/media/speeches/2012/2012-02-16.asp.

74   UN High Commissioner for Refugees, *UNHCR Submission on Bill C-31: Protecting Canada's Immigration System Act* (May 2012), online: UNHCR http://unhcr.ca/beta/wp-content/uploads/2014/10/RPT-2012-05-08-billc31-submission-e.pdf at para 8.

75   See Canadian Association of Refugee Lawyers, Press Release, "Designated Foreign Nationals Regime" (6 December 2012), online: http://carldevelopment.zenutech.com/our-work/issues/DFNR#Press%20Release%20Backgrounder.

ii) The Process for DFN Refugee Claimants

Unlike DCO refugee claimants, DFN refugee claimants are subject to the same timelines and procedural rules as regular refugee claimants.[76] Like DCO refugee claimants, however, restrictions have been placed on their access to different processes and alternative remedies.

Restrictions are outlined as follows. First, DFN claimants are not eligible to apply for temporary resident permits[77] or travel documents.[78] Second, DFN claimants cannot access the Refugee Appeal Division at the Immigration and Refugee Board.[79] Third, this category of claimants cannot benefit from an automatic stay of removal should they choose to judicially review a negative refugee determination.[80] Fourth, DFN claimants are barred from making a humanitarian and compassionate (H&C) grounds application for five years after a determination of a refugee claim or five years after they have been designated.[81] If a claimant becomes a designated foreign national after submitting an H&C application, the processing of the application can be suspended and the minister may refuse to consider the request.[82] DFN claimants are subject to the same restrictions on accessing a pre-removal risk assessment as regular refugee claimants; they are barred from making an application for twelve months after a negative refugee decision.[83] Finally, designated foreign nationals are subject to reporting requirements to an officer.[84]

In addition, designated foreign nationals face a further sanction[85]: mandatory arrest and detention or an issuance of a warrant to arrest and detain. A designated foreign national who is sixteen years of age or older on the day of arrival will be detained upon entry or if designated after entry will be subject to arrest and detention.[86]

---

76   See *Regulations*, above note 8, s 159.9(2), where a claim is referred to the Refugee Protection Division within sixty days of the claim being made.

77   *IRPA*, above note 4, s 24(5).

78   *Ibid*, s 31.1. Judicial review is the only resource. For more information, see Chapter 16.

79   *Ibid*, s 110(2)(a).

80   *Regulations*, above note 8, s 231(2).

81   *IRPA*, above note 4, s 25(1.01).

82   *Ibid*, s 25(1.02)–(1.03); see also ss 58(4), 58.1, 98.1, 11(1.3), 20.2(3), and 24(7); *Regulations*, above note 8, s 174.1(1): A further one-year delay may be added to the five-year period if the applicant fails to comply with terms and conditions imposed upon him.

83   *IRPA*, above note 4, s 112(2). See Chapter 11 for more information on pre-removal risk assessments.

84   *Regulations*, above note 8, s 174.1: This section sets out the reporting requirements for DFNs.

85   See Chapter 15 on the mechanics of enforcement.

86   *IRPA*, above note 4, s 55(3.1).

As noted in Chapter 15, detention review procedures for designated foreign nationals differ from those made available to others. The timing of reviews differs significantly,[87] and there are fewer legislative barriers to keeping designated foreign nationals in prolonged detention.[88] For example, an officer's discretion to order release after the first detention review is removed, and release is permitted only by special application to the minister, if the refugee claim has been determined or if the Immigration Division orders release.[89]

iii) Implications for DFN Refugee Claimants

DFN claimants, like DCO claimants, are subject to an expedited process geared to remove those who have received a negative refugee decision, even if a full resolution has not been made through judicial review of the Federal Court. They are also subject to severe and arguably arbitrary measures, such as mandatory detention with reviews occurring between lengthy time lags. Undoubtedly, these measures will be challenged in the courts.

h) Other Refugee Claimants

Refugee claimants who are neither designated foreign nationals nor from a designated country of origin are also subject to recent significant changes, such as new timelines and determination procedures. Formerly, refugee claimants could submit their application within twenty-eight days. The new system requires claimants to submit their documents within fifteen days of receiving the BOC and other forms.[90] Under the previous system, while hearings were scheduled, on average, between eighteen and twenty months from the date the application

---

87 *Ibid*, ss 57 and 57.1: Instead of detention reviews after forty-eight hours, seven days, then every thirty days after that, DFNs get their first detention review within the first fourteen days but not again until six months have elapsed.

88 *Ibid*, s 58: At the fourteen-day and six-month detention reviews, the person shall be released unless the Immigration Division determines that the usual criteria are satisfied. Identity is also a ground, but it is now less onerous; previously, not only did the minister need to be of the opinion that the person's identity has not yet been established but also that either the detainee was not being cooperative with efforts to establish his identity or the minister was not making reasonable efforts to establish his identity. Now only the minister's opinion is required. Most important, the Immigration Division may now no longer consider any other factors in ordering release, something that appears to prevent consideration of s 248 of the *Regulations* (alternatives to release).

89 *IRPA*, above note 4, s 56.

90 *Regulations*, above note 8, s 159.8(2).

was submitted, under the new system, claimants will now appear before the RPD within sixty days of submitting a claim.[91]

Beyond the procedural changes, refugee claimants who have been denied protection at the RPD are now barred for twelve months from submitting an application for permanent residence on humanitarian and compassionate grounds and also from seeking a pre-removal risk assessment.[92]

The implications of such changes are yet to be fully exposed, but there are anecdotal reports that the new refugee determination system is failing some claimants. For example, the Canadian Council for Refugees (CCR) reports that short timelines are causing high levels of stress and leaving little time for claimants to prepare themselves adequately for their hearing; the short timelines are particularly problematic for vulnerable claimants, such as survivors of torture and people with health problems or disabilities.[93] Beyond that, the CCR also reports on the increased difficulty in obtaining legal representation, interpretive assistance, or essential documentary evidence within the short timelines. When forced to travel to different centres to present themselves and their children, claimants may have difficulties with arranging travel and obtaining child care at the RPD.[94] As a result of these and other difficulties, claimants depend heavily on community organizations not funded by the government to provide extensive support to persons navigating the new refugee system.[95]

i) Hearings at the Refugee Protection Division (RPD) of the Immigration and Refugee Board (IRB)

i) Preliminaries

a. Dates and Times of RPD Hearings

All eligible refugee claimants are provided the opportunity to present their claim at the RPD. As noted, DCO claimants will get a hearing date

---

91   *Ibid*, s 159.9(1).

92   *IRPA*, above note 4, ss 25 and 112(2). See Chapters 11 & 12 for more information.

93   Canadian Council for Refugees, *New Refugee System – One Year On* (9 December 2013), online: CCR http://ccrweb.ca/sites/ccrweb.ca/files/refugee-system-one-year-on.pdf.

94   Canadian Council for Refugees, *The Experience of Refugee Claimants at Refugee Hearings in the New System* (April 2014), online: CCR http://ccrweb.ca/en/refugee-hearing-report-2014.

95   *Ibid*.

between thirty and forty-five days of submitting their claim[96] while all others will receive a date within sixty days of submitting their claim.[97] The RPD will notify, in writing, the claimant and other parties wishing to participate in the hearing of the date, time, and location of the proceeding.[98]

Claimants may make an application to change the date or time of a proceeding.[99] Such an application must be made without delay and at least three days before a hearing is to be scheduled.[100] The date and time of proceedings may be changed for a variety of reasons, such as to accommodate vulnerable persons or to recognize factors outside the party's control.[101] As well, allowance may be made where the claimant does not have counsel or is unable to provide dates when her counsel would be available to attend a hearing.[102]

b.   Submitting Documentary Evidence

Claimants must submit any documentary evidence at least ten days before their refugee hearing or five days if they are responding to another document that was provided by another party.[103] This means that DCO claimants have twenty to thirty-five days after submitting their claims. Other claimants have fifty days after submitting their claims to provide documentary evidence. Claimants must be organized and well prepared in order to meet these deadlines.

The *RPD Rules* set out how documentary evidence or submissions must be provided to the RPD and all other participating parties.[104] The RPD itself may choose to rely on documentary evidence, and if so,

---

96 See Section A(3)(f), above in this chapter.

97 See also *RPD Rules*, above note 10, s 3, where it sets out parameters and considerations an officer must be mindful of when setting dates for a RPD hearing; *Regulations*, above note 8, s 159.9(1), which sets out the timelines: thirty days for DCO claims made inland; forty-five days for DCO claims made at a port of entry; sixty days for all other claims.

98 *RPD Rules*, above note 10, s 25(1); *Regulations*, above note 8, s 168(a). Section 164 of the *Regulations* provides that, with the RPD's discretion, a hearing can be conducted by teleconference.

99 *RPD Rules*, above note 10, ss 50 and 54.

100 *Ibid*, s 54(2). Section 54(3) recognizes the possibility that the party making the application may not have been able to make an application before the date of the hearing and allows for oral applications at the hearing.

101 *Ibid*, s 54(4). See also ss 54(6)–(8) indicating that if the reason is medical, medical certificates must be provided.

102 *Ibid*, s 54(5).

103 *Ibid*, s 34(3).

104 *Ibid*, ss 31–32 and 37–39: In particular, the documents must be written in either English or French or a translation must be provided with a translator's certificate; a list of documents must be provided; and documents must be page numbered.

disclosure of such documents must be provided to each party, including country documentation prepared by the RPD.

Where a party brings a document to the hearing or wishes to introduce one not previously disclosed to the RPD, after the hearing, an application must be made either orally or in writing to have it received.[105] The board member has the discretion to allow the admission of the document during the hearing after assessing its relevance and probative value,[106] whether it is new evidence,[107] and whether the party made reasonable efforts to provide it within the time limits.[108]

c.   Obtaining Medical Evidence and Vulnerable Persons Applications

Obtaining a medical opinion or evidence may be crucial to the refugee determination process. Not only may such evidence corroborate the claimant's testimony, but it also may provide a basis for how a board member may want to approach the claim. For example, in *Feleke v Canada*, the Federal Court identified two ways in which a psychological assessment may aid an claimant: (a) it may corroborate the applicant's story and (b) it may provide an explanation for inconsistencies in the applicant's evidence.[109]

Recent caselaw has raised questions regarding how the RPD should treat medical evidence introduced by claimants. In *Czesak v Canada (Minister of Citizenship and Immigration)*, the Division considered one of the medical reports provided by the claimant as inconclusive and also did not accept the diagnosis reported in the report.[110] In *Czesak*, Annis J stated: "I am of the view that decision-makers should be wary of reliance upon forensic expert evidence obtained for the purpose of litigation, unless it is subject to some form of validation."[111] Dismissing in a wholesale fashion professional opinion about the medical conditions that a claimant suffers seems not only unfair, but unhelpful to the refugee determination process. Further, in calling for a "rigorous validation process under court procedures"[112] in this context, Annis J ignores the fact that refugee determinations take place in a more informal setting and are subject to less stringent rules of evidence. Given the recent changes in the timelines associated with obtaining evidence for hear-

---

105 *Ibid*, ss 36 and 43.
106 *Ibid*, ss 36(a) and 43(3)(a).
107 *Ibid*, ss 36(b) and 43(3)(b).
108 *Ibid*, ss 36(c) and 43(3)(c).
109 2007 FC 539.
110 2013 FC 1149 at para 29 [*Czesak*].
111 *Ibid* at para 37.
112 *Ibid* at para 38.

ings before the RPD, it is hard to see how a process of validating expert opinion can be incorporated. Justice Annis has envisioned "procedures intended to validate expert opinions" that would "include the early exchange of reports, by which I mean that normally there is a rebuttal report as a first line of validation" and where "[t]he parties are normally entitled to obtain extensive background information on the drafting of the reports, including production of correspondence between lawyers and experts and knowing whether there are other reports in existence not being relied upon" and "the opportunity to assess the reliability of the expert opinions under cross-examination by competent lawyers."[113] Such an expectation is unrealistic where most refugee hearings commence forty-five to sixty days after a claim is submitted. Without such a process, Annis J advocates that expert opinions should be rejected or given little weight if refugee claimants provide them.[114] This seems unduly burdensome given the informal processes established under the legislation.

Justice Annis's view is not endorsed by others and has been rejected by refugee law experts worldwide. According to "Guidelines on the Judicial Approach to Expert Medical Evidence" by the International Association of Refugee Law Judges, expert medical reports should serve one or more of the following roles:

- to substantiate claims of ill-treatment;
- to establish a correlation between physical or psychological injuries and the alleged torture or ill-treatment;
- to explain a claimant's difficulties in giving evidence or recounting events by
  (a) providing possible explanation(s) for inconsistencies and/or contradictions within a claimant's narrative of events;
  (b) providing possible explanation(s) for reticence or reluctance in divulging a full account of events, for example delay in divulging allegations of sexual assault and/or other forms of violence directed against an individual;
- to address the possible effect of removal and return to the country of origin upon a person's physical or mental well-being or that of a family member;
- to assess treatment needs;

---

113 *Ibid* at para 39.
114 *Ibid* at para 40.

- to reduce the need for the claimant to give testimony about traumatic events.[115]

Beyond that, the Guidelines also specify that "[e]xpert medical evidence should be treated as an integral element of all the evidence considered in establishing the facts," that the dismissal of expert medical evidence should be "accompanied by appropriate reasoning," and that a "decision-maker, as a layperson, should not attempt to substitute his or her own opinion in preference to that of a reliable expert."[116]

Beyond corroborating the factual basis of a claim, expert medical evidence could be sought and provided to support a "vulnerable person's application," an application outlining the difficulties the claimant may have in attending and performing at the RPD and requesting any accommodation to help the RPD in gathering evidence from the claimant.[117] The Chairperson Guideline[118] titled "Procedures with Respect to Vulnerable Persons Appearing before the IRB" (Vulnerable Persons Guideline) acts as "an aid to the assessment of evidence"[119] and defines vulnerable persons as

> . . . individuals whose ability to present their cases before the IRB is severely impaired. Such persons may include, but would not be limited to, the mentally ill, minors, the elderly, victims of torture, survivors of genocide and crimes against humanity, women who have suffered gender-related persecution, and individuals who have been victims of persecution based on sexual orientation and gender identity.[120]

---

115 International Association of Refugee Law Judges, *Guidelines on the Judicial Approach to Expert Medical Evidence* (18 September 1997), online: IARLJ www.iarlj.org/general/images/stories/working_parties/guidelines/medical-evidenceguidelinesfinaljun2010rw.pdf at para 3.1.

116 *Ibid* at para 6.1.

117 Immigration and Refugee Board of Canada, Chairperson Guideline 8: *Procedures with Respect to Vulnerable Persons Appearing before the IRB* (15 December 2012), online: www.irb-cisr.gc.ca/Eng/BoaCom/references/pol/guidir/Pages/GuideDir08.aspx, s 2.4 [*Guideline on Vulnerable Persons*].

118 For more information regarding Chairperson Guidelines, see Chapter 2.

119 See, for example, *Saleh v Canada (Minister of Citizenship and Immigration)*, 2005 FC 1074 at para 7; *Gilles v Canada (Minister of Citizenship and Immigration)*, 2011 FC 7 at para 17; *Philistin v Canada (Minister of Public Safety and Emergency Preparedness)*, 2011 FC 1333 at para 14.

120 *Guideline on Vulnerable Persons*, above note 117, s 2.1. See also Janet Cleveland, "The Guideline on Procedures with Respect to Vulnerable Persons Appearing before the Immigration and Refugee Board of Canada: A Critical Overview" (2008) 25 *Refuge* 119, discussing the shortcomings of the definition of *vulnerable* under the Guideline.

The IRB "has a broad discretion to tailor procedures to meet the particular needs of a vulnerable person" which includes providing evidence by videoconferencing or other means, allowing a support person to participate in a hearing, creating a more informal setting in the hearing, varying the order of questioning, excluding non-parties from the hearing room, providing a board member or interpreter of a particular gender, explaining the IRB processes to the vulnerable person, and making other procedural accommodations.[121] Any person can raise the issue of vulnerability with the RPD whether it be the claimant, the claimant's counsel, the board member, or the minister's representative, but the Guidelines do note that "counsel . . . is best placed to bring the vulnerability to the attention of the IRB."[122] Further, although an application may be made at any time, it is best to advise the RPD as soon as practically possible so that accommodations can be made before a hearing date.

It is challenging to obtain medical expert opinion, to identify whether a claimant needs accommodation, and to put together a vulnerable person's application given the timelines that are imposed. There will no doubt be applications for judicial review alleging that claimants are not given sufficient opportunity to show that accommodation is necessary. The Federal Court has already held that whether or not the Guideline on Vulnerable Persons is applied correctly is an issue of procedural fairness and that where an individual's vulnerabilities are apparent in the record, the IRB must take these vulnerabilities into account.[123]

d.   Notice of Constitutional Questions

A party wishing to challenge the constitutional validity, applicability, or operability of a legislative provision must provide notice no later than ten days before the date of the hearing.[124]

ii)   *Who May Participate in a Hearing?*

a.   The Board Member

A single IRB member will be present to question the claimant, run the hearing, and make a determination.[125]

---

121   *Guideline on Vulnerable Persons*, above note 117, s 4.2.
122   *Ibid*, s 7.3.
123   *FAM v Canada (Minister of Citizenship and Immigration)*, 2013 FC 574.
124   *IRPA*, above note 4, s 66: Section 66 lists the form and content of the notice and how that notice must be provided to various parties.
125   *Regulations*, above note 8, s 163.

b.   The Minister or Ministerial Representatives

Either the minister of Citizenship and Immigration or the minister of Public Safety and Emergency Preparedness or representatives may appear at a hearing.[126] Officials from Citizenship and Immigration Canada may also participate in hearings to challenge a claimant's credibility. Often, such participation may be arranged through written submissions or documentation, but occasionally officials from the department may appear at a hearing. Officers from the Canada Border Services Agency (CBSA) may also participate. The minister may seek to participate, for example, in order to argue that a claimant should be excluded from refugee protection.[127]

c.   Observers

Observers from the UNHCR or employees with the IRB, such as interpreters or trainees, may attend without making a formal request.[128] Others who wish to attend may be excluded if the board member is of the opinion that their attendance may impede the proceeding.[129] Observers must also be mindful that proceedings at the RPD are confidential.[130]

d.   Interpreters

Interpreters play a crucial role in refugee hearings. Claimants can choose to have their hearings in either English or French and can change the language of proceeding by notifying the RPD and the minister in writing ten days before the date of the hearing.[131] If a claimant needs an interpreter, the claimant can notify the officer at the time she submits her refugee claim and specify the language and dialect she wants interpretation services for.[132] Otherwise, a claimant has ten days prior to the hearing to notify the RPD she needs an interpreter or wants to change the language of interpretation.[133] In *Lamme v Canada (Minister of Citizenship and Immigration)*, the Federal Court held that the general standard to be met with respect to the quality of interpretation is

---

126 *Ibid*, ss 23 and 29: The minister must notify the RPD of the minister's intention to intervene no later than ten days from receiving the BOC. The *RPD Rules*, above note 10, s 29, set out the content of the notice that the minister must provide.

127 For persons excluded from refugee protection, see Chapter 10.

128 *RPD Rules*, above note 10, s 58.

129 *Ibid*, ss 58(1)–(2).

130 *Ibid*, s 58(3).

131 *Ibid*, ss 17–18.

132 *Ibid*, s 19(1).

133 *Ibid*, ss 19(2)–(4): This applies to witnesses whose testimony may need interpretation.

that it must be continuous, precise, impartial, and contemporaneous.[134] In addition, for the interpretation to meet these standards, it must be established that the applicant understood the interpretation and adequately expressed himself through the interpreter.[135] Typically, at the beginning of a hearing, interpreters will be introduced and will take an oath or affirmation to interpret accurately.[136] The board member may evaluate whether the claimant is able to understand the interpreter. Problems arising from interpretation can give rise to a breach in procedural fairness where an issue with interpretation was raised at the earliest opportunity.[137]

e.   Designated Representatives

A representative may be designated for any claimant if the person is under eighteen years of age whose claim is not joined to that of a parent or legal guardian[138] or if he is unable to appreciate the nature of the proceedings.[139] Either an officer of the RPD or counsel of the claimant

---

134 2005 FC 1336 [*Lamme*]; see also *Vakulenko v Canada (Minister of Citizenship and Immigration)*, 2014 FC 667, where the court held that there is an obligation to give a refugee claimant the opportunity to provide submissions during a spot audit of an interpreter.

135 *Lamme*, above note 134.

136 *RPD Rules*, above note 10, s 19(5).

137 See, for example, *Mohammadian v Canada (Minister of Citizenship and Immigration)*, [2000] 3 FC 371 (TD), aff'd 2001 FCA 191, where the court held that, in general terms, the standard of interpretation is high but not so high as perfection. In particular, interpretation should be continuous, precise, impartial, competent, and contemporaneous; *Singh v Canada (Citizenship and Immigration)*, 2007 FC 267 at para 36, where the court held that competency of translation requires that the interpretation must be of a high enough quality to ensure that justice is done and seen to be done; *Saravia v Canada (Minister of Citizenship and Immigration)*, 2005 FC 1296.

138 *RPD Rules*, above note 10, ss 20(1)–(2); *Regulations*, above note 8, s 167(2); *Hillary v Canada (Minister of Citizenship and Immigration)*, 2011 FCA 51: Typically, where a claimant is represented by counsel, it is only in the most unusual circumstances where a panel may be obligated to inquire as to the claimant's ability to understand the nature of the proceedings and whether the claimant needs a designated representative; *Duale v Canada (Minister of Citizenship and Immigration)*, 2004 FC 150: The obligation to designate a representative for a claimant arises at the earliest time at which the RPD becomes aware of facts that reveal the need for the designated representative.

139 *RPD Rules*, above note 10, ss 20(1) and (5): When determining whether a claimant or protected person is able to appreciate the nature of the proceedings, the RPD must consider factors such as the person's ability to understand the reason for the proceedings and to instruct counsel; the person's statements and behaviour at the proceedings; expert evidence, if any, on the person's intellectual or

can request, in writing, that a designated representative be appointed.[140] For a person to qualify as a designated representative, the individual must be eighteen years of age or older;[141] understand the nature of the proceedings;[142] be willing and able to act in the best interests of the claimant or protected person;[143] and not have any interests that conflict with those of the claimant or protected person.[144] The board member may assess the person nominated to be the designated representative to determine whether he is able to fulfill the responsibilities and is fully informed of the responsibilities.[145] Those responsibilities include deciding whether to retain counsel and instructing counsel or assisting the represented person in instructing counsel;[146] making decisions regarding the claim or application or assisting the person in doing so;[147] informing the represented person of the stages and procedures in the determination process;[148] assisting in gathering evidence and providing evidence;[149] protecting the interests of the represented person;[150] informing and consulting the represented person about decisions regarding the case;[151] and filing and perfecting appeals to the Refugee Appeal Division, if required.[152] The designation may end when the person reaches eighteen years of age or when the board member is of the opinion that the representative is no longer required.[153]

f.   Claimants, Witnesses, and Their Representatives

Claimants must attend the hearing.[154] The RPD will automatically join the claim of a claimant to a claim made by a claimant's spouse, common law partner, child, parent, legal guardian, brother, sister, grandchild,

---

physical faculties or mental condition; and whether the person has had a representative designated for the proceedings in another division of the IRB.

140   *Ibid*, ss 20(1) and (3).
141   *Ibid*, s 20(4)(a).
142   *Ibid*, s 20(4)(b).
143   *Ibid*, s 20(4)(c).
144   *Ibid*, s 20(4)(d).
145   *Ibid*, s 20(9).
146   *Ibid*, s 20(10)(a).
147   *Ibid*, s 20(10)(b).
148   *Ibid*, s 20(10)(c).
149   *Ibid*, s 20(10)(d).
150   *Ibid*, s 20(10)(e).
151   *Ibid*, s 20(10)(f).
152   *Ibid*, s 20(10)(g).
153   *Ibid*, ss 20(7)–(8).
154   *IRPA*, above note 4, s 164. Hearings may be conducted by means of live telecommunication.

or grandparent unless it is not practicable to do so.[155] Applications to join or separate claims be made, and the factors used to evaluate whether the application should be granted include whether the claims involve similar questions of fact or law, whether it would promote the efficient administration of RPD work, and whether it would cause an injustice.[156]

If claimants wish to bring witnesses to the hearing, they must provide the RPD and participating parties with notice and information about the witness at least ten days prior to the hearing.[157] While a board member has the discretion to allow a witness to testify without notice being given, the board member may deny a request to allow a witness to testify after evaluating the relevance and probative value of the proposed testimony and the reason why the witness information was not provided in the timelines specified in the *RPD Rules*.[158]

Claimants also have this right,[159] but do not necessarily have a right to be notified of the right to counsel.[160] While this right is not absolute, the RPD may be mindful of the difficulties claimants may have to obtain timely representation.[161] For example, there may be a breach of procedural fairness where a claimant is denied a full and fair hearing as a result of inaction or negligence on the part of the claimant's incompetent counsel.[162] Absent negligence or incompetence, however,

---

155 *RPD Rules*, above note 10, s 55(1).

156 *Ibid*, s 56.

157 *Ibid*, s 44. Section 45 also gives the power for the RPD to order a summons to compel a person to testify at it.

158 *Ibid*, ss 44(4)–(5).

159 *Regulations*, above note 8, s 167(1).

160 *Cha v Canada (Minister of Citizenship and Immigration)*, 2006 FCA 126 at para 54, where the Court of Appeal held that absent a *Charter* right to counsel for detention and arrest, there is no right to be notified of the right to counsel.

161 *Charles v Canada (Minister of Citizenship and Immigration)*, 2011 FC 852; *Malette v Canada (Minister of Citizenship and Immigration)*, 2005 FC 1400; *Mervilus v Canada (Minister of Citizenship and Immigration)*, 2004 FC 1206 at para 25:

The following principles can therefore be drawn from the case law: although the right to counsel is not absolute in an administrative proceeding, refusing an individual the possibility to retain counsel by not allowing a postponement is reviewable if the following factors are in play: the case is complex, the consequences of the decision are serious, the individual does not have the resources — whether in terms of intellect or legal knowledge — to properly represent his interests.

162 *Thamotharampillai v Canada (Minister of Citizenship and Immigration)*, 2011 FC 438; *Shirvan v Canada (Minister of Citizenship and Immigration)*, 2005 FC 1509 [*Shirvan*]: Former counsel must be given notice that allegations of incompetence and/or negligence are being made about their representation of a claimant; *Robles v Canada (Minister of Citizenship and Immigration)*, 2003 FCT 374: The

claimants unfortunately bear the consequences of hiring poor coun-sel.[163]

iii) Before the Hearing

In most cases, the board member will introduce all persons present in the hearing, explain that the hearing will be recorded but that the hearing is in-camera,[164] and identify the documentary evidence. A short pre-hearing conference may be held where counsel, officers, and the board member may identify the issues or main questions that need to be addressed.[165] This meeting is helpful in keeping the hearing focused on the main issues that the board member wants to resolve and in identifying for the claimant and the claimant's counsel what questions the board member may want answered.

iv) During the Hearing

Although the RPD is an administrative tribunal not bound by the strict rules and procedures one would find in court, the *RPD Rules*[166] regulate such aspects of the process as the choice of language for the hearing, designation of a representative for a claimant, disclosure of information and documents, witnesses, making of applications, vacating of a claim, abandoning of a claim, and other elements.[167]

At the beginning of a hearing, an oath or affirmation will be administered to the claimant. Typically, if the minister is not a party, the board member will begin the hearing by questioning the claimant or any witness present.[168] If the minister is present and has intervened on the issue of exclusion[169] or if there is an application to vacate or cease

---

claimant must show a factual foundation to find that prejudice resulted from incompetence of counsel.

163 *Hak v Canada (Minister of Citizenship and Immigration)*, 2005 FC 1488; *Shirvan*, above note 162, where the court held that, while former counsel was inexperienced and unfamiliar with hearing procedures, the claimants were nevertheless able to present their case to the RPD.

164 *RPD Rules*, above note 10, ss 21(4)–(5): The RPD is not to disclose personal or other information unless it is satisfied that there is not a serious possibility that disclosing the information will endanger the life, liberty, or security of any person; or disclosing the information is not likely to cause an injustice. If the Division intends to make information public, they must give notice to the claimant. Applications can be made under s 57 to have the hearings proceed publicly.

165 *Ibid*, s 24.

166 *Ibid*.

167 *Ibid*.

168 *Ibid*, s 10(1).

169 *Ibid*, s 10(2).

refugee protection,[170] then any witness, including the claimant, will be questioned first by the minister, then by the board member, then by claimant's counsel. If the minister is present but has not intervened on the issue of exclusion, then the board member will question any witness, including the claimant, first; then, the minister has the opportunity to ask questions and then, the claimant's counsel does.[171]

The claimant may request some accommodation, such as changing the order of questioning or having limits to questioning imposed, only in exceptional circumstances. A claimant may ask that her counsel question the claimant before other parties by asking for accommodations through a vulnerable persons application,[172] which can be made in writing or orally.[173] Similarly, it is at the discretion of the board member to decide how questions can be limited, taking into account the nature and complexity of the issues and the relevance of the questions.[174]

In *Thamotharem v Canada (Minister of Citizenship and Immigration)*,[175] the Federal Court of Appeal considered whether the standard practice of having the board member question the claimant first (known as "reverse order questioning") violates the principles of natural justice. Counsel for Thamotharem argued that the procedure violated the claimant's right to a fair hearing by denying the claimant the opportunity to be questioned first by his own counsel.[176] Counsel also argued that since the practice of reverse order questioning was demanded by a Chairperson Guideline, it unduly fettered the board member's discretion. The Court of Appeal held that the practice of reverse order questioning is not incompatible with the impartiality required of a member when conducting an inquisitorial hearing.[177] Further, it held that the procedure was not an unlawful fetter on the exercise of the members' discretion as members could deviate from the procedure where facts warrant it.[178]

As a result of the decision in *Thamotharem*, the onus is now on the claimant to ask for accommodation via a vulnerable persons application to vary the procedure where such order of questioning may have

---

170 *Ibid*, s 10(4).
171 *Ibid*, s 10(3). Typically, the only witness in a hearing is the claimant.
172 For more information regarding vulnerable persons applications, see Section A(3)(i)(1)(c), above in this chapter.
173 See *RPD Rules*, above note 10, ss 10(5) and 50.
174 *Ibid*, s 10(6).
175 2007 FCA 198 [*Thamotharem*].
176 *Ibid* at para 3.
177 *Ibid* at para 10.
178 *Ibid* at para 11.

an impact on the claimant's ability to share her story.[179] With today's expedited procedure, claimants may have little opportunity to ask for accommodation.[180]

An experienced board member may have gained "specialized knowledge" on matters related to a particular refugee claim as a result of having presided in other hearings where similar issues were raised. Should a board member wish to rely on this knowledge, the member must give notice of the intention to do so to the claimant and all other parties participating in the hearing, so that they will have an opportunity to dispute it.[181]

After the questioning of witnesses, oral representations may be made by any representative present.[182] A board member may make an oral decision and provide reasons orally at the end of the hearing.[183] In some cases, however, a board member may reserve this right to make a decision if it is impractical given the issues present and the amount of evidence presented at a hearing. In this case, decisions must be made in writing and a notice of decision sent to the claimant.[184] Claimants may request written reasons if they do not receive them.[185]

v)   A Note on Assessing Credibility

Credibility remains at the core of refugee determination. Is the claimant telling the truth? Is the claimant's story plausible? Is the claimant really fearful? The Supreme Court of Canada recognized the import-

---

179   Scholars have discussed the problems associated with this kind of procedure, despite the fact that the refugee hearing is not held in a formal legal setting: France Houle, "*Thamotharem* and Guideline 7 of the IRB: Rethinking the Scope of the Fettering of Discretion Doctrine" (2008) 25 *Refuge* 103; Susan Kneebone, *Refugees, Asylum Seekers and the Rule of Law: Comparative Perspectives* (Cambridge: Cambridge University Press, 2009) at 98; Janet Cleveland, "The Guideline on Procedures with Respect to Vulnerable Persons Appearing before the Immigration and Refugee Board of Canada: A Critical Overview" (2008) 25 *Refuge* 119.

180   Canadian Council for Refugees, *The Experience of Refugee Claimants at Refugee Hearings in the New System* (April 2014), online: CCR http://ccrweb.ca/sites/ ccrweb.ca/files/refugee-hearing-report-2014.pdf: This report highlights the many issues that may face refugee claimants in the new refugee system. One may wish to contrast these vulnerabilities with those recognized in the IRB's guidelines dealing with vulnerable persons to see that accommodations may not be given to certain people.

181   *RPD Rules*, above note 10, s 22.

182   *Ibid*, s 10(7).

183   *Ibid*, s 10(8).

184   *Ibid*, s 67.

185   *Ibid*, s 67(3).

ance of assessing credibility in *Singh* when it held that oral hearings are needed when credibility is at issue.[186]

There is, however, no set or established way to make a credibility finding. In evaluating credibility, decision makers at the IRB have wide latitude in not only managing refugee hearings, but also in resorting to various methods to come to a determination. Further, until recently when the RAD was implemented, there was little oversight over how decision makers make credibility findings. Often, the only recourse was judicial review, and the Federal Court has often taken a deferential approach to credibility findings since it has no direct access to the evidence.

The UNHCR recommends that decision makers resort to a "narrative form of questioning," which includes open-ended questions.[187] It cautions against engaging in extensive examination or knowledge tests with regard to a claimant's circumstances. For example, "knowledge of the claimant's religion may not always be necessary or useful" and "knowledge tests need to take account of individual circumstances, particularly since knowledge of a religion may vary considerably depending on the individual's social, economic or educational background and/ or his or her age or sex."[188] Instead, the UNHCR recommends eliciting information through open-ended questions about a person's individual religious experiences.[189] Although different approaches to their role may be taken by different decision makers, with some scrutinizing claims more closely than others, in general, Canadian jurisprudence recognizes a presumption of truthfulness.[190]

Decision makers need to be careful not to affix rigid labels or stereotypes to claimants nor to determine their credibility based on

---

186 *Singh*, above note 1.

187 UN High Commissioner for Refugees, Guidelines on International Protection No 6: *Religion-Based Refugee Claims under Article 1A(2) of the 1951 Convention and/or the 1967 Protocol relating to the Status of Refugees* (28 April 2004), online: Refworld www.refworld.org/pdfid/4090f9794.pdf at para 29 [UNHCR Guidelines: *Religion-Based Refugee Claims*].

188 *Ibid* at para 28.

189 *Ibid* at para 29:

> . . . such as asking him or her to describe in detail how he or she adopted the religion, the place and manner of worship, or the rituals engaged in, the significance of the religion to the person, or the values he or she believes the religion espouses. For example, the individual may not be able to list the Ten Commandments or name the Twelve Imams, but may be able to indicate an understanding of the religion's basic tenets more generally.

190 *Tar v Canada (Minister of Citizenship and Immigration)*, 2014 FC 767.

pre-fixed but unwarranted generalizations. [191] Hilary Evans Cameron has offered the following analysis:

> Refugee status decision makers typically have unreasonable expectations of what and how people remember. Members of the Refugee Protection Division of Canada's Immigration and Refugee Board (IRB/the Board), for example, often subscribe to the common lay notion that "Memory is like a video recording of your observations that can be played back at will to remind you of what you saw." Yet, even setting aside the effects on memory of trauma and stress, decades of research has established beyond any doubt that human memory is nothing like a video recording, that it is neither as complete nor as stable as this folk theory implies. As a result, decision makers far too often make findings that are as unsound as they are unjust.[192]

Evans Cameron, in her work, highlights common failures of memory that are relevant to the refugee determination process. These include memory for time (dates, duration, frequency, and sequence), common objects, repeated events, peripheral information, names, and verbatim memory. She also discusses common misconceptions on how memory changes over time.[193] Claimants and their counsel may want to alert decision makers of her work to help shape the way credibility findings may be made.[194]

---

191 For example, UN High Commissioner for Refugees, Guidelines on International Protection No 9: *Claims to Refugee Status Based on Sexual Orientation and/or Gender Identity within the Context of Article 1A(2) of the 1951 Convention and/or Its 1967 Protocol relating to the Status of Refugees*, online: UNHCR www.unhcr. org/509136ca9.pdf at paras 3 and 30 [UNHCR Guidelines: *Sexual Orientation*], note:

> LGBTI individuals frequently keep aspects and sometimes large parts of their lives secret. Many will not have lived openly as LGBTI in their country of origin and some may not have had any intimate relationships. Many suppress their sexual orientation and/or gender identity to avoid the severe consequences of discovery, including the risk of incurring harsh criminal penalties, arbitrary house raids, discrimination, societal disapproval, or family exclusion.

It would be improper for a board member to disbelieve a claimant without considering such factors.

192 Hilary Evans Cameron, "Refugee Status Determinations and the Limits of Memory" (2010) 22 *International Journal of Refugee Law* 469 at 469–70.

193 *Ibid.*

194 See also Hilary Evans Cameron, "Risk Theory and 'Subjective Fear': The Role of Risk Perception, Assessment, and Management in Refugee Status Determinations" (2008) 20 *International Journal of Refugee Law* 567.

j)   Withdrawing a Refugee Claim

If a claimant provides notice in writing to the minister of Citizenship and Immigration that he is withdrawing his claim, the refugee claim will be deemed withdrawn as soon as it is received.[195] The effect of withdrawing a claim is that the claim for refugee protection is rejected.[196]

The RPD may refuse to allow a claimant to withdraw a claim if it is of the opinion that the doing so would amount to an abuse of process.[197] Where no substantive evidence has been accepted in a hearing, a claim may be withdrawn by simply notifying the RPD orally or in writing.[198] Where, however substantive evidence has been accepted by the RPD, a claimant must make an application to the RPD to withdraw the claim.[199]

i)   Abandoning a Refugee Claim

There is an onus on the claimant to pursue the refugee claim diligently. Where a claimant fails to appear at a hearing, fails to provide information or communicate with the RPD, or voluntarily leaves Canada,[200] a refugee claim may be deemed abandoned.[201] The effect of abandoning a claim is that the claim for refugee protection is rejected.[202]

Before a claim is deemed abandoned, the RPD must give the claimant an opportunity to explain why he failed to appear, communicate, or provide information to the RPD.[203] Notice of an abandonment hearing must be given,[204] and the opportunity may be provided at an RPD proceeding[205] or by way of a special hearing usually five days after documents/information were to be provided to the RPD or the date of the

---

195 *Regulations*, above note 8, s 170.
196 *Ibid*, s 171.
197 *IRPA*, above note 4, s 168(2).
198 *RPD Rules*, above note 10, s 59(2).
199 *Ibid*, s 59(3). The rules imply that the BOC is not considered "substantive evidence."
200 See *Regulations*, above note 8, s 240: Where a claimant leaves voluntarily when a removal order is enforced under s 240, the applicant is deemed to have abandoned the claim. A claimant who otherwise leaves Canada is also deemed to have abandoned the claim.
201 *Ibid*, s 169; *IRPA*, above note 4, s 168(1); *Gapchenko v Canada (Minister of Citizenship and Immigration)*, 2004 FC 427 [*Gapchenko*].
202 *Regulations*, above note 8, s 171.
203 *RPD Rules*, above note 10, s 65(1); *Revich v Canada (Minister of Citizenship and Immigration)*, 2004 FC 1064 [*Revich*]; *Sharma v Canada (Minister of Citizenship and Immigration)*, 2006 FC 95 [*Sharma*].
204 *Sharma, ibid*: New notice does not have to be given when the claimant changes counsel however.
205 *RPD Rules*, above note 10, s 65(1)(a).

RPD hearing.[206] The board member presiding over the proceeding must consider the explanation given by the claimant[207] and whether the claimant is ready to proceed or continue with the claim or hearing.[208] The question before the RPD in abandonment hearings is whether the claimant truly intended to abandon the claim.[209] The *RPD Rules* provide that, if the board member decides that the claim is not abandoned, the claimant must be prepared to start or continue proceedings the day the decision is made or as soon as possible after that date.[210] If a claimant is unable to proceed that day, the RPD should not sacrifice the right to a full and fair hearing for administrative efficiency.[211]

---

206 *Ibid*, ss 65(1)(b), (2), & (3): A special hearing on the abandonment of the claim for failure to provide a complete Basis of Claim must be held no later than five working days after the day on which the BOC form was due. At the special hearing, the claimant must provide a completed BOC. If the special hearing is on the basis that the claimant failed to appear for a hearing, the abandonment hearing must be held within five days after the day the RPD hearing was originally fixed.

207 *Tajadodi v Canada (Minister of Citizenship and Immigration)*, 2005 FC 1096: The test of "exceptional circumstances" applies to requests for an extension of time to file a personal information form (PIF) or BOC, and those exceptional circumstances are to be among the relevant factors to be considered, but not a decisive test in deciding whether a claim has been abandoned; *Khan v Canada (Minister of Citizenship and Immigration)*, 2005 FC 833: Where claimant's counsel was negligent and there was no contributing negligence or fault on the part of the claimant, an RPD decision not to reopen the claim after it had been declared abandoned can be set aside. This is the case where claimants put their trust in a consultant who led them to believe he would take care of all correspondence with the IRB and would advise them of scheduled proceedings; *Andreoli v Canada (Minister of Citizenship and Immigration)*, 2004 FC 1111: Where the claimants suffered from the carelessness of a third party, a finding that a claim is abandoned is unfair as the claimants cannot be considered true authors of their own misfortune; *Revich*, above note 203: In this case where a claimant provides medical evidence of her state of health, that should be seen as an explanation of why the claim should not be considered abandoned.

208 *RPD Rules*, above note 10, ss 65(4)–(7): If the explanation is one of a medical nature, the claimant must provide a medical certificate.

209 *Revich*, above note 203; *Gapchenko*, above note 201: The question to be asked is whether the refugee claimant's conduct amounts to an expression of intention by that person that he or she did not wish, or had shown no interest, to pursue the refugee claim with diligence; *Anjum v Canada (Minister of Citizenship and Immigration)*, 2004 FC 496.

210 *RPD Rules*, above note 10, s 65(8).

211 *Aslam v Canada (Minister of Citizenship and Immigration)*, 2004 FC 514.

k) Cessation and the *IRPA*, Section 108

The minister of Citizenship and Immigration may apply in writing to the RPD to cease refugee protection.[212] The clause in the *IRPA* authorizing such an application is based on the *Refugee Convention*,[213] article 1C, and states that international protection should not be granted when it is no longer necessary or justified.[214] While the onus is on the minister to provide evidence that refugee protection should cease,[215] while the claimant still has the burden to prove an ongoing fear of return.[216] Where the minister's application is successful, the refugee claim is deemed to be rejected.[217]

Recently, the Federal Court has held that the minister's delegate, in filing a cessation application, owes a duty of procedural fairness, since filing an application is an administrative decision that affects the applicant's interests.[218] Thus, CBSA officers or other immigration officers who actively seek information to form the basis for a cessation application must advise individuals of the purpose of their questions.[219] The court, however, held that there is neither a duty to provide notice nor a duty to provide an opportunity to make submissions before making a cessation application.[220] Further, the court held that a delegate or officer has no duty to consider factors regarding humanitarian and compassionate grounds when preparing a cessation application.[221]

The *IRPA* specifies when refugee protection should cease:

- where the person voluntarily reavails herself of the protection of her country of nationality;[222]

---

212 *IRPA*, above note 4, s 108(2); *RPD Rules*, above note 10, s 64: Section 64(2) sets out the required content of the application, and s 64(3) provides that the application must be provided to the refugee or protected person, as well as the RPD. Note that while the RPD makes a decision on the minister's applications, the Canada Border Services Agency is responsible for administering cessation and vacation decisions.

213 Above note 19.

214 *Romero v Canada (Minister of Citizenship and Immigration)*, 2014 FC 671 at para 37 [*Romero*].

215 *Hasan v Canada (Minister of Citizenship and Immigration)*, 2008 FC 1069 at para 21.

216 *Mileva v Canada (Minister of Employment and Immigration)*, [1991] FCJ No 79 (CA).

217 *IRPA*, above note 4, s 108(3).

218 *Romero*, above note 214 at para 55.

219 *Ibid* at para 78.

220 *Ibid* at para 79.

221 *Ibid* at para 106.

222 *IRPA*, above note 4, s 108(1)(a).

- where the person has voluntarily reacquired his nationality;[223]
- where the person has acquired a new nationality and enjoys the protection of the country or that new nationality;[224]
- where the person has voluntarily become re-established in the country that the person left or remained outside of and in respect of which the person claimed refugee protection in Canada;[225] or
- where the reasons for which the person sought refugee protection have ceased to exist.[226]

There is an exception to the last of these grounds, when a refugee has compelling reasons arising out of previous persecution, torture, treatment, or punishment not to avail himself of the protection of a country, protection will not cease even where the grounds for granting it have ceased to exist.[227] The burden is on the claimant to establish that there are such compelling reasons.[228] It has been held that the situation

---

223 *Ibid*, s 108(1)(b); see *Canada (Minister of Employment and Immigration) v Obstoj*, [1992] 2 FC 739 (CA) [*Obstoj*]; UN High Commissioner for Refugees, *Handbook and Guidelines on Procedures and Criteria for Determining Refugee Status* (December 2011), online: UNHCR www.unhcr.org/3d58e13b4.html at para 128 [UNHCR Handbook].

224 *IRPA*, above note 4, s 108(1)(c); UNHCR Handbook, above note 223 at paras 130–31.

225 *IRPA*, above note 4, s 108(1)(d); UNHCR Handbook, above note 223 at paras 133–34.

226 *IRPA*, above note 4, s 108(1)(e).

227 *IRPA*, *ibid*, s 108(4); *Suleiman v Canada (Minister of Citizenship and Immigration)*, 2004 FC 1125 [*Suleiman*]; *Obstoj*, above note 223; *Brovina v Canada (Minister of Citizenship and Immigration)*, 2004 FC 635: The Federal Court has held that the decision maker must first find that there was a valid refugee or protected person claim and that the reasons for the claim have ceased to exist. It is only then that the IRB should consider whether the nature of the claimant's experience was so appalling that she should not be expected to return; *Elemah v Canada (Minister of Citizenship and Immigration)*, 2001 FCT 779 (TD); *Kulla v Canada (Minister of Citizenship and Immigration)*, 2000 CanLII 16014 (FC): The claimant need not show that the persecution reached a level of atrocious or appalling; rather, the IRB must canvass all documentary and oral evidence to determine whether there are compelling reasons not to return; *Shahid v Canada (Minister of Citizenship and Immigration)* (1995), 89 FTR 106 (TD): The IRB has an obligation to do a proper assessment by considering the persecution, torture, or cruel and unusual punishment suffered by the claimant and whether this constitutes a compelling reason not to return him to this country of origin; *Hassan v Canada (Minister of Employment and Immigration)* (1994), 77 FTR 309(TD); *Arguello-Garcia v Canada (Minister of Employment and Immigration)* (1993), 21 Imm LR (2d) 285 (FCTD).

228 *Yamba v Canada (Minister of Citizenship and Immigration)*, 2000 CanLII 15191 (FCA); *Jiminez v Canada (Minister of Citizenship and Immigration)* (1999), 162

faced by the claimant need not be atrocious or appalling,[229] and the claimant need not suffer specific after-effects such as post-traumatic stress disorder.[230] As well, a political change in the claimant's country is a question of fact that may help determine whether there is prospective risk of persecution, torture, or cruel and unusual punishment, but is not determinative of an application for cessation.[231]

What does it mean to reavail oneself of the protection of one's country of nationality? The Federal Court has held that renewing a passport may, in some circumstances, be accepted as raising a presumption of reavailment,[232] but in other cases, it has held that it is an error to base the decision on this evidence alone.[233] In *Nsende v Canada (Minister of Citizenship and Immigration)*, the court refers to three requirements in making a finding of reavailment:

(a) voluntariness: the refugee must act voluntarily;
(b) intention: the refugee must intend by his action to reavail himself of the protection of the country of his nationality; and
(c) reavailment: the refugee must actually obtain such protection.[234]

In *Cadena v Canada (Minister of Public Safety and Emergency Preparedness)*, the Federal Court held that while a passport application creates a presumption of intention to reavail,[235] proof to the contrary may refute that presumption.[236] In addition, a claimant's intention to travel must be considered but the Federal Court of Appeal has cautioned that the mere fact of returning to a country is not determinative.[237] It has

---

FTR 177 (TD): The claimant need not show that he is suffering continual psychological after-effects from the persecution that he endured in his country of nationality.

229 *Suleiman*, above note 227.
230 *Kotorri v Canada (Minister of Citizenship and Immigration)*, 2005 FC 1195.
231 *Yusuf v Canada (Minister of Employment and Immigration)* (1995), 179 NR 11 (FCA).
232 2012 FC 67 [*Cadena*].
233 *Chandrakumar v Canada (Minister of Employment and Immigration)*, 1997 CanLII 16770 (FCTD).
234 2008 FC 531 at para 13.
235 *Cadena*, above note 232: The court here held that obtaining or renewing a passport may weigh heavily in favour of finding that the claimant voluntarily re-established or reavailed herself to the protection of the country of origin. The exception is a minor, as he cannot form the intention to and therefore cannot re-establish himself in the country of origin.
236 *Ibid* at paras 14–15; see also *RPD File No MB3-01312*, [2013] RPDD No 11.
237 *Shanmugarajah v Canada (Minister of Employment and Immigration)*, [1992] FCJ No 583 (CA).

been held that responding to a family emergency,[238] accessing another country as a necessary part of the process to secure residence somewhere safe,[239] and investigating if the situation in the country has improved[240] are situations that should not be considered as reavailment. On the other hand, the court has accepted that a lengthy stay in a country of origin may constitute reavailment even if it arises because Canadian officials will not allow the person to return[241] and even if the stay takes place under duress.[242] It is interesting to note that the court has understood re-establishment (section 108(1)(d)) and reavailment (section 108(1)(a)) as one and the same.[243]

Finally, the Federal Court has outlined the meaning of a change of circumstances under section 108(1)(e) by looking at three factors:

1)   The change must be of substantial political significance.[244]
2)   There must be reason to believe that the substantial political change is truly effective.[245]
3)   The change of circumstances must be shown to be durable.[246]

---

238   *Starovic v Canada (Minister of Citizenship and Immigration)*, 2012 FC 827 at para 17 [*Starovic*].
239   *Abawaji v Canada (Minister of Citizenship and Immigration)*, 2006 FC 1065.
240   *Revolorio v Canada (Minister of Citizenship and Immigration)*, 2008 FC 1404.
241   *Starovic*, above note 238.
242   Above note 232.
243   *El Kaissi v Canada (Minister of Citizenship and Immigration)*, 2011 FC 1234 at paras 28–29.
244   *Winifred v Canada (Minister of Citizenship and Immigration)*, 2011 FC 827 at para 31:

First, the change must be of substantial political significance, in the sense that the power structure under which persecution was deemed a real possibility no longer exists. The collapse of the persecutory regime, coupled with the holding of genuinely free and democratic elections, the assumption of power by a government committed to human rights, and a guarantee of fair treatment for enemies of the predecessor regime by way of amnesty or otherwise, is the appropriate indicator of a meaningful change of circumstances. It would, in contrast, be premature to consider cessation simply because relative calm has been restored in a country still governed by an oppressive political structure. Similarly, the mere fact that a democratic and safe local or regional government has been established is insufficient insofar as the national government still poses a risk to the refugee.

245   *Ibid*: "Secondly, there must be reason to believe that the substantial political change is truly effective. Because . . . 'there is often a long distance between pledging and doing . . .', it ought not to be assumed that formal change will necessarily be immediately effective . . . ."

246   *Ibid*:

Third, the change of circumstances must be shown to be durable. Cessation is not a decision to be taken lightly on the basis of transitory shifts in the

In essence, the changes must be stable and meaningful.[247]

Recent amendments to the *IRPA* attach a number of significant consequences to a cessation decision. Section 46(1)(c.1) of the *IRPA* establishes that permanent residence may be lost following a cessation decision made by the RPD, except where there has been a change of circumstances under section 108(1)(e).[248] In addition, section 40.1 of the *IRPA* renders a person inadmissible upon cessation of refugee protection, thus making the individual subject to removal.[249] Further, section 21(3) of the *IRPA* bars a protected person from becoming a permanent resident while a minister is pursuing cessation.[250]

Refugee claimants who are subject to a finding of cessation have little recourse. Because a decision is not made in an admissibility hearing or examination, the claimant cannot appeal the decision to the Immigration Appeal Division.[251] As well, the *IRPA* makes clear that there is no appeal of cessation decisions to the Refugee Appeal Division.[252] The only avenue a person may have is to seek leave from the Federal Court to apply for judicial review.[253]

---

political landscape, but should rather be reserved for situations in which there is reason to believe that the positive conversion of the power structure is likely to last. The condition is in keeping with the forward-looking nature of the refugee definition, and avoids the disruption of protection in circumstances where safety may be only a momentary aberration.

247 See *Kovacs v Canada (Minister of Citizenship and Immigration)*, 2010 FC 1003; *Chowdhury v Canada (Minister of Citizenship and Immigration)*, 2008 FC 290; *Barua v Canada (Minister of Citizenship and Immigration)*, 2012 FC 59.

248 *IRPA*, above note 4, s 46(1)(c.1):

> 46. (1) A person loses permanent resident status . . .
> (c.1) on a final determination under subsection 108(2) that their refugee protection has ceased for any of the reasons described in paragraphs 108(1)(*a*) to (*d*).

249 *Ibid*, s 40.1:

> (1) A foreign national is inadmissible on a final determination under subsection 108(2) that their refugee protection has ceased.
> (2) A permanent resident is inadmissible on a final determination that his refugee protection has ceased for any of the reasons described in paragraphs 108(1)(*a*) to (*d*).

250 *Ibid*, s 21(3).

251 *Ibid*, s 63(3).

252 *Ibid*, s 110(2)(c): As a result of having no access to the RAD, the person will not benefit from a statutory stay of removal as well under s 231 of *the Regulations*, above note 8, while seeking a judicial review of a cessation decision.

253 *IRPA*, above note 4, s 72(1). See Chapter 16 for more information about judicial review.

Claimants whose applications for citizenship have otherwise been approved cannot have the granting of citizenship suspended pending an investigation into cessation allegations. In these situations, a claimant can ask the Federal Court for the remedy of *mandamus* to have the citizenship decision take effect.[254] However, the court has yet to grant a *mandamus* for a permanent resident application while a cessation application is in process.[255]

The government has made significant changes to the legislation regarding cessation proceedings. Its policy rationale is to prevent the "abuse" of Canada's generosity and ensure that only vulnerable persons who "genuinely need it" are served by the refugee system.[256] This rationale reflects that government has a deep mistrust of refugee claimants and a poisonous view that refugee claimants are taking advantage of the Canadian refugee system. It also reflects the government's push to increase temporariness to the refugee protection regime. It is curious that there are greater efforts being made to engage in cessation proceedings given that the government has long had the power to punish persons who obtain refugee status through misrepresentation through vacation proceedings, described below.

As a result of these changes to legislation, refugee claimants who find themselves subject to a cessation hearing may argue that there are changed circumstances and urge the decision maker, if they are going to make a decision of cessation, to make a finding under section 108(1)(e) rather than under other sections so that they do not lose their permanent residence status. Further, given the serious implications of a decision, it is likely we will see more cessation decisions being brought for judicial review. These challenges may question the IRB's ability to relinquish status that is subject to Canada's international obligations; whether such a decision breaches the *Charter*, section 7;[257] and whether the decision affects the best interests of a child.

A cessation decision carries further implications. Because a cessation decision means that a person's refugee claim is deemed rejected,

---

254 *Stanizai v Canada (Minister of Citizenship and Immigration)*, 2014 FC 74.

255 *Jaber v Canada (Minister of Citizenship and Immigration)*, 2013 FC 1185.

256 Citizenship and Immigration Canada, Backgrounder, *Deterring Abuse of the Refugee System*, online: CIC www.cic.gc.ca/english/department/media/backgrounders/2012/2012-06-29g.asp.

257 Peter Edelmann, "Cessation of Refugee Status after *PCISA*" (Paper delivered at the CBA National Immigration Conference, Calgary, May 2014): Edelmann suggests referring to *Blencoe v British Columbia (Human Rights Commission)*, 2000 SCC 44, where the Supreme Court recognized that the right to security of the person included protection against state-imposed psychological stress.

she cannot make an application for permanent residence on humanitarian and compassionate grounds for twelve months after the cessation finding unless she falls into one of the limited exceptions listed in section 25 of the *IRPA*.[258] Further, a person subject to a cessation decision is barred from applying for a temporary resident permit for twelve months,[259] is ineligible to apply for a pre-removal risk assessment for twelve months after the cessation finding or thirty-six months if he is from a designated country of origin,[260] and is ineligible for a statutory stay of removal.[261]

l) Vacation

The RPD, on application by the minister of Citizenship and Immigration,[262] may also vacate a decision conferring refugee protection on a person if it finds that the decision was obtained by directly or indirectly misrepresenting or withholding material facts related to the refugee claim.[263] Vacation renders the protected status *void ab initio*. In considering such an application, the RPD must consider any evidence cited in support of the original positive determination and whether such evidence is "tainted" by the material misrepresentation or withholding of facts.[264]

The burden is on the minister of Citizenship and Immigration to prove that there is sufficient new evidence showing a misrepresentation to merit a vacation.[265] Materiality is to be determined on a balance of probabilities in light of the significance of the information not disclosed.

---

258 *IRPA*, above note 4, s 25. See Chapter 12 for more information on humanitarian and compassionate grounds applications.

259 *Ibid*, s 24(4). See Chapter 4 for more information on temporary status.

260 *Ibid*, s 112(2)(b.1). See Chapter 11 for more information on pre-removal risk assessments.

261 *Regulations*, above note 8, s 232.

262 *RPD Rules*, above note 10, s 64, which provides the form and content for the application that needs to be made.

263 *IRPA*, above note 4, s 109(1): See, for example, *Iliev v Canada (Minister of Citizenship and Immigration)*, 2005 FC 395; *Calixto v Canada (Minister of Citizenship and Immigration)*, 2005 FC 1037, in which withholding information regarding a criminal record, a matter that relates to a finding of exclusion or inadmissibility, is found to be material.

264 *Bortey v Canada (Minister of Citizenship and Immigration)*, 2006 FC 190.

265 See *Canada (Minister of Citizenship and Immigration) v Wahab*, 2006 FC 1554 at para 29, where the court outlines some principles to be followed when reviewing an application to vacate:

    a)   Under s. 109(1), to determine if the original decision was made as a result of directly or indirectly misrepresenting or withholding material facts relating to a relevant matter, the RPD must consider all the new evidence put forward by the Minister and the claimant.

Therefore, a falsehood or a misleading answer, which has the effect of foreclosing or averting further inquiries, may be a misrepresentation under the *IRPA*.[266] The Federal Court has held that it is an abuse of process for the minister to proceed with a vacation application at the RPD when the same alleged misrepresentation that led to a finding of inadmissibility in the Immigration Division is under appeal at the Immigration Appeal Division.[267] Although the minister may adduce new evidence, the claimant may not introduce new evidence to show that, notwithstanding the misrepresentation, his claim should be allowed.[268] Despite this limitation, claimants can adduce reply evidence to rebut the minister's allegations.[269] Further, while the minister does not have to disclose exculpatory information in possession of another agency such as the CBSA or the RCMP, the RPD may be required to reopen a vacation application if there arises new evidence that undermines the entire vacation application.[270] Finally, the RPD cannot base a vacation decision on unreliable evidence from the minister and must presume

---

b)   *Mens rea* or the intention of the claimant is not relevant to the finding to be made under s. 109(1).

c)   As the extent and nature of the material misrepresentation or withholding may be relevant to its ability to exercise its discretion pursuant to section 109(2) of the *IRPA*, the RPD must give sufficient details in its reasons as to which misrepresented or withheld fact(s) it found material and in respect of what relevant matter. Those detailed findings will enable the RPD to consider if a particular claimant is, for example, excluded under section 98 of *IRPA*. Such determination must be made prior to proceeding to the second step set out in s. 109(2) and involves consideration of all the evidence on file, including the new evidence presented by both parties.

d)   The RPD only needs to proceed to the s. 109(2) analysis (step two) if it is satisfied that a claimant is not excluded under section 98 of *IRPA*.

e)   When carrying out the analysis set out in s. 109(2), the RPD may refer to its findings under section 109(1) but only to identify what "old" evidence remains untainted by the withholding or misrepresentation. The RPD may not reassess the "old" evidence in light of new evidence adduced by the Minister or the claimant pursuant to section 109(1). The RPD may not give any weight or even consider the new evidence produced by either party when exercising its discretion pursuant to section 109(2).

266 *Schneeberger v Canada (Minister of Citizenship and Immigration)*, 2003 FC 970.

267 *Thambiturai v Canada (Solicitor General)*, 2006 FC 750.

268 *Canada (Minister of Emergency Preparedness) v Gunasingam*, 2008 FC 181.

269 *Canada (Minister of Citizenship and Immigration) v Ekuban*, 2001 FCT 65; *Coomaraswamy v Canada (Minister of Citizenship and Immigration)*, 2002 FCA 153.

270 *Seyoboka v Canada (Minister of Citizenship and Immigration)*, 2009 FC 104.

that the claimant is credible unless otherwise disproven by the minister.[271]

m) Increases in Cessation and Vacation Applications

The current government has vigorously pursued cessation and vacation applications. Between 2007 and 2011, there were 106 cessation applications and 304 vacation applications.[272] The minister of Public Safety and Emergency Preparedness has set a target of 875 cessation and vacation cases per year.[273] These efforts render the grant of refugee protection in Canada less secure. Further, advocates are asking: "What is this [target] based on? Is there any evidence that there are enough cases to sustain such a high figure every year?" "Particularly in the case of cessation, is there *any* benefit to the Canadian public in pursuing these cases? Does it save us money or make us safer?"[274]

As a result, claimants should be cautioned about hiding something from the RPD that could result in status being revoked at a later date,[275] applying for or renewing a passport of the country of origin, and travelling back to the country of origin; if the claimant must return there, it is important to document and challenge any refusal to allow re-entry into Canada, take precautions in disclosing and reviewing travel history and other information when applying for citizenship, and apply for citizenship at the earliest opportunity.

n) Reopening Refugee Claims

The claimant or the minister may make an application to the RPD to reopen a claim for refugee protection that has been decided or declared abandoned, but must do so before the Refugee Appeal Division (RAD) or the Federal Court has made a final determination.[276]

---

271 *Al-Maari v Canada (Minister of Citizenship and Immigration)*, 2013 FC 1037.

272 Sean Rehaag, Numbers compiled based on data provided by the IRB in ATIP 2012-00019 (updated 12 August 2012), online: http://ccrweb.ca/en/2013-refugee-claim-data.

273 Canada Border Services Agency, Operational Bulletin PRG-2013-59.

274 Sarah Boyd, "Ending Protection: Dealing with (and Avoiding) Applications for Cessation and Vacation" (Paper delivered at the 22nd Annual Immigration Law Summit of the Law Society of Upper Canada, 20 November 2014) at 9.

275 There is no *mens rea* requirement for vacation of refugee status. See *Pearce v Canada (Minister of Citizenship and Immigration)*, 2006 FC 492 at para 36.

276 *RPD Rules*, above note 10, s 62(1); see ss 50, 62(2)–(3), and 63 for form and content of the application.

The sole ground available for granting a reopening application is a failure to observe a principle of natural justice.[277] The rules allow for an allegation that a claimant did not have a full and fair hearing due to the incompetence of the claimant's counsel.[278] Where an application alleges that counsel was incompetent, notice of the application must be given to that counsel.[279]

Factors that the RPD may consider include whether the application to reopen was made in a timely manner and whether there are reasons for any delay in making the application;[280] or reasons why a party may not have appealed to the Refugee Appeal Division or made an application for judicial review at the Federal Court.[281] The RPD must also consider, if there is a pending appeal to the Refugee Appeal Division and/or judicial review to the Federal Court, whether allowing the reopening would be necessary for the timely and efficient processing of a claim.[282] Further, the RPD must consider whether the claimant's conduct really amounted to an expression of his intention to diligently pursue his claim or whether there was an expression to "give up absolutely."[283]

The decision to either grant or dismiss an application to reopen a claim is a final decision where reasons must be provided.[284]

B. THE REFUGEE APPEAL DIVISION (RAD)

The Refugee Appeal Division (RAD) was created in the *IRPA* in 2002. However, for ten years, the relevant sections establishing the Appeal Division were not brought into force. Only with the enactment of the *Protecting Canada's Immigration System Act* in December 2012 did the RAD come into being. Section 110(1) of the *IRPA* sets out the main function for the Division:

---

277 *Ibid*, ss 62(6) and 63(6); *Ahmad v Canada (Minister of Citizenship and Immigration)*, 2005 FC 279: Grounds for judicial review are not valid considerations for reopening a refugee claim at the RPD; *Krishnamoorthy v Canada (Minister of Citizenship and Immigration)*, 2005 FC 237.

278 See, for example, *Osagie v Canada (Minister of Citizenship and Immigration)*, 2004 FC 1368.

279 *RPD Rules*, above note 10, ss 62(4) and 63(4).

280 *Ibid*, ss 62(7)(a) and 63(7)(a).

281 *Ibid*, ss 62(7)(b) and 63(7)(b).

282 *Ibid*, ss 62(9) and 63(9).

283 *Emani v Canada (Minister of Citizenship and Immigration)*, 2009 FC 520; *Matondo v Canada (Minister of Citizenship and Immigration)*, 2005 FC 416.

284 *Shahid v Canada (Minister of Citizenship and Immigration)*, 2004 FC 1607; *Javed v Canada (Minister of Citizenship and Immigration)*, 2004 FC 1458.

110.(1) Subject to subsections (1.1) and (2), a person or the Minister may appeal, in accordance with the rules of the Board, on a question of law, or fact or of mixed law and fact, to the Refugee Appeal Division against a decision of the Refugee Protection Division to allow or reject the person's claim for refugee protection.[285]

Section 110(1) makes an appeal available only against decisions that allow or reject refugee claims. In other words, other applications for protection, such as the pre-removal risk assessment, are not subject to appeal.

1) Eligibility

Section 110(2) of the *IRPA* places restrictions on eligibility to appeal an RPD decision to the RAD. The RAD may not hear an appeal by the following claimants nor from the following decisions:

1) A designated foreign national;[286]
2) Refugee claims determined withdrawn or abandoned;[287]
3) Refugee claims found to have no credible basis or manifestly unfounded;[288]
4) Refugee claims that would have been ineligible but for an exception to the *Safe Third Country Agreement*;[289]
5) A refugee claimant from a designated country of origin;[290]
6) A refugee claim subject to a cessation or vacation decision;[291]
7) A refugee decision made prior to 15 August 2012;[292]
8) A refugee claim that is deemed rejected because an order of surrender for extradition was issued under the *Extradition Act*.[293]

---

285 *IRPA*, above note 4, s 110(1).
286 *Ibid*, s 110(2)(a).
287 *Ibid*, s 110(2)(b).
288 *Ibid*, s 110(2)(c).
289 *Ibid*, ss 110(2)(d) and 102: Currently, the only country designated is the United States. The exceptions to the *Safe Third Country Agreement* are set out in the *Regulations*, above note 8, s 159.1.
290 *IRPA*, above note 4, s 110(2)(d.1).
291 *Ibid*, ss 110(2)(e) & (f).
292 *Ibid*, s 36(1); Order in Council PC 2012-999 (26 July 2012).
293 *IRPA*, above note 4, s 105(4).

2) Process

The *Refugee Appeal Division Rules* set out the process for submitting and processing an appeal.[294] All eligible parties, including the minister, have fifteen days to appeal a decision to RAD after receiving written reasons and the decision[295] and following that, an additional fifteen days to perfect the appeal.[296] The RAD has discretion to grant an extension of time should the appellant need it for reasons of fairness and natural justice.[297] A request for an extension requires a written application to the RAD that should include evidence set out in the form of an affidavit or statutory declaration.[298] The factors that the RAD will consider include these:

(a) whether the application was made in a timely manner and the justification for any delay;

(b) whether there is an arguable case;

(c) prejudice to the Minister if the application was granted; and

(d) the nature and complexity of the appeal.[299]

Since section 6(5) of the *RAD Rules* requires that the appellant's record accompany any application for extension of time to file the appellant's record, it appears a request for an extension cannot be made in advance.[300] As a result, appellants may want to file an incomplete record and follow up with any additional documents with an application explaining the delay.[301]

---

294 *Refugee Appeal Division Rules*, SOR/2012-257 [*RAD Rules*]: Although the rules on their face appear repetitive on the same list of requirements, various types of filings differ and procedures may prove consequential. It is important to pay close attention to the specific rules and procedures which may apply to the claimant. For example, service on the minister is required for some documents but not others.

295 *Regulations*, above note 8, ss 110(2.1) and 159.91(1)(a); *RAD Rules*, above note 294, ss 2(1) and 31: The appellant must provide three copies of the written notice of appeal, and the RAD appeal must be filed in the registry of the same region as the RPD decision being appealed.

296 *Regulations*, above note 8, s 159.91(1)(b); *RAD Rules*, above note 294, s 3: Two copies of the appellant's record must be filed, and the appellant need not serve the minister.

297 *Regulations*, above note 8, s 159.91(2).

298 *RAD Rules*, above note 294, ss 6 and 37.

299 *Ibid*, s 6(7).

300 *Ibid*, s 6(5).

301 *Ibid*, s 29.

The minister may intervene in an appeal at any time before the RAD makes a decision.[302] The appellant may file a record in reply to the minister's intervention within fifteen days of the minister filing a notice of intervention or further documents,[303] and such a reply can address only the grounds raised by the minister.[304]

As noted by Peter Edelmann, the rules and the process set out for the RAD reveal a "recurring theme" of the "asymmetrical nature of the severe restrictions placed on the claimant versus enormous flexibility for the Minister."[305] For example, the "Minister can file documents at any time, is not limited in the types of evidence to be filed and, aside from the filing of Minister's appeals, would not appear to be affected by many timelines."[306]

3) Submitting New Evidence

While new evidence may be presented before the RAD, it must either be in response to evidence presented by the minister[307] or meet the same threshold set out for new evidence in pre-removal risk assessments:[308]

> 110(4) On appeal, the person who is the subject of the appeal may present only evidence that arose after the rejection of their claim or that was not reasonably available, or that the person could not reasonably have been expected in the circumstances to have presented, at the time of the rejection.[309]

In stark contrast to the provision governing refugee claimants, the minister is not limited by this rule on new evidence, even where the minister participated in the refugee hearing at the RPD.

Because the test for new evidence is identical to that used in pre-removal risk assessments, it is prudent to examine the approach set out in *Raza*, which highlights a number of factors, including credibility,[310]

---

302 *Ibid*, s 4(1); *Regulations*, above note 8, ss 171(a.1) and (a.2).

303 *RAD Rules*, above note 294, s 5(5).

304 *Ibid*, s 5(2)(d)(i).

305 Peter Edelmann, *Refugee Appeal Division* (Paper delivered at the Continuing Legal Education Conference of Refugee Lawyers Groups, Vancouver, 3 March 2012), online: http://refugeelawyers.net/4b_Edelmann.pdf at 4.

306 *Ibid*.

307 *IRPA*, above note 4, s 110(5).

308 *Ibid*, s 113; see also *Raza v Canada (Minister of Citizenship and Immigration)*, 2007 FCA 385 [*Raza*]. See Chapter 11.

309 *IRPA*, above note 4, s 110(4).

310 *Raza*, above note 308 at para 13: "Credibility: Is the evidence credible, considering its source and the circumstances in which it came into existence? If not, the evidence need not be considered."

relevance,[311] newness,[312] materiality,[313] and express statutory conditions.[314]

So far, the RAD has approached the admission of new evidence and, therefore, the adherence to the *Raza* decision in two ways. First, in some cases, the Division has applied the factors in *Raza* without any modification.[315] In other cases, it has used the *Raza* factors but modified them to be sensitive to the particular context.[316] Cases that have taken a modified approach note that the RAD must be concerned not only with the timing of new evidence, but also with its quality and, in particular, whether the new evidence could affect the outcome of the RAD appeal.

There will undoubtedly be several cases seeking judicial review of RAD decisions relating to the issue of the admission of new evidence. In the recent case of *Singh v Canada (Minister of Citizenship and Immigration)*, the Federal Court held that the restriction on the admission

---

311 *Ibid*: "Relevance: Is the evidence relevant to the PRRA [pre-removal risk assessment] application, in the sense that it is capable of proving or disproving a fact that is relevant to the claim for protection? If not, the evidence need not be considered."

312 *Ibid*:

Newness: Is the evidence new in the sense that it is capable of:
   (a) proving the current state of affairs in the country of removal or an event that occurred or a circumstance that arose after the hearing in the RPD, or
   (b) proving a fact that was unknown to the refugee claimant at the time of the RPD hearing, or
   (c) contradicting a finding of fact by the RPD (including a credibility finding)? If not, the evidence need not be considered.

313 *Ibid*: "Materiality: Is the evidence material, in the sense that the refugee claim probably would have succeeded if the evidence had been made available to the RPD? If not, the evidence need not be considered."

314 *Ibid*: "Express statutory conditions:
   (a) If the evidence is capable of proving only an event that occurred or circumstances that arose prior to the RPD hearing, then has the applicant established either that the evidence was not reasonably available to him or her for presentation at the RPD hearing, or that he or she could not reasonably have been expected in the circumstances to have presented the evidence at the RPD hearing? If not, the evidence need not be considered.
   (b) If the evidence is capable of proving an event that occurred or circumstances that arose after the RPD hearing, then the evidence must be considered (unless it is rejected because it is not credible, not relevant, not new or not material)."

315 See, for example, *X (Re)*, 2014 CanLII 24199 (CA IRB); *X (Re)*, 2014 CanLII 55520 (CA IRB); *X (Re)*, 2014 CanLII 60409 (CA IRB).

316 See, for example, *X (Re)*, 2014 CanLII 33085 (CA IRB); *X (Re)*, 2014 CanLII 20447 (CA IRB); *X (Re)*, 2014 CanLII 24188 (CA IRB); *X (Re)*, 2014 CanLII 60411 (CA IRB); *X (Re)*, 2014 CanLII 60386 (CA IRB).

of evidence to new evidence in the context of pre-removal risk assessments is not entirely transferable to an appeal before the RAD and that leeway should be provided to appellants to respond to evidentiary weaknesses that the RPD may have found in the record.[317]

Thus, where the *Raza* factors have been cited, a claimant may challenge the decision by citing the differences between the processes of the Refugee Appeal Division and of pre-removal risk assessments, the limited timelines of the refugee determination process at the RPD and the RAD, and the importance of the evidence for the appeal.

4) Paper-Based and Oral Hearings

The *IRPA* has restricted the RAD to hearing appeals primarily by paper unless specified factors are met. In particular, section 110(6) of the *IRPA* states:

> 110(6) The Refugee Appeal Division may hold a hearing if, in its opinion, there is documentary evidence referred to in subsection (3)
>
> (a) that raises a serious issue with respect to the credibility of the person who is the subject of the appeal;
>
> (b) that is central to the decision with respect to the refugee protection claim; and
>
> (c) that, if accepted, would justify allowing or rejecting the refugee protection claim.[318]

In addition to this provision, the Supreme Court's decision in *Singh* will be a guiding force to ensure that a hearing will be provided on the basis of procedural fairness where credibility is at issue.[319]

For paper-based appeals, the RAD is required to make a decision within ninety days of the appeal being perfected.[320] The Division has the power to confirm[321] or substitute[322] an RPD decision, or refer a matter back to the RPD for a new hearing.[323]

---

317 2014 FC 1022.

318 *IRPA*, above note 4, s 110(6): The criteria are almost identical to those in s 167 of the *Regulations*, above note 8, which deals with pre-removal risk assessment hearings.

319 *Singh*, above note 1.

320 *Regulations*, above note 8, s 159.92(1).

321 *IRPA*, above note 4, s 111(1)(a).

322 *Ibid*, s 111(1)(b).

323 *Ibid*, s 111(1)(c).

5) Standard of Review or Intervention at the Refugee Appeal Division

At this early stage in the history of the RAD, it is still unclear what its role is in relation to both the RPD and to the Federal Court. The Federal Court seems divided on whether the RAD is a true appeal body or whether it is required to review RPD decisions according to a particular standard of review or intervention. Thus, the main question occupying both the RAD and the Federal Court is whether the RAD's primary purpose is to correct errors made by the RPD or to focus on the mandate of refugee protection.[324]

In the case of *Iyamuremye v Canada (Minister of Citizenship and Immigration)*,[325] the Federal Court held that

> . . . it would be absurd, and contrary to subsection 110(3) of the [*IRPA*] to task the Refugee Appeal Division (RAD) of the Immigration and Refugee Board with re-examining, for every instance, whether the claimants are in fact refugees or persons in need of protection . . . .
>
> It is clear from the case law that an appellate body cannot substitute

---

324 At the 22nd Immigration Law Summit of the Law Society of Upper Canada (on 20 November 2014), Anthony Prakash Navaneelan took part in a panel titled "The Refugee Appeal Division: Where Are We Now?" He framed the question in the following manner:

> There are four provisions in the *IRPA* that are in conflict with one another. This has created no clarity to the problem: section 162 gives exclusive and sole jurisdiction to the RAD to decide questions of fact which is a bold and direct way that the board can draw its own conclusions. This is confirmed by section 111, which allows the RAD to conduct independent assessments with three types of remedial powers including confirming the RPD decision, substituting its own opinion or returning the matter to the RPD. What is confusing is that section 111(2) allows the RAD to return the matter to the RPD only if it has found an error whereas section 111(1)(b) allows the RAD to substitute its own opinion without a requirement to find an error. There are four approaches to the question of what standard of intervention should be used by the RAD. Two are modeled on the understanding that the RAD's role is to correct errors and either turning to a standard of reasonableness or palpable or overriding error. Two other approaches are modeled on the understanding that the RAD's main role is to determine whether refugee protection is warranted and therefore calls for a hybrid appeal or *de novo* appeals similar to the IAD. So far, the Federal Court has not endorsed the view of a *de novo* appeal. Despite the finding in *Spasoja c Canada (Citoyennete et Immigration)*, 2014 CF 913 that uses a standard of invervention of palpable and overriding error, in general, the Federal Court is moving away from endorsing this standard of intervention. *Huruglica* has endorsed the hybrid appeal approach and this has precipitated interesting debates.

325 2014 FC 494.

its own reasoning for that of a specialized tribunal of first instance, the tribunal of fact, having the advantage of having heard *viva voce* testimony . . . unless the trial judge made a "palpable and overriding error" that led to the erroneous result.[326]

On the other hand, in *Alvarez v Canada (Minister of Citizenship and Immigration)* and *Eng v Canada (Minister of Citizenship and Immigration)*, the court stated that

Parliament conferred a true appellate function on the RAD, a specialized (if not overspecialized) tribunal, which sits on appeal of the decisions of another administrative tribunal.

and that

. . . the RAD misinterpreted its role as an appeal body in holding that its role was merely to assess, against a standard of reasonableness, whether the RPD's decision is within a range of possible, acceptable outcomes.[327]

In the more recent case of *Huruglica v Canada (Minister of Citizenship and Immigration)*, the Federal Court had the benefit of hearing submissions from interveners on the issue of the RAD's appellate functions.[328] The court held that the RAD serves more of an appellate function rather than a judicial review function:

In considering the nature of the review to be conducted by the RAD, if the RAD simply reviews RPD decisions for reasonableness, then its appellate role is curtailed. It would merely duplicate what occurs on a judicial review. Further, if the RAD only performed a duplicative role to that of the Federal Court, it would be inconsistent with the creation of the RAD and the extensive legislative framework of the IRPA.[329]

. . .

It flows that in creating an internal appellate body, within the executive branch of government, the principle of standard of review, a function of the division of powers between the executive and the judiciary, is of lesser importance and applicability. The traditional standard of review analysis is not required.[330]

326 *Ibid* at para 1.
327 2014 FC 702 at paras 28 and 33; 2014 FC 711 at paras 29 and 34.
328 2014 FC 799 [*Huruglica*].
329 *Ibid* at para 39.
330 *Ibid* at para 43.

In making this finding the court referred to comments in parliamentary debate that adverted to the creation of a "full fact-based appeal"[331] and the broad remedial powers of the RAD, particularly the ability to substitute a determination.[332]

It appears that the Federal Court is signalling that it views RAD functions and powers to be other than a mere replication of the judicial review function of the Federal Court and that it must weigh evidence itself and conduct its own assessments.[333] In particular, the court in *Huruglica* endorses the approach that the RAD can conduct its own independent assessment of whether refugee protection is warranted where non-credibility issues are raised in appeal. Where, however, credibility issues are raised, the court in *Huruglica* carefully proposed that the RAD should "recognize and respect" credibility findings of the RPD. Taking great pains to avoid using the language of "deference" and "reasonableness," this pronouncement has left the door open for decision makers to either apply the standard of reasonableness when examining credibility findings, or to reject applying any standard of review at all and revisit the issue of credibility themselves. Questions related to RAD jurisdiction have been certified under section 74(d) of the *IRPA* in the case of *Huruglica*, and the Federal Court of Appeal will, it is hoped, weigh in and clarify the inconsistent approach the Federal Court has presented through various cases thus far. In more recent cases, the RAD has adopted the decision in *Huruglica*.[334]

6) Recourse from RAD Decisions

Parties who are unsatisfied with a RAD decision can seek judicial review of the decision at the Federal Court.[335] Prior to a decision being made at the Federal Court, an appellant can also apply to reopen an appeal on the basis that there was a failure to observe a principle of natural justice.[336] As the courts clarify the RAD's role and function, issues of procedural fairness may be raised more often if the courts move to-

---

331 *Ibid* at para 40.

332 *Ibid* at paras 46–47; *IRPA*, above note 4, s 111(1).

333 *Yetna v Canada (Minister of Citizenship and Immigration)*, 2014 FC 858; *Njeukam v Canada (Citizenship and Immigration)*, 2014 FC 859; *Spasoja v Canada (Minister of Citizenship and Immigration)*, 2014 FC 913.

334 *X (Re)*, 2014 CanLII 66650 (CA IRB); *X (Re)*, 2014 CanLII 64251 (CA IRB).

335 *IRPA*, above note 4, s 72: Judicial review cannot be undertaken until any and all appeals have been undertaken. See Chapter 16 for more information on judicial review.

336 *RAD Rules*, above note 294, s 49; *IRPA*, *ibid*, s 171.1.

wards an approach of recognizing the RAD as a body that determines refugee protection, rather than simply a review body looking to correct errors.

The minister may apply for judicial review of a RAD decision even if the minister did not intervene at the RPD or the RAD.[337]

C. APPLICATIONS FOR PERMANENT RESIDENT STATUS

Subject to some exceptions,[338] section 21(2) of the *IRPA* provides

> . . . a person whose application for protection has been finally determined by the Board to be a Convention refugee or to be a person in need of protection, or a person whose application for protection has been allowed by the Minister, becomes . . . a permanent resident if the officer is satisfied that they have made their application in accordance with the regulations and that they are not inadmissible on any ground referred to in section 34 or 35, subsection 36(1) or section 37 or 38.[339]

The regulations specify that applicants may include family members in their applications, but the same criteria of inadmissibility apply to them.

As noted, a designated foreign national is not eligible to apply for permanent resident status for at least five years.[340]

---

337 *Ibid*, s 73.
338 Thus, a person who fits under s 112(3) of the *IRPA* is ineligible. See Chapter 14.
339 *IRPA*, above note 4, s 21(2). See Chapter 14 for more information about inadmissibility.
340 *Ibid*, s 20.2.

CHAPTER 10

CONVENTION REFUGEES AND PERSONS IN NEED OF PROTECTION

A. INTRODUCTION

Sections 96 and 97 of the *Immigration and Refugee Protection Act (IRPA)*[1] provide the backbone to refugee law in Canada. This chapter first analyzes section 96, which incorporates into Canadian law the definition of *refugee* found in the *Convention and Protocol on the Status of Refugees.*[2] It then examines section 97, which identifies persons in Canada who are in need of protection and incorporates into domestic law international obligations imposed by the *Convention Against Torture and Other Cruel, Inhuman or Degrading Treatment or Punishment.*[3] Subsequently, it analyzes section 98 of the *IRPA*, which imposes qualifications on protection by defining those who should be excluded.

B. SECTION 96

Section 96 of the *IRPA* states:

---

1   *Immigration and Refugee Protection Act*, SC 2001, c 27 [*IRPA*].
2   *Convention relating to the Status of Refugees*, 28 July 1951, 189 UNTS 137 (entered into force 22 April 1954) [*Refugee Convention*]; *Protocol relating to the Status of Refugees*, 31 January 1967, 606 UNTS 267 (entered into force 4 October 1967) [*Protocol*].
3   10 December 1984, Can TS 1987 No 36, 23 ILM 1027 [*Convention against Torture*].

96. Convention refugee – A Convention refugee is a person who, by reason of a well-founded fear of persecution for reasons of race, religion, nationality, membership in a particular social group or political opinion,

(a) is outside each of their countries of nationality and is unable or, by reason of that fear, unwilling to avail themself of the protection of each of those countries; or

(b) not having a country of nationality, is outside the country of their former habitual residence and is unable or, by reason of that fear, unwilling to return to that country.

Beyond the requirement of being outside the country of origin, this definition rests on four principal elements: (1) the claimant's well-founded fear; (2) of persecution; (3) for reasons of any of the five enumerated grounds; and (4) the availability of state protection. These four elements are analyzed in detail below.

1) A Well-Founded Fear

The decision of the Supreme Court of Canada in *Canada (AG) v Ward*[4] provides a framework to use when establishing the definitional requirement of a well-founded fear. In *Ward*, La Forest J describes a "bipartite test" involving subjective and objective components: "(1) the claimant must subjectively fear persecution; and (2) this fear must be well-founded in an objective sense."[5] Justice La Forest reproduced the analysis articulated by Heald J at the Federal Court of Appeal:

> The subjective component relates to the existence of the fear of persecution in the mind of the refugee. The objective component requires that the refugee's fear be evaluated objectively to determine if there is a valid basis for that fear.[6]

---

4   [1993] 2 SCR 689 [*Ward*].

5   *Ibid* at 723; see also *Chan v Canada (Minister of Employment and Immigration)*, [1995] 3 SCR 593 at para 119 [*Chan*].

6   *Ward*, above note 4 at 723; see also UN High Commissioner for Refugees, *Handbook and Guidelines on Procedures and Criteria for Determining Refugee Status* (December 2011), online: UNHCR www.unhcr.org/3d58e13b4.html at para 38 [UNHCR Handbook]:

> To the element of fear — a state of mind and a subjective condition — is added the qualification 'well-founded.' This implies that it is not only the frame of mind of the person concerned that determines refugee status, but that this frame of mind must be supported by an objective situation. The term 'well-founded fear' therefore contains a subjective and an objective element, and in

In more recent cases, the bipartite approach has become entrenched. In a frequently cited case, *Kamana v Canada (Minister of Citizenship and Immigration)*,[7] it was stated that "[t]he lack of evidence going to the subjective element of the claim is a fatal flaw which in and of itself warrants dismissal of the claim, since both elements of the refugee definition — subjective and objective — must be met."[8] However, the need for an inquiry into whether a claimant has a subjective fear of persecution is a matter of some controversy. It appears to disqualify claimants who are either too immature or intellectually unable to appreciate the risks to which they are subject, yet who are in extreme need of protection because they face a risk of persecution in their country of origin.[9] That Canadian courts' adamant position that evidence of a subjective fear is a threshold requirement on which the success of a claim may depend is quite puzzling. It can perhaps be explained by the fact that, in the vast majority of cases, the claim is based on an allegation of subjective fear and the apprehension of danger, and when this allegation is not made out, the decision maker sees reason to reject the claim outright. In such cases, the claim is being rejected essentially because the claimant's general credibility is found to be wanting. The claimant's statement of the reason for his departure is rejected in favour of an alternative explanation that may be based not on his oral testimony but on his actions[10] where, for example, he failed to offer a good reason for delaying in fleeing from the alleged danger or failed to explain why he did not seek help from sources closer or more readily available.[11] Where, of course, a claimant can provide an explanation for

---

determining whether well-founded fear exists, both elements must be taken into consideration.

7   [1999] FCJ No 1695 (TD).

8   *Ibid* at para 10.

9   See James C Hathaway & William S Hicks, "Is There a Subjective Element in the Refugee Convention's Requirement of 'Well-Founded Fear'?" (2005) 26 *Michigan Journal of International Law* 505.

10 See, for example, *Subramaniyathas v Canada (Minister of Citizenship and Immigration)*, 2014 FC 583, where the court held that the Refugee Protection Division cannot be speculative when making plausibility findings related to the credibility of the claimant's story.

11 See, for example, *Huerta v Canada (Minister of Employment and Immigration)*, [1993] FCJ No 271 (CA): The court focused on the claimant's conduct before she left, specifically that the claimant continued to work, taking steps to contest her dismissal and get her position reinstated, that she continued to attend classes, and that when she arrived in Canada as a tourist, there was a delay in making a refugee claim; see also *Ilie v Canada (Minister of Citizenship and Immigration)* (1994), 88 FTR 220 (TD), where the claimant provided explanations as to why he did not claim refugee protection in countries he travelled through before

her actions, decision makers may take them into account when assessing credibility.[12]

However, the fact that the courts are willing to reject some claims on the basis that the claimant lacks subjective fear should not entail that an honest claimant who is unable to appreciate the high level of danger that objectively exists should not be offered protection where a representative makes the claim on her behalf. Where it is determined that a claimant does indeed require protection from persecution but where the claimant has not based the claim on a fear that has been found not to exist, there is no reason to reject the claim. For example, where a child has been sent out of a country by others who fear that she will be persecuted, the child's lack of fear should not jeopardize the claim. Subjective fear should not be regarded as an essential element of the definition. Instead, it should be regarded as a device that permits an inquiry into the claimant's reasons for seeking protection. It is a factor that will usually need to be shown on the balance of probabilities to justify why the individual is seeking protection. Only where the claimant cites beliefs or anxieties as the relevant reason will a finding that there is no subjective fear — that the claim is based on a ruse — be a reason for denying the claim.

In addition to establishing that she has a subjective fear, the claimant must also demonstrate that it is grounded in objective reality. The claim is thus evaluated against the context or background of the situation, including country conditions, the laws within the country, and such matters as the claimant's character, background, influence, wealth, and personality. At this stage of analysis, the claimant must prove that there are grounds for her fear.[13] The evaluation carries with it a forward-looking projection: there must be grounds for fearing future persecution. Claimants who have suffered past persecution cannot

---

coming to Canada and his delay in making a claim, but the board member was not convinced of his explanations.

12 See, for example, *El Naem v Canada (Minister of Citizenship and Immigration)* (1997), 126 FTR 15 (TD), where the claimant provided an explanation of why he did not seek refugee protection in another country he was in before coming to Canada, and the board member accepted this. The court placed emphasis on the claimant's age and the fact he was a foreigner in the transit country not familiar with its customs and language. In *Nel v Canada (Minister of Citizenship and Immigration)*, 2014 FC 842, the court held that a claimant's explanation for not having claimed protection in another country before coming to Canada — that she was choosing the best chance of success — was one that should not have been summarily dismissed by the Immigration and Refugee Board (IRB).

13 *Salibian v Canada (Minister of Employment and Immigration)*, [1990] 3 FC 250 (CA) [*Salibian*].

rely on a presumption that their fear is well founded. Evidence of past persecution can inform only whether there is a reasonable chance that persecution will occur if the claimant were to return.[14]

As stated by the Federal Court, when establishing an objective basis for her fear, the claimant need not prove that it is more likely than not that persecution will occur; rather, she need show only that more than a mere possibility of persecution exists.[15] The question to be answered is this: Is there a reasonable chance that persecution would occur were the claimant returned to the country of origin?[16] It is not necessary for the claimant to show he has suffered or would, in certainty, suffer persecution, but there must be more than a minimal possibility of persecution.[17] Nevertheless, the claimant is required to establish on a balance of probabilities any facts that give rise to the belief that there is a reasonable chance of future persecution. On a balance of probabilities, it must also be established that the claimant has a subjective fear.[18]

In summary, it is possible for a claim to be rejected on one of two distinct grounds: first, that the decision maker does not believe that the claimant fears persecution; and second, that the decision maker, while willing to conclude that the claimant does fear persecution, is unwilling to conclude that the fear is justifiable in light of the available evidence.

2) Persecution

As the UN High Commissioner for Refugees (UNHCR) has explained: "There is no universally accepted definition of 'persecution,' and various attempts to formulate such a definition have met with little success."[19] Despite the lack of an all-encompassing or simple explanation of what amounts to persecution, there are parameters, principles, and elements upon which a finding of persecution may be based. This section aims

---

14   *Fernandopulle v Canada (Minister of Citizenship and Immigration)*, 2005 FCA 91.

15   *Adjei v Canada (Minister of Employment and Immigration)*, [1989] 2 FC 680 (CA) [*Adjei*].

16   *Ibid* at para 6.

17   *Ponniah v Canada (Minister of Employment and Immigration)* (1991), 132 NR 32 (FCA).

18   *Chan*, above note 5 at para 120; *Adjei*, above note 15, where the Federal Court stated that the standard is a balance of probabilities for proving an objectively well-founded fear.

19   UNHCR Handbook, above note 6 at para 51; James C Hathaway, *The Law of Refugee Status* (Toronto: Butterworths, 1991) at 104–5: Hathaway defines persecution as sustained or systemic violation of basic human rights demonstrative of a failure of state protection.

to discern and outline these factors to bring greater clarity to the Canadian definition of a refugee.

a) Prospectivity

As emphasized above, the core question in determining whether a person merits refugee protection is whether there is *prospective* risk to the refugee claimant. Thus, the question can be framed in this way: What predicament would the applicant face if he were returned to the country of origin?[20] Where a future negative consequence depends on the future conduct of the claimant, the normative question that must be addressed is whether the claimant should be expected to refrain from that conduct. Doing this requires a fact-specific inquiry and an evaluative judgment. Where a person may be able to avoid severe mistreatment by not speaking in public, or by not practising his religion, or by being discreet about his intimate same-sex relationships, he may be found to face the risk of persecution.[21]

b) Discrimination and Harassment as Persecution

It is widely accepted that discrimination alone does not amount to persecution[22] and that the existence of discriminatory laws will not in itself constitute persecution.[23] As the UNHCR Handbook puts it, "a distinction should be made between discrimination resulting merely in preferential treatment and discrimination amounting to persecution because, in aggregate or of itself, it seriously restricts the claimant's enjoyment of fundamental human rights."[24] Nevertheless, the UNHCR

---

20 UN High Commissioner for Refugees, Guidelines on International Protection No 9: *Claims to Refugee Status Based on Sexual Orientation and/or Gender Identity within the Context of Article 1A(2) of the 1951 Convention and/or Its 1967 Protocol relating to the Status of Refugees*, online: UNHCR www.unhcr.org/509136ca9.pdf at para 32 [UNHCR Guidelines re Sexual Orientation].

21 *Ibid.*

22 UNHCR Handbook, above note 6 at paras 53 & 54: For example, "Persons who receive less favourable treatment as a result of differences are not necessarily victims of discrimination." See also UNHCR, Guidelines on International Protection: *Religion-Based Refugee Claims under Article 1A(2) of the 1951 Convention and/or the 1967 Protocol relating to the Status of Refugees*, online: Refworld www.refworld.org/pdfid/4090f9794.pdf [UNHCR Guidelines on Religion-Based Refugee Claims] at para 17: "Even though discrimination for reasons of religion is prohibited under international human rights law, all discrimination does not necessarily rise to the level required for recognition of refugee status."

23 UNHCR Guidelines on Religion-Based Refugee Claims, *ibid* at para 18: "An assessment of the implementation of such laws and their effects is in any case crucial to establishing persecution."

24 *Ibid* at para 17.

Handbook asserts that discrimination or harassment can amount to persecution where combined with other "adverse effects" or where measures of "discrimination lead to consequences of a substantially prejudicial nature for the person concerned."[25] For example, discrimination may amount to persecution when serious restrictions are placed on a person's right to earn her livelihood, to practise his religion, or have access to educational facilities.[26] The UNHCR Handbook also states that, even where measures of discrimination are, in themselves, not of a serious character, they may still give rise to a reasonable fear of persecution if they produce, in the mind of the person, "a feeling of apprehension and insecurity as regards his future existence."[27]

It is important that, when deciphering whether discrimination amounts to persecution, the discrimination and its effects are considered in light of all of the circumstances that face the claimant in the country of origin.[28]

c) Punishment or Prosecution as Persecution

As with discrimination, neither the existence of a punitive law nor past or future prosecution under such a law is, in and of itself, persecution.[29] As the UNHCR states, "An assessment of the implementation of such laws and their effect is in any case crucial to establishing persecution."[30] The assessment must be "fact-based, focusing on both the individual and the contextual circumstances of the case" taking into account the "legal system in the country concerned, including any relevant legislation, its interpretation, application and actual impact on the applicant."[31]

Persons fleeing from prosecution or punishment may be seen as ordinary fugitives from the law. The onus is on the claimant to show otherwise.[32] Thus, ordinary laws of general application are presumed to be valid and neutral, and it is incumbent upon the claimant to show that the law or its administration is persecutory.[33] In this respect, it is not enough for a claimant to show that a regime is generally oppressive

---

25 *Ibid*; UNHCR Guidelines re Sexual Orientation, above note 20 at para 17.
26 UNHCR Handbook, above note 6 at para 54.
27 *Ibid* at para 55.
28 *Ibid*.
29 *Ibid* at para 56; UNHCR Guidelines on Religion-Based Refugee Claims, above note 22 at para 18.
30 *Ibid*.
31 UNHCR Guidelines re Sexual Orientation, above note 20 at para 27.
32 UNHCR Handbook, above note 6 at para 56; *Zolfagharkhani v Canada (Minister of Employment and Immigration)*, [1993] 3 FC 540 at para 21 (CA) [*Zolfagharkhani*].
33 *Ibid* at para 22.

but rather, that the law in question is persecutory in relation to the enumerated ground on which the claim is premised.[34] Nevertheless, the Federal Court has stated that a law is not one of general application if its application is so draconian as to be completely disproportionate to its objective.[35]

Claimants can meet their burden by showing that the prosecution or punishment they face is excessive or by showing that they are being prosecuted or suffering punishment for engaging in legitimate acts protected by the enumerated grounds of the refugee definition.[36] For example, a person may succeed by claiming that she is being punished for being LGBTIQ and that engaging in same-sex relations may lead to prosecution and punishment in the forms of the death penalty, imprisonment, or severe corporal punishment.[37] If a less severe sanction is identified, it may be more challenging to characterize the law as a form of persecution.

When arguing that prosecution and punishment are equivalent to persecution, the claimant may need to demonstrate that the laws in question are not "in conformity with accepted human rights standards."[38] When evaluating the laws of the country of origin, not only are international human rights instruments used as benchmarks, but Canadian laws may be used as a yardstick also.[39]

Where the law itself is not problematic, the application of the law may be excessively discriminatory, or it may be enforced selectively and therefore amount to persecution.[40] For example, an offence against "public order" applied to the distribution of pamphlets could be characterized as persecuting individuals on the basis of their political opinion.[41] Further, even if a discriminatory law is rarely or irregularly enforced, its existence could lead to an intolerable predicament

---

34   *Ibid* at para 23.

35   *Cheung v Canada (Minister of Employment and Immigration)*, [1993] 2 FC 314 (CA) [*Cheung*]; *Fathi-Rad v Canada (Secretary of State)* (1994), 77 FTR 41 (TD); *Lin v Canada (Minister of Citizenship and Immigration)*, 2014 FC 746.

36   UNHCR Handbook, above note 6 at para 57.

37   UNHCR Guidelines re Sexual Orientation, above note 20 at para 26.

38   UNHCR Handbook, above note 6 at para 58.

39   *Ibid* at para 60; UNHCR Guidelines re Sexual Orientation, above note 20 at para 26.

40   UNHCR Handbook, above note 6 at para 59.

41   *Ibid*; UNHCR Guidelines re Sexual Orientation, above note 20 at para 29: "Even where consensual same-sex relations are not criminalized by specific provisions, laws of general application, for example, public morality or public order laws (loitering, for example) may be selectively applied and enforced against LGBTI individuals in a discriminatory manner, making life intolerable for the claimant, and thus amounting to persecution."

for certain claimants. For example, the criminalization of same-sex relations can create or contribute to an oppressive atmosphere of intolerance and generate a threat of prosecution, thus creating opportunities for blackmail and extortion or the promotion of political rhetoric that can expose claimants to risk of persecutory harm.[42]

In some countries a stiff penalty is imposed on nationals who depart from the country or remain abroad without authorization. If sufficiently severe, this penalty may be recognized as a form of persecution if it can be shown that the reason or motive for leaving or remaining outside the country of origin is tied to one of the enumerated grounds in the refugee definition.[43] On the other hand, if the person can, without hardship, avoid the penalty by remaining at home, this may be regarded as sufficient to defeat a claim. Thus, in *Valentin v Canada (Minister of Employment and Immigration)*,[44] when Marceau J of the Federal Court of Appeal considered the claim of a person who faced up to five years of imprisonment for exiting the country without authorization, he stated:

> I will say, first, that while in humanitarian terms I am very much inclined to sympathize with the idea of granting refugee status to everyone who faces criminal sanctions such as those imposed by section 109 of the Czech Criminal Code, in practical and legal terms the idea seems to me to be illogical and without any rational basis. Neither the international Convention nor our Act, which is based on it, as I understand it, had in mind the protection of people who, having been subjected to no persecution to date, themselves created a cause to fear persecution by freely, of their own accord and with no reason, making themselves liable to punishment for violating a criminal law of general application. I would add, with due respect for the very widely held contrary opinion, that the idea does not appear to me even to be supported by the fact that the transgression was motivated by some dissatisfaction of a political nature.

Finally, it is important to note that the mere existence of legislation protecting certain freedoms or human rights does not demonstrate or prove that individuals are protected; in many cases, such legislation may not be implemented in practice.[45]

---

42   *Ibid* at para 27.

43   UNHCR Handbook, above note 6 at para 61.

44   [1991] 3 FC 390. This decision has frequently been cited favorably. For example, see *Salcedo v Canada (Minister of Citizenship and Immigration)*, 2014 FC 822.

45   UNHCR Guidelines on Religion-Based Refugee Claims, above note 22 at para 18.

d) Economic Migrants versus Refugees

Neither the *Refugee Convention* nor the *IRPA* recognizes persons who have moved exclusively for economic considerations as refugees.[46] Nevertheless, the UNHCR has stated that "[t]he distinction between an economic migrant and a refugee is, however, sometimes blurred in the same way as the distinction between economic and political measures in an applicant's country of origin is not always clear."[47] For example, economic measures taken by a government could have a discriminatory impact amounting to persecution. Economic actions could destroy the economic existence of a population that may be dominated by an ethnic or religious group.[48] Thus, a person making a refugee claim based on economic measures should highlight how those measures constitute more than mere economic policy or objectives and demonstrate any underlying ideological or political motivation, and the serious consequences flowing from such policies.[49]

e) Agents of Persecution

The refugee definition recognizes that persecution can emanate from both state and non-state actors.[50] For example, the state may be the agent of persecution by enacting or enforcing legislation or policies.[51] Further, individual acts of "rogue" state agents may, in some circumstances, be considered as state persecution,[52] particularly where the state agent is a member of the police or other agencies that purport to protect people.[53] In other cases, the state may be implicated in the persecution of the claimant by condoning or ignoring the persecution emanating from sections of the population in the country of origin who do not respect the existing laws and standards established by the state.[54]

---

46   UNHCR Handbook, above note 6 at para 62.
47   *Ibid* at para 63; see, for example, *He v Canada (Minister of Employment and Immigration)* (1994), 78 FTR 313 (TD).
48   UNHCR Handbook, above note 6 at para 63.
49   *Ibid* at para 64.
50   UNHCR Guidelines re Sexual Orientation, above note 20 at para 34.
51   *Ibid*: "State persecution may be perpetrated, for example, through the criminalization of consensual same-sex conduct and the enforcement of associated laws, or as a result of harm inflicted by officials of the State or those under the control of the State, such as the police or the military."
52   *Ibid.*
53   *Ibid.*
54   UNHCR Handbook, above note 6 at para 65; see, for example, *Chabira v Canada (Minister of Citizenship and Immigration)* (1994), 27 Imm LR (2d) 75 (TD) [*Chabira*].

The leading case of *Ward* held that "state complicity in persecution is not a prerequisite to a valid refugee claim."[55] Thus, a wide range of parties could be considered agents of persecution in a refugee claim. In situations where the agent of persecution is not a state agent, "persecution is established where the State is unable or unwilling to provide protection against such harm."[56] Non-state persecutors may include family members, neighbours, or any person in the broader community, as well as paramilitary, rebel, or other armed groups, gangs, and vigilantes.[57]

f) Cumulative Grounds

Persecution may be made out more easily where it is shown that a claimant has been a victim or will be a victim of cumulative or systemic actions.[58] However, it is not a requirement that persecution be cumulative. Indeed, persecution may be constituted by a single event. Where there is a confluence of actions and consequences due to an intersection of reasons or grounds (such as race and political opinion), this may fortify a claim that one faces persecution.[59] Singular acts of discrimination or harassment, for example, may not amount to persecution by themselves, but when taken together and examined at a systemic level, they could evince a level of severity sufficient to constitute persecution.[60]

g) Individual versus Group Persecution

In order to be granted refugee protection, a claimant need not show that she was personally a target.[61] A claimant can succeed by showing that he has a fear that stems from "reprehensible acts committed or likely to be committed against members of a group to which he belonged."[62] Thus, while the refugee protection system is concerned with particular

---

55   *Ward*, above note 4 at 713.
56   UNHCR Guidelines re Sexual Orientation, above note 20 at para 35.
57   *Ibid.*
58   UNHCR Handbook, above note 6 at para 55; *Ward*, above note 4 at 713.
59   UNHCR Handbook, above note 6 at paras 66–67; see also UNHCR Guidelines on Religion-Based Refugee Claims, above note 22 at para 24, which discusses that particular attention should be paid to the impact of gender on religion-based refugee claims.
60   *Bobrik v Canada (Minister of Citizenship and Immigration)* (1994), 85 FTR 13 (TD) [*Bobrik*], where the court held that the aggregate of hostile acts was enough to create a well-founded fear of persecution. See also *Zhou v Canada (Minister of Citizenship and Immigration)*, 2012 FC 1252.
61   *Salibian*, above note 13.
62   *Ibid.*

claimants, sometimes the best evidence that an individual faces sufficient risk of persecution is the treatment afforded similarly situated persons in the country of origin.[63]

The Federal Court of Appeal has, however, cautioned decision makers against using an approach that compares the claimant's risk to the risk of other individuals or groups.[64] Rather, the assessment of risk should be made in a non-comparative manner, by asking whether the claimant faces a risk of sufficiently serious harm that is linked to an enumerated ground regardless of the fact that others may face a more serious risk.[65]

3)   The Five Enumerated Grounds

As the Supreme Court of Canada pointed out in *Ward*, "international refugee law was meant to serve as a 'substitute' for national protection where the latter was not provided" and for this reason, international protection was "qualified by built-in limitations" in the form of the five enumerated grounds.[66] These limitations "reflect the fact that the international community did not intend to offer haven for all suffering individuals."[67]

In order to meet the definition of *refugee*, a person must show a well-founded fear of persecution for reasons of the five enumerated grounds in the *Refugee Convention*.[68] A refugee claimant need not pick or rely on one ground and may demonstrate an intersectional interplay of different grounds.[69] For example, a claimant could be persecuted on grounds of both race and gender, and the combination of such reasons for the persecution may compound the seriousness of the claim. It is therefore advisable that claimants put forward their claim under as many grounds as are applicable.

In analyzing what it means to be persecuted by race, nationality, or religion, the UNHCR has emphasized that, for these three grounds, a decision maker must understand each ground in the widest sense.[70]

---

63   *Ibid.*

64   *Ali v Canada (Minister of Citizenship and Immigration)* (1999), 235 NR 316 at para 4 (FCA); see also *Rajudeen v Canada (Minister of Employment and Immigration)* (1984), 55 NR 129 (FCA).

65   *Ibid.*

66   *Ward*, above note 4 at 731.

67   *Ibid.*

68   UNHCR Handbook, above note 6 at para 66. *Refugee Convention*, above note 2.

69   *Ibid* at para 67.

70   *Ibid* at para 68.

Canadian authorities have maintained that this applies to political opinion also. The five enumerated grounds are explored further below.

a) Race
The UNHCR has stated:

> Race . . . has to be understood in its widest sense to include all kinds of ethnic groups that are referred to as "races" in common usage. Frequently it will also entail membership of a specific social group of common descent forming a minority within a larger population.[71]

Merely belonging to a particular racial group may not be enough to meet the definitional requirement.[72] Membership in a racial group must be shown to be a reason underlying feared persecution.[73]

Similarly, it is also important to remember that discrimination on racial grounds may not always be equivalent to persecution. It can amount to persecution if "a person's human dignity" is affected in a way that is incompatible with human rights or where serious consequences flow from the discrimination.[74]

At its core, this ground recognizes that a person can be a refugee because she faces real and oppressive risks, including substantial violence, because she belongs to a group with race as one defining characteristic.[75]

b) Nationality
As with race, *nationality* also has a broad definition.[76] Often equated in other contexts with citizenship,[77] the term *nationality* in the refugee definition means more:

---

71   *Ibid.*

72   *Ibid* at para 70; see, for example, *Katwaru v Canada (Minister of Citizenship and Immigration)*, 2007 FC 612 [*Katwaru*], where hostility between Afro-Guyanese and Indo-Guyanese communities existed but it was found that there was no clear evidence that crimes directed against one group were racially motivated. However, the Handbook does suggest that in particular, but undefined, circumstances, mere membership may be sufficient to ground a claim.

73   UNHCR Handbook, above note 6 at para 70.

74   *Ibid* at para 69.

75   *Veeravagu v Canada (Minister of Employment and Immigration)*, [1992] FCJ No 468 (CA).

76   *Yang v Canada (Minister of Citizenship and Immigration)*, 2001 FCT 1052 [*Yang*].

77   In *Hanukashvili v Canada (Minister of Citizenship and Immigration)* (1997), 129 FTR 216, the Federal Court Trial Division held that while nationality does not mean the same thing as citizenship, when the word *nationality* is used as one of the five enumerated grounds, it can mean the same thing as citizenship.

The term "nationality" in this context is not to be understood only as "citizenship". It refers also to membership of an ethnic or linguistic group and may occasionally overlap with the term "race". Persecution for reasons of nationality may consist of adverse attitudes and measures directed against a national (ethnic, linguistic) minority and in certain circumstances the fact of belonging to such a minority may in itself give rise to well-founded fear of persecution.[78]

Persecution for reasons of nationality may also overlap with persecution for reasons of political opinion.[79] Further, while this ground may apply more to minority groups, or groups not belonging to the dominant nationality in the country of origin,[80] persecution of a majority group may exist as well.[81]

c)   Religion

Although the *travaux preparatoires* of the *Refugee Convention* reveal that religion-based persecution was regarded as an integral part of the refugee definition, there was no attempt to define the term.[82] The UNHCR recommends that the ground of religion be viewed as a means of protecting the right to freedom of thought, conscience, and belief; it has drawn on numerous international legal instruments for guidance.[83] The UNHCR Handbook states:

> The *Universal Declaration of Human Rights* and the Human Rights Covenant proclaim the right to freedom of thought, conscience and religion, which right includes the freedom of a person to change his

---

78   UNHCR Handbook, above note 6 at para 74.
79   *Ibid* at para 75.
80   See, for example, *Baffoe v Canada (Minister of Citizenship and Immigration)* (1994), 85 FTR 68 (TD): In this case, the IRB ignored the claimant's statements that a land dispute arose because he and his family were not considered nationals and that he experienced problems with the local tribe chief in the past.
81   UNHCR Handbook, above note 6 at para 76.
82   UNHCR Guidelines on Religion-Based Refugee Claims, above note 22 at para 4.
83   *Ibid* at paras 2 and 4:

> In determining religion-based claims, it is therefore useful, *inter alia*, to draw on Article 18 of the 1948 Universal Declaration of Human Rights (the "Universal Declaration") and Articles 18 and 27 of the 1966 International Covenant on Civil and Political Rights (the "International Covenant"). Also relevant are the General Comments issued by the Human Rights Committee, the 1981 Declaration on the Elimination of all Forms of Intolerance and Discrimination based on Religion or Belief, the 1992 Declaration on the Rights of Persons belonging to National or Ethnic, Religious and Linguistic Minorities and the body of reports of the Special Rapporteur on Religious Intolerance.

religion and his freedom to manifest it in public or private, in teaching, practice, worship and observance.[84]

As with nationality and race, religion must also be viewed in the widest sense.[85] On this point the UNHCR refers to decisions of the Human Rights Committee, noting that religion is not limited to "traditional religions or to religions and beliefs with institutional characteristics or practices analogous to those of traditional religions."[86] Similarly, the Federal Court has stated that religion should be broadly interpreted to allow for claims based on a person's religious beliefs, even if those are not part of an organized religion, and include beliefs that reject religion.[87]

Persecution may be viewed as grounded on religion where it is motivated by a person's participation in a religious practice. The right to freedom of religion includes the freedom to demonstrate one's religion or belief in public or private by teaching, practice, worship, and the performance of rites.[88] It also includes the acts of "failing or refusing to observe a religion or to hold any particular religious belief."[89] Thus, religion may involve belief,[90] identity,[91] or a way of life.[92]

---

84   UNHCR Handbook, above note 6 at para 71.

85   *Yang*, above note 76.

86   UNHCR Guidelines on Religion-Based Refugee Claims, above note 22 at para 4; Human Rights Committee, *General Comment No 22*, 20 July 1993, UN doc CCPR/C/21/Rev1/ADD4 (27 September 1993) at para 2.

87   *Yang*, above note 76 at para 13.

88   See, for example, *Fosu v Canada (Minister of Employment and Immigration)* (1994), 90 FTR 182 (TD) [*Fosu*].

89   UNHCR Guidelines on Religion-Based Refugee Claims, above note 22 at para 4.

90   *Ibid* at para 6:

> "Belief," in this context, should be interpreted so as to include theistic, nontheistic and atheistic beliefs. Beliefs may take the form of convictions or values about the divine or ultimate reality or the spiritual destiny of humankind. Claimants may also be considered heretics, apostates, schismatic, pagans or superstitious, even by other adherents of their religious tradition and be persecuted for that reason.

91   *Ibid* at para 7:

> "Identity" is less a matter of theological beliefs than membership of a community that observes or is bound together by common beliefs, rituals, traditions, ethnicity, nationality, or ancestry. A claimant may identify with, or have a sense of belonging to, or be identified by others as belonging to, a particular group or community. In many cases, persecutors are likely to target religious groups that are different from their own because they see that religious identity as part of a threat to their own identity or legitimacy.

92   *Ibid* at para 8:

> For some individuals, "religion" is a vital aspect of their "way of life" and how they relate, either completely or partially, to the world. Their religion

Mere discrimination motivated by a person's adherence to a religion or engagement in a religious practice will be insufficient to find a person a refugee.[93] To amount to persecution on this ground, the conduct in question may take many forms, including prohibition, restrictions, limitations, and punishment or the imposition of serious negative consequences as a result of the practice or membership.[94] Measures may also include forced conversion,[95] forced compliance or conformity with religious practices,[96] and compulsory military service for those who have valid reasons of conscience to not participate.[97]

Further, decision makers should look beyond the face of a conflict or a situation to determine whether there is a "religious tint" or whether the problem faced by the claimant takes on a greater scope such as persecution not just from family members but also from a wider religious community.[98] Where a claimant has escaped persecution in the past by lying to authorities about religious beliefs, a decision maker must consider evidence of the treatment the claimant would suffer if she were to tell the truth.[99] Finally, decision makers cannot expect individuals to give up their religion or conceal their association with a particular religion to avoid persecution in a country of origin, as this would be an affront to their right to freedom of religion.[100]

---

may manifest itself in such activities as the wearing of distinctive clothing or observance of particular religious practices, including observing religious holidays or dietary requirements. Such practices may seem trivial to nonadherents, but may be at the core of the religion for the adherent concerned.

93 UNHCR Handbook, above note 6 at para 73; UNHCR Guidelines on Religion-Based Refugee Claims, above note 22 at para 10: Birth into a particular religious community or a close correlation between race and/or ethnicity and religion could be enough if adherence to that religion is attributed to the individual with regard to persecutory acts directed against a group.

94 UNHCR Handbook, above note 6 at para 72; *Fosu*, above note 88; UNHCR Guidelines on Religion-Based Refugee Claims, above note 22 at paras 12–13: "religious belief, identity, or way of life can be seen as so fundamental to human identity that one should not be compelled to hide, change or renounce this in order to avoid persecution." (See also para 19.)

95 *Ibid* at para 20.

96 *Ibid* at paras 21–23.

97 *Ibid* at paras 25–26.

98 *Chabira*, above note 54.

99 See, for example, *Kazkan v Canada (Minister of Citizenship and Immigration)*, [1997] FCJ No 321 (TD).

100 *Yang*, above note 76.

d) Political Opinion

As with the other enumerated grounds, it is well established that political opinion should be understood in a broad sense.[101] The Supreme Court of Canada confirmed this by stating that political opinion includes "any opinion on any matter in which the machinery of state, government, and policy, may be engaged"[102] As the Federal Court of Appeal has stated, in reference to the Supreme Court's call for a broad definition:

> The need for a broad definition of the concept was justified by the fact that persecution for having expressed a political opinion may originate from a third party without complicity of the state. The Court adopted a broad interpretation of "political opinion" which includes "any opinion on any matter in which the machinery of the state, government, and policy may be engaged". This excerpt from the decision illustrates well the rejection of the narrow definition and the adoption of the general interpretation.[103]

Simply having a political opinion different from those of a government is not sufficient basis for a refugee claim; the refugee claimant must also show that she has a fear of persecution for holding such an opinion.[104] Further, the refugee claimant need not show that the government is the agent of persecution; the claimant may show that she fears persecution by reason of her political opinion from other persons or groups.[105] The state itself may be merely complicit or unable to protect her.[106] Thus, a claimant may be persecuted for having an opinion that the government agrees with.[107]

---

101 *Ward*, above note 4 at 746:

   . . . [I]nternational refugee protection extends to situations where the state is not an accomplice to the persecution, but is unable to protect the claimant. In such cases, it is possible that a claimant may be seen as a threat by a group unrelated and perhaps even opposed to the government because of his or her political viewpoint, perceived or real. The more general interpretation of political opinion . . . reflects more care in embracing situations of this kind.

   See also *Klinko v Canada (Minister of Citizenship and Immigration)*, [2000] 3 FC 327 (CA) [*Klinko*].

102 *Ward*, above note 4 at 746.

103 *Klinko*, above note 101 at para 22.

104 UNHCR Handbook, above note 6 at para 80.

105 *Ibid* at para 83: See also *sur place* claims. The fact that the claimant has refused to avail herself of state protection and concealed her true state of mind may support the claimant's assertions that she fears persecution based on political opinion.

106 *Ward*, above note 4.

107 *Klinko*, above note 101 at para 31: "A political opinion does not cease to be political because the government agrees with it."

Despite the broad nature of the definition of *political opinion*, the Federal Court of Canada has imposed some limitations. For example, in the case of *Asghar v Canada (Minister of Citizenship and Immigration)*, the claimant was a citizen of Pakistan whose father was a police officer. The father had arrested members of a criminal group accused of the murder of another police officer.[108] The members of the criminal group tried to kidnap the claimant, threatened his father, and killed his uncle. At the RPD, the board member found that the claimant had not been threatened by reason of political opinion because the criminal group was not persecuting the father due to his opinion but wanted to prevent him from testifying against the group at a criminal trial. The court held that the father was attacked for carrying out his police duties rather than for an imputed political opinion.[109]

Emerging views in international law may be used to challenge findings similar to those in *Asghar*. As the UNHCR Guidance Note on Refugee Claims Relating to Victims of Organized Gangs states:

> Gang-related refugee claims may also be analysed on the basis of the applicant's actual or imputed political opinion vis-à-vis gangs, and/or the State's policies towards gangs or other segments of society that target gangs (e.g. vigilante groups) . . .
>
>   . . . In certain contexts, expressing objections to the activities of gangs or to the State's gang-related policies may be considered as amounting to an opinion that is critical of the methods and policies of those in power and, thus, constitute a "political opinion" within the meaning of the refugee definition.[110]

Nevertheless, it will be difficult for any claimant to distinguish between being a victim of or threatened with criminal acts or expressing objections to a criminal entity that could amount to political opinion.[111] It appears that in Canadian jurisprudence, both the Refugee Protection Division and the Federal Court have largely avoided the question of whether a claim can be founded on political opinion where a claimant opposes gang-related activities in the home country by examining

---

108 2005 FC 768 [*Asghar*].

109 *Ibid* at para 28.

110 UNHCR, *Guidance Note on Refugee Claims Relating to Victims of Organized Gangs*, online: www.aila.org/content/default.aspx?docid=31688 at paras 45–46.

111 See, for example, *Zacarias v Canada (Minister of Citizenship and Immigration)*, 2011 FC 62, where the issue was raised, but the judicial review was granted on other grounds, namely, that the s 97 analysis on generalized risk was done improperly.

whether section 97 of the *IRPA* applies: whether the claimant faces a personalized or particularized risk.[112]

With regard to the political opinion itself, the UNHCR cautions against assuming first, that it will always be possible to establish a causal link between the opinion expressed and the related measures suffered or feared by the claimant;[113] and second, that the opinion must have been expressed or must be known to the agents of persecution in order to qualify for protection.[114] Indeed, as the Supreme Court of Canada pointed out in *Ward*:

> In many cases, the claimant is not even given the opportunity to articulate his or her beliefs, but these can be perceived from his or her actions. In such situations, the political opinion that constitutes the basis for the claimant's well-founded fear of persecution is said to be imputed to the claimant.[115]

It also follows that "the political opinion ascribed to the claimant and for which he or she fears persecution need not necessarily conform to the claimant's true beliefs" or "be correctly attributed to the claimant."[116] Thus, in examining whether there is well-founded fear, the decision maker should approach the matter from the perspective of the persecutor. The Federal Court has also cautioned against using a "western" or "North-American" interpretation of what constitutes a political opinion. In *Chen v Canada (Minister of Employment and Immigration)*, the court quashed a negative refugee determination where a board member did not find any underlying messages in the satirical drawings by the claimant; it found that the board member had imposed western values in the evaluation of the drawings.[117]

Even where a claimant has not yet expressed strongly held convictions, the UNHCR Handbook suggests that a claim may succeed on the ground that "it may be reasonable to assume that his opinions will sooner or later find expression and that the applicant will as a result, come in conflict with the authorities."[118] Ultimately, the decision maker

---

112 *Ibid*. See also, for example, *Pineda v Canada (Minister of Citizenship and Immigration)*, 2011 FC 81; *Melendez v Canada (Minister of Citizenship and Immigration)*, 2014 FC 700 [*Melendez*]; *Vasquez v Canada (Minister of Citizenship and Immigration)*, 2011 FC 477; and *Diaz v Canada (Minister of Citizenship and Immigration)*, 2011 FC 705; and *IRPA*, above note 1, s 97.

113 UNHCR Handbook, above note 6 at para 81.

114 *Ibid* at paras 82–83; *Ward*, above note 4 at 746: "the political opinion at issue need not have been expressed outright."

115 *Ward, ibid*.

116 *Ibid* at 747.

117 (1993), 70 FTR 241 at para 9 (TD).

118 UNHCR Handbook, above note 6 at para 82.

must evaluate whether an expression of the opinion may result in persecution of the claimant.

Persecutory measures may take the form of prosecution for alleged criminal acts against the state that is nothing more than a pretext for punishing the person for political opinions.[119] The decision maker may need to distinguish between prosecution and punishment that pertains to political opinion and prosecution for politically motivated, but nevertheless criminal acts.[120] When determining whether punishment or prosecution is used to deter particular political opinions, the UNHCR recommends that a decision maker should have regard to the following: "personality of the applicant, his political opinion, the motive behind the act, the nature of the act committed, the nature of the prosecution and its motives" and "the nature of the law on which the prosecution is based."[121]

The challenge of drawing a line between prosecution and punishment and persecution on the basis of political opinion is particularly prominent in cases where conscientious objectors have refused to complete military service. For example, in *Zolfagharkhani*, the court held that the claimant's refusal to participate in military action that involved using chemical weapons against the Kurds would be treated by the Iranian government as an expression of unacceptable political opinion.[122] In *Ates v Canada (Minister of Citizenship and Immigration)*, however, the court found that, while the claimant's refusal to participate in mandatory military service was grounded on political opinion, nevertheless, the Turkish law for prosecuting and punishing the evasion of military service was not inherently persecutory.[123] The court compared the situation to tax evasion: "This is like saying someone who does not believe in the right of the state to tax suffers persecution in Canada for failing to file income tax returns."[124]

The challenge of understanding foreign laws and justice systems when considering claims based on political opinion has also been highlighted in cases where Americans have evaded military duty. These

---

119 *Ibid* at paras 81 and 85.
120 *Ibid* at para 84: "If the prosecution pertains to a punishable act committed out of political motives, and if the anticipated punishment is in conformity with the general law of the country concerned, fear of such prosecution will not in itself make the applicant a refugee." See also *Zolfagharkhani*, above note 32.
121 UNHCR Handbook, above note 6 at para 86.
122 See, for example, *Zolfagharkhani*, above note 32 at para 32.
123 2004 FC 1316 at para 21, aff'd 2005 FCA 322. The other difference may lie in the fact that the claimant in *Zolfagharkhani* did not want to be involved in committing international war crimes with the use of chemical weapons.
124 *Ibid* at para 19 (FC).

cases highlight the need to make a particularized assessment of the facts of each case, no matter which country the claimant comes from. They also raise questions about the adequacy of state protection for individuals with particular political convictions.[125] For example, in *Hinzman v Canada (Minister of Citizenship and Immigration)*, the claimant was an American soldier whose unit was deployed to fight in Iraq. He deserted the army because of his moral objections to the war in Iraq and his belief that American military action in that country was illegal. The RPD denied his claim with a preliminary ruling disallowing the introduction of evidence to show that the war in Iraq was illegal. In the Federal Court, Hinzman sought to have this decision quashed and grounded his arguments on the UNHCR Handbook, paragraphs 170 and 171, which states:

> There are, however, also cases where the necessity to perform military service may be the sole ground for a claim to refugee status, i.e. when a person can show that the performance of military service would have required his participation in military action contrary to his genuine political, religious or moral convictions, or to valid reasons of conscience.
>
> Not every conviction, genuine though it may be, will constitute a sufficient reason for claiming refugee status after desertion or draft-evasion. It is not enough for a person to be in disagreement with his government regarding the political justification for a particular military action. Where, however, the type of military action, with which an individual does not wish to be associated, is condemned by the international community as contrary to basic rules of human conduct, punishment for desertion or draft-evasion could, in the light of all other requirements of the definition, in itself be regarded as persecution.[126]

Justice Mactavish concluded that the claimant did have sincere objections to fighting with the American army in Iraq and that he had brought himself within the terms of paragraph 170. However, she also concluded that his case did not fit within the ambit of paragraph 171. She observed that the claimant himself would not be called upon to commit breaches of international humanitarian law and argued:

---

125 2007 FCA 171 [*Hinzman FCA*]; *Key v Canada (Minister of Citizenship and Immigration)*, 2008 FC 838; *Smith v Canada (Minister of Citizenship and Immigration)*, 2009 FC 1194 [*Smith*]; *Walcott v Canada (Minister of Citizenship and Immigration)*, 2011 FC 415.

126 UNHCR Handbook, above note 6 at paras 170–71.

I am satisfied that when one is dealing with a foot-soldier such as Mr. Hinzman, the assessment of the "military action" that has to be carried out in accordance with paragraph 171 of the *Handbook* relates to the "on the ground" conduct of the soldier in question, and not to the legality of the war itself.

As a consequence, I am satisfied that the Board did not err in finding evidence as to the alleged illegality of the American-led military action in Iraq to be irrelevant to the determination that had to be made by the Refugee Protection Division in this case, in accordance with paragraph 171 of the UNHCR *Handbook*.[127]

At the Federal Court of Appeal, Hinzman's appeal was dismissed on the unrelated ground that state protection was available to him in the United States.[128]

e)   Membership in a "Particular Social Group"

"Particular social group" was inserted into the *Refugee Convention* "to cover any possible lacuna left by the other four groups."[129] Unlike the other enumerated grounds, this ground has not been given a broad liberal interpretation; not every group can qualify as a particular social group. In *Ward*, the Supreme Court of Canada discounted an interpretation that would include "any association bound by some common thread" as this would render superfluous the other grounds of persecution included in the definition.[130] Instead, the Court determined that the meaning to be accorded to the phrase should be informed by human rights and anti-discrimination concepts.[131] Justice La Forest offered the following analysis:

> The meaning assigned to "particular social group" in the Act should take into account the general underlying themes of the defence of human rights and anti-discrimination that form the basis for the international refugee protection initiative. The tests . . . identify three possible categories:

---

127 *Hinzman v Canada (Minister of Citizenship and Immigration)*, 2006 FC 420 at paras 164–65 [*Hinzman*].

128 *Hinzman FCA*, above note 125.

129 *Ward*, above note 4 at 732.

130 *Ibid*; see also *Galvan v Canada (Minister of Citizenship and Immigration)* (2000), 193 FTR 161 (TD) [*Galvan*], wherein the court rejected a broad definition of *particular social group* for these reasons: (1) it would exaggerate the implications of the intention of the framers of the *Refugee Convention*; and (2) it would derogate from the principle that international refugee law was meant to serve as a substitute for national protection where the latter was not provided.

131 *Ibid*; see also *Ward*, above note 4; *Chan*, above note 5; *Cheung*, above note 35.

(1) groups defined by an innate or unchangeable characteristic;
(2) groups whose members voluntarily associate for reasons so fundamental to their human dignity that they should not be forced to forsake the association; and
(3) groups associated by a former voluntary status, unalterable due to its historical permanence.

The first category would embrace individuals fearing persecution on such bases as gender, linguistic background and sexual orientation, while the second would encompass, for example, human rights activists. The third branch is included more because of historical intentions, although it is also relevant to the anti-discrimination influences, in that one's past is an immutable part of the person.[132]

Thus, mere membership in a social group is not sufficient to obtain refugee protection.[133] For example, it has been held that a claimant who fears constant victimization because he is among a group of taxi drivers or wealthy businessmen does not qualify for refugee protection.[134] Moreover, where a person is targeted by an ordinary criminal or, for example, because of something he has done rather than because of an unchangeable characteristic, this may be insufficient to count as membership in a particular social group.[135]

The UNHCR has indicated that a *particular social group* comprises "persons of similar background, habits or social status"[136] and has confirmed the view of the Supreme Court by interpreting the phrase so that it embraces "a group of persons who share a common characteristic other than their risk of being persecuted, or who are perceived as a group by society. The characteristic will often be one which is innate, unchangeable, or which is otherwise fundamental to identity, conscience or the exercise of one's human rights."[137]

---

132 *Ward,* above note 4 at 739.
133 UNHCR Handbook, above note 6 at para 79.
134 *Galvan,* above note 130; *Montchak v Canada (Minister of Citizenship and Immigration),* [1999] FCJ No 1111 (TD).
135 *Mason v Canada (Secretary of State),* [1995] FCJ No 815 (TD); *Gonzales v Canada (Minister of Citizenship and Immigration),* 2002 FCT 345; *Calero v Canada (Minister of Employment and Immigration),* [1994] FCJ No 1159 (TD); *Canada (Minister of Employment and Immigration) v Satiacum* (1989), 99 NR 171 (FCA); *Ababio v Canada (Minister of Employment and Immigration)* (1988), 90 NR 28 (FCA).
136 UNHCR Handbook, above note 6 at para 77.
137 UN High Commissioner for Refugees, Guidelines on International Protection No. 9: *Gender-Related Persecution within the context of Article 1A(2) of the 1951 Convention and/or its 1967 Protocol relating to the Status of Refugees,* HCR/GIP/02/01 (7 May 2002), online: UNHCR www.unhcr.org/3d58ddef4.pdf [UNHCR Gender Guidelines] at para 29.

Particular social groups have included women,[138] families,[139] tribes,[140] and persons identifying with a particular sexual orientation.[141] There is no closed list of what is a particular social group, which allows for the *Refugee Convention* to respond to the evolving nature of refugee protection.[142]

A refugee claimant need not demonstrate that all members of the particular social group are at risk of persecution.[143] Group size does not matter; the fact that the particular social group may consist of a large number of persons — women, for example — is not a reason to refuse refugee protection.[144]

Framing a refugee claim under this enumerated ground also may involve the recognition that the claimant may face persecution on several related grounds, such as race, nationality, or religion. For example, a claimant may want to communicate to decision makers that a gender-sensitive interpretation be given to an enumerated ground.[145]

The next two sections explore two constructed aspects of identity that have provided opportunities for refugee protection under "particular social group": gender and sexual orientation.

---

138 See notes 150–59 and Section B(3)(e)(i), below in this chapter.

139 In *Asghar*, above note 108, the claimant was claiming he was being persecuted because of his relation to his father, a police officer with imputed political opinion against a criminal gang; in *Al-Busaidy v Canada (Minister of Employment and Immigration)* (1992), 139 NR 208 (CA), the court found that the claimant's father might have had a refugee claim that could have supported a derivative claim by the claimant son.

140 See, for example, *Ali v Canada (Minister of Citizenship and Immigration)*, 2008 FC 448; *Traore v Canada (Minister of Citizenship and Immigration)*, 2003 FC 1256; *Mumuni v Canada (Minister of Citizenship and Immigration)*, 2006 FC 1407.

141 See, for example, *Smith*, above note 125. See also Section B(3)(e)(ii), below in this chapter.

142 UN High Commissioner for Refugees, Guidelines on International Protection: *"Membership of a Particular Social Group" within the Context of Article 1A(2) of the 1951 Convention and/or Its 1967 Protocol relating to the Status of Refugees*, HCR/GIP/02/02 (7 May 2002) online: UNHCR www.unhcr.org/3d58de2da.pdf at para 3 [UNHCR Guidelines on PSG].

143 *Ibid* at para 17.

144 *Ibid* at paras 18–19.

145 UNHCR Gender Guidelines, above note 137 at paras 22–28: For example, at para 24: "Persecution for reasons of race may be expressed in different ways against men and women . . . women may be viewed as propagating the ethnic or racial identity and persecuted in a different way, such as through sexual violence or control of reproduction." At para 25: "religion assigns particular roles or behavioural codes to women and men respectively."

i)   Gender

As the UNHCR points out, "[h]istorically, the refugee definition has been interpreted through a framework of male experiences, which has meant that many claims of women and [LGBTQ] persons have gone unrecognized."[146] One can trace this to the fact that gender is not specifically referenced in the refugee definition.[147]

Despite this gap, Canada has been commended for placing gender-related refugee claims within the enumerated ground of particular social group[148] and by creating guidelines for decision makers reviewing gender-related claims.[149] Refugee claims dealing with gender persecution

---

146 *Ibid* at para 5.

147 Audrey Macklin, "Refugee Women and the Imperative of Categories" (1995) 17 *Human Rights Quarterly* 213 at 249 and 252: She finds that the current regime does not go far enough because it fails to "add gender explicitly to the refugee taxonomy." Chantal Tie, "Sex, Gender, and Refugee Protection in Canada under Bill C-11: Are Additional Protections Required in Light of *In re R-A-*?" (2001) 19 *Refuge* 54 at 55: Tie writes:

> Notwithstanding this optimism, there remain a number of analytical difficulties that arise in gender-based claims when we try to fit the specificity of gender persecution into the existing categories of refugee persecution. Because the definition has not been amended to add sex or gender, claimants must show that their persecution is "on account of" their political opinion, race, nationality, or religion, or because of membership in a particular social group.

> Heather Potter, "Gender-Based Persecution: A Challenge to the Canadian Refugee Determination System" (1994) 3 *Dalhousie Journal of Legal Studies* 81; Melanie Randall, "Refugee Law and State Accountability for Violence Against Women: A Comparative Analysis of Legal Approaches to Recognizing Asylum Claims Based on Gender Persecution" (2002) 25 *Harvard Women's Law Journal* 281 at 288–90; Mattie Stevens, "Recognizing Gender-Specific Persecution: A Proposal to Add Gender as a Sixth Refugee Category" (1993) 3 *Cornell Journal of Law & Public Policy* 179.

148 Judith Ramirez, "The Canadian Guidelines on Women Refugee Claimants Fearing Gender-Related Persecution" (1994) 14 *Refuge* 3; Kris Ann Balser Mousette, "Female Genital Mutilation and Refugee Status in the United States – A Step in the Right Direction" (1996) 19 *Boston College International & Comparative Law Review* 353; Walter Long, "Escape from Wonderland: Implementing Canada's Rational Procedures to Evaluate Women's Gender-Related Asylum Claims" (1994) 4 *UCLA Women's Law Journal* 179.

149 Immigration and Refugee Board of Canada, Chairperson Guidelines 4: *Women Refugee Claimants Fearing Gender-Related Persecution* (13 November 1996), online: IRB www.irb-cisr.gc.ca/Eng/BoaCom/references/pol/GuiDir/Pages/GuideDir04.aspx [IRB Gender Guidelines]. See Chapter 2 for more information on the Guidelines provided by the Chairperson of the IRB.

include claims that deal with domestic violence,[150] rape,[151] detention or confinement,[152] beatings,[153] female genital mutilation,[154] forced marriage,[155] forced abortions,[156] forced sterilization,[157] persecution from being a victim of rape or bearing illegitimate children,[158] and harm due to marrying against family wishes.[159]

Recognizing gender-related claims does not come without challenges. Some scholars argue that fitting gender into "particular social group" still provides definitional hurdles for specific kinds of gender-related claims;[160] that the IRB's Gender Guidelines are not all-encompassing or complete;[161] that the current approach in evaluating gender-related

---

150 For example: *Melius v Canada (Minister of Citizenship and Immigration)*, 2013 FC 537; *Varga v Canada (Minister of Citizenship and Immigration)*, 2013 FC 494.

151 For example: *Desire v Canada (Minister of Citizenship and Immigration)*, 2013 FC 167 [*Desire*]; *Raju v Canada (Minister of Citizenship and Immigration)*, 2013 FC 848.

152 For example: *Musleameen v Canada (Minister of Citizenship and Immigration)*, 2010 FC 232; *Latif v Canada (Minister of Citizenship and Immigration)*, 2009 FC 63.

153 For example: *Harinarain v Canada (Minister of Citizenship and Immigration)*, 2012 FC 1519; *Clarke v Canada (Minister of Citizenship and Immigration)*, 2012 FC 1225.

154 For example: *Itua v Canada (Minister of Citizenship and Immigration)*, 2012 FC 631; *Sow v Canada (Minister of Citizenship and Immigration)*, 2011 FC 1313.

155 For example: *Henguva v Canada (Minister of Citizenship and Immigration)*, 2013 FC 483; *Kaniz v Canada (Minister of Citizenship and Immigration)*, 2013 FC 63.

156 For example: *Gecaj v Canada (Minister of Citizenship and Immigration)*, 2012 FC 1369; *Liang v Canada (Minister of Citizenship and Immigration)*, 2013 FC 765.

157 For example: *Cao v Canada (Minister of Citizenship and Immigration)*, 2013 FC 173; *Zheng v Canada (Minister of Citizenship and Immigration)*, 2012 FC 608.

158 For example: *Cornejo v Canada (Minister of Citizenship and Immigration)*, 2010 FC 261; *Ousmer v Canada (Minister of Citizenship and Immigration)*, 2012 FC 222.

159 For example: *Hafeez v Canada (Minister of Citizenship and Immigration)*, 2012 FC 747.

160 Tie, above note 147 at 62; Krista Daley & Ninette Kelley, "Particular Social Group: A Human Rights Based Approach in Canadian Jurisprudence" (2000) 12:2 *International Journal of Refugee Law* 148; Jane Connors, "Legal Aspects of Women as Particular Social Group" (1997) *International Journal of Refugee Law* 159; Deborah Anker, "Refugee Law, Gender and the Human Rights Paradigm" (2002) 15 *Harvard Human Rights Journal* 133; LG Heyman, "Domestic Violence and Asylum: Toward a Working Model of Affirmative State Obligations" (2005) 17:4 *International Journal of Refugee Law* 729; Michelle Foster, "Why We Are Not There Yet: The Particular Challenge of 'Particular Social Group'" in Efrat Arbel, Catherine Dauvergne, & Jenni Millbank, eds, *Gender in Refugee Law: From the Margins to the Centre* (New York: Routledge, 2014) 17; Jenni Millbank, "The Ring of Truth: A Case Study of Credibility Assessment in Particular Social Group Refugee Determinations" (2009) 21 *International Journal of Refugee Law* 1.

161 Nicole LaViolette, "Gender-Related Refugee Claims: Expanding the Scope of the Canadian Guidelines" (2007) 19 *International Journal of Refugee Law* 169; Valerie Oosterveld, "The Canadian Guidelines on Gender-Related Persecution" (1996) 8 *International Journal of Refugee Law* 569.

claims imposes western values on other cultures;[162] and finally, that analyzing gender-related claims under the aegis of particular social group often means that the other applicable grounds such as religion or political opinion have been overlooked.[163] Further, the size of a group has sometimes been used as a basis for refusing to recognize "women" generally as a particular social group.[164] The UNHCR responds to this by stating:

> This argument has no basis in fact or reason, as the other grounds are not bound by this question of size. There should equally be no requirement that the particular social group be cohesive or that members of it voluntarily associate, or that every member of the group is at risk of persecution. It is well-accepted that it should be possible to identify the group independently of the persecution, however discrimination or persecution may be a relevant factor in determining the visibility of the group in a particular context.[165]

Canadian jurisprudence has recognized that decision makers should not only consider gender as a ground under membership in a particular social group, but also that they should consider an intersection of factors relating to gender-based claims, including whether it was objectively unreasonable for the claimant to have sought protection.[166] Further, jurisprudence is increasingly emphasizing that decision makers should act sensitively, following the Gender Guidelines, when interacting with a claimant and assessing her claim.[167]

---

162 See, for example, Sherene Razack, "Domestic Violence as Gender Persecution: Policing the Borders of Nation, Race, and Gender" (1995) 8 *Canadian Journal of Women and the Law* 45 at 49; Macklin, above note 147 at 273; Efrat Arbel, "The Culture of Rights Protection in Canadian Refugee Law: Examining the Domestic Violence Cases" (2003) 58 *McGill Law Journal* 729; Susan Kneebone, "Women within the Refugee Construct: 'Exclusionary Inclusion' in Policy and Practice – The Australian Experience" (2005) 17 *International Journal of Refugee Law* 7; Jenni Millbank & Catherine Dauvergne, "Forced Marriage and the Exoticization of Gendered Harms in United States Asylum Law" (2010) 19 *Columbia Journal of Gender and the Law* 898.

163 UNHCR Gender Guidelines, above note 137 at para 28.

164 *Ibid* at para 31.

165 *Ibid*; see also *Narvaez v Canada (Minister of Citizenship and Immigration)*, [1995] 2 FC 55 (TD); *Dezameau v Canada (Minister of Citizenship and Immigration)*, 2010 FC 559 [*Dezameau*].

166 *Danelia v Canada (Minister of Citizenship and Immigration)*, 2014 FC 707: Factors include the social, cultural, religious, and economic context the claimant finds herself in; *Djubok v Canada (Minister of Citizenship and Immigration)*, 2014 FC 497.

167 See, for example, *Odia v Canada (Minister of Citizenship and Immigration)*, 2014 FC 663.

ii) Sexual Orientation

Persecution of lesbian, gay, bisexual, transgender, intersex, and queer or questioning (LGBTIQ) individuals and those perceived to be LGBTIQ is not a new phenomenon. However the view that sexual orientation and/or gender identity may validly ground a refugee claim has begun to gain greater traction around the world, including in Canada, albeit inconsistently.[168] The UNHCR states that it is

> . . . widely documented that LGBTI individuals are the targets of killings, sexual and gender-based violence, physical attacks, torture, arbitrary detention, accusations of immoral or deviant behaviour, denial of the rights to assembly, expression and information, and discrimination in employment, health and education in all regions around the world. Many countries maintain severe criminal laws for consensual same-sex relations, a number of which stipulate imprisonment, corporal punishment and/or the death penalty.[169]

Like gender, risk of persecution, torture, or death by reason of sexual orientation may intersect other grounds such as nationality, religion, and race.[170] In Canada, claims put forward on the basis of sexual orientation include physical, psychological, and sexual violence;[171] efforts to change someone's sexual orientation or identity;[172] prosecution and

---

168 See, for example, Nicole LaViolette, "Canada Grants Asylum Based on Sexual Orientation" in Lillian Faderman et al, eds, *Great Events from History: Gay, Lesbian, Bisexual, Transgender Events* (Pasadena, CA: Salem Press, 2007); Nicole LaViolette, "UNHCR Guidance Note on Refugee Claims Relating to Sexual Orientation and Gender Identity: A Critical Commentary" (2010) 22 *International Journal of Refugee Law* 173; Nicole LaViolette, "The Immutable Refugees: Sexual Orientation in *Canada (A.G.) v. Ward*" (1997) 55 *University of Toronto Faculty of Law Review* 1.

169 UNHCR Guidelines re Sexual Orientation, above note 20; see International Lesbian, Gay, Bisexual, Trans and Intersex Association, "State-Sponsored Homophobia, A World Survey of Laws Criminalising Same-Sexual Acts between Consenting Adults" (May 2012), online: www.aidsfreeworld.org/Planetaids/~/media/796515F2D74A4158ac599504E042F4A8.pdf.

170 UNHCR Guidelines re Sexual Orientation, above note 20 at paras 3 and 40–50.

171 For example, *Garcia v Canada (Minister of Citizenship and Immigration)*, 2005 FC 807; *Brown v Canada (Minister of Citizenship and Immigration)*, 2011 FC 585.

172 See, for example, *Okoli v Canada (Minister of Citizenship and Immigration)*, 2009 FC 332 [*Okoli*].

detention;[173] threats of death;[174] forced marriage;[175] denial of economic, social, and health rights;[176] and discrimination in employment.[177]

Of vital importance when evaluating such claims is recognizing that a claimant should not be required to change his sexual orientation in order to avoid persecution.[178] Further, the fact that a claimant has not been open about sexual orientation or identity should not be fatal to a claim, but rather can be evidence of the claimant's well-founded fear.[179]

4) State Protection

a) The Canadian Conception of State Protection

One issue that has dominated Canadian refugee law since the early 1990s is the problem of specifying criteria that will identify when refugee claimants must rely on the mechanisms of protection available within their own country of nationality rather than seek protection from another country.[180] In the first edition of his treatise, James Hathaway addressed this question, drew a connection between state protection and a well-founded fear of persecution, and offered an elegant and straightforward analysis:

> Because the risk of persecution will never be definitively measurable, decision-makers should ask only whether the evidence as a whole discloses a risk of persecution which would cause a reasonable person in the claimant's circumstances to reject as insufficient whatever protection her state of origin is able and willing to afford her.[181]

This way of framing the issue reveals that it may be resolved by addressing three separate questions. First, what is the degree and nature of the danger faced by the claimant? Second, what mechanisms of protection are available? Third, would a reasonable person regard the amount of protection as sufficient and rely upon it rather than seek

---

173 See, for example, *Smith*, above note 125.

174 See, for example, *X (Re)*, 2007 CanLII 47398 (CA IRB).

175 See, for example, *X (Re)*, 2013 CanLII 92933 (CA IRB).

176 See, for example, *Diaz v Canada (Minister of Citizenship and Immigration)*, 2008 FC 1243 [*Diaz*].

177 See, for example, *X (Re)*, 2007 CanLII 47398 (CA IRB).

178 *Re R(UW)*, [1991] CRDD No 501 (IRB); *Pizarro v Canada (Minister of Employment and Immigration)* (1994), 75 FTR 120 (TD).

179 *Hernandez v Canada (Minister of Citizenship and Immigration)*, 2007 FC 1297.

180 Between 2009 and 2014 alone this issue has been addressed about 1,200 times by the Federal Court.

181 Hathaway, above note 19 at 80.

an alternative source of security elsewhere? One considers the level of risk created by the agent of persecution and then asks whether this level is diminished by any protective measures made available by state authorities. The approach relies on a device familiar within many other branches of law: the standard of the reasonable person. Where a reasonable person would not put stock in the available sources of security, the claim for a well-founded fear of persecution is established.

The framework articulated by Hathaway has not received much attention or support from the courts in Canada; instead, attention has been put on the decision of the Supreme Court of Canada in *Ward*,[182] which was rendered shortly after the publication of Hathaway's text. In *Ward*, La Forest J offered an alternative approach to the issue, one that is much less straightforward and more convoluted, and ultimately less satisfactory than Hathaway's, but which has nevertheless overshadowed it. Justice La Forest begins his analysis in *Ward* by connecting the idea of a well-founded fear with the absence of state protection. He states:

> [R]egardless of the category under which the claimant falls, the focus [of the definition] is on establishing whether the fear is "well-founded". It is at this stage that the state's inability to protect should be considered.[183]

Justice La Forest is adamant that the claimant need not show that persecution emanates from an agent of the state nor does the claimant have to show a high level of complicity between the persecutor and the state. He observes, "[A]ll parties agree, at a minimum, that state complicity encompasses *an inability to protect*."[184] Thus, the claimant need not show that the state was actually involved in the persecution, or that it had a persecutory intent. It is the mere absence of state protection that supports a refugee claim.

Justice La Forest then outlines a complex set of principles and procedures to guide decision makers. First, he states a presumption in favour of the claimant:

> Having established that the claimant has a fear, the Board is, in my view, entitled to presume that persecution will be *likely*, and the fear *well-founded*, if there is an absence of state protection. The presumption goes to the heart of the inquiry, which is whether there is a likelihood of persecution. But I see nothing wrong with this, if the Board is satisfied that there is a legitimate fear, and an established inability

---

182 *Ward*, above note 4.
183 *Ibid* at 712.
184 *Ibid* at 719 [emphasis added].

of the state to assuage those fears through effective protection. The presumption is not a great leap. Having established the existence of a fear and a state's inability to assuage those fears, it is not assuming too much to say that the fear is well-founded.[185]

Although its meaning is not wholly pellucid, this passage seems to indicate that claimants can make their case by simply showing that their fear is legitimate — presumably by pointing to the substantial nature of the threat that they face — and by then pointing to the absence of any protection from the state. However, in summarizing his position, La Forest J proposes a more generous account that makes no reference to the "legitimacy" of the claimant's fear. He states: "A subjective fear of persecution combined with state inability to protect the claimant creates a presumption that the fear is well-founded."[186]

This rewording would suggest that where claimants show that there is an absence of state protection, their subjective fear should be sufficient to ground their claim unless other evidence reveals that the fear lacks an objective basis. In other words, where there is no state protection from persecution, it is presumptively reasonable to fear that one will be persecuted, unless there is evidence to show that it is unlikely. Justice La Forest takes pains to temper this presumption by explaining that, in most circumstances, it is very difficult for claimants to show that there is an absence of state protection. He states: "The danger that this presumption will operate too broadly is tempered by a requirement that clear and convincing proof of a state's inability to protect must be advanced."[187]

He modifies this further by saying "[a]bsent a situation of a complete breakdown of state apparatus . . . it should be assumed that the state is capable of protecting a claimant."[188] As a rationale, La Forest J suggests that states "should be presumed capable of protecting their citizens" as the "[s]ecurity of nationals is, after all, the essence of sovereignty."[189] He also observes that this presumption

> . . . serves to reinforce the underlying rationale of international protection as a surrogate, coming into play where no alternative remains to the claimant. Refugee claims were never meant to allow a claimant

---

185 *Ibid* at 722 [emphasis added].
186 *Ibid* at 726.
187 *Ibid*.
188 *Ibid* at 725.
189 *Ibid*.

to seek out better protection than that from which he or she benefits already.[190]

This second presumption is, in turn, tempered by further observations on how claimants may prove the state's inability to protect. Justice La Forest states:

> clear and convincing confirmation of a state's inability to protect must be provided. For example, a claimant might advance testimony of similarly situated individuals let down by the state protection arrangement or the claimant's testimony of past personal incidents in which state protection did not materialize.[191]

In addition, he makes observations on the need to seek state protection:

> Like Hathaway, I prefer to formulate this aspect of the test for fear of persecution as follows: only in situations in which state protection "might reasonably have been forthcoming", will the claimant's failure to approach the state for protection defeat his claim. Put another way, the claimant will not meet the definition of "Convention refugee" where it is objectively unreasonable for the claimant not to have sought the protection of his home authorities; otherwise, the claimant need not literally approach the state.[192]

One may summarize the position expressed by La Forest J as follows:

1) Where one proves absence of state protection and the existence of a legitimate fear of persecution, one will have proven a well-founded fear of persecution unless it is shown that one's fears are not objectively grounded.

2) In the absence of a complete breakdown of state machinery, there is a presumption that states are able to protect their nationals.

3) To defeat this presumption one must introduce clear and convincing evidence of an inability to protect.[193]

---

190 *Ibid* at 726.

191 *Ibid* at 724–25.

192 *Ibid* at 724.

193 See, for example, *Balogh v Canada (Minister of Citizenship and Immigration)*, 2014 FC 771; and *Montoya v Canada (Minister of Citizenship and Immigration)*, 2014 FC 808. In most cases, claimants will want to present objective documentary or expert evidence illustrating the lack of state protection. A plethora of jurisprudence calls for decision makers to consider evidence put forward regarding the issue of state protection. Persecution may derive from other parties but also because of the failure or inability of the state to effectively protect the claimant. See *Zalzali v Canada (Minister of Employment and Immigration)*, [1991] 3 FC 605 (CA).

4) Unless it is objectively unreasonable to seek state protection, the failure to do so will defeat a refugee claim.
5) Anecdotal evidence of state failure whether from one's own experience, from that of similarly situated persons, or from generalized documentary sources may serve as "clear and convincing evidence" to ground the claim or justify the failure to seek state protection.

b) Multiple Nationalities

In cases where the claimant has multiple nationalities, these principles will apply in relation to each state. As La Forest J explains, "the rationale underlying international refugee protection is to serve as 'surrogate' shelter coming into play only upon a failure of national support."[194]

This requirement of addressing the availability of state protection extends to situations where a claimant may be able to obtain citizenship of a state that she does not currently possess.[195] How much of a link does a claimant need to have to a country before she could be considered as possessing its nationality? This question was answered to some extent in the case of *Katkova v Canada (Minister of Citizenship and Immigration)*.[196] The claimant was an Eastern European Jew, and at issue was the question whether Israel should be considered a country of nationality due to Israel's law of return.[197] The Federal Court observed that the desire to settle in Israel is a requirement for settling in Israel and that, in this case, the claimant clearly stated she did not want to go to Israel. The court went further and held that, for a person to possess the nationality of a particular country, there must be a "genuine connection" or "physical link" with the state, and that nationality is a "legal bond" having as its basis a "social fact of attachment," a "genuine connection of existence, interests and sentiments" bundled together with reciprocal rights and duties. In this case, the court held that the mere fact of being Jewish was not enough to create a genuine link between Israel and the claimant. Further, the court noted that the

---

194 *Ward*, above note 4 at 752.
195 *Williams v Canada (Minister of Citizenship and Immigration)*, 2005 FCA 126 [Williams].
196 (1997), 130 FTR 192 (TD) [*Katkova*].
197 The relevant provision of Israeli Law No 5710-1950, *The Law of Return*, provides:

2 (b) An Oleh's visa shall be granted to every Jew who has expressed his desire to settle in Israel, unless the Minister of Immigration is satisfied that the applicant
(1) is engaged in an activity directed against the Jewish people; or
(2) is likely to endanger public health or the security of the State; or
(3) is a person with a criminal past, likely to endanger public welfare.

law of return does not apply automatically. It requires an exercise of discretion by both an Israeli office and the applicant.[198]

Katkova can be contrasted with the case of *Williams*.[199] In this case, the claimant was born in Rwanda to a Rwandan father and a Ugandan mother. As a result, he was born a Rwandan citizen and a Ugandan citizen.[200] The claimant had dual nationality until 2000 when he reached the age of eighteen years old. According to Ugandan law a citizen of Uganda ceased to retain that status, if upon attaining the age of eighteen years, he voluntarily acquired or retained the citizenship of a country other than Uganda.[201] A person could reacquire Ugandan citizenship, according to the constitution, by renouncing his other citizenship, in this case, the Rwandan citizenship.[202] The Refugee Protection Division held the claimant could avail himself of protection in Uganda because of the availability of Ugandan citizenship by renouncing Rwandan citizenship.[203] In judicial review, while the Federal Court held that the plain reading of section 96 of the *IRPA* did not include "potential countries of nationality,"[204] the Federal Court of Appeal held otherwise:

> The condition of not having a country of nationality must be one that is beyond the power of the applicant to control.
>
> The true test, in my view, is the following: if it is within the control of the applicant to acquire the citizenship of a country with respect to which he has no well-founded fear of persecution, the claim for refugee status will be denied.[205]

The Court of Appeal elaborated by stating that the unwillingness of an applicant to take steps to gain state protection in another country will be fatal to a claim unless that unwillingness results from the very fear of persecution.[206] Thus "countries of nationalities" in section 96 includes "potential countries of nationalities"[207] and claimants may be expected to make efforts to acquire protection or citizenship in their

---

198 See also *Wanchuk v Canada (Minister of Citizenship and Immigration)*, 2014 FC 885.
199 *Williams*, above note 195.
200 *Ibid* at para 3.
201 *Ibid* at para 4.
202 *Ibid* at para 5.
203 *Ibid* at paras 7–8.
204 *Ibid* at para 10.
205 *Ibid* at para 22.
206 *Ibid*.
207 *Ibid* at para 25.

potential countries of nationalities[208] even if it means renouncing citizenship of another country.[209]

The government has developed this approach with North Korean refugee claimants on the ground that they can obtain nationality and, therefore, state protection from South Korea. In the past, the Federal Court has rejected the notion that a North Korean can obtain South Korean nationality. For example, in the case of *Kim v Canada (Minister of Citizenship and Immigration)*, the court acknowledged that the "question for consideration in the present circumstances is whether South Korea provides refuge, and if so, under what circumstances and does that preclude a refugee claim being successfully made by the Applicants in Canada."[210] The court held that "the extent to which a refugee claimant can 'control' the award of citizenship in another country becomes a critical issue" which requires an examination of the "laws, jurisprudence, practice and politics of that country."[211] In *Kim*, the court found that on the evidence, obtaining South Korean nationality "is by no means 'automatic' or 'within the control' of the Applicants" and that "North Koreans are *not* automatically accepted."[212] Despite this 2010 decision, the government has actively challenged decisions granting refugee status to North Koreans on the ground that they could obtain South Korean nationality.[213] Further, the RAD has held contrary to the *Kim* finding that the "evidence is significantly different than that which was before the RPD and the Federal Court in *Kim*" and that "unlike the objective evidence cited in *Kim*," the information suggests that "North Koreans are in fact deemed to be nationals of South Korea."[214]

---

208 *Ibid* at para 27.

209 *Ibid* at paras 28–32: The claimant argued that he would be forced to renounce his Rwandan citizenship; however, the Court of Appeal did not see that the claimant would be forced to renounce citizenship, but that his choice not to renounce will have certain consequences. The court also noted that, in this case, the claimant would not become stateless.

210 2010 FC 720 at para 4 [*Kim*].

211 *Ibid* at para 8.

212 *Ibid* at para 15 [emphasis in original].

213 Jeremy Nuttall, "Canada Slammed Door Shut to North Korean Escapees" *The Tyee* (11 September 2014), online: http://thetyee.ca/News/2014/09/11/North-Korean-Refugees/; Carol Goar, "Welcome Mat for North Koreans Yanked by Jason Kenney" *Toronto Star* (12 July 2013), online: www.thestar.com/opinion/commentary/2013/07/12/welcome_mat_for_north_koreans_yanked_by_jason_kenney_goar.html; Nicholas Keung, "Canada Closing Door on North Korean Refugees" *Toronto Star* (15 December 2013), online: www.thestar.com/news/immigration/2013/12/15/canada_closing_door_on_north_korean_refugees.html.

214 *X (Re)*, 2013 CanLII 76469 at para 60 (CA IRB).

The recent approach towards North Koreans taken by the current government and IRB decision makers is troubling for two main reasons. First, as one opposition member of Parliament stated, "If people from North Korea are not given status as refugees, it's difficult to imagine what kind of country one would have to come from to qualify."[215] Second, recent caselaw reinforces the notion that a claimant's willingness and desire to obtain or seek nationality of another country is not salient when determining whether the claimant could obtain state protection from another country. Rather, the factual finding of which nationalities the claimant possesses is understood, in Canada, to encompass those claimants that *have access to and are entitled to* and not simply those that are willing to obtain or currently possess other nationality.

c)   The Adequacy of State Protection

Some problematic aspects of the approach developed by La Forest J in *Ward* soon became apparent. The issue of state protection has sparked sharp divisions within the Federal Court, divisions that have not yet been fully resolved.

First, judges offered very different assessments about the level of state protection that could defeat a claim. Justice La Forest had presented state protection as an all-or-nothing element. It is either present or absent, and a refugee claim can succeed only if it is absent. Later cases raised the possibility of differing levels of protection and the need to assess the sufficiency of the level available. In some cases, it was decided that, where a state had made serious efforts to address social problems that gave rise to the risk of persecution, then sufficient state protection should be found to exist. This view has been frequently buttressed by the assertion that no state can offer perfect protection and that therefore anecdotal evidence that authorities had been unable to offer protection on particular occasions would be insufficient to meet the burden of showing with clear and convincing evidence that the state was unable to protect.

A good example of this view is found in *TA6-07453*,[216] an IRB decision rendered in 2007 and identified by the Board as a "persuasive decision": [217]

---

215 Nuttall, above note 213.

216 Immigration and Refugee Board of Canada, Persuasive Decision TA6-07453 (26 November 2007), online: IRB www.irb-cisr.gc.ca/Eng/BoaCom/references/pol/persuas/Pages/TA607453.aspx.

217 See online: www.irb-cisr.gc.ca/Eng/NewsNouv/NewNou/2014/Pages/TA607453-VA9-2166rev.aspx, where this status of persuasive decision was revoked in November 2014.

Evidence that protection being offered is not necessarily perfect is not clear and convincing proof of the state's inability to protect its citizens, as no government can guarantee the protection of all its citizens at all times. However, where a state is in effective control of its territory, has military, police and civil authority in place and makes serious efforts to protect its citizens, the mere fact it is not always successful at doing so will not be enough to justify a claim that the victims are unable to avail themselves of protection.[218]

A different view was adopted in *Bobrik*, where Tremblay-Lamer J stated:

Thus, even when the state is willing to protect its citizens, a claimant will meet the criteria for refugee status if the protection being offered is ineffective. A state must actually provide protection, and not merely indicate a willingness to help. Where the evidence reveals that a claimant has experienced many incidents of harassment and/or discrimination without being effectively defended by the state, the presumption operates and it can be concluded that the state may be willing but unable to protect the claimant.[219]

This view however soon met strong opposition. In *Smirnov v Canada (Secretary of State)*, Gibson J stated:

With great respect, I conclude that Madame Justice Tremblay-Lamer sets too high a standard for state protection, a standard that would, in many circumstances, be difficult to attain even in this country. It is a reality of modern-day life that protection offered is sometimes ineffective. Many incidents of harassment and/or discrimination can be effected in a manner that renders effective investigation and protection very difficult . . . . Random assaults, such as those suffered by the applicants, where the assailants are unknown to the victim and there are no independent witnesses are also difficult to effectively investigate and protect against. In all such circumstances, even the most effective, well-resourced and highly motivated police forces will have difficulty providing effective protection. This Court should not impose on other states a standard of "effective" protection that police forces in our own country, regrettably, sometimes only aspire to.[220]

---

218 As authority, the board member cited *Canada (Minister of Employment and Immigration) v Villafranca* (1992), 18 Imm LR (2d) 130 (FCA) [footnotes omitted].
219 *Bobrik*, above note 60 at para 13.
220 [1995] 1 FC 780 (TD).

More recently Crampton J has tried to settle this issue by holding that a state is required to provide adequate protection. In *Cosgun v Canada (Minister of Citizenship and Immigration)*, he states:

> . . . the law is now well-settled that the appropriate test for assessing state protection is whether a country is able and willing to provide adequate protection. In short, a claimant for protection under sections 96 or 97 of the *IRPA* must establish, with clear and convincing evidence, and on a balance of probabilities, the inability or unwillingness of the state to provide adequate protection.[221]

He continued by analyzing the meaning of adequacy as follows:

> To demonstrate inadequate state protection, "it is not enough for a claimant merely to show that his government has not always been effective at protecting persons in his particular situation." (*Villafranca*, above, at 132). Rather, it must be demonstrated that the state is so weak or corrupt that there are extensive shortcomings in its ability or willingness to provide state protection either to the public at large or to persons *similarly situated* to the claimant, in terms of race, religion, nationality, political opinion, social group, age, ethnic origin, etc. For example, if a 70 year-old woman claims a risk of persecution or physical harm, it would not be particularly helpful for her to adduce evidence of inadequate state protection of males or young activists. Moreover, it would not be sufficient for her to simply adduce evidence that the state protection that has been afforded to persons similarly situated to her has been somewhat ineffective. In this case, the Applicant's failure to provide sufficient information regarding the state's inability to provide adequate protection to either the public at large or to persons similarly situated to her was fatal.[222]

In *Majoros v Canada (Minister of Citizenship and Immigration)*, Zinn J offered this analysis:

> I adopt Justice Mosley's statement of the law in this regard in *Meza Varela v Canada (Minister of Citizenship & Immigration)*, 2011 FC 1364 at para 16: "Any efforts must have 'actually translated into adequate state protection' at the operational level." Or, as I put it in *Orgona v Canada (Minister of Citizenship and Immigration)*, 2012 FC 1438 at para 11: "Actions, not good intentions prove that protection from persecution is available." At the same time, state protection need not rise to the level of perfection. That a state is unable to provide adequate

---

221 2010 FC 400 at para 52 [*Cosgun*].
222 *Ibid* at para 55 [emphasis in original].

protection, assessed at the operational level, can be proved with whatever evidence is sufficiently convincing, including documentary evidence.[223]

Thus, the current approach to state protection identifies "operational adequacy" as the key. This seems to take us quite far from the *Ward* analysis and back to the ideas expressed by Hathaway so many years before, cited at the beginning of this section. However, in the attempts to unpack the idea of operational inadequacy, one again sees differences of opinion. In *Cosgun*, Crampton J states:

> To establish that state protection is inadequate, it must be demonstrated that such protection is significantly less adequate than it is in established democracies. Accordingly, it will not be sufficient to adduce evidence of the types of shortcomings or gaps in the provision of state protection that remain in Canada or other developed countries.[224]

Underlying these statements one may infer a view about the nature of surrogate protection. Justice Crampton appears to be promoting the idea that no one is entitled to a higher level of protection than may be obtained in an "established democracy." Expressed differently, he appears to be promoting the view that one cannot be a refugee from a liberal democracy. Such a view, however, is not self-evident and needs to be defended. Although Canada and the United States may offer similar levels of protection to their citizenry, it may be the case that a Canadian can be safer in the United States (and an American in Canada) because their persecutor would find it difficult to cross the border. It is by no means obvious that we should not provide the additional safety to such individuals, yet that is exactly what we achieve by holding that one must rely on one's own state for protection where it meets the standard of an established democracy.

In sum, advocates for refugee claimants can find some caselaw support for the following propositions when it comes to evaluating whether there is state protection:

1) A state must actually provide protection and not merely indicate a willingness to help.[225]
2) On the other hand, where the state or its agents, such as police, have the ability to provide state protection but are not willing or

---

223 2013 FC 421 at para 12 [*Majoros*].
224 *Cosgun*, above note 221 at para 56.
225 *Bobrik*, above note 60.

choose not to provide this protection, this is ineffective state protection.[226]

3) A claimant cannot be expected to rely on existing legislation or procedural frameworks if, in actuality, the protection is not provided.[227] Effective state protection is comprised of serious efforts made by a state at the operational level.[228] Further, the existence of anti-discrimination laws or the presence of non-governmental organizations helping persons similar to the claimant should not be taken as forms of effective state protection as societal attitudes may not be in line with the law, authorities may still not enforce the law, and continued risk may still exist.[229] A *de facto* existence of protection must exist before state protection can truly be found in any given case.

4) Finally, what is effective depends on what is appropriate in the circumstances. A certain kind of protection that may be sufficient for one individual in a country may not suffice for a different individual facing a different kind of persecution in the same country.[230] An individualized inquiry is needed.

d) The Obligation to Seek State Protection

The democratic nature of the state has also been considered in a second context. Decision makers have offered differing analyses of the situations in which a claimant must seek state protection and of how concentrated his efforts must be. Where an individual has failed to seek out state protection, it is clear that some decision makers consider this sufficient to defeat a claim. Indeed, in some cases, even those who have sought out protection will fail because their efforts have been considered inadequate. In *Kadenko v Canada (Minister of Citizenship and Immigration)*, the Federal Court of Appeal expressed the view that the degree of effort to obtain state protection will fluctuate according to the level of democracy found in the state in question:

> When the state in question is a democratic state, the claimant must do more than simply show that he or she went to see some member of the police force and that his or her efforts were unsuccessful. The

---

226 *Elcock v Canada (Minister of Citizenship and Immigration)*, 1999 CanLII 8680 (FCTD).

227 *Ibid.*

228 *Garcia v Canada (Minister of Citizenship and Immigration)*, 2007 FC 79 [*Garcia*].

229 UNHCR Guidelines re Sexual Orientation, above note 20 at paras 37 and 51; *Garcia*, above note 228; *Molnar v Canada (Minister of Citizenship and Immigration)*, 2002 FCT 1081.

230 *Mendivil v Canada (Secretary of State)* (1994), 167 NR 91 (FCA).

burden of proof that rests on the claimant is, in a way, directly proportional to the level of the democracy of the state in question: the more democratic the state's institutions, the more the claimant must have done to exhaust all courses of action open to him or her.[231]

A similar view has also been adopted by the Federal Court of Appeal in *Hinzman*:

> The presumption of state protection described in *Ward*, therefore, applies equally to cases where an individual claims to fear persecution by non-state entities and to cases where the state is alleged to be a persecutor. This is particularly so where the home state is a democratic country like the United States. We must respect the ability of the United States to protect the sincerely held beliefs of its citizens. Only where there is clear and convincing evidence that such protections are unavailable or ineffective such that state conduct amounts to persecution will this country be able to extend its refugee protections to the claimants.
>
> . . .
>
> Reading all these authorities together, a claimant coming from a democratic country will have a heavy burden when attempting to show that he should not have been required to exhaust all of the recourses available to him domestically before claiming refugee status. In view of the fact that the United States is a democracy that has adopted a comprehensive scheme to ensure those who object to military service are dealt with fairly, I conclude that the appellants have adduced insufficient support to satisfy this high threshold. Therefore, I find that it was objectively unreasonable for the appellants to have failed to take significant steps to attempt to obtain protection in the United States before claiming refugee status in Canada.[232]

In *Cosgun*, Crampton J confirmed this approach.[233] This burden of proof remains the same regardless of the country being assessed, although the evidentiary burden required to rebut the presumption of adequate state protection will increase with the level of democracy of the state in question.

In *Majoros*, on the other hand, Zinn J exposes a problem with the demand that one require a claimant to seek out state protection. He

---

231 (1996), 143 DLR (4th) 532 at para 5 (FCA).
232 *Hinzman FCA*, above note 125 at paras 54 and 57.
233 *Cosgun*, above note 221.

notes that, in some circumstances, it might be pointless to expect individuals to do so:

> Where persecution is widespread and indiscriminate, and unless a claimant is repeatedly targeted by the same individual(s), I fail to understand how it can be said that individual attempts to engage the authorities will have significant, persuasive evidentiary value as to the state's ability to protect against future, indiscriminate violence. In those cases, documentary evidence, rather than individual attempts to seek protection, is more relevant to the state protection analysis. As discussed below, the Board in this case did review the documentary evidence; however, one cannot escape the conclusion reading the decision as a whole that the applicants' perceived inadequate attempts to engage the police not only figured prominently, but were decisive in the Board's analysis. That legal error — which is to place a *legal* burden of seeking state protection on a refugee claimant — is unreasonable and itself sufficient to warrant granting this application.[234]

Justice Zinn's point is powerful. Where one does not know the identity of a persecutor and where the persecution is likely to come from many independent sources, at any random moment, it is difficult to know what a visit to the police would achieve. In addition, one may question why the democratic nature of a government should be regarded as increasing the burden. In *Tar v Canada (Minister of Citizenship and Immigration)*, for example, Russell J states:

> I also agree with the Applicants that the Board relies too heavily on the fact of Hungary's being a nominal "democracy" instead of looking at what form democracy actually takes in Hungary and whether the assumptions it carries about state protection for minorities such as the Roma can be equated with the international norms that are applicable to refugee law.[235]

Justice Russell's emphasis on the actual form of a democracy is important. It is the commitment to the rule of law and the development of an effective and uncorrupted police force, rather than the practice of selecting leaders by democratic election, that will determine the level of security enjoyed by individuals. The point has also been recognized in *Katwaru* where Teitelbaum J states:

---

234 *Majoros*, above note 223 at para 16 [emphasis in original].
235 2014 FC 767 at para 78.

The Board also relied on *Kadenko* . . . for the proposition that the burden for the claimant to prove an absence of state protection is directly proportional to the level of democracy of the state. *Democracy alone does not guarantee effective state protection*; it is merely an indicator of the likely effectiveness of a state institution. In the present case, the evidence indicates that the Guyana Police Force is a very weak institution that is having real difficulties responding to the high levels of violent crime that exist in the Country as a whole. The Board is required to do more than determine whether a country has a democratic political system and must assess the quality of the institutions that provide state protection.[236]

A further problem that has been identified is that of defining a democracy and specifying the relevance of democratic characteristics when assessing state protection. As Liew has observed:

The . . . discussion [surrounding the definition of democracy] that academics and researchers are having illustrates that the finding that a state is democratic is not "uncontroversial" or "beyond reasonable dispute." As well, there is no capability of "immediate and accurate demonstration by resort to readily accessible sources of indisputable accuracy," . . . to define democracy, let alone identify whether a country is democratic.

Second, beyond the problem of defining democracy, and defining which states belong in that definition, one needs to question whether this is a factor that helps in determining whether the presumption of state protection is rebutted in a particular case. Academics such

---

236 *Katwaru*, above note 72 at para 21 [emphasis in original]. See also *Garcia*, above note 228 at para 16, wherein Campbell J states:

For example, when a woman calls the police at 3:00 am to say that her estranged husband is coming through the window, the question is, are the police ready, willing, and able to make serious efforts to arrive in time to protect her from being killed? While it is true that even the best trained, educated, and properly motivated police force might not arrive in time, the test for "serious efforts" will only be met where it is established that the force's capability and expertise is developed well enough to make a credible, earnest attempt to do so, from both the perspective of the woman involved and the concerned community. The same test applies to the help that a woman might be expected to receive at the complaint counter at a local police station. That is, are the police capable of accepting and acting on her complaint in a credible and earnest manner? Indeed, in my opinion, this is the test that should not only be applied to a state's "serious efforts" to protect women but should be accepted as the appropriate test with respect to all protection contexts.

as Zakaria have challenged the idyllic notion that democracy brings with it the rule of law and systemic protections. As well, academics such as Faundez and Robinson question whether democracies today provide the protections of civil, social, and economic rights that are often assumed to be associated with democratic countries. The larger picture is that while we as advocates and adjudicators in the Canadian refugee system are seeking ways to get to a determination in an efficient and easy-to-use manner, the democracy factor does neither. Instead, it is distorting our notions of what is effective state protection . . . .[237]

Evidence of the practices of police forces, and consideration of how reasonable they are and whether they meet standards that can be expected, is what should determine whether a person faces an acceptable risk of persecution. Even where a claimant comes from a nominal democracy, it will be important to base her claim on documentary comparative evidence about police practices. Indeed, even if a country is identified as a "strong democracy," vulnerable groups such as persons identified as LGBTIQ or minorities, such as a racial minority, may be subject to differential treatment with regard to state protection. In many circumstances, such evidence should outweigh any counter evidence focusing on the fact that the claimant omitted to seek help.

5) Internal Flight Alternative (IFA)

The question of internal flight alternative (IFA) asks objectively whether it would be reasonable for the refugee claimant to relocate to an area in the country of origin where the feared risk of persecution would not exist for the claimant; where the claimant could receive state protection; or where the claimant could live a normal life.[238]

The concept of internal flight alternative (IFA) or, as it is sometimes known, internal relocation alternative, is not a "stand-alone principle of refugee law, nor is it an independent test in the determination of

---

237 Jamie Liew, "Creating Higher Burdens: The Presumption of State Protection in Democratic Countries" (2009) 26 *Refuge* 207 at 217.

238 UNHCR Guidelines re Sexual Orientation, above note 20 at para 51; *Thirunavukkarasu v Canada (Minister of Employment and Immigration)*, [1994] 1 FC 589 (CA) [*Thirunavukkarasu*]. The question one can ask is this: Given the persecution in the claimant's part of the country, is it objectively reasonable to expect him to seek safety in a different part of the country, or would it be unduly harsh to expect this person, who is being persecuted in one part of the country, to move to another less hostile part of the country before seeking refugee status abroad?

refugee status."[239] Indeed, it is not mentioned or explicitly referred to in the *Refugee Convention*. In Canada, jurisprudence supports the notion that internal flight alternative is located in the state protection analysis of the refugee definition.[240] As the Federal Court of Appeal has stated, it is neither a legal doctrine nor a defence, but a convenient, shorthand way of describing a fact situation in which a person may be in danger of persecution in one part of the country but not in another; IFA is thus inherent in the definition of Convention refugee.[241]

An important requirement of procedural fairness must be met before internal flight alternative can be raised as an issue. The onus is on the board member or the party wishing to raise the possibility of an internal flight alternative to give notice to the claimant and expressly identify the possible IFA location.[242] The refugee claimant must be provided with an adequate opportunity to respond both to the idea of relocation and to the proposed area.[243] Since the question of whether the person merits protection is a prospective or forward-looking one, the question is whether the proposed area provides a meaningful alternative in the future.[244] The IRB must be satisfied on a balance of probabilities that there is no serious possibility of the claimant being persecuted in the alternative location.[245] Further, the proposed alternative cannot be speculative or theoretical; it must be realistically accessible and any barriers reasonably surmountable.[246]

The question of whether there is a viable internal flight alternative is a factual determination based on the consideration of several variables. The UNHCR advocates engaging in a two-step analysis when evaluating whether an internal flight alternative exists. The first step

---

239 UN High Commissioner for Refugees, Guidelines on International Protection: *"Internal Flight or Relocation Alternative" within the Context of Article 1A(2) of the 1951 Convention and/or 1967 Protocol relating to the Status of Refugees*, HCR/GIP/03/04 (23 July 2003), online: www.unhcr-centraleurope.org/pdf/resources/legal-documents/unhcr-handbooks-recommendations-and-guidelines/unhcr-guidelines-on-the-internal-flight-or-relocation-alternative-2003.html) at para 2 [UNHCR Guidelines on IFA].

240 *Ibid* at para 3: Some jurisdictions outside Canada have located it in the well-founded fear part of the refugee definition. The UNHCR says these approaches are not contradictory since the definition includes a holistic test.

241 *Thirunavukkarasu*, above note 238.

242 UNHCR Guidelines on IFA, above note 239 at para 6; *Rasaratnam v Canada (Minister of Employment and Immigration)*, [1992] 1 FC 706 (CA) [*Rasaratnam*]; *Thirunavukkarasu*, above note 238.

243 *Ibid.*

244 UNHCR Guidelines on IFA, above note 239 at para 8.

245 *Rasaratnam*, above note 242 *Thirunavukkarasu*, above note 238.

246 *Thirunavukkarasu, ibid.*

consists of a relevance analysis and questions whether an alternative is even relevant given the type of persecution the claimant fears.[247] For example, if the country of origin criminalizes same-sex relations and enforces said legislation, it can be assumed that such laws are applicable in the entire country, and therefore the consideration of an internal flight alternative is irrelevant to the claim.[248] Nor would an alternative exist if the claimant is required to conceal his sexual orientation.[249] Some questions a decision maker may ask under this branch of the analysis include these: Is the area of relocation practically, safely, and legally accessible to the claimant?[250] Is the agent of persecution the state?[251] Would the claimant be exposed to a risk of being persecuted or other serious harm upon relocation?[252]

The second step, the reasonableness analysis, requires a decision maker to assess whether return to the place of relocation would cause undue hardship.[253] Under this step, the decision maker must examine the applicant's personal circumstances, such as the existence of past persecution, whether it is safe and secure for the person to get to the location, and whether the location could provide a life that respects the claimant's human rights and economic survival.[254]

---

247 UNHCR Guidelines re Sexual Orientation, above note 20 at paras 52–53; UNHCR Guidelines on IFA, above note 239 at para 7.

248 UNHCR Guidelines re Sexual Orientation, above note 20 at para 53.

249 See, for example, *Okoli*, above note 172 at paras 36–37 and 39; *Diaz*, above note 176 at paras 35–36.

250 UNHCR Guidelines on IFA, above note 239 at paras 10–12.

251 *Ibid* at paras 13–17.

252 *Ibid* at paras 18–21.

253 See *Ranganathan v Canada (Minister of Citizenship and Immigration)*, [2001] 2 FC 164 (CA): In this case, the court held that nothing less than providing evidence of the existence of conditions that would jeopardize the life and safety of the claimant in travelling or temporarily relocating to a safe area would be needed to dismiss an IFA. Further, the court held that some hardship may be reasonable given that it requires a person to relocate. The court looked at factors such as whether the claimants had relatives in the internal flight alternative.

254 UNHCR Guidelines re Sexual Orientation, above note 20 at para 56; UNHCR Guidelines on IFA, above note 239 at paras 7 and 24–30; see *Okoli*, above note 172, wherein the court held that the claimant cannot be expected to conceal his sexual orientation; *Diaz*, above note 176, wherein the court held that there were systemic barriers of employment and health care for HIV-positive Mexicans in the proposed IFA; *Li v Canada (Minister of Citizenship and Immigration)*, 2014 FC 811 at para 1: "When a state participates in that which amounts to persecution, an Internal Flight Alternative (IFA) is not an option."

C. SECTION 97

Section 97 of the *IRPA* is the lesser-known sister of section 96 and forms Canada's complementary protection in its inland refugee protection regime. Before its introduction in 2002, recognition of risk to a refugee claimant outside of the five enumerated grounds in the *Refugee Convention* was provided only through safety mechanisms designed to comply with international human rights obligations through pre-removal risk procedures.[255] Essentially, if the IRB had denied a claim, the denied claimant could be assessed prior to being removed from Canada and obtain permanent or temporary status to stay in Canada if there was a risk of the claimant returning to torture, death, or cruel and unusual punishment.[256]

Not until 2002 were formal changes made to the refugee definition in Canada and to the jurisdiction of the RPD.[257] The Legislative Summary of Bill C-11 refers to the addition of section 97 to the *IRPA* as an "expansion" and a "consolidation" of decisions regarding "risk,"[258]

---

255 Jessica Reekie, *Complementary Refugee Protection in Canada: The History and Application of Section 97 of the* Immigration and Refugee Protection Act (November 2006), online: Gilbert + Tobin Centre of Public Law www.gtcentre.unsw.edu.au/sites/gtcentre.unsw.edu.au/files/Pt%203%20Canada%20final.pdf at 37.

256 Auditor General of Canada, *1997 December Report of the Auditor General of Canada*, online: Office of the Auditor General of Canada www.gnb.ca/OAG-BVG/1997/1997-e.asp at 25.19, wherein the report stated: "If their claims are denied, they may avoid removal if the Department considers that, under the Post-Determination Refugee Claimants in Canada Class (see paragraph 25.117), they would still be at serious risk if they returned to their home country." See also para 25.117 wherein the report stated:

> Under the Minister's discretionary power to create classes of persons to single out for special treatment, a class of persons called the Post-Determination Refugee Claimants in Canada Class was created by regulation in 1993. It was designed to protect claimants who fail to meet the Convention's definition of refugee but who nonetheless would face personal risk of harm if forced to leave Canada. Establishment of this class formalized a practice that the Department had used since 1989. According to the stated criteria, the risk must be compelling — consisting of a threat to life, extreme sanctions or inhumane treatment— and it must be personal — that is, directed at the individual rather than based on a generalized situation of risk in the country. The objective in this case is different from the Department's when it assesses the general conditions in a country to determine if carrying out removals to that country would be justified.

257 *IRPA*, above note 1.

258 Canada, Law and Government Division, *Legislative Summary of Bill C-11* (Report LS-397E) by Jay Sinha & Margaret Young (26 March 2001), online: http://publications.gc.ca/Collection-R/LoPBdP/LS/371/c11-e.htm.

which recognizes Canada's obligations to protect people under the *Convention against Torture*.[259] Section 97 states:

> 97. PERSON IN NEED OF PROTECTION – (1) A person in need of protection is a person in Canada whose removal to their country or countries of nationality or, if they do not have a country of nationality, their country of former habitual residence, would subject them personally
>
> (a) to a danger, believed on substantial grounds to exist, of torture within the meaning of Article 1 of the Convention Against Torture; or
>
> (b) to a risk to their life or to a risk of cruel and unusual treatment or punishment if
>> (i) the person is unable or, because of that risk, unwilling to avail themselves of the protection of that country,
>> (ii) the risk would be faced by the person in every part of that country and is not faced generally by other individuals in or from that country,
>> (iii) the risk is not inherent or incidental to lawful sanctions, unless imposed in disregard of accepted international standards, and
>> (iv) the risk is not caused by the inability of that country to provide adequate health or medical care.
>
> (2) PERSON IN NEED OF PROTECTION – A person in Canada who is a member of a class of persons prescribed by the regulations as being in need of protection is also a person in need of protection.[260]

The insertion of section 97 into Canada's refugee definition is significant, despite the fact it was part of a consolidation of the refugee determination process. While section 96 implements Canada's obligations under the *Refugee Convention*, section 97 implements Canada's obligations under the *Convention against Torture*[261] and ensures that a full assessment of risks listed in the *Convention against Torture* is done during the refugee determination process, rather than as an *ad hoc* assessment just before removal. With its place firmly entrenched in

---

259 Above note 3; see also Nicole LaViolette, "The *Immigration and Refugee Protection Act* and the International Definition of Torture" (2004) 35 *Immigration Law Reports* (3d) 59.

260 *IRPA*, above note 1, s 97.

261 Above note 3.

Canada's refugee definition, decision makers have a duty to consider section 97 when reviewing refugee claims.[262]

As a result of the difference in focus and rationale for providing protection, Canadian jurisprudence recognizes that separate analyses of each section must be conducted in claims before the IRB.[263] There are also other important reasons for conducting separate analyses when claimants present their claims as justifying protection under both sections 96 and 97 or either.

First, while both sections 96 and 97 require a standard of proof on the balance of probabilities, what this means for each section differs. For example, section 96 requires a "reasonable chance of persecution" be made out by the claimant,[264] whereas section 97 calls for a higher legal test: torture, death, or unusual and undeserved treatment must be shown to be more probable than not.[265]

Second, while section 96 requires a bipartite analysis of examining both the subjective and objective elements of well-founded fear of persecution,[266] section 97 focuses more on an objective assessment of risk.[267]

Finally, section 97 has its own built-in limitations to obtaining protection. In section 96, the requirement of a nexus to one of the five enumerated grounds provides the limitation. In section 97, on the other hand, section 97(1)(b)(ii) provides a frequently used limitation known as "generalized risk."[268] The subsection states that protection

---

262 *Selvarajah v Canada (Minister of Citizenship and Immigration)*, 2014 FC 769; *Balachandran v Canada (Minister of Citizenship and Immigration)*, 2014 FC 800.

263 For example: *Desire*, above note 151; *Guerrero v Canada (Minister of Citizenship and Immigration)*, 2011 FC 1210 at para 26: To be found to be a person in need of protection under s 97, a claimant in Canada must establish three things: (a) that she would be personally subjected to a risk to her life or a risk of torture or cruel and unusual treatment or punishment if returned to her country of origin; (b) that she would face the personal risk in every part of her country; and (c) that the personal risk she faces is not faced generally by other individuals in or from that country.

264 *Adjei*, above note 15.

265 *Li v Canada (Minister of Citizenship and Immigration)*, 2005 FCA 1.

266 *Ward*, above note 4.

267 *Ustaoglu v Canada (Minister of Citizenship and Immigration*, 2003 FC 1009; *Shah v Canada (Minister of Citizenship and Immigration)*, 2003 FC 1121; *Nyathi v Canada (Minister of Citizenship and Immigration)*, 2003 FC 1119; *Sanchez v Canada (Minister of Citizenship and Immigration)*, 2007 FCA 99.

268 *Correa v Canada (Minister of Citizenship and Immigration)*, 2014 FC 252 at paras 27 and 46: If the claimant does not face a personal risk of the types of harms described in s 97, that ends the s 97(1)(b)(ii) analysis; *Portillo v Canada (Minister of Citizenship and Immigration)*, 2012 FC 678 at paras 40–41:

will be given where "the risk would be faced by the person in every part of that country *and is not faced generally by other individuals in or from that country*."[269] This limitation highlights a significant difference between sections 96 and 97, namely, that while a person claiming under section 96 can rely on evidence of similarly situated persons to show prospective risk of persecution,[270] such evidence may deny a claimant protection under section 97, since the requirement under section 97 is that the risk be personalized and individualized.[271]

Canadian jurisprudence has provided neither a clear nor a consistent picture of what is "generalized risk" nor a clear, well-defined idea of the types of situations in which a person can obtain protection under section 97.[272] Decision making has revealed two problematic trends when "generalized" risk is involved.[273] First, some decision makers interpret the limitation as a reason to deny protection for certain types of claims, including those that may merit section 96 protection.[274] For example, gender-based claims have been denied on the basis that many

---

[T]he essential starting point for the required analysis under section 97 of *IRPA* is to first appropriately determine the nature of the risk faced by the claimant. This requires an assessment of whether the claimant faces an ongoing or future risk (i.e. whether he or she continues to face a "personalized risk"), what the risk is, whether such risk is one of cruel and unusual treatment or punishment and the basis for the risk . . . . The next required step in the analysis under section 97 of *IRPA*, after the risk has been appropriately characterized, is the comparison of the correctly-described risk faced by the claimant to that faced by a significant group in the country to determine whether the risks are of the same nature and degree. If the risk is not the same, then the claimant will be entitled to protection under section 97 of *IRPA*.

269 *IRPA*, above note 1, s 97(1)(b)(ii).

270 *Salibian*, above note 13.

271 *Prophète v Canada (Minister of Citizenship and Immigration)*, 2009 FCA 31 [*Prophète*]; *Turton v Canada (Minister of Citizenship and Immigration)*, 2011 FC 1244.

272 See, for example, the following cases in contrast to those below: *Soimin v Canada (Minister of Citizenship and Immigration)*, 2009 FC 218; *Cyriaque v Canada (Minister of Citizenship and Immigration)*, 2010 FC 1077 at para 13; *Frederic v Canada (Minister of Citizenship and Immigration)*, 2010 FC 1100 at para 10; *Luc v Canada (Minister of Citizenship and Immigration)*, 2010 FC 826 at paras 25–26.

273 See Jamie Liew, "Taking It Personally: Delimiting Gender-Based Refugee Claims Using the Complementary Protection Provision in Canada" (2014) 26 *Canadian Journal of Women and the Law* 300.

274 For example: *Michel v Canada (Minister of Citizenship and Immigration)*, 2010 FC 159 [*Michel*]; *Dezameau*, above note 165; *Josile v Canada (Minister of Citizenship and Immigration)*, 2011 FC 39; *Spencer v Canada (Minister of Citizenship and Immigration)*, 2011 FC 397; *Belle v Canada (Minister of Citizenship and Immigration)*, 2012 FC 1181; *Gutierrez v Canada (Minister of Citizenship and Immigration)*, 2011 FC 1055.

women suffer from the risk (for example, victims of domestic abuse).[275] Second, some decision makers rely on fact-dependent findings that the risk is experienced by large groups of people in a particular country to evade their duty to examine whether there is a personalized or individualized risk associated with the particular claimant.[276]

Despite the limitations imposed in the legislation and the difficulties some decision makers have in conducting section 97 analyses, claimants, if they have an opportunity, should present their case within this alternative framework and remind decision makers of their duty to evaluate section 96 and 97 claims separately.

D. SECTION 98 AND EXCLUSION

Section 98 of the IRPA implements the *Refugee Convention*'s provisions that exclude from protection persons who would otherwise be eligible. Section 98 states:

> 98. Exclusion – Refugee Convention – A person referred to in section E or F of Article 1 of the Refugee Convention is not a Convention refugee or a person in need of protection.[277]

Articles 1E and F of the *Refugee Convention* state:

> E. This Convention shall not apply to a person who is recognized by the competent authorities of the country in which he has taken residence as having the rights and obligations which are attached to the possession of the nationality of that country.

> F. The provisions of this Convention shall not apply to any person with respect to whom there are serious reasons for considering that:

---

275 Liew, above note 273.

276 For example: *Dieujuste-Phanor v Canada (Minister of Citizenship and Immigration)*, 2011 FC 186; *Michel*, above note 274; *Munoz v Canada (Minister of Citizenship and Immigration)*, 2010 FC 238; *Surajnarain v Canada (Minister of Citizenship and Immigration)*, 2008 FC 1165; *De Parada v Canada (Minister of Citizenship and Immigration)*, 2009 FC 845; *Gabriel v Canada (Minister of Citizenship and Immigration)*, 2009 FC 1170; *Prophète*, above note 271; *Osorio v Canada (Minister of Citizenship and Immigration)*, 2005 FC 1459; *Melendez*, above note 112; *Ore v Canada (Minister of Citizenship and Immigration)*, 2014 FC 642: Here the court stated that the fact the claimant may initially have been subject to a generalized act of crime did not mean that his subsequent personal targeting was excluded from consideration under s 97.

277 *IRPA*, above note 1, s 98.

(a)   he has committed a crime against peace, a war crime, or a crime against humanity, as defined in the international instruments drawn up to make provision in respect of such crimes;

(b)   he has committed a serious non-political crime outside the country of refuge prior to his admission to that country as a refugee;

(c)   he has been guilty of acts contrary to the purposes and principles of the United Nations.[278]

It is important to distinguish between the concept of exclusion, outlined in section 98 of the *IRPA*, and the criteria of inadmissibility, found in the *IRPA*, sections 35 to 42.[279] While both aim to prevent particular persons who have committed serious crimes from obtaining refugee protection, the processes involved, and the finding of exclusion versus inadmissibility, are entirely separate and distinct. The criteria of inadmissibility apply to any non-citizen whose status in Canada is at issue while exclusion arises in the context of a refugee hearing. For example, a person found to be inadmissible to Canada is not eligible for a refugee hearing,[280] whereas the issue of exclusion usually arises after the claimant has been found to be eligible for a refugee hearing and the claim is before a board member.

1)   *Refugee Convention*, Article 1E

Article 1E recognizes the surrogate nature of refugee protection; that protection is not needed if a person can avail herself of state protection in another country.[281] Canadian jurisprudence identifies the aim of this article as preventing or deterring refugee claimants from asylum shopping.[282]

The onus is on the minister of Public Safety and Emergency Preparedness to demonstrate that the claimant enjoys the rights and obligations of a national in another state.[283] These rights include the right

---

278   *Ibid*, Schedule. It is important to note that section 98 qualifies both section 96 and section 97, even though the *Convention against Torture* on which section 97 is based does not make provision for qualifications or exceptions.

279   For more information on inadmissibility, see Chapter 14.

280   *IRPA*, above note 1, s 101(1)(f).

281   See, for example, *Zeng v Canada (Minister of Citizenship and Immigration)*, 2010 FCA 118 [*Zeng*].

282   *Ibid* at para 19; UN High Commissioner for Refugees, *Note on the Interpretation of Article 1E of the 1951 Convention relating to the Status of Refugees* (March 2009), online: Refworld www.refworld.org/docid/49c3a3d12.html [UNHCR Interpretation Note on Article 1E]; *Ward*, above note 4 at para 51: Claimants are not entitled to seek better protection than that from which they already benefit.

283   *Mai v Canada (Minister of Citizenship and Immigration)*, 2010 FC 192 at paras 34–35.

to return to the country of residence; to work or study without restriction; and to have access to social services.[284] As well, the status must have been intact at the time the claimant arrived in Canada and at the time the refugee determination is being made.[285]

When determining whether to exclude a claimant on the basis of article 1E, the UNHCR recommends a two-step analysis. First, it must be determined that the claimant has taken residency in another country with which article 1E can apply.[286] Second, it must be determined whether the claimant is currently recognized in that country as having rights and obligations associated with nationality, including protection from deportation, expulsion, and refoulement to a third country.[287]

Once the minister has demonstrated a *prima facie* case that the claimant may return to a different state and enjoy full rights there, the onus shifts to the claimant to show why he cannot enjoy or regain the rights of residence.[288] If the minister fails to establish a *prima facie* case, the IRB may still balance and consider various factors to determine whether the claimant could return to the identified state.[289]

2) *Refugee Convention*, Article 1F

While article 1E excludes persons who do not *need* protection, article 1F excludes persons who do not *deserve* protection. The *Refugee Convention* excludes three limited categories of persons from refugee status in article 1F. The main impetus behind including such a provision in the *Refugee Convention* was a concern that serious criminals should not evade prosecution and punishment for their crimes by claiming asylum, but also the concern that states would not want to be bound to admit serious criminals as refugees into their states, viewing such persons as undeserving of protection.[290] Thus, "the

---

284 *Vifansi v Canada (Minister of Citizenship and Immigration)*, 2003 FCT 284 at para 27.
285 *Zeng*, above note 281 at para 34.
286 *Ward*, above note 4; UNHCR Interpretation Note on Article 1E, above note 282 at paras 9–11.
287 *Ibid* at paras 6 and 13; *IRPA*, above note 1, s 115.
288 *Ramadan v Canada (Minister of Citizenship and Immigration)*, 2010 FC 1093 at para 18.
289 *Zeng*, above note 281 at para 28.
290 UNHCR, *Background Note on the Application of the Exclusion Clauses: Article 1F of the 1951 Convention relating to the Status of Refugees*, HCR/GIP/03/05 (4 September 2003) at para 4 [UNHCR Background Note]; James Hathaway & Michelle Foster, *The Law of Refugee Status*, 2d ed (Cambridge: Cambridge University Press, 2014) at 525; *Zrig v Canada (Minister of Citizenship and Immigration)*, 2003 FCA 178 at paras 118–19 [*Zrig*]; *Febles v Canada (Citizenship and*

Refugee Convention's commitment to refugee protection is broad, but not unbounded," balancing the humanitarian goals of the *Convention* with concern to protect the integrity of the international refugee protection system. [291]

While article 1F outlines the crimes that serve as the reason for a denial of protection, it is important to note that assessing exclusion during a refugee hearing is not akin to a determination of guilt or innocence in a criminal court or tribunal, [292] as the purpose of article 1F is to "exclude *ab initio* those who are not *bona fide* refugees at the time of their claim for refugee status." [293] Because the exclusion clauses represent exceptions to guaranteed human rights, [294] the UNHCR has advised that the exclusion clauses be interpreted restrictively and applied with caution. [295]

The issue of exclusion can arise during a refugee hearing. [296] The onus of establishing that a refugee claimant should be excluded under article 1F falls on the minister of Public Safety and Emergency Preparedness. [297] The refugee claimant must be given notice by the minister

---

Immigration), 2014 SCC 68 at para 62 [*Febles*]: The Federal Court of Appeal held that it is clear from the *travaux preparatoires* that the drafters did not intend to limit the exclusion provision to fugitives from justice.

291 *Ezokola v Canada (Minister of Citizenship and Immigration)*, 2013 SCC 40 at paras 33–36 [*Ezokola*]; see also *Sivakumar v Canada (Minister of Employment and Immigration)*, [1994] 1 FC 433 at 445 (CA) [*Sivakumar*]; *Zrig*, above note 290 at para 118; *Pushpanathan v Canada (Minister of Citizenship and Immigration)*, [1998] 1 SCR 982 at para 63 [*Pushpanathan*]; UN High Commissioner for Refugees, *Guideline on International Protection: Application of the Exclusion Clauses: Article 1F of the 1951 Convention relating to the Status of Refugees*, HCR/GIP/03/05 (4 September 2003) at para 7 [UNHCR Guideline on Exclusion]: The UNHCR finds the exclusion articles as exhaustive, meaning that states cannot exclude *bona fide* refugees for any other reasons that are not listed in the *Convention*. However, the interpretation of how exhaustive the articles are is subject to domestic interpretation and incorporation.

292 *Ezokola*, above note 291 at paras 38–39: The court here noted that refugee hearings are less formal than criminal trials and are also not bound by traditional rules of evidence.

293 *Pushpanathan*, above note 291 at para 58.

294 See, for example, the *Universal Declaration of Human Rights*, GA Res 217(III), UN GAOR, 3d Sess, Supp No 13, UN Doc A/810 (1948) 71 at art 14, which protects the right to live free from persecution.

295 UNHCR Background Note, above note 290 at para 4.

296 UNHCR Handbook, above note 6 at para 141, provides that refugee status may be rendered after an exclusion decision has been made. In Canada, this could be achieved by making an application to vacate the decision. For more details on vacation, see Chapter 9.

297 *Murillo v Canada (Minister of Citizenship and Immigration)*, 2008 FC 966 at para 24.

if there is an intention to argue that exclusion is applicable. For article 1F, the burden of proof is low; the minister must prove that there are "serious reasons for considering" that the claimant has committed the serious crime listed in article 1F.[298] This standard is remarkably lower than the criminal law standard of beyond a reasonable doubt and also the civil law standard of balance of probabilities. The standard consists of compelling and credible information that provides an objective basis for findings of fact.[299] It is important to note that when applying the "reasonable grounds to believe" standard, it applies only to questions of fact.[300]

a) Article 1F(a) and Crime against Peace, War Crime, or Crime against Humanity

The following definition of *crime against peace* can be found in the 1845 London Agreement: "planning, preparation, initiation or waging of a war of aggression or a war in violation of international treaties, agreements or assurances."[301]

To determine the meaning of *war crime* or *crime against humanity*, claimants can look to section 6 of the *Crimes against Humanity and War Crimes Act* among other international sources of law.[302]

---

298 *Mugasera v Canada (Minister of Citizenship and Immigration)*, 2005 SCC 40 at para 115 [*Mugasera*]: "In imposing this standard in the *Immigration Act* in respect of war crimes and crimes against humanity, Parliament has made clear that these most serious crimes deserve extraordinary condemnation. As a result, no person will be admissible to Canada if there are reasonable grounds to believe that he or she has committed a crime against humanity, even if the crime is not made out on a higher standard of proof." *Sivakumar*, above note 291 at 445, where the court held that it is more than mere suspicion; *Chiau v Canada (Minister of Citizenship and Immigration)*, [2001] 2 FC 297 at para 60 (CA); *Sabour v Canada (Minister of Citizenship and Immigration)* (2000), 9 Imm LR (3d) 61 (FCTD): Reasonable grounds will exist where there is an objective basis for the belief which is founded on compelling and credible information.

299 *Mugasera*, above note 298 at para 117.

300 *Ibid* at para 116; *Moreno v Canada (Minister of Employment and Immigration)*, [1994] 1 FC 298 at 311 (CA).

301 United Nations, *Agreement for the Prosecution and Punishment of the Major War Criminals of the European Axis, and Charter of the International Military Tribunal*, 8 August 1945, 82 UNTS 280, online: International Committee of the Red Cross www.icrc.org/ihl/INTRO/350?OpenDocument [London Agreement]; see also *Hinzman*, above note 127 at para 142, where the court held that only those capable of planning, preparing, initiating, and waging wars of aggression may be culpable for crimes against peace.

302 SC 2000, c 24, s 6: *crime against humanity* means murder, extermination, enslavement, deportation, imprisonment, torture, sexual violence, persecution, or any other inhumane act or omission that is committed against any civilian

For the purposes of article 1F(a), the Supreme Court of Canada has outlined four elements in the crime against humanity:

1. An enumerated proscribed act was committed (this involves showing that the accused committed the criminal act and had the requisite guilty state of mind for the underlying act);
2. The act was committed as part of a widespread or systemic attack;
3. The attack was directed against any civilian population or any identifiable group of persons; and
4. The person committing the proscribed act knew of the attack and knew or took the risk that his or her act comprised a part of that attack.[303]

A decision maker may begin an assessment of exclusion under article 1F(a) by asking whether the claimant was directly involved in the commission of a crime against peace, a war crime, or a crime against humanity. In other words, was he the actual perpetrator of the crime? If not, was the claimant indirectly involved in the commission of the crime? Many cases on exclusion deal with the latter scenario where a claimant may be indirectly involved in the commission of the crime.

Before the Supreme Court of Canada issued its decision in *Ezokola*, the Canadian approach to dealing with individuals who may be indirectly involved in the commission of a crime was broad reaching. The leading case was *Ramirez v Canada (Minister of Employment and Immigration)* which held that complicity required a "shared common purpose" with the perpetrators of the crime or "personal and knowing participation in persecutorial acts" and that mere membership *could* constitute complicity if the claimant had membership in an organization

population or any identifiable group and that, at the time and in the place of its commission, constitutes a crime against humanity according to customary international law or conventional international law or by virtue of its being criminal according to the general principles of law recognized by the community of nations, whether or not it constitutes a contravention of the law in force at the time and in the place of its commission; *war crime* means an act or omission committed during an armed conflict that, at the time and in the place of its commission, constitutes a war crime according to customary international law or conventional international law applicable to armed conflicts, whether or not it constitutes a contravention of the law in force at the time and in the place of its commission. See also the *Geneva Conventions*, set out in Schedules I to IV of the *Geneva Conventions Act*, RSC 1985, c G-3, for example.

303 *Mugasera*, above note 298 at para 119.

with a limited brutal purpose.[304] Further, in the case of *Sivakumar*, an inference of complicity could be drawn from the claimant's rank or position.[305]

Ezokola clarified the test for complicity in Canadian refugee law:

> To exclude a claimant from the definition of "refugee" by virtue of art. 1F(a), there must be serious reasons for considering that the claimant has voluntarily made a significant and knowing contribution to the organization's crime or criminal purpose.[306]

The Court emphasized that "voluntarily" means without duress or coercion. As well, the Court highlighted the importance of the requirement of a "significant contribution" as being "critical to prevent an unreasonable extension of the notion of criminal participation in international criminal law."[307] In particular, the Court, with regard to knowing contribution to the crime or criminal purpose, explained that, "[t]o be complicit in crimes committed by the government, the official must be aware of the government's crime or criminal purpose and aware that his or her *conduct* will assist in the furtherance of the crime or criminal purpose"[308] and that "unless an individual has control or responsibility over the individuals committing international crimes, he or she cannot be complicit by simply remaining in his or her position without protest."[309] The Court then provided a list of factors to serve as a guide in assessing whether an individual has voluntarily made a significant and knowing contribution to a crime or criminal purpose:

(i)   the size and nature of the organization;

(ii) the part of the organization with which the refugee claimant was most directly concerned;

(iii) the refugee claimant's duties and activities within the organization;

(iv) the refugee claimant's position or rank in the organization;

(v)   the length of time the refugee claimant was in the organization, particularly after acquiring knowledge of the group's crime or criminal purpose; and

---

304 *Ramirez v Canada (Minister of Employment and Immigration)*, [1992] 2 FC 306 (CA) [*Ramirez*].

305 *Sivakumar*, above note 291.

306 *Ezokola*, above note 291 at para 84.

307 *Ibid* at para 88.

308 *Ibid* at para 89 [emphasis in original].

309 *Ibid* at para 82.

(vi) the method by which the refugee claimant was recruited and the refugee claimant's opportunity to leave the organization.[310]

While the Court should be lauded for clarifying the issue of complicity in the commission of crimes and rejecting the Federal Court of Appeal's approach that mere membership in a group can lead to a finding of exclusion, the criteria listed above may open the door for future decision makers to return to previous practice. Evaluating the claimant's position and rank in the organization alongside the claimant's length of time in an organization could lead decision makers to resort to the practice advocated in *Ramirez*, where mere membership may be enough. Advocates would be wise to accentuate the portion of the *Ezokola* decision that discusses what it means to significantly contribute to a crime.

b) Article 1F(b) and Serious Non-political Crimes

Article 1F(b) aims to prevent persons who have committed serious non-political crimes from obtaining refugee protection. As with article 1F(a), the aim is to protect civilians in the country of refuge and to ensure that persons hoping to escape criminal charges in their home country do not evade prosecution.[311]

The UNHCR has provided that

> [i]n determining whether an offence is "non-political" or is, on the contrary, a "political" crime, regard should be given in the first place to its nature and purpose i.e. whether it has been committed out of genuine political motives and not merely for personal reasons or gain. There should be a close and direct causal link between the crime committed and its alleged political purpose and object. The political element of the offence should also outweigh its common-law character. This would not be the case if the acts committed are grossly out of proportion to the alleged objective.[312]

Thus, the questions that a decision maker will want to pose are as follows: Was there an objective, rational connection between the crime and achieving a realistic political goal, such as defeating or over-

---

310 *Ibid* at para 91.

311 *Pushpanathan*, above note 291 at para 73: Art 1F(b) "is generally meant to prevent ordinary criminals extraditable by treaty from seeking refugee status, but that the exclusion is limited to serious crimes committed before entry in the state of asylum."

312 UNHCR Handbook, above note 6 at para 152.

throwing a corrupt government, and were the means used to achieve the goal proportionate to that legitimate political objective?[313]

When considering the seriousness of a non-political crime, the Federal Court of Appeal has held that an evaluation must look at (a) the elements of the crime; (b) the mode of prosecution; (c) the penalty prescribed; (d) the facts; and (e) the mitigating and aggravating circumstances underlying the conviction.[314] Thus, "whatever presumption of seriousness may attach to a crime . . . that presumption may be rebutted by references to the above factors."[315] The Court of Appeal also pointed out, however, that there should be no consideration of factors extraneous to the facts and circumstances underlying the conviction, such as the risk of persecution, as that is to be assessed when considering whether refugee protection should be given.[316]

A recurring issue in Canadian jurisprudence has been whether or not the IRB has an obligation to consider whether a refugee claimant who had committed a serious crime was rehabilitated and posed a present danger in making a finding of exclusion. Recently, in the case of *Febles*, the Supreme Court of Canada held that the plain words of the exclusion clause do not indicate that article 1F(b) applies only to fugitives, or that factors such as current lack of dangerousness or post-crime expiation or rehabilitation are to be considered or balanced against the seriousness of the crime.[317] As a result, the Court affirmed that article 1F(b) applies to anyone who has ever committed a serious non-political crime outside the country of refuge prior to her admission to that country as a refugee.[318]

c)   Article 1F(c) and Acts Contrary to Purposes of the United Nations

Article 1F(c) provides no definition for "principles and purposes" of the United Nations, and while we can take guidance from the *Charter of the United Nations* as to what the purposes and principles of the organization are, the *Charter of the United Nations* provides limited guidance on the application of article 1F(c) to actions of refugee claimants.[319]

---

313 See also *Gil v Canada (Minister of Citizenship and Immigration)*, [1995] 1 FC 508 at paras 28–29, 33–36, and 44 (CA).

314 *Jayasekara v Canada (Minister of Citizenship and Immigration)*, 2008 FCA 404 at para 44.

315 *Ibid.*

316 *Ibid.*

317 *Febles*, above note 290 at para 17.

318 *Ibid* at para 18.

319 United Nations, *Charter of the United Nations*, 24 October 1945, 1 UNTS XVI, arts 1 & 2.

In the case of *Pushpanathan*, the Supreme Court of Canada stated that the purpose of article 1F(c) is "to exclude those individuals responsible for serious, sustained or systemic violations of fundamental human rights which amount to persecution in a non-war setting."[320] In what amounts to actions contrary to the purposes of the United Nations, the Court stated that the "guiding principle is that where there is consensus in international law that particular acts constitute sufficiently serious and sustained violations of fundamental human rights as to amount to persecution, or are explicitly recognized as contrary to the purposes and principles of the United Nations, then Article 1F(c) will be applicable."[321] Acts can be identified as contrary to the purposes of the United Nations by consulting widely accepted international agreements or United Nations resolutions or by looking at determinations of international courts.[322]

The Court also referred to an inferred qualification on article 1F(c), namely, that the perpetrator must be a person in a position of power, but not necessarily a state actor.[323] Cases involving article 1F(c) have involved incitement to genocide,[324] complicity in crimes against humanity,[325] membership in a terrorist organization,[326] and child abduction.[327]

3) After a Finding of Exclusion

The only recourse for a refugee claimant after a finding of exclusion has been made is judicial review at the Federal Court.[328] When findings of exclusion are made, a state cannot simply remove the person due to international obligations preventing refoulement.[329] Excluded refugee claimants can apply for a pre-removal risk assessment (examined in Chapter 11).

---

320 *Pushpanathan*, above note 291 at para 64.
321 *Ibid* at para 65.
322 *Ibid* at paras 66–67.
323 *Ibid* at para 68.
324 *X (Re)*, 2012 CanLII 99423 (CA IRB).
325 *X (Re)*, 2012 CanLII 95544 (CA IRB).
326 *Rathinasigngam v Canada (Minister of Citizenship and Immigration)*, 2006 FC 988.
327 *YLH (Re)*, [2006] RPDD No 238 (CA IRB).
328 *Pushpanathan*, above note 291 at para 50; *Febles*, above note 290. See Chapter 16 for more information on judicial review.
329 *IRPA*, above note 1, s 115.

E. *SUR PLACE* CLAIMS

As emphasized above, past persecution is not a prerequisite for refugee status.[330] Indeed, the requirement is not whether the claimant has experienced persecution but whether the claimant will face prospective persecution, torture, or death should she return to her country of origin.[331] The claimant need not show that authorities or the agents of persecution knew about the claimant's identity or have an inclination to mistreat the claimant prior to leaving the country.

Sur place claims arise in situations where a claimant may not have a well-founded fear of persecution upon leaving the country of origin, but due to her actions or a change of circumstances, may have obtained a well-founded fear outside the country of origin.[332] *Sur place* claims may arise, for example, in a situation where an individual converted religions after departing from the country of origin,[333] identified himself as LGBTIQ after arriving in a country of asylum,[334] or was labelled as "criminal" outside his country of origin.[335] Thus, the fear of persecution arises or finds expression while an individual is away from the country of origin.

As the Federal Court has stated, in assessing the claimant's risk of return, in the context of a *sur place* claim, it is necessary to consider evidence of the claimant's activities while in Canada independently from the motives that gave rise to the *sur place* claim (such as a conversion to a particular religion).[336] Thus, even if the motives of the claimant are not sincere, the consequences of the activities that give rise to the fear may, nonetheless, be sufficient to find a well-founded fear of persecution.[337]

---

330 UNHCR Guideline re Sexual Orientation, above note 20 at para 18.

331 *Ibid*.

332 See contemporary examples in the *Sun Sea* and *Ocean Lady* cases: *Canada (Minister of Citizenship and Immigration) v B344*, 2013 FC 447; *Canada (Minister of Citizenship and Immigration) v B420*, 2013 FC 321; *Canada (Minister of Citizenship and Immigration) v B472*, 2013 FC 151; *Canada (Minister of Citizenship and Immigration) v B380*, 2012 FC 1334.

333 UNHCR Guidelines on Religion-Based Refugee Claims, above note 22 at para 34: "Such a claim may also arise if a claimant marries someone of another religion in the country of asylum or educates his or her children in that other religion there and the country of origin would use this as the basis for persecution."

334 UNHCR Guidelines re Sexual Orientation, above note 20 at para 57.

335 See above note 332.

336 *Ejtehadian v Canada (Minister of Citizenship and Immigration)*, 2007 FC 158 at para 11.

337 See *ibid*; *Hu v Canada (Minister of Citizenship and Immigration)*, 2012 FC 544; *Li v Canada (Minister of Citizenship and Immigration)*, 2012 FC 998; and *Chen*

F. CONCLUSION

Over the course of twenty-five years, in an increasingly adversarial setting, the IRB and the judiciary have struggled with the task of determining who is a Convention refugee or a person in need of protection. Various factors have increased the difficulty of the task and have contributed to a system generating many confusing and inconsistent refugee determinations. The open-endedness of the language used in sections 96, 97, and 98 of the *IRPA* has provided a context of uncertainty and doubt as decision makers struggle to define, for example, the contours of persecution, the essential idea behind membership in a group, or the meaning of a generalized risk. Different decision makers have different ideas about the steps a person should take to obtain protection within the country of origin before seeking protection elsewhere. Various expectations can be seen in cases where claimants have experienced significant threats from domestic partners or criminal groups, and have been offered little support from authorities. There has also been heated controversy about the characteristics of those who should be excluded from the definition, which, to some extent, has been settled, at least temporarily, by interventions from the Supreme Court. Moreover, as outlined earlier, one can discern a deep divide about the nature of the values that underlie the very commitment to refugee protection, with ideas of entitlement competing against those of generosity.

In this context, it is unsurprising that refugee law has evolved haphazardly and in a manner marked by inconsistency and widely varying rates of acceptance among decision makers. In a world of diminishing generosity and growing suspicion of abuse of the system, where use of prejudicial rhetoric persists, the refugee's fate will increasingly depend on her lawyer's ability to kindle and rekindle the idea that Canada has committed itself to an international regime based not on governmental largesse, but on the entitlement of all individuals to be protected from sustained abuse.

---

v Canada (Minister of Citizenship and Immigration), 2014 FC 749. However, see, for example, the case of *Su v Canada (Minister of Citizenship and Immigration)*, 2013 FC 518 at para 18, wherein the court stated that it is not improper for the IRB to consider an applicant's motive for practising a religion that the applicant converted to in order to assess the genuineness of the claimant's claimed beliefs. Yet even if the beliefs may not be genuine, this does not take away the IRB's duty to assess whether there is a *sur place* claim.

CHAPTER 11

PRE-REMOVAL RISK ASSESSMENTS AND REFOULEMENT

A. INTRODUCTION

The principle of non-refoulement prohibits states from returning a person to a country where that person would face specified risks. This precept has been codified in both the *Refugee Convention*[1] and the *Convention against Torture*.[2] Canada's obligation to uphold this principle is incorporated into domestic law via the *Immigration and Refugee Protection Act (IRPA)*, section 115(1),[3] which not only expresses adherence to the two conventions but also aims to meet the obligation to protect the life, liberty, and security of the person guaranteed in section 7 of the *Charter of Rights and Freedoms*.[4] Section 115(1) provides that a Convention refugee or a protected person cannot be removed from Canada to a country where he would be at risk of persecution for enumerated reasons or at risk of torture, death, or cruel and unusual punishment.[5]

In order to meet these international commitments and constitutional guarantees, Canada has established the pre-removal risk as-

---

1   *Convention Relating to the Status of Refugees,* 28 July 1951, 189 UNTS 150 (entered into force 22 April 1954), art 33 [*Refugee Convention*].

2   *Convention against Torture and Other Cruel, Inhuman or Degrading Treatment or Punishment,* 10 December 1984, 1465 UNTS 85 (entered into force 26 June 1987), art 3 [*Convention against Torture*].

3   *Immigration and Refugee Protection Act,* SC 2001, c 27, s 115(1) [*IRPA*].

4   *Canadian Charter of Rights and Freedoms,* s 7, Part I of the *Constitution Act, 1982,* being Schedule B to the *Canada Act 1982* (UK), 1982, c 11 [*Charter*].

5   *IRPA,* above note 3.

sessment (PRRA). The assessment is designed to operate as a fail-safe mechanism to ensure that individuals who are denied access to protected status through other means are not removed without consideration of the risks they may face.

Foreign nationals may be removed from Canada when their authorization to remain as temporary residents expires,[6] or when they have been found to be inadmissible.[7] Permanent residents may also lose their status and be forced to leave Canada if their status was conditional and they failed to meet a condition,[8] if their status was gained through fraud or misrepresentation,[9] if they fail to meet the residency obligation,[10] or if they are found to be inadmissible on grounds of security, human rights violations, or serious criminality.[11] Further, certain Canadian citizens may have their Canadian citizenship stripped and find themselves subject to removal to a country where they may hold another nationality.[12]

In general, when a person has been identified as removable, a pre-removal risk assessment will usually be made available prior to the removal. This application is often the last that an individual may make in a bid to stay in Canada. It can trigger a regulatory stay of removal that will remain in effect until the application has been rejected.[13]

While article 3 of the *Convention against Torture* expresses the principle of non-refoulement as an absolute principle, both the *Refugee Convention* and section 115(2) of the *IRPA* admit exceptions to the principle and define circumstances where persons *may* be returned to face torture and other risks.[14] This qualified stance has been upheld

---

6 *Immigration and Refugee Protection Regulations*, SOR/2002-227, s 183(2) [*Regulations*]. See Chapter 4 for more information on temporary status.

7 *IRPA*, above note 3, s 45(d). See Chapter 14 for more information on inadmissibility.

8 See, for example, *Regulations*, above note 6, s 72.1, which outlines conditions of permanent residency for spouses who come under the family class. Those who do not complete the two-year conditional residency requirement may be subject to removal.

9 *IRPA*, above note 3, s 40.

10 *Ibid*, s 28.

11 *Ibid*, ss 34–41.

12 *Citizenship Act*, RSC 1985, c C-29, s 10, which provides the legislative framework for revoking citizenship and parameters or conditions surrounding revocation.

13 *Regulations*, above note 6, s 232. See also ss 165–66: However, where a person applies at a port of entry, it will not trigger a stay (s 166). Similarly, no stay will be triggered when the person reapplies for a PRRA having already been rejected (s 165). This matter will be discussed further below.

14 *Refugee Convention*, above note 1, arts 1F and 33(2); *IRPA*, above note 3, s 115(2). Unlike the *Convention against Torture*, above note 2, the *Refugee Convention*, arts 1F and 33(2), and the *IRPA*, s 115(2), recognize exceptions to the principle

by the Supreme Court of Canada. In *Suresh*,[15] the Court held that there could be exceptional circumstances that may justify a return to torture.[16] It therefore declined to hold that section 115(2) was unconstitutional.

In addition, and equally troubling, there are cases where Canadian law permits the removal of individuals from Canada without any inquiry into the risks that they may face. The right to apply for a pre-removal risk assessment is not granted to every person who is being removed. As outlined below, an assessment is made available only to individuals in specified categories, including persons found ineligible to make a refugee claim before the Immigration and Refugee Board (IRB) because of inadmissibility on a serious ground and persons subject to security certificates.[17] It is also made available to some individuals whose refugee claim before the IRB has already been rejected, although severe restrictions are applied in such cases.

After a positive assessment, some applicants will be granted refugee or protected person status and will be offered the opportunity to apply for permanent residence. However, those who have previously been found to be inadmissible on the most serious grounds will receive a temporary reprieve in the form of a further stay of removal. Of course, a negative pre-removal risk assessment leads to a resumption of removal arrangements.

When the *IRPA* first came into force in 2002, the PRRA application was promoted as an effective protection device because it instituted a risk assessment immediately prior to the execution of a removal order. The previous risk determination processes had assessed similar risks but had incorporated a problematic time lapse between the assessment and actual removal, during which country conditions could change.[18] However, over the years the effectiveness of the pre-removal risk assessment has been called into question and has induced serious skepticism. Few individuals have received a positive PRRA evaluation. At best, only about 3 percent of persons are granted either a temporary stay or protected status through the assessment.[19] The Canadian Council

---

of non-refoulement where persons may be denied protection despite a risk of torture or other cruel and unusual punishment, including death.

15   *Suresh v Canada (Minister of Citizenship and Immigration)*, 2002 SCC 1 [*Suresh*].

16   *Ibid* at para 76.

17   *IRPA*, above note 3, ss 34–37.

18   Martin Jones & Sasha Baglay, *Refugee Law* (Toronto: Irwin Law, 2007) at 332.

19   See, for example, *Nalliah v Canada (Solicitor General)*, 2004 FC 1649 [*Nalliah*], where Snider J commented that of all the applications processed, only about 3 percent of all PRRA decisions were favourable. See also Kristina Dragaitis, "PRRA Bar Outline" (Presented at the 22nd Annual Immigration Law Summit of the Law Society of Upper Canada, 20 November 2014) at Appendix A, which

for Refugees has expressed concern that there has been "inconsistent application by PRRA decision-makers in the consideration of what constitutes sufficient evidence and expert evidence" and "insufficient guidelines for PRRA decision-makers with respect to how they are to evaluate evidence."[20] Additionally, under the guise of reducing delays and streamlining the system,[21] several exceptions have been introduced to further limit access to the pre-removal risk assessment, thereby reducing its effectiveness and raising questions about Canada's willingness and its capacity to meet the legal obligations established in the *Convention against Torture*, the *Refugee Convention*, and the *Charter of Rights and Freedoms*.

B. GENERAL ELIGIBILITY FOR A PRE-REMOVAL RISK ASSESSMENT

Subject to a list of specific exemptions, the *IRPA* allows persons in Canada who are either subject to a removal order that is in force or named in a security certificate to apply for a pre-removal risk assessment unless refugee protection has already been conferred by the Refugee Protection Division (RPD) or unless they have been recognized as a Convention refugee by another country.[22] Persons eligible for a pre-removal risk assessment usually fall into one of five categories:

1) Persons whose claim for refugee protection has been denied, withdrawn, or abandoned;[23]

---

includes information from Citizenship and Immigration Canada revealing that only 1.6 percent of failed refugee claimants received a positive PRRA decision between 2005 and 2012.

20   Canadian Council for Refugees, *PRRA and International Law* (November 2004), online: CCR http://ccrweb.ca/en/res/prra-and-international-law.

21   See, for example, *House of Commons Debates,* 41st Parl, 1st Sess, No 126 (17 May 2012) at 15:20, where Jason Kenney stated during the debate on Bill C-31:

The measure was intended to simplify the refugee system, eliminate duplication and expedite the removal of failed refugee claimants. The government proposed an amendment that extended this ban to three years for failed refugee claimants from countries that generally do not produce refugees. The extension of the bar for these claimants is aimed at addressing existing process vulnerabilities that lead to misuse by those who are not in need of protection. It would facilitate the removals of those individuals not in need of Canada's protection, without the requirement to conduct a redundant second risk assessment.

22   *IRPA,* above note 3, ss 112(1) and 77(1).

23   *Ibid,* ss 112(1) and (3); see also, for example, *Ikechi v Canada (Minister of Citizenship and Immigration),* 2013 FC 361; *Kabeya v Canada (Minister of Citizenship and*

2) Persons whose claim for refugee protection has been denied, who have left, and then returned to Canada;[24]

3) Persons who are ineligible for refugee determination at the Immigration and Refugee Board;[25]

4) Persons who wish to apply for protection before removal from Canada who have not made a previous claim for refugee protection;[26] and

5) Persons who have made a previous PRRA application but were denied and are making a repeat PRRA application.[27]

Immigration), 2012 FC 697; *Terenteva v Canada (Minister of Citizenship and Immigration)*, 2012 FC 1431; *Tenzin v Canada (Minister of Citizenship and Immigration)*, 2009 FC 1010; *Selvarasa v Canada (Minister of Citizenship and Immigration)*, 2008 FC 1169; *Fan v Canada (Minister of Citizenship and Immigration)*, 2004 FC 1692; and *Thang v Canada (Solicitor General)*, 2004 FC 457.

24   IRPA, above note 3, ss 112(1) and (3); see also, for example, *Molnar v Canada (Minister of Citizenship and Immigration)*, 2012 FC 577, where the applicant left Canada to care for an ailing parent prior to determination of a refugee claim, making him ineligible for another refugee claim; the applicant submitted a PRRA when he returned to Canada. See also *Varadi v Canada (Minister of Citizenship and Immigration)*, 2013 FC 407; *Thiyagarajah v Canada (Minister of Citizenship and Immigration)*, 2010 FC 1015; and *Sen v Canada (Minister of Citizenship and Immigration)*, 2005 FC 2.

25   IRPA, above note 3, ss 112(1) and (3); see also, for example, *Burton v Canada (Minister of Citizenship and Immigration)*, 2013 FC 549; and *Sinniah v Canada (Minister of Citizenship and Immigration)*, 2011 FC 1285.

26   IRPA, above note 3, s 112(1); see also, for example, *Fordyce v Canada (Minister of Citizenship and Immigration)*, 2009 FC 556, where a stay of removal was granted. The serious issues identified included whether the port-of-entry officer offered a PRRA to the applicant at the port of entry to persons who did not seek or were ineligible for refugee protection. See also *Prieto v Canada (Minister of Citizenship and Immigration)*, 2010 FC 253 [*Prieto*], where the applicant was arrested at a port of entry and was issued a PRRA. In *Hernandez v Canada (Minister of Public Safety and Emergency Preparedness)*, 2012 FC 1417, the applicant had listed his refugee status in the United States and was subject to deportation to Cuba. The applicant was found to be ineligible for a refugee hearing as he was subject to an inadmissibility finding. At para 41, the court discusses that persons inadmissible for engaging in serious criminality are still able to apply for a PRRA, albeit in a limited manner.

27   Regulations, above note 6, s 165; see also, for example, *Gorzsas v Canada (Minister of Public Safety and Emergency Preparedness)*, 2008 FC 1060, where a gay male Roma from Hungary was unsuccessful on his first PRRA and submitted a second PRRA based on new evidence of his diagnosis as HIV positive and his sexual orientation; *Hall (Litigation guardian of) v Canada (Minister of Citizenship and Immigration)*, 2008 FC 865, where the second PRRA included new medical evidence. Note that this category of persons also includes persons who are ineligible for refugee determinations, have made a PRRA, left Canada, and returned

C. INELIGIBILITY FOR A PRE-REMOVAL RISK ASSESSMENT

Those listed as ineligible[28] to apply for a pre-removal risk assessment include

1) Persons who have already been granted refugee or protected person status;[29]
2) Persons who have been found to be ineligible to apply to the IRB for refugee determination because they came to Canada from a safe third country;[30]
3) Persons who have earlier made a refugee claim to the IRB or an earlier application for a pre-removal risk assessment that was rejected — such individuals are ineligible to apply until a specified time has passed: the period is longer (thirty-six months instead of twelve months) where the individual's country of origin has been designated;[31] and
4) Persons subject to procedures under the *Extradition Act*.[32]

Each of these categories of ineligible persons is examined in turn.

1) Refugees or Protected Persons

In general, refugees or protected persons are not eligible to apply for a pre-removal risk assessment because they have already obtained protection.[33] An application in most circumstances would be redundant. This category includes both individuals who gained their protected status in Canada and also those who obtained Convention refugee status or protected person status in another country.

However, as in the case of *Suresh*, situations can arise where the removal process in Canada is triggered after the conferral of protection.

---

for a second PRRA: *Yakut v Canada (Minister of Citizenship and Immigration)*, 2009 FC 1190 [*Yakut*].

28   *IRPA*, above note 3, s 112(2). Section 112(2) contains all of the exceptions to the principle of non-refoulement found in s 112(1).
29   *Ibid*, s 115(1).
30   *Ibid*, s 112(2)(b).
31   *Ibid*, ss 112(2), 112(2)(b.1), and 112(2)(c). Persons that fall under s (b) are prohibited from applying for one year unless they are found inadmissible or if their refugee claims were vacated, abandoned, or withdrawn. In the case of persons who come from designated countries subject to s 109.1(1), the period of ineligibility extends to thirty-six months.
32   *Ibid*, s 112(2)(a).
33   *Ibid*, s 112(1).

Section 115(2) of the *IRPA* allows for such removal. Before it is effected, the risks that the individual faces must be assessed and weighed against other considerations.[34] There may also be situations where a person who has obtained protected status in a third country may be unwilling to return there because of risks she would face there. The principle of non-refoulement would apply to such individuals, and they may apply for a risk assessment relating to that country.[35] These non-refoulement assessments, or section 115(1) cases, offer an assessment of the risk in the country that had offered protection.[36] This category of risk assessment will be discussed below.

2) Persons Arriving via a Safe Third Country

A safe third country is a country that has been designated by the minister of Citizenship and Immigration as a country where an individual, passing through that country, could have made a claim for refugee protection.[37] The only country that has thus far been designated as a safe third country is the United States.[38]

Persons arriving via a safe third country, as designated under the *Regulations*, are in most circumstances ineligible for a pre-removal risk assessment[39] and ineligible to make a claim before the Refugee Protection Division. However, the Safe Third Country Agreement applies only

---

34   See *Suresh*, above note 15.

35   *IRPA*, above note 3, s 115(1).

36   *Ibid*; see, for example, *Kandasamy v Canada (Minister of Citizenship and Immigration)*, 2011 FC 716, where a Sri Lankan citizen who had obtained non-immigrant refugee status for one year in Mexico applied for protection under s 115(1) of the *IRPA* because he feared being persecuted as a member of a visible minority group and being victimized by criminal elements and corrupt police.

37   *IRPA*, above note 3, s 102(2). This provision sets out the criteria for designating a country as a safe third country. Criteria include whether the country is a party to and respects the obligations of the *Refugee Convention* and is a party to the *Convention against Torture*, whether the country adheres to international human rights norms, and whether it is a party to a Safe Third Country Agreement with Canada. Persons who have a family member within Canada, however, are exempted from the designation.

38   *Agreement between the Government of Canada and the Government of the United States of America for Cooperation in the Examination of Refugee Status Claims from Nationals of Third Countries* (29 December 2004), online: Refworld www.refworld. org/docid/42d7b9944.html [Safe Third Country Agreement]. See also *Regulations*, above note 6, ss 159.1–159.7.

39   *IRPA*, above note 3, s 112(2)(b).

to individuals who enter Canada at a port of entry at the land border.[40] It does not apply to individuals who have family members in Canada, as defined in the *Regulations*.[41] This has far-reaching implications. For example, if a stateless person, who has no family in Canada, arrives at a port of entry via the United States, she will not be eligible for a pre-removal risk assessment.

Previously, applicants who came through a safe third country and who were found ineligible for a refugee hearing did have access to a risk assessment.[42] The current denial of a risk assessment to persons in this category raises the question whether Canada is upholding its obligations under the *Refugee Convention* and the *Convention against Torture*. In particular, Canada is increasingly relying upon other countries, in this case, the United States, to conduct proper risk assessments. It is unclear whether the outsourcing of such assessments has been evaluated with sufficient care by Canada to determine whether the proper assessments are done in the so-called safe third country. It is also unclear whether Canada is providing an adequate safety net to ensure that persons are not returned to risks of persecution, death, torture, and cruel and unusual punishment. The inaccessibility of both the refugee determination process and the pre-removal risk assessment for this category of persons is alarming because it means that large groups of persons coming through the United States may not be properly assessed and, therefore, may be returned to risks Canada is obligated to protect persons against.[43]

3) Previously Rejected Refugee Claimants and PRRA Applicants

As discussed below, those who have previously made a refugee claim or an application for a pre-removal risk assessment that was rejected are time-barred from making a PRRA application. Interestingly, the time bar does not apply where the refugee claim was rejected on grounds

---

40   *Regulations*, above note 6, s 159.4. Thus, individuals who have crossed the border at a place not designated as a port of entry are not subject to the Safe Third Country Agreement.

41   *Ibid*, s 159.5. The *Regulations* define *family* broadly to include a spouse or common-law partner, a legal guardian, and any of the following persons, namely, a child, father, mother, brother, sister, grandfather, grandmother, grandchild, uncle, aunt, nephew, or niece.

42   See, for example, *Sivapatham v Canada (Minister of Citizenship and Immigration)*, 2010 FC 314.

43   See *Canadian Council for Refugees v Canada*, 2006 FC 1046.

of exclusion[44] or where the claim is deemed to be rejected after a vacation application.[45] The time bar, where it does apply, is usually twelve months. It is thirty-six months for individuals from designated countries of origin.[46]

4) Persons Arriving from a Designated Country of Origin[47]

As outlined in Chapter 9, a *designated country of origin* is a country designated[48] by the minister of Citizenship and Immigration because the minister believes that it is comparatively safe and that a person from that country is less likely to face persecution, torture, death, or cruel and unusual punishment if returned there.[49]

Persons from a designated country of origin are not eligible to apply for a pre-removal risk assessment for thirty-six months after a final decision of a refugee claim or a final PRRA decision. The policy rationale has been explained in this way: "Since a person's risk of return will have been assessed by the Refugee Protection Division at the Immigration and Refugee Board of Canada (IRB), and with most failed claims, the Refugee Appeal Division, a further risk assessment is not necessary."[50] Despite this, the minister of Citizenship and Immigration may exempt certain nationals from the time bar on accessing a pre-removal risk assessment.[51]

5) Persons Subject to the *Extradition Act*

Those subject to an extradition proceeding are not eligible for a pre-removal risk assessment. Under the *Extradition Act*, extradition proceedings begin when an authority to proceed (ATP) is issued after the

---

44   See *IRPA*, above note 3, s 98. For more information on exclusion, see Chapter 10.

45   *IRPA*, above note 3, s 109. For more information on vacation, see Chapter 9.

46   *IRPA*, above note 3, s 109.1.

47   For more information on designated countries of origin, see Chapter 9.

48   *IRPA*, above note 3, s 109.1. The section outlines the criteria upon which the minister can designate a country of origin. These include the rate at which the RPD has rejected claims from the specified country and whether there is an independent judiciary or a democratic system in the specified country.

49   Canada has designated several countries *designated countries of origin*, online: Citizenship and Immigration Canada www.cic.gc.ca/english/refugees/reform-safe.asp.

50   Citizenship and Immigration Canada, "Limits on Pre-removal Risk Assessments and Applications for Humanitarian and Compassionate Consideration," online: CIC www.cic.gc.ca/english/refugees/reform-ppra.asp.

51   *IRPA*, above note 3, s 112(2.1).

Department of Justice has established that there is sufficient documentation from the requesting country to proceed with an extradition.[52] A confirmation of the ATP is sent to Citizenship and Immigration Canada.[53] Once the ATP is issued, the affected person is no longer eligible for a pre-removal risk assessment.[54] If an application is pending when an ATP is issued, the application is suspended until a determination regarding whether to extradite the applicant is made by the minister of Justice.[55] If the minister of justice orders the surrender of an applicant under the *Extradition Act*, consideration of the application is terminated.[56] If, however, the applicant is discharged under the *Extradition Act*, the application will continue to be processed.[57]

D. NOTIFICATION OF ELIGIBILITY AS A PREREQUISITE

In most cases, a person cannot apply for a pre-removal risk assessment without first receiving notification of entitlement to do so.[58] As outlined by Citizenship and Immigration Canada, those whose refugee claims have been rejected by the IRB will first receive a CIC document titled *Advance Information Regarding the Pre-removal Risk Assessment*, which describes the assessment and informs the individual that he may be entitled to apply.[59]

Notification is usually given in person. The *Regulations* state the obvious by providing that it should be given before the person's removal from Canada.[60] A removals officer will find the individual to be "removal ready," meaning that the person has exhausted any recourse that would also trigger a statutory or regulatory stay.[61] The individual will

---

52 *Extradition Act*, SC 1999, c 18, s 15.
53 Citizenship and Immigration Canada, "Processing Pre-removal Risk Assessment Applications: Intake," online: CIC www.cic.gc.ca/english/resources/tools/refugees/prra/intake.asp ["PRRA Manual"].
54 *IRPA*, above note 3, s 112(2)(a).
55 *Ibid*, s 112(1.2)(b).
56 *Ibid*, s 112(1.5).
57 *Ibid*, s 112 (1.6).
58 *Ibid*, s 160(1). Of course, those exempted from applying in the first place cannot apply: see *Regulations*, above note 6, s 112(2).
59 "PRRA Manual," above note 53.
60 *IRPA*, above note 3, s 160(3)(a).
61 *Ibid*, s 48(1): "Removal ready" status is established by ensuring that there are no impediments to removal under the *IRPA*, *ibid*, ss 49(1), 49(2), and 50; or *Regulations*, above note 6, ss 230–33.

then receive notification to appear at a Canada Border Services Agency (CBSA) office to meet with a removals officer.[62] The removals officer will provide the eligible person with a PRRA application kit.[63] Persons receiving the application kit will have fifteen days from receiving the application to submit it.[64] A further fifteen days after the application is submitted will be given for a person to prepare and send in submissions for the application.[65]

In some cases, individuals will receive notification of eligibility in the mail.[66] In such cases an additional seven days are added to the first fifteen days given to submit a PRRA application to account for time the notice spent in transit.[67]

Where a foreign national has been found to be inadmissible at a port of entry and has been issued a removal order, that person may apply for a pre-removal risk assessment without notification that she is entitled to do so. Likewise, those who have previously but unsuccessfully applied may reapply without receiving notification of eligibility by submitting a PRRA application form and accompanying written submissions.[68] Those who have withdrawn or abandoned previous PRRA applications are also able to reapply since withdrawn or abandoned applications are considered as rejected applications.[69] The reapplication may be made only after a required temporal limitation has elapsed. Persons who have received a negative PRRA decision must wait twelve or thirty-six months (depending on their country of origin and other applicable factors) before submitting their next application.[70]

Persons named in a security certificate will receive notification of their eligibility to apply for a pre-removal risk assessment after a summary of evidence has been filed in the Federal Court.[71]

---

62 *Ibid*, s 160(4)(a).
63 "PRRA Manual," above note 53.
64 *Regulations*, above note 6, s 162.
65 *Ibid*, s 163.
66 *Ibid*, s 160(4)(b).
67 *Ibid*, s 160(4)(b).
68 *Ibid*, s 165.
69 *Ibid*, s 171.
70 *IRPA*, above note 3, s 112(2)(b.1).
71 *Regulations*, above note 6, s 160(3)(b); for more information on security certificates, see Chapter 15.

E. PROCEDURAL VARIATIONS AND SCOPE OF INQUIRY

1) Persons at the Port of Entry

As noted, persons who are subject to an effective removal order at the port of entry because they are inadmissible may still be eligible for a risk assessment. Such persons must ask for the risk assessment at the port of entry immediately and must submit the application with submissions immediately as well.[72] The application will not stay any removal order that has been issued.[73] In effect, persons in this category must seek a judicial stay of removal to avoid the execution of a removal order.

Often, persons do not approach a port of entry with a lawyer or with knowledge of their eligibility for a pre-removal risk assessment. Such persons are highly dependent upon the officer they meet at the port of entry who may or may not advise the persons of their right to apply. The discretionary nature of notice of a pre-removal risk assessment at the port of entry raises questions as to whether Canada is denying entry to persons who may deserve protection through such a risk assessment.

2) Refused Refugee Claimants and Repeat PRRA Applicants

As noted above, persons who have been denied protection through a refugee claim or PRRA application are eligible for a first or subsequent pre-removal risk assessment subject to two main limitations: the temporal limitation and the new evidence rule.

a) The Time Bar

In reality, the twelve- and thirty-six-month bars prohibit failed refugee claimants and PRRA applicants from enjoying the benefit of one final risk assessment before a removal order is executed against them. Certain nationals are not subject to the time bar as the minister can exempt persons from particular countries from it.[74] Where no exemption

---

72   *Regulations*, above note 6, s 166.

73   *Ibid.*

74   IRPA, above note 3, s 112(2.1). See "PRRA Manual," above note 53: Currently, nationals from the following countries are exempted: Central African Republic, Egypt, Guinea-Bissau, Libya, Mali, Somalia, South Sudan, Sudan, and Syria. It

applies, a person may find herself removal ready before the twelve- or thirty-six-month bar since the final determination of the refugee claim or PRRA application has passed. The temporal limitations render the pre-removal risk assessment ineffective or non-existent for a potentially vulnerable population.

Although a person may ask an officer to use personal discretion to defer removal until the person becomes eligible for a pre-removal risk assessment, the provision dealing with the execution of a removal order requires that it be enforced "as soon as possible," giving little flexibility to an officer to exercise personal discretion.[75] In the face of such restrictions, lawyers will no doubt pursue judicial determination that the temporal limitations violate the *Charter of Rights and Freedoms*. In volatile countries, circumstances may change rapidly. To deny a risk assessment for a lengthy period is to increase the risk that the decision to return an individual will be based on flawed outdated information. In time we will see whether the courts accept that the life, liberty, or security of a person is affected by the inability to access this risk assessment prior to removal.[76]

---

is prudent to check with Citizenship and Immigration Canada as to the updated list and the effective dates of exemption.

75 *IRPA*, above note 3, s 48(2); previously, this subsection provided that the order be enforced "as soon as reasonably practicable." Even this earlier wording was held by the Federal Court of Appeal to grant limited discretion. *Baron v Canada (Minister of Public Safety and Emergency Preparedness)*, 2009 FCA 81 at para 49; see also *Simoes v Canada (Minister of Citizenship and Immigration)* (2000), 187 FTR 219 at para 12 (TD); and *Wang v Canada (Minister of Citizenship and Immigration)*, 2001 FCT 148 [*Wang*].

76 See the decisions of *Savunthararasa v Canada (Minister of Public Safety and Emergency Preparedness)*, 2014 FC 1074 [*Savunthararasa*], and *Peter v Canada (Minister of Public Safety and Emergency Preparedness)*, 2014 FC 1073 [*Peter*], where Annis J of the Federal Court dismissed the judicial reviews challenging the constitutionality of the twelve-month bar to apply for a PRRA. Two questions were certified as being of general importance: "Does the prohibition contained in section 112(2)(b.1) of the *Immigration and Refugee Protection Act* against bringing a Pre-Removal Risk Assessment application until 12 months have passed since the claim for refugee protection was last rejected infringe section 7 of the *Charter*?" and "If not, does the present removals process, employed within 12 months of a refugee claim being last rejected, when determining whether to defer removal at the request of an unsuccessful refugee claimant for the purpose of permitting a Pre-Removal Risk Assessment application to be advanced infringe section 7 of the *Charter*?"

b) The New Evidence Rule

Failed refugee claimants and PRRA applicants may submit only new evidence for consideration in the PRRA application.[77] New evidence qualifies as evidence that arose after the rejection of the refugee claim[78] or PRRA application or evidence that was not reasonably available when the refugee claim was being heard or PRRA application submitted.[79] The applicant is required to identify the evidence and indicate how it relates to him.[80] The scope of the new evidence rule will be discussed below.

Thus, for refugee claimants or rejected PRRA applicants, subsequent PRRA applications are assessed only in terms of risk factors arising since the last assessment took place, whether it be at the RPD or in a previous risk assessment.[81] Finally, it is important to note that a regulatory stay of removal is not available for failed refugee claimants or rejected PRRA applicants when they submit a subsequent PRRA application.[82]

3) Persons Ineligible to Make a Refugee Claim

Persons who are ineligible to make a refugee claim because they are inadmissible on the grounds of serious criminality or subject to a security certificate are subject to different PRRA rules and processes.[83] What is common among applications that fall into this category is that, even if an officer finds in favour of the applicant, the positive determination does not lead to the conferral of refugee or protected person status. Rather, the determination simply grants a stay of removal, which can be revoked at any time, if circumstances in the person's country of origin change.[84] Two classes of person fall within this category.

a) Inadmissible Persons

For persons who are inadmissible on grounds of serious criminality, organized criminality, national security, or violations of international humanitarian law, different procedures are followed and the pre-

---

77 *IRPA*, above note 3, s 113(a); see also *Raza v Canada (Minister of Citizenship and Immigration)*, 2007 FCA 385 [*Raza*]; *Kaybaki v Canada (Solicitor General of Canada)*, 2004 FC 32 at para 11.

78 *IRPA*, above note 3.

79 *Ibid.*

80 *Regulations*, above note 6, s 161(2).

81 *IRPA*, above note 3, s 113(a).

82 *Ibid*, s 165.

83 *Ibid*, s 112(3).

84 *Ibid*, s 114(1)(b).

removal risk assessment will have a limited scope.[85] Those who are inadmissible on these grounds will not be assessed against all the risks listed in Canada's refugee definitions.[86] An astonishingly complex set of rules has been established to deal with such cases. The general rule is that the assessment will examine only whether the person is subject to a risk listed in section 97 of the *IRPA*, that is to say, the risk of torture, death, or cruel and unusual treatment or punishment.[87] In addition, the general rule provides that the risks that the individual faces will be balanced against either subsection 113(d)(i), a judgment about whether he is a danger to the public in Canada where he is inadmissible on grounds of serious criminality[88] or, subsection 113(d)(ii), where he is inadmissible on any of the other serious grounds, against a judgment whether "they should be refused because of the nature and severity of acts committed by the applicant or because of the danger that the applicant constitutes to the security of Canada."[89] This general approach is qualified. In exceptional circumstances, a different set of factors will be applied:

> 113(e) in the case of the following applicants, consideration shall be on the basis of sections 96 to 98 and subparagraph (d)(i) or (ii), as the case may be:
>
> (i)   an applicant who is determined to be inadmissible on grounds of serious criminality with respect to a conviction in Canada punishable by a maximum term of imprisonment of at least 10 years for which a term of imprisonment of less than two years — or no term of imprisonment — was imposed, and
>
> (ii) an applicant who is determined to be inadmissible on grounds of serious criminality with respect to a conviction of an offence outside Canada that, if committed in Canada, would constitute an offence under an Act of Parliament punishable by a maximum term of imprisonment of at least 10 years, unless they are found to be a person referred to in section F of Article 1 of the Refugee Convention.

Not only is the language of this *IRPA* provision unduly prolix and its objective difficult to discern, but it is also drafted to include a *non-sequitur*. Since both the subparagraphs in section 113(e) refer to grounds of serious criminality, it makes no sense to cross-reference

---

85   *Ibid*, s 112(3).
86   *Regulations*, above note 6, s 172(2).
87   *Ibid*; *IRPA*, above note 3, ss 113(d) & (e).
88   *Ibid*, s 113(d)(i).
89   *Ibid*, s 113(d)(ii).

both subparagraphs 113(d)(i) and 113(d(ii). Only the former applies to cases of serious criminality.

The balance between providing surrogate protection and preserving the security interests of Canada will continue to merit judicial attention. The seminal case dealing with persons in this category is the *Suresh* case.[90] *Suresh* dealt with an individual who obtained refugee protection in Canada but was unable to obtain permanent residence status as the government of Canada found Suresh to be inadmissible based on security grounds due to his membership in the Liberation Tigers of Tamil Eelam (LTTE) in Sri Lanka.[91] The government initiated proceedings to remove Suresh under the removal regime of the former *IRPA*, and Suresh provided submissions and documentary evidence on the torture, disappearances, and killings of members of the LTTE.[92] When the case reached the Supreme Court of Canada, the Court was wrestling with the scope of Canada's obligations under section 7 of the *Charter of Rights and Freedoms* in Canada's decision to remove a recognized refugee to a place where he could be subject to a risk to life and torture. The Court held that Suresh should have been provided with the procedural safeguards necessary to protect his section 7 right to life and not torture.[93] Since this decision, the Court has left open the door to allow Canada to remove persons to a risk of life and torture where there are exceptional circumstances.[94] The parameters of exceptional circumstances are yet to be circumscribed.

b) Persons Subject to Security Certificates

As explained in Chapter 15, permanent residents and foreign nationals may be subject to a security certificate[95] signed by the minister of Citizenship and Immigration and the minister of Public Safety and Emergency Preparedness alleging that they have reasonable grounds to believe that the person is inadmissible on grounds of security, violations of human or international rights, serious criminality, or organized criminality.[96] With few exceptions, all proceedings to which the named person is party are adjourned until a judge of the Federal Court

---

90 *Suresh*, above note 15.
91 *IRPA*, above note 3, s 40.1.
92 *Suresh*, above note 15.
93 *Ibid.*
94 See *Sogi v Canada (Minister of Citizenship and Immigration)*, 2004 FC 853; *Re Jaballah*, 2006 FC 1230.
95 *IRPA*, above note 3, s 77. For more information on security certificates, see Chapter 15.
96 *IRPA, ibid.*

determines whether the security certificate is reasonable. One of the exceptions is the pre-removal risk assessment.[97] A person may apply for an assessment within fifteen days of receiving notice that she is entitled to do so.[98] Since the security certificate is deemed to be a removal order only after it is found to be reasonable, this allows the decision balancing risk and danger to be made prior to the removal order coming into force.

4) Non-refoulement Assessments (Section 115(1) Cases)

For Convention refugees or protected persons who are facing a return to a state which may have given them protected status, a pre-removal risk assessment will focus on whether an affected person faces persecution, torture, or cruel and unusual punishment if returned there. Typically, a removals officer will notify the person that he is eligible for such an assessment and give the person thirty days to make submissions in support of the notion that risks in the country signify that the person deserves protected status.[99] If no submissions are filed, the removal process will proceed. If submissions are received, a risk assessment will be done, and a recommendation will be provided by a PRRA officer to the removals officer.[100] The removals officer uses his discretion based upon the assessment provided.[101] If the removals officer decides not to remove the person, the removal will be suspended temporarily and is subject to review if circumstances change.[102]

5) Regulatory Stay of Removal

After a person is notified that she is entitled to a pre-removal risk assessment, a regulatory stay of removal is executed against the removal order against her.[103] The stay is maintained from the time that the notice is given at least until the fifteen-day deadline for submitting a

---

97   *Ibid*, s 77(3).
98   *Regulations*, above note 6, s 160(3), requires that notice of the right to seek a PRRA be given to the person named in the security certificate at the time the certificate is issued.
99   *Ibid*, ss 160–61 and 164.
100 PRRA Manual, above note 53.
101 *IRPA*, above note 3, 112(1).
102 *Ibid*, s 114(1)(b).
103 *Regulations*, above note 6, ss 162 and 232. In the two circumstances where a notification is not required (where a person is applying at a port of entry and reapplying after a negative PRRA), there will be no mandatory stay.

PRRA application lapses.[104] Should an applicant miss the fifteen-day deadline, she may still submit the application but will not benefit from a stay of the removal order.[105] Thus, it is imperative that an application be submitted on time.

The regulatory stay renders the removal order inoperable until a PRRA decision has been made.[106] The *Regulations* specify that a stay is effective until the earliest of one of the following events:

1) Citizenship and Immigration Canada receives notification in writing that the person does not intend to apply for a risk assessment.[107]
2) An application is not properly submitted under the given timeline of fifteen days after notification.[108]
3) The application is rejected.[109]
4) An application is granted and the person has obtained permanent residence status or has been denied permanent residence status.[110]
5) The expiry of the period (180 days) under which a permanent residence application must be made when an application is granted and the person has not made an application for permanent residence.[111]
6) The minister of Citizenship and Immigration uses ministerial discretion to cancel the stay after examining the situation where an applicant was granted a pre-removal risk assessment but was inadmissible on grounds of criminality, security, violating human or international rights, or organized criminality.[112]

The failure to apply for permanent residence or the denial of an application for permanent residence does not affect the person's status as a protected person, but it may affect whether she is subject to a stay of removal.[113]

The minister of Citizenship and Immigration may also reconsider a stay of removal at any time if circumstances surrounding the granting of the stay have changed.[114] For example, obtaining assurances from the country to which the applicant will be removed that the applicant would not be subject to torture, death, or cruel and unusual punish-

---

104 *Ibid*, s 162.
105 *Ibid*, s 163.
106 *Ibid*, s 232.
107 *Ibid*, s 232(a).
108 *Ibid*, s 232(b).
109 *Ibid*, s 232(c).
110 *Ibid*, s 232(e).
111 *Ibid*, s 232(e).
112 *Ibid*, s 232(f); *IRPA*, ss 112(3) and 114(2).
113 *Regulations*, above note 6, s 232(e).
114 *IRPA*, above note 3, s 114(2).

ment may qualify.[115] However, the Federal Court has questioned the practice of relying upon such assurances, putting the onus on the PRRA officer to ensure that the assurances are meaningful and reliable.[116]

When re-examining a stay of removal, the minister of Citizenship and Immigration must give notice of the re-examination,[117] provide a written assessment as to whether there are any risks of torture, death, or cruel and unusual punishment,[118] and assess whether the applicant is a danger to the public or security of Canada, or whether the nature and severity of the acts committed by the applicant merit a decision to deny protection under the risk assessment.[119] The minister and ministerial delegate must also consider any written submissions provided by the applicant.[120] These written submissions are to be submitted within fifteen days of receiving the assessments of the minister or ministerial delegate.[121]

Those ineligible for a regulatory stay of removal include persons who have missed the application deadline of fifteen days,[122] persons making subsequent PRRA applications,[123] and persons at the port of entry.[124] In these cases, an applicant may request a deferral of removal from the minister of Public Safety and Emergency Preparedness or the minister's delegate.[125] The decision to defer removal is discretionary and can be judicially reviewed.[126] When interpreting the previous requirement that orders be enforced as soon as reasonably practical, the Federal Court identified the following factors as relevant:

---

115 See, for example, *Jaballah v Canada (Minister of Citizenship and Immigration)*, 2004 FCA 257.

116 *Lai v Canada (Minister of Citizenship and Immigration)*, 2007 FC 361.

117 *Regulations*, above note 6, s 173(1)(a).

118 *Ibid*, s 173(1)(b).

119 *Ibid*, s 173(1)(c).

120 *Ibid*, s 173(2).

121 *Ibid*.

122 *Ibid*, s 163.

123 *Ibid*, s 165.

124 *Ibid*, s 166.

125 *IRPA*, above note 3, s 48. For further information, see Chapter 15.

126 See text above at footnote 75. As noted, s 48(2) of the *IRPA* now requires that an order be enforced as soon as possible. Previously, it required that an order be enforced as soon as reasonably practical.

1) The existence of a pending permanent residence application on humanitarian and compassionate grounds that was filed in a timely manner;
2) Medical problems;
3) Arrangement of travel documents; and
4) Threats to personal safety.[127]

In essence, the court held that Parliament did not intend ministerial delegates to exercise discretion in a manner that would effectively deprive an applicant of the recourse Parliament had made available.[128] It is unclear what, if any, factors will be relevant under the new wording of section 48(2) that requires an order to be enforced as soon as possible. The issue is discussed in more detail in Chapter 15.

If an applicant cannot secure a deferral for removal, he or she can seek a stay of removal from the Federal Court.[129] Stays of removal are interlocutory or injunctive relief and therefore are subject to the same legal tests as other injunctions. The three-part test includes examining whether there are serious issues to be determined, irreparable harm likely to be suffered on a balance of probabilities, and whether the balance of convenience favours the applicant.[130]

6) Evidence and Submissions

a) Applicant's Burden to Provide Evidence and Submissions

The onus is on an applicant to provide evidence and make submissions with regard to the risks present in the country to which the applicant may be returned.[131] As explained above, where a refugee claim has been

---

127 *Boniowski v Canada (Minister of Citizenship and Immigration)*, 2004 FC 1161 (decided before the words of s 48 were changed).

128 *Shpati v Canada (Minister of Public Safety and Emergency Preparedness)*, 2010 FC 367; *Lin v Canada (Minister of Public Safety and Emergency Preparedness)*, 2011 FC 771.

129 See, for example, *Yakut*, above note 27. See Chapter 16 for more information on judicial review.

130 For more information, see Chapter 16 and its section on remedies.

131 See, for example, *Ivakhnenko v Canada (Solicitor General)*, 2004 FC 1249; *Selliah v Canada (Minister of Citizenship and Immigration)*, 2004 FC 872; *Ormankaya v Canada (Minister of Citizenship and Immigration)*, 2010 FC 1089; *Ibrahim v Canada (Minister of Citizenship and Immigration)*, 2014 FC 837; and *Sufaj v Canada (Minister of Citizenship and Immigration)*, 2014 FC 373. These cases may be qualified by the decision in *Hassaballa v Canada (Minister of Citizenship and Immigration)*, 2007 FC 489, where the court held that the PRRA officer has a duty to consider the most recent sources of information and cannot simply rely upon evidence provided by the applicant. This duty places a positive

denied or an earlier PRRA application has been unsuccessful, the applicant may only provide evidence not reasonably available at the time or evidence that arose after their refugee or previous PRRA determinations.[132] This limitation may be explained as a device to promote the values underlying the principles of *res judicata* and issue estoppel espousing the notion that a conclusive decision should not be reopened unless it is in the interests of justice to do so.[133]

The problem of determining whether evidence is "new" or "not reasonably available" at the time earlier applications were considered has provided the courts with many opportunities for normative analysis.[134] The seminal case is *Raza*,[135] where the Federal Court of Appeal identified a list of factors that should be considered when determining whether to admit evidence in a PRRA application. Justice Sharlow analyzed the statutory language as follows:

> Paragraph 113(*a*) asks a number of questions, some expressly and some by necessary implication, about the proposed new evidence. I summarize those questions as follows:
>
> 1.   Credibility: Is the evidence credible, considering its source and the circumstances in which it came into existence? If not, the evidence need not be considered.

---

obligation the PRRA officer to seek out current and relevant information upon which to base a decision.

132   See discussion in Section E(2), above in this chapter. See also *Yansane v Canada (Minister of Citizenship and Immigration)*, 2009 FC 1242 [*Yansane*]: The court quashed a negative PRRA decision where the officer neglected to review the new evidence.

133   See, for example, *Kouka v Canada (Minister of Citizenship and Immigration)*, 2006 FC 1236 at paras 14–15; *Quiroga v Canada (Minister of Citizenship and Immigration)*, 2006 FC 1306; *Voloshina v Canada (Minister of Citizenship and Immigration)*, 2008 FC 1202; *Roberto v Canada (Minister of Citizenship and Immigration)*, 2009 FC 180; *Orozco v Canada (Minister of Citizenship and Immigration)*, 2006 FC 1426; *Yansane v Canada (Minister of Citizenship and Immigration)*, 2008 FC 1213; *Kaba v Canada (Minister of Citizenship and Immigration)*, 2007 FC 647; *Eid v Canada (Minister of Citizenship and Immigration)*, 2010 FC 639; *Hausleitner v Canada (Minister of Citizenship and Immigration)*, 2005 FC 641 [*Hausleitner*]; *Casseus v Canada (Minister of Citizenship and Immigration)*, 2003 FCT 472; and *Chowdhury v Canada (Minister of Citizenship and Immigration)*, 2003 FC 1050.

134   See, for example, *Jessamy v Canada (Minister of Citizenship and Immigration)*, 2009 FC 20; *Yansane*, above note 132; and *Elezi v Canada (Minister of Citizenship and Immigration)*, 2007 FC 240.

135   *Raza*, above note 77.

2. Relevance: Is the evidence relevant to the PRRA application, in the sense that it is capable of proving or disproving a fact that is relevant to the claim for protection? If not, the evidence need not be considered.

3. Newness: Is the evidence new in the sense that it is capable of:

   (a) proving the current state of affairs in the country of removal or an event that occurred or a circumstance that arose after the hearing in the RPD, or

   (b) proving a fact that was unknown to the refugee claimant at the time of the RPD hearing, or

   (c) contradicting a finding of fact by the RPD (including a credibility finding)?

   If not, the evidence need not be considered.

4. Materiality: Is the evidence material, in the sense that the refugee claim probably would have succeeded if the evidence had been made available to the RPD? If not, the evidence need not be considered.

5. Express statutory conditions:

   (a) If the evidence is capable of proving only an event that occurred or circumstances that arose prior to the RPD hearing, then has the applicant established either that the evidence was not reasonably available to him or her for presentation at the RPD hearing, or that he or she could not reasonably have been expected in the circumstances to have presented the evidence at the RPD hearing? If not, the evidence need not be considered.

   (b) If the evidence is capable of proving an event that occurred or circumstances that arose after the RPD hearing, then the evidence must be considered (unless it is rejected because it is not credible, not relevant, not new or not material).[136]

To be considered as new, the evidence must meet at least one of the three criteria of newness.[137] If the evidence relates to events that arose after a previous refugee or PRRA determination, then an officer is obligated to consider the evidence.[138] If, however, the evidence deals with circumstances arising prior to the determination of a refugee claim or a PRRA application, the officer must focus on the reasonable availability of the evidence. In particular, the officer must ask whether

---

136 *Ibid* at para 13.

137 *IRPA*, above note 3, s 113(a); see, for example, *Ayach v Canada (Minister of Citizenship and Immigration)*, 2010 FC 1023 [*Ayach*].

138 *IRPA*, above note 3, s 113.

the evidence was reasonably available to the applicant or whether the applicant could reasonably have been expected to provide it in prior applications. If this question is answered affirmatively, then the officer must ask if the evidence is material or capable of leading the officer to a different conclusion than the one reached by prior decision makers at the IRB or a prior pre-removal risk assessment. In essence, is the evidence so relevant that it could lead to a positive determination?[139]

The Federal Court has added to this analysis by holding that where an applicant has been diligent in securing information, it is inappropriate to rely on a strict interpretation of section 113(a).[140] In addition it has provided further guideposts. For example, the court has held that "the fact that the evidence post-dates the hearing does not *per se* make it new evidence, likewise evidence that refers to an old risk should not be rejected as 'not new.'"[141] Thus, there is no presumption that evidence should not be considered simply because it existed prior to a refugee or PRRA determination. Along the same lines, the court has held that, where a report may have existed before a refugee determination was made, an applicant cannot be faulted for not having found it when the IRB did not find it and therefore include it in its documentation package.[142] Further, PRRA officers must consider new risks that may have arisen over time.[143] Officers have a duty to consider all possible grounds of fear.[144]

The court has also discussed the importance of assessing explanations that an applicant may offer for failing to provide evidence earlier. In *Selduz v Canada (Minister of Citizenship and Immigration)*, the court acknowledged that an arrest warrant was issued two weeks before an IRB decision was made, but the court found that the officer failed to consider that it may not have been reasonable for the warrant to be filed as evidence before the IRB within the available time.[145] Further, an officer has a duty to provide within her reasons for denying the admission of evidence an account of why the explanation was not sufficient. In *Selduz*, the court held that, "if the officer was aware that an

---

139 See, for example, *de Torres v Canada (Minister of Citizenship and Immigration)*, 2009 FC 208.

140 *Komahe v Canada (Minister of Citizenship and Immigration)*, 2006 FC 1521.

141 *Jessamy v Canada (Minister of Citizenship and Immigration)*, 2010 FC 489 at para 21.

142 *Sanchez v Canada (Minister of Citizenship and Immigration)*, 2009 FC 101 [Sanchez].

143 *Zemo v Canada (Minister of Citizenship and Immigration)*, 2010 FC 800 [Zemo].

144 *Boroumand v Canada (Minister of Citizenship and Immigration)*, 2007 FC 1219 [Boroumand].

145 2009 FC 361.

explanation had been provided and found the explanation inadequate, his reasons should have reflected this finding, particularly in light of the probative nature of the document."[146] Thus, a PRRA officer must have regard for the evidence before him. In *Ayach*, the court cautioned against summarily dismissing evidence, whether it arose before or after prior determinations.[147]

b)   PRRA Officer's Duty to Disclose Adverse Extrinsic Information

PRRA officers have a duty to disclose adverse information to the applicant. As a matter of procedural fairness, where a PRRA officer intends to use or rely upon evidence or information that would affect the risk assessment, the officer must give the applicant the opportunity to respond.[148] This duty, however, is limited.

The PRRA Manual provides the following guidelines on disclosure:

> Subject to the following paragraph, officers will retain discretion with regard to whether a document should be shared with the applicant prior to rendering a decision, if it can be demonstrated that the document is "publicly accessible" ["publicly accessible" documents should originate with reliable sources, and should be available at sites directly related to the source, rather than through cross-references from other sites, the reliability of which may not be as well established];
>
> Where a document post-dates the submission of the applicant, or where the date of publication is not clearly indicated, officers will share with the applicant, prior to rendering a decision, any document that shows changes in the country conditions that could affect the decision;[149]

This guidance is based on a decision by the Federal Court of Appeal. In *Mancia v Canada (Minister of Citizenship and Immigration)*,[150] Décary JA held:

(a)   with respect to documents relied upon from public sources in relation to general country conditions which were available and

---

146   *Ibid* at para 17; see also *DP v Canada (Minister of Citizenship and Immigration)*, 2010 FC 533.

147   *Ayach*, above note 137.

148   See *Duda v Canada (Minister of Citizenship and Immigration)*, 2010 FC 512; *Ramanathan v Canada (Minister of Citizenship and Immigration)*, 2008 FC 843; *Kumarasamy v Canada (Minister of Citizenship and Immigration)*, 2008 FC 597 [*Kumarasamy*].

149   "PRRA Manual," above note 53.

150   [1998] 3 FC 461 (CA).

accessible at Documentation Centres at the time submissions were made by an applicant, fairness does not require the post claims determination officer to disclose them in advance of determining the matter;

(b) with respect to documents relied upon from public sources in relation to general country conditions which became available and accessible after the filing of an applicant's submissions, fairness requires disclosure by the post claims determination officer where they are novel and significant and where they evidence changes in the general country conditions that may affect the decision.[151]

In *Zamora v Canada (Minister of Citizenship and Immigration)*,[152] Harrington J addressed whether an officer may rely on information available on the Internet without disclosure:

> [Previous cases have not] addressed the issue of the internet. I cannot believe an applicant can anticipate what documents the officer may retrieve from the internet, some of which may be of doubtful validity, when there are over a million to choose from!
>
> The documents in question were not standard documents such as Human Rights Watch, Amnesty International or country reports issued under governmental authority, but rather the result of specific research on the internet carried out by the PRRA officer. That research, including such documents she may have found were beneficial to Mr. Aguilar Zamora, should have been disclosed and he should have been given an opportunity to respond. It cannot be said with any confidence that the documents were not novel, or significant.[153]

In *Kumarasamy*,[154] the PRRA officer relied on reports released two months subsequent to the application being made. The reports provided novel and significant information used in making the decision. The court found that there was a duty on the part of the officer to provide an opportunity to respond to such novel and significant arguments.

---

151 *Ibid* at para 27.
152 2004 FC 1414.
153 *Ibid* at paras 17 & 18.
154 *Kumarasamy*, above note 148.

7) Assessment

a) Oral Hearing

Unlike refugee claimants before the IRB, not all PRRA applicants will be afforded the opportunity to participate in an oral hearing. Provisions in the *IRPA* provide discretion to the minister of Citizenship and Immigration to determine whether an oral hearing should be made available to a PRRA applicant.[155] As with a refugee determination, a hearing is imperative where credibility is a concern and where credibility findings go to the heart of the determination.[156] Section 167 of the *Regulations* list a number of factors that must be assessed:

1) Does the evidence raise a serious issue of the applicant's credibility?[157]
2) Is the evidence central to the decision?[158]
3) Would the evidence support a positive PRRA decision?[159]

The Federal Court has held that it would be a clear violation of principles of fairness and fundamental justice for a PRRA officer to make an adverse credibility finding against the applicant without an oral hearing.[160] In *Tekie v Canada (Minister of Citizenship and Immigration)*,[161] Phelan J offers a very broad interpretation of section 167:

> In my view, section 167 becomes operative where credibility is an issue which could result in a negative PRRA decision. The intent of the provision is to allow an Applicant to face any credibility concern which may be put in issue.

---

155 *IRPA*, above note 3, s 113(b).

156 See *Singh v Canada (Minister of Employment and Immigration)*, [1985] 1 SCR 177 at para 59; *Shafi v Canada (Minister of Citizenship and Immigration)*, 2005 FC 714 at para 22; *Liban v Canada (Minister of Citizenship and Immigration)*, 2008 FC 1252; *Puerta v Canada (Minister of Citizenship and Immigration)*, 2010 FC 464; *Cho v Canada (Minister of Citizenship and Immigration)*, 2010 FC 1299; *G(DJD) v Canada (Minister of Public Safety and Emergency Preparedness)*, 2010 FC 765; *Zemo*, above note 143; *Hamadi v Canada (Minister of Citizenship and Immigration)*, 2011 FC 317.

157 *Regulations*, above note 6, s 167(a).

158 *Ibid*, s 167(b).

159 *Ibid*, s 167(c).

160 See, for example, *Prieto*, above note 26 at paras 43–44, where the court found that an oral hearing was needed for a proper assessment of the subjective component of the applicant's fear; *Kaberuka v Canada (Minister of Citizenship and Immigration)*, [1995] 3 FC 252 (TD).

161 2005 FC 27 at para 16.

When a hearing is found to be necessary, the *Regulations* specify that a person must be given notice of the hearing and the issues of fact to be raised during the hearing.[162] The applicant must respond to questions posed by the officer, and the applicant may have a lawyer present to assist him in the hearing.[163]

b) Issues and Considerations

The following section briefly outlines issues and considerations that PRRA officers evaluate in PRRA applications.

i) Evaluations under the IRPA, Sections 96 and 97

With the exception of those found inadmissible or subject to a security certificate, risk assessments consider the grounds provided in both sections 96 and 97 of the *IRPA*. However, the evaluation of whether the application raises issues that merit section 96 and 97 protections is limited to considering evidence that has been raised after a failed refugee claim or earlier failed risk assessment.[164] Despite the fact that PRRA officers are often evaluating applications on the same grounds as board members at an RPD hearing at the IRB, some jurisprudence has posited that PRRA applications are not meant to be a reconsideration of IRB decisions,[165] while others consider the pre-removal risk assessment to be an extension of a refugee determination.[166]

Where section 97 of the *IRPA* applies to the applicant, an assessment in this category also includes the evaluation of whether the applicant is a danger to the public[167] or security of Canada[168] or whether the nature and severity of the acts committed by the applicant merit a decision to deny protection under the pre-removal risk assessment.[169] If the decision maker finds the applicant does not fit within section 97 of the *IRPA*, the decision maker is not required to provide an assessment as to whether the applicant is a danger to the public or security of Canada, or whether the nature and severity of the acts committed by

---

162   *Regulations*, above note 6, ss 168(a)–(b).
163   *Ibid*, s 168(c).
164   See Section C(3), above in this chapter.
165   *Hausleitner*, above note 133; *Raza*, above note 77 at para 12; *Kadjo v Canada (Minister of Citizenship and Immigration)*, 2010 FC 1050 at para 12; *Sohanpal v Canada (Minister of Citizenship and Immigration)*, 2013 FC 454 at para 24.
166   See, for example, *Savunthararasa*, above note 76.
167   *IRPA*, above note 3, s 113(d)(i); *Regulations*, above note 6, s 172(2)(b).
168   *IRPA*, above note 3, s 113(d)(ii); *Regulations*, above note 6, s 172(2)(b).
169   *Ibid*.

the applicant merit a decision to deny protection under the pre-removal risk assessment — the risk assessment is simply rejected.[170]

ii) Evaluations under Only Section 97 of the IRPA

Persons who are inadmissible on grounds of serious criminality, violations of human or international rights, or organized crime, or are subject to security certificates under section 77 of the IRPA are not eligible for a full risk assessment.[171] Instead, the pre-removal risk assessment for such persons is a narrow examination that is limited to grounds set out in section 97 of the IRPA.[172] If the risks identified fit within section 97, a positive PRRA decision may be granted. Such a grant will lead only to a stay of removal until the conditions in the person's country of nationality allow for a reconsideration of the state.[173]

iii) Evaluating Exclusion under Section 98 of the IRPA

It is important to note that a PRRA officer has the jurisdiction to find an applicant excluded under section 98 of the IRPA.[174] This exclusion can be based on a finding that the applicant has residency in another country and there is available state protection in that country or that there are serious reasons for believing that the applicant was complicit with or committed a war crime, crime against humanity, or a serious non-political crime; is a member of a terrorist organization; or is guilty of acts contrary to the purposes and principles of the United Nations.[175]

iv) Best Interests of the Children

Unlike applications made on humanitarian and compassionate grounds, the PRRA application does not need to assess the best interests of the children.[176] Nonetheless, a risk assessment can include consideration of the children attached to the applicant, the risks they face, or the risks that may arise because of the existence of the children. For example, in the case of *Campos v Canada (Minister of Citizenship and Immigration)*, the court quashed a PRRA decision where the officer did not consider

---

170   *Regulations*, above note 6, s 172(4).

171   See *IRPA*, above note 3, s 112(3); *Regulations*, above note 6, s 172.

172   *Regulations*, ibid, s 172(2)(a); *IRPA*, above note 3, s 97; see also, for example, *Boroumand*, above note 144.

173   *Regulations*, above note 6, s 232.

174   *IRPA*, above note 3, s 98; see *Li v Canada (Minister of Citizenship and Immigration)*, 2009 FC 623 at para 55, rev'd 2010 FCA 75, leave to appeal to SCC refused, [2010] SCCA No 183.

175   *IRPA*, above note 3, s 98; *Refugee Convention*, above note 1, arts 1E & 1F.

176   *Varga v Canada (Minister of Citizenship and Immigration)*, 2006 FCA 394 at para 20; *Ammar v Canada (Minister or Citizenship and Immigration)*, 2006 FC 1041.

the applicant to be at a heightened risk of harm from a former spouse due to the fact that her child was not her former spouse's child.[177] The court held that the officer should have considered this factor when evaluating the risk to the applicant.

v) Humanitarian and Compassionate Grounds

Applications for permanent residence on humanitarian and compassionate grounds can be forwarded to PRRA officers if risk of return was raised in the application.[178] In such cases, the PRRA officers will review the application to ensure a risk assessment is done. However, outside humanitarian and compassionate grounds applications, PRRA officers are not mandated to consider humanitarian and compassionate factors.[179] Strictly speaking, PRRA applications are restricted to risk assessments.

vi) Country of Removal

In order to be successful, PRRA applicants must provide information and submissions regarding any and all countries that they may be removed to. Section 241(1) provides a guide to determine which country applicants may focus on.[180] An applicant can be removed to the country from which she came to Canada;[181] the country in which he last permanently resided before coming to Canada;[182] a country of which she is a national or citizen;[183] or the country of birth.[184] If none of the countries identified will authorize the applicant to enter, another country that will authorize entry may be selected.[185]

---

177 2008 FC 556 at para 8; *Kakonyi v Canada (Minister of Public Safety and Emergency Preparedness)*, 2008 FC 1410 at para 38.

178 *IRPA*, above note 3, s 25(1).

179 See *Kim v Canada (Minister of Citizenship and Immigration)*, 2005 FC 437 at para 70:

> I find that PRRA officers need not consider humanitarian and compassionate factors in making their decisions. There is no discretion afforded to a PRRA officer in making a risk assessment. Either the officer is satisfied that the risk factors alleged exist and are sufficiently serious to grant protection, or the officer is not satisfied. The PRRA inquiry and decision-making process does not take into account factors other than risk. In any case, there is a better forum for the consideration of humanitarian and compassionate factors: the H&C determination mechanism.

180 *Regulations*, above note 6, s 241(1).

181 *Ibid*, s 241(1)(a).

182 *Ibid*, s 241(1)(b).

183 *Ibid*, s 241(1)(c).

184 *Ibid*, s 241(1)(d).

185 *Ibid*, s 241(2).

F. DECISIONS AND APPEALS

1) Decision Final When Delivered

A decision is not final until it is delivered or communicated to the applicant.[186] Thus, a PRRA officer has an obligation to consider all evidence and submissions provided until the decision is delivered.[187] Where a decision is sent by mail and not given by hand to the applicant, the applicant is deemed to have received the decision seven days after the day on which the decision was sent to the last address the applicant provided to Citizenship and Immigration Canada.[188] Applicants can request the reasons or justification for allowing or rejecting the risk assessment. The minister of Citizenship and Immigration or ministerial delegate will provide a copy of file notes or other written reasons upon request.[189]

2) Positive PRRA Decisions

Where a PRRA application has been granted, unless the applicant falls into one of the categories of persons restricted by s 112(3) of the *IRPA*, namely, those found inadmissible,[190] excludable,[191] or named in a security certificate,[192] the person will be granted refugee protection.[193] Subsequently, the applicant may apply for permanent residence status.[194] Those excluded by section 112(3) will not benefit from protection or permanent residence status but are granted a stay of removal which may be evaluated at any time should there be changes in the circumstances of the country to which they would be removed.[195]

---

186 *Ibid*, s 172(3).
187 *Chudal v Canada (Minister of Citizenship and Immigration)*, 2005 FC 1073.
188 *Regulations*, above note 6, s 172(3).
189 *Ibid*, s 174.
190 *IRPA*, above note 3, s 112(3)(a): inadmissible on grounds of security, violating human or international rights or organized criminality; s 112(3)(b): inadmissible on grounds of serious criminality.
191 *Ibid*, s 112(3)(c).
192 *Ibid*, ss 77(1) and 112(3)(d).
193 *Ibid*, s 114(1)(a).
194 *Ibid*, ss 21(2) and 112(1)(a).
195 *Ibid*, s 114(1)(b).

3) Deemed Rejected Decisions

There are three situations in which a risk assessment is deemed to have been rejected. They include where the minister of Citizenship and Immigration vacates a positive PRRA decision and where an applicant either abandons or withdraws an application.

a) Vacation

The minister of Public Safety and Emergency Preparedness can apply to vacate a positive PRRA decision if "the Minister is of the opinion that a decision to allow an application for protection was obtained as a result of directly or indirectly misrepresenting or withholding material facts on a relevant matter."[196] If a decision is vacated, the decision is also nullified, and the application is deemed to have been rejected.[197] If a person was granted permanent resident status as a result of the positive PRRA decision, the permanent resident status is also automatically nullified.[198]

While the legislation is silent regarding the procedures that the minister must follow to vacate a PRRA decision, administrative law principles of procedural fairness come into play. Any affected persons must be given notice of the application to vacate, as well as notice to appear at the vacation hearing.[199] In *Seyoboka v Canada (Minister of Citizenship and Immigration)*, it was held that a high level of procedural fairness is required in vacation proceedings.[200]

b) Abandonment

A PRRA application will be declared abandoned in two situations. The first is where an applicant fails to appear at a hearing.[201] The application is not abandoned until the applicant does not show up to a second subsequent hearing. If an applicant does not show up to the first scheduled hearing, a notice will be sent to the applicant regarding the second subsequent hearing. A failure to appear at the second hearing will lead to a declaration of abandonment of the PRRA application.[202] The second situation arises where an applicant voluntarily departs from Canada.[203]

---

196 *Ibid*, s 114(3).
197 *Ibid*, s 114(4).
198 *Ibid*, s 46.
199 See, for example, *Regulations*, above note 6, s 173; *Refugee Protection Division Rules*, SOR/2012-256, s 64.
200 2009 FC 104 at para 35.
201 *Regulations*, above note 6, s 169(a).
202 *Ibid*.
203 *Ibid*, s 169(b).

In this instance, the applicant is deemed to have ceased pursuing the application. The result is the same in both cases: the stay of removal will no longer apply and the application is deemed rejected.[204]

c) Withdrawal

A PRRA application can be withdrawn at any time by notifying the minister of Citizenship and Immigration in writing.[205] The application will be deemed withdrawn, and therefore rejected, upon receipt of the notice.[206]

4) Judicial Review

Applicants who receive a negative pre-removal risk assessment have only one method of recourse. They may apply for leave to seek judicial review of the decision to the Federal Court.[207] The regulatory stay of removal, however, ends with a negative PRRA decision. Thus, the application for leave must be accompanied by a motion seeking a judicial stay of removal to prevent the applicant from being removed from Canada before the court has rendered a decision in the judicial review.[208]

G. CONCLUSION: THE EROSION OF THE PRINCIPLE OF NON-REFOULEMENT

The barriers to applying for a pre-removal risk assessment have grown to an extent that it has now been rendered unavailable to large numbers of persons seeking to avoid being removed from Canada to their country of origin. Time restrictions, limitations on evidence that can be submitted, the grounds upon which an application may be assessed — all of these PRRA aspects have been narrowed, leaving few people fully eligible for a complete risk assessment. Coupled with the astonishingly low acceptance rates,[209] this raises the question whether the risk

---

204 *Ibid*, s 171.

205 *Ibid*, s 170.

206 *Ibid*, s 171.

207 *Federal Courts Act*, RSC 1985, c F-7, s 18(1). See Chapter 16 for more information on judicial review.

208 See, for example, *Sanchez*, above note 142; *Srignanavel v Canada (Minister of Public Safety and Emergency Preparedness)*, IMM-13055-12 (28 December 2012); and *Aguilar v Canada (Minister of Public Safety and Emergency Preparedness)*, IMM-478-12 (21 January 2013).

209 See, for example, *Nalliah*, above note 19, where Snider J commented that of all the applications processed, only about 3 percent of PRRA decisions were

assessment is functioning to ensure that Canada is meeting domestic and international obligations to prevent persons from being returned to various risks in their country of origin. Recent changes to the timelines, in effect, bar many persons from a risk assessment prior to removal, thereby raising the question whether Canada is sending people to places where they would be facing torture, death, or other cruel and unusual punishment. Indeed, even where one is afforded the opportunity to present evidence and submissions for a risk assessment, it may be limited to a narrow set of concerns couched under the umbrella of new evidence or circumstances. This is exacerbated by the criteria by which persons are denied the opportunity to have a risk assessment, particularly the criterion that renders ineligible some applicants who arrived via the United States. This criterion and the qualifications imposed on it have an arbitrary quality.

Counsel will have opportunities to challenge these new barriers. Indeed, the constitutionality of the bar to a pre-removal risk assessment for persons currently ineligible has already been raised.[210] In most recent cases, the issue is arising in motions for a stay of removal. Counsel have argued that a stay is required in order for an opportunity for pre-removal risk assessments to be completed.[211] The constitutionality of the PRRA bar has been considered as a "serious issue" and the possibility of removal before a risk assessment, as "irreparable harm" — two requirements for a stay of removal.[212]

The current government has defended the measures and tools put in place to limit access to the risk assessment, arguing that the system has simply been streamlined and that there still exists a framework under which Canada is meeting its domestic and international obligations. In the meantime, many persons will be removed, and we may never know if they would have qualified for protection under the pre-removal risk assessment.

---

favourable. See also Dragaitis, above note 19 at Appendix A, which includes information from Citizenship and Immigration Canada revealing that only 1.6 percent of failed refugee claimants received a positive PRRA decision between 2005 and 2012.

210 See the decisions of *Savunthararasa*, above note 76, and *Peter*, above note 76, where Annis J dismissed the judicial reviews challenging the constitutionality of the twelve-month bar to apply for a PRRA. Two questions were certified as questions of general importance

211 *Ibid.*

212 *Ibid.*

CHAPTER 12

APPLICATIONS MADE ON HUMANITARIAN AND COMPASSIONATE GROUNDS

A. THE HUMANITARIAN AND COMPASSIONATE (H&C) GROUNDS ASSESSMENT

The humanitarian and compassionate (H&C) grounds assessment is a discretionary device that introduces flexibility into immigration decision-making. It allows for the grant of "permanent resident status or a permanent resident visa to certain foreign nationals who would otherwise not qualify in any class."[1] The assessment enhances the attainment of the objectives of the *Immigration and Refugee Protection Act* (*IRPA*)[2] by allowing an immigration officer to weigh the reasons for admission instead of merely applying the rules found in the *IRPA* and the *Regulations*.[3]

While the IRPA provides various opportunities for H&C grounds to be considered by various decision makers, this chapter will focus on

---

1   Citizenship and Immigration Canada, "Humanitarian and Compassionate Consideration," online: CIC www.cic.gc.ca/english/resources/tools/perm/hc/index. asp [Manual: "H&C Consideration"].

2   *Immigration and Refugee Protection Act*, SC 2001, c 27 [*IRPA*].

3   Citizenship and Immigration Canada, "Humanitarian and Compassionate: Assessment of Applicants' Submissions," online: CIC www.cic.gc.ca/english/ resources/tools/perm/hc/tools/evaluation.asp [Manual: "H&C Assessment"].

the assessment found at section 25 and section 25.1 of the IRPA.[4] Sections 25(1) and 25.1(1) of the *IRPA* outline the situations in which an H&C assessment is appropriate.[5] They deal with three distinct cases: (1) applications made in Canada; (2) applications made outside Canada; and (3) cases where the minister acting on her own initiative may consider the particular circumstances of a person. Where the application is made in Canada, the minister must consider the request and may grant it where she is of the opinion that she is justified in doing so by H&C considerations, taking into account the best interests of any child directly affected.[6] For applications made outside Canada, the minister *may* consider the request and may grant it for the same reason.

A person may not have more than one H&C application pending simultaneously.[7]

The discretionary nature of the H&C assessment is the very reason that it is seen to be an "exceptional measure" or a "special grant of an exemption from a requirement" of the *IRPA*, not as an "alternative means of applying for permanent residence status in Canada."[8] Whereas formerly, the H&C application was regarded as a process to obtain an exemption from the normal expectation that persons apply for permanent residence from *outside* Canada, it is now regarded as simply an exceptional mode of obtaining permanent resident status.[9]

---

4   See for example, *IRPA*, above note 2, s 65 (the Immigration Appeal Division), s 67 (the Immigration Appeal Division), s 68 (the Immigration Appeal Division), and s 69 (the Minister).

5   *IRPA*, above note 2, ss 25(1) and 25.1.

6   *Ibid*, s 25(1).

7   *Ibid*, s 25(1.2)(a).

8   Manual: "H&C Assessment," above note 3; see also *Singh v Canada (Minister of Citizenship and Immigration)*, 2009 FC 11 at para 14 [*Singh*]; *Doumbouya v Canada (Minister of Citizenship and Immigration)*, 2007 FC 1186 [*Doumbouya*]; and *Quiroa v Canada (Minister of Citizenship and Immigration)*, 2007 FC 495.

9   *IRPA*, above note 2, ss 6 and 11(1); see also *Doumbouya*, above note 8 at para 8; *Akinbowale v Canada (Minister of Citizenship and Immigration)*, 2007 FC 1221 at paras 14 and 24; *Djerroud v Canada (Minister of Citizenship and Immigration)*, 2007 FC 981 at para 32.

B. ELIGIBILITY

1) Foreign Nationals Who Do Not Meet the *IRPA* Requirements

Foreign nationals who do not meet the requirements of the *IRPA* or its regulations may make an H&C application.[10] For example, as outlined in earlier chapters, there are only limited avenues for a foreign national to apply for permanent resident status from within Canada.[11] In most circumstances, the legislation envisages that foreign nationals will first apply for a permanent resident visa while outside Canada. The H&C assessment is one avenue by which a person may seek to be exempt from the normal requirement that one apply for permanent resident status from outside Canada.

2) Inadmissible Persons

In addition, persons who are inadmissible may make a request for H&C consideration in order to overcome their inadmissibility. Section 25(1) of the *IRPA* specifically excludes persons who are inadmissible under sections 34, 35, and 37.[12] Section 34 finds persons inadmissible on security grounds and includes acts of espionage and terrorism.[13] Section 35 deals with inadmissibility on grounds of violating human or international rights and includes war crimes and crimes against humanity.[14] Section 37 posits a person can be found inadmissible on grounds of organized criminality.[15]

3) Refugee Claimants and the Twelve-Month Bar

Refugee claimants[16] face particular restrictions. Before 28 June 2012, refugee claimants were able to make concurrent applications for refugee protection and for permanent residence on H&C grounds.[17] Today,

---

10   *IRPA*, above note 2, s 25(1).
11   See Chapters 5 and 6.
12   *IRPA*, above note 2, s 25(1). See Chapter 12.
13   *Ibid*, s 34.
14   *Ibid*, s 35.
15   *Ibid*, s 36.
16   *Ibid*, s 25(1.02). See Chapters 9 & 10.
17   Citizenship and Immigration Canada, "Operational Bulletin 440-B" (15 August 2013), online: CIC www.cic.gc.ca/english/resources/manuals/bulletins/2013/ob440B.asp.

concurrent applications are not permitted.[18] If a person has made a claim for refugee protection that is pending before the Refugee Protection Division (RPD) or Refugee Appeal Division (RAD) at the Immigration and Refugee Board (IRB), an H&C application will not be examined.[19] Further, after a determination has been made at the RPD or RAD, a refugee claimant is not eligible to make an H&C application until twelve months after the final determination of a refugee claim where the resolution is one of abandonment, withdrawal, or rejection.[20]

After submitting a claim, a refugee claimant may choose to withdraw it in order to submit an H&C application, if he meets one requirement: the claim must be withdrawn before any evidence is heard by the RPD.[21] The choice to withdraw a claim to submit an H&C application is fraught with risk, however. Where a refugee claimant enjoys the benefit of a *de facto* stay of removal while the refugee claim is pending[22] and a regulatory stay of removal while seeking judicial review of a negative refugee determination,[23] an H&C applicant does not.

The effect of the twelve-month bar is that refugee claimants are excluded from the complementary protection provided by a grant of status on H&C grounds. Refugee claimants are thus forced to guess and gamble as to whether it is in their best interest to submit a refugee claim or an H&C application.

In reality, unsuccessful refugee claimants may never have an opportunity to make a viable H&C application. Removal processes are triggered the instant a refugee claim has been rejected, withdrawn, or abandoned. The delay of twelve months allows removals officers to proceed with removal, thereby denying failed refugee claimants any other route for obtaining status in Canada. While technically true that an H&C application can be made outside the country, the likelihood of providing a viable or successful application is diminished because certain important criteria will not be met. For example, it will be difficult to fulfill requirements regarding establishment in Canada once the person is removed from Canada.

---

18   *IRPA*, above note 2, ss 25(1.2)(b) & (c).

19   *Ibid*, s 25(1.2)(b).

20   *Ibid*, s 25(1.2)(c).

21   *Ibid*.

22   *Immigration and Refugee Protection Regulations*, SOR/2002-227, s 228(3) [*Regulations*], which specifies that refugee claimants are subject to departure orders that will not be enforced until a determination has been made at the IRB.

23   *Ibid*, ss 231(1) and 233: A stay is available only where the minister is of the opinion that a stay is justifiable on H&C grounds.

There are some exceptions to the rule prohibiting H&C applications within the twelve-month time frame following the rejection, abandonment, or withdrawal of a refugee claim. Refugee claimants who fall into one of the two exceptional categories may file an application for an assessment on H&C grounds within the twelve-month period following a final decision on their refugee claim.[24] The two exceptions are as follows:

1) persons subject to a risk to their life in the country of nationality or former habitual residence due to inadequate health or medical care;[25] and

2) persons whose removal would have an adverse effect on the best interests of a child affected.[26]

For those that do not meet the exceptions, the twelve-month bar is a harsh tool that excludes classes of persons that might otherwise benefit from an H&C application. The twelve-month bar assumes that persons who receive a negative refugee decision do not have *bona fide* reasons to request exemption from the provisions in the *IRPA*. The time limitation also assumes that failed refugee claimants are simply seeking to have their claim reheard. This notion is based on the view that H&C applications assess the same factors as refugee hearings. However, the criteria considered in refugee determination differ significantly from those considered in an H&C assessment.[27] Risks recognized in section 96 or 97 are not evaluated in H&C assessments. An H&C application does not provide an individual with a second chance under the same criteria. A refugee claimant who does not satisfy section 96 or 97 of the *IRPA* may nevertheless have suffered or may be likely to suffer different forms of hardship that may be reason to grant status on humanitarian and compassionate grounds. The twelve-month bar, however, blocks any possibility of reviewing an applicant's situation in this light.

4) Persons under a Removal Order with No Statutory Stay

Applicants under a removal order may submit an H&C application, but unlike most applicants submitting pre-removal risk assessments

---

24   *Ibid*, s 25(1.2).
25   *Ibid*, s 25(1.2)(a).
26   *Ibid*, s 25(1.2)(b).
27   See Chapter 9, which discusses inland refugee claims. See also Section D(3), below in this chapter, which outlines the H&C criteria in general. See, for example, *Kanthasamy*, below note 101.

(PRRA),[28] these applicants will not enjoy the benefit of a stay of removal.[29] An applicant will have her application processed and is entitled to a decision, but is not able to stay in Canada as a result of a pending application, unless exceptional circumstances warrant a stay of removal.[30]

Where an applicant is removed prior to any assessment being made on an H&C application, the H&C application will be considered after removal.[31] An applicant who receives a positive assessment and is otherwise not inadmissible to Canada may be allowed to return to Canada for further processing.[32]

5) Designated Foreign Nationals and the Five-Year Bar[33]

Designated foreign nationals are barred from making an application for permanent residence on H&C grounds until five years after they have received a final refugee determination,[34] a final PRRA decision, or in any other case,[35] after being designated.[36] Where a person has submitted an H&C application and subsequently becomes a designated foreign national, the H&C application is suspended if the person has also

---

28   See Chapter 11 on pre-removal risk assessments.

29   *Regulations*, above note 22, ss 162 and 232, outline regulatory stays of removals for PRRA applicants. Note that in the two circumstances where a notification of eligibility for a pre-removal risk of assessment is not required (where a person is applying at a port of entry and where someone is reapplying after a negative PRRA decision), there will be no mandatory stay. See Chapter 11.

30   *Ibid*, s 233: the minister can make a stay of removal if she finds it is justified by H&C considerations or by public policy considerations; see *Firsova v Canada (Minister of Citizenship and Immigration)*, 2003 FC 933 at para 6; *Thirunavukkarasu v Canada (Minister of Citizenship and Immigration)*, 2003 FC 1075 at para 4; and *Wynne v Canada (Minister of Citizenship and Immigration)*, 2010 FC 440 at para 24, where the court discusses that there must be exceptional circumstances to warrant a stay where an H&C application is pending.

31   Citizenship and Immigration Canada, "Humanitarian and Compassionate Consideration Stage 1 Processing in Canada: Applicants under a Removal Order," online: CIC www.cic.gc.ca/english/resources/tools/perm/hc/processing/canada/removal.asp [Manual: "Applicants under a Removal Order"].

32   *Regulations*, above note 22, s 67; Citizenship and Immigration Canada, "Humanitarian and Compassionate Consideration in Canada: Positive Stage 1 Assessment – Applicant Has Left Canada," online: CIC www.cic.gc.ca/english/resources/tools/perm/hc/processing/canada/left-1.asp [Manual: "Applicant Has Left Canada"].

33   For more information on designated foreign nationals, see Chapter 9 on inland refugees.

34   *IRPA*, above note 2, s 25(1.01)(a).

35   *Ibid*, s 25(1.01)(b).

36   *Ibid*, s 25(1.01)(c).

made a refugee claim and/or PRRA application and has not received a final determination within the last five years,[37] or has been a designated foreign national for less than five years.[38]

As discussed above,[39] being barred from making an H&C application has serious consequences for potential applicants.

6) Ministerial Instructions and H&C Applications

The minister of Citizenship and Immigration has issued instructions that provide:

> **No Humanitarian and Compassionate requests to overcome requirements of Ministerial Instructions**
> Requests made on the basis of Humanitarian and Compassionate grounds from outside Canada that accompany any permanent resident application affected by Ministerial Instructions but not identified for processing under the Instructions will not be processed.[40]

As a result of this instruction, it appears that foreign nationals may not seek H&C exemption from the requirements found in ministerial instructions[41] that identify criteria governing applications for a permanent resident visa.[42]

7) Permanent Residents or Canadian Citizens

Persons who already have permanent resident or citizenship status lack any need to apply for an H&C assessment as they enjoy all the rights accorded to their status. There are no additional rights to be gained from obtaining an exemption through an H&C application. However, those who have lost their permanent resident or citizenship status are eligible to make an H&C application.

---

37   *Ibid*, ss 25(1.02)(a) & (b).
38   *Ibid*, s 25(1.02)(c).
39   See Section B(3), above in this chapter.
40   Minister of Citizenship and Immigration Canada, Updated Ministerial Instructions, *Canada Gazette* (30 June 2012), online: http://gazette.gc.ca/rp-pr/p1/2012/2012-06-30/html/notice-avis-eng.html#d118.
41   For more information on ministerial instructions, see Chapter 2.
42   See the *IRPA*, above note 2, s 87.3(4), which states: "Officers and persons authorized to exercise the powers of the Minister under section 25 shall comply with any instructions before processing an application or request or when processing one. If an application or request is not processed, it may be retained, returned or otherwise disposed of in accordance with the instructions of the Minister."

8) Spouse or Common Law Partner of a Canadian or Permanent Resident

Spouses or common law partners of Canadian citizens or permanent residents may apply for permanent resident status based on their status as a spouse or common law partner.[43] There are instances where a spouse or common law partner, however, may not satisfy the eligibility requirements for the spouse or common law partner class. In such cases, they may submit H&C applications to ask that they be exempt from the applicable requirements.

Where an H&C applicant is a spouse or common law partner of a sponsor[44] and cohabits with that sponsor in Canada,[45] Citizenship and Immigration Canada (CIC) has adopted the policy of processing the applications as sponsorship applications under the spouse or common law partner in Canada class.[46] Where a sponsor is not in Canada[47] or where the spouse or common law partner is not in Canada,[48] however, the application will be processed as an H&C application and not under the spouse or common law partner in Canada class.[49] In all cases, the applicant must make an explicit request for consideration of H&C grounds.[50] An officer is not obligated to review H&C grounds where an applicant fails to make the explicit request.

---

43   *Regulations*, above note 22, ss 123–24.

44   See *ibid*, s 130: Sponsors are persons who are Canadian citizens or permanent residents over the age of eighteen and reside in Canada. A person residing outside Canada can be a sponsor only if he is a Canadian citizen and will reside in Canada once the sponsored person becomes a permanent resident. Further, if the sponsor had been sponsored herself, she must have resided as a permanent resident for five years immediately preceding the day on which she submits a sponsorship application. For more information, see Chapter 6.

45   *Ibid*, ss 124(a)–(b).

46   Citizenship and Immigration Canada, Operational Manual IP 8: *Spouse or Common Law Partner in Canada Class*, online: CIC www.cic.gc.ca/english/resources/manuals/ip/ip08-eng.pdf at 5.1.

47   *Regulations*, above note 22, s 124(a).

48   *Ibid*, s 124(b).

49   Citizenship and Immigration Canada, "The Humanitarian and Compassionate Assessment: Dealing with Family Relationships," online: CIC www.cic.gc.ca/english/resources/tools/perm/hc/processing/family.asp. The manual notes that the applicant, not the sponsor, must request that the application be reviewed on H&C grounds in both cases where the sponsor is not eligible to sponsor or the applicant does not meet the *IRPA* or the *Regulations*.

50   Citizenship and Immigration Canada, "Humanitarian and Compassionate Consideration Stage 1 Processing in Canada: Applicants with Family Relationships," online: CIC www.cic.gc.ca/english/resources/tools/perm/hc/processing/canada/fam.asp.

C. PROCESS

An application for permanent residence on H&C grounds must comply with the requirements listed in the *IRPA*, section 25, and the *Regulations* in order to be assessed.[51] An applicant must be prepared to pay fees associated with the application and provide the pertinent forms and written material to support the application.

1) Fees

An applicant must pay the applicable fee in order for the application to be assessed.[52] Persons who are exempt from paying fees include protected persons and their family members, which include Convention refugees under section 96 of the *IRPA* or protected persons under section 97 of the *IRPA*.[53] Dependent children of any Canadian citizens or permanent residents who are the principal applicants of an H&C application are also exempt from paying fees.[54]

Where the minister has on his own initiative undertaken an H&C assessment, he may exempt an applicant from paying applicable fees.[55] While a minister is obliged to consider a request for exemption from the requirement to pay a fee, the Federal Court of Appeal has held that the failure to grant the request or the failure of the government to legislate exemptions for indigent applicants in Canada does not infringe the *Charter of Rights and Freedoms*, sections 7 and 15; the rule of law; or the common law constitutional right of access to the courts.[56]

2) Paper Application

An H&C application must be made in writing.[57] In the case of a person requesting to remain in Canada, the application must accompany an

---

51   *IRPA*, above note 2, s 175(1).
52   *Ibid*, s 25(1.03); *Regulations*, above note 22, ss 295(1)(c) and 307. For an applicant to remain in Canada as a permanent resident, currently, the fees are as follows: principal applicant ($550); family member of principal applicant who is a spouse or common law partner ($550); and family member of a principal applicant who is a dependent child ($150).
53   *IRPA*, above note 2, s 95(2); *Regulations*, above note 22, ss 295(2) and 301(1.1).
54   Citizenship and Immigration Canada, "Guide 5291 — Humanitarian and Compassionate Considerations" (21 November 2014), online: CIC www.cic.gc.ca/english/information/applications/guides/5291ETOC.asp#5291E5.
55   *IRPA*, above note 2, s 25.1(2).
56   *Toussaint v Canada (Minister of Citizenship and Immigration)*, 2011 FCA 146.
57   *Regulations*, above note 22, s 66.

application for permanent residence.[58] For persons outside Canada, the application must accompany an application for a permanent resident visa.[59]

Although officers have the discretion to interview an applicant, they are not required to do so even when there are ambiguities in an application.[60] Only when an officer has given reason for the applicant to believe that there is a legitimate expectation for an interview or where an officer makes a finding solely on credibility may an officer need to conduct an interview.[61]

In the Supreme Court of Canada case of *Baker v Canada (Minister of Citizenship and Immigration)*, L'Heureux-Dubé J analyzed the issue thus:

> [A]n oral hearing is not a general requirement for H&C decisions. An interview is not essential for the information relevant to an H&C application to be put before an immigration officer, so that the humanitarian and compassionate considerations presented may be considered in their entirety and in a fair manner. In this case, the appellant had the opportunity to put forward, in written form through her lawyer, information about her situation, her children, and their emotional dependence on her, and documentation in support of her application . . . . These documents were before the decision-makers, and they contained the information relevant to making this decision. Taking all the factors relevant to determining the content of the duty of fairness into account, the lack of an oral hearing or notice of such a hearing did not, in my opinion, constitute a violation of the requirements of procedural fairness . . . .[62]

---

58   *Ibid.*

59   *Ibid.*

60   See, for example, *Tharmaseelan v Canada (Minister of Citizenship and Immigration)*, 2003 FCT 694 at para 11, where the court stated: "It cannot be the case that Immigration Officers who are under no obligation to interview H & C applicants are under an obligation to take the initiative and update the facts which might support an applicant's H & C application." See also *Kuhathasan v Canada (Minister of Citizenship and Immigration)*, 2008 FC 457 at para 34, where the court stated, "There is no statutory right to an oral interview and no obligation to interview applicants in order to clarify ambiguities in an application."

61   See, for example, *Rafieyan v Canada (Minister of Citizenship and Immigration)*, 2007 FC 727 at para 37, where the court stated: "A legitimate expectation of an interview in these circumstances would have to be based on a clear, unambiguous and unqualified representation." See also *Duka v Canada (Minister of Citizenship and Immigration)*, 2010 FC 1071 at para 13, where the court stated that "an oral interview may have been required where the impugned decision is based on an adverse credibility finding."

62   [1999] 2 SCR 817 at para 34 [*Baker*].

While an officer may not be obligated to interview or meet with the applicant and his family, when the officer does, the officer may not rely unduly on the information obtained in the interview without assessing the documentary evidence submitted.[63]

3) Onus on Applicant

The onus is on the applicant to present reasons why the minister or ministerial delegate should exempt the applicant from the regular requirements under the *IRPA*.[64] An applicant must be clear in explaining what hardship she would face if not granted an exemption. There is no obligation on the part of the decision maker to elicit information or investigate whether certain grounds are not applicable.[65] The onus is entirely upon the applicant to provide evidence and submissions as to which H&C factors are alive in the application and why they justify granting an exemption.[66]

Although the applicant has the burden to provide pertinent information, an officer may consider extrinsic or third party evidence. According to principles of procedural fairness, the officer owes a duty to the applicant to disclose the use of extrinsic evidence and provide an opportunity for the applicant to respond to such evidence.[67]

---

63 See, for example, *Terigho v Canada (Minister of Citizenship and Immigration)*, 2006 FC 835 at para 9.

64 See, for example, *Thandal v Canada (Minister of Citizenship and Immigration)*, 2008 FC 489 at para 9, where the court stated, "It is well established that an applicant has the burden of establishing her case." See also *Gallardo v Canada (Minister of Citizenship and Immigration)*, 2003 FCT 45 at para 28, where the court stated, "As stated in the Immigration Manual, and is well-known to counsel, the applicants bear the onus of satisfying the decision-maker that their personal circumstances are such that the hardship of having to obtain an immigration visa from outside of Canada would be an unusual and undeserved or disproportionate hardship." Other examples: *Owusu v Canada (Minister of Citizenship and Immigration)*, 2003 FCT 94 at para 11; *Robertson v Canada (Minister of Citizenship and Immigration)*, 2002 FCT 763 at para 12.

65 *Ibid.*

66 *Ibid.*

67 See, for example, *Phillip v Canada (Minister of Citizenship and Immigration)*, 2008 FC 19 at para 9; and *Tikaprasad v Canada (Minister of Citizenship and Immigration)*, 2005 FC 843 at para 10.

4) Temporary Resident Permit (TRP)

Applicants who do not have valid status may be advised to apply for a temporary resident permit (TRP)[68] in conjunction with the H&C application. Where an applicant makes a TRP request, it must be considered, and a failure to do so is a reviewable error.[69] Reasons for denying a temporary resident permit, however, can be based on the same grounds as those of a decision for an H&C application.[70]

5) Assessing Officer

An application may be assessed by a delegate of the minister of Citizenship and Immigration. In *Krotov v Canada (Minister of Citizenship and Immigration)*, where the applicant's H&C application and pre-removal risk assessment (PRRA) were both denied, the same officer made both the H&C assessment and the risk assessment.[71] Krotov challenged the minister's authority to delegate decision-making power over his H&C application to an officer of the Canada Border Services Agency (CBSA), arguing that the officer was not under the direction of the minister. On judicial review, the Federal Court found that the minister could delegate authority to a CBSA officer to assess an H&C application.[72]

In the case of *Oshurova v Canada (Minister of Citizenship and Immigration)*, the applicant did not challenge the appropriateness of a CBSA officer as the delegate but argued that the delegation of two separate applications by the same person (H&C and PRRA applications) to the same officer raised a reasonable apprehension of bias. The Federal Court of Appeal rejected the argument.[73]

6) Two-Step Assessment Process

Ministerial guidelines specify that once an applicant is determined eligible to make an H&C application, the assessment goes through two steps.[74] The first step involves an assessment of the humanitarian and

---

68   See Chapter 4.

69   See, for example, *Shah v Canada (Minister of Citizenship and Immigration)*, 2011 FC 1269 at para 77.

70   See, for example, *Ferraro v Canada (Minister of Citizenship and Immigration)*, 2011 FC 801 at para 25.

71   2005 FC 438.

72   *Ibid.*

73   2006 FCA 301.

74   Citizenship and Immigration Canada, "Humanitarian and Compassionate: Processing in-Canada Applications," online: CIC www.cic.gc.ca/english/resources/

compassionate grounds. At the second stage, a decision is made on whether permanent resident status (for applicants in Canada) or a visa (for those outside Canada) should be granted.

This two-step process has been challenged unsuccessfully in the Federal Court. In *Espino v Canada (Minister of Citizenship and Immigration)*, the court found that this assessment process is not contrary to the *IRPA* or its regulations and is supportable within the intent and terms of the legislation.[75]

a) Stage 1: Approval in Principle

The first assessment determines whether the H&C application may be approved in principle. At this stage, the decision maker decides whether there are sufficient humanitarian and compassionate grounds to grant an exemption. The standard of proof an officer uses is the civil standard of balance of probabilities, asking whether it is more likely than not that the evidence presented is true.[76]

Where an applicant receives a negative first-stage decision, the H&C application is denied.[77] Where approval in principle has been granted at the first stage, the applicant will be notified that the exemption from eligibility criteria has been granted, but that the applicant and his dependants still need to meet admissibility requirements in a permanent residence application.[78] Applicants are either given temporary resident status, granted an extension in their temporary resident status, or allowed to apply for a new temporary resident permit as a result of this

---

tools/perm/hc/processing/canada/index.asp [Manual: "Processing in-Canada Applications"]; and Citizenship and Immigration Canada, "Humanitarian and Compassionate: Processing Applications from outside Canada," online: CIC www.cic.gc.ca/english/resources/tools/perm/hc/processing/out/index.asp.

75   2007 FC 74.

76   See, for example, *Chekroun v Canada (Minister of Citizenship and Immigration)*, 2013 FC 737 at para 94 [*Chekroun*]; Citizenship and Immigration Canada, "Humanitarian and Compassionate Consideration Stage 1 Processing in Canada: All Applicants," online: CIC www.cic.gc.ca/english/resources/tools/perm/hc/processing/canada/all.asp.

77   Citizenship and Immigration Canada, Humanitarian and Compassionate Consideration Stage 1 Approval in Canada: "Procedures following a Negative Stage 1 Assessment," online: CIC www.cic.gc.ca/english/resources/tools/perm/hc/processing/canada/negative-1.asp.

78   Citizenship and Immigration Canada, Humanitarian and Compassionate Consideration Stage 1 Approval in Canada: "General Procedures following a Positive Stage 1 Assessment," online: CIC www.cic.gc.ca/english/resources/tools/perm/hc/processing/canada/positive-1.asp.

first-stage approval.[79] The applicant enjoys a regulatory stay of removal until a decision has been rendered on the application for permanent residence.[80]

Stage 1 approval is an interim decision and, therefore, should any significant information or evidence come to the attention of a decision maker affecting the stage 1 approval, such as the breakdown of a relationship, an officer may consider the evidence and revisit the approval.[81]

Applicants who receive stage 1 approval should be cautioned about leaving Canada. Stage 1 approval provides only temporary resident status; there is no guarantee that permanent resident status will be given. Stage 1 approval leads to some relief so that the applicant can obtain temporary resident status and a stay of removal. Applicants who travel outside Canada after a positive stage 1 assessment may not be readmitted. Readmission into Canada is at the discretion of the border official at the port of entry. Applicants are therefore advised in their notification that "if you leave Canada, there is no guarantee that you will be readmitted to continue with this application."[82]

For applicants who have complied with a removal order and left Canada before a stage 1 decision, a stage 1 approval in an H&C application does not guarantee that the applicants will be readmitted because readmission into Canada is at the discretion of the border official.[83] Applicants outside Canada will receive notification of their stage 1 approval from a local visa office.[84]

b) Stage 2: Assessing Permanent Residence Eligibility

Stage 2 begins the processing of an application for permanent residence or, where the individual is outside Canada, an application for a permanent resident visa. The officer in evaluating such applications deter-

---

79   *Ibid*; Citizenship and Immigration Canada, Humanitarian and Compassionate Consideration Stage 1 Approval in Canada: "Positive Stage 1 Assessment — Interim Documentation," online: CIC www.cic.gc.ca/english/resources/tools/perm/hc/processing/canada/documentation-interim.asp; *Regulations*, above note 22, ss 207(d) and 215(1)(g): At this point, the application for permanent residence begins to be processed, and the applicant can apply for a work permit and/or a study permit.

80   *Ibid*, s 233.

81   See, for example, *Abbott v Canada (Citizenship and Immigration)*, 2011 FC 344 at para 47.

82   *Regulations*, above note 22, s 63(b).

83   Manual: "Applicant Has Left Canada," above note 32; see *Regulations*, above note 22, s 238.

84   *Ibid*.

mines if the applicant is otherwise admissible and meets all other *IRPA* requirements, including the requirements for permanent residency.

At this stage, applicants and their family members will undergo medical, security, and criminal checks to assess whether they meet with admissibility requirements.[85] Family members abroad will undergo similar checks via a visa office.[86]

7) Final Examination

Where the application has been made in Canada, the final step to an approved H&C application is a mandatory interview where an officer verifies documents, identification, and information.[87] Where there is information that there are outstanding issues, an officer may postpone this interview. Outstanding issues may include the incomplete examination of family members for admissibility purposes, outstanding criminal charges, and questions as to whether the applicant and her family receive social assistance (if they did not receive an exemption for this factor).[88] Should applicants fail to attend the interview, the application for permanent residence may be refused.[89]

D. EVALUATING THE APPLICATION

1) Balancing Flexibility and Consistency

Citizenship and Immigration Canada recommends to its officers that when exercising the discretionary power delegated to them by the minister, they should also place value on consistency of decisions: "Effective decision-making in H&C cases involves striking a balance between

---

85 See, for example, *IRPA*, above note 2, ss 15–16 and 21(1); *Regulations*, above note 22, ss 29–42 (medical examinations) and ss 12.1 and 13–13.11 (security and criminal information).

86 See, for example, *ibid*, s 30, which lists who is exempt from medical examinations. Those not listed in s 30 must undergo a medical examination.

87 *IRPA*, above note 2, s 21(1); Citizenship and Immigration Canada, "Humanitarian and Compassionate Consideration in Canada: Processing the Application for Permanent Residence Stage 2 Assessment," online: CIC www.cic.gc.ca/english/resources/tools/perm/hc/processing/canada/positive-2.asp.

88 *Ibid*.

89 Manual: "Processing in-Canada Applications," above note 74: "If correspondence is returned or applicant does not respond, check that the correct address was used and if applicable that counsel was copied. The application must be processed through to a decision (i.e. approval or refusal)."

certainty and consistency on the one hand and of flexibility to deal with the specific facts of a case, on the other."[90] Decision makers may turn not only to legislation and subordinate legislation, but also to policy statements, guidelines, manuals, and handbooks to aid them in making a decision.[91]

2) Standard of Proof

An applicant will normally be required to prove the facts on which the application is based on the balance of probabilities. The officer will ask, is it more likely than not that the evidence or information is true?[92]

Citizenship and Immigration's operational manual provides the following guide:

> Once all elements of the case have been determined, using the appropriate standard of proof, assess all facts in the application and decide whether a refusal to grant the request for an exemption would, more likely than not, result in unusual and underserved or disproportionate hardship.[93]

This rule is tempered by the standards that apply when determining whether a person is inadmissible. A lower standard of proof may, in some circumstances, be used to evaluate the application. The officer may ask whether there are reasonable grounds to believe that the applicant is inadmissible.[94] For example, a person may be determined to be inadmissible on grounds of criminality under section 36 of the *IRPA* where there are reasonable grounds to believe that the individual has committed a crime.

After determining whether the information and evidence provided in the application are trustworthy, an officer will then determine whether a denial of the application will result in unusual, undeserved, or disproportionate hardship.

---

90 Citizenship and Immigration Canada, "The Humanitarian and Compassionate Assessment: Balance between Discretion and Consistency," online: CIC www.cic.gc.ca/english/resources/tools/perm/hc/processing/balance.asp.

91 *Baker*, above note 62; *Thamotharem v Canada (Minister of Citizenship and Immigration)*, 2007 FCA 198.

92 See, for example, *Chekroun*, above note 76 at para 94; *Jamshedji v Canada (Minister of Citizenship and Immigration)*, [2011] IADD No 2985 at para 7 (CA IRB).

93 Citizenship and Immigration Canada, "The Humanitarian and Compassionate Assessment: Threshold of Proof," online: CIC www.cic.gc.ca/english/resources/tools/perm/hc/processing/proof.asp.

94 *IRPA*, above note 2, s 33; see also ss 34–37. See Chapter 14.

3) Criteria

Although the language of "humanitarian" and "compassionate" suggests a broad, open-ended discretionary power, the officer's choices are circumscribed by legislative requirements to examine various factors to see if they support the conclusion that the applicant should be exempted from the requirements in the *IRPA*. Officers are mandated to take a global perspective in assessing the various factors that inform a decision; no single criterion outweighs any other.[95] An officer has a duty to look at all of the applicant's personal circumstances, including the beliefs and motivations of the applicant.[96] The following are some of the key factors that decision makers should consider when evaluating an application.

a) Hardship

Many applications made by foreign nationals in Canada hinge on the claim that the applicant would face unusual, undeserved, or disproportionate hardship if required to either file an application from outside Canada or be forced to leave Canada.[97] Outside Canada, applications may be based on the claim that an individual would face hardship if not granted an exemption or a visa.[98] The operational manual provides some assistance on what is meant by "unusual, undeserved or disproportionate." It defines *unusual* and *undeserved hardship* as follows:

- The hardship faced by the applicant (if they were not granted the requested exemption) must be, in most cases, unusual. In other words, a hardship not anticipated or addressed by the *Act* or *Regulations*; and
- The hardship faced by the applicant (if they were not granted the requested exemption) must be undeserved so in most cases, the result of circumstances beyond the person's control.[99]

---

95 *Begum v Canada (Minister of Citizenship and Immigration)*, 2013 FC 265 at para 20, where the court stated, "The weighing of a particular factor . . . is for the Officer to determine"; *Gomez v Canada (Minister of Citizenship and Immigration)*, 2010 FC 1301 at para 29.

96 *Hinzman v Canada (Minister of Citizenship and Immigration)*, 2010 FCA 177.

97 *Doumbouya*, above note 8 at para 8; *Paul v Canada (Minister of Citizenship and Immigration)*, 2013 FC 1081; *Ek v Canada (Minister of Citizenship and Immigration)*, 2003 FCT 526.

98 Citizenship and Immigration Canada, "The Humanitarian and Compassionate Assessment: Hardship and the H&C Assessment," online: CIC www.cic.gc.ca/english/resources/tools/perm/hc/processing/hardship.asp.

99 *Ibid.*

The operational manual defines *disproportionate hardship* in this way:

> Sufficient humanitarian and compassionate grounds may also exist in cases that do not meet the "unusual and undeserved" criteria but where the hardship of not being granted the requested exemption(s) would have an unreasonable impact on the applicant due to their personal circumstances.[100]

The operational manual also provides a list of factors that a decision maker may consider when determining whether there is sufficient hardship:

1) factors in the applicant's country of origin, including but not limited to medical inadequacies and discrimination that does not amount to persecution, harassment, or other hardships described in sections 96 and 97 of the *IRPA*;[101]
2) establishment in Canada, ties to Canada, or the applicant's inability to leave Canada, which can lead to establishment;[102]
3) best interests of any children affected by the application;[103]
4) family violence considerations;[104]
5) consequences of the separation of relatives;[105] and
6) health considerations.[106]

The Federal Court has stated that "[h]ardship that is inherent in having to leave Canada is not enough."[107] Similarly, hardship consequent on a separation from family and friends or the leaving of employment or residence will not necessarily merit an exemption from

---

100 *Ibid.*
101 *Ibid*; see *White v Canada (Minister of Citizenship and Immigration)*, 2011 FC 1043 at para 34; *Bagwandeen v Canada (Minister of Citizenship and Immigration)*, 2005 FC 661 at para 16; *George v Canada (Minister of Citizenship and Immigration)*, 2007 FC 1315 at paras 16–18; *Kanthasamy v Canada (Minister of Citizenship and Immigration)*, 2013 FC 802 at paras 19 and 37 [*Kanthasamy*].
102 Establishment: *Judnarine v Canada (Minister of Citizenship and Immigration)*, 2013 FC 82 at para 31; ties: *Diabate v Canada (Minister of Citizenship and Immigration)*, 2013 FC 129 at para 28; inability to leave: *Bansal v Canada (Minister of Citizenship and Immigration)*, 2006 FC 226 [*Bansal*].
103 *Leobrera v Canada (Minister of Citizenship and Immigration)*, 2010 FC 587 [*Leobrera*]; *Hawthorne v Canada (Minister of Citizenship and Immigration)*, 2002 FCA 475 [*Hawthorne*].
104 *Swartz v Canada (Minister of Citizenship and Immigration)*, 2002 FCT 268.
105 *Matthias v Canada (Minister of Citizenship and Immigration)*, 2014 FC 1053.
106 *Ashraf v Canada (Minister of Citizenship and Immigration)*, 2013 FC 1160.
107 *Singh*, above note 8 at para 20; *Doumbouya*, above note 8 at para 10.

the *IRPA*.[108] Hardship must be more than an "inconvenience," and the applicant must meet a "high threshold" when requesting an exemption from the *IRPA*.[109]

It is important to note that the *IRPA* distinguishes between hardship and the types of risk that may ground a refugee claim and a pre-removal risk assessment.[110]

i) Hardship in Country of Origin

a. Excluding Persecution or Torture

In June 2010, Parliament passed amendments to the *IRPA* that reduced the discretionary powers of a decision maker reviewing an H&C application.[111] Section 25(1.3) states:

> (1.3) Non-application of certain factors – In examining the request of a foreign national in Canada, the Minister may not consider the factors that are taken into account in the determination of whether a person is a Convention refugee under section 96 or a person in need of protection under subsection 97(1) but must consider elements related to the hardships that affect the foreign national.[112]

Although an applicant is able to present evidence of risks under sections 96 and 97 in a pre-removal risk assessment (PRRA), eliminating the discretion to review such risks in an H&C application is severely detrimental to applicants and unnecessarily restrictive. It would appear that the government views the evaluation of factors under sections 96 and 97 in H&C applications as an improper opportunity for an applicant to have a refugee claim reassessed. This perspective, however, conflates the refugee determination process and the H&C application process. Each process is entirely distinct. As discussed in more detail below, hardship under an H&C application requires a different assessment than a risk assessment. By excluding the evidence of risks under sections 96 and 97 in an H&C application, an officer is given only a partial picture of the individual's life. It is also unlikely that the H&C assessment has been rendered more efficient by excluding this evidence.

---

108 *Williams v Canada (Minister of Citizenship and Immigration)*, 2006 FC 1474 [*Williams*].

109 *Ibid.*

110 *Kanthasamy*, above note 101 at para 16; *Thalang v Canada (Minister of Citizenship and Immigration)*, 2008 FC 340.

111 Canada, Bill C-11, *An Act to amend the Immigration and Refugee Protection Act and the Federal Courts Act*, 3rd Sess, 40th Parl, 2010 (assented to 29 June 2010), SC 2010, c 8.

112 *IRPA*, above note 2, s 25(1.3).

The task of distinguishing which factors should be considered and which should not is both difficult and time consuming.

In the face of the legislative constraint, applicants will benefit by characterizing issues they will face in their home country as hardship rather than as risks, and also by trying to describe the hardship in a way that avoids the language found in sections 96 and 97 of the *IRPA*. The Federal Court has attempted, with limited success, to develop a test to be used to distinguish between hardship and the risks in question.[113] For example, in the case of *Ba v Canada (Minister of Citizenship and Immigration)*, the court states:

> While PRRA and H&C applications take risk into account, the manner in which they are assessed is quite different. In the context of a PRRA, "risk" as per section 97 of *IRPA* involves assessing whether the applicant would be personally subjected to a danger of torture or to a risk to life or to cruel and unusual treatment or punishment.
>
> In an H&C application, however, risk should be addressed as but one of the factors relevant to determining whether the applicant would face unusual, and undeserved or disproportionate hardship. Thus the focus is on hardship, which has a risk component, not on risk as such.
>
> In general terms, it is more difficult for a PRRA applicant to establish risk than it is for an H&C applicant to establish hardship.[114]

Thus, applicants should include all details of any kind of risk of harm that would contribute to their submissions for hardship but focus on the consequential hardships ensuing as a result of facing the risks in question.

b.   Discrimination *Not* Amounting to Persecution

Discrimination that does not amount to persecution may fall within the ambit of section 25(1.3). An officer may consider whether discrimination itself amounts to hardship.[115] The Supreme Court of Canada has described discrimination as

---

113 *Sha'er v Canada (Minister of Citizenship and Immigration)*, 2007 FC 231 at paras 8–9 [*Sha'er*]; *Pinter v Canada (Minister of Citizenship and Immigration)*, 2005 FC 296 at para 304; *Ramirez v Canada (Minister of Citizenship and Immigration)*, 2006 FC 1404 at paras 42 and 47; *Sahota v Canada (Minister of Citizenship and Immigration)*, 2007 FC 651 at para 12; *Pacia v Canada (Minister of Citizenship and Immigration)*, 2008 FC 804 at paras 12–13.

114 2009 FC 287 at para 37 [footnotes omitted]; see also *Melchor v Canada (Minister of Citizenship and Immigration)*, 2004 FC 1327 at para 16; and *Dharamraj v Canada (Minister of Citizenship and Immigration)*, 2006 FC 674.

115 *Sha'er*, above note 113; *Kanthasamy*, above note 101.

a distinction, whether intentional or not but based on grounds relating to personal characteristics of the individual or group, which has the effect of imposing burdens, obligations, or disadvantages on such individual or group not imposed upon others, or which withholds or limits access to opportunities, benefits, and advantages available to other members of society. Distinctions based on personal characteristics attributed to an individual solely on the basis of association with a group will rarely escape the charge of discrimination, while those based on an individual's merits and capacities will rarely be so classed.[116]

It has been held that discrimination can amount to persecution if it is "serious" or "persistent" such that it violates a fundamental human right and leads to grave personal consequences.[117] However, an applicant could face discrimination that does not amount to persecution. Discrimination could manifest in isolated incidents or permeate systemically. A series of discriminatory events that do not give rise to persecution must be considered cumulatively.[118] Applicants face the bizarre and indefensible burden of showing that they face discrimination that will be sufficiently serious to cause hardship but insufficiently serious to count as persecution. For those with failed refugee claims, the fact that the risks assessed were found to be undeserving of refugee protection should bolster the view that there are significant hardships that should be assessed in an H&C application.

Applicants should provide information about any discrimination experienced in the past and also their perspective as to prospective discrimination. They should supplement this evidence with documentary evidence detailing discrimination against similarly situated persons and address whether or not there are any avenues for recourse. Applicants should also provide information about the prospect of relocating within the country of origin and whether that would affect the prospective chance of experiencing discrimination.

c.   Generalized Risk as Hardship

Aside from distinguishing any discrimination from persecution, an applicant may also be well advised to distinguish generalized risk from persecution. Doing so will distinguish the risk he may face from the risks enumerated in section 97 of the *IRPA* and thereby allow a decision maker to assess them in an H&C application.

---

116 *Law Society of British Columbia v Andrews*, [1989] 1 SCR 143 at para 37.
117 *Stephenson v Canada (Minister of Citizenship and Immigration)*, 2011 FC 932 at para 41.
118 *Divakaran v Canada (Minister of Citizenship and Immigration)*, 2011 FC 633.

Section 97 of the *IRPA* provides that a person can be deemed a person in need of protection if there is a risk of torture, death, and cruel and unusual punishment. Section 97, however, provides a caveat: the risk cannot be "faced generally by other individuals in or from that country."[119] While this may be problematic in framing a refugee claim, arguably this exception demarcates risks that can be assessed in an H&C application. Applicants should endeavour to make use of this distinction.

The Federal Court has confirmed that this tack is advisable. In a series of cases, the court has ruled that hardship faced by H&C applicants need not be individualized or personalized. While personalized risk or hardship is not an irrelevant consideration in an H&C application, decision makers must also take into account the generalized nature of the hardship the applicant may face.[120] In *Caliskan v Canada (Minister of Citizenship and Immigration)*, Hughes J has even advocated the abandonment of the distinction between personalized and generalized risks:

> I conclude that the Guidelines got it right in construing how the amended provisions of section 25 of *IRPA* are to be interpreted. We are to abandon the old lingo and jurisprudence respecting personalized and generalized risk and focus upon the hardship to the individual. Included within the broader exercise in considering such hardship is consideration of "adverse country conditions that have a direct negative impact on the applicant."[121]

d. Other Adverse Country Conditions

An applicant may also provide information relating to the general conditions in the country, including information relating to the effectiveness of state protection. Although state protection is not a determinative factor in H&C applications, an officer still must review and assess whether it has sufficient impact on the applicant's circumstances to warrant granting an exemption from the requirements in the *IRPA*.[122]

e. Lack of Critical Health or Medical Care

In their applications, applicants may assert that they will endure hardship should they return to their country of origin because they suffer

---

119 *IRPA*, above note 2, s 97(1)(b)(ii).

120 See *Barrak v Canada (Minister of Citizenship and Immigration)*, 2008 FC 962 at paras 32–34; and *Ramsawak v Canada (Minister of Citizenship and Immigration)*, 2009 FC 636 at para 30.

121 2012 FC 1190 at para 22.

122 *Walcott v Canada (Minister of Citizenship and Immigration)*, 2011 FC 415.

from a medical, health, or mental condition and there is inadequate treatment in that country.[123] To allow an officer to weigh this factor properly, an applicant should provide evidence that the applicant suffers from the medical, health, or mental condition as well as evidence that the treatment needed for the condition is unavailable or difficult to obtain. To meet their burden, applicants can provide letters or reports from doctors confirming the diagnosis of the condition, the needed treatment, and most important, that the treatment is vital to their well-being.[124] In addition, applicants should provide documentary evidence from relevant health authorities or health/medical organizations in the country of origin confirming that acceptable treatment is not available.[125]

An officer may look to other resources for information on the availability of treatment. In those cases, evidence gathered to counter an applicant's claim must be disclosed to the applicant, and the applicant must be given a chance to respond.[126]

Where medical services are available in the country of origin, applicants may choose to acknowledge this and explain why they are not accessible or appropriate. In some cases, applicants may explain that the services are prohibitively expensive, that medicines are not available, or that the conditions or treatment are not safe. If such factors are substantiated, an officer must weigh or consider them. Where an applicant does not acknowledge the existence of services and there is no evidence to support the notion that there would be hardship upon the applicant because of a medical, health, or mental condition, it is open to an officer to find no hardship.

ii)   Hardship Caused by Denial of Entry or Removal from Canada

a.   De Facto Family Member

Hardship can result where the applicant is not permitted to enter or remain in Canada. It may occur where the applicant is found to be a de facto family member of a Canadian citizen or permanent resident.[127]

---

123 Y Sotomayor v Canada (Minister of Citizenship and Immigration), 2013 FC 962 at para 38 [Sotomayor].

124 Citizenship and Immigration Canada, "The Humanitarian and Compassionate Assessment: Hardship and the H&C Assessment: Inability of a Country to Provide Medical Treatment," online: CIC www.cic.gc.ca/english/resources/tools/perm/hc/processing/hardship.asp.

125 Ibid.

126 Lovo v Canada (Minister of Citizenship and Immigration) (1995), 102 FTR 211 (TD).

127 See, for example, Frank v Canada (Minister of Citizenship and Immigration), 2010 FC 270 at paras 26–29; John v Canada (Minister of Citizenship and Immigration),

De facto family members are those that "would have difficulty meeting financial or emotional needs without the support and assistance of the family unit in Canada" and must be in a "genuine dependent" relationship.[128] To determine whether such a relationship exists, the officer may consider the following factors: whether the dependency is *bona fide*; the level of dependency; the stability of the relationship; the duration of the relationship; the ability and willingness of the family in Canada to provide support; the applicant's other alternatives, such as family outside Canada who are able and willing to provide support; documentary evidence about the relationship, such as joint bank accounts or properties or wills; and the degree of establishment in Canada.[129]

In assessing whether an applicant should be considered a family member under the family reunification goals of the *IRPA*, an officer must not unduly fetter his discretion by failing to consider family members who are neither parents nor children.[130] The category of *de facto* family members can include any person who has an emotional or other kind of dependency on a person in Canada.[131] The Federal Court has highlighted the H&C application as a venue to recognize and examine extenuating circumstances and the fragility of the human condition.[132]

iii) Hardship If Required to Apply from Outside Canada

An applicant may also present information and evidence showing there would be hardship for the applicant to apply for permanent residence from outside Canada. For example, in the case of *Kaur v Canada (Minister of Citizenship and Immigration)*, an applicant had not been a part of her family's permanent residence application because she was not considered a dependant.[133] Although her family enjoyed permanent residence status, she did not disclose the fact she had lived most of her life either in the United States or Canada.[134] Her H&C application was denied, and in judicial review, the Federal Court held that there had been no proper assessment of the hardship the applicant would face should she be required to return to India to apply for permanent residence.[135]

2010 FC 85 at paras 12–15 [*John*]; and *Da Silva v Canada (Minister of Citizenship and Immigration)*, 2011 FC 347.

128 *John*, above note 127 at para 12.

129 *Ibid.*

130 *Koromila v Canada (Minister of Citizenship and Immigration)*, 2009 FC 393 at paras 64–67.

131 *Ibid.*

132 *Yu v Canada (Minister of Citizenship and Immigration)*, 2006 FC 956, involving twin sisters.

133 2012 FC 964.

134 *Ibid* at para 3.

135 *Ibid* at para 8.

The court indicated the officer did not look at how long the process might take or explore the applicant's opportunities to adapt given she did not speak the language or have experience with the culture of India, especially the restrictive view towards single women.[136]

a.   Establishment in Canada

Where an applicant has spent time in Canada, an immigration officer may consider the extent of the person's establishment. The more an applicant has become integrated into Canadian society, the stronger the reason for concluding that hardship would follow removal. Factors that an officer may look to in determining whether there is significant establishment include these:

1)   the amount of time the applicant has lived in Canada;[137]
2)   whether the applicant can communicate in English or French and efforts to improve language skills;[138]
3)   the applicant's efforts to improve education or work skills while in Canada;[139]
4)   the number of, kind of contact with, and relationships with family members and relatives legally in Canada;[140]
5)   whether the applicant is married to a Canadian citizen;[141]
6)   whether the applicant has Canadian-born children;[142]
7)   the number of and types of connections the applicant has with other Canadians;[143] and
8)   the applicant's community involvement or volunteer work.[144]

Factors that may illustrate a lack of establishment include the following:

1)   the amount of time the applicant collected social assistance;[145]

---

136   *Ibid.*
137   See *Espino v Canada (Minister of Citizenship and Immigration)*, 2006 FC 1255 [*Espino*], where the officer failed to consider the fact that the applicant had been in Canada for fifteen years, nine of which she spent working but waiting for her permanent residence application to be processed.
138   See *Latifi v Canada (Minister of Citizenship and Immigration)*, 2007 FC 338.
139   See *Noh v Canada (Minister of Citizenship and Immigration)*, 2012 FC 529.
140   See *John*, above note 127.
141   See *Ebonka v Canada (Minister of Citizenship and Immigration)*, 2009 FC 80.
142   *Baker*, above note 62.
143   See *Chekroun*, above note 76 at para 89.
144   See *Pramauntanyath v Canada (Minister of Citizenship and Immigration)*, 2005 FC 604.
145   See *John v Canada (Minister of Citizenship and Immigration)*, 2006 FC 1422, where the applicant had been receiving social assistance for a number of years

2) the amount of contact or time spent with the applicant's country of origin and family outside Canada;[146]
3) the existence of assets abroad;[147] and
4) family, especially children, living in the applicant's home country.[148]

In addition, an important factor for consideration is the applicant's financial self-sufficiency. Applicants can show such establishment by providing letters from past and present employers, pay stubs, income tax assessments, mortgage statements, and bank statements, for example.

In order to show general establishment, an applicant may also submit letters from individuals in the community attesting that they know the applicant and can give an account of the applicant's activities, perspectives, plans, and intentions. For example, an applicant may submit letters from teachers, professors, employers, co-workers, volunteer coordinators, counsellors, religious leaders, and other community members. Such letters will be more effective where they are not perfunctory but contain personal and anecdotal details to give context to the application and where they convey the sense that the applicant has not only integrated into Canadian society, but has actively contributed to the community, through work, volunteer activities, and religious affiliations and to the lives of relatives and friends, or otherwise. Equally effective are letters that illustrate how the applicant has invested in life in Canada and made a commitment to build long-lasting relationships with people, organizations, or the community.

The Federal Court has held that credit must be given to applicants for the initiative and work undertaken to establish themselves.[149] An officer should not reject an application on the ground that the applicant purchased a home and made investments in Canada with the knowledge that he may have to leave Canada one day.[150] The court stated:

---

and her situation was unlikely to change. The officer denied her H&C application and the court dismissed the judicial review.

146 See *Kawtharani v Canada (Minister of Citizenship and Immigration)*, 2006 FC 162 at para 8.

147 See *Singh v Canada (Minister of Citizenship and Immigration)*, 2013 FC 295 at para 19.

148 See *El Thaher v Canada (Minister of Citizenship and Immigration)*, 2012 FC 1439 at para 55.

149 See *Espino*, above note 137, where an applicant worked on valid work permits as a live-in caregiver and applied for permanent resident status which was refused after nine years of processing. In the interim the applicant built a career with a prominent bank. The court found a lack of analysis with regard to the fact that the applicant was a single woman of fifty-one years who had not lived in the Philippines for fifteen years.

150 *Sebbe v Canada (Minister of Citizenship and Immigration)*, 2012 FC 813.

Is every investment, purchase, business established, residence purchased, etc. to be discounted on the basis that it was done knowing that it might have to be given up or left behind? Is the Officer suggesting that it is the preference of Canadians that failed claimants do nothing to succeed and support themselves while in Canada? Is he suggesting that any steps taken to succeed will be worthless, because they knew that they were subject to removal? In my view, the answers to these questions show that it is entirely irrelevant whether the person knew he or she was subject to removal when they took steps to establish themselves and their families in Canada . . . . Given the time frame most of these applicants spend in Canada, it is unrealistic to presume that they would put their lives on hold awaiting the final decision.[151]

Thus, the proper factor here is what steps the applicants took that illustrate establishment, not what knowledge the applicants had when taking those steps to establishment. Nor may an officer discount what an applicant has "done by crediting the Canadian immigration and refugee system for having given them the time to do these things without giving credit for the initiatives they undertook."[152]

Aside from the factors that are within the applicant's control, an officer may review other factors that have contributed not only to the applicant's lengthy sojourn in Canada, but also to the applicant's reasons for establishing himself in Canada. Such circumstances may arise where the applicant's country of origin is considered unsafe due to war, civil unrest, and environmental disaster meriting a suspension of removals to that country.[153] Further, an applicant may be waiting in earnest for a decision on an immigration application.[154] Where, however, an applicant had the ability to leave Canada but did not do so or thwarted

---

151 *Ibid* at para 23.

152 *Ibid* at paras 21–23.

153 Citizenship and Immigration Canada, "The Humanitarian and Compassionate Assessment: Establishment in Canada: What Is Meant by Circumstances beyond the Applicant's Control?," online: CIC www.cic.gc.ca/english/resources/tools/perm/hc/processing/establishment.asp [Manual: "Circumstances beyond Applicant's Control"]; see *Regulations*, above note 22, s 230; *Lalane v Canada (Minister of Citizenship and Immigration)*, 2009 FC 6 at para 39.

154 Manual: "Circumstances beyond Applicant's Control," above note 153; *Bansal*, above note 102 at paras 28–30, where the applicant had co-operated with removals officials trying to arrange his departure from Canada but could not obtain a valid passport; *Espino*, above note 137.

efforts to remove her, an officer may consider these factors as militating against an exemption on H&C grounds.[155]

b) Best Interests of the Child

i) Baker

The seminal case of *Baker* brought to the fore the importance of considering the interests of children connected to the principal applicant when assessing an H&C application.[156] Mavis Baker was a Jamaican woman who came to Canada as a visitor in 1981 and worked as a live-in domestic worker for eleven years. While in Canada, she had four children. Baker was ordered deported in 1992 after it was determined that she overstayed her visitor's visa and had also worked without a valid work permit in Canada. In 1993, Baker made an H&C application. Among other considerations, Baker asked the decision maker to consider the fact that she was the sole caregiver for two of her Canadian-born children and that her other two Canadian-born children depended on her for emotional support. She also provided documentary evidence to show that she would suffer emotional hardship if she were separated from her children.[157] Baker's application was denied.[158]

When an appeal of a judicial review reached the Supreme Court of Canada, L'Heureux-Dubé J held that while deference is usually accorded to an immigration officer, the approach indicated in the officer's notes was unreasonable and "completely dismissive" of the interests of Baker's children.[159] In particular, L'Heureux-Dubé J emphasized that the exercise of discretionary power under the *IRPA* should be based on "*compassionate* or *humanitarian* considerations" and that these "words and their meaning must be central in determining whether an individual H & C decision was a reasonable exercise of the power conferred by Parliament."[160] In speaking specifically of the factor of the best interests of the children, she stated:

---

155 Manual: "Circumstances beyond Applicant's Control," above note 153: Circumstances not beyond the applicant's control include these: an applicant "in Canada for a number of years, is unwilling to sign or provide information for a passport application," "wilfully loses or destroys their travel document(s)," and "goes 'underground' and remains in Canada illegally"; *Legault v Canada (Minister of Citizenship and Immigration)*, 2002 FCA 125 [*Legault*].

156 *Baker*, above note 62.

157 *Ibid* at para 2.

158 *Ibid.*

159 *Ibid* at paras 62–65.

160 *Ibid* at para 66 [emphasis in original].

for the exercise of the discretion to fall within the standard of reasonableness, the decision-maker should consider children's best interests as an important factor, give them substantial weight, and be alert, alive and sensitive to them. That is not to say that children's best interests must always outweigh other considerations, or that there will not be other reasons for denying an H & C claim even when children's interests are given this consideration. However, where the interests of children are minimized, in a manner inconsistent with Canada's humanitarian and compassionate tradition and the Minister's guidelines, the decision will be unreasonable.[161]

This decision led to the inclusion in the *IRPA* of the requirement to consider the best interests of the child as a requirement for consideration in H&C applications.[162] Thus, the examination of the best interests of a child is now a statutory obligation that applies to any child directly affected, whether Canadian or foreign born within or outside Canada under the age of eighteen.[163] The relationship between the applicant and a child need not be that of parent and child but could be another relationship.[164] For example, the principal applicant may be a grandparent who is the primary caregiver of the child.[165]

ii) Alert, Alive, and Sensitive

Despite the explicit obligation to consider the interests of children in an H&C application, the decision of *Baker* did not give much guidance on the ways in which a decision maker should be "alert, alive and sensitive" to a child's circumstances.

The Federal Court of Appeal has since been clear that an applicant is not entitled to an affirmative H&C application simply because the best interests of a child favour that result. The best interests of the

---

161 *Ibid* at para 75.

162 *IRPA*, above note 2, s 25.

163 In *Moya v Canada (Minister of Citizenship and Immigration)*, 2012 FC 971 at para 17, the court held that children ages eighteen and twenty were not children and therefore did not need to be considered under the "best interests of the child" but certified the question of whether a child spoken of in the *IRPA*, s 25, is restricted to a person under the age of eighteen years. See also *Regulations*, above note 22, s 2, which now defines *dependent child* as a person under nineteen years old.

164 See *Kwon v Canada (Minister of Citizenship and Immigration)*, 2012 FC 50 [*Kwon*], where the applicants were grandparents; *Momcilovic v Canada (Minister of Citizenship and Immigration)*, 2005 FC 79, where the applicant asked the officer to consider the best interests of children the applicant works for as a caregiver and is close to.

165 *Kwon*, above note 164.

child are an important *but not a determinative* factor.[166] For example, the commission of serious criminal offences may outweigh the factor of a child's best interests.[167]

In addition, the Federal Court has stated that the children's interests must be well identified and defined and examined with much attention.[168] An officer cannot superficially touch on or marginalize the best interests of the children but must properly analyze the consequences they will face should an applicant not be granted permanent resident status.[169] Mere recognition of a bond between the applicant and a child is not enough. Rather, there must be a meaningful and critical analysis of the best interests of the children in their real life situation.[170] This analysis cannot be done in a vacuum, but must be "consistent with "Canada's humanitarian and compassionate tradition."[171] The focus should be on the child and the child's needs, not what is best for the family.[172] Decision makers should also concentrate on both the harms and the benefits of a decision to children involved.[173] In some cases, an officer may be required "to obtain further information concerning the best interests of the Canadian born children if the officer believed the information presented by the applicant to be insufficient to assess the best interests of the children."[174] It has, however, been held that where the applicant's references to children affected by the application are too oblique, cursory, and obscure, there will not be a positive obligation imposed on an officer to inquire further about the best interests of the children.[175] Indeed, it is recommended to officers that the obligation to be alert, alive, and sensitive to the interests of children "only arises when it is sufficiently clear from the material submitted . . . that an application relies in whole, or at least in part" on the factor.[176]

---

166 *Kisana v Canada (Minister of Citizenship and Immigration)*, 2009 FCA 189 [*Kisana*]; *Singh v Canada (Minister of Citizenship and Immigration)*, 2005 FC 718 [*Singh, 2005*].

167 *Legault*, above note 155.

168 *Ibid* at paras 12 and 31; *Hawthorne*, above note 103 at para 32; *Zazai v Canada (Minister of Citizenship and Immigration)*, 2012 FC 162 at paras 51–52 [*Zazai*].

169 *Hawthorne*, above note 103; *Zazai*, above note 168; *Gelaw v Canada (Minister of Citizenship and Immigration)*, 2010 FC 1120 at para 30.

170 *Kolosovs v Canada (Minister of Citizenship and Immigration)*, 2008 FC 165 at para 14 [*Kolosovs*]; *Singh, 2005*, above note 166 at para 14.

171 *Duque v Canada (Minister of Citizenship and Immigration)*, 2007 FC 1367 at para 32.

172 *Alie v Canada (Minister of Citizenship and Immigration)*, 2008 FC 925 at para 1.

173 *Ibid* at para 8.

174 *Del Cid v Canada (Minister of Citizenship and Immigration)*, 2006 FC 326 at para 30.

175 *Owusu v Canada (Minister of Citizenship and Immigration)*, 2004 FCA 38.

176 *Ibid* at para 5.

In *Gill v Canada (Minister of Citizenship and Immigration)*, Campbell J at the Federal Court identified two steps that must be taken to adequately assess the best interests of a child.[177] The first step is to identify and analyze potential factors that would have an impact on the child's best interest.[178] The factors may include those identified in the operational manual but also factors identified in family law legislation, such as Ontario's *Children's Law Reform Act*.[179] The officer must make a choice between the options available for the child.[180]

In *Kisana*, however, Nadon JA at the Federal Court of Appeal observed that it is inappropriate to import the best interests of the child framework used in custody and access cases into immigration applications because although the child's best interests are determinative in family law cases, they are only one factor to be weighed in immigration cases.[181] In the same case, in separate reasons, Trudel JA confirmed this point and also expressed the view that being alert, alive, and sensitive means taking into account the vulnerabilities of the child when he or she is being interviewed.[182] During interviews, an officer should ask age-appropriate questions, keeping in mind the linguistic, cognitive, and emotional differences between children and adults.[183]

iii) A Balancing of Factors

What are the factors a decision maker will consider when examining the best interests of a child? In *Gordon v Goertz*, McLachlin J stated, "The multitude of factors that may impinge on the child's best interest make a measure of indeterminacy inevitable" and "a more precise test would risk sacrificing the child's best interests to expediency and certainty."[184] The list that follows thus includes only some elements for consideration:

1) the age of the child;[185]
2) the level of dependency between the child and the H&C applicant or the child and sponsor;[186]

---

177 2008 FC 613.
178 *Ibid* at para 17.
179 *Ibid* at para 18.
180 *Ibid* at para 20.
181 *Kisana*, above note 166 at para 37.
182 *Ibid* at para 72.
183 *Ibid* at para 68.
184 [1996] 2 SCR 27 at para 20.
185 *Leobrera*, above note 103 at para 3.
186 *Benyk v Canada (Minister of Citizenship and Immigration)*, 2009 FC 950 at para 9.

3) the degree of the child's establishment in Canada;[187]
4) the child's links to the country in relation to which the H&C assessment is being considered;[188]
5) the conditions of that country and the potential impact on the child;[189]
6) medical issues or special needs the child may have;[190]
7) the impact on the child's education;[191] and
8) matters related to the child's gender.[192]

Applicants should document and provide supporting information or evidence related to any of the factors that could tip the balance in favour of an applicant. The Federal Court, however, recognizes that if, on the facts, it would be obvious that the departure of an applicant would deprive the children affected of emotional, psychological support, expert opinions are not required.[193] Despite this, if an applicant is able to provide documentation, such as medical or health reports, counselling reports, or letters from various individuals, it will help.

iv) Test Is Not Unusual, Undeserved, or Disproportionate Hardship
In assessing the hardship the child will suffer, the court has stated that the best interests of the child are not only relevant where basic necessities will be denied, but that the officer must consider hardship beyond basic necessities.[194] The Federal Court has emphasized that the assessment of the best interests of the child is based on considerations different from those used in a hardship assessment. Where an officer applies the wrong test in assessing the best interests of the child, this is a reviewable error: including the test of unusual, undeserved, and disproportionate hardship in the analysis of the best interests of the child

---

187 *Sylvester v Canada (Minister of Citizenship and Immigration)*, 2012 FC 17 at para 61; Kolosovs, above note 170 at para 9.
188 *Idehen v Canada (Minister of Citizenship and Immigration)*, 2012 FC 1148 at para 20; *Guadeloupe v Canada (Minister of Citizenship and Immigration)*, 2008 FC 1190.
189 *Hawthorne*, above note 103.
190 *Kimotho v Canada (Minister of Citizenship and Immigration)*, 2005 FC 1004.
191 *Okoye v Canada (Minister of Citizenship and Immigration)*, 2008 FC 1133 at para 15 [*Okoye*].
192 *Awolope v Canada (Minister of Citizenship and Immigration)*, 2010 FC 540 at paras 46–47, where the officer erred by not considering whether there would be physical risk of tribal mutilation to the Canadian-born child and a physical risk of female mutilation.
193 *Kwon*, above note 164 at para 16.
194 *Pokhan v Canada (Minister of Citizenship and Immigration)*, 2012 FC 1453.

is incorrect.[195] Hardship that may be experienced by children need not meet the threshold of unusual and undeserved hardship.[196] Similarly, the court has found that it is an error to use an "irreparable harm" standard in considering the best interests of a child.[197]

v) For Children within Canada

An officer must consider all proposed situations that the children may face, including staying in Canada without the applicant and accompanying the applicant to the applicant's home country.[198] When reviewing the latter the officer should consider consequences such as any possible detriment to the child's education[199] and separation from other family members who have valid status in Canada.[200]

In addition, an officer may need to examine the consequences to a child should she stay in Canada without the applicant: these include the economic consequences facing the child.[201] It is important to keep in mind that H&C applications are distinct from other applications (such as refugee determination and PRRA). In this sense, the Federal Court has stated that an officer cannot rely on the future possibility of a pre-removal risk assessment to negate the duty to do a proper analysis of the best interests of a child.[202]

vi) For Children outside Canada

Where a child is not residing in Canada, the Federal Court has stated that the current situation of the child is not the starting point for an analysis of the child's best interests.[203] An officer has a duty to look beyond the status quo to determine whether it is sufficient for a child

---

195 *Williams*, above note 108; *Beharry v Canada (Minister of Citizenship and Immigration)*, 2011 FC 110 at para 11 [*Beharry*]; *Sinniah v Canada (Minister of Citizenship and Immigration)*, 2011 FC 1285 at para 52 [*Sinniah*]; *Mangru v Canada (Minister of Citizenship and Immigration)*, 2011 FC 779 at paras 22–25 [*Mangru*].

196 *Beharry*, above note 195 at para 13; *Sinniah*, above note 195 at para 64; *Mangru*, above note 195 at para 24.

197 *Arulraj v Canada (Minister of Citizenship and Immigration)*, 2006 FC 529 at para 14.

198 *Kobita v Canada (Minister of Citizenship and Immigration)*, 2012 FC 1479 at para 53 [*Kobita*]; *Cordeiro v Canada (Minister of Citizenship and Immigration)*, 2004 FC 1231 at paras 21–24 [*Cordeiro*]; *Charles v Canada (Citizenship and Immigration)*, 2014 FC 772 at para 61.

199 *Ranji v Canada (Minister of Public Safety and Emergency Preparedness)*, 2008 FC 521 at paras 36–37; *Okoye*, above note 191.

200 *Saliaj v Canada (Minister of Citizenship and Immigration)*, 2004 FC 499 at para 8; *Cordeiro*, above note 198.

201 *Hawthorne*, above note 103.

202 *Zazai*, above note 168 at para 60.

203 *Kobita*, above note 198 at para 52.

and to consider other options, including life in Canada.[204] Further, the court has held that there is no need to find that the children were suffering undue hardship before considering whether their best interests could be met by moving to Canada.[205]

As with children in Canada, the officer must examine and consider all the alternatives and also the most probable outcome should a particular decision be rendered.[206] In *Ferrer*, an officer assessing the best interests of children who were living in the Philippines considered only the possibility of the children remaining in the Philippines with either the father providing for them financially or the father living with them in the Philippines.[207] The officer neglected to consider the alternative of the children living in Canada with the father and benefiting from the financial status of the father in Canada.[208] The Federal Court quashed the decision because of this failure.

c) Undeclared Family Members[209]

Section 117(9) of the *Regulations* enumerates the relationships that will be considered as excluded when determining who is a member of the family class.[210] Specifically, the provision states:

> A foreign national shall not be considered a member of the family class by virtue of their relationship to a sponsor if

> (d) subject to subsection 10, the sponsor previously made an application for permanent residence and became a permanent resident and, at the time of that application, the foreign national was a non-accompanying family member of the sponsor and was not examined.[211]

In effect, if a foreign national has neglected to declare a person as a family member in any documentation for any application for status in Canada (and in effect failed to have them examined by an immigration officer), the person is deemed not part of the family for the purposes of sponsorship. Persons who face a lifetime bar from sponsoring such a family member may nevertheless apply for an exemption from the *Regulations*, section 117(9)(d), in an H&C application.

---

204 *Ibid* at para 53.
205 *Ibid* at para 52.
206 *Ferrer v Canada (Minister of Citizenship and Immigration)*, 2009 FC 356 [*Ferrer*].
207 *Ibid* at para 2.
208 *Ibid* at para 5.
209 For more information on "family members" and "members of the family class," see Chapter 6.
210 *Regulations*, above note 22, s 117(9)(d).
211 *Ibid*.

In assessing whether to grant an exemption to section 117(9)(d), an officer must consider the submissions and explanation of an applicant surrounding the circumstances of the non-disclosure of a family member.[212] While the onus and burden are on the applicant to provide such evidence and explanation, the officer must not simply apply the *IRPA* strictly but must recognize that an H&C application requires the assessment of whether an applicant may be permitted to move forward in a process despite having breached a statutory requirement.[213]

Further, such a request for exemption from section 117(9)(d) should not be confined to the reasons for the omission but also speak to the hardship on the family member who was not disclosed; a balancing of factors will, nevertheless, occur in such an assessment.[214]

In *de Guzman v Canada (Minister of Citizenship and Immigration)*[215] Evans JA addressed the question whether section 117(9)(d), which ostensibly prevents parents from sponsoring and thus living with their children, contravened Canada's obligations under the *Convention on the Rights of the Child*. He determined that it did not but only because the provision was qualified by the *IRPA*, section 25, which allowed for a full inquiry into the circumstances of the case. Subsequently in *Sultana*, Montigny J commented on the important role played by section 25:

> [O]ne must not forget that the presence of s. 25 in the *IRPA* has been found to guard against *IRPA* non-compliance with the international human rights instruments to which Canada is signatory due to paragraph 117(9)(d): *de Guzman v. Canada (Minister of Citizenship and Immigration)*. If that provision is to be meaningful, Immigration officers must do more than pay lip service to the H&C factors brought forward by an applicant, and must truly assess them with a view to deciding whether they are sufficient to counterbalance the harsh provision of paragraph 117(9)(d).[216]

Despite this, section 117(9)(d) is a harsh antidote in the federal government's efforts to combat misrepresentation and fraud, one that

---

212 *Odicho v Canada (Minister of Citizenship and Immigration)*, 2008 FC 1039 at paras 14–16.
213 *Ibid.*
214 *Sultana v Canada (Minister of Citizenship and Immigration)*, 2009 FC 533 [*Sultana*].
215 2005 FCA 436 at paras 102–9. At para 107, Evan JA states, "the discretion conferred on the Minister by section 25 enables *IRPA* to be administered in a compliant manner."
216 *Sultana*, above note 214 at para 25.

scholars and advocates have deemed excessive and overbroad.[217] The use of H&C applications to temper the automatic lifetime exclusion of family members has not always been effective, rendering the objective of the *IRPA* aiming to reunify families as an empty promise for some.[218]

d) Inadmissibility

Foreign nationals who are inadmissible under the *IRPA* (except for those under sections 34, 35, and 37) may submit an H&C application to be exempt from the provision that identifies them as inadmissible. Once an exemption is granted, the person affected is no longer considered inadmissible on that ground associated with the person.[219] The relief through an H&C application is thus a powerful one for persons who are inadmissible.

The onus is on the inadmissible applicant to request and justify an exemption. An officer has discretion to refuse the application if there arise inadmissibility issues that have not been addressed in the application.[220] Further, where applicable, if an applicant has a pending situation, such as an ongoing criminal trial, that may affect an admissibility assessment, the onus is on the applicant to seek a deferral of a decision until matters are settled.[221] As with all other evidence, the onus is on the applicant to provide evidence and rationale for the deferral, and to provide information when circumstances are finalized.

The operational manual identifies that where inadmissibility is raised by the applicant, it should be addressed at the first stage of the

---

217 Jamie Liew, "Violence and the Form: The Ultrahazardous Activity of Excluding Children in Canada's Immigration Family Class" *Gender and Sexuality Law* (14 February 2011), online: http://blogs.law.columbia.edu/genderandsexualitylawblog/2011/02/14/new-from-gsl-online-violence-and-the-form-the-ultrahazardous-activity-of-excluding-children-in-canada%E2%80%99s-immigration-family-class/; Canadian Council for Refugees, *Submission on 117(9)(d)* (7 June 2007), online: CCR http://ccrweb.ca/files/excludedfam.pdf; Canadian Council for Refugees, *Families Never to Be United: Excluded Family Members* (April 2008), online: CCR http://ccrweb.ca/sites/ccrweb.ca/files/static-files/documents/famexcluprofilsEN.pdf.

218 *Kisana*, above note 166.

219 *IRPA*, above note 2, s 25. See Chapter 14.

220 *IRPA, ibid*, s 25.1(1); *Regulations*, above note 22, ss 67(b)–(c) and 68(b)–(c); Citizenship and Immigration Canada, "Humanitarian and Compassionate: Dealing with Inadmissibility," online: www.cic.gc.ca/english/resources/tools/perm/hc/processing/admiss/index.asp [Manual: "Inadmissibility"].

221 *Johnson v Canada (Minister of Citizenship and Immigration)*, 2008 FC 2 at para 35 [*Johnson*].

H&C process.[222] However, inadmissibilities can and will be addressed at the second stage. The operational manual provides:

> Inadmissibilities should be considered at the stage at which they are known by the decision maker and in the overall context of the H&C factors put forward by the applicant. In other words, determine whether the H&C factors are sufficient to warrant a waiver of the inadmissibility. Any known inadmissibility should be assessed and the exemption granted, refused or the case referred to the delegated decision maker for consideration of an exemption.
>
> Example: an applicant requests an exemption from a medical inadmissibility. As the decision maker knows about the inadmissibility at the time of the Stage 1 assessment, they must consider granting an exemption from the medical inadmissibility at that time.[223]

In some circumstances, however, it is important to delay consideration of inadmissibility until the second stage. For example, in *Wong v Canada (Minister of Citizenship and Immigration)*, the applicant had been issued a removal order because of criminal activities. He made an H&C application. At the first stage of the assessment the officer had placed great weight on the fact that he suffered from schizophrenia and was inadmissible on health grounds. The Federal Court held that the consideration of inadmissibility on health grounds should have been deferred to stage 2 as it more appropriately affects a determination of admissibility under stage 2.[224]

The following sections review some factors that a decision maker may consider when deciding whether to waive inadmissibility in an application.

i) Criminal Charges Outstanding

The *IRPA* stipulates that an applicant may be inadmissible due to criminality.[225] Where an applicant faces outstanding criminal charges either in Canada or another country, the onus is on the applicant to provide information to demonstrate that, regardless of the criminal charge, he is still deserving of an exemption.[226] There are various ways in which an applicant may frame such a submission. The officer has the discretion to grant an exemption if the criminal charge involves a minor and single incident of criminality, such as shoplifting, or if the officer believes that the charge will result in a favourable outcome before the

---

222 Manual: "Inadmissibility," above note 220.
223 *Ibid.*
224 2006 FC 1410.
225 *IRPA*, above note 2, ss 34, 36, and 37.
226 *Kharrat v Canada (Minister of Citizenship and Immigration)*, 2007 FC 842 at para 23.

courts within a short time.[227] If, however, the applicant is facing a serious charge such as attempted murder of a family member and/or it appears it will be some time before the matter of the charge is resolved, the officer may either choose to deny the H&C application or wait until the court renders a decision.[228]

In some cases, where criminal charges may be more serious, an applicant may want to ask an officer for a deferral of a decision until matters are settled. In this way, the applicant does not have to fear that a decision is rendered in the interim without the benefit of knowing what will come of a criminal charge. In doing so, an applicant may avoid a need to send in a new H&C application with new information of the settlement of the criminal matter. The onus is on the applicant to request such a deferral and to provide evidence and reasons for such a deferral.[229] The applicant also has the burden of informing the officer when matters have been settled.[230]

ii)   Rehabilitation or Record Suspension?

Where the issue of criminal inadmissibility has been raised by the applicant, the officer may determine if the applicant is eligible to apply for either rehabilitation or a record suspension and may inform the applicant of the various options available. Nonetheless, the officer is not obliged to inform the applicant of such options. Applicants should not wait for an officer to advise, but prior to submitting an H&C application, should seek out various avenues to obtain help in receiving rehabilitative services, such as counselling, and provide evidence of such efforts. Similarly, if applicants are eligible, they should also submit record suspension applications and provide evidence of the same. Such efforts may be viewed as compelling H&C factors that may shift a balance towards allowing the application rather than denying it.[231]

---

227   Citizenship and Immigration Canada, "Humanitarian and Compassionate: Criminal Inadmissibilities – A36(1) and A36(2)," online: CIC www.cic.gc.ca/english/resources/tools/perm/hc/processing/admiss/crim.asp [Manual: "Criminal Inadmissibilities"]. See also *Avila v Canada (Minister of Citizenship and Immigration)*, 2009 FC 13, where the reviewing officer unjustifiably relied on the criminal charges to deny the H&C application.
228   Manual: "Criminal Inadmissibilities," above note 227.
229   *Johnson*, above note 221.
230   *Ibid.*
231   *BL v Canada (Minister of Citizenship and Immigration)*, 2012 FC 538.

iii) Health Inadmissibility
A person who is inadmissible on grounds of a health condition may also make an H&C application to be granted an exemption. Applicants may wish to have an assessment made by their own doctors included in the application, as well as expert opinion as to why being returned to their home country with their health issue may be a hardship. Compelling reasons may include that access to medication, services, or treatment may be non-existent or difficult to obtain in the country to which the applicant would return to;[232] or that the applicant needs support from family members or other medical practitioners in Canada.[233] Hardship related to health or medical reasons is not confined to cases of physical disability. Should the applicant suffer from a mental illness or disability, the applicable reports or opinions should be provided.[234]

Where an applicant faces inadmissibility due to excessive demand on health or social services, the applicant may want to address the perceived burden on services in the H&C application and provide compelling reasons why the applicant may not, in fact, pose a huge demand on services or how the applicant plans to alleviate such a demand.[235]

iv) Inadmissible Family Member
In the case of an application where one family member may be inadmissible for medical, criminal, and/or security reasons, an application may be denied to an entire family, or the particular family member may be denied, whether the inadmissible applicant intends to immigrate or not.[236] Thus, serious consequences can result in the finding that a family member is inadmissible. An officer may make this decision relying upon information provided in the H&C application or information received

---

232 See *Kambo v Canada (Minister of Citizenship and Immigration)*, 2012 FC 872; and *Yusufzai v Canada (Minister of Citizenship and Immigration)*, 2005 FC 113.

233 See *Sotomayor*, above note 123, where the minor applicant faced institutionalization in Mexico if returned with her mother or institutionalization in Canada if she were to remain in Canada alone.

234 *Zambrano v Canada (Minister of Citizenship and Immigration)*, 2008 FC 481, where the applicant failed to provide sufficient evidence of an ongoing medical diagnosis or treatment.

235 See Citizenship and Immigration Canada, "Operational Bulletin 063" (24 September 2008), online: CIC www.cic.gc.ca/english/resources/manuals/bulletins/2008/ob063.asp; Citizenship and Immigration Canada, "Operational Bulletin 063B (Expired)" (29 July 2009), online: www.cic.gc.ca/english/resources/manuals/bulletins/2009/ob063b.asp; *Rosenberry v Canada (Minister of Citizenship and Immigration)*, 2012 FC 521 at para 65.

236 *IRPA*, above note 2, s 42; *Regulations*, above note 22, ss 23, 69–69.1, 70(1)(e), and 72(1)(e)(i).

from the visa office that verified the information of the family members outside Canada.[237] If, however, a decision is made using third-party information, the officer has a duty to disclose this information to the applicant and give the applicant an opportunity to respond.[238]

An officer has the discretion to waive the requirement that a family member be examined.[239] Applicants can also ask an officer for an exemption from the requirement in the *IRPA* that the family member overcome inadmissibility provisions.[240] Applicants with inadmissible family members may consider strategically making efforts to have the family member examined and providing submissions as to why there are H&C grounds that outweigh the family member's inadmissibility. In other cases, some applicants consider excluding the family member altogether to preserve a viable application. This decision should not be taken lightly.

e) Waiving of Other Criteria

H&C applications can ask for relief in a variety of ways. An applicant may ask to be exempt from the normal procedure required to make an application for permanent residence.[241] For example, an applicant who has worked as a live-in caregiver but not through the live-in caregiver program can ask to be exempt from the requirement to hold a live-in caregiver program work permit to be eligible for an application for permanent residence.[242]

---

237 Citizenship and Immigration Canada, "Humanitarian and Compassionate: Inadmissibility of Family Members (A42)," online: CIC www.cic.gc.ca/english/resources/tools/perm/hc/processing/admiss/fam.asp.
238 *Kim v Canada (Minister of Citizenship and Immigration)*, 2005 FC 1357.
239 *Regulations*, above note 22, ss 30(1) and 38.
240 *Sandramoorthy v Canada (Minister of Citizenship and Immigration)*, 2011 FC 358.
241 *Jacob v Canada (Minister of Citizenship and Immigration)*, 2012 FC 1382: In this case, the applicant had applied within Canada and did not notice his work permit was not under the live-in caregiver program. He provided an explanation and was denied. The Federal Court found that the officer did not consider the purpose of the regulatory scheme underlying the program, which was to encourage people to come to fill a void in Canada and in consideration of their commitment to work, to guarantee participants permanent residence.
242 *Ibid.*

E. RECOURSE AFTER A NEGATIVE DECISION

1) Request for Reconsideration

Where applicants have received a decision denying them an exemption under an H&C application, they may submit a request for reconsideration. This request should be made in writing and include submissions as to why the decision should be reconsidered.

An officer is more likely to revisit a decision where there is a compelling reason to do so. Recognizing that stage 1 approvals are interim decisions, an officer should consider whether there is new or undiscovered significant information or evidence that would change the decision.[243] Reconsideration, however, is not confined to interim decisions. The Federal Court of Appeal has stated that "the principle of *functus officio* does not strictly apply in non-adjudicative administrative proceedings and that, in appropriate circumstances, discretion does exist to enable an administrative decision-maker to reconsider his or her decision."[244] While the court did not find it useful to provide a "definitive list of the specific circumstances in which a decision-maker has such discretion to reconsider," the court did accentuate the importance of a decision maker recognizing the existence of discretion to reconsider.[245]

In practice, while an officer may have discretion to reconsider a final H&C decision, such reconsiderations are undertaken only in "exceptional circumstances."[246] Citizenship and Immigration Canada has identified the following as relevant considerations when assessing a request for reconsideration:

- Whether the decision-maker failed to comply with the principles of natural justice or procedural fairness when the decision was made.
- Whether the applicant has requested correction of a clerical or other error (e.g. a decision was made by an officer who did not have the delegated authority).
- If new evidence is submitted by an applicant, is the evidence based on new facts (i.e. facts that arose after the original decision was

---

243 Citizenship and Immigration Canada, "The Humanitarian and Compassionate Assessment: Reconsideration of a Negative H&C Decision," online: CIC www.cic.gc.ca/english/resources/tools/perm/hc/processing/reconsider.asp [Manual: "Reconsideration"].

244 *Canada (Minister of Citizenship and Immigration) v Kurukkal*, 2010 FCA 230 at para 3.

245 *Ibid* at paras 3–4.

246 Manual: "Reconsideration," above note 243.

made and communicated to the applicant) and is it material and reliable. Decide whether that evidence would be more appropriately considered in the context of a new application.

- When additional evidence is presented that was available at the time of the original decision, consider why it was not submitted at the time of the original application. Determine whether that evidence is material and reliable.
- The passage of time between the date of the original decision and the date of the reconsideration.
- Whether there were any concerns regarding fraud or misrepresentation relating to a material fact, in the original decision or with the new submissions.
- If there is a negative decision from the Federal Court after judicial review, you may refuse to re-open if there are no extenuating factors to warrant reconsideration.[247]

Applicants seeking a reconsideration should make a request in writing and speak to any of the above factors and other reasons why an officer should take a second look at the application.

2) Judicial Review

Where an applicant receives a negative decision and may have received a denial in the reconsideration of an application, the final recourse for the applicant is to seek judicial review of the decision at the Federal Court.[248]

F. H&C: AN ALTERNATE REMEDY

The inception of the discretionary power available under an H&C assessment had initially brought some hope to advocates who thought it might significantly ease the harshness of the immigration system for any applicant. In reality, while a decision maker has discretion, the power has been constrained increasingly over time by policy guidelines and legislative changes designed to restrict an officer's discretion. As a result, H&C applications do not have a high success rate. According to one access-to-information request, in 2011, 64 percent of H&C appli-

---

247 *Ibid.*
248 *Federal Courts Act*, RSC 1985, c F-7, s 18(1); *IRPA*, above note 2, s 72(1). See Chapter 16.

cations were denied.[249] Further, acceptance rates of such applications have declined steadily since 2002 at 56 percent to 2011 at 36 percent.[250] The decline in accepting H&C applications is not expected to change. Recent changes in legislation show that the Canadian government is willing to take a more explicit role in dictating what officers should be looking at and how, further diluting the effect of this avenue of relief. The thin approach to exercising discretion under the H&C regime is problematic because it challenges the basic assumption that an H&C application should serve as an alternative remedy for those who cannot pass through regular channels. When applications in various immigration programs, such as refugee claimants and sponsors of family members, have challenged a number of immigration criteria and processes on the ground that they do not conform to principles of procedural fairness nor to the *Charter*, the government has successfully responded by pointing to the H&C assessment as a viable alternate remedy. However, as this chapter reveals, through legislative change and judicial interpretations that have limted the scope of inquiry, the capacity of the H&C assessment to offer such a true alternative is shrinking. Nevertheless, dissatisfaction with the process is increasing and as a result of continuing challenges this trend may be reversed.

---

249 Citizenship and Immigration Canada, DWS (FOSS) Finalized H&C Applications and Removals as of 29 June 2012 (requested by Andrea Asbil, 3 August 2012).
250 *Ibid.*

CHAPTER 13

CITIZENSHIP STATUS

A. INTRODUCTION

This chapter outlines a brief history of the development of Canadian citizenship law and then examines the criteria for obtaining citizenship, the rights and responsibilities that attach, and the processes by which one may lose the legal status that signifies full membership in our national community.

B. THE EMERGENCE OF CANADIAN CITIZENSHIP

As explained in Chapter 1, until 1947, the position of Canada within the British empire determined that the basic legal status enjoyed by Canadians was that of British subject. In the nineteenth century, the Dominion Parliament, acting under its constitutional authority over aliens and naturalization,[1] had enacted various Naturalization Acts which provided that individuals who swore allegiance to the monarch could become "local" British subjects; it had not, however, undertaken to identify a local citizenry. Indeed, as Mervyn Jones has argued, be-

---

1   *Constitution Act, 1867* (UK), 30 & 31 Vict, c 3, s 91(25), reprinted in RSC 1985, Appendix II, No 5.

fore the enactment of the *Statute of Westminster*² in 1931, the Canadian government probably did not have the authority to amend the law of nationality that accorded the status of British subject to individuals born in a territory of the British empire.³

Nevertheless, the Dominion Parliament introduced the concept of citizenship into Canadian law in 1910. The *Immigration Act* of that year made reference to citizens as one group of individuals who were entitled to enter and remain in Canada even if they belonged to a prohibited class. The other group with the entitlement was those with Canadian domicile.⁴

The Act defined a citizen as (a) a person born in Canada who had not become an alien; (b) a British subject domiciled in Canada; or (c) a person naturalized in Canada not having lost domicile or become an alien.⁵ There was no need for the drafters of the legislation to have used the term *citizen* for its limited purpose of identifying who had rights to enter and remain in Canada. They could easily have framed the legislation to include the various subgroups without introducing the more generic term *citizen*. Clive Parry, however, has suggested that one can discern an underlying intent of the Canadian Parliament to assert its authority to identify individuals as Canadian citizens while not threatening a confrontation with the Imperial Parliament in London.⁶ This was, in other words, an early intimation of what was to follow. Although it did not displace the status of British subject, citizenship had entered the legal lexicon.

The *Immigration Act* was later supplemented by the *Canadian Nationals Act*,⁷ but again, the legislation was not a grandiose assertion of sovereignty; the sole purpose in defining Canadian nationals was to allow Canada to be represented at the International Court of Justice (the rule of the Court was that a country could nominate only its own nationals as judges).

Not until after the Second World War, did the Canadian Parliament recognize more abstract and fundamental reasons for formalizing the status of citizenship. Redefining the relationship between the state and the people came to be regarded as a way of promoting national unity and social cohesion. The idea of personal allegiance to the monarch

2   *Statute of Westminster*, (1931) (UK), 22 & 23 Geo V, c 4.
3   J Mervyn Jones, *British Nationality Law* (Oxford: Clarendon Press, 1956) at 87.
4   *Immigration Act*, SC 1910, c 27, s 3.
5   *Ibid*, s 2.
6   Clive Parry, *Nationality and Citizenship Laws of the Commonwealth and of the Republic of Ireland* (London: Stevens and Sons, 1957) at 451.
7   *Canadian Nationals Act*, SC 1910, c 4.

was replaced by the underlying notion that a set of common bonds united each individual with others who held the same status. In the legal imagination, the sovereignty of the citizenry replaced the sovereignty of the monarch.

The *Canadian Citizenship Act*, enacted in 1946 but which came into force in 1947, maintained many of the distinctions that had been recognized at common law.[8] Thus, a person born outside Canada took the citizenship of the father unless he was born out of wedlock in which case he took the citizenship of the mother. In addition, the Act applied retrospectively to individuals who were born before it came into force. It did not, however, make mention of the definition of *citizenship* found in the 1910 *Immigration Act*. Many of those whom it made citizens already had that status. The earlier definition began to lose its relevance as, from this point onwards, immigration legislation used the 1947 Act as its reference point.

Significant complexities resulted from the 1947 Act. For example, an illegitimate child born overseas to a Canadian father serving in the military forces during the Second World War and coming to Canada shortly after the war was not recognized as a Canadian citizen even though he became domiciled in Canada.[9] Persons born outside Canada after the Act came into force became citizens only if their birth was registered within two years. Such individuals would lose their status unless they made a declaration of retention within a year of attaining the age of twenty-one. These and similar measures created room for many to slip between cracks and unwittingly lose or not gain citizenship. Moreover, although holding multiple nationalities was initially permitted, this rule was soon amended to strip Canadians of citizenship if they (or their father, if they were children) acquired citizenship elsewhere. A generation of what came to be known as "lost Canadians" was created.

Eventually, a new *Citizenship Act* was passed in 1977, which addressed some of these anomalies.[10] This Act has remained the cornerstone of today's law and has undergone a number of revisions. One major change was to consolidate citizen classes and declare naturalized and native-born citizens equal in terms of their entitlements, powers, rights, and privileges, as well as their obligations, duties, and liabilities.[11] In the last decade, we have seen a number of amendments to this Act, many introduced to remedy past unfairness. In 2009, the

---

8   *Canadian Citizenship Act*, SC 1946, c 15 [1947 Act].
9   *Taylor v Canada (Minister of Citizenship and Immigration)*, 2007 FCA 349.
10 *Citizenship Act*, SC 1974-75-76, c 108; RSC 1985, c C-29.
11 *Ibid.*

legislature tried to fix many problematic and unfair effects of the legislation, but it did not address the case of those whose claim to status could be traced to events that occurred prior to the coming into force of the 1947 Act. As outlined below, the legislature eventually addressed the predicament of such individuals in 2014.

Currently, the *Citizenship Act* is undergoing a series of staggered changes. In June 2014, the *Strengthening Canadian Citizenship Act* received Royal Assent and became law.[12] Some of its provisions retroactively addressed the predicament of individuals whose status had been inadequately defined by the 1947 law, some of which have been given a retroactive effect. Other provisions, such as those that have handed greater decision-making power to the minister, have come into force by order in council. Yet others will not come into force until at least a year after the Act is law. The statute has stirred controversy; its title is seen by some as an Orwellian attempt to camouflage measures whose real aim is to dilute the security previously enjoyed by citizens by rendering them subject to harsh governmental restriction.[13] Moreover, the measures introduced to make citizenship more difficult to obtain (the primary method of "strengthening" the status) and easier to lose have been attacked as arbitrary and discriminatory. These critiques are examined in more detail below.

C. OBTAINING CITIZENSHIP

Canadian citizenship can be acquired in three ways: (1) by birth in Canada, (2) by birth outside Canada to a Canadian parent, or (3) by naturalization.[14]

1) Birth in Canada

A person who is born in Canada is a Canadian citizen.[15] Exceptions to this rule exist, but they are less extensive than in many jurisdictions where a parent's status in the country has some bearing on whether the newborn is granted citizenship. Concern is often expressed that we should restrict access to citizenship by birth to prevent outsiders from

---

12 *Strengthening Canadian Citizenship Act*, SC 2014 c 22 [2014 Act].
13 See Canadian Association of Refugee Lawyers, Press Release, "New Citizenship Act Threatens Rights of All Canadians" (6 May 2014), online: CARL Lawyers www.carl-acaadr.ca/articles/75.
14 *Citizenship Act*, above note 10, s 3.
15 *Ibid*, s 3(1)(a).

abusing this basic mode of gaining status. The terms *passport baby* and *birth tourists* have been coined to refer to the feared abuse and exploitation of our basic rule for granting membership in the polity; however, advocates of restriction have been unable to substantiate their fears with credible evidence of widespread abuse.

Most exceptions that exist are found in section 3(2) of the *Citizenship Act* which provides that a person born in Canada is not a citizen if, for example, the parent was a diplomat.[16] The government has recently attempted to deport an individual who was born in Canada but who, it believes, fits into this category.[17]

2) Birth to a Canadian Parent outside Canada

The long-established mode of acquiring citizenship by being born to a Canadian outside Canada was limited in 2009 to first-generation children born outside Canada.[18] Where a person, who has acquired citizenship by being born to a Canadian outside Canada, has a child who is also born outside Canada, the child will *not* be Canadian. A child born outside Canada will gain citizenship by descent only if the parent was born in Canada or has naturalized as a Canadian.[19] This "first generation" rule does not apply to a person if one or both of the person's parents, either biological or adoptive, or grandparents were, at the time of birth or adoption, employed outside Canada with the Canadian Armed Forces or the federal or provincial public service.[20]

The first-generation rule can be understood most clearly by considering the situation of four children: the first is born outside Canada to

---

16   *Ibid*, s 3(2): The section provides that a person is not a citizen if

> at the time of his birth, neither of his parents was a citizen or lawfully admitted to Canada for permanent residence and either of his parents was
> (a)   a diplomatic or consular officer or other representative or employee in Canada of a foreign government;
> (b)   an employee in the service of a person referred to in paragraph (a); or
> (c)   an officer or employee in Canada of a specialized agency of the United Nations or an officer or employee in Canada of any other international organization to whom there are granted, by or under any Act of Parliament, diplomatic privileges and immunities certified by the Minister of Foreign Affairs to be equivalent to those granted to a person or persons referred to in paragraph (a).

17   See *Budlakoti v Canada (Citizenship and Immigration)*, 2014 FC 855. An appeal of this decision was heard at the Federal Court of Appeal on 26 May 2015.

18   *Citizenship Act*, above note 10, s 3(3).

19   *Ibid*. For more information about naturalization, see Section C(3), below in this chapter.

20   *Ibid*, s 3(5).

a parent born in Canada; the second is born outside Canada to a parent who naturalized after acquiring Canadian permanent resident status; the third is born outside Canada to a parent who acquired citizenship by being born outside Canada to a Canadian parent; and the fourth is born to a parent who is a member of the armed forces who was born outside Canada to a Canadian parent. Only the third is not a Canadian citizen.

The amendment to the *Citizenship Act* that limited citizenship by birth to the first generation was prompted by an incident in which Canadian passport holders were evacuated from Lebanon during a war in July 2006.[21] The incident prompted outcry from a vocal group, upset that individuals who did not live in Canada were able to rely on taxpayers to subsidize their flight from danger. Ironically, this incident, which sparked the legislative amendment, did not involve people who gained their citizenship by descent. It did, however, bring to light the racialized perspectives that inform our citizenship policy.[22]

The case of *Canada (Minister of Citizenship and Immigration) v Kandola* raises interesting questions of what it means to be "born to a Canadian parent" in order to qualify for citizenship.[23] Kandola was conceived through *in vitro* fertilization using anonymous donors for both the sperm and eggs to create embryos.[24] Kandola's parents sought out this technique because "they were infertile and incapable of making a genetic contribution of their own."[25] Kandola's mother carried the embryo and gave birth to the girl in India. At the time of Kandola's birth, her father was a Canadian citizen and her mother had "undertaken steps to become a permanent resident through the sponsorship process."[26] Both parents were listed on Kandola's birth certificate, and adoption was thus not an option. The opportunity to obtain citizenship as a result of adoption was closed off.[27]

At issue in Kandola's application for a citizenship certificate was whether she should be recognized as a Canadian citizen by being "born

---

21   See Standing Senate Committee on Foreign Affairs and International Trade, "The Evacuation of Canadians from Lebanon in July 2006: Implications for the Government of Canada" by Senator Consiglio Di Nino & Senator Peter Stollery (May 2007), online: Parliament of Canada www.parl.gc.ca/content/sen/committee/391/fore/rep/rep12may07-e.pdf.

22   Lois Harder & Lyubov Zhyznomirska, "Claims of Belonging: Recent Tales of Trouble in Canadian Citizenship" (2012) 12 *Ethnicities* 293.

23   2014 FCA 85 [*Kandola*].

24   *Ibid* at para 7.

25   *Ibid*.

26   *Ibid* at para 6.

27   *Ibid* at para 51.

to a Canadian parent" despite the fact she had no genetic connection with either parent. In her application, the officer reviewing her case held that she could not acquire citizenship by descent. The Federal Court disagreed, and the minister of Citizenship and Immigration appealed the matter to the Federal Court of Appeal.

When interpreting the term *parent* in section 3(1)(b) of the *Citizenship Act*, the Federal Court of Appeal adopted a strict approach, looking for the "grammatical and ordinary sense" of the meaning of *parent* within the context of the legislation, including its shared meaning in the French text of the legislation. The court acknowledged that Kandola had a legal parent–child relationship with both her father and mother, but nevertheless held that she was not eligible for citizenship by descent since it determined that the term *parent* should be restricted to those who are genetically related to the child or those that have a "blood connection" with the child.[28] It suggested that this might include the "gestational mother" who need not have a genetic link to the child. In sum, the Court of Appeal's decision recognized that one must be a "blood relative" in order to qualify for citizenship by birth.

Justices Mainville of the Court of Appeal, in dissent, and Blanch of the Federal Court took a broader contextual and purposive approach to interpreting the word *parent*, positing that all that is needed is the legal connection rather than the biological or genetic one.[29] Justice Mainville, however, also offered an argument, based on a strict construction of the statute, that *parent* should not be defined solely by blood connection:

> I note that had Parliament intended to use the term "parent" exclusively in its biological or genetic sense, it would not have been necessary to expressly exclude adoptive parents from the ambit of paragraph 3(1)(*b*). By specifically adding the word "other than a parent who adopted him" ("mais non un parent adoptif" in the French version of the 1977 Act), Parliament has clearly indicated that the notion of "parent" which it uses in that paragraph is intended to refer to a legally recognized parent. Indeed, an adoptive parent has no genetic or biological link with his or her adopted child, but is nevertheless a "parent" under the legal meaning of the term. Had only a biological or genetic link been intended, that exclusion would have not been required, or the words used would have been quite different.[30]

---

28   *Ibid* at para 80.
29   *Ibid* at paras 95–99.
30   *Ibid* at para 100.

The majority's interpretation of *parent* may be defended on the ground that granting citizenship at the moment of birth to a child with no blood connection to the parents could offer incentive to potential parents to use this mode of obtaining children rather than adopting them, thereby permitting them to circumvent the requirements for granting citizenship to adopted children found in the *Citizenship Act*, section 5.1. Nevertheless, with the evolving advances to technology in reproductive health, it is hard to reconcile the Court of Appeal's decision with the lived realities of families in Canada today.

a) Special Circumstances: Adopted Children

In 2007, following a determination by the Federal Court that differential treatment between children born to Canadian parents and children adopted by Canadian parents abroad violated section 15 of the *Charter of Rights and Freedom*,[31] the *Citizenship Act* was amended to allow children adopted abroad by a Canadian parent to be granted citizenship without having to go through the naturalization process.[32] Parents of adopted children may apply immediately for citizenship for the child rather than submit sponsorship and permanent resident applications.[33] The legislation provides that citizenship will be granted to a minor child only if the adoption

1)   is in the best interests of the child;[34]
2)   creates a genuine relationship of parent and child;[35]
3)   is in accordance with the laws of the place where the adoption took place and the laws of the country of residence of the adopting citizen;[36]

---

31   *Worthington v Canada (Minister of Citizenship and Immigration)*, 2008 FC 409; *Canadian Charter of Rights and Freedoms*, Part 1 of the *Constitution Act, 1982*, being Schedule B to the *Canada Act 1982* (UK), 1982, c 11 [*Charter*].

32   *Citizenship Act*, above note 10, s 2(1): "child" includes a child adopted or legitimized in accordance with the laws of the place where the adoption or legitimation took place (see also *ibid*, s 5.1). See Citizenship and Immigration Canada, News Release, "Canada Makes It Easier for Children Adopted Overseas to Become Canadian Citizens" (20 December 2007), online: http://goo.gl/V2htV8. It is important to note that there are slightly different procedures for Quebec adoptions as provided for in the *Citizenship Act*, s 5.1(3). For further analysis, see Chapter 6.

33   *Ibid*.

34   *Citizenship Act*, above note 10, s 5.1(1)(a).

35   *Ibid*, s 5.1(1)(b).

36   *Ibid*, s 5.1(1)(c).

4) does not occur in a manner that circumvented the legal requirements for international adoptions;[37] and

5) is not entered into primarily for the purpose of acquiring immigration status.[38]

Ironically, children who have gained their citizenship at the moment of adoption, rather than through naturalization, have been placed in a worse position in the sense that they are not able to pass on their status to any child who is born or adopted overseas, because of the first generation rule.[39] An adopted child who gained citizenship by naturalization can pass on the status to a child who is born or adopted overseas.[40]

b) Special Circumstances: "Lost Canadians"

The self-identified "lost Canadians," mentioned above, lost or were denied citizenship because of provisions in earlier citizenship legislation despite their close connections to Canada.[41] Through a series of amendments, the *Citizenship Act* has addressed the concerns of some of these individuals. The most recent amendments, made in 2014, aim to ensure that various persons born before 1 January 1947, the date when the first citizenship legislation came into force, are recognized as citizens.[42] In effect, the changes give retroactive Canadian citizenship to individuals born or naturalized in Canada, as well as British subjects residing in Canada before 1 January 1947 who were not eligible

---

37 *Ibid*, s 5.1(1)(c.1).

38 *Ibid*, ss 5.1(1)(d) and 5.1(2)(b). For adult children or persons adopted who are eighteen years or older, citizenship will be granted if

- there was a genuine relationship of parent and child before the child attained the age of eighteen and at the time of adoption;
- the adoption was in accordance with the laws of the place where the adoption took place and the laws of the country of residence of the adopting citizen;
- the adoption did not occur in a manner that circumvented the legal requirements for international adoptions; and
- and the adoption was not entered into primarily for the purpose of acquiring immigration status.

39 *Ibid*, s 3(3).

40 *Ibid*.

41 Some had been born in Canada but had lost their citizenship when their father had taken out citizenship elsewhere. According to the laws then in operation, which did not tolerate such dual nationality, both father and child automatically lost their status. Others were born illegitimately outside Canada to Canadian fathers and "war brides." Yet others, "border babies," were born in the United States because there were inadequate hospital facilities in their locale.

42 *2014 Act*, above note 12, s 2(2). These provisions received Royal Assent on 19 June 2014 but have yet to come into force. The Governor in Council will set the date.

for citizenship when the earlier *Canadian Citizenship Act* took effect. For first-generation children born outside Canada of parents who will obtain citizenship due to their "lost Canadian" status, citizenship will be retroactively granted from the date of the child's birth if it happened after 1 January 1947.[43]

However, not all "lost Canadians" are eligible for citizenship. For example, persons who, before 1 January 1947, made a declaration of alienage or who had their status as British subject revoked do not qualify.[44]

3) Naturalization

Permanent residents may acquire citizenship through the process known as naturalization if they meet a number of requirements. The requirements now in force have been modified in significant ways by the 2014 amendments, although some of these changes have not yet come into force. It is expected that this will be completed in 2015.

Section 5 currently imposes five prerequisites (apart from the requirement that one make an application). There is an age requirement: a person who is aged eighteen and who meets the other requirements shall be granted citizenship.[45] The Act, however, does give the minister of Citizenship and Immigration the discretion to waive the age requirement.[46] There is also a residency requirement,[47] a language requirement,[48] a knowledge of Canada requirement,[49] and a requirement that one not be under a removal order or subject to a declaration by the Governor in Council that one is a threat to security or part of organized criminal activity.[50] Both the current and the new regime requirements will be discussed, in turn, below. It is important to consult with the legislation and CIC to check which requirements are in place.

a) The Current Residency Requirement

Under the law currently in force, the residency requirement is three years of residence in Canada in the four years immediately prior to

---

43   *Ibid*, s 2(5). For those in Newfoundland, the retroactive date of citizenship commences on 1 April 1949. The new amendments protect the eligibility of citizenship for children of "lost Canadians" even if the parent is deceased.

44   See *Citizenship Act*, above note 10, s 3(1)(f).

45   *Ibid*, s 5(1)(b).

46   *Ibid*, s 5(3)(b).

47   *Ibid*, s 5(1)(c).

48   *Ibid*, s 5(1)(d).

49   *Ibid*, s 5(1)(e).

50   *Ibid*, s 5(1)(f).

the date of application.[51] Specific rules outline how the days are to be counted. The Act provides:

(i) for every day during which the person was resident in Canada before his lawful admission to Canada for permanent residence the person shall be deemed to have accumulated one-half of a day of residence, and

(ii) for every day during which the person was resident in Canada after his lawful admission to Canada for permanent residence the person shall be deemed to have accumulated one day of residence.[52]

Moreover, other provisions set out that some days, specifically days spent in prison, on parole, or under probation, will not count towards this requirement.[53]

The residency requirement has been the spark for numerous court challenges. These have stemmed from the failure of Parliament to define the term *residence* in the legislation and disagreement among Federal Court judges and citizenship judges about what the proper test should be. Some have adopted a physical presence test.[54] Others have shown more sympathy to the mobility needs of permanent residents who are often required to travel for business or family reasons. This latter group of judges has adhered to a test of residence that does not regard physical presence as determinative. The most influential version of this approach formulated the following list of questions to assist in determining whether Canada is the place where the applicant "regularly, normally or customarily" lives and to assess the quality of the applicant's connection with Canada:[55]

(1) Was the individual physically present in Canada for a long period prior to recent absences which occurred immediately before the application for citizenship?

(2) Where do the applicant's family and dependants reside?

(3) Does the pattern of physical presence in Canada indicate a returning home or merely visiting the country?

(4) What is the extent of the physical absences? Are they a few days short of the residency requirement or extensive?

---

51 *Ibid*, s 5(1)(c).
52 *Ibid*.
53 *Ibid*, s 21.
54 *Re Pourghasemi* (1993), 62 FTR 122 (TD).
55 *Re Koo*, [1993] 1 FC 286 (TD).

(5) Are the physical absences caused by clear temporary situations such as employment as a missionary abroad, following a course of study abroad as a student, accepting temporary employment abroad, or accompanying a spouse who has accepted temporary employment abroad?

(6) What is the quality of the connection with Canada? Is it more substantial than that which exists with any other country?[56]

b) The New Physical Presence Test

Under the new regime, due to come into force in 2015, physical presence becomes part of the residency requirement in Canada.[57] The new rule requires that one must have been physically present in Canada as a permanent resident for at least 1,460 days (four years) out of the previous six years and at least 183 days per year for four years out of the previous six years.[58]

By introducing a physical presence test, the 2014 amendments have relieved the uncertainty occasioned by the existence of different residency tests. However, it is hard to justify the legislature's selection of a rigid requirement since it does not respect either the hardships that may be induced by requiring people to remain in Canada or the fact that there are many ways to build connections with Canadian society without being in the country. Those who have family members abroad and are hoping to reunite with them in Canada will feel this most sharply. Moreover, the increase in the time that must pass before citizenship may be acquired will magnify hardship already experienced by those seeking citizenship, exacerbated by the fact that under the new rules, applicants are no longer able to use time spent in Canada as non-permanent residents to meet the physical presence requirement. The effect of this change will be experienced most sharply by refugee claimants who will no longer be able to count the time spent while they wait for permanent residence to be granted.

c) The New Requirement That Income Taxes Be Filed

Changes to the legislation impose the requirement of filing taxes; one must have met any requirement to file a tax return in respect of four taxation years within the six years immediately before the date of making an application.[59]

---

56 *Ibid* at 287.
57 2014 Act, above note 12, s 3(1).
58 *Ibid.* This will replace *Citizenship Act*, above note 10, ss 5(1)(c)–(e).
59 2014 Act, above note 12.

The new requirement that one file income tax returns has an arbitrary quality. There are penalties already included in the tax laws that aim to deter individuals from omitting to file. The new requirement takes one characteristic of the "good" citizen — a willingness to pay taxes on time — and imposes it as a prerequisite for gaining citizenship. One can think of many other such characteristics, such as payments of fines, voluntary contributions to charities, and engagement in community activities, which are not included. The selection of tax filing as a requirement suggests an implicit xenophobic attitude that those who have not yet sworn an oath of allegiance are likely to cheat unless their future status is made to depend on their not doing so.

d) The New Requirement of an Intention to Reside in Canada
The 2014 changes to the *Citizenship Act* have also introduced a more ambiguous requirement: that an applicant show an intention to continue to reside in Canada, or if not in Canada, to engage in employment or have a spouse or common law partner engaged in employment outside Canada with the Canadian Armed Forces or the federal or provincial government.[60] Concern has been expressed that a future government may rely on this provision to strip citizenship from individuals who have acquired the status through naturalization but who then depart from Canada for a time. The later decision to leave may be regarded as evidence that the citizen misrepresented his intention when making the application.[61] By way of contrast, those who gained their status by birth in Canada have no grounds for fearing that they may lose their status by deciding to spend extended periods outside the country. This requirement erroneously presupposes that only Canadians residing in Canada full-time contribute to Canadian society.

e) Adequate Knowledge of an Official Language
Adults are required to demonstrate adequate knowledge of one of the official languages in Canada.[62] Previously, the language requirement was applied only to persons between eighteen and fifty-four years of age.[63] The new amendments extend the age range: fourteen to sixty-four years of age.[64]

---

60   *Ibid*, ss 3(1) & (2).
61   *Immigration and Refugee Protection Act*, SC 2001, c 27, s 40; see also Chapter 14 for more information on inadmissibility.
62   *Citizenship Act*, above note 10, s 5(1)(d).
63   Citizenship and Immigration Canada, CIT 0002: *Application for Canadian Citizenship under Subsection 5(1) – Adults 18 Years of Age and Older*, online: CIC www.cic. gc.ca/english/information/applications/guides/CIT0002ETOC.asp [CIT 0002].
64   2014 Act, above note 12, s 3(1).

In November 2012, changes were made to the means by which one can demonstrate knowledge of English or French.[65] Before this date, applicants demonstrated their language ability by interacting with CIC staff. The rules were amended to diminish flexibility and the discretionary power of CIC staff and require more objective proof of language ability at the time of application.[66] This change may create economic difficulties for those who may not have access to formal language training or educational services.

Currently, one can demonstrate language ability by submitting documentation such as test results or other evidence to prove that the criteria set out in section 14 of the *Citizenship Regulations* are met.[67] The official language criteria require the applicant to demonstrate competence in basic communication by taking part in short, routine conversations about everyday topics;[68] understanding simple instructions and directions;[69] using basic grammar;[70] and using vocabulary adequate for routine oral communication.[71]

While this requirement may pose less of a challenge for skilled workers, it will be a significant hurdle for family members of skilled workers and migrants from certain parts of the world, signalling Canada's preferences for the kind of migrants it prefers to admit.[72] In March 2013, the minister of Citizenship and Immigration announced that more newcomers will be expected to be fluent in one of the official languages before their arrival in Canada.[73]

f) Adequate Knowledge of Canada and Citizenship Criteria

Adequate knowledge of Canada and the responsibilities and privileges of citizenship are assessed by administering a series of questions to

---

65 *Regulations Amending the Citizenship Regulations*, SOR/2012-178 [*Amending Regulations*]. This document amends ss 3(4) and 14 of the *Citizenship Regulations*, SOR/93-246. The new rule requires applicants to show objective evidence that they meet the language requirements at the time of application. This evidence includes results of a CIC-approved third-party test; evidence of secondary or post-secondary education in an official language; or evidence of achieving an appropriate level in certain government-funded training programs.

66 CIT 0002, above note 63.

67 *Citizenship Regulations*, above note 65, s 3(1)(e).

68 *Ibid*, s 14(a).

69 *Ibid*, s 14(b).

70 *Ibid*, s 14(c).

71 *Ibid*, s 14(d).

72 For more information on the application requirements for skilled workers, see Chapter 5.

73 Rachel Décoste, "Welcome to Canada, But Only if You're Fluent" (21 March 2012), online: Huffington Post www.huffingtonpost.ca/rachel-decoste/canada-immigration-kenney_b_1370638.html. See *Immigration and Refugee Protection Regulations*, SOR/2002-227, s 75(2)(d).

applicants within the same age range as for the language requirement.[74] Applicants may be questioned in an oral or written format, or through both forms. These questions must be "fair and reasonable."[75]

The questions regarding knowledge of Canada deal with the following subject matters:

1) Canadian political and military history;[76]
2) Canadian social and cultural history;[77]
3) Canadian physical and political geography;[78]
4) Canadian system of government as a constitutional monarchy;[79] and
5) other topics relating to characteristics of Canada.[80]

The questions dealing with the responsibilities and privileges of citizenship include these subjects:

1) participation in the Canadian democratic process;[81]
2) participation in Canadian society, including volunteerism, respect for the environment, and the protection of Canada's natural, cultural, and architectural heritage;[82]
3) respect for the rights, freedoms, and obligations set out in the laws of Canada;[83] and
4) other responsibilities and privileges.[84]

In 2011, the citizenship test and the study guide used by persons to prepare for the test were amended.[85] The guide, titled *Discover Canada*, was updated to include an emphasis on democratic principles, recognition of equal treatment for gay and lesbian persons, the notion that forced marriage is not tolerated, information about the War of 1812, and information on trade, economic growth, and outstanding cultural

---

74 CIT 0002, above note 63; 2014 Act, above note 12, s 3(1). Currently the age range is between eighteen and fifty-four years, but under the new regime, the range is between fourteen and sixty-four years.

75 *Re Petti*, [1994] FCJ No 558 (TD).

76 *Citizenship Regulations*, above note 65, s 15(1)(a).

77 *Ibid*, s 15(1)(b).

78 *Ibid*, s 15(1)(c).

79 *Ibid*, s 15(1)(d).

80 *Ibid*, s 15(1)(e).

81 *Ibid*, s 15(2)(a).

82 *Ibid*, s 15(2)(b).

83 *Ibid*, s 15(2)(c).

84 *Ibid*, s 15(2)(d).

85 *Ibid*, s 15; Citizenship and Immigration Canada, Operational Bulletin 244: *Amendments to the Citizenship Regulations and Updated Guidelines Regarding the Citizenship Test* (13 October 2010), online: CIC www.cic.gc.ca/english/resources/manuals/bulletins/2010/ob244.asp.

figures.[86] Since these changes have come into effect, the failure rate has jumped from just 4 percent in 2009 (prior to the changes) to nearly 15 percent in 2011.[87] Nearly half of the Afghan-born immigrants who took the test failed, compared to only 21 percent in 2009.[88] Only 2 percent of immigrants born in Australia, England, and the United States failed last year.[89] Some argue that the failure rates indicate that the test is skewed towards immigrants of particular types coming from certain parts of the world; specifically, those coming from English- or French-speaking countries or countries that have a similar culture to Canada have a greater chance of passing the test. Critics question the function of the test and the government's current understanding of who deserves citizenship. They also say that the test now functions as a *de facto* language test.[90]

In 2013, a further change was made to the process of taking the citizenship test. Where an applicant has failed a test, she can retake the test instead of waiting months for an appointment with a citizenship judge.[91]

g) Waiving of the Language and Knowledge Requirements

The requirements concerning knowledge of an official language and of Canada may be waived by the minister of Citizenship and Immigration on compassionate grounds after reviewing a person's particular circumstances.[92] Until an amendment that took effect in August 2014, a citizenship judge was able to recommend an exercise of discretion pursuant to the *Citizenship Act*. This authority has now been repealed.[93] In these cases, the citizenship judge used to consider the circumstances of the applicant, including the applicant's age, literacy, employment history,

---

86 Citizenship and Immigration Canada, News Release, "Updated *Discover Canada* Citizenship Study Guide Now Available" (14 March 2011), online: http://news. gc.ca/web/article-en.do?nid=595679.

87 Carys Mills, "How Applicants Are Stumbling on the Final Step to Becoming Canadians" *The Globe and Mail* (29 June 2012), online: www.theglobeandmail. com/news/national/how-applicants-are-stumbling-on-the-final-step-to-becoming-canadians/article4382633/.

88 *Ibid.*

89 *Ibid.*

90 *Ibid.*

91 Citizenship and Immigration Canada, "What Happens if I Fail the Written Citizenship Test?" (7 November 2014), online: CIC Help Centre, www.cic.gc.ca/english/helpcentre/answer.asp?q=361&t=5.

92 *Citizenship Act*, above note 10, s 5(3)(a).

93 Bill C-24, *An Act to amend the Citizenship Act and to make consequential amendments to other Acts*, 2nd Sess, 41st Parl, 2013, s 13.

and presence of a mental disability or physical health issues that may prevent the applicant from acquiring the necessary knowledge to pass the test.[94] Ministerial discretion is now the only way that the language and knowledge requirements can be waived, showing a mistrust of how citizenship judges exercised their discretion in the past.[95]

h) Process

Prior to the amendments of 2014, which, in this case, did come into force in August 2014, the decision whether an individual met the required criteria was placed in the hands of a citizenship judge. Citizenship judges now play only an ancillary role; it is a delegate of the minister who determines whether the requirements have been met.[96] The matter may be referred to a citizenship judge only where the minister's delegate is not satisfied that the applicant meets the residency requirement.[97] With new rules of residence being introduced, it is likely that the role of the judge will diminish further. Formerly, an appeal by either the minister or the applicant could be made to the Federal Court. Under the new provisions, the appeal process has been replaced by a process which allows the applicant to apply for leave to seek judicial review.[98]

The minister has discretion to suspend processing an application until a determination has been made on a removal order.[99] Previously, a citizenship judge could suspend the processing. In the past, applicants challenged the jurisdiction of the citizenship judge in these situations by asking for relief in the form of a writ of *mandamus* to force the minister to administer the citizenship oath or a citizenship judge to rule on

---

94   *Re Weiss*, [1998] FCJ No 123 (TD); *Re Hokayem* (1990), 37 FTR 49 (TD).

95   *Chiu v Canada (Minister of Citizenship and Immigration)* (1997), 140 FTR 254 (TD).

96   *Citizenship Act*, above note 10, ss 5, 13–13.2, and 14; *Amending Regulations*, above note 65. The Regulatory Impact Analysis Statement for the *Amending Regulations* states:

> Specifically, the Act puts in place a new decision-making model that streamlines the citizenship grant application process by limiting duplication of review by citizenship officers and the citizenship judge, and having the Minister decide on most grants of citizenship. Judges will continue to preside over citizenship ceremonies, and continue with outreach activities to engage the public about the rights and responsibilities of citizenship. The legislation also strengthens the authority for officials to consider an application as abandoned if an applicant fails to comply with a request of information or to attend an interview.

97   *Citizenship Act*, above note 10, s 14.

98   *Ibid*, s 22.1–22.4. See Chapter 16 for more information about judicial review.

99   *Ibid*, s 13(1)(b).

an application. *Mandamus* may be issued where there is an unreasonable delay in processing the application, including the completion of inquiries by the Canadian Security Intelligence Service (CSIS).[100] In most of these cases, the applicants were at various stages of inadmissibility proceedings and failed to make out the condition precedent required for the writ to be granted.[101]

i) Oath or Affirmation of Citizenship

To acquire citizenship by naturalization, an applicant must also swear an oath or make an affirmation before a citizenship judge or someone authorized by the minister.[102] The oath must be taken by persons fourteen years or older[103] at a citizenship ceremony.[104] The oath requires applicants to swear allegiance to Canada's head of state, the Queen, and her successors.[105]

The oath of allegiance set out in the Schedule of the *Citizenship Act* has been vigorously challenged as unconstitutional by one applicant, in particular: Charles Roach. In 1992 Roach filed an action with the Federal Court that the oath of citizenship violated his freedoms

---

100 *Conille v Canada (Minister of Citizenship and Immigration)*, [1999] 2 FC 33 (TD); *Latrache v Canada (Minister of Citizenship and Immigration)* (2001), 201 FTR 234 (TD). On *mandamus*, see Chapter 16.

101 *Victoria v Canada (Minister of Citizenship and Immigration)*, 2006 FC 857 at para 30; *Golestaney v Canada (Minister of Citizenship and Immigration)*, 2005 FC 1736 at para 17.

102 *Citizenship Act*, above note 10, s 3(1)(c); *Citizenship Regulations*, above note 65, ss 19(1), 22, and 24: An oath can be taken in front of the following persons in Canada: a registrar, a citizenship judge, a citizenship officer, a commissioner for taking oaths, a notary public, or a justice of the peace. Outside Canada, an oath can be taken in front of a foreign service officer, a judge, a magistrate, an officer of a court of justice, or a commissioner authorized to administer oaths in the country in which the person is living.

103 *Citizenship Act*, above note 10, s 3(1)(c). Sections 5(5)–(6) provide that, in certain circumstances, the oath of citizenship is not required. For example, persons who gain citizenship by reason of statelessness and a bloodline connection to Canada are not required to swear allegiance to Canada's head of state. Sections 5(3)(b)(iv) and 5(3)(c) of the *Citizenship Act* provide that the minister has the ability to waive the oath-taking requirement where the person gaining citizenship does not have the ability to understand the significance of the oath by reason of mental disability, or is a minor.

104 *Citizenship Regulations*, above note 65, s 19(2).

105 *Citizenship Act*, above note 10, s 24; Schedule to the *Citizenship Act*: The oath states: "I swear (*or* affirm) that I will be faithful and bear true allegiance to Her Majesty Queen Elizabeth the Second, Queen of Canada, Her Heirs and Successors, and that I will faithfully observe the laws of Canada and fulfil my duties as a Canadian citizen."

of conscience and expression, and equality rights under the *Charter*, and argued that compelling the oath was akin to cruel and unusual punishment.[106] Both the Federal Court and the Court of Appeal held that the oath to "be faithful and bear true allegiance to Her Majesty Queen Elizabeth the Second, Queen of Canada, Her Heirs and Successors" did not to violate Roach's rights under the *Charter*.[107] Both courts confirmed the oath itself is derived from the Constitution and its recognition of the Queen as the head of state in Canada and that the relief sought was a matter for Parliament to determine.[108]

This issue was raised again in the courts in 2005 when Roach initiated a class action lawsuit alleging that the oath "forces the plaintiffs to express allegiance and faithfulness to a royal family and/or monarchial form of government and to disavow republican thoughts and activity or their religious, cultural or moral beliefs."[109] Roach argued that the oath infringed rights under sections 2 and 15(1) of the *Charter*.[110] The most recent ruling was given by the Ontario Superior Court in September 2013 that the compelled speech of the oath does violate freedom of expression; however, it is justifiable under section 1 of the *Charter*.[111]

Further, in 2011, then-minister of Citizenship and Immigration, Jason Kenney, stated, "[t]he citizenship oath is a quintessentially public act. It is a public declaration that you are joining the Canadian family and it must be taken freely and openly,"[112] thus justifying the imposition of the demand that the individual's face be uncovered and visible when taking the oath. Although some argue that this policy attempts to infuse some neutrality or gender equality in our secular society, others posit that this approach does not take a balanced approach to the freedom of religion and also presents an orientalist or parochial vision of society.[113] This debate will no doubt continue, as it has in other legal spheres.

---

106 *Roach v Canada (Minister of State for Multiculturalism and Culture)* (1992), 53 FTR 241, 88 DLR (4th) 225.

107 *Roach v Canada (Minister of State for Multiculturalism and Citizenship)*, [1994] 2 FC 406 (CA).

108 *Ibid* at paras 5 and 25.

109 *Roach v Ontario (AG)*, 2012 ONSC 3521 at para 6.

110 *Ibid*.

111 *McAteer v Canada (AG)*, 2013 ONSC 5895.

112 Kim Mackrael & Les Perreaux, "Muslim Women Must Show Faces when Taking Citizenship Oath" *The Globe and Mail* (12 December 2011), online: www.theglobeandmail.com/news/politics/muslim-women-must-show-faces-when-taking-citizenship-oath/article2267972.

113 See, for example, Pascale Fournier & Erica See, "The 'Naked Face' of Secular Exclusion: Bill 94 and the Privatization of Belief" (2012) 30 *Windsor Yearbook of Access to Justice* 63.

j) Barriers to Acquiring Citizenship

Not everyone who meets the requirements listed under the *Citizenship Act* and its regulations is able to acquire citizenship through naturalization. Section 22 excludes applicants on grounds of criminality, including paroled inmates, persons under a probation order, and persons detained in a penitentiary, jail, reformatory, or prison.[114] The 2014 amendments to the *Citizenship Act* have added several other categories of person who will be denied citizenship: these include individuals convicted of crimes outside Canada and those who have had their citizenship revoked.[115] Additionally, if the applicant has been convicted of an indictable offence either during the four-year period immediately preceding the date of the application or the period between the date of the application and the date the person would have been granted citizenship, the applicant will be denied citizenship.[116] This criterion includes offences committed outside Canada that, if committed in Canada, would constitute indictable offences, regardless of whether the person was pardoned or granted amnesty.[117]

Another future subsection will deny citizenship to permanent residents who have been convicted of treason with a sentence to life imprisonment or high treason,[118] convicted of terrorism or an offence outside Canada that would constitute terrorism in Canada,[119] convicted of various offences under the *National Defence Act* or *Security of Information Act*,[120] or served as a member of an armed force or organized armed group that engaged in armed conflict with Canada.[121] The minister is authorized to decide that the provision will not apply in specific cases where this is warranted by exceptional circumstances.[122]

If the minister has reasonable grounds to believe that a person has engaged in activity that constitutes a threat to the security of Canada or is involved in organized criminal activity, she may make a report to the Security Intelligence Review Committee (SIRC) outlining her concerns.[123] The allegations are investigated by SIRC and its findings are reported to the Governor in Council. Where the Governor in Council

---

114 *Citizenship Act*, above note 10, s 22(a).
115 2014 Act, above note 12, s 19.
116 *Ibid*, s 19(3).
117 *Ibid*.
118 *Ibid*, s 19(4)(a).
119 *Ibid*, s 19(4)(b).
120 *Ibid*, ss 19(4)(c)–(h).
121 *Ibid*, s 19(4)(i).
122 *Ibid*, s 19(5).
123 *Citizenship Act*, above note 10, ss 19(1)–(4).

declares that there are such reasonable grounds, the individual shall not be granted citizenship.[124]

D. RIGHTS AND RESPONSIBILITIES

1) In General

The *Citizenship Act* specifies that all citizens are entitled to the same rights and obligations regardless of how citizenship was obtained.[125] Citizenship and Immigration Canada identifies the following as responsibilities associated with Canadian citizenship:

- Obeying the law — One of Canada's founding principles is the rule of law. Individuals and governments are regulated by laws and not by arbitrary actions. No person or group is above the law.
- Taking responsibility for oneself and one's family — Getting a job, taking care of one's family and working hard in keeping with one's abilities are important Canadian values. Work contributes to personal dignity and self-respect, and to Canada's prosperity.
- Serving on a jury — When called to do so, you are legally required to serve. Serving on a jury is a privilege that makes the justice system work as it depends on impartial juries made up of citizens.
- Voting in elections — The right to vote comes with a responsibility to vote in federal, provincial or territorial and local elections.
- Helping others in the community — Millions of volunteers freely donate their time to help others without pay — helping people in need, assisting at your child's school, volunteering at a food bank or other charity, or encouraging newcomers to integrate. Volunteering is an excellent way to gain useful skills and develop friends and contacts.
- Protecting and enjoying our heritage and environment — Every citizen has a role to play in avoiding waste and pollution while protecting Canada's natural, cultural and architectural heritage for future generations.[126]

---

124 *Ibid*, s 20.
125 *Ibid*, s 6.
126 Citizenship and Immigration Canada, "Rights and Responsibilities of Citizenship," *Discover Canada*, online: CIC www.cic.gc.ca/english/resources/publications/discover/section-04.asp.

The majority of the rights outlined in the *Charter* are equally applicable to all persons in Canada regardless of their citizenship status.[127] The few sections of the *Charter* that explicitly exclude non-citizens are provisions that deal with democratic rights,[128] mobility rights,[129] and language of instruction.[130]

Human rights legislation, such as the *Ontario Human Rights Code*, for example, also makes distinctions between citizens and non-citizens.[131] While the Preamble of the Ontario Code indicates that the Code is applicable to all persons regardless of status in Canada[132] and that various sections of the Code call for freedom from discrimination based on citizenship,[133] the Code also allows for Canadian citizenship to be a requirement, qualification, or consideration imposed or authorized by law.[134] An exception to the latter includes requirements for gaining citizenship.[135]

2) Passports

All citizens are eligible to apply for a passport. The issuance of a passport stems from authority under royal prerogative rather than through an act of Parliament. The power to issue passports is found in an order in council called the *Canadian Passport Order*.[136] Recent changes to the order have granted the authority to issue passports to the minister of Citizenship and Immigration.[137]

A passport is the single most important document in identification, providing information on nationality and other matters. The document also serves to facilitate mobility rights found under section 6 of

---

127 *Singh v Canada (Minister of Employment and Immigration)*, [1985] 1 SCR 177; *Law Society of British Columbia v Andrews*, [1989] 1 SCR 143. See also Catherine Dauvergne, "How the *Charter* Has Failed Non-citizens in Canada: Reviewing Thirty Years of Supreme Court of Canada Jurisprudence" (2013) 58 *McGill Law Journal* 663 for a critical perspective.

128 *Charter*, above note 31, ss 3–5.

129 *Ibid*, s 6.

130 *Ibid*, s 23.

131 *Human Rights Code*, RSO 1990, c H.19 [Ontario Code].

132 *Ibid*, Preamble.

133 *Ibid*, ss 1–3 and 5–6.

134 *Ibid*, s 16(1).

135 *Ibid*, ss 16(2)–(3).

136 *Canadian Passport Order*, SI/81-86.

137 *Ibid*.

the *Charter*.[138] The courts have noted the critical need of a passport, not just to engage in travel, but also for a citizen to enter Canada.[139]

Passport Canada may revoke or refuse to issue or renew a passport on grounds set out in the *Canadian Passport Order*. Such grounds include failure to submit a complete application,[140] misrepresentation in obtaining a passport,[141] criminality,[142] already possessing a valid passport,[143] and national security grounds.[144]

Whether or not a passport can be denied for reasons of national security has been challenged. In July 2004, Abdurahman Khadr was denied a passport for reasons of the national security of Canada.[145] As this reason was not listed in the *Canadian Passport Order* at the time, the government of Canada invoked royal prerogative to allow the denial of an issuance of a passport. Shortly thereafter, on 22 September 2004, the *Canadian Passport Order* was amended to allow the minister to revoke or refuse a passport on national security grounds.[146]

Khadr sought judicial review of the decision of the minister of Foreign Affairs to refuse the issuance of a passport.[147] The Federal Court ruled that the *Canadian Passport Order* did not give authority to the government to deny Khadr a passport for the reasons given, but also held that if the *Canadian Passport Order* were to be amended, as it now has been, Khadr would likely not be able to challenge the revocation.[148] In 2006, the minister again denied Khadr's application for a passport, this time referring to the amended *Canadian Passport Order*, specifically section 10.1, which cites national security reasons as justification for revoking or refusing an issuance of a passport.[149]

---

138 *Charter*, above note 31, s. 6.
139 *Kamel v Canada (AG)*, 2009 FCA 21 at paras 14–15 [*Kamel 2009*]; *Abdelrazik v Canada (Minister of Foreign Affairs)*, 2009 FC 580 at para 151 [*Abdelrazik*].
140 *Canadian Passport Order*, above note 136, s 9(a)(i).
141 *Ibid*, s 9(a)(ii).
142 *Ibid*, ss 9(b)–(e).
143 *Ibid*, s 9(g).
144 *Ibid*, s 10.1.
145 *Khadr v Canada (AG)*, 2006 FC 727 at para 1 [*Khadr*].
146 *Canadian Passport Order*, above note 136, s. 10.1.
147 *Khadr*, above note 145 at para 1.
148 *Ibid* at para 4.
149 Colin Freeze, "MacKay Again Denies Canadian Passport Despite Directive from Federal Court" *The Globe and Mail* (30 August 2006).

Fateh Kamel was also denied a passport, but under section 10.1 of the *Canadian Passport Order*.[150] His challenge claimed that this section infringed his rights under sections 6, 7, and 8 of the *Charter*.[151] The Federal Court held that section 10.1 did violate his *Charter* rights and was therefore invalid, but suspended the declaration of invalidity for six months in order to allow the government to amend the order.[152] The government appealed the decision successfully. The Federal Court of Appeal held that the denial of a passport on national security grounds complies with the *Charter*.[153]

In 2010, the Federal Court was faced with a case in which the applicant sought judicial assistance to obtain a passport and a means by which to return to Canada. Abousfian Abdelrazik, a Canadian citizen, travelled to Sudan to visit his ailing mother. He was detained and tortured by Sudanese authorities.[154] While Abdelrazik was detained, his Canadian passport expired.[155] Over a number of years, he made numerous requests to obtain a passport and assistance in returning to Canada, but had not received any responses.[156] Despite Abdelrazik accommodating requests to make travel plans to return to Canada, the government denied requests for an emergency passport.[157] Abdelrazik applied to the Federal Court to review the government's decision and argued that the government's non-issuance of a passport violated his mobility rights in section 6 of the *Charter*. The court found that Abdelrazik's section 6 rights were infringed, and the government was directed to issue him an emergency passport to facilitate his return to Canada: ". . . where a citizen is outside Canada, the Government of Canada has a positive obligation to issue an emergency passport to that citizen to permit him or her to enter Canada; otherwise the right guaranteed by the Government of Canada in section 6(1) of the *Charter* is illusory."[158]

---

150 *Canadian Passport Order*, above note 136, s 10.1, which states, "Without limiting the generality of subsections 4(3) and (4) and for greater certainty, the Minister may refuse or revoke a passport if the Minister is of the opinion that such action is necessary for the national security of Canada or another country."

151 *Kamel v Canada (AG)*, 2008 FC 338 at para 2 [*Kamel* 2008]; *Kamel v Canada (AG)*, 2011 FC 1061 at para 7 [*Kamel* 2011].

152 *Kamel* 2008, above note 151 at para 146.

153 *Kamel* 2009, above note 139 at para 19.

154 *Abdelrazik*, above note 139 at para 12.

155 *Ibid* at para 14.

156 *Ibid* at para 33.

157 *Ibid* at paras 38 and 40.

158 *Ibid* at para 152.

The court in *Abdelrazik*, however, qualified its finding by stating that while a refusal to issue a passport is a *prima facie* breach of the citizen's *Charter* right, the government may justify a refusal pursuant to section 1 of the *Charter*.[159] As in the case of *Kamel*, the court held that section 10.1 of the *Canadian Passport Order* was a reasonable state purpose.[160] In *Abdelrazik*, the court reiterated that the reasonableness of denying a passport under section 10.1 must be justified on a case-by-case basis.[161]

E. LOSING CITIZENSHIP

There are two ways in which a person can lose citizenship status in Canada: through renunciation and through revocation.

1) Renunciation

A citizen may renounce his citizenship by application and by meeting a number of pre-conditions.[162] First, the citizen must have citizenship of another country.[163] This requirement aims to prevent a citizen from becoming stateless at the point of renunciation. Second, the citizen must not be subject to a declaration by the Governor in Council that the citizen is believed to be a threat to the security of Canada or part of organized criminal activity.[164] The citizen must be eighteen years or older[165] and also must have the mental capacity to understand the significance of renouncing citizenship.[166] Finally, the citizen must not reside in Canada.[167] The minister has the discretion to waive the requirements of mental capacity or residence in Canada on compassionate grounds.[168] Once an application for renunciation is approved, the minister will issue a certificate of renunciation.[169] The applicant will

---

159 *Ibid.*
160 *Ibid*; *Kamel* 2011, above note 151 at para 113.
161 *Abdelrazik*, above note 139 at para 152.
162 *Re Drinnan*, [1982] FCJ No 709 (TD); *Wodajio v Canada (Minister of Citizenship and Immigration)*, 2004 FC 429.
163 *Citizenship Act*, above note 10, s 9(1)(a).
164 *Ibid*, s 9(1)(b).
165 *Ibid*, s 9(1)(c).
166 *Ibid*, s 9(1)(d).
167 *Ibid*, s 9(1)(e).
168 *Ibid*, s 9(2).
169 *Ibid*, s 9(3).

cease to be a citizen of Canada when the certificate expires or on such date as the certificate may specify.[170]

2) Revocation

Currently, the process of revocation applies only to naturalized citizens.[171] Moreover, the grounds for revocation are severely limited. Under the 2014 amendments, expected to come into force in 2015, the grounds will change. In the following section, the current rules are examined followed by an outline of the rules under the 2014 amendments.

a) The Current Law

Under section 10 of the *Citizenship Act*, revocation of citizenship can be triggered only if it is determined that the person in question has obtained, retained, or resumed citizenship by fraud, false representation, or knowingly concealing material circumstances.[172] There is a presumption that if a person became a permanent resident by false representation, by fraud, or by knowingly concealing material circumstances and subsequently obtained or resumed citizenship because of that status, that person obtained or resumed citizenship by false representation, fraud, or knowingly concealing material circumstances.[173]

The Governor in Council makes the determination on a report submitted by the minister of Citizenship and Immigration.[174] The minister is not permitted to submit a report without giving notice of her intention to do so to the individual in question.[175] In receiving such notice, the individual may request the minister to refer the matter to the Federal Court.[176] The court then decides whether the citizenship has been obtained in the proscribed way.[177] The court's decision is final and may not be appealed.[178] Only after an individual has requested that the matter be referred to the Federal Court and the court has rendered

---

170 *Ibid.*

171 There was an exception between 1947 and 1977, when the *Citizenship Act* allowed the revocation of citizenship of any person found guilty of treason. See *House of Commons Debates*, 41st Parl, 1st Sess, No 212 (15 February 2013) at 1330 (Hon Irwin Cotler).

172 *Citizenship Act*, above note 10, s 10(1).

173 *Ibid*, s 10(2).

174 *Ibid*, s 10(1).

175 *Ibid*, s 18(1).

176 *Ibid*, s 18(1)(a).

177 *Ibid*, s 18(1)(b).

178 *Ibid*, s 10(3).

a decision can the minister submit the report. In the case where the individual has not made the request that the matter be referred to the court, the minister may also submit the report.[179] Where citizenship is revoked, the individual reverts to being a permanent resident and may lose that status if found to be inadmissible.

The ability of the government to revoke legally acquired citizenship creates potential issues in administrative law, constitutional law, international law, and human rights law. The courts have recognized that revocation of citizenship engages section 7 of the *Charter* and therefore must conform to the principles of fundamental justice.[180] However, it has also been held that revocation of citizenship does not constitute cruel or unusual punishment.[181]

In *Canada (Minister of Citizenship and Immigration) v Fast* the Federal Court stated the standard of proof in revocation proceedings is a balance of probabilities.[182] In *Sadiq* this standard was clarified as a "high level of probability."[183]

What kind of misrepresentation is needed to trigger the attention of the minister? In *Oberlander*, being untruthful about membership in a group within the Third Reich was found to be sufficient.[184] Although there may not be enough evidence to find that a person had personally committed any war crimes, the non-disclosure of membership in a particular group or the acquisition of citizenship of another country can give the minister enough reason to revoke citizenship.[185] Most jurisprudence reviewing decisions to revoke citizenship has focused on those accused of being complicit in war crimes during the Second World War.[186] The cases challenge the notion that citizenship acquired by birth enjoys the same privileges as those that are acquired through naturalization. The revocation process illustrates that persons who have acquired citizenship by naturalization are always at risk of losing

---

179 *Ibid*, s 18(1).

180 *Oberlander v Canada (AG)* (2004), 69 OR (3d) 187 at para 45 (SCJ) [*Oberlander*].

181 *Canada v Sadiq*, [1991] 1 FC 757 at 768 (TD) [*Sadiq*].

182 2003 FC 1139 at paras 19 and 25 [*Fast*].

183 *Sadiq*, above note 181 at 765.

184 *Oberlander*, above note 180 at para 6.

185 *Ibid*; *Fast*, above note 182.

186 *Ibid*; see also *Canada (Minister of Citizenship and Immigration) v Odynsky*, 2001 FCT 138; *Canada (Minister of Citizenship and Immigration) v Rogan*, 2011 FC 1007; *Canada (Minister of Citizenship and Immigration) v Katriuk*, [1999] 3 FC 143; *Canada (Minister of Citizenship and Immigration) v Skomatchuk*, 2006 FC 994; *Canada (Minister of Citizenship and Immigration) v Bogutin* (1998), 144 FTR 1 (TD); *Canada (Minister of Citizenship and Immigration) v Dinaburgsky*, 2006 FC 1161.

that status if they are found to have neglected to reveal particular information, despite the fact that the information may be innocuous.

Recently, however, the government has begun to focus more rigorously on others who have not disclosed relevant information, in particular, those who, it believes, have "fabricated residency." Between 1976 and 2011, Canada revoked citizenship from sixty persons. In 2012, twenty-seven persons had their citizenship revoked.[187] Since 2011, 3,100 people have received notice that their citizenship may be revoked, and 5,000 permanent residents have been flagged for additional scrutiny if they apply for citizenship.[188]

b) The New Amendments

The 2014 amendments to the *Citizenship Act*, enacted although not yet in force, introduce multiple grounds for revocation. A new section under the heading "Revocation by Minister – Convictions relating to National Security" has been included.[189]

---

187 Daniel Proussalidis, "Feds Revoke Citizenship of 27 Fraudsters in One Year" *Toronto Sun* (14 September 2013), online www.torontosun.com/2013/09/14/feds-revoke-citizenship-of-27-fraudsters-in-one-year.

188 Gloria Galloway, "Ottawa Revoking Citizenship of More Than 3,000 after Fraud Investigation" *The Globe and Mail* (10 September 2012), online: www.theglobe-andmail.com/news/politics/ottawa-revoking-citizenship-of-more-than-3000-after-fraud-investigation/article4532222/.

189 2014 Act, above note 12, s 10(2): The section reads:

> (2) The Minister may revoke a person's citizenship if the person, before or after the coming into force of this subsection and while the person was a citizen,
>
> (a) was convicted under section 47 of the *Criminal Code* of treason and sentenced to imprisonment for life or was convicted of high treason under that section;
>
> (b) was convicted of a terrorism offence as defined in section 2 of the *Criminal Code* — or an offence outside Canada that, if committed in Canada, would constitute a terrorism offence as defined in that section — and sentenced to at least five years of imprisonment;
>
> (c) was convicted of an offence under any of sections 73 to 76 of the *National Defence Act* and sentenced to imprisonment for life because the person acted traitorously;
>
> (d) was convicted of an offence under section 78 of the *National Defence Act* and sentenced to imprisonment for life;
>
> (e) was convicted of an offence under section 130 of the *National Defence Act* in respect of an act or omission that is punishable under section 47 of the *Criminal Code* and sentenced to imprisonment for life;
>
> (f) was convicted under the *National Defence Act* of a terrorism offence as defined in subsection 2(1) of that Act and sentenced to at least five years of imprisonment;

The minister may also revoke a person's citizenship if he has reasonable grounds to believe that the person served as a member of an armed force or organized armed group that engaged in an armed conflict with Canada.[190] In such a case, after giving notice to the person, the minister must seek a court declaration stating that the person performed these actions.[191] The declaration made by the court will revoke the person's citizenship.[192]

Under the new regime, the minister has the authority to revoke citizenship for fraud or concealing information. Section 10 of the *Citizenship Act* will be replaced by a provision that reads:

> the Minister may revoke a person's citizenship or renunciation of citizenship if the Minister is satisfied on a balance of probabilities that the person has obtained, retained, renounced or resumed his or her citizenship by false representation or fraud or by knowingly concealing material circumstances.[193]

The provision is qualified by another that requires a minister who has reasonable grounds to believe that a person made false representations or knowingly concealed material circumstances relating to serious grounds of inadmissibility to seek a court declaration to that effect, which will revoke the citizenship.[194]

In all cases, before revoking a person's citizenship, the minister must provide written notice specifying that person's right to make written representation, the time period that the representations must be made within as well as the form and manner for doing so, and the grounds on which the minister is relying to make the decision.[195] A hearing may be held if the minister believes it is required.[196] The minister must always provide a decision to revoke a person's citizenship to that person in writing.[197] Previously, the person who received notice

---

(g) was convicted of an offence described in section 16 or 17 of the *Security of Information Act* and sentenced to imprisonment for life; or

(h) was convicted of an offence under section 130 of the *National Defence Act* in respect of an act or omission that is punishable under section 16 or 17 of the *Security of Information Act* and sentenced to imprisonment for life.

190 *Ibid*, s 10.1(2).
191 *Ibid*, s 10.5.
192 *Ibid*, s 10.1(3)(b).
193 *Ibid*, s 10(1).
194 *Ibid*, ss 10.1(1)–(2).
195 *Ibid*, s 10(3).
196 *Ibid*, s 10(4).
197 *Ibid*, s 10(5).

that her citizenship was being revoked had thirty days to request that the matter be referred to the Federal Court to determine whether the grounds of revocation had merit. Requesting referral to the Federal Court is no longer an option for persons facing revocation of citizenship.

The new revocation amendments do not specify that they are applicable only to dual citizens. However, there are further provisions added to protect persons facing revocation from statelessness in certain circumstances.[198] If revoking a person's citizenship renders that person stateless, the citizenship cannot be revoked due to Canada being a signatory of international human rights instruments regarding statelessness.[199] In the event that the revocation of a person's citizenship results in that person being rendered stateless, the burden of proof rests on that person to prove that she is not a citizen of any country for which the minister has reasonable grounds to believe she holds citizenship.[200]

3) Resumption of Citizenship

The *Citizenship Act* allows for the resumption of citizenship.[201] Currently a person is eligible for a resumption of citizenship if he has become a permanent resident and has *resided* in Canada for one year preceding the date of application, is not under a removal order, and is not subject to a revocation order or a declaration under section 20.[202]

Under the new amendments the prerequisites for resumption are more complex. They reflect the new requirements for gaining citizenship. Thus, among other demands, an applicant for resumption must meet a physical presence requirement (365 days in the previous two years) and a requirement of having met any obligation to file income taxes in respect of the preceding year; the applicant must also intend to continue to reside in Canada, if granted citizenship.[203] In addition, the applicant must have met any conditions placed on her permanent resident status.[204]

---

198 *Ibid*, s 10.4(1).
199 *Ibid*.
200 *Ibid*, s 10.4(2).
201 *Citizenship Act*, above note 10, s 11.
202 *Ibid*, s 11(1).
203 2014 Act, above note 12, ss 9(2) and 12.
204 *Ibid*.

F. CONCLUSION

Recent reforms to the *Citizenship Act* render the status of citizenship more difficult to obtain and easier to lose. Canada's citizenship regime privileges those who acquire citizenship by birth in Canada rather than by descent or naturalization. Thus, those who have acquired citizenship by descent may be unable to pass on citizenship by descent. What is more, those who have dual or multiple citizenship and who spend time outside Canada conducting business or maintaining ties with family living abroad may now be at risk of being assessed as to whether they are "genuine" Canadians.

The minister now has unprecedented power to grant and strip citizenship on suspicion that persons have engaged in various kinds of listed "wrongdoing." In taking this power, the current government has shown less trust in citizenship judges and manifests the intent to centralize decision making by concentrating it in the hands of a few. Further, the ease with which one can lose citizenship has rendered it an elevated form of permanent residence.[205]

Aside from the lack of trust in citizenship judges, a lack of trust in foreign nationals is also revealed. Those who have gone through rigorous determination processes to obtain permanent resident status, as a refugee, skilled worker, or sponsored family member, now must embark on further scrutiny and assessment. Such a requirement projects the implied presumption that refugees are likely bogus and that immigrants are likely terrorists or criminals, lying and cheating to enter and stay.

The mistrust extends to the electorate and experts as well. A lack of debate preceded the recent profound changes to citizenship laws. Stakeholders complained that expert witnesses were literally shut out of discussion about the proposed reforms, and time limits were set on debate in Parliament.[206]

Moreover, changes to the language requirement and the widening of the age range for those needing to demonstrate language skills in official languages privilege immigrants of certain kinds. Strict physical presence requirements ignore important personal and economic

---

205 Debra Black, "Immigration Experts Say Bill C-24 Discriminatory and Weakens Citizenship" *Toronto Star* (27 June 2014), online: www.thestar.com/news/immigration/2014/06/27/immigration_experts_say_bill_c24_discriminatory_and_weakens_citizenship.html.

206 Jenny Uechi, "Citizenship Bill Reveals Flaws in Canada's Democratic Process: Critic" *Vancouver Observer* (23 June 2014), online: www.vancouverobserver.com/news/citizenship-bill-reveals-flaws-canadas-democratic-process-critic.

dimensions of global society. Further, the extended ability to revoke citizenship raises questions as to whether the federal government is seeking to use the citizenship regime as a tool to punish or exclude people from Canada. Even something as apparently benign as the subject matters on which applicants are tested may have deleterious effects by privileging a parochial and exclusionary image of Canada.

The full impact that these reforms will have on the fabric of society is unclear and is still a subject for speculation. The normative discourse promoted by the government in which citizenship is assigned only conditionally and its value is founded on its exclusivity has potential to radically influence both our social institutions and our debates about identity, community, and belonging.

PART THREE

ENFORCEMENT

INADMISSIBILITY

A. INTRODUCTION

As outlined in previous chapters, the immigration system aims to attract and facilitate the entry of various classes of people into Canada. At the same time, it establishes mechanisms to ensure that those whose presence is unwelcome are denied entry or are removed. The idea that some individuals are desired while others are not is reflected in the objectives listed in the *Immigration and Refugee Protection Act* (IRPA).[1] On the one hand, there are provisions to facilitate family reunification[2] and to "permit Canada to pursue the maximum social, cultural and economic benefits of immigration."[3] On the other hand, there are provisions to "protect the health and safety of Canadians and to maintain the security of Canada."[4]

Thus, while an applicant may be eligible to obtain status in Canada in the sense that he meets the selection criteria, he may nevertheless be inadmissible. Where a reason exists for barring entry or continued residence, it will usually trump any reason for permitting the person to stay.

---

1   *Immigration and Refugee Protection Act*, SC 2001, c 27, s 3 [*IRPA*].
2   *Ibid*, s 3(1)(d).
3   *Ibid*, s 3(1)(a).
4   *Ibid*, s 3(1)(h).

Over the years, recurring warnings have been included in government publications that, as a society, we face severe and continuing threats from organizations and individuals from beyond our borders. Moreover, a dominant idea that has recently informed and shaped the government's agenda on immigration regulation is that these groups and individuals will be able to perpetrate their mischief more easily unless we police our borders more carefully and impose tougher sanctions on those whom we have permitted to enter but who may have spurned our generosity by engaging in wrongful or irregular conduct. It has become a high priority to expose the possible threats posed by non-citizens who seek to enter or who may have entered the country for illegitimate reasons and to devise and develop effective remedies that will address the risks effectively. As a consequence, we have witnessed substantial modifications to our immigration laws with a new and stronger emphasis being placed on securitization and deterrence. The fact that undeserving victims are also netted in these wide-ranging efforts to diminish the risks appears to be regarded as merely unfortunate and unavoidable collateral damage. This change in emphasis has been noted by the Supreme Court of Canada. In *Medovarski v Canada (Minister of Citizenship and Immigration)*; *Esteban v Canada (Minister of Citizenship and Immigration)*, the Chief Justice observed:

> The objectives as expressed in the *IRPA* indicate an intent to prioritize security. This objective is given effect by preventing the entry of applicants with criminal records, by removing applicants with such records from Canada, and by emphasizing the obligation of permanent residents to behave lawfully while in Canada. This marks a change from the focus in the predecessor statute, which emphasized the successful integration of applicants more than security . . . .[5]

In addition, the government has introduced harsh measures to counter what it identifies as serious attacks on its sovereignty by those who would seek to weaken the fabric of the immigration regime by violating its norms. Expensive and controversial processes have been developed to root out those who have misrepresented their status or ignored the conditions placed upon their entry.

One can trace this development in immigration law in Canada to the statement of Sopinka J in *Canada (Minister of Employment and Immigration) v Chiarelli* that, "[t]he most fundamental principle of immigration law is that non-citizens do not have an unqualified right to enter or remain in the country."[6] This statement has been repeated frequently

---

5   2005 SCC 51 at para 10 [*Medovarski*].
6   [1992] 1 SCR 711 at 733.

in very different circumstances to justify the denial of entry or the removal of both foreign nationals and permanent residents. Despite the influence of Sopinka J's statement, its pedigree and the conclusions to which it has led him are both of questionable merit.[7] Nevertheless, it is undeniable that the idea that admission into Canada is "a privilege determined by statute, regulation or otherwise, and not a matter of right"[8] is the normative approach that currently guides how Canada determines inadmissibility and provides the underlying rationale for the criteria of inadmissibility that are applied.

This chapter focuses on the criteria used to find a person inadmissible, while also highlighting the significance of recent changes introduced in Bill C-43, the *Faster Removal of Foreign Criminals Act*, which came into force in June 2013.[9]

B. GROUNDS OF INADMISSIBILITY

The *IRPA*, sections 34 to 42, sets out ten general grounds of inadmissibility: security (section 34); human or international rights violations (section 35); serious criminality (section 36);[10] organized criminality (section 37); health (section 38); financial reasons (section 39); misrepresentation (section 40); cessation of refugee protection (section 40.1);[11] non-compliance with the *IRPA* (section 41); and inadmissible family member (section 42).[12]

---

7   See Chapter 1, which discusses how Sopinka J's statement relies on a questionable claim of Lord Denning, in *R v Governor of Pentonville Prison* , [1973] 2 All ER 741 at 747 (CA), that "[a]t common law no alien has any right to enter this country except by leave of the Crown . . . . If he comes by leave, the Crown can impose such conditions as it thinks fit" and how various scholars have challenged the validity of this view in the common law.

8   *Toronto Coalition to Stop the War v Canada (Minister of Public Safety and Emergency Preparedness)*, 2009 FC 326 at para 23.

9   SC 2013, c 16.

10   Criminality is included as a subcategory that applies only to foreign nationals. Serious criminality applies to both permanent residents and foreign nationals.

11   This ground of inadmissibility is considered in Chapter 11 dealing with inland refugee determinations.

12   Bill S-7, *An Act to amend the Immigration and Refugee Protection Act, the Civil Marriage Act and the Criminal Code and to make consequential amendments to other Acts*, 2nd Sess, 41st Parl, 2013–2014 (Second Reading in the House of Commons and Referral to Committee 23 March 2015): New additions will be added to this ground of inadmissibility.

1) Facts Arising from Omissions and Facts for Which There Are Reasonable Grounds to Believe They Have Occurred (Section 33)

Section 33 of the *IRPA* is an interpretive provision that provides: "The facts that constitute inadmissibility under sections 34 to 37 include facts arising from omissions and, unless otherwise provided, include facts for which there are reasonable grounds to believe that they have occurred, are occurring or may occur."[13]

In *Almrei (Re)*, Mosley J of the Federal Court discussed the meaning of "reasonable grounds to believe":

> The standard is . . . somewhere between "mere suspicion" and the balance of probabilities. It is higher than the standard applied in the control order cases in the United Kingdom which requires reasonable grounds for <u>suspecting</u> involvement in terrorism related activity . . . . Where the legislation requires "reasonable grounds to believe" a certain fact, the standard has been interpreted as meaning that proof of that fact itself is not required. Evidence that falls short of establishing the fact will be sufficient if it is enough to show reasonable grounds for a belief in the fact . . .[14]

2) Statutory Interpretation and Judicial Review

Immigration officers and members of the Immigration Division of the Immigration and Refugee Board (IRB) have primary responsibility for determining what the language used in sections 34 to 42 means, and deciding whether it applies to the particular individuals who appear before them. The Federal Court has the authority to review the decisions made by these decision makers.[15] The court also must confront the issue whether it should show deference to the interpretive skills and expertise of the first-instance decision makers. Where the primary decision maker has made a finding of fact, the court has been content to show deference to the decision maker by using a standard of reasonableness, rather than a standard of correctness when reviewing the decision. Similarly, it has almost uniformly applied a standard of reasonableness when reviewing a decision of mixed fact and law, which

---

13   *IRPA*, above note 1, s 33.

14   2009 FC 1263 at paras 91 and 94 [*Almrei*]; see also *Mugesera v Canada (Minister of Citizenship and Immigration)*, 2005 SCC 40 [*Mugesera*], and *Jaballah (Re)*, 2010 FC 79.

15   *Federal Courts Act*, RSC 1985, c F-7, s 18(1); *IRPA*, above note 1, s 72(1). See Chapter 16 for information on judicial review.

is a decision whether the law applies to a particular set of facts. The decisions of the court have been less uniform when the issue being reviewed is a pure question of law, which is the issue of construing the statutory language.

In *Canada (Minister of Citizenship and Immigration) v Dhillon*, Snider J outlined the dilemma faced by the court with great clarity while also manifesting her uncertainty about the issue.[16] She noted that the Federal Court of Appeal held that the interpretation of section 37 of the *IRPA* was a question of law subject to review on a standard of correctness.[17] However, since that case, the Supreme Court has decided several cases where it has said that unless the question is one of "central importance to the legal system as a whole and outside the adjudicator's expertise," a tribunal's decision will generally be reviewed on a reasonableness standard.[18] Thus, the standard of review to be selected — correctness or reasonableness — will depend on whether the question is characterized as one of general legal importance: a standard that is vague in the extreme. Justice Snider concluded:

> A finding of inadmissibility due to serious criminality or organized crime has implications for and application to a number of other processes involved in the immigration context. For example, a visa officer in an overseas post must take into account the admissibility of a person applying for permanent residence status . . . . In sum, there are many tribunals or decision-makers who must consider and apply s. 37(1)(b) in their daily jobs. In this sense, the question before me is one of general legal importance.[19]

Justice Snider, however, attached the following caveat: "However, if I am wrong on this question of standard of review, I will also determine whether the interpretation found by the IAD [Immigration Appeal Division] was reasonable."[20]

Thus, the issue of the proper standard of judicial review in relation to these sections of the *IRPA* should be regarded as an open question.

---

16   2012 FC 726 [*Dhillon*].
17   *Sittampalam v Canada (Minister of Citizenship and Immigration)*, 2006 FCA 326 [*Sittampalam*].
18   For example, *Canada (Canadian Human Rights Commission) v Canada (AG)*, 2011 SCC 53.
19   *Dhillon*, above note 16 at para 20.
20   *Ibid* at para 21.

3) Security Risk (Section 34(1))

Section 34(1) of the *IRPA* provides that a foreign national or permanent resident can be found inadmissible on security grounds for engaging in the following activities:

1) espionage that is against Canada or that is contrary to Canada's interests;[21]
2) subversion by force of any government or subversion against a democratic government, institution, or process;[22]
3) terrorism;[23]
4) violence that would or might endanger the lives or safety of persons in Canada;[24]
5) being a danger to the security of Canada;[25] and
6) being a member of an organization that engages in any of the above acts.[26]

Each of these will be considered in turn.

a)   Espionage (Section 34(1)(a))[27]

Neither the *IRPA* nor the *Regulations* defines the term *espionage*. The Operational Manual on Enforcement, however, provides some clarification. *Espionage* is broadly defined as "a method of information gathering by spying; that is, the gathering of information in a surreptitious manner, secretly seeking out information usually from a hostile country to benefit one's own country."[28] The Manual goes further to explain that espionage "against Canada" includes "espionage activities conducted by a foreign state or organization in Canada and/or abroad against any Canadian public or private sector entity on behalf of a foreign government; and activities of a foreign non-state organization against the Government of Canada, but does not include acts of industrial spying between private entities where no government is involved."[29] The

---

21   *IRPA*, above note 1, s 34(1)(a).
22   *Ibid*, ss 34(1)(b)–(b.1).
23   *Ibid*, s 34(1)(c).
24   *Ibid*, s 34(1)(e).
25   *Ibid*, s 34(1)(d).
26   *Ibid*, s 34(1)(f).
27   Amendments to s 34 in the legislation in 2013 separated acts of espionage from acts of subversion.
28   Citizenship and Immigration Canada, Operational Manual ENF 2/OP 18: *Evaluating Inadmissibility*, online: www.cic.gc.ca/english/resources/manuals/enf/enf02-eng.pdf at 20 [OP 18].
29   *Ibid*.

Manual lists four types of activities that could be considered espionage "contrary to Canada's interests":

- Espionage activity committed inside or outside Canada that would have a negative impact on the safety, security or prosperity of Canada. Prosperity of Canada includes but is not limited to the following factors: financial, economic, social, and cultural.
- The espionage activity does not need to be against the state. It could also be against Canadian commercial or other private interests.
- The use of Canadian territory to carry out espionage activities may be contrary to Canada's national security and public safety and therefore contrary to Canada's interests.
- Espionage activity directed against Canada's allies as it may also be contrary to Canada's interests.[30]

The Manual notes that the guidelines "are intended to be dynamic as the concept of what is contrary to Canada's interest may evolve or change over time."[31]

The Federal Court has noted that there is no legal definition to be found either in the *IRPA* or in the caselaw,[32] so it has relied on the plain meaning definition of the word *espionage* using dictionary definitions:

> "Espionage" is simply a method of information gathering — by spying, by acting in a covert way. Its use in the analogous term "industrial espionage" conveys the essence of the matter — information gathering surreptitiously.[33]

This definition has been affirmed in more recent decisions where the court has said, "espionage was simply the covert or surreptitious act of gathering information" and "does not require any element of hostile intent and can be occasioned even when carried out lawfully on behalf of a foreign government or agency."[34] Further, "it does not require a

---

30   *Ibid.*

31   *Ibid.*

32   *Afanasyev v Canada (Minister of Citizenship and Immigration)*, 2010 FC 737 at para 34.

33   *Qu v Canada (Minister of Citizenship and Immigration)*, [2000] 4 FC 71 at 96 (TD) [*Qu* TD], rev'd on other grounds 2001 FCA 399 [*Qu* FCA]; see also *Shandi (Re)* (1991), 51 FTR 252 (TD) [*Shandi*]. This definition has been adopted in more recent cases: *Peer v Canada (Minister of Citizenship and Immigration)*, 2010 FC 752; and *Lennikov v Canada (Minister of Citizenship and Immigration)*, 2007 FC 43 at para 27. The IRB also relied upon the former *Official Secrets Act*.

34   *Afanasyev v Canada (Minister of Citizenship and Immigration)*, 2012 FC 1270 at para 19.

detailed appreciation of how the information may be put to later use by higher authorities."[35]

Despite any precise legal definition for the term *espionage*, the court has found there is no obligation on the part of an officer to set out a precise definition to the applicant.[36] This finding raises the question of how decision makers are supposed to make consistent and "correct" decisions given the lack of precision in the definition. More problematic is the court's view that it is not necessary for a determination of inadmissibility to identify any acts on the part of the applicant; as long as an officer finds that there were reasonable grounds to believe that the applicant was a member or worked in close collaboration with an organization involved in espionage, the applicant can be deemed inadmissible.[37]

b) Subversion by Force of Any Government or Subversion against a Democratic Government, Institution, or Process (Sections 34(1)(b) and (b.1))[38]

As with espionage, the Federal Court has noted, "There is no single definition of subversion by force found in the jurisprudence or the Act,"[39] but the court in *Eyakwe* has pointed out that the "most common definition for subversion is the changing of a government or instigation thereof through the use of force, violence or criminal means."[40] This

---

35   *Ibid*.

36   *Ibid* at para 20.

37   *Vukic v Canada (Minister of Public Safety and Emergency Preparedness)*, 2012 FC 370 at paras 33–34.

38   In 2013, s 34(1)(b.1) was added in Bill C-43.

39   *Eyakwe v Canada (Minister of Citizenship and Immigration)*, 2011 FC 409 at para 30 [*Eyakwe*]; in *Qu TD*, above note 33 at para 25, the Federal Court stated:

> The *Immigration Act* does not contain any definition of espionage or subversion and, as noted, there are no cases on point except the decision of the Immigration Appeal Board in Wenberg, Eric Ray (1968), 4 I.A.C. 292, which stated at page 307: The words "espionage", "sabotage" and "subversive activity" would appear to have no special legal meaning, and they must therefore be given their ordinary meaning.

40   *Eyakwe*, above note 39 at para 30; *Suleyman v Canada (Minister of Citizenship and Immigration)*, 2008 FC 780 at para 63: "accomplishing change by illicit means or for improper purposes related to an organization"; *Shandi*, above note 33 at 258: "[a]ny act that is intended to contribute to the process of overthrowing a government." These cases have been followed by *Maleki v Canada (Minister of Citizenship and Immigration)*, 2012 FC 131 at para 8; *Jalloh v Canada (Minister of Public Safety and Emergency Preparedness)*, 2012 FC 317; *Najafi v Canada (Public Safety and Emergency Preparedness)*, 2013 FC 876; *Canada (Minister of Citizenship and Immigration) v USA*, 2014 FC 416 at para 36; and *Tshimanga v Canada (Minister of Citizenship and Immigration)*, 2014 FC 137 at para 50.

analysis is problematic. By reading the use of force or violence into the meaning of the term *subversion* the court has failed to take account of the fact that the legislature itself distinguishes between subversion and subversion by force. In an earlier decision, the Federal Court adopted a more exacting standard where evidence was presented regarding the definition of *subversion*. In *Al Yamani v Canada (Minister of Citizenship and Immigration) (No 3)*, the court stated:

> The Review Committee appears to have essentially ignored the compelling testimony before it of Professor Whitaker, quoted at some length earlier in these reasons, relating to the elusiveness of the concept subversion and his studied view that the concept involves two essential elements, a clandestine or deceptive element, which would appear to have been identified here, and more importantly, an element of undermining from within.[41]

An applicant may do well to provide expert opinion to finesse the issue of how the term should be defined.

In *Oremade v Canada (Minister of Citizenship and Immigration)*, the court noted that the legislation distinguished between mere subversion and subversion by force and adopted the view that a wide range of activities are included in the notion of "subversion by force":

> [T]he term "by force" is not simply the equivalent of "by violence". "By force" includes coercion or compulsion by violent means, coercion or compulsion by threats to use violent means, and . . . reasonably perceived potential for the use of coercion by violent means.[42]

In addition, the court, in the same case, held that where the focus is on subversion by force, the intention to subvert by force is critical but that the intent is not to be measured solely from the subjective perspective.[43] One can be presumed to have intended the natural consequences of one's acts. What must be determined is whether the use of force in the subversion is more than an accident: was force the intended means by which to affect the overthrow of a government?[44]

The Federal Court of Appeal has also offered extensive analysis of a "democratic institution."[45] The court emphasized that democratic institutions include non-governmental organizations such as trade unions, professional associations, and political parties:

---

41   [2000] 3 FC 433 at para 85 (TD).
42   2005 FC 1077 at para 27.
43   *Ibid* at paras 25–26.
44   *Ibid* at para 29.
45   *Qu* FCA, above note 33.

[B]oth the words "institution" and "process" when qualified by the word "democratic" are capable of a meaning which transcends government.

In Canada, a democratic institution is not limited to a political institution, it includes organized groups who seek through democratic means to influence government policies and decisions.

Canada is a pluralistic society with a variety of autonomous organizations independent of the government and to one and other.

As a free and democratic society, Canada values and protects democratic non-governmental institutions which enhance the participation of individuals and groups in society . . . .

Accordingly, a democratic institution for the purpose of subparagraph 19(1)(f)(i) of the *Immigration Act* consists of a structured group of individuals established in accordance with democratic principles with preset goals and objectives who are engaged in lawful activities in Canada of a political, religious, social or economic nature.[46]

Thus, democratic institutions or processes are not limited to those that exercise political or governmental authority.[47]

c) Terrorism (Section 34(1)(c))

A definition of *terrorism* has been provided by the Supreme Court of Canada in the case of *Suresh v Canada (Minister of Citizenship and Immigration)*:

. . . any act intended to cause death or serious bodily injury to a civilian, or to any other person not taking an active part in the hostilities in a situation of armed conflict, when the purpose of such act, by its nature or context, is to intimidate a population, or to compel a government or an international organization to do or to abstain from doing any act.[48]

---

46   *Ibid* at paras 45–50.

47   *Ibid* at para 52.

48   2002 SCC 1 at para 98 [*Suresh*]; see, for example, *Naeem v Canada (Minister of Citizenship and Immigration)*, 2010 FC 1069: The Court in *Suresh* notes that they did not seek to define terrorism exhaustively (para 93) and also that there is no authoritative definition of terrorism in the then *Immigration Act* or one accepted by the United Nations or a treaty. Quoting intervener Canadian Arab Federation, "the term is open to politicized manipulation, conjecture, and polemical interpretation" (para 94); *Villegas v Canada (Minister of Citizenship and Immigration)*, 2011 FC 105 [*Villegas*]; *Kablawi v Canada (Minister of Citizenship and Immigration)*, 2010 FC 888; *Omer v Canada (Minister of Citizenship and Immigration)*, 2007 FC 478.

As the Federal Court held in *Fuentes v Canada (Minister of Citizenship and Immigration)*, "[t]he definition of terrorism adopted by the Supreme Court of Canada focuses on the protection of civilians — a central element in international humanitarian law . . ."[49] and "by choosing the definition of terrorism it did, the Supreme Court harmonized and gave space to each of the key concepts we find in section 19 [now section 34] of the Act: subversion, terrorism, crimes against humanity, war crimes and ordinary crimes. Each of those concepts are distinct and have separate roles to play in law."[50]

Despite the adherence to the definition in *Suresh*, a decision maker may also rely on the *Criminal Code* definition of terrorism,[51] specifically the definitions of *terrorist activity*[52] and *terrorist group*.[53] As the court in *Khan* stated: "Parliament did adopt a more detailed or different definition in the *Criminal Code*."[54]

Despite the adoption of a broad definition, the Court in *Suresh* did find that "it was not the intention of Parliament to include in the s. 19 [section 34] class of suspect persons those who innocently contribute to or become members of terrorist organizations."[55] This finding however was based on the inclusion of an exception within section 34(2), which exempted "persons who have satisfied the Minister that their admission would not be detrimental to the national interest."[56] As will be discussed below, since section 34(2) has been repealed, the broad approach to defining terrorism may merit further discussion in future cases. Section 34(2) has been replaced with section 42.1 of the *IRPA* but differs in that section 42.1 applies only to foreign nationals.[57]

---

49   2003 FCT 379 at para 56 [*Fuentes*].

50   *Ibid* at para 62.

51   *Criminal Code*, RSC 1985, c C-46, s 83.01(1); *Soe v Canada (Minister of Citizenship and Immigration)*, 2007 FC 671 at paras 19–28: The court found that the *Suresh* definition encompassed the *Criminal Code* definition and was also not overly broad; *Khan v Canada (Minister of Citizenship and Immigration)*, 2005 FC 1053 at para 7 [*Khan*]; *Ali v Canada (Minister of Citizenship and Immigration)*, 2004 FC 1174 at para 58 [*Ali*]; *Mekonen v Canada (Minister of Citizenship and Immigration)*, 2007 FC 1133 at para 28.

52   *Criminal Code*, above note 51, s 83.01 for the meaning of "terrorist activity." See also *R v Khawaja*, 2010 ONCA 862, where the Ontario Court of Appeal found that there is no "armed conflict" exception built into the *Criminal Code* definition of terrorist activity.

53   *Criminal Code*, above note 51, s 83.01 for the meaning of "terrorist group."

54   *Khan*, above note 51 at para 7.

55   *Suresh*, above note 48 at para 110.

56   *Ibid*.

57   *IRPA*, above note 1, s 42.1.

According to *Jalil v Canada (Minister of Citizenship and Immigration)*, decision makers determining whether a person is inadmissible due to engaging in terrorism must first, make a factual determination of "whether there are reasonable grounds to believe that the organization in question committed the acts of violence attributed to it," then second, "determine whether those acts do constitute acts of terrorism."[58] In conducting the second step, an officer must set out the definition of terrorism and also identify any specific executed acts that would meet that definition.[59] An analysis of the evidence is required.[60] The court, however, has stated that once an officer has identified the definition of terrorism to be relied upon, "an extensive analysis is not always required" and "a less than explicit explanation of how the impugned acts constituted terrorism was [acceptable]."[61] In practice, in determining whether a person represents a threat to the security of Canada, the first step is to assess whether she falls within one of the classes listed in section 34: the threshold test.[62] In responding to an officer's concerns about inadmissibility, an applicant may want to set out a definition of terrorism using expert evidence and provide an explanation of why her acts or involvement in a group do not meet that definition.

---

58   *Jalil v Canada (Minister of Citizenship and Immigration)*, 2007 FC 568 at para 18 [*Jalil*]; *Daud v Canada (Minister of Citizenship and Immigration)*, 2008 FC 701 at para 11: In *Daud*, the court was unable to find that the officer's analysis with respect to the second step was unreasonable and held that the existence of general violence does not preclude a determination that an organization engages in terrorism.

59   *Ali*, above note 51 at para 64; *Alemu v Canada (Minister of Citizenship and Immigration)*, 2004 FC 997 at paras 33 and 41 [*Alemu*]: ". . . the decision-maker must specify what acts the organization engaged in, i.e., those referred to in [s. 34(1)] (a), (b) or (c), or any combination thereof. A sweeping statement that merely references paragraph 34(1)(f), without more, will not suffice . . . . A finding of exclusion must provide some basis for the determination regarding the nature of the group and the determination regarding an applicant's membership in the group." *Jalil*, above note 58; *Naeem v Canada (Minister of Citizenship and Immigration)*, 2007 FC 123 at para 46.

60   *Fuentes*, above note 49: The decision maker must make specific findings of fact about what acts the organization engaged in that are contained in either paragraphs 34(1)(a), (b), or (c); *Alemu*, above note 59 at paras 32, 33, and 41.

61   *Mohiuddin v Canada (Minister of Citizenship and Immigration)*, 2010 FC 51 at paras 48 and 61; see also *Jalil*, above note 58 at paras 33–35.

62   *Canada (Minister of Citizenship and Immigration) v Mahjoub*, 2001 FCT 1095 at para 22; *Suresh*, above note 48 at para 62.

d) **Being a Danger to the Security of Canada (Section 34(1)(d)) and Engaging in Acts of Violence That Would or Might Endanger Persons in Canada (Section 34(1)(e))**

While many decision makers will find a person inadmissible on more specific grounds of engaging in espionage, subversion by force, or terrorist activities, section 34 includes the broad notions of "being a danger to the security of Canada" and "engaging in violence" which offer a catch-all that embraces those who might fall outside the more defined categories in section 34. There is no need to show that the applicant was involved in criminal acts or acts of violence to find that she is a danger to the security of Canada.[63] Indeed, the Supreme Court of Canada in *Suresh* also held that the phrase "danger to the security of Canada" be given a "fair, large and liberal interpretation."[64] Nevertheless, a threat that a person may constitute a danger to the security of Canada must be "substantial and based on an objectively reasonable suspicion."[65] In a nutshell:

> a person constitutes a "danger to the security of Canada" if he or she poses a serious threat to the security of Canada, whether direct or indirect, and bearing in mind the fact that the security of one country is often dependent on the security of other nations. The threat must be "serious", in the sense that it must be grounded on objectively reasonable suspicion based on evidence and in the sense that the threatened harm must be substantial rather than negligible.[66]
>
> . . . Moreover, the "security of Canada" cannot be limited to instances where the personal safety of Canadians is concerned. It should logically extend to instances where the integrity of Canada's international relations and obligations are affected.[67]

e) **Being a Member of an Organization (Section 34(1)(f))**

The phrase "being a member of an organization" has received considerable attention from the courts both under section 34(1)(f) and also section 37. Much of the jurisprudence dealing with each of these provisions overlaps.

The Supreme Court of Canada has explored the policy rationale for finding someone inadmissible for "being a member of an organization":

---

63 *Re Zündel*, 2005 FC 295 at para 19 [*Zündel*]. See also *Suresh*, above note 48 at para 85; *Almrei*, above note 14 at paras 99–100.

64 *Suresh*, above note 48 at para 85.

65 *Zündel*, above note 63 at para 19.

66 *Ibid*, quoting *Suresh*, above note 48 at para 90.

67 *Zündel*, above note 63 at para 21, quoting *Suresh v Canada (Minister of Citizenship and Immigration)*, [2000] 2 FC 592 at para 61 (CA).

The objectives as expressed in the *IRPA* indicate an intent to prioritize security. This objective is given effect by preventing the entry of
applicants with criminal records, by removing applicants with such
records from Canada, and by emphasizing the obligation of permanent residents to behave lawfully while in Canada . . . . [T]he objectives of the *IRPA* and its provisions concerning permanent residents,
communicate a strong desire to treat criminals and security threats
less leniently than under the former Act.[68]

"Being a member of an organization" has been accorded a broad
interpretation, and courts have rejected the idea that the test for membership should be based on significant integration in an organization:

> There is no definition of the term "member" in the Act. The courts
> have not established a precise and exhaustive definition of the term.
> In interpreting the term "member" in the former *Immigration Act* . . .
> the Trial Division (as it then was) has said that the term is to be given
> an unrestricted and broad interpretation. The rationale for such an
> approach is set out in *Canada (Minister of Citizenship and Immigra-
> tion) v Singh* (1988), 151 F.T.R. 101 at paragraph 52 (T.D.):
>
> > [52]   The provisions deal with subversion and terrorism. The
> > context in immigration legislation is public safety and national
> > security, the most serious concerns of government. It is trite to say
> > that terrorist organizations do not issue membership cards. There
> > is no formal test for membership and members are not therefore
> > easily identifiable. The Minister of Citizenship and Immigration
> > may, if not detrimental to the national interest, exclude an indi-
> > vidual from the operation of subparagraph 19(1)(f)(iii)(B). I think
> > it is obvious that Parliament intended the term "member" to be
> > given an unrestricted and broad interpretation.[69]

Membership is also not restricted to present membership in an organization. As the Federal Court of Appeal stated in *Sittampalam*, the
legislation "permits a decision-maker to consider past, present and future facts when making a determination as to inadmissibility."[70] Further,

---

68   *Medovarski*, above note 5 at para 10.
69   *Poshteh v Canada (Minister of Citizenship and Immigration)*, 2005 FCA 85 at para
     27 [*Poshteh*]; see also *Sittampalam*, above note 17 at paras 35–36.
70   *Sittampalam, ibid* at para 18. At para 19, the court stated, "If one were to inter-
     pret paragraph 37(1)(a) as including only present membership in an organiza-
     tion, it would, in effect, render section 33 redundant." At para 21, the court
     stated the policy rationale for this broad interpretation: "If one were to interpret
     'being a member' as including only present membership in an organization
     described in paragraph 37(1)(a), this would have a contrary effect, by narrow-

"membership in a terrorist organization or a terrorist group can be either formal or 'membership by association' or 'informal participation.'"[71]

In order to resolve whether an applicant is a member of an organization, the court has held that there is no established test but refers to some factors or criteria including the person's involvement in the organization; the length of time associated with the organization; and the person's degree of commitment to the organization and its objectives.[72]

Despite the broad interpretation of "member in an organization," the Court of Appeal has also made it clear that decision makers should

> . . . consider coercion, duress, or any form of compulsion when assessing membership under section 34(1). Apart from formal membership, the whole point of examining the conduct of someone in the Applicant's position is to ascertain whether the conduct in question was carried out with a view to contributing to the objectives of the

---

ing the scope of persons who are declared inadmissible, thereby increasing the potential risk to Canadian safety." At para 23:

> Such an interpretation would also mean that a former member of the Nazi party in Germany could not be found inadmissible because the Nazi party no longer exists, so that he is no longer a member. It would mean that a member of an international terrorist organization could renounce his or her membership immediately prior to making a refugee claim, and would not be inadmissible because he is not a current member of a terrorist organization. It would also mean that a person who spends ten years as a member of an organization engaged in criminal activities within Canada could withdraw from the organization before being reported under the IRPA and avoid a finding of inadmissibility.

See also *Zündel*, above note 63; and *Hussenu v Canada (Minister of Citizenship and Immigration)*, 2004 FC 283.

71 *TK v Canada (Minister of Public Safety and Emergency Preparedness)*, 2013 FC 327 at para 98 [*TK*]; see also *Kanapathy v Canada (Minister of Public Safety and Emergency Preparedness)*, 2012 FC 459 at para 38 [*Kanapathy*]; and *Kanendra v Canada (Minister of Citizenship and Immigration)*, 2005 FC 923 at paras 21–23. See also *Saleh v Canada (Minister of Citizenship and Immigration)*, 2010 FC 303.

72 *TK*, above note 71 at para 105; *Krishnamoorthy v Canada (Minister of Citizenship and Immigration)*, 2011 FC 1342 at para 23; *Villegas v Canada (Minister of Citizenship and Immigration)*, 2011 FC 105 at para 44; *Gebreab v Canada (Minister of Public Safety and Emergency Preparedness)*, 2009 FC 1213 at para 19. See *Sittampalam*, above note 17 at para 38: The court listed factors such as occupied territory or regular meeting locations alongside those listed in *Thanaratnam v Canada (Minister of Citizenship and Immigration)*, 2004 FC 349 [*Thanaratnam*], rev'd on other grounds, 2005 FCA 122 at para 30: Some factors to consider include identity, leadership, loose hierarchy, and basic organizational structure. The court in *Sittampalam*, above note 17 at para 39, held that it is necessary to adopt a flexible approach in assessing whether the attributes of a particular group meet the requirements of the IRPA.

[organization]. The existence of subsection 34(2) cannot dispense with the need for such an assessment . . . . [T]he availability of ministerial discretion . . . does not relieve the Member from assessing membership in subsection 34(1) . . . and it does not relieve the Court on judicial review of the obligation to review whether a reasonable assessment has been carried out by the Member.[73]

Since section 34(2) has been repealed, this analysis can be applied to its replacement in section 42.1 of the *IRPA*.[74]

The court has also acknowledged that although "Parliament intended that the term 'member' should have an 'unrestricted and broad interpretation,'" some restrictions should be read in. As Mosley J stated in *Toronto Coalition to Stop the War v Canada (Minister of Public Safety and Emergency Preparedness)*:

> The phrase "member of an organization" is not defined in the statute. The courts have not given it a precise and exhaustive definition. It is well-established in the jurisprudence that the term is to be given an unrestricted and broad definition . . . . But an unrestricted and broad definition is not a license to classify anyone who has had any dealings with a terrorist organization as a member of the group. Consideration has to be given to the facts of each case including any evidence pointing away from a finding of membership.[75]

Thus, an applicant whose inadmissibility is being determined on the basis of membership in an organization should introduce all relevant evidence that would clarify the precise nature of her interactions with the organization, including evidence that might indicate constraints on her ability to choose to join or to leave.

With regard to minors, in *Poshteh* the Court of Appeal held that a child over the age of eleven may be held liable for criminal actions, and after reaching the age of fourteen, there is a rebuttable presumption of capacity for criminal intent.[76] But the court also held:

> While a finding of membership in a terrorist organization may be possible for a minor of any age, it would be highly unusual for there to be a finding of membership in the case of a young child, say, under the age of twelve. Although it will depend on the evidence in each case, it would seem self-evident that in the case of such children,

---

73   *TK*, above note 71 at para 114.
74   *IRPA*, above note 1, s 42.1. Section 42.1, unlike s 34(2), applies only to foreign nationals.
75   2010 FC 957 at para 118; see also *Poshteh*, above note 69 at para 38.
76   *Poshteh*, *ibid* at para 49.

the presumption would be that they do not possess the requisite knowledge or mental capacity to understand the nature and effect of their actions. In the case of young children, the age of the child itself would be *prima facie* evidence of an absence of the requisite knowledge or mental capacity. There would be an obligation on the Immigration Division to carefully consider the level of understanding of such a child.[77]

Thus, for the purpose of determining a minor's membership in a terrorist organization, the requisite knowledge or mental capacity will be viewed on a continuum.[78] It will also be open to the minor to raise the issue of duress or coercion.[79]

Finally, there is no requirement that there be evidence that an organization sanctioned or approved of the terrorist or criminal acts; however, an immigration officer may determine whether there is enough evidence to establish that the organization has sanctioned the impugned acts.[80]

f) Listed Terrorist Entities

The minister of Public Safety and Emergency Preparedness has created a list of "terrorist entities" as "a public means of identifying a group or individual as being associated with terrorism."[81] The minister has defined an entity as including "a person, group, trust, partnership or fund, or an unincorporated association or organization"[82] and specifically states, "It is not a crime to be listed"[83] despite the fact that the power to create such a list comes from the *Criminal Code*. Further, the minister does state that there are consequences to being listed: these include the "seizure/restraint and/or forfeiture" of property, and reporting requirements on institutions that have access to such property.[84]

The power to create such a list is found in section 83.05(1) of the *Criminal Code*.[85] The Governor in Council can establish on recommen-

---

77   *Ibid* at para 48.
78   *Ibid* at para 51.
79   *Ibid* at para 52.
80   *Jalil*, above note 58 at para 38.
81   Public Safety Canada, "Listed Terrorist Entities," online: www.publicsafety.gc.ca/cnt/ntnl-scrt/cntr-trrrsm/lstd-ntts/index-eng.aspx.
82   *Criminal Code*, above note 51, s 83.01(1).
83   *Ibid.*
84   *Ibid.*
85   *Ibid*, s 83.05(1):

> The Governor in Council may, by regulation, establish a list on which the Governor in Council may place any entity if, on the recommendation of

dation of the minister of Public Safety and Emergency Preparedness, by regulation, a list of terrorist entities.[86] The minister will make a recommendation that an entity be included on the list where he has reasonable grounds[87] to believe that the entity is either knowingly carrying out or attempting to carry out a terrorist activity[88] or has knowingly acted on behalf of, or at the direction of, or in association with an entity already listed.[89]

A listed entity may make an application in writing to the minister, providing reasons why the minister should recommend to the Governor in Council to remove the entity from the list.[90] If the minister has not made a decision on the application within sixty days of receiving the application, the minister is deemed to have recommended that the entity remain on the list.[91] Such a decision must be communicated to the applicant.[92] The applicant may seek judicial review of the decision within sixty days of receiving notice of the decision of the minister.[93] During judicial review, a judge "must examine, in private, any security or criminal intelligence reports considered in listing the applicant and hear any other evidence or information that may be presented" by the minister.[94] Information presented by the minister may or may not be shared in the presence of the applicant, depending on whether the "information would injure national security or endanger the safety of any person."[95] The judge, however, will provide the applicant with a summary of information available to the judge without disclosing information that would "injure national security or endanger the safety of any person" and give the applicant an opportunity to be heard before a decision is made.[96] If an applicant is unsuccessful, the entity cannot

---

the Minister of Public Safety and Emergency Preparedness, the Governor in Council is satisfied that there are reasonable grounds to believe that (a) the entity has knowingly carried out, attempted to carry out, participated in or facilitated a terrorist activity; or (b) the entity is knowingly acting on behalf of, at the direction of or in association with an entity referred to in paragraph (a).

86   *Ibid.*
87   *Ibid*, s 83.05(1.1).
88   *Ibid*, s 83.05(1)(a).
89   *Ibid*, s 83.05(1)(b).
90   *Ibid*, s 83.05(2).
91   *Ibid*, s 83.05(3).
92   *Ibid*, s 83.05(4).
93   *Ibid*, s 83.05(5).
94   *Ibid*, s 83.05(6)(a). A *judge* means the Chief Justice of the Federal Court or a judge of that court designated by the Chief Justice (s 83.05(11)).
95   *Ibid.*
96   *Ibid*, ss 83.05(6)(c) and (d).

make another application unless there is a material change in circumstances.[97] The minister must review the list every two years to determine whether an entity should remain a listed entity.[98]

g) Alternative Remedies

As discussed above, the court has relied upon the existence of "alternative remedies" or legislative avenues upon which an applicant can ask for exemption or relief from findings of inadmissibility to justify the broad interpretations of various terms in section 34, but also a strict or harsh approach to implementing section 34. The most common alternative remedy was included in section 34(2),[99] which was repealed in 2013.[100] It stated: "(2) The matters referred to in subsection (1) do not constitute inadmissibility in respect of a permanent resident or a foreign national who satisfies the Minister that their presence in Canada would not be detrimental to the national interest."[101]

The removal of this avenue of request to the minister is significant for two reasons: first, it was seen as an "alternative remedy" that would serve to protect applicants finding themselves subject to inadmissibility under section 34;[102] and second, it permitted a broad interpretation of the terms *espionage, subversion, being a member in an organization*,[103] and *terrorism*, for example, given that there was an avenue to ask for exemption from inadmissibility under this section.[104]

---

97 *Ibid*, s 83.05(8).

98 *Ibid*, s 83.05(9).

99 See, for example, *Poshteh*, above note 69 at para 28.

100 *Faster Removal of Foreign Criminals Act*, above note 9, s 13(3).

101 *IRPA*, above note 1, s 34(2), as repealed by the *Faster Removal of Foreign Criminals Act*, above note 9, s 13(3).

102 *Kanapathy*, above note 71 at para 39: Mactavish J stated:

> I acknowledge Mr. Kanapathy's argument that a certain amount of interaction with the LTTE may have been inevitable in LTTE-controlled areas of northern Sri Lanka during the period in question. However, it seems to me that those submissions may be better advanced in the context of an application for a Ministerial exemption under subsection 34(2) of *Immigration and Refugee Protection Act*.

103 See, for example, *Sittampalam*, above note 17 at para 28, where the Federal Court of Appeal stated in response to the broad interpretation of being a member in an organization as including past membership: "Subsection 37(2) of the *IRPA* is intended to alleviate the harshness of the inadmissibility rule where, as the appellant suggests, there is evidence of a person's genuine withdrawal from membership."

104 See, for example, *Stables v Canada (Minister of Citizenship and Immigration)*, 2011 FC 1319 at para 35; *TK*, above note 71 at para 112: ". . . if the result seems harsh, subsection 34(2) can be called into play. The rationale for this position

As the Federal Court of Appeal stated in *Poshteh*:

> ... under subsection 34(2) of the *Immigration and Refugee Protection Act*, membership in a terrorist organization does not constitute inadmissibility if the individual in question satisfies the Minister that their presence in Canada would not be detrimental to the national interest .... Thus, under subsection 34(2), the Minister has the discretion to exclude the individual from the operation of paragraph 34(1)(f).[105]

Section 42.1 of the *IRPA* has replaced section 34(2):

(1) The Minister may, on application by a foreign national, declare that the matters referred to in section 34, paragraphs 35(1)(b) and (c) and subsection 37(1) do not constitute inadmissibility in respect of the foreign national if they satisfy the Minister that it is not contrary to the national interest.

(2) The Minister may, on the Minister's own initiative, declare that the matters referred to in section 34, paragraphs 35(1)(b) and (c) and subsections 37(1) do not constitute inadmissibility in respect of a foreign national if the Minister is satisfied that it is not contrary to the national interest.

(3) In determining whether to make a declaration, the Minister may only take into account national security and public safety considerations, but in his or her analysis, is not limited to considering the danger that the foreign national presents to the public or the security of Canada.[106]

This new provision fails to refer to permanent residents. It also does not provide restrictions on what the minister may take into account when considering whether an individual should be exempted from inadmissibility under section 34. The changes to the legislation raise serious questions about the impact of a finding of inadmissibility under section 34.

---

is that subsection 34(1) is intended to cast a very broad net to capture conduct that is inimical to Canada's interests." See also *Agraira v Canada (Minister of Public Safety and Emergency Preparedness)*, 2011 FCA 103 at para 64: "There may be other cases in which persons who would otherwise be caught by subsection 34(1) of the *IRPA* may justify their conduct in such a way as to escape the consequences of inadmissibility. For example, those who could persuade the Minister that their participation in a terrorist organization was coerced might well benefit from ministerial relief."

105 *Poshteh*, above note 69 at para 28.
106 *IRPA*, above note 1, s 42.1.

4) Human or International Rights Violations (Section 35)

Section 35 provides that a permanent resident or a foreign national is inadmissible for violating human or international rights and includes, within its ambit, acts committed outside Canada that constitute a crime against humanity or war crime.[107] In the following sections, each of the main components of this ground of inadmissibility is examined in turn.

a) Committing an Act outside Canada That Constitutes an Offence under the *Crimes against Humanity and War Crimes Act* (Section 35(1)(a))

In the seminal case of *Mugesera*, the Supreme Court of Canada identifies the components of crimes against humanity.[108] The Court states that crimes against humanity as defined have two elements, "(1) a criminal act; and (2) a guilty mind," both of which must be considered.[109]

The "criminal act of a crime against humanity is made up of three essential elements: (1) one of the enumerated proscribed acts is com-

---

107 *Ibid*, ss 35(1)(a) & (b).
108 *Mugesera*, above note 14. The court applied the definition of a crime against humanity found in an earlier version of the *Criminal Code* that was in force immediately prior to the enactment of the *Crimes against Humanity and War Crimes Act*, SC 2000, c 24. It stated that the differences introduced by the new legislation were not material to the decision. Sections 4(3) and 6(3) of the current legislation provide:

> *"crime against humanity"* means murder, extermination, enslavement, deportation, imprisonment, torture, sexual violence, persecution or any other inhumane act or omission that is committed against any civilian population or any identifiable group and that, at the time and in the place of its commission, constitutes a crime against humanity according to customary international law or conventional international law or by virtue of its being criminal according to the general principles of law recognized by the community of nations, whether or not it constitutes a contravention of the law in force at the time and in the place of its commission.
>
> *"genocide"* means an act or omission committed with intent to destroy, in whole or in part, an identifiable group of persons, as such, that, at the time and in the place of its commission, constitutes genocide according to customary international law or conventional international law or by virtue of its being criminal according to the general principles of law recognized by the community of nations, whether or not it constitutes a contravention of the law in force at the time and in the place of its commission.
>
> *"war crime"* means an act or omission committed during an armed conflict that, at the time and in the place of its commission, constitutes a war crime according to customary international law or conventional international law applicable to armed conflicts, whether or not it constitutes a contravention of the law in force at the time and in the place of its commission.

109 *Mugesera*, above note 14 at para 127.

mitted; (2) the act occurs as part of a widespread or systematic attack; and (3) the attack is directed against any civilian population or any identifiable group."[110]

The first of these elements requires one to consult the proscribed acts that "represent the different ways in which a crime against humanity can be committed."[111] Both the physical and mental elements of the underlying act must be made out.[112] In addition, the act must contravene international law,[113] which "tells us that the enumerated acts will become crimes against humanity if they are committed *as part of a widespread or systematic attack directed against any civilian population or any identifiable group*."[114] The Court clarified that "[a]n attack need be only widespread *or* systematic," not both.[115] The nature of the attack will be "determined by examining the means, methods, resources and results of the attack upon a civilian population."[116] Further, it is the attack, not the act of the accused that needs to be widespread or systematic.[117] The Court also confirmed that there is "no additional requirement for a state or other policy [to be] behind the attack."[118] As well, "a link must be demonstrated between the act and the attack which compels inter-

---

110 *Ibid* at para 128.

111 *Ibid* at para 129: The crimes include murder, extermination, enslavement, deportation, persecution, or any other inhumane act or omission.

112 *Ibid* at para 130:

> For instance, where the accused is charged with murder as a crime against humanity, the accused must (1) have caused the death of another person, and (2) have intended to cause the person's death or to inflict grievous bodily harm that he or she knew was likely to result in death. Once this has been established, the court will go on to consider whether the murder was committed in the context of a widespread or systematic attack directed against a civilian population or an identifiable group . . . .

In *Mugesera*, the court considered whether the underlying crimes of persecution by hate speech and counselling of murder were made out.

113 *Ibid* at para 150. See *Zazai v Canada (Minister of Citizenship and Immigration)*, 2005 FCA 303, where the court decided that complicity is not a crime in common law and under Canadian criminal law but is rather a mode or means of committing a crime, and therefore cannot constitute an underlying offence.

114 *Mugesera*, above note 14 at para 151: The Court stated, "This additional contextual requirement is what distinguishes a crime against humanity from an ordinary crime . . . ."

115 *Ibid* at para 156 [emphasis in original].

116 *Ibid*.

117 *Ibid*: "Even a single act may constitute a crime against humanity as long as the attack it forms a part of is widespread or systematic and is directed against a civilian population . . . ."

118 *Ibid* at para 158.

national scrutiny"[119] and this "link may be expressed in many ways."[120] The act undertaken does not need to be an essential or officially sanctioned part of the attack; it is enough that it was undertaken as part of the attack.[121]

The "mere existence of a systematic attack is not sufficient": "The attack must also be directed against a civilian population."[122] In discussing what is meant by *population*, the Court noted it refers to a "relatively large group of people who share distinctive features which identify them as targets of the attack."[123]

With regard to the mental element, the Court explained that the mental element of the underlying act must be made out,[124] but that discriminatory intent is not needed unless the underlying act takes the form of persecution.[125]

The Court held that "[i]t is now well settled that in addition to the *mens rea* for the underlying act, the accused must have knowledge of the attack and must know that his or her acts comprise part of it *or* take the risk that his or her acts will comprise part of it."[126] Motive is irrelevant.[127] Knowledge can be factually implied from the circumstances by looking at "the accused's position in a military or government hierarchy, public knowledge about the existence of the attack, the scale of violence and the general historical and political environment in which the acts occurred."[128] However, subjective knowledge must be shown in the sense that the accused must have actual knowledge of the attack and "must know that his or her actions are part of the attack or at least take the risk that they are part of the attack."[129]

As will be discussed below, an applicant who has been convicted, but pardoned or rehabilitated will escape a finding of inadmissibility based on criminality. However, such an exemption may not exist where the ground of inadmissibility is based on commission of a crime

---

119 *Ibid* at para 164.
120 *Ibid* at para 165.
121 *Ibid* at para 167.
122 *Ibid* at para 161: "This means that the civilian population must be 'the primary object of the attack,' and not merely a collateral victim of it."
123 *Ibid* at paras 161–62: "A prototypical example of a civilian population would be a particular national, ethnic or religious group."
124 *Ibid*.
125 *Ibid* at para 172.
126 *Ibid* at para 173.
127 *Ibid* at para 174: "It is important to stress that the person committing the act need only be cognizant of the link between his or her act and the attack."
128 *Ibid* at para 175.
129 *Ibid* at para 176.

against humanity. Legislation is silent on the matter. In *Varela v Canada (Minister of Citizenship and Immigration)*, Harrington J addressed the issue and took into account Guidelines of the United Nations High Commissioner for Refugees (UNHCR) relating to exclusion of individuals from the refugee definition.[130] The Guidelines suggested that the exclusion clauses might no longer be justified where expiation of the crime is considered to have taken place but that some crimes are so grave and heinous that the exclusion is still justified despite the existence of a pardon or an amnesty. Justice Harrington, in this case, found the conduct of the individual so grave (participation in a death squad) that the judge ruled that the amnesty granted to the applicant should not negate his inadmissibility.[131]

b) Being a Prescribed Senior Official in a Government That Has Engaged in Terrorism, Human Rights Violations, Genocide, War Crime, or Crime against Humanity (Section 35(1)(b))

Section 16 of the *Regulations* defines a *prescribed senior official* as "a person who, by virtue of the position they hold or held, is or was able to exert significant influence on the exercise of government power or is or was able to benefit from their position."[132] Prescribed senior officials include heads of state or government;[133] members of cabinet or governing council;[134] senior advisers to heads of state, cabinet, or governing council;[135] senior members of the public service;[136] senior members of the military, intelligence, and internal security services;[137] ambassadors and senior diplomatic officials;[138] and members of the judiciary.[139]

---

130 2008 FC 436. See UNHCR, Guidelines on International Protection: *Application of the Exclusion Clauses: Article 1F of the 1951 Convention relating to the Status of Refugees* (4 September 2003), online: www.refworld.org/pdfid/3f5857684.pdf.

131 *Ibid*; note that on appeal (*Varela v Canada (Minister of Citizenship and Immigration)*, 2009 FCA 145), the court addressed the question whether a pardon or general amnesty should be taken into account in considering whether a person is inadmissible on grounds of violating human or international rights, and unhelpfully concluded at para 42, "It would be difficult to say that a relevant factor — surely a general amnesty is a relevant factor — should not be taken into account in determining admissibility under the Act."

132 *Immigration and Refugee Protection Regulations*, SOR/2002-227, s 16 [*Regulations*].

133 *Ibid*, s 16(a).

134 *Ibid*, s 16(b).

135 *Ibid*, s 16(c).

136 *Ibid*, s 16(d).

137 *Ibid*, s 16(e).

138 *Ibid*, s 16(f).

139 *Ibid*, s 16(g).

Under section 35(1)(b), the minister of Public Safety and Emergency Preparedness has the authority to designate regimes. A person cannot be found to be inadmissible under section 35(1)(b) "unless the government concerned has been designated by the Minister as a regime that has been involved in terrorism, systemic or gross human rights violations, or genocide, a war crime or a crime against humanity."[140] Previously, the War Crimes Section of the Department of Justice kept a list of the designated regimes.[141] With the inception of section 35(1)(c) in the legislation, there was no longer any need to keep an updated list as the designated regimes list mirrored the list of countries that faced sanctions from Canada.[142] A recent list of countries facing sanctions may be found online on the website of the Department of Foreign Affairs, Trade and Development Canada.[143]

The Federal Court has endorsed the view that once the applicant is shown to be a senior official in a government that has been designated by the minister, a finding of inadmissibility follows automatically.[144] The court appears to adopt the absolute liability approach; no defences based on lack of complicity in crimes against humanity or human rights violations can rebut the presumption of inadmissibility where the individual is a prescribed senior official of a designated regime.[145] Thus, simply serving as a senior official of a designated regime is enough, and it is a non-rebuttable presumption.

Citizenship and Immigration Canada's Operational Manual pertaining to war crimes and crimes against humanity rationalizes this legislative non-rebuttable presumption: "[A]lthough such persons may never have personally participated in terrorism or gross human rights abuses, they nevertheless must share and accept the responsibility for such practices."[146] The Manual also classifies persons who can be found

---

140 OP 18, above note 28.

141 See, for example, Canada Border Services Agency, *Canada's Program on Crimes against Humanity and War Crimes*, 12th Report, 2008–2011 [archived], online: CBSA http://cbsa.gc.ca/security-securite/wc-cg/wc-cg2011-eng.html.

142 See policy rationale in Parliament of Canada, *Bill C-11: The Immigration and Refugee Protection Act*, LS-397E (31 January 2002), online: www.parl.gc.ca/About/Parliament/LegislativeSummaries/bills_ls.asp?source=library_prb&ls=C11&Parl=37&Ses=1&Language=E&Mode=1#D.%C2%A0%20Division%204txt at Part I, Section D.

143 The current list can be found online: www.international.gc.ca/sanctions/countries-pays/index.aspx?lang=eng [Sanctions].

144 *Segasayo v Canada (Minister of Citizenship and Immigration)*, 2010 FC 173.

145 *Ibid.*

146 Citizenship and Immigration Canada, ENF 18: *War Crimes and Crimes against Humanity*, online: CIC www.cic.gc.ca/english/resources/manuals/enf/enf18-eng.pdf at 3.1 [CIC: "War Crimes"].

inadmissible under section 35(1)(b) into three categories in which different evidentiary requirements need to be met.[147]

Thus, applicants facing a finding of inadmissibility under this section should focus on their role in a designated regime and build their case on an absence of seniority.[148] Expert evidence may be useful in explaining to decision makers the nature of the applicant's employment and whether it could be considered a senior position, especially where the viewpoint is that the position is in the "top half of the organization."[149] Providing evidence of the applicant's position is all the more important because the Federal Court has held that even where an applicant may have held an administrative position, the inquiry may not end there as the decision maker can "scrutinize labels carefully."[150]

c) Restricted by Sanctions (Section 35(1)(c))

A foreign national may be found to be inadmissible where Canada has imposed sanctions to that effect. For example, in February and March 2014, Canada imposed travel and economic sanctions on senior government officials of the Yanukovych government in Ukraine[151] and on

---

147 See ibid at 8.2; see also Habeeb v Canada (Minister of Citizenship and Immigration), 2011 FC 253, where the Federal Court accepts the three categories as appropriate ways to assess inadmissibility under s 35(1)(b) of the IRPA, and Younis v Canada (Minister of Citizenship and Immigration), 2010 FC 1157 at para 25, where the court accepts the approach in s 8.2 of CIC: "War Crimes," which provides that, "[i]f it can be demonstrated that the position is in the top half of the organization, the position can be considered senior." See also Hamidi v Canada (Minister of Citizenship and Immigration), 2006 FC 333; Nezam v Canada (Minister of Citizenship and Immigration), 2005 FC 446; and Holway v Canada (Minister of Citizenship and Immigration), 2006 FC 309 [Holway].

148 See, for example, Lutfi v Canada (Minister of Citizenship and Immigration), 2005 FC 1391, where it was held that the decision maker failed to examine the hierarchy of the military in question.

149 Ismail v Canada (Minister of Citizenship and Immigration), 2006 FC 987 at para 18; see, for example, Salahaldin v Canada (Minister of Citizenship and Immigration), 2014 FC 51 at para 5: In this case, the Federal Court held that an officer's decision that the applicant was a senior official in a designated regime as a result of his work and his contact with the minister was unreasonable because evidence showed that the applicant's access to the minister was only by reason of his part-time position on a project; he was never a ministry official and had no title within the ministry.

150 Holway, above note 147 at para 23: "It is important in this context to scrutinize labels carefully. Labels can block analysis."

151 Kathryrn Blaze Carlson, "Canada Imposes New Sanctions on Senior Ukrainian Officials" The Globe and Mail (20 February 2014), online: www.theglobeandmail.com/news/politics/canada-new-ecnomoic-sanctions-ukraine/article16997843/.

Russian senior officials.[152] Canada keeps a running list of sanctions measures against various countries.[153]

5) Serious Criminality, Criminality, and Organized Criminality

Sections 36 and 37 provide criminality as grounds for inadmissibility. In particular, section 36(1) enunciates the ground of serious criminality, section 36(2) provides for the ground of criminality, and section 37 provides the ground of organized criminality. Each will be examined more closely in turn.

a) Serious Criminality (Section 36(1))

A permanent resident or a foreign national can be found inadmissible on the ground of serious criminality for

1) having been convicted in Canada of an offence punishable by a maximum term of imprisonment of at least ten years or more or of an offence for which a term of imprisonment of more than six months has been imposed;[154]

2) having been convicted of an offence outside Canada that, if committed in Canada, would constitute an offence punishable by a maximum term of imprisonment of at least ten years;[155] or

3) committing an act outside Canada that is an offence in the place it was committed and that if committed in Canada would constitute an offence punishable by a maximum term of imprisonment of at least ten years.[156]

The *IRPA* attaches an important qualification to the third ground. Specifically, the legislation provides that "a determination of whether a permanent resident has committed an act described in [section 36] (1) (c) must be based on a balance of probabilities"[157] and excludes persons found or deemed to be rehabilitated[158] or young offenders.[159]

---

152 Prime Minister of Canada Stephen Harper, Backgrounder: "Sanctions List" (17 March 2014), online: www.pm.gc.ca/eng/news/2014/03/17/sanctions-list.

153 See above note 143.

154 *IRPA*, above note 1, s 36(1)(a).

155 *Ibid*, s 36(1)(b).

156 *Ibid*, s 36(1)(c).

157 *Ibid*, s 36(3)(d).

158 *Ibid*, s 36(3)(c).

159 *Ibid*, s 36(3)(e).

The use of the maximum penalty as the decisive factor for determining whether a person is inadmissible on this ground is noteworthy. A permanent resident may be found inadmissible and lose his status where he is found guilty of the offence in question. Even harsher is the possibility that he may lose his status because his conduct outside Canada can be classified as falling within a definition found in Canada's *Criminal Code* without any actual determination of guilt. Any extenuating circumstances that may be considered at the sentencing stage of a criminal trial are deemed to be irrelevant in an admissibility hearing. The distinction between criminality and serious criminality is determined by the classification of the offence rather than by the level of culpability, and by the technical description of the conduct rather than by the assessment of the level of wrongdoing. The section introduces the Orwellian practice of labelling as serious criminals those individuals whose conduct is only minimally transgressive.

b)   Criminality (Section 36(2))

Section 36(2) of the *IRPA* specifies that a foreign national is inadmissible on grounds of criminality for

1) having been convicted in Canada of an indictable offence or two summary offences not arising out of a single occurrence;[160]
2) having been convicted outside Canada of an offence that, if committed in Canada, would constitute an indictable offence or two summary offences not arising out of a single occurrence that, if committed in Canada, would constitute offences here;[161]
3) committing an act outside Canada that is an offence in the place where it was committed and that, if committed in Canada, would constitute an indictable offence in Canada;[162] or
4) committing, on entering Canada, an offence.[163]

It is important to note a few things. First, this provision applies only to foreign nationals and not to permanent residents. It is thus distinguishable from the provisions dealing with serious criminality. Second, the legislation specifies that if an offence can be prosecuted either summarily or by way of indictment, the offence is deemed to be an indictable offence, even if it was prosecuted summarily.[164] It is the potential for prosecution under indictment that grounds the deter-

---

160   *Ibid*, s 36(2)(a).
161   *Ibid*, s 36(2)(b).
162   *Ibid*, s 36(2)(c).
163   *Ibid*, s 36(2)(d).
164   *Ibid*, s 36(3)(a).

mination of inadmissibility rather than the actual mode of prosecution chosen.

The following sections focus on some of the complexities raised by section 36.

i)   Equivalency of Foreign Offences

The *IRPA* has deliberately included foreign offences and convictions within the ambit of criminal inadmissibility that requires an inquiry into whether the act committed *outside* Canada would be regarded as criminal *within* Canada. This inquiry is often referred to as an examination into "equivalency." Section 36 introduces the thorny question of equivalency. The task, as the Federal Court has stated, is one where, "[t]he foreign and Canadian laws in question must be interpreted to determine whether or not the two offences are equivalent, based on how the respective offences are constructed."[165] There is some authority that indicates that the question of equivalency is a question of law and that an immigration officer must interpret the foreign and Canadian law correctly.[166] However, in other contexts, where an officer is required to determine questions of foreign law (where, for example, the validity of a foreign marriage is at issue), the view is often stated that questions of foreign law are actually questions of fact, which may be reviewed according to a standard of reasonableness rather than a standard of correctness.

In *Hill v Canada (Minister of Employment and Immigration)* the Federal Court of Appeal has explained that there are three ways to determine whether an offence committed outside Canada is equivalent to a requisite offence in Canada:

> [F]irst by a comparison of the precise wording in each statute both through documents and, if available, through the evidence of an expert or experts in the foreign law and determining therefrom the *essential ingredients* of the respective offences. Two, by examining the evidence adduced before the adjudicator, both oral and documentary, to *ascertain whether . . . ingredients* of the offence in Canada had been proved in the foreign proceedings, whether precisely described in the initiating documents or in the statutory provisions in the same words or not. Third, by a combination of the two.[167]

---

165   *Kharchi v Canada (Minister of Citizenship and Immigration)*, 2006 FC 1160 at para 29 [*Kharchi*].

166   *Ibid.*

167   (1987), 73 NR 315 at 320 (FCA) [emphasis added].

Thus, the primary question when determining equivalency is whether the offence committed abroad has the essential elements of an equivalent offence in Canada:

> Whatever the names given the offences or the words used in defining them, one must determine the essential elements of each and be satisfied that these essential elements correspond. One must, of course, expect differences in the wording of statutory offences in different countries.[168]

The Federal Court has also stated that the law does not require that offences be identical in every aspect.[169] Rather, what is required is "essentially the similarity of definitions of offences."[170] Thus, the offences must be compared to determine whether they are sufficiently similar, regardless of how the terminology used to define the crime:

> I believe that it would be most consistent with the purposes of the statute, and not inconsistent with the jurisprudence of this Court, to conclude that what equivalency of offences requires is essentially the similarity of definitions of offences. A definition is similar if it involves similar criteria for establishing that an offence has occurred, whether those criteria are manifested in "elements" (in the narrow sense) or "defences" in the two sets of laws. In my view the definition of an offence involves the elements and defences particular to that offence, or perhaps to that class of offences. For the purpose of subparagraph 19(2)(a.1)(i) of the *Immigration Act* it is not necessary to compare all the general principles of criminal responsibility in the two systems: what is being examined is the comparability of offences, not the comparability of possible convictions in the two countries.[171]

Thus, the Federal Court of Appeal has distinguished between the elements of an offence and the procedural or evidentiary rules used to determine guilt. Even if a person is more or less likely to be convicted of an offence in a jurisdiction outside Canada because the rules of evidence are less lax or stricter, this is irrelevant in an admissibility proceeding. What is important is that the "essential ingredients" or "elements" of the offences correspond. It is not important that the in-

---

168 *Brannson v Canada (Minister of Employment and Immigration)*, [1981] 2 FC 141 at para 38 (CA); see also *Kharchi*, above note 165 at para 34.
169 *Wang v Canada (Minister of Citizenship and Immigration)*, 2011 FC 1510.
170 *Ibid* at para 34.
171 *Li v Canada (Minister of Citizenship and Immigration)*, [1997] 1 FC 235 at para 18 (CA); see also *Kharchi*, above note 165 at para 35.

dividual would probably not have been convicted if she had been tried in Canada.

ii) *Equivalency between Acts Committed outside Canada with Acts Committed inside Canada under Sections 36(1)(c) and 36(2)(c)*

In making a finding under sections 36(1)(c) and 36(2)(c), an officer must first determine whether the act constitutes an offence in the foreign jurisdiction, then provide critical analysis as to how it could constitute an offence in Canada.[172] In making the determinations, where an applicant provides expert opinion as to whether the offence was made out in the foreign jurisdiction, or whether it constitutes an offence in Canada, an officer must consider credible and well-articulated opinions from experts whose credentials are not in dispute.[173]

Caselaw reveals that a conviction is not required for a finding of inadmissibility under serious criminality.[174] The court in *Magtibay*[175] held that it was clear Parliament intended to allow for the inadmissibility of a permanent resident or foreign national not only on conviction but also on the commission of certain acts. Thus, even in a case where charges were dropped, an officer can review the evidence and still determine that the criminal act occurred despite the difficulties in prosecuting or pursuing a charge in Canada.[176]

iii) *"Term of Imprisonment" (Section 36(1))*

What constitutes a "term of imprisonment"? Both the Federal Court and the Immigration Appeal Division have counted pre-sentencing detention as part of the term of imprisonment, indicating it was the intention of Parliament to calculate the term in this way.[177] Conditional sentences, however, may not be considered "terms of imprisonment" as the court has stated that "the fact that a conditional sentence is described as a sentence of imprisonment in general terms in the [Criminal]

---

172 *Zeon v Canada (Minister of Citizenship and Immigration)*, 2005 FC 1338 at para 10; *Wang v Canada (Minister of Citizenship and Immigration)*, 2007 FC 1188 at para 9; *Farenas v Canada (Minister of Citizenship and Immigration)*, 2011 FC 660 at para 28.
173 *Xiao v Canada (Minister of Citizenship and Immigration)*, 2009 FC 195 at para 26.
174 *Magtibay v Canada (Minister of Citizenship and Immigration)*, 2005 FC 397 [*Magtibay*].
175 *Ibid*.
176 *Bankole v Canada (Minister of Citizenship and Immigration)*, 2011 FC 373.
177 *Shepherd v Canada (Minister of Citizenship and Immigration)*, 2005 FC 1033; *Cheddesingh v Canada (Minister of Citizenship and Immigration)*, 2006 FC 124; *Nguyen v Canada (Minister of Citizenship and Immigration)*, 2010 FC 30 at para 20. Note that much of the jurisprudence interpreting the phrase "term of imprisonment" also deals with the *IRPA*, above note 1, s 64.

Code does not necessarily mean it should be considered to be a sentence of imprisonment in other statutes such as *IRPA*" and that "courts impose conditional sentences on persons who are not regarded as serious criminals."[178] This finding, however, will likely be appealed and challenged by the federal government. Therefore, when advising persons who have had conditional sentences imposed, it may be prudent to note that a conditional sentence of six months or more may be considered a term of imprisonment. Further, with the passage of the *Faster Removal of Foreign Criminals Act*,[179] it is important to note that persons with conditional sentences may not have a right to appeal a resulting deportation order to the Immigration Appeal Division.

iv) Discharges, Record Suspensions, and Rehabilitation

Section 36(3)(b) provides that inadmissibility grounded on criminality cannot be based on a conviction in respect of which a record suspension has been ordered and has not been revoked or ceased to have effect under the *Criminal Records Act* or where there has been a final determination of an acquittal.[180] Thus, persons granted a record suspension (previously known as a pardon) or an absolute or conditional discharge will not be found to be inadmissible.[181] The explanation for this is that the *Criminal Code* has made it clear that an accused who has been granted an absolute or conditional discharge is deemed not to have been convicted,[182] and those who have been granted a record suspension are deemed to have been rehabilitated.

178　*Tran v Canada (Minister of Public Safety and Emergency Preparedness)*, 2014 FC 1040 at paras 9–10. The federal government will likely appeal this decision and therefore the current understanding of term of imprisonment in relation to conditional sentences may change.

179　Above note 9.

180　*IRPA*, above note 1, s 36(3)(b).

181　Some persons are not eligible for a record suspension, those convicted of sexual offences involving children among them.

182　*Criminal Code*, above note 51, s 730:

　　(1)　Where an accused, other than an organization, pleads guilty to or is found guilty of an offence, other than an offence for which a minimum punishment is prescribed by law or an offence punishable by imprisonment for fourteen years or for life, the court before which the accused appears may, if it considers it to be in the best interests of the accused and not contrary to the public interest, instead of convicting the accused, by order direct that the accused be discharged absolutely or on the conditions prescribed in a probation order made under subsection 731(2).

　　(2)　. . .

v) "Having Been Convicted" (Sections 36(1)(a) and (b))

The case of *Burgon v Canada (Minister of Employment and Immigration)* identifies some of the difficulties raised by the fact that a conviction is a prerequisite for inadmissibility.[183] In *Burgon*, the applicant was being sponsored by her Canadian spouse. She had pleaded guilty in England to conspiracy to supply a controlled drug and was given a suspended sentence. After the sponsorship application was submitted, the applicant received an English discharge order. Her criminal record was thereby cleared completely. The Federal Court of Appeal held that Canadian criminal law policy had evolved to allow judges to impose absolute and conditional discharges, which have the effect of deeming the accused not to have been convicted of an offence in question. The court acknowledged that similar measures had been adopted in the United Kingdom. It then interpreted the phrase "having been convicted" as excluding convictions that had been expunged, reasoning that if Parliament created the means by which a conviction could be erased by legislation, then that conviction was not meant to be treated in the same way as a conviction that had not been erased. Further, the court emphasized the underlying similarities in the law within the two jurisdictions and concluded there was no reason to thwart the legislative intent. Having made these findings, the court held that the applicant was not inadmissible.

The Federal Court in *Barnett v Canada (Minister of Citizenship and Immigration)* has confirmed and expanded the approach outlined in *Burgon*.[184] Once again the applicant had been deemed not to have a conviction under English law. The court stated that where another country, whose legal system is based on similar foundations and values as our own, has enacted legislation that reflects goals and objectives analogous to those encompassed within our own system, then that law should be accorded respect and recognized for the purposes of Canadian immigration law. The court stated that the question is not whether Canada has identical legislation in place but whether the underlying rationale of the foreign legislation is consistent with some fundamental principle of justice recognized in Canada.

---

(3) Where a court directs under subsection (1) that an offender be discharged of an offence, the offender shall be deemed not to have been convicted of the offence . . . .

183 (1991), 78 DLR (4th) 103 (FCA) [*Burgon*].

184 *Barnett v Canada (Minister of Citizenship and Immigration)* (1996), 109 FTR 154 (TD).

vi) Rehabilitation (Section 36(3)(c))

The *IRPA* recognizes that persons who have committed or have been convicted of an offence outside Canada may have been rehabilitated.[185] Where this is found to be the case, neither the conviction nor the criminal offence will be a ground of inadmissibility. The determination of rehabilitation may be based on an individualized inquiry or may be based solely on general factors that justify deeming the person to be rehabilitated. The purpose of the individualized inquiry is "to allow the Minister to take into consideration the unique facts of each particular case and to consider whether the overall situation warrants a finding that the individual has been rehabilitated."[186] Decision makers will look at the nature of the offence; the circumstances under which it was committed; the length of time that has elapsed; and whether there have been previous or subsequent offences.[187] They are required to engage in forward-looking analysis and must not fixate on past criminal activity.[188] The question to be asked is prospective: whether there is a likelihood of the applicant committing or being involved in criminal or unlawful activity.[189] Decision makers also have a duty to examine mitigating factors; where there is supporting documentation or evidence that an applicant has not committed or been convicted of offences for a lengthy time, and also that the applicant has demonstrated rehabilitation, such evidence must be considered when determining whether acts or convictions should be considered.[190]

A determination of deemed rehabilitation will be based on the length of time after the conviction or the completion of a sentence during which there has been no further criminal activity.[191] Deemed rehabilitation periods vary according to the type of offence committed. In general, if a person has been convicted of an offence outside Canada that would be an indictable offence punishable by a maximum term of imprisonment of ten years or less in Canada, a person will not be deemed rehabilitated until at least ten years after completion of the sentence imposed and will not be eligible to apply for rehabilitation until

---

185 *IRPA*, above note 1, s 36(3)(c).

186 *Hadad v Canada (Minister of Citizenship and Immigration)*, 2011 FC 1503 at para 43 [*Hadad*], quoting Rouleau J in *Aviles v Canada (Minister of Citizenship and Immigration)*, 2005 FC 1369 at para 18.

187 *Hadad*, above note 186.

188 *Ibid* at para 44.

189 *Ibid* at para 45.

190 *Kok v Canada (Minister of Citizenship and Immigration)*, 2005 FC 77.

191 *IRPA*, above note 1, s 36(3)(c); *Regulations*, above note 132, ss 17–18.

five years after the completion of the sentence imposed.[192] Individuals who have been convicted of two or more offences outside Canada that, if committed in Canada, would constitute summary conviction offences, would not be deemed rehabilitated until at least five years after the sentences imposed were served or to be served.[193] Finally, those that have committed an offence which, if committed in Canada, would constitute an indictable offence punishable by a maximum term of ten years or less, will not be deemed rehabilitated until at least ten years have elapsed since the day of the commission of the offence and they have not been convicted of an offence within that period of time.[194]

a.   The Ten-Year Term of Imprisonment Bar on Rehabilitation
Under section 18 of the *Regulations*, persons who have been convicted of or have committed a crime punishable by ten years or more in Canada cannot be deemed to be rehabilitated for the purposes of admissibility.[195] Where the *Criminal Code* provides a term of imprisonment "not exceeding 10 years," this qualifies as falling within the maximum term of "less than 10 years" for the purposes of rehabilitation under section 18 of the *Regulations*.[196]

vii) *Record Suspensions (Formerly Known as "Pardons")*
Persons who have a criminal record must seek a record suspension, formerly known as a "pardon," from the Parole Board of Canada before being considered rehabilitated and therefore admissible to Canada.[197] Pardons obtained outside Canada may be helpful as well.[198] The Federal Court of Appeal has held that:

---

192 *Regulations, ibid,* s 18(2)(a).
193 *Ibid,* s 18(2)(b).
194 *Ibid,* s 18(2)(c).
195 *Ibid,* s 18.
196 *Sun v Canada (Minister of Citizenship and Immigration),* 2011 FC 708.
197 Once an applicant is eligible, has completed all of his sentences, and the applicable waiting period has passed, the applicant can apply for a record suspension. The process has ten steps: (1) get criminal record from RCMP in Ottawa and, if required, proof of conviction documents; (2) get court information; (3) get military conduct sheet; (4) get local police record check(s); (5) get proof of citizenship or immigration documents; (6) get photocopy of document to support identity; (7) fill in Schedule 1 Exception form; (8) fill in Record Suspension Application form; (9) fill in Measureable Benefit/Sustained Rehabilitation form; and (10) complete checklist, and mail application and documents with $631 (CDN) processing fee. More detailed information can be found online at http://pbc-clcc.gc.ca/prdons/pardoninstr-eng.pdf.
198 *Canada (Minister of Citizenship and Immigration) v Saini,* 2001 FCA 311.

. . . three elements must be established before a foreign discharge or pardon may be recognized: (1) the foreign legal system as a whole must be similar to that of Canada; (2) the aim, content and effect of the specific foreign law must be similar to Canadian law; and (3) there must be no valid reason not to recognize the effect of the foreign law . . . .[199]

Thus, as legislation is silent on the treatment of foreign pardons, such discharges are not "automatically recognized" and the gravity of the offence can be considered in deciding whether to give effect to a foreign pardon.[200] The Federal Court of Appeal has stated that an applicant seeking to use a foreign discharge as a means to avoid inadmissibility should present how the three elements listed above are met.[201]

viii) Young Offenders

Convictions arising under the *Young Offenders Act*[202] and sentences arising under the *Youth Criminal Justice Act (YCJA)*[203] are exempt from consideration when determining inadmissibility.[204] Where a young person has been convicted under the *YCJA*, officers and the Immigration Appeal Division (IAD) have an obligation to determine whether an applicant's juvenile conviction is releasable under the *YCJA*.[205] However, where an order was made to transfer charges from the youth court to ordinary court, the applicant will not be considered to have been tried under the *Young Offenders Act* and, therefore, convictions stemming from such charges can be used to find the applicant inadmissible.[206]

ix) Multiple Permissible Entries in Canada after Conviction

An applicant should not rely on the fact that, after being convicted of an offence, he has been admitted to Canada multiple times in the past without incident. Past decisions to permit entry into Canada are not a

---

199 *Ibid* at para 24.
200 *Ibid* at para 45.
201 *Ibid* at para 48.
202 The *Young Offenders Act* [repealed 2002, c 1, s 199] was repealed in 2003 with the passing of the *Youth Criminal Justice Act*, SC 2002, c 1 [*YCJA*].
203 *YCJA*, *ibid*.
204 See *IRPA*, above note 1, ss 36(3)(e)(ii) & (iii), which state that inadmissibility under ss 36(1) & (2) cannot be based on an offence for which a permanent resident or foreign national is found guilty under the *Young Offenders Act* or received a sentence under the *YCJA*.
205 *Younis v Canada (Citizenship and Immigration)*, 2008 FC 944.
206 *Tessma v Canada (Minister of Citizenship and Immigration)*, 2003 FC 1126.

factor listed under section 36(3) that may render an otherwise inadmissible person admissible.[207]

x)   No Automatic Obligation to Defer pending Criminal Proceedings

Where an applicant has initiated an appeal against a criminal conviction, there is no obligation on the part of the decision maker to defer reaching a decision with regard to inadmissibility.[208] The Federal Court has held this to be the case because one may file a new application if circumstances later change as a result of a successful appeal.[209] Further, the court reasoned that an applicant can always ask for a deferral.[210] Thus, an applicant awaiting a resolution to a criminal appeal must be proactive and ask for a deferral, outlining the specifics of the appeal and any information on timelines associated with the proceeding. Without such a request, there is no obligation on the part of the officer to delay implementing the scheme of the IRPA.[211]

c) Organized Criminality (Section 37(1))

A permanent resident or foreign national is inadmissible on grounds of organized criminality for

(a) being a member of an organization that is believed on reasonable grounds to be or to have been engaged in activity that is part of a pattern of criminal activity planned and organized by a number of persons acting in concert in furtherance of the commission of an offence punishable under an Act of Parliament by way of indictment, or in furtherance of the commission of an offence outside Canada that, if committed in Canada, would constitute such an offence, or engaging in activity that is part of such a pattern; or

(b) engaging, in the context of transnational crime, in activities such as people smuggling, trafficking in persons or money laundering.

Those who have entered Canada with the assistance of a person who is involved in organized criminality are exempt from a finding of

---

207 *Aksenova v Canada (Minister of Public Safety and Emergency Preparedness)*, 2006 FC 557 at para 16.

208 *Johnson v Canada (Minister of Citizenship and Immigration)*, 2008 FC 2.

209 *Ibid* at para 22.

210 *Ibid* at para 35. In Johnson's case, he did not request a deferral until his appeal was dealt with, and the court was not ready to impose an obligation without such a request.

211 *Ibid*.

inadmissibility based on this ground.[212] Thus, at least in this respect, persons who are "smuggled into Canada are not penalized as a result of their mode of entry."[213]

i)   "Being a Member of an Organization" (Section 37(1)(a))

The phrase "membership in an organization" appears in both section 37 and section 34. Thus, jurisprudence dealing with this issue under section 34 should be read alongside jurisprudence under section 37.

The Federal Court of Appeal has identified a number of factors that help in determining whether someone is a member of a criminal organization:

1) The legislation is "broad enough to enable Canada to protect its national security by excluding, not only those intending to commit crimes here, but also those whose presence in Canada may be used to strengthen a criminal organization or to advance its purposes."[214]

2) A "person's participation in a legitimate business, knowing it is controlled by a criminal organization, in some circumstances may support a reasonable belief that the person is a member of the criminal organization itself."[215]

3) "Reasonable grounds" is a standard of proof that falls short of balance of probabilities but connotes a "bona fide belief in a serious possibility based on credible evidence."[216]

The Federal Court has acknowledged that the IRPA neither defines the term *member* nor stipulates a test for belonging to an organization.[217] It has also noted that the courts have developed inconsistent tests to determine whether someone is a member of a criminal organ-

---

212 *IRPA*, above note 1, s 37(2).

213 *B010 v Canada (Minister of Citizenship and Immigration)*, 2013 FCA 87 at para 86, leave to appeal to SCC granted, [2013] SCCA No 220 [*B010*]. The appeal was heard by the Supreme Court of Canada 16 February 2015 and judgment was reserved. Those individuals who are smuggled into Canada and are designated under s 20.1 of the *IRPA* are, however, subject to different treatment. For more information, see Chapter 9 on inland refugee determinations.

214 *Chiau v Canada (Minister of Citizenship and Immigration*, [2001] 2 FC 297 at para 58.

215 *Ibid* at para 59.

216 *Ibid* at para 60; see also *Canada (AG) v Jolly*, [1975] FC 216 (CA). For more information, see Section B(1), above in this chapter, which discusses facts arising from omissions or for which there are reasonable grounds to believe they have occurred (s 33).

217 *Castelly v Canada (Minister of Citizenship and Immigration)*, 2008 FC 788 at para 42 [*Castelly*].

ization.[218] However, the Federal Court of Appeal has stipulated clearly that "a member of an organization" includes a person who is not currently a member, but has been a member in the past.[219] Further, it has stipulated the word *organization* is to be given a broad, unrestricted interpretation.[220] While no precise definition can be established, the factors listed in *Thanaratnam* are helpful, keeping in mind that no element is essential.[221] Criminal organizational structures vary, and the definition of *organization* must reflect this. As well, the Federal Court has held that it is not necessary for an applicant to take part personally in serious crimes; it is enough for an applicant to have direct knowledge of criminal activity by other members of the organization.[222]

ii) "Engaging, in the Context of Transnational Crime, in Activities" (Section 37(1)(b))

The Federal Court and the Federal Court of Appeal have examined the scope of section 37(1)(b) and, in particular, the nature of "activities" to which it refers. In the case of *Dhillon*, the Federal Court held that the inclusion of the words *such as* within the provision implied that its application was not limited to the crimes of people smuggling, trafficking in persons, and money laundering.[223] The question at issue in the case was whether drug smuggling is a transnational crime within the meaning of section 37(1)(b). The court concluded that a textual, contextual, and purposive approach to interpretation led to the conclusion that it was. The issue was important because, under section 64 of the *IRPA*, a person inadmissible under section 36(1)(b) may still have access to an

---

218 *Ibid.*

219 *Ibid; Sittampalam*, above note 17. The court has addressed the standard of proof, holding that it is not necessary to prove that the person belongs to a criminal organization but that it is sufficient to have reasonable grounds to believe that he or she was a member of such an organization.

220 *Ibid.*

221 *Thanaratnam*, above note 72 at para 38. Some of these factors include
   - involvement directly or indirectly in a gang-related crime or incident;
   - acknowledgment of gang membership or gang association;
   - identification as a gang member or gang associate by physical evidence;
   - identification as a gang member or gang associate by reliable source information;
   - police information provided or received as the result of directly observed association with other known gang members or gang associates;
   - common or symbolic gang identifier(s) or paraphernalia; and
   - previous court findings including, but not limited to, sworn testimonies that the person is a gang member or associate.

222 *Castelly*, above note 217.

223 Above note 16.

appeal at the Immigration Appeal Division if sentenced to less than two years, whereas those found inadmissible under section 37 do not.

The Federal Court has, however, held that mere knowledge of the fact that fellow passengers on a boat are not in possession of the required visa or other legal documents to enter Canada is insufficient to find an applicant engaged in an activity under section 37(1)(b).[224] The court went further and held that such a conclusion is even less reasonable where the applicant acted to protect himself against hunger, illness, and other difficulties in the journey. Here, what is important to consider is the applicant's level of engagement, and the nature of the applicant's dependence vis-à-vis the alleged smugglers.[225]

iii) "People Smuggling" (Section 37(1)(b))

The meaning of the term people smuggling, as used in section 37(1)(b) has been considered in cases involving Sri Lankan migrants who arrived in Canada on board the MV *Sun Sea* in August 2010. In *B010*, the Federal Court of Appeal held that it was appropriate to define *people smuggling* in terms of the offence created by section 117 of the *IRPA*, the provision that prohibits human smuggling and trafficking.[226] This provision does not include a requirement that one receive a "material benefit" for the offence to be complete.[227] The court went further and

---

224 *B306 v Canada (Minister of Public Safety and Emergency Preparedness)*, 2012 FC 1282, rev'd 2013 FCA 262, leave to appeal to SCC granted, [2014] SCCA No 22. The appeal was heard by the Supreme Court of Canada 16 February 2015 and judgment was reserved. The Federal Court of Appeal at para 143 did not answer the certified question:

> For the application of paragraph 37(1)(b) and section 117 of the *IRPA*, is there a distinction to be made between aiding and abetting the coming into Canada of one or more persons who are not in possession of a visa, passport or other document required by the *IRPA*, as opposed to aiding and abetting the smugglers while within a vessel and in the course of being smuggled? In other words, in what circumstances would the definition of people smuggling in paragraph 37(1)(b) of the *IRPA* extend to the offences referred to in section 131 of the *IRPA*?

It remains to be seen whether the Supreme Court of Canada will clarify what activities are covered under s 37(1)(b).

225 *Ibid.*

226 *B010*, above note 213 at para 8; *IRPA*, above note 1, s 117:

> (1) Organizing entry into Canada — No person shall organize, induce, aid or abet the coming into Canada of one or more persons knowing that, or being reckless as to whether, their coming into Canada is or would be in contravention of this Act.

227 *B010*, above note 213 at para 8; *Canada (Minister of Public Safety and Emergency Preparedness) v JP*, 2013 FCA 262, leave to appeal to SCC granted, [2014]

held that "defining the term 'people smuggling' by reference to section 117 of the *IRPA* does not place Canada in breach of the *Refugee Convention* because a finding of inadmissibility is not the equivalent of removal or refoulement" since "[s]ignificant protections remain available to the person found inadmissible."[228] The court, in a different case, *JP*, also held that the provision does not violate section 7 of the *Charter* as section 7 could not be engaged in the admissibility process but only later, in the removals process.[229] Our understanding of what is included in "people smuggling" may be clarified when the aforementioned cases are heard at the Supreme Court of Canada.

iv) Precarious Distinction between Finding of Inadmissibility and Removal
Various decisions of the Federal Court have highlighted the fact that an applicant may pursue a number of avenues after a finding of inadmissibility but before a removal order is executed.[230] However, recent changes in the legislation have limited these opportinities and have cast doubt on whether meaningful alternative remedies will be available. For example, a group, such as the Sri Lankan migrants who arrived by boat, can now be designated by the minister as an irregular arrival and its members deemed to be designated foreign nationals.[231] The minister may make this designation either on the basis that it is easier to estab-

---

SCCA No 22 [*JP*]. The appeal was heard by the Supreme Court of Canada 16 February 2015 and judgment was reserved. In *JP*, the Federal Court of Appeal concluded, as it had in *B010*, that individuals need not obtain a material benefit from a smuggling event in order to be found inadmissible under s 37 and that the applicable standard of review is reasonableness notwithstanding the fact that a decision may involve interpreting international conventions, treaties, and protocols. The difference between *JP* and *B010*, however, is that the court in *B010* did not consider the constitutionality of s 37 and, namely, whether it would offend s 7 of the *Charter* because its application would bar refugee claimants from having their claims heard before the Refugee Protection Division. The court dismissed the constitutional arguments, stating that s 7 is not engaged in the admissibility process; it is engaged only later in the removals process.

228 *B010*, above note 213 at para 91.
229 *JP*, above note 227 at para 120.
230 *B010*, above note 213 at paras 89–90: In this case, the court stated,

Examples of procedures potentially available to B010 and B072 include an application for ministerial relief pursuant to paragraph 37(2)(*a*) of the Act, an application for ministerial relief on humanitarian and compassionate grounds pursuant to section 25 of the Act, and a pre-removal risk assessment on subsection 97(1) grounds pursuant to section 112 of the Act.

See also *Németh v Canada*, 2010 SCC 56 at para 50; and *Poshteh*, above note 69 at para 63.
231 *IRPA*, above note 1, s 20.1. See Chapter 9 for information on designated foreign nationals.

lish their identity or their inadmissibility as a group or on the basis that there are reasonable grounds to suspect human smuggling or terrorist activity.[232] Being deemed a "designated foreign national," however, has serious implications, including the inability to obtain a temporary resident permit,[233] the inability to obtain a stay of removal,[234] no access to the Refugee Appeal Division,[235] and, in some cases, no access to the Immigration Appeal Division.[236] These restrictions will provide future challenges for courts that have relied on the notion that there are supplementary remedies or processes for applicants who have been found inadmissible on the basis of criminality.

v) Relying on a Conviction

It is important for applicants to note that a conviction may not be determinative under section 37(1). In *Tang v Canada (Minister of Citizenship and Immigration)*, the Federal Court held that a conviction for claiming to be a member of an organization may be insufficient to ground an inadmissibility decision.[237] Justice Phelan stated:

> As a general proposition, a conviction may form the basis for a conclusion of inadmissibility but does not necessarily always do so. A conviction may form that basis where there is reason to believe that the allegations on which the conviction is based are a true statement of facts. However, to rely upon a conviction does require an inquiry into the meaning of the conviction and may engage an analysis of the circumstances surrounding it. For example, a plea bargain may raise different considerations than a finding of guilt after a trial.[238]

In the case at bar, the conviction arose from a guilty plea with a minimal penalty, and there were circumstances surrounding the facts, in Phelan J's opinion, that could lead one to believe that the applicant had a limited role or that he was not a true member of the organization. It is interesting to note that Phelan J referred to the fact that the government had permitted Tang to enter Canada on several occasions, which belied its stated belief that he was a member of a triad. He stated:

> [I]f the Respondent had "a *bona fide* belief" that Tang was or had been a member of a triad, the Respondent had that belief since 1997 and

---

232 *Ibid.*
233 See *ibid*, s 24.
234 See *Regulations*, above note 132, ss 231–33.
235 See *IRPA*, above note 1, s 110(2).
236 See *ibid*, s 64.
237 *Tang v Canada (Minister of Citizenship and Immigration)*, 2009 FC 292.
238 *Ibid* at para 19.

yet continued to permit Tang to enter Canada on a regular basis. The Respondent's actions and acquiescence belie its stated belief.[239]

6) Health (Section 38)

Section 38 of the *IRPA* provides that a foreign national may be found inadmissible for reasons of ill health. There are three distinct grounds under which a finding of inadmissibility can be made: if the health condition (a) is likely to be a danger to public health; (b) is likely to be a danger to public safety; or (c) might reasonably be expected to cause excessive demand on health or social services.[240] Although the legislative distinction between "likelihood" and "reasonable expectation" appears to indicate that the latter is a lower standard, in *Hiramen v Canada (Minister of Employment and Immigration)*, the Federal Court has held that the mere possibility of a health condition causing excessive demand is not enough. An opinion on reasonable expectation must be couched in the language of probability.[241] It is also important to note that none of these grounds of inadmissibility applies to permanent residents.

Foreign nationals who apply for permanent status will undergo a medical examination prior to coming to Canada; however, certain members of the family class, namely, spouses, common law partners, and children, as well as Convention refugees and protected persons and their family members, cannot be found inadmissible on the basis of excessive demand on health or social services.[242] Those seeking temporary status are required to do so only in limited circumstances outlined in the *Regulations*.[243] Those required to undergo a medical examination include

1) foreign nationals seeking to work in an occupation in which the protection of public health is essential;[244]

---

239 *Ibid* at para 24.
240 *IRPA*, above note 1, s 38(1).
241 (1986), 65 NR 67 (FCA).
242 *IRPA*, above note 1, s 38(2).
243 *Ibid*, s 16; *Regulations*, above note 132, s 30. See Citizenship and Immigration Canada, "Medical Requirements," online: CIC www.cic.gc.ca/english/resources/tools/medic/index.asp [Operational Manual: Medical Requirements].
244 *Regulations*, above note 132, s 30(1)(a)(ii).

2) foreign nationals seeking to enter Canada or applying for a renewal of their work or study permit or authorization to stay in Canada as a temporary resident in excess of six consecutive months;[245]
3) foreign nationals who have stayed in Canada for a period of six consecutive months or longer;[246]
4) foreign nationals who officers have reasonable grounds to believe are inadmissible based on health grounds;[247] and
5) foreign nationals claiming refugee status or protected person status.[248]

Some foreign nationals are exempted from a medical exam.[249]

a) Medical Examination and Obtaining Evidence

Persons required to undergo medical examinations attend at their own expense. Typically, a medical examination may include a physical and mental examination, a review of past medical history, laboratory and diagnostic tests, and a medical assessment of records.[250] Applicants who pass their medical examination receive a medical certificate that is valid for twelve months.[251] Such certificates indicate that if the foreign national does have a medical condition, it will not pose a danger to public health or safety and is not reasonably expected to cause excessive demand.[252] Examinations are conducted by designated medical practitioners or panel physicians designated by Citizenship and Immigration Canada.

---

245 *Ibid*, s 30(1)(a)(iii)(A).
246 *Ibid*, s 30(1)(a)(iii)(B).
247 *Ibid*, s 30(1)(a)(iv).
248 *Ibid*, ss 30(1)(a)(v) & (vi).
249 See *ibid*, ss 186(b) and 30(1): The classes of foreign nationals that may benefit from such an exemption include foreign representatives and their family members who are carrying out official duties as a diplomatic agent, consular officer, or official unless they are engaging in secondary employment; members of visiting armed forces of a country that is designated in the *Visiting Forces Act* who are carrying out official duties and are not seeking to engage in secondary employment and are not a civilian component of the armed forces; family members of protected persons not included in the protected persons' applications to remain in Canada as permanent residents; non-accompanying family members of a foreign national who has applied for refugee protection outside Canada; and foreign nationals who are in the live-in caregiver class applying for permanent residence.
250 *Regulations,* above note 132, s 29.
251 *Ibid*, s 30(3).
252 *Ibid*.

An officer reviewing whether a person is inadmissible with regard to health may obtain evidence by collecting medical certificates, copies of records giving assessments of a person's health condition, media articles, scholarly journals, and expert evidence.[253] Evidence of medical inadmissibility for a temporary resident application may not be used to refuse a permanent resident application on the basis of medical inadmissibility.[254] A more thorough examination and analysis of the application needs to be done. However, evidence of medical inadmissibility in a permanent resident application can be used to find a temporary resident applicant inadmissible on the same grounds.[255]

b) Danger to Public Health (Section 38(1)(a))

Citizenship and Immigration Canada specifies conditions that are "likely to be a danger to public health":

> Active Pulmonary Tuberculosis (TB) and untreated Syphilis are considered a danger to public health. If the foreign national has either or both of these conditions, they will likely be found inadmissible on the grounds of danger to public safety, unless the foreign national is treated according to Canadian standards. Although the Human immunodeficiency virus (HIV) is not considered a danger to public health, CIC is committed to public health risk mitigation, and provides foreign nationals with HIV with important information that can reduce the risk of transmission.[256]

Often, if a foreign national suffers from a communicable disease, she may be found inadmissible under section 38(1)(a). Before concluding whether a foreign national's health condition is likely to be a danger to public health, an officer assessing the health condition must consider any report made by a health practitioner or medical laboratory with respect to the foreign national;[257] the communicability of any disease that the foreign national is affected by or carries;[258] and the impact the disease may have on other persons living in Canada.[259]

---

253 Citizenship and Immigration Canada, Operational Manual ENF 1: *Inadmissibility*, online: CIC www.cic.gc.ca/English/resources/manuals/enf/enf01-eng.pdf at 45.
254 Citizenship and Immigration Canada, Operational Manual ENF 2: *Evaluating Inadmissibility*, online: CIC www.cic.gc.ca/English/resources/manuals/enf/enf02-eng.pdf at 27.
255 *Ibid.*
256 Operational Manual: Medical Requirements, above note 243.
257 *Regulations*, above note 132, s 31(a).
258 *Ibid*, s 31(b).
259 *Ibid*, s 31(c).

c) Danger to Public Safety (Section 38(1)(b))

A foreign national is inadmissible on health grounds if his health condition is likely to be a danger to public safety.[260] Citizenship and Immigration Canada also specifies what could constitute a danger to public safety:

> Health conditions that are likely to cause a danger to public safety include serious uncontrolled and/or uncontrollable mental health problems such as:
> - certain impulsive sociopathic behaviour disorders;
> - some aberrant sexual disorders such as pedophilia;
> - certain paranoid states or some organic brain syndromes associated with violence or risk of harm to others;
> - applicants with substance abuse leading to antisocial behaviours such as violence, and impaired driving; and
> - other types of hostile, disruptive behaviour.[261]

Before concluding whether a foreign national's health condition might reasonably be expected to pose a danger to public safety, an officer who is assessing the foreign national's health condition must consider any reports made by a health practitioner or medical laboratory with respect to the foreign national,[262] and the risk of sudden incapacity or of unpredictable or violent behaviour of the foreign national that would create a danger to the health or safety of persons living in Canada.[263]

d) Excessive Demand on Health or Social Services

Excessive demand is defined in section 1(1) of the *Regulations*:

> (a) a demand on health services or social services for which the anticipated costs would likely exceed average Canadian per capital health services and social services costs over a period of five consecutive years immediately following the most recent medical examination required under paragraph 16(2)(b) of the Act, unless there is evidence that significant costs are likely to be incurred beyond that period, in which case the period is no more than 10 consecutive years; or
> (b) a demand on health services or social services that would add to existing waiting lists and would increase the rate of mortality

---

260 *IRPA*, above note 1, s 38(1)(b).
261 Operational Manual: Medical Requirements, above note 243.
262 *Regulations*, above note 132, s 33(a).
263 *Ibid*, s 33(b).

and morbidity in Canada as a result of an inability to provide timely services to Canadian citizens or permanent residents.[264]

Before concluding that a foreign national's health condition might reasonably be expected to cause excessive demand, an officer must consider any reports made by a health practitioner or medical laboratory with respect to the foreign national,[265] and any condition identified by the medical examination.[266]

i)   Exceeding the Total Cost of an Average Canadian over Five Years

A visa officer and medical officer are required to provide a precise calculation of health or social services costs over a five-year period, comparing that with the average Canadian.[267] Despite this requirement, where it seems obvious that an applicant may exceed the total cost of the average Canadian per capita over a period of five years, an exact estimate may not be warranted.[268] In *Kirec v Canada (Minister of Citizenship and Immigration)*, the Federal Court held that despite the failure to provide an exact dollar amount of all services, it was reasonable, under the circumstances, for the medical officer to conclude that the total cost would be in excess of the average Canadian over five years.[269] Nevertheless, an applicant facing a finding of excessive demands on services may be well advised to provide her own assessment to counter any evidence that there may be excessive demands on services. This onus of providing information to the officer will be discussed in further detail below.

---

264 *Ibid*, s 1(1). *Health services* and *social services* are also defined under s 1(1) of the *Regulations*:
- "health services" means any health services for which the majority of the funds are contributed by governments, including the services of family physicians, medical specialists, nurses, chiropractors and physiotherapists, laboratory services and the supply of pharmaceutical or hospital care.
- "social services" means any social services, such as home care, specialized residence and residential services, special education services, social and vocational rehabilitation services, personal support services and the provision of devices related to those services,
  - (a) that are intended to assist a person in functioning physically, emotionally, socially, psychologically or vocationally; and
  - (b) for which the majority of the funding, including funding that provides direct or indirect financial support to an assisted person, is contributed by governments, either directly or through publicly-funded agencies.

265 *Ibid*, s 34(a).

266 *Ibid*, s 34(b).

267 *Cohen v Canada (Minister of Citizenship and Immigration)*, 2006 FC 804.

268 2006 FC 800.

269 *Ibid*.

ii) Problematic Distinction between Social and Health Services

In the seminal case of *Hilewitz* v *Canada* (*Minister of Citizenship and Immigration*), the Supreme Court of Canada held that an applicant's ability and willingness to attenuate the excessive burden on the public purse that would otherwise be created was a relevant factor to determine whether the condition could reasonably be expected to cause excessive demands on the system.[270] In *Hilewitz*, the applicant applied for permanent residence under the "investor" category and was denied because he had a dependent child who suffered from an intellectual disability that might reasonably have been expected to cause excessive demands on social services.[271] At issue was whether the resources of the family should be disregarded in determining whether their child with a disability would create an undue burden on Canadian social services. The Court held that, if there is evidence to show the applicant is self-sufficient or if the family is able to support the person financially or emotionally without additional services, then the applicant should be deemed admissible.[272] An individualized assessment of all the circumstances of the case is needed, coupled with a comparative evaluation of the individual's requirements.[273] In this case, the Court considered the fact that the applicant had applied under a category that required him to have substantial financial resources to apply and therefore found that it would be inappropriate for an officer to consider his financial ability for the application but not for the admissibility of the child with a disability.[274]

From *Hilewitz* it is clear that an officer must engage in "individualized assessments" and that immigration law, as it stands, does not automatically impede entry for all persons who are subject to intellectual disability, regardless of family support or assistance, and regardless of whether they pose any reasonable likelihood of excessively burdening Canada's social services.[275] In particular, the Court stated, "[t]his means that the individual, not administrative convenience, is the interpretive focus"[276] and that "[t]he clear legislative threshold provides that to be denied admission, the individual's medical condition 'would' or 'might reasonably be expected' to result in an excessive public burden" rather

---

270 2005 SCC 57 [*Hilewitz*].
271 *Ibid*: This was considered under what is now known as s 38(1)(c) but then was s 19(1)(a)(ii).
272 *Ibid* at para 61.
273 *Ibid* at para 57.
274 *Ibid* at para 40.
275 *Ibid* at para 57.
276 *Ibid*.

than a "remote possibility."[277] The Court chastised the officer for conjecturing that there were possible contingencies to negate a family's future ability to pay or absorb the burden of a child's disabilities, such as bankruptcy, mobility, school closure, or a parent's death.[278]

The Federal Court has followed the reasoning in *Hilewitz*, finding in other cases that the applicant's willingness and ability to bear costs is a relevant factor in overcoming inadmissibility based on excessive demand on health[279] or social services.[280] However, the Federal Court has raised a distinction between considering the ability to attenuate the burden on health services as opposed to social services.[281] In *Lee*, the applicant had health conditions that were expected to cause excessive demands on Canada's health services. The applicant argued that, as an entrepreneur with considerable net worth, he would be able to cover the costs of his health care if admitted into Canada.[282] The officer denied the application and at judicial review at the Federal Court, the applicant relied on the *Hilewitz* case to argue that the officer did not consider the applicant's ability to pay for his own health services. The Federal Court distinguished *Hilewitz* from this case by stating that *Hilewitz* was concerned with the ability to pay for social services, not health services.[283] The Federal Court relied on the notion that Canada's health-care system is largely public and that there was no private health care that would be available, thereby making the applicant automatically available to access public health care.[284]

Despite the *Lee* decision, the Federal Court has recognized that some areas of health services may borrow from the *Hilewitz* analysis. In *Companioni v Canada (Minister of Citizenship and Immigration)*, the court dealt with the issue of whether the cost of out-patient prescriptions

---

277 *Ibid* at para 58.
278 *Ibid* at para 68.
279 *Hossain v Canada (Minister of Citizenship and Immigration)*, 2006 FC 475.
280 *Sarkar v Canada (Minister of Citizenship and Immigration)*, 2006 FC 1556; *Vashishat v Canada (Minister of Citizenship and Immigration)*, 2008 FC 1346 [*Vashishat*]; *Parmar v Canada (Minister of Citizenship and Immigration)*, 2010 FC 723; *Sapru v Canada (Minister of Citizenship and Immigration)*, 2011 FCA 35 [*Sapru*]: In this case, the court highlighted the importance of performing an individualized assessment of all the circumstances and doing a comparative evaluation of the individual's requirements. An assessment as to the likely demands on the system is also needed.
281 *Lee v Canada (Minister of Citizenship and Immigration)*, 2006 FC 1461 [*Lee*]; see also *Jafarian v Canada (Minister of Citizenship and Immigration)*, 2010 FC 40 [*Jafarian*].
282 *Lee*, above note 281 at para 2.
283 *Ibid* at para 6.
284 *Ibid* at para 7.

constitutes an excessive demand on health services.[285] Here the court acknowledged that there are provincial differences in the supply of social services and out-patient drugs by provinces. The court found that, in general, provinces are entitled to recover most, if not all, of the costs of social services from those who can afford them, but the costs of drugs would be paid by the province, and the promises not to access the program are not enforceable.[286] It appears that, while some cases focus on the inability to enforce commitments people may make to use alternative sources or to not use the provincial sources of prescription drug care, others follow the *Hilewitz* principle: if there is evidence to show an applicant is self-sufficient or the applicant's family is able to support a person financially or emotionally, then that person can be found to be admissible.[287] Thus, where an applicant has a private, personal, or employment insurance policy that could cover prescription drug costs, inadmissibility can be overcome.[288] Further, where it can be identified that the province has a reimbursement mechanism for health or social services, this must be taken into account when deciding whether inadmissibility can be overcome; a decision maker cannot take for granted that a distinction may exist between health and social services but must look at the proposed plan and whether such a reimbursement mechanism truly exists in the province where the applicants intend to live.[289]

iii) Overcoming the Ground of Inadmissibility Based on Excessive Demand on Services

The Federal Court has also clarified the burden of proof upon the applicant. In *Airapetyan v Canada (Minister of Citizenship and Immigration)*, the Federal Court held that the applicant must provide evidence to show that she is supported by family financially to be found admissible and that it is up to the applicant to rebut the presumption that she is inadmissible on this basis.[290]

---

285 *Companioni v Canada (Minister of Citizenship and Immigration)*, 2009 FC 1315 [*Companioni*]; *Jafarian*, above note 281. *Rashid v Canada (Minister of Citizenship and Immigration)*, 2010 FC 157; *Bichari v Canada (Minister of Citizenship and Immigration)*, 2010 FC 127 [*Bichari*]. There is of course a distinction as to how each province deals with costs of services, whether social or health, and the differences should be considered in the context of each case.

286 *Ibid.*

287 *Companioni*, above note 285.

288 *Ibid.*

289 *Cuarte v Canada (Minister of Citizenship and Immigration)*, 2012 FC 261: Where the *Saskatchewan Education Act* does not establish a mechanism allowing reimbursement, but it is possible to voluntarily enter an agreement with the school board to contribute to expenses, the Federal Court held that the possibility of a voluntary agreement must be considered.

290 2007 FC 42 [*Airapetyan*].

In addition, one may counter evidence of excessive demand on health or social services by demonstrating or providing proposals on how the costs may be mitigated by personal financial means or other mechanisms. Thus, individualized assessments are mandated not only in arriving at the cost estimate to compare to a Canadian average, but also in reviewing whether inadmissibility can be overcome.[291] Medical officers must provide adequate information for the visa or immigration officer to make their assessment, and insufficient information cannot be saved by the visa or immigration officer's reasoning.[292] On the other hand, immigration or visa officers must consult with medical officers on issues assigned to medical officers and cannot simply rely upon their own assessment.[293]

Despite the requirement to conduct an individualized assessment, the Federal Court has held that the use of research or statistical information to help determine the future state of a person with a particular condition may not be improper if there is no other medical information from personal history or otherwise.[294] The onus is on the applicant not only to make out his case, but also to provide evidence on the extent of the medical condition, the progression of the illness, the plan or proposals to support the inadmissible person, or the availability of care in the applicant's home country.[295] The Federal Court has been clear that an officer (whether visa or medical officer) is not obligated to seek out information about the applicant's ability and intent to mitigate excessive demands but that in meeting the duty of procedural fairness, an officer should provide a fairness letter that clearly sets out all the relevant concerns and offer a genuine opportunity to meaningfully respond to all of the concerns of the medical or immigration officer.[296] Where evidence is provided and it is contrary to the conclusion that the officer

---

291 *Colaco v Canada (Minister of Citizenship and Immigration)*, 2007 FCA 282; *Aguinaldo v Canada (Minister of Citizenship and Immigration)*, 2010 FC 682 [*Aguinaldo*]: In this case, the Federal Court held that the visa officer made unsubstantiated assumptions about the costs of living and the expenses associated with the proposed plans of the applicant that were not based in any inquiry or evidence.

292 *Sapru*, above note 280; *Cramer v Canada (Minister of Citizenship and Immigration)*, 2011 FC 854.

293 *Lawrence v Canada (Minister of Citizenship and Immigration)*, 2012 FC 1523.

294 *Mazhari v Canada (Minister of Citizenship and Immigration)*, 2010 FC 467.

295 *Bichari*, above note 285; *Sharma v Canada (Minister of Citizenship and Immigration)*, 2010 FC 398.

296 *Sapru*, above note 280; *Villegas*, above note 48; *Firouz-Abadi v Canada (Minister of Citizenship and Immigration)*, 2011 FC 835.

reaches, the officer has a duty to provide reasons why the evidence was discounted.[297]

Willingness of the applicant to overcome inadmissibility based on excessive demand is not enough; the applicant must show that there is an ability and capacity to pay or provide alternatives.[298] Such plans and proposals must be clear, not speculative.[299] Further, the applicant may argue that there is no reasonable expectation of excessive demand due to the family's willingness and ability to contribute time and resources that will substitute for those provided by public services.[300] Thus, the ability to pay is not the only way in which one can overcome this ground of inadmissibility; demand on services and not mere eligibility must be considered.[301] There may be cases, however, where assisting or volunteering may not be enough. For example, in *Newton-Juliard v Canada (Minister of Citizenship and Immigration)*, the Federal Court held that volunteering at a publicly funded school was difficult to quantify and proposals for private insurance for health care did nothing to alleviate any demand on social services.[302]

It is important to recognize that an applicant does not need to show zero demand on services; some demand is acceptable, and a full analysis of the applicant's situation, proposed plan, and other factors must be examined carefully and cannot be ignored.[303] The court has held that where an officer has characterized pejoratively actions taken by an applicant, judicial review may be warranted. In *Ma v Canada (Minister of Citizenship and Immigration)*, an officer unduly focused on the fact that the applicant's child was enrolled in public school but then was enrolled in a private school.[304] The officer found that the recent enrollment in private school raised the question of whether the enrollment was done for the purposes of securing immigration status rather than as part of a genuine plan to assume responsibility for the costs of the child's special education services. The court here held that the inference rested upon a tenuous factual underpinning and was a reviewable error.[305]

---

297 *Sharpe v Canada (Minister of Citizenship and Immigration)*, 2011 FC 21.

298 *Airapetyan*, above note 290.

299 *Chaudhry v Canada (Minister of Citizenship and Immigration)*, 2011 FC 22; *Villegas*, above note 48. This decision turned on lack of notice to the applicant about the concern that the plans presented were unclear.

300 *Vashishat*, above note 280.

301 *Ibid.*

302 2006 FC 177.

303 *Sökmen v Canada (Minister of Citizenship and Immigration)*, 2011 FC 47.

304 2009 FC 1042.

305 *Ibid.*

iv) Humanitarian and Compassionate Grounds

Where an application for permanent residence has been made on humanitarian and compassionate (H&C) grounds,[306] to what extent should the ground of inadmissibility due to excessive demand be overcome by H&C grounds? In *Bichari*, the Federal Court held that the standard on H&C applications cannot be whether the applicant will get better or more affordable treatment in Canada as, if this were the case, then virtually all medically inadmissible persons would be entitled to stay.[307] On the other hand, this does not mean that H&C grounds never play a role. In the case of *Aguinaldo*, a citizen of the Philippines who had worked for several years as a nurse in a remote hospital north of Saskatoon applied for permanent residence status so that her husband and son could immigrate to Canada.[308] The visa officer denied the application after finding the applicant's son had autism and therefore could pose an excessive demand on health or social services. While granting the judicial review on other grounds, Harrington J *in obiter* stated:

> I refuse to accept that Canadian immigration law is so rigid as to deny the inhabitants of a northern community the services of a desperately-needed nurse because her son's condition may pose a demand on social services that the applicable payor government would, if necessary, be happy to absorb. Our immigration law creates at least three possible paths to a favourable outcome. First, she may have the ability and intent to offset these costs per *Hilewitz*. Second, s. 24 of *IRPA* allows an officer to issue a temporary resident permit which can lead to permanent residence. Finally, s. 25 of *IRPA* allows the Minister to grant a foreign national permanent residence status or an exemption from any applicable criteria, if of the opinion that such is justified by humanitarian and compassionate considerations, taking into account the best interests of the child directly affected. Is it in Jon's best interests that he only be able to see his mother a few weeks a year? Is it in the best interest of the community of La Loche, which desperately needs Mrs. Aguinaldo's services, that she pack up her bags in frustration and go home to her family?[309]

Justice Harrington raises the possibility that applicants may ask for exemptions from a finding of inadmissibility based on H&C grounds where factors militate. An applicant seeking such an exemption should set out how Canada would benefit from the presence of the applicant,

---

306 See Chapter 12.

307 *Bichari*, above note 285.

308 *Aguinaldo*, above note 291.

309 *Ibid* at para 12.

while demonstrating that the possible demand on services may be off-set or diminished in some capacity.

v)   Change in Circumstances

If a medical condition changes or improves in the course of the application, such evidence may be put forward by the applicant and may be considered. However, where an applicant provides such evidence during an appeal of an application at the Immigration Appeal Division (IAD), the Federal Court has held that the medical condition at the time the visa officer refused the application was the only relevant one, and subsequent improvement was only relevant as to whether special relief should be granted on appeal.[310] Thus, it is vitally important for any applicant to provide up-to-date information on a medical condition as soon as possible before such evidence may be foreclosed.

7)   Financial Reasons (Section 39)

A foreign national (and not a permanent resident) can be found inadmissible for financial reasons if he is or will be unable or unwilling to support himself or any other person who is dependent on him. If a foreign national can satisfy an officer that adequate arrangements for care and support, not involving social assistance, are in place, then inadmissibility on this ground may not apply.[311] Convention refugees and protected persons are exempted from this ground of inadmissibility.[312]

The Federal Court has held that social assistance is a flexible term that can include "public assistance, in the form of government subsidized housing" or benefits from a disability program.[313] In order to avoid being found inadmissible for financial reasons, applicants must show that adequate arrangements for their care and support have been made other than those that involve social assistance. If an officer has any such concerns, she must raise them with the applicant and give the latter an opportunity to address them.

There appears to be a lack of legislative consistency between this provision and the provisions governing family reunification. In some cases where members of the family class are being sponsored, the sponsor may be exempt from the minimum necessary income require-

---

310   *Mohamed v Canada (Minister of Employment and Immigration)*, [1986] 3 FC 90 (CA); *Vazirizadeh v Canada (Minister of Citizenship and Immigration)*, 2009 FC 807.
311   OP 18, above note 28 at 27.
312   *Regulations*, above note 132, s 21.
313   *Delisa v Canada (Minister of Citizenship and Immigration)*, 2010 FC 88.

ment.[314] However, the member of the family class could still be found inadmissible on section 39 grounds, thereby negating any effect of the exemption provided in a family reunification scheme.

Some cases that fall under section 39 may pertain to a non-accompanying family member who may be inadmissible on health grounds because he may pose excessive demand on health or social services.[315] To avoid being caught under this provision, applicants may have to undertake to renounce the right to sponsor the non-accompanying family member or provide a credible plan for mitigating the excessive demand.[316]

8) Misrepresentation (Section 40)

A permanent resident or foreign national may be found to be inadmissible for any of four types of misrepresentation:

1) for directly or indirectly misrepresenting or withholding material facts relating to a relevant matter that induces or could induce an error in the administration of the *IRPA*;[317]
2) for being or having been sponsored by a person deemed inadmissible for misrepresentation;[318]
3) for misrepresenting or withholding material facts relating to a refugee claim, after which there is a finding to that effect and a refugee decision is vacated;[319] and
4) for obtaining citizenship by false representation, fraud, or knowingly concealing material facts.[320]

Recent changes in legislation through the *Faster Removal of Foreign Criminals Act* will extend the duration of inadmissibility on this ground from two to five years.[321] During that period, a person cannot apply for permanent residence.[322]

---

314 See *Regulations*, above note 132, s 133(4), in the case of sponsoring spouses, common law partners, conjugal partners, or a dependent child.

315 See, for example, *Zhang v Canada (Minister of Citizenship and Immigration)*, 2012 FC 1093.

316 For more analysis of the issue of inadmissibility for health reasons, see Section B(6), above in this chapter.

317 *IRPA*, above note 1, s 40(1)(a).

318 *Ibid*, s 40(1)(b).

319 *Ibid*, ss 40(1)(c) and 109; see, for example, *Calixto v Canada (Minister of Citizenship and Immigration)*, 2005 FC 1037.

320 *IRPA*, above note 1, s 40(1)(d); *Citizenship Act*, RSC 1985, c C-29, s 10(2).

321 *Faster Removal of Foreign Criminals Act*, above note 9, s 16(1) (but not in force at time of writing).

322 *Ibid*, s 16(3).

a) Directly or Indirectly Misrepresenting or Withholding Material Facts

An applicant may be found to be inadmissible for misrepresenting on a wide variety of facts or situations associated with an application. Misrepresentation on many kinds of information may be embraced by this provision. For example, the Federal Court has found that misrepresentations on the source of an applicant's funds,[323] on whether the applicant had previously submitted and been denied permanent residence,[324] and on the death or timing of death of a parent[325] all concern material facts.

Nevertheless, the Federal Court has required decision makers to conduct an analysis of the materiality of the facts that are alleged to have been misrepresented or withheld. For example, in *Ali v Canada (Minister of Citizenship and Immigration)*, the court was not convinced that a fraudulent school record should be considered material since the applicant's age, identity, and family relationships were not in doubt prior to the detection of the misrepresentation.[326] Thus, an officer's failure to conduct a proper analysis with regard to materiality of alleged misrepresentations will amount to a reviewable error.[327]

In *Baro v Canada (Minister of Citizenship and Immigration)*, a Canadian citizen sponsored her spouse. In his application for permanent residence, the applicant did not disclose to having a previous marriage or the fact that, having lost touch with his spouse entirely, he had sought a court order in the Philippines declaring her to be presumed dead.[328] The applicant's sponsor, or second wife, notified immigration officials that she learned, on a visit to the Philippines, that the applicant's first wife had reappeared. The applicant was thereafter found inadmissible for misrepresentation and withholding of material facts. The Federal Court stated that an applicant has a "duty of candour," which requires the disclosure of material facts, and that this duty extends to information regarding the change of marital status. Thus, an innocent failure to provide material information can result in a finding of inadmissibility. A finding of inadmissibility on this basis can be avoided only if the applicant can show that he honestly and reasonably believed that he was not withholding material information.[329] The court accentuated

---

323 *Zhang v Canada (Minister of Citizenship and Immigration)*, 2005 FC 1313.
324 *Koo v Canada (Minister of Citizenship and Immigration)*, 2008 FC 931 [*Koo*].
325 *Mukamutara v Canada (Minister of Citizenship and Immigration)*, 2008 FC 451 [*Mukamutara*].
326 2008 FC 166.
327 *Koo*, above note 324 at para 38; *Mukamutara*, above note 325.
328 2007 FC 1299.
329 *Ibid*.

the importance of information about marital history because spousal sponsorship is based on the applicant's marital status and its genuineness. In this case, the inadmissibility finding was upheld.

Is an applicant required to disclose information that has not been sought by an examining officer? In *Bodine v Canada (Minister of Citizenship and Immigration)*, the Federal Court held that while there is no duty to spontaneously disclose any fact that could possibly be relevant, the surrounding circumstances will inform what is pertinent.[330]

Despite the duty of candour, the Federal Court, in *Koo*, held that where inadvertent errors were made in an application, but where the applicant was nevertheless forthcoming and honest with his dealings with immigration officers, misrepresentation cannot be found.[331]

The concept of misrepresentation and its breadth of application is further analyzed in *Khan v Canada (Minister of Citizenship and Immigration)*.[332] In this case, an applicant was denied permanent residence as a skilled worker as a result of a misrepresentation in an application that had been prepared by his immigration consultant. While the applicant corrected the error before the decision on the application was made, the Federal Court held that misrepresentation applies to misrepresentation at any time and that a broad interpretation is demanded in the legislation. Justice O'Keefe stated:

> I acknowledge that this case presents a unique situation as the misrepresentation was clarified before the decision was rendered. However, to adopt the applicant's interpretation would lead to a situation whereby individuals could knowingly make a misrepresentation, but not be found inadmissible under paragraph 40(1)(a) so long as they clarified the misrepresentation right before a decision was rendered. I agree with the respondent that such an interpretation could result in a situation whereby only misrepresentations "caught" by the visa officer during an interview would be clarified; therefore, leaving a high potential for abuse of the Act.[333]

Despite such broad interpretations of "misrepresentation" and "withholding of material facts," the court also calls on decision makers to take a contextual approach to their analysis. In the case of *Maruquin v Canada (Minister of Citizenship and Immigration)*, a couple was approved as permanent residents to Canada.[334] Prior to their visas being

---

330 2008 FC 848.
331 *Koo*, above note 324 at para 38.
332 2008 FC 512.
333 *Ibid* at para 27.
334 2007 FC 1349.

issued, but twenty-one months after the birth of their child, the couple informed immigration officials of the birth. The couple's application for permanent residence was then refused for failing to disclose the birth of their son in a timely fashion. The Federal Court held that the non-disclosure of the information should not be characterized as withholding of a material fact that induced or could have induced an error in the administration of the *IRPA* because in the end, the son's birth was disclosed prior to any legal requirement to do so in the *Regulations*. Further, the court held that there was no evidence that the information was withheld or that there was any incentive not to disclose the birth of the child.

Similarly, in *Walia v Canada (Minister of Citizenship and Immigration)*, the Federal Court held that if a finding of inadmissibility is made, there must be evidence in the record to establish the facts that were misrepresented or withheld.[335] In this case, the applicant had indicated she was divorced and not cohabiting with her former husband. An officer visiting the applicant discovered she was living with her former husband. However, the court indicated that sharing a residence is different from cohabitation, which has been interpreted as meaning a marriage-like relationship, and the evidence on the record fell short of establishing this.

9) Failure to Comply with the *IRPA* (Section 41)

A foreign national can be found inadmissible for an act or omission that directly or indirectly contravenes the *IRPA*.[336] A permanent resident can be found inadmissible only for failing to comply with section 27(2) or section 28. The former of these would cover contravention of the terms and conditions imposed either when gaining status in Canada or at a later time, for example, when a removal order has been conditionally stayed.[337] The latter covers failure to meet residency obligations.[338] Section 28(2)(c) provides that "a determination by an officer that humanitarian and compassionate considerations relating to a permanent resident, taking into account the best interests of a child directly affected by the determination, justify the retention of permanent resident status overcomes any breach of the residency obligation prior to the determination." Section 63(4) provides that a permanent resident may

---

335 2008 FC 486.

336 *IRPA*, above note 1, s 41(a).

337 *Mand v Canada (Minister of Citizenship and Immigration)*, 2005 FC 1637.

338 See, for example, *El Idrissi v Canada (Minister of Citizenship and Immigration)*, 2005 FC 1105; *Yu v Canada (Minister of Citizenship and Immigration)*, 2005 FC 1323; and *Ikhuiwu v Canada (Minister of Citizenship and Immigration)*, 2008 FC 35.

appeal to the Immigration Appeal Division against a decision made outside Canada on the residency obligation. In such a case the permanent resident will be issued a travel document to allow her to return to Canada to make the appeal.[339]

10) Inadmissible Family Member (Section 42)

A foreign national, other than a Convention refugee or protected person, is inadmissible on the ground of having an inadmissible accompanying family member, or in prescribed circumstances,[340] an inadmissible non-accompanying family member.[341] Foreign nationals who are accompanying family members of an inadmissible person are rendered inadmissible as well.[342] The exception to findings of inadmissibility on this ground will not be made if an applicant is seeking temporary residence. Further, an applicant for temporary residence will be inadmissible only if the family member is inadmissible under sections 34, 35, and 37.[343]

C. INADMISSIBILITY AND *CHARTER* RIGHTS

The Federal Court of Appeal has held that a determination of whether a person is inadmissible to Canada does not engage an individual's section 7 *Charter* rights because "a number of proceedings may yet take place before he reaches the stage at which his deportation from Canada may occur."[344] As noted earlier, this finding may be tested in future cases as changes in the both the *IRPA* and the *Regulations* will challenge the notion that there are "alternative remedies" or processes by which a person may prevent removal from Canada.[345] Indeed, in *Poshteh*, the court relies on now-repealed section 34(2) as a proceeding that

---

339 *IRPA*, above note 1, s 31(3).

340 See *Regulations*, above note 132, s 23, which defines prescribed circumstances related to family members. In short, the provision lists categories of non-accompanying family members as spouses, common law partners, and dependent children of both the foreign national and the dependent child of the foreign national.

341 *IRPA*, above note 1, s 42(1)(a).

342 *Ibid*, s 42(1)(b).

343 *Ibid*, s 42(2).

344 *Poshteh*, above note 69 at para 63; see also *Barrera v Canada (Minister of Employment and Immigration)*, [1993] 2 FC 3 (CA).

345 See Section B(3)(g), above in this chapter, which discusses alternative remedies and the differences between repealed s 34(2) and s 42.1 of the *IRPA*. See also, for

takes place after the finding of inadmissibility.[346] This is no longer a viable alternative for persons today. Further, other remedies or processes, such as H&C applications, PRRA applications, stays of removals, and access to the Immigration Appeal Division or the Refugee Appeal Division may be out of reach for persons in various categories.[347] Such persons may be exposed to a violation of section 7 rights due to the lack of available "alternative remedies" or proceedings.

D. CONCLUSION: THE INCREASE IN SECURITIZATION OF OUR BORDERS

The attempt to achieve high levels of security through Canada's immigration policy brings with it the danger that Canada is sacrificing other important objectives, including our obligation to provide safe haven for refugees.[348] As can be gleaned from this chapter, Canada has made a sharp turn towards developing and enforcing increased anti-terrorism and security measures, and has done so at the expense of vulnerable refugees and to the detriment of long-established commitments and aspirations such as family reunification. According broad unrestricted meanings to the language of inadmissibility is but one manifestation of a general trend that is also revealed in the procedural mechanisms that lead to exclusion and removal, to be examined in Chapter 15.[349] Cumu-

---

example, the recent amendment to s 25 of the *IRPA*, which proscribes the grant of permanent residence to individuals who are inadmissible under s 34.

346 *Poshteh*, above note 69 at para 63.

347 See, for examples, *IRPA*, above note 1, s 109.1, dealing with persons coming from designated countries of origin; s 20.1, dealing with designated foreign nationals; s 25, dealing with exceptions to who can make applications on H&C grounds; s 112(2), dealing with exceptions on who can make pre-removal risk assessment applications; s 110(2), dealing with who has access to the Refugee Appeal Division; ss 64(1)–(2), dealing with who has access to the Immigration Appeal Division; and *Regulations*, above note 132, ss 231–33, dealing with who can obtain stays of removals.

348 *Ibid.*

349 See Efrat Arbel & Alletta Brenner, *Bordering on Failure: Canada-U.S. Border Policy and the Politics of Refugee Exclusion* (26 November 2013), online: Harvard and Immigration Refugee Clinic http://harvardimmigrationclinic.files.wordpress.com/2013/11/bordering-on-failure-harvard-immigration-and-refugee-law-clinical-program1.pdf at 2:

> The Multiple Borders Strategy is a broad strategy that re-charts Canada's borders for the purposes of enhanced migration regulation. Its stated goal is to "push the border out" — outside the edge of Canadian territory — to facilitate Canada's ability to intercept improperly documented persons as far away

latively, the shifts in our practices of statutory interpretation, exclusion and removal have "ushered in a public tolerance for discretionary government actions aimed at 'outsiders.'"[350] These changes will call into question the extent to which *Charter* rights are engaged, especially now that many persons will no longer have access to alternative remedies or processes. Our practices will test the reach of our *Charter*, but will also shape the future of Canada's immigration policies.

---

from Canada's territorial borders as possible . . . . Canada enacts measures that deter and deflect the arrival of asylum seekers at each of the external borderlines marked by the Multiple Borders Strategy: countries of origin; visa screening points; airline check-in points; points of initial embarkation; transit areas; points of final embarkation; and points of final arrival. These measures include offshore screening, visa restrictions, carrier sanctions, and other interdiction measures . . . . Together, these measures systematically close Canada's borders to asylum seekers, making it harder for asylum seekers to lawfully reach Canada's territorial frontiers . . . .

350 Catherine Dauvergne, "Evaluating Canada's New *Immigration and Refugee Protection Act* in Its Global Context" (2003) 41 *Alberta Law Review* 725 at 735.

CHAPTER 15

THE MECHANICS OF ENFORCEMENT

A. INTRODUCTION

While recognizing that enforcement techniques are implemented outside our territorial borders to prevent the arrival of unwanted visitors and migrants,[1] the focus of this chapter is on the enforcement measures that are implemented within Canada. The chapter outlines the processes of decision making that may precede a person's removal from Canada. When a person presents himself to an officer of the Canada Border Services Agency (CBSA)[2] at a port of entry, a decision must be made regarding whether the individual should be allowed to come into Canada, whether conditions should be attached to the entry, whether the individual should be detained while a decision is pending, whether the person should be removed from Canada, and if removable, what the terms of possible re-entry should be. These decisions will be based on assessments of the person's status and of any evidence of inadmis-

---

1 See Francois Crépeau & Delphine Nakache, "Controlling Irregular Migration in Canada: Reconciling Security Concerns with Human Rights Concerns" (2006) 12: 1 *IRPP Choices*, online: Social Science Research Network http://ssrn.com/ abstract=1516626. For example, migration integrity officers have been stationed overseas to prevent undocumented or suspicious individuals boarding planes to Canada; sanctions have been placed on transportation companies that have permitted improperly documented passengers to load; and security checks of visa applicants are undertaken.

2 For more information about the Canada Border Services Agency, see Chapter 2.

sibility. Similarly, a person already in Canada may come to the notice of a CBSA officer, who may initiate inquiries into their status and into possible grounds for holding them to be inadmissible, and then may initiate removal proceedings.[3]

B. REMOVAL FROM CANADA

1) Enforcing the *Immigration and Refugee Protection Act* and Its Regulations

The minister of Public Safety and Emergency Preparedness, along with the Canada Border Services Agency (CBSA), is primarily in charge of enforcing Canada's immigration regime. (For more information, see Chapter 2.)

2) The Removal Order

The primary tool of enforcement within the immigration regime is the removal order. A permanent resident loses her status when a removal order against her comes into force; she reverts to being a foreign national.[4] As well, temporary residents may be subject to a removal order at the end of the period for which they are authorized to stay in Canada, when their temporary resident permit is cancelled, or for other reasons.[5] In general, where a removal order is enforceable, the order must be enforced as soon as possible; the foreign national must leave Canada immediately.[6] Where a removal order has been enforced, the individual may not return to Canada unless authorized by an officer "or in other prescribed circumstances."[7]

---

3   Such persons could include, for example, refugee claimants who were denied refugee protection, who have exhausted all avenues of appeal and alternative remedies, and who have stayed in Canada beyond the authorized period, or visitors who had valid status but who have stayed beyond the authorized period on their visa.

4   *Immigration and Refugee Protection Act*, SC 2001, c 27, s 46(1)(c) [*IRPA*].

5   *Ibid*, s 47. Section 47(b) gives the power to an officer or the Immigration Division to determine that temporary resident status is lost if a foreign national fails to comply with any *IRPA* requirements.

6   *Ibid*, s 48(2). Section 48(1) specifies that a removal order is enforceable if it has come into force and is not stayed. See Section E, below in this chapter, on the discussion of stays.

7   *Ibid*, s 52(1).

The *Regulations* identify three types of removal order: (1) a departure order,[8] (2) an exclusion order,[9] and (3) a deportation order.[10] They also prescribe different circumstances permitting a person's return to Canada for each type of order that has been made.[11]

Where a *deportation order* has been issued and enforced, the subject may not return to Canada without written authorization.[12] Where an *exclusion order* has been issued, the subject requires written authorization to return to Canada within a year of the enforcement of the order.[13] Where a *departure order* has been issued, the subject may return without written authorization, if the other requirements of the *IRPA* and its *Regulations* are met.[14] A foreign national who has been issued a departure order must meet specified conditions within thirty days, failing which, the order becomes a deportation order.[15] Conditions include appearing before an officer at a port of entry to verify departure from Canada, obtaining a certificate of departure from Citizenship and Immigration Canada (CIC), and departing from Canada.[16] Justice Harrington, in *Sahakyan v Canada (Minister of Citizenship and Immigration)*, has described effectively the impact of this rule.[17] His reasons begin as follows:

> When you are told to get out of Canada, you better get going! Sergey Sahakyan was a little slow in leaving Canada after his refugee claim was turned down. Because he should have left three months earlier, he may never get back in, even though he now holds the right papers.
>
> He has been selected for permanent residence by Québec, pursuant to a Federal–Provincial agreement. Had he left Canada when he

---

8   *Immigration and Refugee Protection Regulations*, 2002 SOR/2002-227, s 224 [*Regulations*].

9   *Ibid*, s 225.

10 *Ibid*, s 226.

11 *Ibid*, s 223.

12 *Ibid*, s 226.

13 *Ibid*, s 225(1). See also *ibid*, s 225(2): However, where the order has been issued because of misrepresentation, the relevant period of time is two years. Under changes introduced by the *Faster Removal of Foreign Criminals Act*, SC 2013, c 16, s 16(1), not yet in force, the period is increased to five years.

14 *Regulations*, above note 8, s 224. See s 229(2), which provides that a refugee claimant is issued a departure order once the claim has been determined eligible to be referred to the Refugee Protection Division.

15 *Ibid*, s 224(2).

16 *Ibid*, ss 240(1)(a)–(c). See also s 224 (c): If the individual is detained during a thirty-day period, the time limit is suspended until the day of release.

17 2004 FC 1542.

should, he would be entitled to be here as of right. Now a Canadian visa officer will not let him back in.[18]

The type of removal order that is issued depends solely on the ground of inadmissibility that underlies its issuance.[19] As noted above, the grounds of inadmissibility do not reflect an assessment of individual culpability. No room is made available for leniency that might reflect the individual's actual degree of wrongdoing. For example, it is the fact that an offence is punishable by ten years of imprisonment that renders an offender inadmissible on grounds of serious criminality.[20] If an individual is found to be inadmissible on this ground, a deportation order will be issued with no weight given to mitigating factors or to the level of involvement in the wrongdoing. A minor accessory is treated in similar fashion to the actual perpetrator.

Sections 228 and 229 of the *Regulations* determine which removal orders attach to which grounds of inadmissibility. Section 228 is limited in application to foreign nationals. As noted, the exclusion order issued on grounds of misrepresentation is anomalous because of the extended period of time during which a person must seek authorization for re-entry.[21]

3) The Process of Removal

a) The Section 44 Report

i) Issuing a Section 44 Report
The process of removal normally begins with the issuance of a report by a CBSA officer in which he identifies grounds for believing that the individual in question is inadmissible.[22] The report is transmitted to a second officer, acting as the delegate of the minister of Public Safety and Emergency Preparedness, for consideration.[23] In some circumstances,

---

18   *Ibid* at paras 1 & 2. See para 24 where Harrington J ultimately found in favour of Sahakyan on the ground that the officer did not provide the applicant with sufficient opportunity to explain his delay in departing from Canada.
19   *Regulations*, above note 8, ss 228 & 229. For more information about inadmissibility, see Chapter 14.
20   *IRPA*, above note 4, s 36.
21   *Regulations*, above note 8, ss 225(2) and 229(1)(h): However, where the order has been issued because of misrepresentation, the relevant period is two years. Under changes introduced by the *Faster Removal of Foreign Criminals Act*, above note 13, s 16(1), not yet in force, the period is increased to five years.
22   *IRPA*, above note 4, s 44(1).
23   *Ibid*.

this second officer has the authority to issue a removal order.[24] In other cases, a removal order may be issued only by the Immigration Division (ID) of the Immigration and Refugee Board (IRB).[25] The ground of inadmissibility and the status of the individual determine which body shall make the decision. The division of powers is delineated relatively precisely, and jurisdictional disputes are not common.[26]

ii) Section 44 Report against Family Members

The *IRPA* renders inadmissible the family member of a foreign national found to be inadmissible.[27] The *Regulations* also include family members of foreign nationals within a report and a removal order:

> **227.** (1) For the purposes of section 42 of the Act, a report prepared under subsection 44(1) of the Act against a foreign national is also a report against the foreign national's family members in Canada.
>
> (2) A removal order made by the Immigration Division against a foreign national is also a removal order against their family members in Canada to whom subsection (1) applies if

---

24 These circumstances are listed in *Regulations*, above note 8, s 228(1); *IRPA*, above note 4, s 44(2) provides:

> If the Minister is of the opinion that the report is well-founded, the Minister may refer the report to the Immigration Division for an admissibility hearing, except in the case of a permanent resident who is inadmissible solely on the grounds that they have failed to comply with the residency obligation under section 28 and except, in the circumstances prescribed by the regulations, in the case of a foreign national. In those cases, the Minister may make a removal order.

25 *Regulations*, above note 8, s 229.

26 However, in *Canada (Public Safety and Emergency Preparedness) v Barci*, 2010 CanLII 85379 (CA IRB), a jurisdictional dispute did arise. The minister of Public Safety and Emergency Preparedness had referred a report to the Immigration Division alleging that Barci was inadmissible pursuant to s 29(2) of the *IRPA* for failing to leave Canada by the end of the period authorized for his stay. Specific reference is made to overstays in s 228(1)(c)(iv) of the *Regulations*, above note 8. However, the minister argued that the case also fell within s 229(1)(n), which refers to individuals who "are inadmissible under paragraph 41(a) of the Act *for any other failure to comply with the Act*" [emphasis added]. Locating the individual in this group would grant jurisdiction to the Immigration Division. It would also permit the Division to issue a deportation order under the terms of s 229(3)(a), which deals with repeat offenders. Such an option is not available to the minister's delegate acting under s 228. Board member Tessler declined to accept the minister's arguments, basing his reasons on the principle of statutory interpretation known as "implied exclusion": by specifying overstays in one section the legislature may be presumed to have excluded them from the more general provisions of the other section.

27 *IRPA*, above note 4, s 42.

(a)   an officer informed the family member of the report, that they
are the subject of an admissibility hearing and of their right to
make submissions and be represented, at their own expense, at
the admissibility hearing; and

(b)   the family member is subject to a decision of the Immigration
Division that they are inadmissible under section 42 of the Act
on grounds of the inadmissibility of the foreign national.[28]

iii) An Officer's Discretion in Issuing Section 44 Reports

The wording used in section 44 of the *IRPA* has created some interpretive difficulties that have been brought to the Federal Court and the
Federal Court of Appeal. In both subsections (1) and (2), the word *may*
is used to define the officer's authority. Subsection (1) provides:

> An officer who is of the opinion that a permanent resident or a for-
> eign national who is in Canada is inadmissible *may* prepare a report
> setting out the relevant facts . . .[29]

Subsection (2) reads:

> If the Minister is of the opinion that the report is well-founded, the
> Minister *may* refer the report to the Immigration Division for an ad-
> missibility hearing . . . .[30]

On first sight, it might be thought that the use of the word *may*
indicates a legislative intent to give broad discretion to the officer and
the minister's delegate to either prepare the report (or not) in the first
case, or to refer the report (or not) in the second. If such discretion
existed, it would be possible for the officer or the delegate to prevent
the removal process from starting or to bring it to a halt, thus allowing
an inadmissible individual to remain in the country even where the
ground of inadmissibility is of the most serious type. One reason for
recognizing such discretion has already been alluded to: the grounds of
inadmissibility do not reflect accurately the culpability of the particular
individual. They are rough-and-ready categories that can encompass a
wide range of wrongdoers or a wide range of personal circumstances.

The judicial response to this issue has been inconsistent. In *Hernandez v Canada (Minister of Citizenship and Immigration)*, the applicant
had arrived in Canada as a permanent resident in 1985, at the age of
twelve.[31] In 2003, he was convicted and sentenced to thirty months of

---

28   *Regulations*, above note 8, s 227.
29   *IRPA*, above note 4, s 44(1) [emphasis added].
30   *Ibid*, s 44(2) [emphasis added].
31   2005 FC 429 at para 1.

imprisonment for possession of cocaine for the purposes of trafficking, an offence that potentially carries a life sentence.[32] Justice Snider's interpretation of the word *may* was influenced by comments made by an assistant deputy minister to a parliamentary committee about the drafting of the *IRPA*:

> Under Bill C-11 [s. 44(1)], the officer investigating the case of a permanent resident with serious criminality has new discretion right at the front end of the process not to write a report recommending that enforcement action be taken. The recommendation about looking at whether or not to consider writing a report is only taken after all the factors have considered, after all the individual circumstances of the permanent resident have been considered. The length of time in Canada, the presence of family in Canada, the seriousness of the crime, the circumstances surrounding the commission of the offence, and so on, are all factors taken into account before a decision is taken, and will continue to be factors taken into account before a decision is taken.[33]

She concluded:

> These comments could not be clearer; CIC believed that, under subsections 44(1) and (2), both the immigration officer and the Minister's delegate would take all the circumstances into account prior to engaging the removal process — specifically in the case of serious criminality.[34]

Justice Snider also took note of the fact that the operational manual contains extensive advice to officers on how to exercise their discretion under section 44.[35]

In *Cha v Canada (Minister of Citizenship and Immigration)*,[36] Décary JA concluded:

> To the extent that Lemieux J. suggested that the Minister's delegate could look at the gravity of the offence, and the particular circumstances of Mr. Cha and his conviction in determining not to issue the removal order, he was in error. It is simply not open to the Minister's delegate to indirectly or collaterally go beyond the actual conviction.

---

32   *Ibid.*
33   *Ibid* at para 18.
34   *Ibid* at para 19.
35   *Ibid* at paras 20–25.
36   2006 FCA 126 [*Cha*].

To do so would ignore Parliament's clearly expressed intent that the breaking of the condition of non-criminality be determinative . . . .

Should a foreign national wish to invoke humanitarian and compassionate considerations, he would be at liberty to make a request to the Minister pursuant to sections 25 of the Act . . . .[37]

In arriving at this conclusion, Décary JA made some comments on the word *may* in section 44 of the *IRPA:*

In *Ruby v. Canada (Solicitor General),* . . . Létourneau J.A. reminded us that the use of the word "may" is often a signal that a margin of discretion is given to an administrative decision maker. It can sometimes be read in context as "must" or "shall", thereby rebutting the presumptive rule in section 11 of the *Interpretation Act* . . . that "may" is permissive. It can also be read as no more than a signal from the legislator that an official is being empowered to do something. Even when "may" is read as granting discretion, all grants of discretion are not created equal: depending on the purpose and object of the legislation, there may be considerable discretion, or there may be little.[38]

Justice Décary also identified that the meaning of the word *may* could change when different grounds of inadmissibility were raised:

The scope of the discretion, therefore, may end up varying depending on the grounds alleged, on whether the person concerned is a permanent resident or a foreign national and on whether the report is referred or not to the Immigration Division. There may be room for discretion in some cases, and none in others. This is why it was wise to use the term "may".[39]

Justice Décary noted as well that the position of a foreign national, the status of the applicant in the case at bar, was different from that of a permanent resident:

I appreciate that before the Standing Committee the Minister and senior bureaucrats have expressed the view that personal circumstances of the offender would be considered at the front end of the process before any decision is taken to remove them from Canada (see *Hernandez* at paragraph 18). I also appreciate that the Manual contains some statements to the same effect (see *Hernandez* at paragraphs

---

37   *Ibid* at paras 39–40.
38   *Ibid* at para 19.
39   *Ibid* at para 22.

20–23). However, these views and statements were all expressed or made in respect of permanent residents convicted of serious offences in Canada. No such assurances were given by specific reference to foreign nationals. I need not, therefore, decide what weight, if any, I would have given to such assurances in the circumstances of the present case. Whether weight was properly given to such assurances in *Hernandez* (where the issue was the scope of the Minister's delegate's discretion to refer a report of inadmissibility in respect of a permanent resident to the Immigration Division), is a question better left for another day.[40]

In *Monge Monge v Canada (Minister of Public Safety and Emergency Preparedness)* Harrington J has offered an extensive analysis of these two cases.[41] The applicant in this case had been a permanent resident for sixteen years and had been convicted of twenty-seven offences, including armed robbery and dangerous driving.[42] Before coming to Canada he had been put into an orphanage by state authorities in Poland where, he claimed, he had endured sexual and physical abuse. He was later adopted and then immigrated to Canada. He threatened to kill his adoptive parents and was put into the care of British Columbia's Ministry of Children and Family Development. He lived in foster and group homes and became addicted to drugs and alcohol.[43] The CBSA officer had found him to be inadmissible and had forwarded a report to the minister's delegate who, in turn, concurred and forwarded the report to the Immigration Division, which issued a removal order.[44] Justice Harrington noted that the individual had no access to an appeal to the Immigration Appeal Division but also noted that pursuant to section 25 of the *IRPA*, he could apply for temporary or permanent resident status from within Canada on humanitarian and compassionate grounds.[45] However, he concluded as follows:

> Given the divergence in the jurisprudence, it would be inappropriate for me to say anything more than is necessary to dispose of this particular case. Either the Minister's delegate had discretion . . . or she did not. Either she had the discretion to refer the subject of a well-founded report to an admissibility hearing or she did not. It is not

---

40 *Ibid* at para 41.
41 2009 FC 809.
42 *Ibid* at para 2.
43 *Ibid* at para 13.
44 *Ibid* at para 5.
45 *Ibid* at paras 7 and 37.

necessary for me to say. . . . [I]f she had that discretion, she exercised it reasonably.[46]

One may summarize these decisions by saying that the Federal Court of Appeal has determined that, while they may have discretion in relation to permanent residents, neither the CBSA officer nor the minister's delegate has discretion not to forward a report dealing with the criminality of a foreign national, or where relevant, not to issue the removal order. On the other hand, the Federal Court has been unwilling to extend the reasoning underlying this conclusion to cases concerning permanent residents. It has, in fact, developed a wholly different and incompatible account of the meaning of the provisions found in section 44.

iv) An Officer's Duty to Follow Principles of Procedural Fairness

A further interesting point is raised in *Cha* and some later cases.[47] It relates to the level of procedural fairness that must be accorded when a determination of inadmissibility is being made. In *Cha*, Décary JA held that the "failure to notify Mr. Cha of the purpose of the interview with the immigration officer" was a breach of procedural fairness.[48] However, this finding and the account of how Cha was treated were not enough to find in favour of Cha; the deportation order was restored against him. Justice Décary's judgment on this matter is quite chilling:

> The sequence of events is revealing. Mr. Cha was called by Mr. Yelle, the immigration officer, sometime before March 14, 2003 and informed that the purpose of the interview scheduled for March 17, 2003, was to discuss his criminal conviction. Mr. Cha was not informed that his status as a foreign national authorized to be in Canada would be questioned.
>
> On March 17, 2003 Mr. Cha was interviewed by Mr. Yelle. The interview started at 9:05 a.m. and ended at 9:30 a.m. Mr. Yelle immediately prepared an inadmissibility report.
>
> The report was immediately sent to Ms. Perreault, the Minister's delegate. Ms. Perreault interviewed Mr. Cha 20 minutes later. The interview lasted from 9:50 a.m. to 10:30 a.m., at which time Mr. Cha was informed that a deportation order was being issued against him.

---

46 *Ibid* at paras 32 & 33.
47 For example, *Nagalingam v Canada (Public Safety and Emergency Preparedness)*, 2012 FC 1411. *Cha*, above note 36.
48 *Cha, ibid* at para 62.

In these circumstances it was open to Lemieux J. to find that the absence of a proper notice of the purpose of the first meeting with the immigration officer, amounted to a breach of the duty of fairness.

This is not, however, the end of the matter. Breaches of the duty of fairness do not automatically lead to the setting aside of an administrative decision (see *Mobil Oil Canada Ltd. v. Canada-Newfoundland Offshore Petroleum Board*, [1994] 1 S.C.R. 202, at page 228; *Correia* at paragraph 36). Mr. Cha was represented by counsel in the Federal Court. In the affidavit he filed in support of his application for judicial review, he recognized that he had been convicted because he "was over the legal limit for alcohol" (appeal book, at page 13). He or his counsel did not suggest that he had been pardoned, that the offence fell under the *Young Offenders Act* or that he was under 18 years of age or unable to appreciate the nature of the proceeding. As a new hearing before a different Minister's delegate could only result, again, in the issuance of a deportation order, to order a new hearing would be an exercise in futility.[49]

The conclusion, namely, that a violation of the principles of fairness should be allowed to stand when it is believed that the ultimate decision was unaffected, bases the value of these principles on their instrumental utility alone. No weight is given to the notion that it is inherently valuable to accord respect to individuals who appear before the law if for no other reason than that they are entitled to know what is happening to them. A different view has been expressed by the Supreme Court of Canada in *Cardinal v Kent Institution*:[50]

> The right to a fair hearing must be regarded as an independent, unqualified right which finds its essential justification in the sense of procedural justice which any person affected by an administrative decision is entitled to have. It is not for a court to deny that right and sense of justice on the basis of speculation as to what the result might have been had there been a hearing.[51]

Similarly, in a famous quotation, Megarry LJ has noted the difficulty of ignoring procedural fairness in an open-and-shut case:

> As everybody who has anything to do with the law well knows, the path of the law is strewn with examples of open and shut cases which, somehow, were not; of unanswerable charges which, in the event,

---

49   *Ibid* at paras 63–67.
50   [1985] 2 SCR 643 [*Cardinal*].
51   *Ibid* at para 23.

were completely answered; of inexplicable conduct which was fully explained; of fixed and unalterable determinations that, by discussion, suffered a change. Nor are those with any knowledge of human nature who pause to think for a moment likely to underestimate the feelings of resentment of those who find that a decision against them has been made without their being afforded any opportunity to influence the course of events.[52]

Closer to home and to the matter at hand, in *Persaud v Canada (Minister of Citizenship and Immigration)*,[53] Hughes J has offered a narrower interpretation of the *Mobil Oil* decision on which Décary JA relied in *Cha*. He acknowledges the decision in *Cardinal* and argues thus:

> The point being made by the Supreme Court is that where a breach of natural justice or procedural fairness has been found the Court cannot refuse to send it back because it supposes that the case would be found to be futile. A rare exception exists where the remedy sought would not be relevant in the context of the matter presently before the Court.
>
> Here the remedy being sought by the Applicant is precisely the remedy affected by the lack of natural justice and procedural fairness. The Panel should not presume what the result would be nor should it prejudge the case as hopeless.[54]

b) Admissibility Hearings before the Immigration Division (ID)

Where a report has been forwarded to the board member, an admissibility hearing will be held before an ID member according to terms specified in relevant sections of the *IRPA* and the *Immigration Division Rules*.[55]

i) Public and Private Admissibility Hearings

In most cases, the hearing will be open to the public,[56] unless the Immigration Division considers it necessary to ensure the confidentiality of the proceedings by considering the following:

(i) a serious possibility that the life, liberty or security of a person will be endangered if the proceeding is held in public,

---

52 *John v Rees*, [1970] Ch 345 at 402.
53 2011 FC 31.
54 *Ibid* at paras 19 & 20.
55 *IRPA*, above note 4, ss 162–69 and 173; *Immigration Division Rules*, SOR/2002-229 [*ID Rules*].
56 *IRPA*, above note 4, s 166(a).

(ii) a real and substantial risk to the fairness of the proceeding such
that the need to prevent disclosure outweighs the societal interest that the proceeding be conducted in public, or
(iii) a real and substantial risk that matters involving public security
will be disclosed.[57]

In addition, proceedings must be held in the absence of the public "if they concern a person who is the subject of a proceeding before
the Refugee Protection Division or the Refugee Appeal Division that is
pending or who has made an application for protection to the Minister
that is pending."[58] However, this provision is qualified by the following,
which allows the board member to open up proceedings:

(d) on application or on its own initiative, the Division may conduct
a proceeding in public, or take any other measure that it considers
necessary to ensure the appropriate access to the proceedings if, after
having considered all available alternate measures and the factors set
out in paragraph (b), the Division is satisfied that it is appropriate to
do so.[59]

The ID Rules also provide the opportunity to make an application to
have the proceedings conducted in private[60] or in public.[61]

ii)   The Parties to an Admissibility Hearing

The admissibility hearing is adversarial in nature with counsel for the
minister presenting the grounds for the reports prepared by the Canada
Border Services Agency.[62] The individual who is the subject of the proceedings is also entitled to be represented by counsel.[63] Where needed,
an interpreter is made available.[64] Where the individual is under the
age of eighteen or is unable to appreciate the nature of the proceedings,
a designated representative, whose role is to assist the individual in
presenting evidence and instructing counsel, is provided.[65] In addition,
the chair of the IRB has prepared the guideline Procedures with Respect
to Vulnerable Persons Appearing before the IRB, which identifies various
accommodations that may be made, including the following:

---

57   Ibid, s 166(b).
58   Ibid, s 166(c.1).
59   Ibid, s 166(d).
60   ID Rules, above note 55, s 45.
61   Ibid, s 46.
62   Ibid, s 3.
63   IRPA, above note 4, s 167(1).
64   ID Rules, above note 55, ss 3(h) and 17.
65   IRPA, above note 4, s 167(2); see also Chapter 9.

- allowing the vulnerable person to provide evidence by videoconference or other means;
- allowing a support person to participate in a hearing;
- creating a more informal setting for a hearing;
- varying the order of questioning;
- excluding non-parties from the hearing room;
- providing a panel and interpreter of a particular gender;
- explaining IRB processes to the vulnerable person; and
- allowing any other procedural accommodations that may be reasonable in the circumstances.[66]

iii) Evidence in an Admissibility Hearing

The Immigration Division is not bound by any legal or technical rules of evidence;[67] however, at a hearing, each party may call witnesses, who may be examined and cross-examined.[68] In *Cheung v Canada (Minister of Employment and Immigration)* (decided under the former Act), the Federal Court of Appeal quashed a decision of a decision maker when he based the decision on a statutory declaration provided by an officer and refused to allow the applicant to call the officer as a witness.[69] The declaration contained admissions made by the applicant to the officer. Chief Justice Thurlow held that there were no good grounds for denying the applicant the right to call the officer as a witness.[70] Justice Urie offered a different account of why the decision was wrong. He stated:

> While it is true that the evidentiary rules applicable in trials in courts of law need not be followed . . . with the rigidity that is required in such courts and while an Adjudicator is, by the Act, entitled to receive and base his decision on evidence which he considers to be credible and trustworthy, he ought to exercise great care in the weight which he attaches to the kind of evidence tendered in this inquiry.[71]

---

66   Immigration and Refugee Board of Canada, Chairperson Guideline 8: *Procedures with Respect to Vulnerable Persons Appearing before the IRB* (15 December 2012), online: IRB www.irb-cisr.gc.ca/Eng/BoaCom/references/pol/guidir/Pages/GuideDir08.aspx.

67   *IRPA*, above note 4, s 173(c). For the Immigration Appeal Division, see s 175(1)(b).

68   *ID Rules*, above note 55, s 32.

69   [1981] 2 FC 764 (CA).

70   *Ibid* at para 11.

71   *Ibid* at para 26.

Justice Urie went on to stress that it was incumbent on the adjudicator (the title formerly given to those in charge of admissibility hearings) to use the best evidence available.[72]

In *Thanabalasingham v Canada (Minister of Citizenship and Immigration)*, the Immigration Appeal Division considered what is meant by "not bound by any legal or technical rules of evidence."[73] Board member Sangmuah made the following points:

> It is agreed that the IAD may receive and consider evidence it considers credible or trustworthy and the appellant concedes that the IAD may receive and consider hearsay evidence. Nonetheless, the appellant insists that evidence that is not sworn or given orally is *ipso facto* not credible or trustworthy. This position is not supported by the jurisprudence. The jurisprudence makes it abundantly clear that the IAD is not bound by legal or technical rules of evidence. The Supreme Court of Canada noted in *Chieu* that the IAD has liberal rules of evidence. If the IAD is not bound by any rules of evidence, then it cannot simply refuse to admit credible evidence because it is not sworn, not given orally, or was not subject to cross-examination. The appellant confuses the admissibility of the evidence with the weight to be given to the evidence after it has been tested . . . .
>
> Having said that, the fact the IAD is not bound by any rules of evidence does not mean it cannot use a legal rule of evidence if it assists in its determination of whether a document or other evidence is credible or trustworthy . . . .
>
> The panel agrees with the appellant that, although the IAD has liberal rules of evidence, there are some limits that the IAD must respect. These limits are however few. The limits that come readily to my mind are relevance and fairness.
>
> If evidence proffered is not relevant to any issues to be decided by the IAD, then it is inadmissible. It serves no purpose and may lead the IAD into a different inquiry than that which it is obliged to conduct. The task of determining relevance is not always simple and sometimes, if not often, raises a natural justice issue: the right of a person affected by a decision to be heard. In *Université de Québec à Trois Rivières v. Larocque,* the Supreme Court of Canada . . . was unanimous in cautioning against the "reckless rejection of relevant evidence."[74]

---

72   *Ibid.*
73   (2003), 34 Imm LR (3d) 132 (IAD) [*Thanabalasingham*]; IRPA, above note 4, s 175(1)(b).
74   *Thanabalasingham,* above note 73 at paras 18–21.

The *IRPA* grants the minister a general power that may be exercised in many proceedings, including an admissibility hearing, to make an application that information not be disclosed.[75] This power and the rules qualifying the possible responses of the decision maker are discussed below.

iv) The Burden of Proof and Decisions from the Immigration Division

At the conclusion of the hearing, the board member is bound to make one of the decisions listed in section 45 of the *IRPA*:

> 45. The Immigration Division, at the conclusion of an admissibility hearing, shall make one of the following decisions:
>
> (a) recognize the right to enter Canada of a Canadian citizen within the meaning of the *Citizenship Act*, a person registered as an Indian under the *Indian Act* or a permanent resident;
>
> (b) grant permanent resident status or temporary resident status to a foreign national if it is satisfied that the foreign national meets the requirements of this Act;
>
> (c) authorize a permanent resident or a foreign national, with or without conditions, to enter Canada for further examination; or
>
> (d) make the applicable removal order against a foreign national who has not been authorized to enter Canada, if it is not satisfied that the foreign national is not inadmissible, or against a foreign national who has been authorized to enter Canada or a permanent resident, if it is satisfied that the foreign national or the permanent resident is inadmissible.[76]

Section 45(d) gives an indication of who has the burden of proof in a hearing. It indicates that foreign nationals seeking to enter Canada must satisfy the member of the Immigration Division of the Immigration and Refugee Board that they are not inadmissible. Where, however, the case relates to a foreign national who has been granted status in Canada or a permanent resident, the board member must be satisfied that the person is inadmissible. The inference to be drawn is that the onus in these cases lies on the minister.

---

75   *IRPA*, above note 4, s 78.
76   *Ibid*, s 45.

C. DETENTION AND DETENTION REVIEW

1) Detention

a) Shortcomings of Detention of Non-citizens in Canada

The *IRPA* defines the situations in which a foreign national may and, in some cases, must be detained.[77] The very practice of detaining non-citizens while their status and entitlement to remain in Canada is in question, the nature of the facilities in which they are held, the conditions of their detention, and the staggering costs of detention[78] are all factors that have gained significant public attention and have generated critical and concerned intercessions by established organizations. For example, in a scathing confidential report made available through an access-to-information request in 2014, the Canadian Red Cross, which provides independent monitoring of detention facilities, upbraided the Canada Border Services Agency and identified a lengthy list of shortcomings.[79] The report estimated that 3,952 immigration detainees were held in correctional institutions in 2012, intermixed with the criminal population.[80] As reported in *The Globe and Mail*, the report revealed:

> In Alberta and Quebec correctional facilities, overcrowding was "a persistent concern," including triple-bunking — three people in a cell intended for one — and detainees sleeping on mattresses on the floor with limited personal space.
>
> In 2012, an estimated 291 minors were detained under immigration law — 288 in federal facilities and three in provincial ones. However, it cautioned the numbers may actually be higher.
>
> Inspectors found the border agency had no facility that could appropriately accommodate a complete family unit of mother, father and children — or a father with child — without having to separate family members.[81]

Delphine Nakache reveals a similar litany of problems in a report prepared for the United Nations High Commissioner for Refugees

---

77 *Ibid*, s 55.
78 In 2013–14 the costs of detention were $55,195,949. See House of Commons, *Order Paper*, 41st Parl, 2nd Sess, No 97 (5 June 2014) [Order Paper June 2014].
79 Jim Bronskill, "Red Cross Probe Finds Cramped Conditions for Immigration Detainees" *The Globe and Mail* (25 September 2014), online: www.theglobeand-mail.com/news/national/red-cross-probe-finds-cramped-conditions-for-immigration-detainees/article20783417/#dashboard/follows/.
80 *Ibid*.
81 *Ibid*.

(UNHCR) in 2011.[82] Nakache reports a dramatic increase in the time that immigrants were detained in 2009–10 compared with 2005 and also a large disparity among the different regions of Canada in the use of detention in similar types of cases.[83] She outlines the principles of international law that govern the detention of migrants and concludes:

> [I]nternational human rights law has issued a set of principles relating to immigration detention. When put together, these principles establish that: immigration detention should be the exception rather than the rule; that detention, to be justified, must be in accordance with law and must not be arbitrary and that the conditions of detention be humane.[84]

She puts particular emphasis on the stipulation that "detained migrants should be 'held in specifically designed centres in conditions tailored to their legal status and catering for their particular needs.'"[85] It may, of course, also be argued that our detention practices violate an individual's constitutional right not to be subjected to cruel and

---

82 Delphine Nakache, *The Human and Financial Cost of Detention of Asylum-Seekers in Canada*, UN High Commissioner for Refugees (December 2011), online: UNHCR www.refworld.org/docid/4fafc44c2J.html.

83 *Ibid* at 41; see Order Paper June 2014, above note 78, where most recent figures suggest that the length is still increasing. In 2009–10, the average length of detention prior to removal was thirty-two days; in 2013–14, it was thirty-seven days.

84 Nakache, above note 82 at 26; see also Global Detention Project, *Canada Detention Profile*, online: www.globaldetentionproject.org/countries/americas/canada/introduction.html, which notes the following on its website:

> Many of Canada's detention practices compare unfavourably to those of other key destination countries. Thus, for example, although there are widely recognized international human rights norms against using criminal facilities for the purposes of immigration detention, Canada remains one of only a handful of major industrialized countries to make widespread — and, in the case of Canada, increasing — use of prisons to confine non-citizens in administrative detention, where immigration detainees tend to be mixed with the regular prison population. As the Global Detention Project has found in other federal systems like Switzerland and Germany, Canada's use of local prisons makes accessing up-to-date information about detention activities extraordinarily difficult, raising questions about the overall transparency of the Canadian detention estate. Also, in contrast to other major detaining countries, Canada has no institutionalized framework for independent monitoring of detention conditions and making reports on these conditions publicly available. Additionally, Canada's lack of detention time limits places the country in the company of a dwindling number of states.

85 Nakache, above note 82 at 24, quoting an ICJ publication.

unusual treatment, guaranteed by section 12 of the *Canadian Charter of Rights and Freedoms*.[86]

The case of Lucia Vega Jimenez is a reminder of the alarming treatment to which immigration detainees are subjected and the lack of oversight of those in their charge. Since 2000, nine people have died in immigration detention, most of which were held in a provincial jail or non-CBSA facility, and until Lucia's case, the Canada Border Services Agency did not tell anyone when immigration detainees died in custody.[87] Lucia Vega Jimenez was a Mexican who committed suicide while being held at a CBSA airport holding cell in December 2013.[88] The Canada Border Services Agency did not publicly disclose details of her death, and members of the Mexican-Canadian community came forward to question the manner in which she died and why her death was not disclosed.[89] An inquest was held to investigate the death, and it was revealed that staff failed to complete the multiple required room checks and that non-CBSA staff were managing immigration detainees; CBSA efforts to avoid answering questions about the death were also described.[90] The inquest made a number of recommendations, including civilian oversight, access to lawyers and translators, and "dedicated, above-ground holding centres for detainees that feature natural light, ventilation and outside access."[91] It remains to be seen whether these recommendations will become a reality.

b) Decisions to Detain or Release an Individual

i) *The Standard Used*
Section 55 of the *IRPA* authorizes a CBSA officer to detain foreign nationals and permanent residents where she has *reasonable grounds to*

---

86   Part 1 of the *Constitution Act, 1982*, being Schedule B to the *Canada Act 1982* (UK), 1982, c 11 [*Charter*].

87   Leslie Young, "Deaths in Detention: CBSA's Fatal Failure to Learn from Its Mistakes" *Global News* (5 November 2014), online: http://globalnews.ca/news/1649523/deaths-in-detention-cbsas-fatal-failure-to-learn-from-its-mistakes/.

88   Tara Carman, "Lucia Vega Jimenez: Border Services Information Censorship Exposed" *Vancouver Sun* (3 December 2014), online: www.vancouversun.com/news/Lucia+Vega+Jimenez+Border+services+information+censorship+expos ed/10437597/story.html.

89   Young, above note 87.

90   Carman, above note 88; Tara Carman & Matthew Robinson, "CBSA Should Staff Its Own Detention Centre: BC Coroner's Inquest" *Ottawa Citizen* (10 June 2014), online: www.ottawacitizen.com/news/CBSA+should+staff+detention+cent re+coroner+inquest+updated+with+video/10271559/story.html.

91   Carman & Robinson, *ibid*.

believe that the individual in question is inadmissible to Canada and is either a danger to the public or unlikely to appear for immigration processes, such as examination, hearing, or removal.[92] A warrant is required for the detention of a permanent resident but may not be necessary for some foreign nationals.[93] Under section 55(2), the officer may detain a foreign national where the person has not satisfied the officer as to his identity.[94] Section 55(3) also states that, at a port of entry, a CBSA officer may detain a foreign national or a permanent resident where it is necessary to complete the immigration examination, or where the officer has *reasonable grounds to suspect* that the person is inadmissible on grounds of security, violating human or international rights, serious criminality, criminality or organized criminality.[95] It should be noted that whereas sections 55(1) and (2) refer to the need to have "*reasonable grounds to believe*," section 55(3) refers to "*reasonable grounds to suspect*" [emphasis added] a seemingly *lower* standard. In *Mugesera v Canada (Minister of Citizenship and Immigration)*, the Court distinguished the two phrases as follows:

> The FCA has found, and we agree, that the "reasonable grounds to believe" standard requires something more than mere suspicion, but less than the standard applicable in civil matters of proof on the balance of probabilities . . . . In essence, reasonable grounds will exist where there is an objective basis for the belief which is based on compelling and credible information . . . .[96]

ii) Detention Reviews

a. Overview

Where a foreign national or permanent resident has been detained, notice must be provided to the IRB's Immigration Division without delay.[97] In most circumstances, the Division must review the detention order

---

92 *IRPA*, above note 4, s 55.
93 *Ibid*, ss 55(1)–(2). Section 55(2) specifies, "An officer may, without a warrant, arrest and detain a foreign national, other than a protected person" under certain conditions listed in the section.
94 *Ibid*, s 55(2).
95 *Ibid*, 55(3). The *Protecting Canada's Immigration System Act*, SC 2012, c 17, assented to on 28 June 2012, introduced this broad array of grounds for detention at a port of entry. Previously, unless the individual was suspected to be inadmissible on grounds of security or violating human or international rights, the detention could be justified only on the grounds mentioned in sections 55(1) & (2) — danger, flight risk, or, in the case of a foreign national, identity.
96 2005 SCC 40 at para 114.
97 *IRPA*, above note 4, s 55(4).

within forty-eight hours, with a second review to follow within seven days.[98] Subsequently, reviews follow at least once every thirty days.[99]

The purpose of the detention review is to determine whether there continue to be reasons for the individual to be held.[100] Section 58 of the *IRPA* specifies when a person held in detention should not be released:

> **58.** (1) The Immigration Division shall order the release of a permanent resident or a foreign national unless it is satisfied, taking into account prescribed factors, that
>
> (*a*) they are a danger to the public;
>
> (*b*) they are unlikely to appear for examination, an admissibility hearing, removal from Canada, or at a proceeding that could lead to the making of a removal order by the Minister under subsection 44(2);
>
> (*c*) the Minister is taking necessary steps to inquire into a reasonable suspicion that they are inadmissible on grounds of security, violating human or international rights, serious criminality, criminality or organized criminality;
>
> (*d*) the Minister is of the opinion that the identity of the foreign national . . . has not been, but may be, established and they have not reasonably cooperated with the Minister by providing relevant information for the purpose of establishing their identity or the Minister is making reasonable efforts to establish their identity.[101]

The *Regulations* specify the factors that must be taken into account when a decision to detain is being made on the various grounds.[102] In

---

98 *Ibid*, ss 57(1)–(2). See also s 57.1, which provides the exceptional case where the detained person is a designated foreign national or where the individual is detained under a security certificate. These cases are considered in detail in Section F(2), below in this chapter.

99 *Ibid*, s 57(2).

100 See *ibid*, ss 58 and 58.1, for reasons why persons may not be released from detention.

101 *Ibid*, s 58.

102 *Regulations*, above note 8, ss 244–50. Section 244 lists the following factors: (a) whether the person will appear for examination, a hearing, a scheduled removal, or a proceeding where a removal order could be made; (b) whether the person is a danger to the public; and (c) whether the person's identity has been established. Section 245 looks at factors that may identify whether a person is a flight risk, such as compliance with previous departure orders and conditions imposed on the person's entry, release, or stay of removal, appearances at immigration or criminal proceedings, attempts to avoid examination or custody, involvement with people smuggling or trafficking operations, and strength

addition, the chairperson of the IRB has prepared a useful guideline on the reasons for detention and on the considerations that should be given weight on review.[103] In *Sahin v Canada (Minister of Citizenship and Immigration)*, Rothstein J asserted strongly that detention could not be indefinite.[104] He made the following remarks on what should be considered when detention is being reviewed:

> To assist adjudicators I offer some observations on what should be taken into account by them . . . . The following list, which, of course, is not exhaustive of all considerations, seems to me to at least address the more obvious ones. Needless to say, the considerations relevant to a specific case, and the weight to be placed upon them, will depend upon the circumstances of the case.
>
> (1) Reasons for the detention, i.e. is the applicant considered a danger to the public or is there a concern that he would not appear for removal. I would think that there is a stronger case for continuing a long detention when an individual is considered a danger to the public.
>
> (2) Length of time in detention and length of time detention will likely continue. If an individual has been held in detention for some time as in the case at bar, and a further lengthy detention

---

of ties to a community in Canada. Section 246 looks at factors that may help identify whether the person could be a danger to the public. For example, is the person associated with a criminal organization, engaged in people smuggling or trafficking of persons, or with a criminal conviction? Section 247 lists factors that one may consider to discern whether identity has been established. Section 248 lists other factors, such as, among others, the reason for the detention, length of time in detention, and existence of alternatives to detention. Section 249 lists special considerations applicable to minor children.

103 Immigration and Refugee Board of Canada, Chairperson Guideline 2: *Detention* (5 June 2013), online: www.irb-cisr.gc.ca/Eng/BoaCom/references/pol/GuiDir/Pages/GuideDir02.aspx; see also Citizenship and Immigration Canada, ENF 20: *Detention*, online: CIC www.cic.gc.ca/English/resources/manuals/enf/enf20-eng.pdf. This operational manual on detention also provides details on the procedures that must be followed by CBSA officers and the factors that must be taken into account.

104 [1995] 1 FC 214 (TD) [*Sahin*]. Justice Rothstein's remarks on this issue are cited by the Supreme Court in *Charkaoui v Canada (Citizenship and Immigration)*, 2007 SCC 9 at para 108 [*Charkaoui*]:

> In *Sahin*, Rothstein J had occasion to examine a situation of ongoing detention (for reasons unrelated to national security) under the *Immigration Act*. He concluded that "what amounts to an indefinite detention for a lengthy period of time may, in an appropriate case, constitute a deprivation of liberty that is not in accordance with the principles of fundamental justice."

is anticipated, or if future detention time cannot be ascertained, I would think that these facts would tend to favour release.

(3) Has the applicant or the respondent caused any delay or has either not been as diligent as reasonably possible. Unexplained delay and even unexplained lack of diligence should count against the offending party.

(4) The availability, effectiveness and appropriateness of alternatives to detention such as outright release, bail bond, periodic reporting, confinement to a particular location or geographic area, the requirement to report changes of address or telephone numbers, detention in a form that could be less restrictive to the individual, etc.[105]

b. Interpretation of Section 58

Some interesting cases have been sparked by section 58 of the *IRPA*. Many have concerned the detention of hundreds of Sri Lankans who arrived in two boats: the *Ocean Lady* in October 2009 and the MV *Sun Sea* in August 2010. For example, in *Canada (Citizenship and Immigration) v X*, the Federal Court reviewed the decision of board member Nupponen who had ordered the release of a detainee.[106] The minister had formed the suspicion that the detainee and other individuals on the same boat were inadmissible on security grounds.[107] The minister relied on "expert" evidence that the board member found lacking in credibility because the close connection between the witness and the Sri Lankan government raised "more than just a slight basic apprehension of bias."[108] Justice Barnes quashed the decision and argued as follows:

> A plain reading of this provision indicates that the Board is required to extend deference to the Minister in the exercise of its mandate under ss. 58(1)(c). Unlike ss. 58(1)(a) and (b), ss. 58(1)(c) and (d) refer respectively to the Minister's "suspicion" and to the Minister's "opinion." Both of these latter provisions involve situations of ongoing investigation by the Minister into unresolved concerns about security, admissibility or identity.
>
> If it was intended by Parliament that the Board was entitled under ss. 58(1)(c) to carry out a *de novo* assessment of the available evidence and to decide for itself whether a reasonable suspicion exists, no purpose would be served by referring to the Minister. If that was the

---

105 *Sahin, ibid* at para 30.
106 2010 FC 112.
107 *Ibid* at para 2.
108 *Ibid* at para 5.

intent, this section would have been written in a manner consistent with ss. 58(1)(a) and (b) which do provide for an independent assessment of the evidence by the Board.

Although the statutory interposition of the Minister was intended to require the Board to pay deference to the Minister's view of the evidence, that is not to say that the Minister is entitled to form a suspicion on the strength of bare intuition or pure speculation. A reasonable suspicion is one which is supported by objectively ascertainable facts that are capable of judicial assessment . . . .

The question that must be answered by the Board is not whether the evidence relied upon by the Minister is true or compelling, but whether that evidence is reasonably capable of supporting the Minister's suspicion of potential inadmissibility . . . .

The significant error in the Board's approach to the evidence in this case is that it effectively usurped the Minister's role to weigh the available evidence in formulating a suspicion. The Board apparently thought that it was entitled to conduct an assessment of the credibility of the Respondent and of the Minister's expert witness and to substitute its views of that evidence for those of the Minister. Having then found the Respondent to be credible (notwithstanding several obvious problems with that evidence) and Dr. Gunaratna not to be credible, the Board concluded that no reasonable suspicion remained.

In reviewing the available evidence, the Board lost sight of the proper focus of its enquiry which was to consider whether the Minister was taking necessary steps to verify a reasonable suspicion of inadmissibility. The question was not whether this ship was actually controlled by the LTTE — a fact which the Board acknowledged as a possibility — or whether the Respondent was actually a past or present member of the LTTE, but rather, whether there was sufficient evidence to support the Minister's suspicion that he was inadmissible on security grounds and whether the Minister was still undertaking the necessary investigation in support of that suspicion.[109]

The interpretation of section 58 offered by Barnes J is highly contentious. Where a suspicion is based on evidence that is identified as biased, it is arguably unreasonable, yet it would appear that Barnes J does not think that a board member should make an assessment of such matters. Justice Barnes's decision was appealed to the Federal Court of Appeal, where Nadon JA noted that the detainee had been released before Barnes J had rendered his decision, a fact that convinced

---

109 *Ibid* at paras 13–18.

him not to entertain the appeal.[110] As a result, the Federal Court decision stands. It may be that it will stand for some time since, if the issue arises again in a future case, the government may prevent the issue from being considered on appeal by releasing the individual in question, thus rendering the issue in the case at bar moot.

The rules relating to the review of detention where the establishment of identity of a foreign national is at issue are also worthy of particular attention. Section 58(1)(d) of the *IRPA* appears to establish a two-part test for determining whether an individual should be released. In the first part, it is the minister's opinion of whether identity has been established that will determine the outcome of the review rather than the board member's. In the second part, one of two factors needs to be established: either that the individual has not reasonably co-operated with the minister or that the minister is making reasonable efforts to establish identity.

c.   Detention Where Identity Is in Question

The *Regulations* identify the following as factors to be taken into account in cases where identity is in question:

(a)   the foreign national's cooperation in providing evidence of their identity, or assisting the Department in obtaining evidence of their identity, in providing the date and place of their birth as well as the names of their mother and father or providing detailed information on the itinerary they followed in travelling to Canada or in completing an application for a travel document;

(b)   in the case of a foreign national who makes a claim for refugee protection, the possibility of obtaining identity documents or information without divulging personal information to government officials of their country of nationality or, if there is no country of nationality, their country of former habitual residence;

(c)   the destruction of identity or travel documents, or the use of fraudulent documents in order to mislead the Department, and the circumstances under which the foreign national acted;

(d)   the provision of contradictory information with respect to identity at the time of an application to the Department; and

(e)   the existence of documents that contradict information provided by the foreign national with respect to their identity.[111]

---

110   *X v Canada (Citizenship and Immigration)*, 2011 FCA 27.
111   *Regulations*, above note 8, s 247.

The Canadian Council for Refugees (CCR) has expressed concern about this basis of review. In a submission to the United Nations Working Group on Arbitrary Detention, it has stated:

> The Immigration Division is required to [assess whether] the Minister is making "reasonable efforts to establish" the detainee's identity. After 48 hours and even after a subsequent 7 days the Immigration Division will generally conclude that insufficient time has passed to allow it to conclude that the Minister's efforts are not reasonable. The Immigration Division tends to accept CBSA's position about what needs to be done in order to establish identity, which usually involves obtaining documents and submitting them for expertise, and/or making inquiries in Canada and abroad. These procedures routinely take at least several days, and more often several weeks. Thus, even if the detainee is brought before an independent tribunal, the review of the detention is not meaningful when the tribunal is so constrained that it has little choice but to maintain detention.
>
> Furthermore, the CCR is concerned about the potential for abuse of power when the law requires that the Immigration Division rely on the Minister's opinion. In such a case, there is no legal check on the Minister detaining individuals for improper reasons, such as the person's nationality or religion, or for the Minister's political convenience, or even on the basis of the personal antipathy of the Minister's delegate towards the detainee.[112]

d. Where Release May Not Be Immediately Granted

Where the Immigration Division has ordered that a detainee be released, it is nevertheless possible that the individual will remain in detention. The minister may make a motion to the Federal Court seeking an order that the release be stayed while an application for judicial review of the decision is being considered. As for any application for a stay, the party making the motion must satisfy the court on three issues: that a serious issue has been raised, that irreparable harm is risked if the stay is not granted, and that the balance of convenience is in favour of the party making the motion.[113] In the course of granting such a motion in relation to one of the MV *Sun Sea* arrivals, Lemieux J noted:

---

112 Canadian Council for Refugees, *Submission to the UN Working Group on Arbitrary Detention for Consideration in "Guiding Principles on the Right of Anyone Deprived of His or Her Liberty to Challenge the Legality of the Detention in Court": Country Submission: Canada* (20 January 2014), online: CCR http://ccrweb.ca/files/wgad-submission-jan-2014.pdf.

113 *Toth v Canada (Minister of Employment and Immigration)* (1988), 86 NR 302 (FCA). For more information about stays, see Section E, below in this chapter, and Chapter 16 on judicial review.

[T]here is a rapidly fast growing jurisprudence from the Court on stay of release from detention applications by the Minister arising out of the *Sun Sea* claimants where the identity of the individual is not in question but where the Minister seeks continued detention on the unlikely to appear ground in the context of a section 44 referral for an admissibility hearing based on the allegation the individual is a person described in paragraph 34(1)(f) of the *IRPA*, as in the case here. If those cases are substantially similar the principle of judicial comity applies.[114]

Justice Lemieux subsequently reviewed several MV *Sun Sea* decisions where the minister had been granted a stay of release. He then applied the three-part test for granting a stay and concluded with the following observation:

Irreparable harm flows for the reasons given by my colleagues on the impact of the public interest in the context of the administration of Canada's immigration laws and the balance of convenience favours the Minister as it maintains the *status quo*. Having said this I readily realize the Respondent's liberty interests are at stake and, under normal circumstances, release might be justified. But the manner in which the Respondent arrived in Canada as part of a large smuggling operation tips the balance for the Minister.[115]

In another case, *Canada (Minister of Citizenship and Immigration) v B456*, Harrington J developed the idea that the mode of arrival is a relevant factor to be taken into account:

Counsel for B456 submitted that it should make no difference how one arrives in Canada. I disagree. Although all the hearings relating to those on board the *Sun Sea* naturally focus on immigration and refugee law, it cannot be forgotten that the *Sun Sea* is a ship and that the admiralty jurisdiction of this Court is also in issue. The (UK) *Colonial Courts of Admiralty Act, 1890*, 53 & 54 Vic, c 27, gives this

---

114 *Canada (Minister of Citizenship and Immigration) v B236*, 2010 FC 1339 at para 20 [*B236*]. Justice Lemieux, quoting himself in *Almrei v Canada (Minister of Citizenship and Immigration)*, 2007 FC 1025 at para 61 [*Almrei*], explained the principle as follows:

> The principle of judicial comity is well-recognized by the judiciary in Canada. Applied to decisions rendered by judges of the Federal Court, the principle is to the effect that a substantially similar decision rendered by a judge of this Court should be followed in the interest of advancing certainty in the law.

115 *B236*, above note 114 at para 37.

Court jurisdiction over prize and ships engaged in the slave trade. An undocumented ship such as the *Sun Sea*, which has violated a plethora of international and Canadian laws, faces a rebuttable presumption that she is engaged either in piracy or in the slave trade. The English admirals did not take kindly to such activities. Neither should we.[116]

Unfortunately, Harrington J does not provide quantitative data that might support the conclusion that such a presumption is justified.

e. Detention of Children

One major qualification of section 58 is found in section 60 which affirms as a matter of principle that "a minor child shall be detained only as a measure of last resort, taking into account the other applicable grounds and criteria including the best interests of the child."[117] The *Regulations* confirm that special considerations apply to the detention of children under eighteen.[118]

Despite this special consideration, hundreds of children are being detained in Canada, and exact numbers are hard to confirm since children are not tracked as detainees but as accompanying their parents.[119] Furthermore, while children may not be detained, the alternative is not appealing; parents who are detained have the choice of bringing their children into detention with them or giving them to the Children's Aid Society.[120] As with the provisions discussed below, challenges to these provisions in the courts may examine the question of whether the detention of children, or their separation from detained parents, infringe their *Charter* rights.

---

116 2011 FC 439 at para 26.

117 *IRPA*, above note 4, s 60.

118 *Regulations*, above note 8, s 249: The conditions specified are as follows:
   (a) the availability of alternative arrangements with local child-care agencies or child protection services for the care and protection of the minor children;
   (b) the anticipated length of detention;
   (c) the risk of continued control by the human smugglers or traffickers who brought the children to Canada;
   (d) the type of detention facility envisaged and the conditions of detention;
   (e) the availability of accommodation that allows for the segregation of the minor children from adult detainees who are not the parent of or the adult legally responsible for the detained minor children; and
   (f) the availability of services in the detention facility, including education, counselling and recreation.

119 End Immigration Detention Network, *Indefinite, Arbitrary and Unfair: The Truth about Immigration Detention in Canada* (June 2014), online: http://endimmigrationdetention.files.wordpress.com/2014/06/truth-about-detention-report_eidn.pdf.

120 *Ibid.*

f.   Designated Foreign Nationals[121]

In response to the arrival of the MV *Sun Sea*, the Canadian government introduced amendments to the *IRPA* that significantly alter the enforcement regime that applies to foreign nationals of particular categories. A new category, that of "designated foreign national," has been created. It is defined in vague and imprecise language, and the minister is given the authority to determine whether a particular individual fits within the category. The basis of the designation is that the individual belongs to a "group" whose mode of arrival is adjudged improper. The key provision is section 20.1 of the *IRPA*, which provides:

> 20.1 (1) The Minister may, by order, having regard to the public interest, designate as an irregular arrival the arrival in Canada of a group of persons if he or she
>
> (a)   is of the opinion that examinations of the persons in the group, particularly for the purpose of establishing identity or determining inadmissibility — and any investigations concerning persons in the group — cannot be conducted in a timely manner; or
>
> (b)   has reasonable grounds to suspect that, in relation to the arrival in Canada of the group, there has been, or will be, a contravention of subsection 117(1) [the provision proscribing human smuggling] for profit, or for the benefit of, at the direction of or in association with a criminal organization or terrorist group.
>
> (2) When a designation is made under subsection (1), a foreign national . . . who is part of the group whose arrival is the subject of the designation becomes a designated foreign national unless, on arrival, they hold the visa or other document required under the regulations and, on examination, the officer is satisfied that they are not inadmissible.[122]

Designated foreign nationals are subject to different rules of procedure and face severe substantive consequences. One of the most severe consequences that attaches to designation is that detention is mandatory, even for young people between the ages of sixteen and eighteen:

> 55.3(1) If a designation is made under subsection 20.1(1), an officer must
>
> (a)   detain, on their entry into Canada, a foreign national who, as a result of the designation, is a designated foreign national and

---

121   For more information on designated foreign nationals, see Chapter 9 on the refugee determination process in Canada.

122   *IRPA*, above note 4, s 20.1.

who is 16 years of age or older on the day of the arrival that is the subject of the designation; or

(b) arrest and detain without a warrant — or issue a warrant for the arrest and detention of — a foreign national who, after their entry into Canada, becomes a designated foreign national as a result of the designation and who was 16 years of age or older on the day of the arrival that is the subject of the designation.[123]

It is difficult, probably impossible, to reconcile this measure with section 60 of the *IRPA*, which identifies that detention of minors should be a last resort, and with the *Convention on the Rights of the Child*, article 1 of which states:

For the purposes of the present Convention, a child means every human being below the age of eighteen years unless under the law applicable to the child, majority is attained earlier.[124]

According to section 56(2) of the *IRPA*, designated foreign nationals must be detained until

(a) a final determination is made to allow their claim for refugee protection or application for protection;

(b) they are released as a result of the Immigration Division ordering their release under section 58; or

(c) they are released as a result of the Minister ordering their release under section 58.1[125]

In addition, the timelines for detention reviews are different for designated foreign nationals: the first review must be within fourteen days.[126] A subsequent review must not take place until six months have elapsed.[127] The differential treatment of persons, particularly children, under this category will no doubt be challenged in the courts. While it may be made out that such measures infringe *Charter* rights of those detained, an important question will be whether the government's rationale and implementation will survive a judicial assessment under section 1 of the *Charter*.

---

123 *Ibid*, s 55.3(1). Other severe consequences imposed on designated foreign nationals who make refugee claims are discussed below.

124 *Convention on the Rights of the Child*, 20 November 1989, 1577 UNTS 3.

125 *IRPA*, above note 4, s 56(2).

126 *Ibid*, s 57.1(1).

127 *Ibid*, s 57.1(2). It is likely that six months was selected as the appropriate time because the Supreme Court of Canada had suggested that such a term may be appropriate in relation to individuals held under a security certificate. See *Charkaoui*, above note 104 at para 8.

D. APPEALING A REMOVAL ORDER

The *IRPA* grants the right to appeal the issuance of a removal order to three groups of individuals: foreign nationals who hold a permanent resident visa, permanent residents, and protected persons.[128] In addition, the minister may appeal a decision by the Immigration Division not to make a removal order.[129] Thus, foreign nationals who have not been issued a permanent resident visa do not have the right to appeal a removal order. They must seek judicial review of the decision.[130]

The IRB's Immigration Appeal Division (IAD) has jurisdiction to hear appeals; however, section 64 of the *IRPA* limits access by providing:

(1) No appeal may be made to the Immigration Appeal Division by a foreign national or their sponsor or by a permanent resident if the foreign national or permanent resident has been found to be inadmissible on grounds of security, violating human or international rights, serious criminality or organized criminality.

(2) For the purpose of subsection (1), serious criminality must be with respect to a crime that was punished in Canada by a term of imprisonment of at least six months or that is described in paragraph 36(1)(b) or (c).[131]

The IAD may allow an appeal, stay a removal order and impose conditions, or dismiss an appeal.[132] The Division has the discretion not only to allow the appeal but also to set aside the original decision and to substitute it with the decision that should have been made, including the making of a removal order.[133] Where it chooses not to provide its own decision, the Division can also refer the matter to another decision maker for reconsideration.[134] To allow an appeal, the *IRPA* stipulates that the IAD must be satisfied that the decision appealed is wrong in law, fact, or mixed law and fact[135] or violates a principle of natural

---

128 *IRPA*, above note 4, s 63(3). Where an officer outside Canada has decided that a permanent resident has not met the residency obligation, that decision may also be appealed.

129 *Ibid*, s 63(5).

130 *Ibid*, s 72(1).

131 *Ibid*, s 64. This definition was introduced by the *Faster Removal of Foreign Criminals Act*, above note 13.

132 *IRPA*, above note 4, s 67(2).

133 *Ibid*.

134 *Ibid*. See Chapter 16 on judicial review.

135 *Ibid*, s 67(1)(a).

justice,[136] or that special relief is merited in light of humanitarian and compassionate considerations, including the best interests of any children affected.[137]

To issue a stay of removal order, the IAD must be satisfied that this special relief is warranted in light of all circumstances in the case, taking into account humanitarian and compassionate considerations, including the best interests of a child affected.[138] In staying a removal order, the Division must impose any conditions that the *IRPA* and its *Regulations* prescribe and any others that it deems necessary or vary or cancel any non-prescribed conditions.[139] Section 251 of the *Regulations* provides that the following conditions must be imposed on the individual:

(a) to inform the Department and the Immigration Appeal Division in writing in advance of any change in the person's address;

(b) to provide a copy of their passport or travel document to the Department or, if they do not hold a passport or travel document, to complete an application for a passport or a travel document and to provide the application to the Department;

(c) to apply for an extension of the validity period of any passport or travel document before it expires, and to provide a copy of the extended passport or document to the Department;

(d) to not commit any criminal offences;[140]

(e) if they are charged with a criminal offence, to immediately report that fact in writing to the Department; and

(f) if they are convicted of a criminal offence, to immediately report that fact in writing to the Department and the Division.[141]

The IAD has the power to cancel the stay or reconsider the appeal on its own initiative.[142]

---

136 *Ibid*, s 67(1)(b).

137 *Ibid*, s 67(1)(c).

138 *Ibid*, s 68(1). For more information on H&C considerations and the "best interests of the child," see Chapter 12.

139 *Ibid*, ss 68(2)(a)–(c).

140 See *ibid*, s 68(4). Where a criminal offence is committed, the stay is automatically revoked and the removal order stands. Section 68(4) provides:

> If the Immigration Appeal Division has stayed a removal order against a permanent resident or a foreign national who was found inadmissible on grounds of serious criminality or criminality, and they are convicted of another offence referred to in subsection 36(1), the stay is cancelled by operation of law and the appeal is terminated.

141 *Regulations*, above note 8, s 251.

142 *IRPA*, above note 4, ss 68(2)(d) & (3).

It can be seen from the above description of the appeal process that the IRB may rely on humanitarian and compassionate grounds when allowing an appeal or staying a removal order. When such decisions are made, the Division will frequently refer to the *Ribic* factors as factors that should influence the decision whether such grounds exist.[143] *Ribic v Canada (Minister of Employment and Immigration)* involved a person appealing a deportation order for having committed a criminal offence. The IAD, as it was then, listed the following as the factors to be considered when exercising its discretion:

- the seriousness of the offence;
- the possibility of rehabilitation and progress towards it;
- the length of time spent in Canada and the degree of establishment;
- family in Canada and the dislocation that would be caused by deportation;
- the support available to the appellant from family and the community; and
- the level of hardship that would be caused to the appellant by return to the country of nationality.[144]

E. STATUTORY STAYS

1) Where Removal Orders Are Stayed Due to a Continuing Appeal or Application

Individuals under a removal order who either have no right of appeal to the IAD or whose appeal has been dismissed, have a limited number of opportunities to avoid removal. They may apply for a pre-removal risk assessment;[145] apply for permanent residence on humanitarian and compassionate grounds;[146] or apply for a temporary resident permit.[147] They may also apply to the Federal Court for leave to apply for judicial review of any of the decisions that led to the issuance of the order or,

---

143 [1985] IABD No 4.

144 *Ibid* at para 14.

145 *IRPA*, above note 4, s 112; see Chapter 11 for more information on pre-removal risk assessments.

146 *IRPA*, above note 4, s 25; see Chapter 12 for more information on permanent residence applications on humanitarian and compassionate grounds.

147 *IRPA*, above note 4, ss 24(1)–(2); see Chapter 4 for more information on temporary resident permits.

where relevant, to the dismissal of their appeal.[148] In some cases where an application for leave for judicial review is made, the removal order will be automatically stayed until the matter is determined.[149] These cases occur within the refugee determination process when an individual applies for judicial review after her appeal to the RAD has been dismissed. In another group of cases, no stay is available and the order may be enforced before the application is determined.[150] In these cases, the individual is required to apply to the court for a stay.[151] These applications and the stays that may be available are considered in the next chapters.

2) Where Removal Orders Are Stayed Independent of Further Appeal or Application

Section 50 of the *IRPA* recognizes five situations in which a removal order is stayed that are not dependent on a further application being made by the person named in the removal order.[152] The first is where a judicial decision would be directly contravened by the enforcement of the removal order.[153] The limits of this provision are unclear, but it has become evident that the Federal Court is inclined to interpret it very narrowly. In *Blake v Canada (Minister of Public Safety and Emergency Preparedness)*, a permanent resident was under a removal order on account of various criminal convictions.[154] The central issue was whether orders issued by the Ontario Court of Justice granting her custody of her children and prohibiting their removal from Ontario gave rise to a statutory stay of removal for the purposes of subsection 50(a) of the *IRPA*.[155] Following an earlier decision,[156] Heneghen J concluded that it did not, and based her conclusion on the following reasoning:

> The first matter to be addressed here is the legislative context which governs the Applicant's status. She is a permanent resident who is

---

148 *IRPA*, above note 4, s 72(1); see Chapter 16 for more information on judicial review.
149 *Regulations*, above note 8, s 231(2).
150 *Ibid*, s 231(3). These provisions outline that persons who are inadmissible on a number of grounds are not eligible for a stay of removal. See also s 231(2), which provides that designated foreign nationals and individuals from designated countries of origin cannot benefit from an automatic stay of removal.
151 For more information, see Chapter 16 on judicial review.
152 *IRPA*, above note 4, s 50.
153 *Ibid*, s 50(a).
154 2008 FC 572 [*Blake*].
155 *Ibid* at para 1.
156 *Alexander v Canada (Solicitor General)*, 2005 FC 1147.

the subject of a removal order made pursuant to the former Act. She is subject to the requirements of immigration law. In that regard, I refer to the decision of the Supreme Court of Canada in *Chiarelli* at 733–734, where Justice Sopinka said the following:

> Thus Parliament has the right to adopt an immigration policy and to enact legislation prescribing the conditions under which non-citizens will be permitted to enter and remain in Canada . . . .

The scheme of the Act is to regulate the entry of non-citizens into Canada. At the same time the Act identifies, as one of its objectives, the reunification of families, that is in paragraph 3(1)(d). The Act also refers to respect for international conventions in paragraph 3(3)(f). However, the Courts have repeatedly ruled that the best interests of the children are not paramount in the scheme of immigration law . . . .

The Act does not contemplate that the making of a custody order *per se* will give rise to a statutory stay pursuant to subsection 50(a). The Custody and Non-Removal Order in question was made pursuant to a provincial statute, that is, the CLRA [*Children's Law Reform Act*] of Ontario. The intent, purpose and scope of that legislation do not trump the legislative scheme set out in the Act. Insofar as the Order in question arises under a statutory scheme enacted by the Province of Ontario for the purposes and objectives that are unrelated to the purposes of the Act, this Court is not required to apply provincial law . . . .

In the scheme of the Act, only Canadian citizens and permanent residents have an unqualified right to remain in Canada. Permanent residents may be removed, under certain circumstances. The Applicant, as a result of criminal activities and convictions, became vulnerable to removal. Once the Removal Order against her became effective, the Respondent was obliged to discharge his statutory duty, pursuant to section 48 to effect that removal . . . , unless that removal was stayed by an order of the Court or by operation of law. This statutory obligation cannot be displaced by the making of a custody order, pursuant to another statutory scheme.

The Custody and Non-Removal Order made on February 16, 2005 by Mr. Justice Scully pursuant to the CLRA is not an "order" that gives rise to a stay pursuant to section 50 of the Act.[157]

This lengthy analysis says little more than that a removal order is not stayed by a custody order because that type of order is not contemplated by the statute. The *IRPA*, however, contemplates that the

---

157 *Blake,* above note 154 at paras 54–61.

fast removal of a criminal will be stayed in some circumstances. It is unclear from this passage why the issuance of an order proscribing the removal of the applicant's children is not one of those circumstances.

Section 50(b) provides a second circumstance where an order is stayed, namely, in the case of a foreign national sentenced to a term of imprisonment in Canada, until the sentence is completed.[158] The general practice, with some qualifications noted in the *Regulations*, is that a criminal will serve his sentence before he is removed.[159] Section 50(c) of the *IRPA* covers the case where the Immigration Appeal Division has issued a stay.[160] Section 50(d) addresses the circumstances where a stay is granted to a person granted protection after a pre-removal risk assessment is conducted.[161] Finally, section 50(e) stays a removal order "for the duration of a stay imposed by the Minister."[162] To understand this final provision one must turn to section 230(1) of the *Regulations*, which provides:

> The Minister may impose a stay on removal orders with respect to a country or a place if the circumstances in that country or place pose a generalized risk to the entire civilian population as a result of
>
> (a) an armed conflict within the country or place;
> (b) an environmental disaster resulting in a substantial temporary disruption of living conditions; or
> (c) any situation that is temporary and generalized.[163]

This section does not however apply to individuals who are inadmissible on the most serious grounds.[164] A temporary suspension of removals has been imposed on removals to Afghanistan, Democratic Republic of the Congo, and Iraq.[165] In addition, administrative deferrals of removals are in effect for Somalia (three regions), Syria, the Gaza Strip, Mali, and as of June 2014, the Central African Republic.[166]

---

158 *IRPA*, above note 4, s 50(b).
159 *Regulations*, above note 8, s 234.
160 *IRPA*, above note 4, s 50(c).
161 *Ibid*, ss 50(d) and 112(3). Section 50(d) applies to a few classes of persons who are inadmissible to Canada on various grounds, excluded on the basis of art 1F of the *Convention relating to the Status of Refugees*, 28 July 1951, 189 UNTS 137 (entered into force 22 April 1954), or named in a security certificate.
162 *IRPA*, above note 4, s 50(e).
163 *Regulations*, above note 8, s 230(1).
164 *Ibid*, s 230(3).
165 Order Paper June 2014, above note 78.
166 *Ibid*.

In December 2014, Haiti and Zimbabwe were removed from the list of countries where temporary suspension of removals was imposed.[167] The rationale for lifting the temporary suspension of removals to these two countries was stated as follows:

> Haitians and Zimbabweans have demonstrated tremendous courage in recovering from the earthquake of 2010 and years of political instability. After a thorough review of country conditions, the Government of Canada is lifting the temporary suspension of removals to these countries as others of international allies have already done . . . .
>
> Canada is one of the most generous countries in the world, and we have extended that generosity for over 10 years to Haitians and Zimbabweans by allowing them to stay in Canada because of unsafe conditions in their home countries. With the temporary suspension now lifted, the uncertainty has ended and Haitians and Zimbabweans will have the opportunity to apply to make Canada their permanent home.[168]

---

167 Government of Canada, News Release, "Temporary Suspension of Removals Lifted for Haiti and Zimbabwe" (1 December 2014), online: http://news.gc.ca/web/article-en.do?nid=910599.

168 *Ibid*. See also Government of Canada, Backgrounder: *Temporary Suspension of Removals (TSRs)* (1 December 2014), online: http://news.gc.ca/web/article-en.do?nid=910579, where further rationale was provided:

> A thorough review and consultations revealed that a generalized risk to the civilian population no longer exists in Haiti and Zimbabwe. The review found that
>
> In Haiti (TSR imposed in 2004):
> * Haiti is not in a state of war or extreme civil strife.
> * International humanitarian and security assistance continues, and the Government of Canada has committed more than $1 billion towards Haiti since 2006. That assistance is helping to stabilize the conditions in this country.
> * Internally displaced persons are being resettled into safer housing.
> * General living conditions, political stability and the level of security have improved.
> * Other countries, such as France, Brazil, Peru, Ecuador and French Guiana are removing individuals to Haiti.
> * There are regular international flights to and from Haiti and a significant number of Haitians travel back and forth between Haiti and Canada.
>
> In Zimbabwe (TSR imposed in 2002):
> * Zimbabwe is not in a state of war or extreme civil strife.
> * International humanitarian assistance is available.
> * Internally displaced persons and refugees are returning to their homes.

This move to delist Haiti and Zimbabwe is curious given that no change in conditions in the two countries precipitated the move. Further, the statement by the federal government that "uncertainty has ended" and Haitians and Zimbabweans will be able to make Canada their "permanent home" is misleading. Some individuals who enjoy the temporary suspension may not meet any requirements under the *IRPA* or its *Regulations* to qualify for permanent residence, or may have applied already and have been denied. Thus, in some cases, this lifting of the temporary suspension of removals will mean the removal of persons to precarious environments and conditions in Haiti and Zimbabwe. This move is a further signal on the part of the federal government that it is narrowing the avenues of protection to migrants from unstable parts of the world.

F. THE ENFORCEMENT OF A REMOVAL ORDER

1) Enforcing Removal

a) "As Soon as Possible"

Section 49 of the *IRPA* provides that a removal order comes into force on the latest of the following dates:

   (*a*) the day the removal order is made, if there is no right to appeal;

   (*b*) the day the appeal period expires, if there is a right to appeal and no appeal is made; and

   (*c*) the day of the final determination of the appeal, if an appeal is made.[169]

Section 48 provides

   (1) A removal order is enforceable if it has come into force and is not stayed.

   (2) If a removal order is enforceable, the foreign national against whom it was made must leave Canada immediately and the order must be enforced as soon as possible.[170]

- Other countries, such as the U.S., Australia, the U.K. and South Africa, are removing individuals to Zimbabwe.
- There are regular international flights to and from Zimbabwe.

169 *IRPA*, above note 4, s 49. Note that the section recognizes that a removal order imposed on a refugee claimant is conditional.

170 *Ibid*, s 48.

The phrase "as soon as possible" was added to section 48(2) of the *IRPA* in 2012. Formerly, the requirement had been that the order must be enforced "as soon as reasonably practicable." The previous wording gave rise to challenges that, in particular circumstances, the officer had not exercised properly the discretion to defer the enforcement of the order. In several cases, individuals applied to the Federal Court for leave to apply for judicial review and would also seek a judicial stay of removal.[171] The practice of seeking an administrative deferral of enforcement and then seeking judicial review of a negative decision continues. However, in *Legnin v Canada (Minister of Citizenship and Immigration)*,[172] Annis J has commented on how the practice may be affected by the new wording in the provision:

> It is noted that there appears to be a developing jurisprudence in the Federal Court suggesting that the December 15, 2012 amendment to s. 48(2) further narrows the scope of the Court's already limited discretion by requiring the removal to be executed "as soon as possible", as opposed to the former wording "as reasonably practicable".
>
> I would agree that the amendment is intended to convey the need to minimize delays in executing removal orders. Given that the applicants have already benefited from two deferrals of their removal, the need for compliance with s. 48(2) would appear to be heightened.[173]

Although it is agreed that the deferral officer's discretion is very limited and that accordingly, the officer is not required to make a humanitarian and compassionate review, there is authority that deferral officers must show that they are alive and alert to the short-term interests of any child directly affected.[174]

It should be recognized that the enforcement of a removal order may not only meet with expected resistance from the individual involved, but from extreme measures on the part of the government. In 1990, then-minister of Immigration Barbara McDougall disclosed that deportees leaving Canada by plane, train, bus, or boat are liable to be drugged and was quoted as saying that the practice was "not a violation of anything as far as I can tell you."[175]

---

171   See *Varga v Canada (Minister of Citizenship and Immigration)*, 2006 FCA 394 [*Varga*].

172   2013 FC 869.

173   *Ibid* at paras 23–24.

174   *Martinez v Canada (Public Safety and Emergency Preparedness)*, 2013 FC 1256; *Varga*, above note 171.

175   Associated Press, "Canada: Deportees Are Drugged" (9 May 1990), online: *Chicago Tribune* http://archives.chicagotribune.com/1990/05/09/page/47/article/canada-deportees-are-drugged.

More recently, in July 2013, Khurshid Awan was at a meeting with CBSA officers when she suffered a heart attack and was brought to the emergency wing at a Montreal hospital.[176] CBSA officers attended the hospital to place Awan under arrest to remove her from Canada the following day. Doctors, however, prevented the officers from removing Awan from hospital, telling them that the woman could not fly for six weeks following her heart attack. Khurshid Awan sought sanctuary at an Anglican church to avoid being removed from Canada. It was only after the leader of the Opposition intervened that the arrest order was rescinded.[177]

b) Removal to Torture

Canadian law that permits individuals to be deported to a country where they face the risk of torture is out of step with international law and practice. The problematic provision is section 115(2) of the *IRPA*:

> **115.** (1) A protected person or a person who is recognized as a Convention refugee by another country to which the person may be returned shall not be removed from Canada to a country where they would be at risk of persecution for reasons of race, religion, nationality, membership in a particular social group or political opinion or at risk of torture or cruel and unusual treatment or punishment.
>
> (2) Subsection (1) does not apply in the case of a person
>
> (*a*) who is inadmissible on grounds of serious criminality and who constitutes, in the opinion of the Minister, a danger to the public in Canada; or
>
> (*b*) who is inadmissible on grounds of security, violating human or international rights or organized criminality if, in the opinion of the Minister, the person should not be allowed to remain in Canada on the basis of the nature and severity of acts committed or of danger to the security of Canada.[178]

In *Suresh v Canada (Minister of Citizenship and Immigration)*, the Supreme Court of Canada considered an earlier version of this sec-

---

176 Michael Boyer, "Pakistani Woman Facing Deportation after Heart Attack" *CJAD 800 AM Radio* (25 July 2013), online: www.cjad.com/CJADLocalNews/entry.aspx?BlogEntryID=10571623.

177 *Ibid.*

178 *IRPA*, above note 4, s 115.

tion[179] and concluded that, although this section was inconsistent with non-derogable norms of international law, nevertheless, it was not unconstitutional under section 7 of the *Charter*.[180] The Court concluded:

> Canadian jurisprudence does not suggest that Canada may never deport a person to face treatment elsewhere that would be unconstitutional if imposed by Canada directly, on Canadian soil. To repeat, the appropriate approach is essentially one of balancing. The outcome will depend not only on considerations inherent in the general context but also on considerations related to the circumstances and condition of the particular person whom the government seeks to expel. On the one hand stands the state's genuine interest in combatting terrorism, preventing Canada from becoming a safe haven for terrorists, and protecting public security. On the other hand stands Canada's constitutional commitment to liberty and fair process. This said, Canadian jurisprudence suggests that this balance will usually come down against expelling a person to face torture elsewhere.[181]

The Court in *Suresh* also determined that courts should show deference to ministerial decisions relating to the degree of danger to the public or to security created by the presence of the individual in question and relating to the risk faced by the individual in the country to which she may be deported.[182] The Court may not reweigh the factors considered by the minister, but may intervene if the decision is not supported by the evidence or fails to consider the appropriate factors.[183]

Human Rights Watch has reported that "[t]o date, Canada has yet to invoke the *Suresh* exception to remove a person acknowledged to be at risk of torture."[184] However, it is the federal government's practice to seek diplomatic assurances from other countries that they will not engage in torture and ill-treatment, even though the "government

---

179 *Suresh v Canada (Minister of Citizenship and Immigration)*, 2002 SCC 1 [*Suresh*]. Note that the earlier version of the provision did not refer to the nature and severity of previous acts as being a ground for removal.

180 *Suresh*, *ibid* at paras 75 and 79: The Court concluded "that the better view is that international law rejects deportation to torture, even where national security interests are at stake."

181 *Ibid* at para 58.

182 *Ibid* at para 41.

183 *Ibid* at para 39.

184 Human Rights Watch, *Cases Involving Diplomatic Assurances against Torture* (January 2007), online: HRW www.hrw.org/sites/default/files/reports/eu0107.pdf at 6.

has acknowledged that such assurances are not reliable."[185] As Human Rights Watch points out, "One can only assume that by securing assurances for controversial deportations, the Canadian government is seeking to avoid invoking the disturbing 'exception' carved out by the *Suresh* court."[186] It is important to note that the *Suresh* exception applies only to cases where the government *acknowledges* that there is a possibility of torture awaiting an individual upon return.[187]

c) CBSA's Most Wanted List

The current government is taking more active measures to enforce the *IRPA* and its *Regulations*. The Canada Border Services Agency has issued a public "Most Wanted" list of individuals who "have been determined to be inadmissible to Canada and are the subject of an active Canada-wide arrest warrant."[188] The agency has defended the program, stating, "By publicizing the identities of these individuals, the CBSA is enlisting the help of the public in identifying these individuals and reporting any relevant information to the CBSA."[189]

While the list has been successful in leading the agency to make about seventy arrests, the federal privacy commissioner found the list as "potentially misleading" the public by using the term *war criminal* to describe individuals on the list despite the fact that no one on the list was ever charged or convicted of a war crime.[190] Further, this

---

185 *Ibid* at 7: "The government of Canada sought diplomatic assurances against torture and ill-treatment from the government of Morocco in the *Charkaoui* case, the government of Egypt in the *Mahjoub* case, and the government of Algeria in the *Harkat* case." See also Human Rights Watch, *Still at Risk* (April 2005), online: HRW www.hrw.org/sites/default/files/reports/eca0405.pdf at 54 [*Still at Risk*], where there was credible evidence that called into question the extent to which Egypt would honour its assurances.

186 *Still at Risk, ibid* at 48.

187 There have been cases where Canada has deported persons to torture. See, for example, *Benhmuda v Canada (Minister of Citizenship and Immigration)*, 2012 FC 1222. Benhmuda was deported from Canada back to Libya in 2008, imprisoned, and tortured. Benhmuda and his family fled to a refugee camp in Malta where the United Nations High Commissioner for Refugees declared the family to be refugees and asked Canada to take them back. Canada claimed that the family had been taking advantage of the welfare system and denied the request. The decision was judicially reviewed by the Federal Court, and the case was sent to another visa officer to reassess. Visas were then granted.

188 Canada Border Services Agency, "Wanted by the CBSA," online: CBSA www.cbsa-asfc.gc.ca/wc-cg/menu-eng.html.

189 *Ibid.*

190 Michael Friscolanti, "Wanted, But Not Here: In a Bid to Deport Suspected War Criminals and Gangsters, Ottawa Finds Itself in a Catch-22" *Maclean's* (27 May 2014), online: www.macleans.ca/politics/wanted-but-not-here/.

enforcement mechanism has produced the paradoxical consequence of creating reasons why persons on the list *cannot* be deported. By publicly branding persons as both war criminals and suspected terrorists, the list makes such persons prime targets for torture if returned to their home country.[191]

One report has exposed the current government's recognition of this quandary:

> Even before the list went live, it was a question that concerned senior bureaucrats: By finally identifying the border agency's most-wanted fugitives, would the Stephen Harper government actually jeopardize its chances of deporting some of them? A CBSA briefing note, since disclosed under the Access to Information Act, specifically warned that the "release of this information would highlight a person's case to the public, potentially leading to the person being at risk when removed." The Conservatives went ahead anyway, clearly convinced that the benefits of the list — as both a law-enforcement tool and a public relations strategy — outweighed any potential pitfalls.[192]

Further, the list has brought to light questions regarding how the Canada Border Services Agency is tracking down those subject to removal. *Maclean's* magazine tracked down one man on the list who was already removed and outside Canada; the man claims that the list has destroyed his livelihood due to the public nature of the unproven allegations made against him on the list.[193]

d) Sanctuary

Khurshid Awan, in the case described above, sought sanctuary in a church to avoid being removed from Canada. While not recognized in the *IRPA* or its *Regulations*, the practice of giving sanctuary and recognizing sanctuary is arguably a type of customary law in Canada that is tolerated but not condoned by the current government.

Originating from ancient medieval European law, ancient Greek and Roman law, Catholic canon law, and from the Arab practices of *ijara* and *aman*, sanctuary is the practice of granting temporary immunity to fugitives within sacred places.[194] In Canada, sanctuary is

---

191 *Ibid.*

192 *Ibid.*

193 Michael Friscolanti, "Maclean's Tracked Down an Accused War Criminal Ottawa Couldn't Find" *Maclean's* (9 January 2014), online: www.macleans.ca/news/world/macleans-tracked-down-an-accused-war-criminal-ottawa-couldnt-find/.

194 Karen Musalo, Jennifer Moore, & Richard Boswell, eds, "The International Origins of Refugee Law" in *Refugee Law & Policy*, 3d ed (Durham, NC: Carolina

often seen as a measure of last resort, where individuals have exhausted all other means of preventing their removal from Canada.[195] Sanctuary, however, is an imperfect remedy for foreign nationals avoiding removal as it renders people prisoners within the physical premises of a religious institution for an unlimited time without any guarantee that there may arise a resolution allowing the person to live freely with status within Canada. A person in sanctuary puts his life in limbo, resulting in significant loss of personal freedom and choice, of privacy, of costs, and of energy. For example, Iranian Amir Kazemian lived in sanctuary for nearly three years, while ex-KGB agent Mikhail Lennikov and US Iraq war veteran Rodney Watson have spent more than five years in sanctuary.[196] Perhaps because of this, and the lower number of positive outcomes from Canadian sanctuary, sanctuary incidents have decreased.[197] Officially, while the Canadian government has respected the boundaries that sanctuary places between the foreign national and enforcement officers, the government has also stated that it is against the practice of seeking sanctuary as a means to avoid removal as it undermines the immigration program's integrity.[198] Indeed, the current federal government is taking a stricter approach to sanctuary, deciding to "wait out" and exhaust individuals in sanctuary and those giving

---

Academic Press, 2007) 1 at 2–3; Sean Rehaag, "Bordering on Legality: Canadian Church Sanctuary and the Rule of Law" (2009) 26 *Refuge* 43 at 43.

195 Randy Lippert, "Rethinking Sanctuary: The Canadian Context, 1983–2003" (2005) 39 *International Migration Review* 381 at 391; Randy Lippert, *Sanctuary, Sovereignty, Sacrifice: Canadian Sanctuary Incidents, Power, and Law* (Vancouver: University of British Columbia Press, 2005) at 42.

196 Staff, "Iranian Refugee Now a Free Man: Lived Three Years in Sanctuary" *Anglican Journal* (1 April 2007), online: www.anglicanjournal.com; Carmen Hamilton, "Reasonable Doubt: Seeking Sanctuary? Better Hope the Public Is on Your Side" (11 October 2013), online: www.straight.com.

197 Randy Lippert, "Wither Sanctuary" (2009) 26 *Refuge* 57 at 57.

198 House of Commons, Standing Committee on Citizenship and Immigration, *15th Report of the Standing Committee on Citizenship and Immigration, "Safeguarding Asylum — Sustaining Canada's Commitments to Refugees"* (17 October 2007). There are two recorded incidents where officials have arrested individuals in sanctuary. The first was in 2004, when an Algerian man was arrested in a Quebec sanctuary for breaching his bail conditions. This case may be different because he was likely arrested due to his criminal warrant and not his removal order. The second incident took place in 2007, when police arrested an Iranian man living in a church sanctuary. The man had called police after receiving harassing phone calls. Here, the police were responding to the man's call rather than forcibly entering the church. Eventually, both men received permanent resident status in Canada (Canadian Sanctuary Network, "The Legal Implications of Offering Sanctuary" (30 May 2014), online: sanctuarycanada.ca at 5) [Sanctuary Network, "Legal Implications"].

sanctuary to enforce removal orders rather than endure public criticism or publicity in violating sanctuary.[199] For those in sanctuary, all they can do is wait and try to bring their plight to the attention of those who can sway decision makers.

2) Security Certificates and Concealed Evidence

Woven into the removal processes outlined in the *IRPA* is an enforcement mechanism that permits the government to bypass the normal requirements that regulate the removal of non-citizens from Canada. The security certificate, first introduced into Canadian law in 1978, is a seldom-used device. According to the Department of Public Safety and Emergency Preparedness, a certificate is issued "only in exceptional circumstances where the information to determine the case cannot be disclosed without endangering the safety of any person or national security."[200] This account, however, is inadequate. As outlined below, the *IRPA* allows for evidence to be kept secret within the normal processes of removal. It is more likely that a security certificate will be issued when the ministers involved wish to avoid sending the case to an independent decision maker and seek to avoid the normal practices of judicial review.

A security certificate is a document signed by both the minister of Public Safety and Emergency Preparedness and the minister of Citizenship and Immigration.[201] It states that a named permanent resident or foreign national is inadmissible on grounds of security, violating human

---

199 Kristen Marshall, "Offering Sanctuary to Failed Refugee Claimants in Canada" (2014) 48 *Forced Migration Review* 38; Michael Creal, "What Is Entailed in Offering Sanctuary? Findings from a Consultation Held at Romero House Toronto, November 2007" (2009) 26 *Refuge* 71 at 71; see Citizenship and Immigration Canada, ENF 10: *Removals*, online: www.cic.gc.ca/english/resources/manuals/enf/enf10-eng.pdf at 33, where it cautions CBSA officers against entering a place of sanctuary except in exceptional circumstances because of negative publicity. See also the *IRPA*, above note 4, ss 48(2) and 124, which provides that an individual may face penalties of up to two years in prison and a $50,000 fine for violating an enforceable removal order. These penalties are rarely imposed on those taking sanctuary due to the public optics of doing so. Further, the *IRPA*, ss 126 to 131, provides that those assisting someone to violate the Act may face up to five years in prison and a $100,000 fine. See also Sanctuary Network, "Legal Implications," above note 198 at 6. So far the Canadian government has not charged or convicted any church or religious organization for providing sanctuary to foreign nationals.

200 Public Safety Canada, "Security Certificates," online: Government of Canada www.publicsafety.gc.ca/cnt/ntnl-scrt/cntr-trrrsm/scrt-crtfcts-eng.aspx.

201 *IRPA*, above note 4, s 77(1).

or international rights, serious criminality, or organized criminality.[202] Section 33 of the *IRPA* confirms obliquely that ministers must have reasonable grounds to believe that the individual is inadmissible.[203] In *Re Almrei*, Mosley J unpacked the requirement of "reasonable grounds" as follows:

> The standard is . . . somewhere between "mere suspicion" and the balance of probabilities. It is higher than the standard applied in the control order cases in the United Kingdom which requires reasonable grounds for *suspecting* involvement in terrorism related activity: see for example *Secretary of State for the Home Department v. AF and Another*, [2009] UKHL 28 (*SSHD v. AF*), at paragraphs 62–63. The *habeas corpus* proceedings relating to Guantanamo detainees are being conducted in the U.S. District Court on a preponderance of the evidence standard: *Al Mutairi v. United States*, 2009 WL 2364173, (D.D.C. July 29, 2009).[204]

Having signed it, the minister of Public Safety and Emergency Preparedness is required to refer the certificate to the Federal Court, along with the information on which it is based and an expurgated summary of that information that is intended to enable the person named in the certificate to be reasonably informed of the case made by the minister.[205] A Federal Court judge is tasked with determining whether the certificate is reasonable.[206] If it is found to be so, then the certificate "is conclusive proof that the person named in it is inadmissible and is a removal order that is in force without it being necessary to hold or continue an examination or admissibility hearing."[207]

As with the ordinary processes of determining inadmissibility, the *IRPA* provides for detention when a security certificate has been signed. The two ministers may issue a warrant for the individual's arrest if "they have reasonable grounds to believe that the person is a danger to national security or to the safety of any person or is unlikely to appear at a proceeding or for removal."[208] Until it is determined whether the

---

202 *Ibid.*
203 Section 33 provides: The facts that constitute inadmissibility under ss 34–37 include facts arising from omissions and, unless otherwise provided, facts for which there are reasonable grounds to believe that they have occurred, are occurring, or may occur.
204 2009 FC 1263 at para 91.
205 *IRPA*, above note 4, ss 77(1) & (2).
206 *Ibid,* s 88.
207 *Ibid,* s 80.
208 *Ibid,* s 81.

certificate is reasonable, the reasons for detention must be reviewed within forty-eight hours followed by subsequent reviews, each within six months of the preceding one. Where a certificate is found to be reasonable and the individual continues to be detained, the reasons for the detention may be reviewed every six months.[209] Where detention is reviewed, the judge is required to order the person's detention to be continued if satisfied that the person's release under conditions would be injurious to national security or endanger the safety of any person, or that, if released under conditions, the person would be unlikely to appear at a proceeding or for removal; otherwise, the judge is required to order the release of the person but may attach conditions considered appropriate.[210]

The current rules governing the issuance and review of security certificates and accompanying detention are a direct response to the Supreme Court of Canada's decision in *Charkaoui*, in which the Court declared that central aspects of both the former process of determining that a certificate was reasonable and the former process of detention review were unconstitutional — they violated section 7 of the *Charter* and were not saved by section 1.[211] Section 7, which guarantees the right to life, liberty, and security of the person and the right not to be deprived thereof unless in accordance with the principles of fundamental justice, was deemed to be engaged since individuals named in a security certificate were subject to automatic detention until 120 days after the certificate was found to be reasonable.[212] The right to security of the person was also found to be engaged because a person subject to a certificate loses the protection of section 115 of the *IRPA*.[213] In reaching this decision, the Court observed:

> While the deportation of a non-citizen in the immigration context may not *in itself* engage s. 7 of the *Charter*, some features associated with deportation, such as detention in the course of the certificate process or the prospect of deportation to torture, may do so.[214]

The Court then proceeded to describe the processes that were being followed and why they failed to respect the principles of fundamental justice:

---

209 *Ibid*, s 82.
210 *Ibid*, s 82(5).
211 *Charkaoui*, above note 104.
212 *Ibid* at para 13.
213 *Ibid* at para 14.
214 *Ibid* at para 17.

When reviewing the certificate, the judge sees all the material relied on by the government. But if the government claims confidentiality for certain material, the judge cannot share this material with the named person. The judge must make his or her decision without hearing any objections the named person might be able to make, were he or she granted access to the whole of the record. Part of the hearing may be held *in camera*, with only the judge and the government lawyers in the room. The named person is not there. His or her lawyer is not there. There is no one to speak for the person or to test the evidence put against him or her.

These circumstances may give rise to a perception that the designated judge under the *IRPA* may not be entirely independent and impartial as between the state and the person named in the certificate . . . .

Three related concerns arise with respect to independence and impartiality. First is the concern that the *IRPA* may be perceived to deprive the judge of his or her independent judicial role and co-opt the judge as an agent of the executive branch of government. Second is the concern that the designated judge functions as an investigative officer rather than a judge. Third is the concern that the judge, whose role includes compensating for the fact that the named person may not have access to material and may not be present at the hearing, will become associated with this person's case . . . .

The judge, working under the constraints imposed by the *IRPA*, simply cannot fill the vacuum left by the removal of the traditional guarantees of a fair hearing. The judge sees only what the ministers put before him or her. The judge, knowing nothing else about the case, is not in a position to identify errors, find omissions or assess the credibility and truthfulness of the information in the way the named person would be. Although the judge may ask questions of the named person when the hearing is reopened, the judge is prevented from asking questions that might disclose the protected information. Likewise, since the named person does not know what has been put against him or her, he or she does not know what the designated judge needs to hear. If the judge cannot provide the named person with a summary of the information that is sufficient to enable the person to know the case to meet, then the judge cannot be satisfied that the information before him or her is sufficient or reliable. Despite the judge's best efforts to question the government's witnesses and scrutinize the documentary evidence, he or she is placed in the situation of asking questions and ultimately deciding the issues on the basis of incomplete and potentially unreliable information.[215]

The Court also noted that there were less intrusive alternatives that could reconcile security concerns and procedural rights. In particular, it noted the system of special advocates that had been adopted in the United Kingdom.[216]

In relation to the detention provisions, the Court held that the absence of a review provision until 120 days after the certificate was found to be reasonable violated a number of sections of the *Charter*, in particular, section 9, which guarantees freedom from arbitrary detention.[217] The rules in place allowed review of detention for permanent residents within forty-eight hours, but this opportunity was not made available to foreign nationals. The Court argued thus:

> It is clear that there may be a need for some flexibility regarding the period for which a suspected terrorist may be detained. Confronted with a terrorist threat, state officials may need to act immediately, in the absence of a fully documented case. It may take some time to verify and document the threat. Where state officials act expeditiously, the failure to meet an arbitrary target of a fixed number of hours should not mean the automatic release of the person, who may well be dangerous. However, this cannot justify the complete denial of a timely detention review. Permanent residents who pose a danger to national security are also meant to be removed expeditiously. If this objective can be pursued while providing permanent residents with a mandatory detention review within 48 hours, then how can a denial of review for foreign nationals for 120 days after the certificate is confirmed be considered a minimal impairment?
>
> I conclude that the lack of timely review of the detention of foreign nationals violates s. 9 and s. 10(c) and cannot be saved by section 1.[218]

---

215 *Ibid* at paras 35, 36, 37, and 63.
216 *Ibid* at paras 80–83.
217 *Ibid* at para 91.
218 *Ibid* at paras 93 & 94. See *Regulations*, above note 8, s 248, which provides that one must consider the following five, non-exclusive factors in determining whether conditional release would be injurious to national security or make it likely that the person would abscond:

   1) Reasons for detention,
   2) Length of detention,
   3) Reasons for delay in deportation,
   4) Anticipated future length of detention, and
   5) Availability of alternatives to detention.

The Court suspended the declaration of unconstitutionality for one year to provide the legislature with adequate time to remedy the Act, and in response, the measures now found in sections 76 to 87.2 were introduced.[219] They include both detention reviews and a system of special advocates similar to that found in the United Kingdom.

The salient aspects of the current process may be summarized as follows. Both in proceedings in which a judge is determining the reasonableness of a certificate and in proceedings in which detention is being reviewed, the following restrictions, paraphrased from section 83, are placed on the judge:

1) the judge shall proceed as informally and expeditiously as the circumstances and considerations of fairness and natural justice permit;

2) the judge shall appoint a person to act as a special advocate in the proceeding after hearing representations from the named individual and the minister and after giving particular consideration and weight to the preferences of the named individual;

3) at any time the judge may, on the judge's own motion — and shall, on each request of the minister — hear evidence in the absence of the public and of the named individual and their counsel if, in the judge's opinion, its disclosure could be injurious to national security or endanger the safety of any person;

4) the judge shall ensure the confidentiality of evidence provided by the minister if, in the judge's opinion, its disclosure would be injurious to national security or endanger the safety of any person;

5) the judge shall ensure that the named individual is provided with a summary of evidence that enables them to be reasonably informed of the case made by the minister but that does not include anything that, in the judge's opinion, would be injurious to national security or endanger the safety of any person if disclosed;

6) the judge shall ensure the confidentiality of all evidence that is withdrawn by the minister;

7) the judge shall provide the named individual and the minister with an opportunity to be heard;

8) the judge may receive into evidence anything that, in the judge's opinion, is reliable and appropriate, even if it is inadmissible in a court of law, and may base a decision on that evidence;

9) the judge may base a decision on evidence even if a summary of that evidence is not provided to the named individual; and

---

219 *Charkaoui*, above note 104 at para 140; *IRPA*, above note 4, ss 76–87.2.

10) the judge shall not base a decision on information or other evidence provided by the minister, and shall return it to the minister, if the judge determines that it is not relevant or if the minister withdraws it.[220]

In *Canada (Citizenship and Immigration) v Harkat*, the constitutionality of these provisions was challenged on two central grounds.[221] First, Harkat challenged the special advocate system as insufficient to ensure fair representation, and second, he challenged the process of providing summaries of information to the named person.[222]

The role of the special advocate is outlined in the *IRPA*, sections 85.1 to 85.6.[223] In her majority opinion McLachlin CJ offered the following summary:

> The judge must appoint one or more special advocates to protect the interests of the named person in closed hearings. These hearings are held *in camera* and *ex parte*, in order to permit the Minister to present information and evidence the public disclosure of which could be injurious to national security or endanger the safety of a person . . . .
>
> Special advocates are security-cleared lawyers whose role is to protect the interests of the named person and "to make up so far as possible for the [named person's] own exclusion from the evidentiary process": S. Sedley, "Terrorism and Security: Back to the Future?", in D. Cole, F. Fabbrini and A. Vedaschi, eds., *Secrecy, National Security and the Vindication of Constitutional Law* (2013), 13, at p. 16. During the closed hearings, they perform the functions that the named person's counsel (the "public counsel") performs in the open hearings. They do so by challenging the Minister's claims that information or evidence should not be disclosed, and by testing the relevance, reliability, and sufficiency of the secret evidence . . . . They are active participants in the closed hearings. They may make submissions and cross-examine witnesses who appear in those hearings . . . . The *IRPA* scheme also provides that the special advocates may "exercise, with the judge's authorization, any other powers that are necessary to protect the interests" of the named person . . . .
>
> No solicitor-client relationship exists between the special advocates and the named person. However, solicitor-client privilege is deemed to apply to exchanges between the special advocates and the named person, provided that those exchanges would attract solicitor-

---

220 *IRPA, ibid*, s 83.
221 2014 SCC 37 [*Harkat*].
222 *Ibid* at para 3.
223 *IRPA*, above note 4, ss 85.1–85.6.

client privilege at common law .... As Lutfy C.J. put it, "[a]s between special advocates and named persons, Division 9 protects information and not relationships .... The information that passes between them, absent the solicitor and client relationship, is deemed to be protected": *Almrei (Re)*, [2009] 3 F.C.R. 497, at paras. 56–57.

Strict communication rules apply to special advocates, in order to prevent the inadvertent disclosure of sensitive information. After the special advocates are provided with the confidential information and evidence, they "may, during the remainder of the proceeding, communicate with another person about the proceeding only with the judge's authorization and subject to any conditions that the judge considers appropriate" .... Read plainly, "this prohibition covers all information about the proceeding from both public and private sessions, including any testimony given in the absence of the public and the named person and their counsel": *Almrei*, at para. 16. By contrast, any other person — such as the ministers' counsel or the court personnel in attendance at closed hearings — is subject to significantly fewer restrictions on communication. Other persons must refrain from communicating about the proceedings only (i) if that person has had a court-authorized communication with the special advocates and the judge has specifically prohibited that person from communicating with anyone else about the proceeding, or (ii) if the communication would disclose the content of a closed hearing ....[224]

Harkat also argued that the vague and general summaries would not allow a named person to know and meet the case against that person. He challenged the ability of the judge to rely on hearsay evidence and identified as particularly problematic the provision that allows a judge to base a decision on information or evidence of which the named person has not been informed in summary form.[225]

The Supreme Court held that the scheme established by the *IRPA* passed constitutional muster.[226] The critical factor in this determination is the discretion given to the judge to ensure that, in the circumstances of any given case, the individual is treated fairly. In her conclusion, McLachlin CJ places significant responsibilities on the judge designated to make the decision:

> The *IRPA* scheme does not provide a perfect process. However, it meets the requirements of procedural fairness that are guaranteed by

---

224 *Harkat*, above note 221 at paras 34–37.
225 *Ibid* at paras 20 and 28.
226 *Ibid* at para 110.

section 7 of the *Charter*. The discretion granted to designated judges is the crucial ingredient that allows the proceedings to remain fair from beginning to end. Designated judges must ensure that the named person receives sufficient disclosure of the information and evidence to be able to give meaningful instructions to his public counsel and meaningful guidance to his special advocates, must refuse to admit evidence that is unreliable or whose probative value is outweighed by its prejudicial effects, and must take a liberal approach towards authorizing communications by the special advocates. And in cases where the inherent limitations of the *IRPA* scheme create procedural unfairness, designated judges must exercise their discretion under s. 24(1) of the *Charter* to grant an appropriate remedy.[227]

In the course of setting out her reasons for accepting the special advocate system, the Chief Justice is punctilious about emphasizing that the judge must implement the system in a way that accorded with fundamental values:

> The designated judge can ensure that the special advocates function as closely as possible to ordinary counsel in a public hearing. The restrictions on communications are designed to avert *serious* risks of disclosure of information or evidence whose disclosure would be injurious to national security or to the safety of any person. While the *IRPA* scheme requires the judge to minimize risks of inadvertent disclosure of information, the judge must also give special advocates significant latitude. The special advocates are competent and security-cleared lawyers, who take their professional and statutory obligations seriously. They have the ability to distinguish between the public and confidential aspects of their case. The judge should take a liberal approach in authorizing communications and only refuse authorization where the Minister has demonstrated, on a balance of probabilities, a real — as opposed to a speculative — risk of injurious disclosure.[228]

The Chief Justice also recognizes the potential of a minister over-estimating the need for security and confidentiality:

> Only information and evidence that raises a *serious* risk of injury to national security or danger to the safety of a person can be withheld from the named person. The judge must ensure throughout the

---

227 *Ibid.*
228 *Ibid* at para 70.

proceedings that the Minister does not cast too wide a net with his claims of confidentiality . . . .

The judge must be vigilant and skeptical with respect to the Minister's claims of confidentiality. Courts have commented on the government's tendency to exaggerate claims of national security confidentiality . . . .[229]

In response to the challenge that section 83(1)(i) was unconstitutional because it appears to allow a decision to be made with no disclosure of the case against the named individual, the Chief Justice denied that the scheme allows for this possibility. She argued:

> *Charkaoui I* makes clear that there is an incompressible minimum amount of disclosure that the named person must receive in order for the scheme to comply with s. 7 of the *Charter*. He or she must receive sufficient disclosure to know and meet the case against him or her.
>
> Parliament amended the *IRPA* scheme with the intent of making it compliant with the s. 7 requirements expounded in *Charkaoui I*, and it should be interpreted in light of this intention: *R. v. Ahmad*, 2011 SCC 6, [2011] 1 S.C.R. 110, at paras. 28-29. The *IRPA* scheme's requirement that the named person be "reasonably informed" ("*suffisamment informé*") of the Minister's case should be read as a recognition that the named person must receive an incompressible minimum amount of disclosure.
>
> Under the *IRPA* scheme, a named person is "reasonably informed" if he has personally received sufficient disclosure to be able to give meaningful instructions to his public counsel and meaningful guidance and information to his special advocates which will allow them to challenge the information and evidence relied upon by the Minister in the closed hearings. Indeed, the named person's ability to answer the Minister's case hinges on the effectiveness of the special advocates, which in turn depends on the special advocates being provided with meaningful guidance and information. As the House of Lords of the United Kingdom put it in referring to disclosure under the British special advocates regime, the named person
>
>> must be given sufficient information about the allegations against him to enable him to give effective instructions in relation to those allegations . . . . Where . . . the open material consists purely of general assertions and the case . . . is based solely or to a decisive degree on closed materials the requirements of a fair trial will not

---

229 *Ibid* at paras 61 and 63 [emphasis in original].

be satisfied, however cogent the case based on the closed materials may be . . . .

. . . At the very least, the named person must know the essence of the information and evidence supporting the allegations. This excludes the scenario where the named person receives no disclosure whatsoever of essential information or evidence.

The *IRPA* scheme is silent as to what happens if there is an irreconcilable tension between the requirement that the named person be "reasonably informed", on the one hand, and the imperative that sensitive information not be disclosed, on the other. The *IRPA* scheme does not provide that the "reasonably informed" standard can be compromised. But nor does it provide that sensitive information can be disclosed where this is absolutely necessary in order for the "reasonably informed" standard to be met.

In my view, the necessary outcome of situations where there is an irreconcilable tension is that the Minister must withdraw the information or evidence whose non-disclosure prevents the named person from being reasonably informed. In some cases, this may effectively compel the Minister to put an end to the proceedings.

To hold that the Minister can rely on essential information and evidence of which the named person cannot be reasonably informed would force the judge to violate the responsibility expressly placed on him by the statute, i.e. his duty to ensure that the named person remain reasonably informed throughout the proceedings. It cannot have been Parliament's intent to design a scheme in which the judge is required to violate the responsibilities placed upon him. Consequently, the *IRPA* scheme must be interpreted as precluding the Minister from bringing a case in respect of which the named person cannot be kept reasonably informed.[230]

It is clear from the tenor of the views expressed that it is only with grudging reluctance that the Supreme Court has allowed the security certificate regime to stand. It is also clear that, in future cases, the decisions of designated judges should be scrutinized closely to ensure that the principles of procedural fairness are not sacrificed to the overzealous pursuit of concealment and confidentiality in the name of protecting public security.

---

230 *Ibid* at paras 54–60.

3) Human Smuggling and Human Trafficking

Another aspect of the enforcement regime is worthy of attention. Recognizing that human smuggling and human trafficking have become organized and lucrative endeavours that may contribute to human misery, harm, and, indeed, death, the United Nations in November 2000 adopted the *Convention against Transnational Organized Crime*[231] and two Protocols — the *Protocol against Smuggling of Migrants by Land, Sea and Air*[232] and the *Protocol to Prevent, Suppress and Punish Trafficking in Persons, Especially Women and Children (Trafficking Protocol)*.[233] Article 6(1)(a) of the *Smuggling Protocol*[234] and article 5(1) of the *Trafficking Protocol*[235] require state parties to enact domestic legislation criminalizing human smuggling. Canada ratified the convention and protocols in 2002 prior to enacting the *IRPA*, which includes sections proscribing smuggling and trafficking, attaching severe penalties.[236] In addition, the offence of trafficking was included in the *Criminal Code*.[237]

The offence of human smuggling and the attached penalties are found in section 117 of the *IRPA*.[238] Significantly, the offence is defined quite differently from the way it is defined in the *Smuggling Protocol*. Article 3 provides:

---

231 *United Nations Convention against Transnational Organized Crime*, 15 November 2000, 2225 UNTS 209.

232 *Protocol against the Smuggling of Migrants by Land, Sea and Air, supplementing the United Nations Convention against Transnational Organized Crime*, 15 November 2000, 2241 UNTS 507 [*Smuggling Protocol*].

233 *Protocol to Prevent, Suppress and Punish Trafficking in Persons, Especially Women and Children, supplementing the United Nations Convention against Transnational Organized Crime*, 15 November 2000, 2237 UNTS 319 [*Trafficking Protocol*].

234 *Smuggling Protocol*, above note 232, art 6(1)(a).

235 *Trafficking Protocol*, above note 233, art 5(1).

236 See United Nations Treaty Collection, *Status as at 5 May 2015 for the United Nations Convention against Transnational Organized Crime*, online: https://treaties.un.org/pages/ViewDetails.aspx?src=TREATY&mtdsg_no=XVIII-12&chapter=18&lang=en: Canada ratified this convention on 13 May 2002; United Nations Treaty Collection, *Status as at 5 May 2015 for the Protocol against the Smuggling of Migrants by Land, Sea and Air*, online: https://treaties.un.org/pages/viewdetails.aspx?src=ind&mtdsg_no=xviii-12-b&chapter=18&lang=en: Canada ratified this protocol on 13 May 2002; United Nations Treaty Collection, *Status as at 5 May 2015 for the Protocol to Prevent, Suppress and Punish Trafficking in Persons, Especially Women and Children*, online: https://treaties.un.org/pages/viewdetails.aspx?src=ind&mtdsg_no=xviii-12-a&chapter=18&lang=en: Canada ratified this protocol on 13 May 2002.

237 *Criminal Code*, RSC 1985, c C-46, ss 279.01 and 279.011.

238 *IRPA*, above note 4, s 117.

"Smuggling of migrants" shall mean the procurement, in order to obtain, directly or indirectly, a financial or other material benefit, of the illegal entry of a person into a State Party of which the person is not a national or a permanent resident.[239]

By way of contrast it is defined in the *IRPA* as follows:

117(1) No person shall knowingly organize, induce, aid or abet the coming into Canada of one or more persons knowing that, or being reckless as to whether, their coming into Canada is or would be in contravention of this Act.[240]

The omission in the latter definition of a requirement that there be a purpose of obtaining material benefit has led to a court challenge. In *R v Appulonappa*, the accused, who had arrived in Canada with seventy-two others on board the MV *Ocean Lady* in 2009, were charged with "human smuggling" under section 117.[241] They argued that this section infringed section 7 of the *Charter* on the ground of overbreadth.[242] The overbreadth doctrine has been explained by the Supreme Court of Canada in *Canada (AG) v Bedford* in the following way:

Overbreadth deals with a law that is so broad in scope that it includes *some* conduct that bears no relation to its purpose. In this sense, the law is arbitrary *in part*. At its core, overbreadth addresses the situation where there is no rational connection between the purposes of the law and *some*, but not all, of its impacts. For instance, the law at issue in *Demers* required unfit accused to attend repeated review board hearings. The law was only disconnected from its purpose insofar as it applied to permanently unfit accused; for temporarily unfit accused, the effects were related to the purpose.

Overbreadth allows courts to recognize that the law is rational in some cases, but that it overreaches in its effect in others. Despite this recognition of the scope of the law as a whole, the focus remains on the individual and whether the effect on the individual is rationally connected to the law's purpose. For example, where a law is drawn broadly and targets some conduct that bears no relation to its purpose in order to make enforcement more practical, there is still no connection between the purpose of the law and its effect on the

---

239   *Smuggling Protocol*, above note 232, art 3(a).
240   *IRPA*, above note 4, s 117(1).
241   2014 BCCA 163 [*Appulonappa*].
242   *Ibid* at para 3.

specific individual. Enforcement practicality may be a justification for an overbroad law, to be analyzed under s. 1 of the *Charter.*[243]

The four accused in *Appulonappa* argued that section 117 was overbroad since its words would apply to both family members bringing their children into the country or humanitarian organizations assisting refugees to receive Canada's protection as well as to international smugglers.[244] The British Columbia Court of Appeal rejected the challenge on the ground that the purpose of section 117 was not solely to meet the country's obligations under the *Smuggling Protocol*; it also aimed to fulfill a more general purpose:

> [T]he primary legislative objective of s. 117 is rooted in the historical domestic concern of Parliament, as sovereign, with border control. The provision is directed at preventing any individual from arranging the unlawful entry of undocumented migrants into Canada. This in turn serves a number of secondary aims, including combatting international human smuggling, and addresses multiple domestic concerns, some of which are reflected in ss. 3(1)(*f*), (*h*) and (*i*) and (2)(*a*), (*b*), (*e*), (*g*), and (*h*) of the *IRPA.*[245]

The Supreme Court of Canada heard an appeal to this case on 7 February 2015 and reserved judgment.[246] The appeal was considered alongside appeals dealing with the meaning of the term *human smuggling* as a ground of inadmissibility.[247]

The offence of human trafficking is defined in section 118 of the *IRPA*:

> 118(1) No person shall knowingly organize the coming into Canada of one or more persons by means of abduction, fraud, deception or use or threat of force or coercion.[248]

It is unclear whether the offence is complete where arrangements have been made to bring a person into Canada but where the person has not yet arrived. A separate broader definition which does not refer to entering the country is found in the *Criminal Code*, section 279.01(1):

---

243 *Canada (AG) v Bedford*, 2013 SCC 72 at paras 112–13 [emphasis in original].
244 *Appulonappa*, above note 241 at para 3.
245 *Ibid* at para 114.
246 [2014] SCCA No 283 (leave granted 9 October 2014).
247 *Ibid.* The appeal will be heard with the following cases with docket numbers: *B010 v Minister of Citizenship and Immigration* (35388), *Jesus Rodriguez Hernandez v Minister of Public Safety and Emergency Preparedness* (35677), *B306 v Minister of Public Safety and Emergency Preparedness* (35685), and *JP et al v Minister of Public Safety and Emergency Preparedness* (35688).
248 *IRPA*, above note 4, s 118(1).

Every person who *recruits, transports, transfers, receives, holds, conceals or harbours* a person, or *exercises control, direction or influence over the movements* of a person, *for the purpose of exploiting* them or facilitating their exploitation is guilty of an indictable offence and liable

(a)   to imprisonment for life if they kidnap, commit an aggravated assault or aggravated sexual assault against, or cause death to, the victim during the commission of the offence; or

(b)   to imprisonment for a term of not more than fourteen years in any other case.[249]

Neither of these definitions is as broad or as detailed as the definition found in article 3 of the *Trafficking Protocol*, which addresses difficulties that may arise where there is consent and makes special mention of the position of children. It does raise a problem also found in the *Criminal Code* definition — that of interpreting the term *exploitation* — but also attempts to address it:

(a)   "Trafficking in persons" shall mean the recruitment, transportation, transfer, harbouring or receipt of persons, by means of the threat or use of force or other forms of coercion, of abduction, of fraud, of deception, of the abuse of power or of a position of vulnerability or of the giving or receiving of payments or benefits to achieve the consent of a person having control over another person, for the purpose of exploitation. Exploitation shall include, at a minimum, the exploitation of the prostitution of others or other forms of sexual exploitation, forced labour or services, slavery or practices similar to slavery, servitude or the removal of organs;

(b)   The consent of a victim of trafficking in persons to the intended exploitation set forth in subparagraph (a) of this article shall be irrelevant where any of the means set forth in subparagraph (a) have been used;

(c)   The recruitment, transportation, transfer, harbouring or receipt of a child for the purpose of exploitation shall be considered "trafficking in persons" even if this does not involve any of the means set forth in subparagraph (a) of this article.[250]

---

249   *Criminal Code*, above note 237, s 279.01(1) [emphasis added].
250   *Smuggling Protocol*, above note 232, art 3.

G. CONCLUSION

The current government is enforcing the *IRPA* and its *Regulations* with more vigour than ever before, amending legislation to widen the reasons for removal, to deny stays of removals, and to give more power to the minister to deem persons inadmissible. In a democracy, the ballot box provides the most significant outlet through which discontent with government policies may be shown. However, those affected the most by the new measures have no access to this device. They may be removed before any public complaint can be lodged either formally or informally. Moreover, the removal of persons from Canada is often conducted in the shadows without proper and effective oversight; it is based on allegations and suspicions that the person has committed a wrong. By relying on flimsy evidence and single-minded motivation, Canada risks infringing its most serious obligations under international law: to protect the human rights of those within Canada, and to ensure that persons are not removed to torture, death, or cruel and unusual punishment.

PART FOUR

JUDICIAL SUPERVISION

CHAPTER 16

JUDICIAL REVIEW

A. INTRODUCTION

Our legal system has long relied on the judiciary to supervise and oversee the workings of government. As a measure of last resort, we have depended on the courts to ensure that government officials remain within the limits of the law and that sufficient regard has been shown for the interests of individuals who are affected by the exercise of power. The doctrine of the rule of law requires that governmental officials respect and work within set boundaries, even when granted wide discretion; it requires that they pay heed to the human impact of their decisions and acknowledge that those affected by a future decision should have an opportunity to influence how it should be made. Of course, government departments frequently create internal mechanisms to ensure that officials remain within the proper, legally defined limits. Independent and impartial supervision, however, has long been recognized as a vital part of the judicial function that provides an ultimate protection from overzealous officialdom.

Individuals who have been required to negotiate the byzantine labyrinths created by our immigration laws and who, along the way, have experienced arbitrary and oppressive exercises of power have been able to turn to the courts for redress. Judicial review will no doubt become an increasingly important mechanism since recent legislation has denied many groups access to internal mechanisms and appeals. Where these exclusions are in effect, judicial review may be the only opportunity for some individuals to raise serious issues regarding the unfairness of the process to which they have been subject, or the impropriety of a decision relating to their status in Canada. This chapter provides a brief overview of the process of judicial review, of the grounds that may support an application, and of the remedies an applicant may seek.

B. THE FEDERAL COURT

The Federal Court is a statutory body created in 1971 under the authority of section 101 of the *Constitution Act, 1867* for the "better administration of the laws of Canada."[1] The court is a successor to the Exchequer Court of Canada, which was established in 1875.[2]

As a result of its statutory origins, the Federal Court has no inherent jurisdiction. Thus, the court will have jurisdiction over a matter only if it has been conferred either by the *Federal Courts Act*[3] or by other legislation.[4] The *Immigration and Refugee Protection Act* (*IRPA*) provides that, "with respect to any matter — a decision, determination or order made, a measure taken or a question raised" under the *IRPA* can be subject to a judicial review by the Federal Court.[5] Interestingly, if there is a conflict between provisions in the *Federal Courts Act* and provisions in the *IRPA*, the *IRPA* prevails.[6]

According to the *Federal Courts Act*, the court consists of a Chief Justice and thirty-six other judges.[7] The Federal Court website reveals that there are currently thirty-four full-time judges, seven supernumerary judges, and five prothonotaries.[8] Until 2003, the Federal Court of

---

1   (UK), 30 & 21 Vict, c 3, s 101, reprinted in RSC 1985, Appendix II, No 5.
2   Gus Van Harten, Gerald Heckman, & David Mullan, *Administrative Law: Cases, Text and Materials*, 6th ed (Toronto: Emond Montgomery, 2010) at 1043 [Van Harten et al].
3   RSC 1985, c F-7.
4   Van Harten et al, above note 2 at 1051.
5   *Immigration and Refugee Protection Act*, SC 2001, c 27, s 72(1) [*IRPA*].
6   *Ibid*, s 75.
7   *Federal Courts Act*, above note 3, s 5.1(1).
8   *Ibid*, s 12. Prothonotaries hear matters set out in rule 51 of the *Federal Courts Rules*, SOR/98-106. They are full judicial officers, appointed under s 12 of the *Federal Courts Act*, who exert many of the Federal Court judges' powers and functions. (See Federal Court, "Judges and Prothonotaries" (12 December 2012), online: cas-ncr-nter03.cas-satj.gc.ca/portal/page/portal/fc_cf_en/Bio; see *Felipa v Canada (Minister of Citizenship and Immigration)*, 2011 FCA 272, which held that the Chief Justice does not have the authority under s 10(1.1) of the *Federal*

Canada consisted of two divisions: an Appeal Division and a Trial Division. In 2003, the *Federal Courts Act* was amended, and these divisions became two separate courts: the Federal Court of Appeal and the Federal Court.

C. THE PROCESS OF JUDICIAL REVIEW

1) Commencing an Application for Judicial Review

Section 72(1) of the *IRPA* provides: "Judicial review by the Federal Court with respect to any matter — a decision, determination or order made, a measure taken or a question raised — under this Act is commenced by making an application for leave to the Court."[9]

Hence, numerous matters are subject to judicial review, including the following examples: refugee decisions,[10] decisions to continue the detention of a person following a detention review[11] or to impose conditions on a person released from detention,[12] decisions on applications for permanent or temporary residence,[13] decisions on inadmissibility,[14] and decisions on pre-removal risk assessments.[15] In effect, any individual who has made an application under the *IRPA* or has been subject to a determination under the *IRPA* may submit an application for leave to the Federal Court and thereby commence the process of judicial review. The minister of Citizenship and Immigration or the minister of Public Safety and Emergency Preparedness may also make an application for leave.

With respect to an application seeking review of a decision of the Refugee Appeal Division (RAD) of the Immigration and Refugee Board (IRB), section 73 explicitly grants the minister the power to make an application for leave, whether or not the minister took part in the proceedings at the IRB's Refugee Protection Division (RPD) or RAD.[16] As well, section 70(2) implicitly recognizes the minister's power to apply

---

Courts Act to request that a retired judge of a superior court act as a deputy judge of the Federal Court after attaining the age of seventy-five.

9   *IRPA*, above note 5, s 72(1). Any matter includes a decision, determination, or order made, a measure taken, or a question raised.

10   *Ibid*, s 198.

11   *Ibid*, s 82(3).

12   *Ibid*, s 82(4).

13   *Ibid*, s 72(1).

14   *Ibid*.

15   *Ibid*.

16   *Ibid*, s 73.

for leave in relation to decisions by the IRB's Immigration Appeal Division (IAD) by providing:

> If the Minister makes an application for leave to commence an application for judicial review of a decision of the Immigration Appeal Division with respect to a permanent resident or a foreign national, an examination of the permanent resident or the foreign national under this Act is suspended until the final determination of the application.[17]

Before making an application for leave, the relevant party must have exhausted any rights of appeal provided by the *IRPA*.[18] Thus, if an individual has the right to appeal to the IAD[19] or the RAD,[20] those avenues must first be explored and exhausted. In some circumstances, a person may be able to apply to a decision maker to have a matter reopened. Should an applicant make such a request while pursuing a judicial review concurrently, and should the Federal Court make a final determination, the decision maker in the other venue cannot reopen the matter on any grounds.[21]

The decision maker at first instance, whether it is an officer or a tribunal, has only a limited role in judicial review proceedings. The respondent is not the officer or tribunal that made the determination that is the subject of the judicial review.[22] Thus, even where there is a right to participate, an administrative actor's role is limited to an explanatory role with reference to the record and to making representations relating to jurisdiction.[23] He will not be recognized as an intervenor and will be denied the opportunity to raise or speak to substantive issues.

In most cases, if the applicant is an individual who is directly affected by the decision of an immigration officer, board, or tribunal, the respondent in an application for judicial review will be the minister of Citizenship and Immigration or the minister of Public Safety and

---

17   *Ibid*, s 70(2).

18   *Ibid*, s 72(2)(a).

19   *Ibid*, s 63; in *Somodi v Canada (Minister of Citizenship and Immigration)*, 2009 FCA 288, the Federal Court of Appeal answered the following certified question affirmatively: Does s 72 of the *IRPA* bar an application for judicial review by the applicant of a spousal application, while the sponsor exercises the rights of appeal pursuant to s 63 of the *IRPA*?

20   *IRPA*, above note 5, s 110.

21   *Ibid*, s 170.2, with respect to the RPD; and s 171.1, with respect to the RAD.

22   *Federal Courts Rules*, above note 8, s 303(1)(a).

23   *Li v Canada (Minister of Citizenship and Immigration)*, 2004 FCA 267.

Emergency Preparedness.[24] Where the applicant cannot identify the appropriate respondent, the Attorney General of Canada may be named.[25]

2) Serving and Filing a Notice of Application for Leave

A party seeking judicial review must serve on the respondent and file in the Registry of the Federal Court a notice of application for leave within specific time periods. Service of an application for leave is effected by serving a certified copy of the application for leave on the respondent. For a matter arising within Canada, a party must serve and file the notice of application for leave within fifteen days of being notified of the decision.[26] For a matter arising outside Canada, the applicant must serve and file the notice of application within sixty days of being notified of the decision.[27]

An applicant who needs an extension of time for filing and serving the notice of application must file a motion requesting such an extension, and a judge of the Federal Court,[28] after reviewing the matter in a summary way without personal appearance,[29] may, for special reasons, allow it.[30] The following factors will be taken into account:

1) whether the applicant has a continuing intention to pursue the application;
2) whether the application has some merit;
3) whether any prejudice to the respondent arises from the delay; and
4) whether a reasonable explanation for delay exists.[31]

There is no appeal from a decision regarding an extension of time.[32]

Where an applicant has received a decision, but not the reasons for the decision, she should file a notice of application for leave within the allotted timelines, indicating that no reasons for the decision have been received and that the applicant is requesting the reasons for the decision.[33]

---

24 *Federal Courts Rules*, above note 8, s 303(1).
25 *Ibid*, s 303(2).
26 *IRPA*, above note 5, s 72(2)(b).
27 *Ibid*.
28 *Ibid*, ss 8(2) and 369.
29 *Ibid*, s 72(2)(d).
30 *Ibid*, s 72(2)(c).
31 *Canada (AG) v Hennelly* (1999), 244 NR 399 (FCA).
32 *IRPA*, above note 5, s 72(2)(e).
33 *Federal Courts Citizenship, Immigration and Refugee Protection Rules*, SOR/93-22, s 9 [*Federal Courts Immigration Rules*].

The respondent in the matter has ten days, after receiving the notice of application for leave, to serve the applicant and file with the Federal Court a notice of appearance.[34] Where a request has been made, the respondent must also ensure that a copy of the reasons for the decision is sent to the applicant.

3) Perfecting an Application for Leave

To perfect an application for leave, the applicant must serve on the respondent and file an application record with the Registry of the Federal Court. The applicant must serve an application record on the respondent and must file it with proof of service within thirty days from the date she receives the reasons for the decision (if they were not received prior to filing the notice of application)[35] or thirty days from the date of filing the application.[36] An extension of time may be requested via a written motion to the Federal Court, and the decision cannot be appealed.[37]

The application record, which includes a supporting affidavit based on personal knowledge of the applicant in the judicial review, is often used to bring within the court record evidence brought before the decision maker at first instance to establish the fact of the application and the decision rendered.[38] The application record also includes the application for leave,[39] the decision under review,[40] the reasons for the decision,[41] a memorandum of argument,[42] and proof of service to the other parties.[43]

The respondent must serve affidavits and a memorandum of argument within thirty days after receiving the application record.[44] The applicant will have an opportunity to serve and file a reply within ten days of receiving the respondent's memorandum of argument.[45]

---

34   *Ibid*, s 8.
35   *Ibid*, s 10(1)(b).
36   *Ibid*, s 10(1)(a).
37   IRPA, above note 5, s 72(2)(e); *Yohalingam v Canada (Minister of Citizenship and Immigration)*, 2003 FCT 540.
38   *Federal Courts Immigration Rules*, above note 33, ss 10(2)(d) and 12; in *Sarmis v Canada (Minister of Citizenship and Immigration)*, 2004 FC 110, the court held that the failure to submit affidavits based on personal knowledge is not automatically fatal to an application for judicial review; third-party affidavits may be sufficient to establish the fact of the application and its rejection.
39   *Federal Courts Immigration Rules*, above note 33, s 10(2)(a).
40   *Ibid*, s 10(2)(b).
41   *Ibid*, s 10(2)(c).
42   *Ibid*, s 10(2)(e).
43   *Ibid*, s 10(2).
44   *Ibid*, s 11.
45   *Ibid*, s 13.

4) Obtaining Leave

The first hurdle that an applicant faces is that of obtaining leave to have the judicial review application considered by a judge of the Federal Court. An application for leave will be considered and either granted or denied without personal appearance by the parties involved. Seeking an oral hearing or motion to argue leave is not only discouraged by the court, but understood as "antithetical" to the legislation.[46] A single judge reviews the notice of application, application record, respondent's memorandum, and the reply to make a decision.[47] The decision to grant or deny leave cannot be appealed.[48] Applicants, however, may bring a motion for reconsideration where the denial of leave is inconsistent with any reasons provided, or where a matter that should have been dealt with in denying leave was overlooked or accidentally omitted.[49] The practical reality, however, is that it is extremely difficult to demonstrate that the leave decision overlooked or accidentally omitted an aspect of the case. In general, the Federal Court has interpreted the scope for reconsideration quite narrowly.[50]

The test for granting leave is not set in the legislation or in any of the rules governing judicial review of immigration matters. As the Federal Court noted in *Hinton v Canada (Minister of Citizenship and Immigration)*, "[t]he parameters which should influence a judge's discretion are not set out. There is very little guiding jurisprudence, which is not surprising given that reasons are usually not provided and that the decision cannot be appealed."[51]

What is clear from Federal Court jurisprudence is that the onus is on the applicant to present a case for leave to be granted. An applicant need

---

46 IRPA, above note 5, s 72(2)(d); in *Padda v Canada (Minister of Citizenship and Immigration)*, 2006 FC 995 at para 6, the court held that, "To allow an applicant to obtain an oral hearing for an interlocutory motion in a leave application that is intended to be conducted entirely in writing appears antithetical to the statutory and regulatory objectives of efficiency and expediency." Thus, as a rule, the registry should seek directions from the court with respect to any motion in an immigration leave application that is not brought in writing pursuant to rule 369 of the *Federal Courts Rules*.

47 *Federal Courts Immigration Rules*, above note 33, s 14.

48 IRPA, above note 5, s 72(2)(e).

49 *Federal Courts Rules*, above note 8, s 397.

50 See, for example, *Key v Canada (Minister of Citizenship and Immigration)*, 2011 FC 92; *Dan v Canada (Minister of Citizenship and Immigration)* (2000), 189 FTR 301 (TD).

51 2008 FC 1007 at para 15.

not establish that the decision maker has erred in law,[52] but caselaw indicates that the applicant must raise a "serious question" to be determined or a "reasonable" or "fairly arguable" case that the decision maker has erred.[53] However formulated, the test is meant to be highly permissive.[54] Thus, leave should be granted unless it is clear that the judicial review application has no reasonable chance of success, where it is so obvious that the application must fail, or where a determination on the merits is unnecessary.[55]

In reality, decisions regarding leave do not always reflect the permissive approach cited in the jurisprudence. Thus, while the step of obtaining leave seems benign, scholars and advocates have questioned the fairness of the leave requirement. As Gerald Heckman writes:

> [T]he leave requirement was enacted to prevent individuals from abusing the judicial review remedy by flooding the Federal Court with unmeritorious applications for review, and to allocate scarce judicial resources to meritorious applications by allowing others to be screened out quickly . . . .
>
> The first objective of the leave requirement appears to be based on an assumption that the proportion of abusive or unmeritorious judicial review applications filed by applicants under the Immigration

---

52   See, for example, *Level v Canada (Minister of Citizenship and Immigration)*, 2010 FC 251 at para 58: "While the leave judge determines if there is a serious question to be tried, it is the judge on judicial review who has the opportunity to fully consider and weigh the merits of the application . . . [O]n leave to commence an application, the merits of the parties' arguments are not to be considered."

53   *Wu v Canada (Minister of Immigration)*, [1989] 2 FC 175; *Bains v Canada (Minister of Employment and Immigration)* (1990), 109 NR 239 at paras 1 and 3 (FCA):

> The only question to be considered in disposing of an application for leave . . . is whether or not a fairly arguable case is disclosed for the relief proposed to be sought if leave were to be granted . . . [T]he requirement for leave is in reality the other side of the coin of the traditional jurisdiction to summarily terminate proceedings that dispose no reasonably arguable case.

54   *Canadian Council for Refugees v Canada*, 2006 FC 1046 at para 20: "[T]he standard for granting an Order permitting judicial review is low. The matter at that point is to be dealt with in a summary way. The standard on a leave application is whether or not a fairly arguable case is disclosed"; *Sunarti v Canada (Minister of Citizenship and Immigration)*, 2011 FC 191 at para 14.

55   *Saleh v Canada (Minister of Employment and Immigration)*, [1989] FCJ No 825 (TD): "I am satisfied that on an application for leave one should grant such a request unless it is plain and obvious that the applicant would have no reasonable chance of succeeding"; *Mina v Canada (Minister of Citizenship and Immigration)*, 2010 FC 1182 at para 6: "In an application for leave and for judicial review, a serious, arguable case with serious issues must be submitted."

Act, mostly refugee claimants and other non-citizens, is unusually high. The second objective of the leave requirement and that of the certification requirement are premised on the assumption that the high volume of judicial review applications under the Act and resulting appeals warrants the implementation of a filter mechanism.[56]

After reviewing whether the leave requirement violates section 15 of the *Canadian Charter of Rights and Freedoms*,[57] Heckman concludes:

A contextual analysis of the differential treatment imposed by the leave and certification requirements in the Immigration Act suggests that these measures discriminate in a substantive sense by perpetuating the view that non-citizens, who suffer from a pre-existing disadvantage in Canadian society, are disproportionately more likely than citizens to abuse the judicial review remedy and are thus less worthy of recognition as human beings and members of Canadian society.[58]

Despite Heckman's assessment, the constitutionality of the leave requirement was upheld in *Krishnapillai v Canada (Minister of Citizenship and Immigration)*,[59] where the Federal Court of Appeal stated:

There is no doubt that the right to apply for leave is a right of access to courts. Leave requirement is a usual procedure in Canadian law and it is, in Canadian terms, an accepted form of access to the courts of the country. No suggestions were made that in Canada refugees do not have free access to the leave requirement procedure within the meaning of the Convention . . . .

. . . [J]udicial decisions are not subject to the requirement of giving formal reasons . . . and in my view . . . with respect to the requirement that in certain circumstances reasons be provided for administrative decisions, leads to the import of such a requirement with respect to judicial decisions denying leave to seek judicial review.

The attack on the constitutionality of the leave requirement prescribed by . . . the Immigration Act has no chance of success.[60]

---

56   Gerald Heckman, "Unfinished Business: *Baker* and the Constitutionality of the Leave and Certification Requirements under the *Immigration Act*" (2002) 27 *Queens Law Journal* 683 at paras 75–76 [Heckman].

57   Part 1 of the *Constitution Act, 1982*, being Schedule B to the *Canada Act 1982* (UK), 1982, c 11 [*Charter*].

58   Heckman, above note 56 at para 96.

59   2001 FCA 378.

60   *Ibid* at paras 32 and 35–36.

Beyond the constitutionality of the leave requirement, empirical evidence gathered by Sean Rehaag has raised important questions about how judges have been applying the tests for granting leave. Rehaag writes:

> The central finding of the study is that leave decisions hinge partly on which judge is assigned to decide the application. There were massive unexplained variations in leave grant rates . . . . It seems clear that some applications which could well succeed before most JR judges are prevented from reaching the merits stage by the fact that some leave judges are predisposed to deny leave. This is deeply troubling in light of the fact that leave decisions are the determinative step in the vast majority of applications . . . , and the fact that a large proportion of applications that pass the leave stage end up succeeding on the merits . . . .[61]

Rehaag's study confirms findings in earlier research over the last twenty years[62] and raises doubts about the efficacy of the current leave regime. He discusses possible reforms to address the various concerns raised by the study, including abolishing the leave requirement,[63] reforming the leave requirement,[64] and clarifying the test for leave.[65] The case for immediate reform is powerful.[66]

5) Hearings at the Federal Court

When leave is granted, applicants will receive a copy of an order outlining the date of a hearing and also dates and instructions for further

---

61   Sean Rehaag, "Judicial Review of Refugee Determinations: The Luck of the Draw?" (2012) 38 *Queens Law Journal* 1 at 30. See also at 25–26:

> The most remarkable finding of the study is the enormous variation in the leave grant rates of judges in perfected applications brought by refugee claimants . . . . For example, Campbell J granted leave in 77.97% of the applications he decided, whereas Crampton J (now the Chief Justice) granted leave only 1.36% of the time. In other words, though both judges decided over 200 applications, refugee claimants were an incredible 57.33 times as likely to obtain leave from Campbell J as from Crampton J . . . .

62   *Ibid* at 50.
63   *Ibid* at 34.
64   *Ibid* at 39.
65   *Ibid* at 41.
66   *Ibid* at 50. Rehaag notes that there is inevitably some degree of variability across judges as they are human beings, but still argues that the level of variability is unfair and unsustainable.

filings if necessary.[67] It is possible to obtain adjournments for hearings before the Federal Court but only in exceptional circumstances. Requests to adjourn must be made to the Associate Chief Justice and should be made promptly after the fixing of a hearing date.[68]

The Federal Court holds sittings across the country throughout the year.[69] The sittings are open to the public unless, for special reasons, the court directs otherwise.[70] In general, one judge is assigned to hear a judicial review.

6) Automatic or Statutory Stays of Removal

Some persons subject to removal orders may benefit from a statutory stay of removal if they have commenced an application for leave and judicial review.[71] However, those in the following categories are ineligible for a statutory stay of removal:

1) designated foreign nationals;[72]
2) persons from designated countries of origin;[73]
3) those inadmissible on grounds of serious criminality;[74]
4) those who reside or sojourn in the United States or St. Pierre and Miquelon, and are the subject of a report prepared under subsection 44(1) of the *IRPA*;[75]
5) those subject to an extradition order;[76]
6) those who have decisions from the Refugee Protection Division that found their claims to be "manifestly unfounded" or with "no credible basis."[77]

---

67 Federal Court, "Judicial Review (Immigration) Practice Guide" (23 August 2012), online: cas-ncr-nter03.cas-satj.gc.ca/portal/page/portal/fc_cf_en/Practice_Guide_Immigration.
68 *Dydyuk v Canada (Minister of Citizenship and Immigration)*, 2003 FCT 717.
69 Federal Court, "Hearing Lists" (23 August 2012), online: cas-ncr-nter03.cas-satj.gc.ca/portal/page/portal/fc_cf_en/Hearing_Lists.
70 *Ibid.*
71 *Immigration and Refugee Protection Regulations*, SOR/2002-227, s 231(2) [*Regulations*]. See Section F(2)(c), below in this chapter, for more information on injunctions and Chapter 15 for more information on judicial stays.
72 *Ibid.*
73 *Ibid.*
74 *Ibid*, s 231(3)(a).
75 *Ibid*, s 231(3)(b).
76 *Extradition Act*, SC 1999, c 18, s 40, deems the Minister of Justice as having jurisdiction over extradition proceedings and needing only to consult the Minister of Citizenship and Immigration before making an order of extradition.
77 *Regulations Amending the Immigration and Refugee Protection Regulations*, PC 2012-1631, (2012) C Gaz II, 2632, s 319(3).

D. GROUNDS FOR RELIEF

The Federal Court does not have jurisdiction to second-guess or substitute its own decision for that of the decision maker whose decision is under review. Its role is to police the boundaries and procedures within which decision makers operate. In this way, judicial review differs from an appeal.

Section 18.1(4) of the *Federal Courts Act* provides the grounds of review:

> (4) The Federal Court may grant relief under subsection (3) if it is satisfied that the federal board, commission or other tribunal
>
> (a)   acted without jurisdiction, acted beyond its jurisdiction or refused to exercise its jurisdiction;
> (b)   failed to observe a principle of natural justice, procedural fairness or other procedure that it was required by law to observe;
> (c)   erred in law in making a decision or an order, whether or not the error appears on the face of the record;
> (d)   based its decision or order on an erroneous finding of fact that it made in a perverse or capricious manner or without regard for the material before it;
> (e)   acted, or failed to act, by reason of fraud or perjured evidence; or
> (f)   acted in any other way that was contrary to law.[78]

One can classify these grounds under five headings.

The first focuses on a *procedural aspect* of the decision under review; the court will intervene when a procedural error, such as neglecting to give the claimant an opportunity to present her case, has been made.[79]

The second includes *errors of law*, where the decision maker based the decision under review on a misapprehension of the applicable law.[80] For example, where the issue is whether a person qualifies for refugee protection, a question of law could include what counts as persecution under section 96 of the *IRPA*.

The third includes *abuses of discretion*, where a decision maker exercised judgment improperly by failing to take into account relevant factors, by taking into account irrelevant factors, or by acting arbitrarily or in bad faith.[81]

---

78   *Federal Courts Act*, above note 3, s 18.1(4).
79   *Ibid*, s 18.1(4)(b).
80   *Ibid*, ss 18.1(4)(a) and (c).
81   *Ibid*, ss 18.1(4)(e)–(f).

The fourth includes *errors of fact*, where the decision maker made findings not based on the evidence provided or that were based on a misunderstanding of that evidence.[82]

Finally, a fifth category includes what are often called *questions of mixed fact and law*, where the decision maker has misapplied an abstract legal concept to a particular fact situation. For example, the inquiry into whether a particular individual suffered persecution will involve both factual questions (what happened to him) and legal questions (what are the legal requirements for something to count as persecution).

E. STANDARDS OF REVIEW

In the pivotal case of *Canada (Minister of Citizenship and Immigration) v Khosa*,[83] the Supreme Court of Canada examined the language of section 18.1 of the *Federal Courts Act* and concluded that the section

> sets out threshold grounds which permit but do not require the court to grant relief. Whether or not the court should exercise its discretion in favour of the application will depend on the court's appreciation of the respective roles of the courts and the administration as well as the "circumstances of each case."[84]

The Court determined that the Federal Court may have reason to apply a different standard of review in different types of cases.[85] Citing its earlier decision in *Dunsmuir v New Brunswick*,[86] the Supreme Court of Canada stated:

> Courts, while exercising their constitutional functions of judicial review, must be sensitive not only to the need to uphold the rule of law, but also to the necessity of avoiding undue interference with the discharge of administrative functions in respect of the matters delegated to administrative bodies by Parliament and legislatures.[87]

A reviewing court may show the required sensitivity to the need not to interfere unduly by showing deference to the administrator's expertise. It may do this by subjecting the decision to less rigorous scrutiny in some types of cases while applying high levels of scrutiny in

---

82   *Ibid*, s 18.1(4)(d).
83   2009 SCC 12 [*Khosa*].
84   *Ibid* at para 36.
85   *Ibid*.
86   2008 SCC 9 [*Dunsmuir*].
87   *Ibid* at para 27; *Khosa*, above note 83 at para 78.

others cases where deference is not called for. As a result of the acceptance of this analysis, one sees, in almost every decision reached by the
Federal Court, a preliminary analysis of the appropriate "standard of
review." Two standards have been recognized: the standard of correctness, which requires the reviewing court to determine that the decision
maker reached the right decision; and the standard of reasonableness.
In *Khosa*, the standard of reasonableness was explained as follows:

> Reasonableness is a single standard that takes its colour from the
> context . . . . Where the reasonableness standard applies, it requires
> deference. Reviewing courts cannot substitute their own apprecia-
> tion of the appropriate solution, but must rather determine if the out-
> come falls within "a range of possible, acceptable outcomes which
> are defensible in respect of the facts and law." . . . There might be
> more than one reasonable outcome. However, as long as the process
> and the outcome fit comfortably with the principles of justification,
> transparency and intelligibility, it is not open to a reviewing court to
> substitute its own view of a preferable outcome.[88]

The next section discusses how these standards are applied in various cases.

1) Applying the Different Standards of Review

a) Reviewing for Procedural Fairness

Common law courts have a long history of intervening where there
has been a failure to provide adequate procedural protection to a party
or where accepted procedures have been disregarded in some way.[89]
They have recognized two main types of procedural rights that vest
in a party who appears before an administrative body: (1) the right to
participate in the decision-making process; and (2) the right to an unbiased decision maker. However, they have faced the continuing challenge of determining in concrete cases the nature of the participation
that should be accorded to a party, and the indicia of bias.

This long common law history of providing procedural safeguards
and the recognition that procedural protection can severely affect important individual interests have convinced the judiciary to apply a
high standard of scrutiny to questions of procedure. Courts have seen
little reason to defer to an administrative body's sense of procedural

---

88   *Khosa*, ibid at para 59.
89   *Cooper v Board of Works for Wandsworth District* (1863), 14 CBNS 180, 143 ER
     414 (CP).

fairness. Some courts have stated categorically that the question of whether adequate procedural safeguards have been provided must always be assessed using a standard of correctness.[90] Debate on the issue, however, continues particularly where the legislature has given the administrative body the authority to control its own process. In the Federal Court of Appeal, Evans JA has attempted to provide a balanced account of the stance that a court should take:

> In short, whether an agency's procedural arrangements, general or specific, comply with the duty of fairness is for a reviewing court to decide on the correctness standard, but in making that determination it must be respectful of the agency's choices. It is thus appropriate for a reviewing court to give weight to the manner in which an agency has sought to balance maximum participation on the one hand, and efficient and effective decision-making on the other. In recognition of the agency's expertise, a degree of deference to an administrator's procedural choice may be particularly important when the procedural model of the agency under review differs significantly from the judicial model with which courts are most familiar.[91]

Justice Evans appears to see no contradiction in saying that, while the decision must be correct, respect for the choices made by the decision maker must also be shown.

In most cases where a court assesses the procedural aspects of a decision, it does so under the guise of interpreting the enabling statute — reading in, where appropriate, the procedural requirements that the legislature must be deemed to have intended to include. Where the statute is explicit, no issue will arise. For example, the *IRPA* leaves nothing to guesswork by providing that a party is entitled to be represented by counsel in proceedings before the IRB.[92] Where the statute is silent, the court will try to discern the procedure that the legislature intended to impose or would have intended had it given the matter thought. It will rely on the inference that the legislature would have intended the procedures to be fair and thus would have intended common law standards of fairness to be incorporated into the statute unless a different view was articulated.

Where the legislature has made it clear that it intended that only limited regard for procedural niceties need be shown, the party calling for greater procedural protections may look elsewhere to locate

---

90   See, for example, *Kambo v Canada (Minister of Citizenship and Immigration)*, 2012 FC 872 at para 24.

91   *Re: Sound v Fitness Industry Council of Canada*, 2014 FCA 48 at para 42.

92   *IRPA*, above note 5, s 167(1).

the source of a right to such protections. Besides the statute and any common law standards that may be read into it, one may look to the *Charter*[93] and the *Canadian Bill of Rights*.[94] Section 7 of the *Charter* has proved helpful because it demands that the principles of fundamental justice be respected where the rights to life, liberty, and security of the person are put in jeopardy.[95] In immigration and refugee law, there are a number of scenarios where section 7 may be identified as germane, for example, where a person is detained, or where a person is facing removal from Canada to persecution, torture, or death. A clear example of the effectiveness of section 7 in the area of immigration and refugee law is provided by the case of *Singh v Canada (Minister of Employment and Immigration)*, which called for an oral hearing to be held whenever issues of credibility arise in refugee determinations.[96] This led to the legislation being changed to provide for statutory recognition as well.[97]

Similarly, sections 1(a) and 2(e) of the *Canadian Bill of Rights* may be a useful legal source.[98] Section 1(a) declares that the right of the individual to life, liberty, security of the person, and enjoyment of property, and the right not to be deprived thereof except by due process of law, has existed and shall continue to exist. Section 2(e) provides that

> no law of Canada shall be construed or applied so as to . . . deprive a person of the right to a fair hearing in accordance with the principles of fundamental justice for the determination of his rights and obligations . . . .

When determining the level of fairness that should be accorded to a party and the concrete nature of the entitlements enjoyed by a party, the judiciary has devised a procrustean solution that allows for a set of floating standards to be applied according to the facts of the case. In the seminal case of *Baker v Canada (Minister of Citizenship and Immigration)*,[99] the Supreme Court of Canada outlined several factors that should be taken into consideration by reviewing courts when deciding what procedures would be consistent with legal principle:

1) the nature of the decision being made and the process followed in making it;

---

93   *Charter*, above note 57
94   SC 1960, c 44 [*Bill of Rights*].
95   *Charter*, above note 57.
96   [1985] 1 SCR 177 [*Singh*].
97   See Chapter 9.
98   *Bill of Rights*, above note 94.
99   [1999] 2 SCR 817 [*Baker*].

2) the nature of the statutory scheme and the term of the statute pursuant to which the body operates;
3) the importance of the decision to the individual(s) affected;
4) the legitimate expectations of the person challenging the decision; and
5) the choices of procedure made by the agency itself.[100]

As a result, it has become clear that where a decision-making process is similar to a criminal or civil law proceeding, courts see increased reason to provide more strict procedural standards. In addition, courts will not impose procedures that will frustrate the decision maker's role as described in the statute. They will take into account the seriousness of the interests at stake and whether any previous representations have been made to a party about the nature of the process to be offered. They will also look at the processes that the decision makers themselves have developed.

After deciding whether certain procedural requirements are needed, the Court will then examine whether such requirements were provided. If procedural requirements were not provided or were inadequately provided, the decision arising from such a procedure may be quashed. There is authority for the position that a decision should be quashed only where rehearing the matter could lead to a different result.[101]

In immigration and refugee law, a number of procedural entitlements have been considered and called for by the courts, including these:

1) the right to notice of a hearing or notice that an issue will be raised at a hearing;[102]
2) the right to disclosure of evidence;[103]

---

100 *Ibid.*
101 See *Cha v Canada (Minister of Citizenship and Immigration)*, 2006 FCA 126. See also Chapter 15 on the mechanics of enforcement, which discusses this case in greater detail.
102 For example, in refugee cases, notice that the question of internal flight alternatives (IFA) must be raised directly with the claimant. See *Rasaratnam v Canada (Minister of Employment and Immigration)* (1991), [1992] 1 FC 706 at 710–11 (CA): "[A] claimant is not to be expected to raise the question of an IFA nor is an allegation that none exists simply to be inferred from the claim itself. The question must be expressly raised at the hearing by the refugee hearing officer or the Board and the claimant afforded the opportunity to address it with evidence and argument."
103 See, for example, *Canada (Minister of Citizenship and Immigration) v Harkat*, 2014 SCC 37, dealing with disclosure issues under the security certificate regime; see also *Chu v Canada (Minister of Citizenship and Immigration)*, 2001 FCA 113, where the court found that there should have been disclosure of a ministerial

3) the right to a decision without undue delay;[104]
4) the right to bring evidence or make submissions, whether oral or written;[105]
5) the right to counsel;[106]
6) the right to be provided with reasons for the decision;[107]
7) the right to have the decision maker rather than a delegate hear the case;[108]

---

opinion report prior to a decision finding the applicant a "danger to the public" under the *IRPA*.

104 See, for example, *Canada (Minister of Citizenship and Immigration) v Dragan*, 2003 FCA 139, regarding immigration applications that were assessed under new criteria in the new *IRPA* and denied. A group of applicants sought to have their applications reviewed under the old Act due to delay in the processing of their applications.

105 For example: For refugee cases, see *Singh*, above note 96; for permanent resident applications on humanitarian and compassionate (H&C) grounds, see *Baker*, above note 99 at para 34: "I agree that an oral hearing is not a general requirement for H&C decisions. An interview is not essential for the information relevant to an H&C application to be put before an immigration officer, so that the humanitarian and compassionate considerations presented may be considered in their entirety and in a fair manner."

106 See, for example, *Dehghani v Canada (Minister of Employment and Immigration)*, [1993] 1 SCR 1053, where an applicant argued he was denied the right to counsel during examinations conducted by immigration officials at a port of entry and that this infringed his s 7 and s 10(b) rights under the *Charter*. The Supreme Court held that, in this situation, there was no right to counsel as the examination was routine information-gathering but did say that a denial of the right to counsel during a hearing could constitute an infringement of the *Charter*. Contrast this decision with *Dragosin v Canada (Minister of Citizenship and Immigration)*, 2003 FCT 81 at para 16, where the Federal Court held that the right to counsel existed the moment the applicant was ordered to be detained. See also *Tokar v Canada (Minister of Citizenship and Immigration)*, 2003 FCT 77, where the court held that the right to counsel is not absolute. Finally, see *Sheikh v Canada (Minister of Citizenship and Immigration)*, [1990] 3 FC 238 (CA): in some cases, incompetent counsel may be a justification to hold that the applicant's procedural entitlements, such as a right to a fair hearing, may have been interfered with.

107 For example, in a judicial review of a permanent resident application on humanitarian and compassionate grounds, see *Lemus v Canada (Minister of Citizenship and Immigration)*, 2014 FCA 114 at paras 37–38 [*Lemus*]: "It follows that it would not be appropriate, in this case, to accept the Minister's invitation and supplement or recast the Officer's reasons to save her decision. This is a situation where the Officer, informed by these reasons of her error and of the proper standard to be applied, might well reach a different result."

108 See, for example, *Monemi v Canada (Solicitor General)*, 2004 FC 1648; *Rai v Canada (Minister of Citizenship and Immigration)*, 2007 FC 12; *Singh v Canada (Minister of Citizenship and Immigration)*, 2013 FC 201, where applicants chal-

8) the right to an unbiased decision maker, and the right to a process that does not create the reasonable apprehension of bias.[109]

b) Reviewing Substantive Aspects of a Decision

An applicant may also request the Federal Court to review the substance of the decision. The court must decide whether to show deference and review the decision using a standard of reasonableness or whether to use the stricter standard of correctness. Recall that judicial review gives the Federal Court limited powers when reviewing a decision made by an immigration decision maker. The court does not engage in *de novo* examinations and thus is reluctant to substitute or supplement decisions that come before it.

The case of *Dunsmuir* provided an influential account of the two standards of review and an analysis of how a court should determine which standard of review to use in any particular case.[110] In fact, it was the decision in *Dunsmuir* that first held that there should be only two standards of review.[111]

In discussing what makes a decision reasonable, the Supreme Court in *Dunsmuir* stated:

> In judicial review, reasonableness is concerned mostly with the existence of justification, transparency and intelligibility within the decision-making process. But it is also concerned with whether the decision

---

lenged the fact that the same immigration officer made decisions on both their PRRA status and H&C applications.

109 Applicants who had their PRRA and H&C applications decided by the same immigration officer have argued unsuccessfully that there was an apprehended bias. See, for example, *Haddad v Canada (Minister of Citizenship and Immigration)*, 2003 FCT 405 at paras 7–8:

> The applicant argues that there is an apprehension of bias because the same officer processed the request for a visa exemption for humanitarian considerations and the PRRA application. This argument cannot be advanced without proof. Moreover this Court has held that a decision-maker who assesses risk twice in a particular case does not by this fact alone demonstrate bias . . . .

In *Xuan v Canada (Minister of Citizenship and Immigration)*, 2013 FC 673, counsel took the interesting approach of putting forth Professor Sean Rehaag's statistics on particular board members to demonstrate bias on the part of the board member. The Federal Court held that statistics alone do not give rise to an apprehension of bias.

110 *Dunsmuir*, above note 86.

111 *Ibid* at para 48: The Court did away with the third standard of review, patent unreasonableness, but stated, "The move towards a single reasonableness standard does not pave the way for a more intrusive review by courts and does not represent a return to pre-*Southam* formalism."

falls within a range of possible, acceptable outcomes which are defensible in respect of the facts and law.[112]

By using reasonableness as the standard of review, a court can show a margin of appreciation for different plausible decisions, according deference to administrative decision makers such as immigration officers and tribunals as long as their decisions fall within the possible range of acceptable outcomes.

How does a court decide when to apply the reasonableness standard or the correctness standard? Where the enabling legislation specifies the standard to be used, this will determine the issue. If, however, the legislation is silent, *Dunsmuir* notes that prior jurisprudence continues to have bearing: that if a particular tribunal or court has determined a particular standard of review for a particular scenario, then that standard may be applied.[113] *Dunsmuir*, however, emphasizes that past decisions should be relied on only where they have "already determined *in a satisfactory manner* the degree of deference to be accorded with regard to a particular category of question."[114] Thus, advocates and applicants may be wise to challenge any existing precedent as "unsatisfactory," particularly in light of ever-changing judicial attitudes to this issue.

Where prior jurisprudence does not provide an answer, the Supreme Court in *Dunsmuir* directs courts to look at the nature of the issue being judicially reviewed. If the error alleged is one of fact, the default approach should be to use a standard of reasonableness. Similarly, if the error is one of mixed fact and law, a standard of reasonableness should be used. Where it is a question of law, the Court outlined a number of considerations. If the error of law is one regarding a constitutional question,[115] a question of central importance to the legal system that is outside the specialized area of law or expertise of the decision maker, or a question of true jurisdiction asking whether a decision maker can act in the way that it has, then the standard of correctness is used.[116]

In addition to these default standards, the Court also pointed to four established contextual factors that had been used pre-*Dunsmuir*

---

112 *Ibid* at para 47.

113 *Ibid* at para 62.

114 *Ibid* [emphasis added]. For example, if the standard of patently unreasonable was determined in previous jurisprudence to be the governing standard of review, this may be reason to review whether the standard continues to stand.

115 See *Doré v Barreau du Quebec*, 2012 SCC 12, and the Supreme Court's discussion regarding how a *Charter* analysis may differ when reviewing administrative law decisions.

116 *Dunsmuir*, above note 86 at paras 54–59.

to determine the proper standard of review. The four variables are as follows:

1) the wording of the legislation (such as the existence of a privative clause or statutory right of appeal);
2) the purpose of the statute and the impugned provision in particular;
3) the area of expertise of the administrative body relative to that of the reviewing court on the issue in question; and
4) the nature of the problem before the administrative body (whether it is a question of law, fact, or mixed fact and law).[117]

Having determined whether reasonableness or correctness is the standard, the last step the court will take is to apply the standard to the decision at hand. If the standard to be applied is correctness, the question to be asked is: was the decision correct? If reasonableness is the standard, then the court will ask whether the decision concerned was justified, transparent, or intelligible. The court will not focus on whether it agrees with the decision, but whether the decision falls into a range of possible outcomes given the legal parameters, the facts, and the evidence before it.

Situations in which a correctness standard has been identified include, for example, the interpretation of article 1F(b) of the *Refugee Convention*;[118] the definition of "membership in a particular social group" within section 96 of the *IRPA*;[119] interpretations of the *Immigration and Refugee Protection Regulations* by visa officers;[120] interpretation of sections 98, 112, and 113 of the *IRPA*;[121] and interpretations of sections 96 and 97 of the *IRPA*.[122]

---

117 *Ibid.*
118 *Febles v Canada (Minister of Citizenship and Immigration)*, 2012 FCA 324; the Supreme Court of Canada, in 2014 SCC 68, assumes the same standard.
119 *Canada (Minister of Citizenship and Immigration) v B472*, 2013 FC 151.
120 *Takeda Canada v Canada (Minister of Health)*, 2013 FCA 13; *Patel v Canada (Minister of Citizenship and Immigration)*, 2011 FCA 187; *Khan v Canada (Minister of Citizenship and Immigration)*, 2011 FCA 339.
121 *Canada (Minister of Citizenship and Immigration) v Li*, 2010 FCA 75.
122 There is inconsistency on whether correctness should be used in interpreting ss 96 and 97; however, where it is argued that interpretation requires the examination of international law, a correctness standard may be accepted by the reviewing judge. See, for example, *Portillo v Canada (Minister of Citizenship and Immigration)*, 2012 FC 678; *Gonzales v Canada (Minister of Citizenship and Immigration)*, 2011 FC 1059; *Innocent v Canada (Minister of Citizenship and Immigration)*, 2009 FC 1019; and *Begum v Canada (Minister of Citizenship and Immigration)*, 2011 FC 10.

On the other hand, the reasonableness standard has been identified in cases where one might have expected the correctness standard to be used. This has occurred, for example, in some cases involving the interpretation of sections 96 and 97 of the *IRPA*[123] and in relation to the interpretation of *people smuggling* in section 37(1)(b) of the *IRPA*.[124] Despite these anomalies, applicants should advocate for a correctness standard to be applied in questions of interpretation of the law, even if it appears to be within the expertise of the decision maker. They may bolster their stance by arguing that the interpretation requires looking at international law and other areas of law such as criminal law.

Other types of decisions dealing with findings of fact or mixed law and fact have been based on a reasonableness standard. For example, cases applying this standard may ask whether the decision maker properly considered humanitarian and compassionate grounds when making a removal order under section 67(1)(c) of the *IRPA*,[125] whether the best interests of the child were properly considered in a permanent residence application on humanitarian and compassionate grounds,[126] and whether an applicant was employed in an occupation identified in the National Occupational Classification (NOC).[127]

There is an overabundance of situations that may trigger a standard of review analysis. A proper mining of the jurisprudence and consideration of the best interests of the applicant should drive which standard may be advocated in a particular case.

c)   Recent Pushback on the Deferential Approach

Since *Dunsmuir*, the Supreme Court of Canada has attempted, on several occasions, to clarify how to identify the appropriate standard of review and how to apply it. As noted above, in *Khosa*, the Supreme Court held that the *Dunsmuir* principles apply to matters that fall within section 18 of the *Federal Courts Act*.[128] Specifically, the Court interpreted section 18 as not imposing a rigid standard of review:

---

123   See, for example, *Guifarro v Canada (Minister of Citizenship and Immigration)*, 2011 FC 182; and *Salvagno v Canada (Minister of Citizenship and Immigration)*, 2011 FC 595.

124   *B010 v Canada (Minister of Citizenship and Immigration)*, 2013 FCA 87.

125   *Khosa*, above note 83 at para 58; *Tian v Canada (Minister of Citizenship and Immigration)*, 2011 FC 1148; *Tai v Canada (Minister of Citizenship and Immigration)*, 2011 FC 248 at para 48.

126   *Singh v Canada (Minister of Citizenship and Immigration)*, 2009 FC 11 at para 21; *Arteaga v Canada (Minister of Citizenship and Immigration)*, 2013 FC 778 at para 18; *Habtenkiel v Canada (Minister of Citizenship and Immigration)*, 2014 FCA 180.

127   *Qin v Canada (Minister of Citizenship and Immigration)*, 2013 FCA 263 at para 26.

128   *Khosa*, above note 83.

It cannot have been Parliament's intent to create by s. 18.1 of the *Federal Courts Act* a single, rigid Procrustean standard of decontextualized review for all "federal board[s], commission[s] or other tribunal[s]", an expression which is defined (in s. 2) to include generally all federal administrative decision makers. A flexible and contextualized approach to s 18.1 obviates the need for Parliament to set customized standards of review for each and every federal decision maker.[129]

More recent decisions of the Supreme Court of Canada have suggested that the Court is taking an increasingly deferential approach to judicial review.[130] In the case of *Newfoundland and Labrador Nurses Union v Newfoundland and Labrador (Treasury Board)*,[131] the Supreme Court discussed the role of reasons in determining whether a decision was reasonable. In particular, the Court reiterated that the role of reasons is to enable reviewing courts to assess whether a given decision falls within a range of reasonable outcomes and thus the adequacy of reasons is not a stand-alone ground for overturning an administrative decision, but serves as a mechanism by which the reasonableness of a decision may be assessed.[132] Further, the Court went so far as to say that a "decision-maker is not required to make an explicit finding on each constituent element, however subordinate, leading to its final conclusion"[133] and that the existence of "an alternative interpretation" does not lead to the conclusion that the decision should be set aside — reviewing judges should pay "respectful attention" to the decision maker's reasons and be cautious about substituting their own.[134] This approach seems to accord less importance than *Dunsmuir* did to the idea that decisions must be transparent.

In furthering the trend towards deference, the Supreme Court, in *Alberta (Information and Privacy Commissioner) v Alberta Teachers' Association*,[135] held that the starting point when determining the standard of review is a presumption of deference;[136] that the correctness standard should apply only to constitutional questions, questions regarding jurisdictional lines between competing specialized tribunals, questions of central importance to the legal system as a whole, and true

---

129 *Ibid* at para 28.
130 See, for example, *Celgene Corp v Canada (AG)*, 2011 SCC 1.
131 2011 SCC 62 [*Newfoundland Nurses*].
132 *Ibid* at para 14.
133 *Ibid* at para 16.
134 *Ibid* at para 17.
135 2011 SCC 61 [*Alberta Teachers*].
136 *Ibid* at para 34.

questions of jurisdiction or *vires*;[137] and finally, that a court must not interfere "if there exists a reasonable basis upon which the decision maker could have decided as it did."[138]

Despite the findings in *Newfoundland Nurses* and *Alberta Teachers*, advocates have been pushing back in the Federal Court with some success. For example, in *Komolafe v Canada (Minister of Citizenship and Immigration)*, the Federal Court stated:

> *Newfoundland Nurses* is not an open invitation to the Court to provide reasons that were not given, nor is it a licence to guess what findings might have been made or to speculate as to what the tribunal might have been thinking. This is particularly so where the reasons are silent on a critical issue. It is ironic that *Newfoundland Nurses*, a case which at its core is about deference and standard of review, is urged as authority for the supervisory court to do the task that the decision maker did not do, to supply the reasons that might have been given and make findings of fact that were not made. This is to turn the jurisprudence on its head. *Newfoundland Nurses* allows reviewing courts to connect the dots on the page where the lines, and the direction they are headed, may readily be drawn. Here, there were no dots on the page.[139]

Similarly, in the case of *Benoit v Canada (Minister of Citizenship and Immigration)*, the Federal Court was not convinced that any amount of "supplementing" to an officer's decision or reasons would suffice.[140] As well, in *Canada (Minister of Citizenship and Immigration) v Grdan*,[141] the Federal Court held that it was not a reviewing judge's job to go through the tribunal record to speculate or reach his own conclusion:

> In the case at bar, we ended up at the hearing looking for evidence in the record and speculating as to what the Board may have meant. The reviewing court is not there "to supply the reasons that might have been given or make findings of fact that were not made". It does not matter that the decision is rendered orally or after deliberations.[142]

---

137 *Ibid* at para 30.
138 *Ibid* at para 53. At para 54, the Court also stated: "[W]hen only limited reasons are required, it is entirely appropriate for courts to consider the reasons that could be offered for the decision when conducting a reasonableness review."
139 2013 FC 431 at para 11.
140 2013 FC 185 at para 5.
141 2014 FC 187.
142 *Ibid* at para 11.

Similarly, in *Lemus*, the Federal Court of Appeal stated, "it would not be appropriate, in this case, to accept the Minister's invitation and supplement or recast the Officer's reasons to save her decision."[143]

In *Nintawat v Canada (Minister of Citizenship and Immigration)*,[144] the Federal Court granted relief, notwithstanding the views expressed in *Newfoundland Nurses* and *Alberta Teachers*, noting that the RPD's decision failed to mention a central issue in a refugee claim and the inadequacy of sufficient reasons that would allow the applicant to understand the basis of the decision. This decision hinges on the court's judgment that the failure to provide adequate reasons breached principles of procedural fairness and thus avoids the question of whether adequate reasons should be provided. As a matter of fairness a party is entitled to sufficient reasons to allow them to know to adjudge whether they should challenge the decision. *Nintawat* identifies an effective gambit that may be employed in response to argument that a reviewing court is permitted to supplement a decision maker's actual reasons with those that it could have relied on.

Applicants and counsel should not abandon the notion that there is a difference between assessing the adequacy of reasons as an element of procedural fairness and assessing whether the reasons are reasonable as an element of substantive judicial review. While some may argue that *Dunsmuir*, *Newfoundland Nurses*, and *Alberta Teachers* did away with this distinction, the Federal Court has resisted this position in the above decisions; many judges do not want to engage in speculations and are asserting that it is the government's obligation to provide reasons.

Thus, while recent cases from the Supreme Court of Canada have reinvigorated an approach of deference in immigration judicial review, there is some resistance from the Federal Court on how deferential they should be. Immigration applicants and their counsel should continue to push the issue and protect what could be the last line of defence against decisions that unreasonably or erroneously deny applicants access to immigration status.

---

143 Above note 107 at para 37.
144 2012 FC 66 [*Nintawat*].

F. REMEDIES AND COSTS

The *Federal Courts Act* provides that the Federal Court has exclusive original jurisdiction to

1) issue an injunction, writ of *certiorari*, writ of prohibition, writ of *mandamus* or writ of *quo warranto*, or grant declaratory relief, against any federal board, commission, or other tribunal; and
2) hear and determine any application or other proceeding for relief in the nature of relief contemplated by [(1) above], including any proceeding brought against the Attorney General of Canada, to obtain relief against a federal board, commission or other tribunal.[145]

Further, "the Federal Court may"

1) order a federal board, commission or other tribunal to do any act or thing it has unlawfully failed or refused to do or has unreasonably delayed in doing; or
2) declare invalid or unlawful, or quash, set aside or set aside and refer back for determination in accordance with such directions as it considers to be appropriate, prohibit or restrain, a decision, order, act or proceeding of a federal board, commission or other tribunal.[146]

Thus, the *Federal Courts Act* "equips the Federal Courts with the same remedies as the provincial superior courts, operating under an unmodified common-law administrative remedy regime."[147]

It significant to note that the *Federal Courts Act* permits the Federal Court to award remedies in a discretionary manner as indicated by the phrase, "the Federal Court may."[148] Indeed, the court has the discretion to refuse to grant a remedy even where one is warranted by the facts of the case.[149] Further, even when one obtains a remedy, it "does not

---

145 *Federal Courts Act*, above note 3, s 18(1).

146 *Ibid*, s 18.1(3).

147 Craig Forcese, "Making a Federal Case out of It: The Federal Court and Administrative Law" in Colleen Flood & Lorne Sossin, eds, *Administrative Law in Context*, 2d ed (Toronto: Emond Montgomery, 2013) 525 at 537–38 [Flood & Sossin].

148 *Federal Courts Act*, above note 3, s 18.1(3); *Canadian Pacific Ltd v Matsqui Indian Band*, [1995] 1 SCR 3 at para 31; Forcese, above note 147 at 538: "As a consequence, the Act 'preserves the traditionally discretionary nature of judicial review.'"

149 See, for example, *Immeubles Port Louis Ltée v Lafontaine (Village)*, [1991] 1 SCR 326; see also Cristie Ford, "Dogs and Tails: Remedies in Administrative Law" in

necessarily mean wider success for the judicial review applicant."[150] For example, the quashing of a decision simply sends the matter back to a different decision maker who may then render an unfavourable decision to the applicant.

As can be gleaned from above, the Federal Court's remedies can be put into two classes: prerogative writs and ordinary remedies. The differences between the two classes are largely historical as the applicant can seek a remedy of either type without the need to embark on different procedures.

1) Prerogative Writs

a) *Certiorari*

Certiorari, in early times, was used by the Court of King's Bench in England to check the jurisdiction of inferior courts and to maintain the supremacy of the royal courts.[151] This prerogative remedy allowed a court to review a record of proceeding to determine if there was an exercise of power in excess of jurisdiction. *Certiorari* is an *ex post facto* remedy that results in the quashing or invalidating of an order or decision.[152] However, as emphasized above, the court cannot substitute its decision for the one it has quashed since the reviewing court often does not have the expertise or authority of the decision maker charged with making the decision. Nevertheless, the Federal Court has the jurisdiction to set aside a decision and to remit it back to a different officer, board member, or delegate to reconsider.[153] In some limited cases, the court may send the decision back with directions, indicating to the next decision maker how to embark on the decision-making process and, in some rare cases, directing the outcome.[154]

Flood & Sossin, above note 147, 85 at 108–12, where she discusses the set of discretionary grounds upon which a remedy may not be granted.

150 Van Harten et al, above note 2 at 1010.

151 Ford, above note 149 at 117.

152 *Ibid.*

153 IRPA, above note 5, s 198. The RPD has jurisdiction to consider decisions that are set aside by the Federal Court.

154 See *Abdelrazik v Canada (Minister of Foreign Affairs)*, 2009 FC 580, wherein the court directed the government to issue an emergency passport. See also, for example, *Ning v Canada (Minister of Citizenship and Immigration)* (2000), 194 FTR 63 at paras 9 and 11 (TD), where the court provided the following directions along with *certiorari*:

(a) The matter will be referred back to a different visa officer for redetermination.

(b) The matter will be referred back on the basis that the selection criteria have already been met.

Even where the legislature has not given a board or decision maker the explicit authority to reopen a matter after it has been quashed and referred back by the Federal Court, the Federal Court of Appeal has held that it nevertheless has the implied authority to do so and rectify the wrongs.[155]

b) Prohibition

As noted in *Nagalingam v Canada (Minister of Public Safety and Emergency Preparedness)*: "One of the objectives of judicial review of the decisions of administrative bodies is to prevent those bodies from doing acts that they do not have the power to do, and one method of doing this . . . is to obtain a writ of prohibition."[156]

Unlike *certiorari*, prohibition is a pre-emptive remedy sought in advance of a decision being made in order to prevent it from being made.[157] In *Psychologist "Y" v Nova Scotia Board of Examiners in Psychology*, Cromwell JA emphasized its discretionary nature: "Prohibition is a drastic remedy. It is to be used only when a tribunal has no authority to undertake (or to continue with) the matter before it. Unless a lack of jurisdiction or a denial of natural justice is clear on the record, prohibition is also a discretionary remedy."[158]

Prohibition aims at prohibiting proceedings or decisions not yet made or executed. The remedy of prohibition has been used to prevent the removal of a person from Canada, but only in rare circumstances.[159] In such cases, the Federal Court has shown a preference for issuing a declaration rather than the stronger remedy of prohibition.

(c) The Applicant's medicals will need to be redone, since they expired in May 1999.

(d) It will be necessary to re-interview the Applicant regarding admissibility. This will be limited to issues of security.

. . .

[T]he visa officer will be prohibited from asking questions to the applicant dealing with issues of security or intelligence matters related to the applicant's employer and/or the Government of China.

155 *Gill v Canada (Minister of Employment and Immigration)*, [1987] 2 FC 425 (CA).

156 *Nagalingam v Canada (Minister of Public Safety and Emergency Preparedness)*, 2012 FC 362 at para 18 [*Nagalingam*], quoting the Federal Court of Appeal in *Canada (AG) v Canada (Commission of Inquiry on the Blood System in Canada - Krever Commission)*, [1997] 2 FC 36.

157 *Ford*, above note 149 at 117; *Nagalingam*, above note 156.

158 2005 NSCA 116 at para 21; see also *Khosa*, above note 83 at para 40.

159 *Nagalingam*, above note 156; *Kalicharan v Canada (Minister of Manpower and Immigration)*, [1976] 2 FC 123 at para 4 (TD).

c) *Mandamus*

Mandamus is a remedy that compels the performance of a public legal duty, which a public authority refuses or neglects to perform although duly called upon to do so.[160] It may be coupled with *certiorari* to get a decision quashed so that the remedy of *mandamus* can then require a decision maker to take a particular action. Thus, the Federal Court may issue an order quashing an immigration decision and sending the matter back to a different decision maker with mandatory instructions. The use of directions ensures that the court does not force a decision maker to take a particular decision but directs a decision maker in the process of how to make the decision.

Requesting a writ of *mandamus* proved to be an effective remedy for a group of applicants who were victims of legislative changes in the *IRPA*, which left their applications in limbo. In the consolidated case of *Dragan v Canada (Minister of Citizenship and Immigration)*,[161] 124 applicants applied for permanent residence in Canada before 28 June 2002, the date on which the *IRPA* came into force and the date on which the former *Immigration Act* and corresponding regulations were repealed.[162] The applicants complained that their applications were refused under the new selection criteria under the new system and sought a *mandamus* to compel the minister of Citizenship and Immigration to review their applications under the previous system.[163] The court found that the majority of the applicants were entitled to have their applications reviewed under the old criteria found in the former system, but that twenty-two applicants who applied during the transitional period and who had notice of the changes to the system were not so entitled.[164] In ordering a *mandamus*, the court reviewed what the remedy provides:

> In *Apotex Inc v Canada (AG)* . . . , the Federal Court of Appeal conducted an extensive review of the jurisprudence relating to *mandamus* and outlined the following conditions that need to be satisfied for the Court to issue a writ of *mandamus*:
>
> (1) There must be a public legal duty to act.
> (2) The duty must be owed to the applicant.

---

160 *Canada (Minister of Manpower and Immigration) v Tsiafakis*, [1977] 2 FC 216 (CA).
161 2003 FCT 211 [*Dragan*].
162 *Ibid* at para 4.
163 *Ibid* at para 5. There were two categories of applicants. The first applied under the old system and the second (comprised of about twenty-two applicants) applied after 2 January 2002 but before 28 June 2002 and therefore had notice of the new selection criteria under the new system.
164 *Ibid* at para 37.

(3) There is a clear right to the performance of that duty, in particular:
   a. The applicant has satisfied all conditions precedent giving rise to the duty;
   b. There was (i) a prior demand for performance of the duty; (ii) a reasonable time to comply with the demand unless refused outright; and (iii) a subsequent refusal which can be either expressed or implied, e.g. unreasonable delay.
(4) No other adequate remedy is available to the applicant.
(5) The order sought will be of some practical value or effect.
(6) The Court in the exercise of discretion finds no equitable bar to the relief sought.
(7) On a "balance of convenience" an order in the nature of *mandamus* should issue.[165]

When applying the criteria to the consolidated applicants, the court granted a *mandamus* for 102 of the applicants, citing as one of the reasons that many of the applicants had waited an inordinate period of time for their immigration application to be processed.[166]

Mandamus has also been successfully sought to compel the minister of Citizenship and Immigration to make a decision regarding applications for permanent residence on humanitarian and compassionate grounds,[167] sponsorship applications,[168] applications for permanent residence after being granted refugee protection,[169] applications for permanent residence in the economic classes,[170] applications for ministerial relief from provisions finding an applicant inadmissible,[171] and

---

165 *Ibid* at para 39; *Kalachnikov v Canada (Minister of Citizenship and Immigration)*, 2003 FCT 777.

166 *Dragan*, above note 161 at para 61.

167 See, for example, *Bakhsh v Canada (Minister of Citizenship and Immigration)*, 2004 FC 1060.

168 See, for example, *Abdolkhaleghi v Canada (Minister of Citizenship and Immigration)*, 2005 FC 729; and *Dhondup v Canada (Minister of Citizenship and Immigration)*, 2011 FC 108.

169 See, for example, *Ahmad v Canada (Minister of Citizenship and Immigration)*, 2012 FC 508; *Shahid v Canada (Minister of Citizenship and Immigration)*, 2010 FC 405; and *Jaber v Canada (Minister of Citizenship and Immigration)*, 2013 FC 1185.

170 See, for example, *Hanano v Canada (Minister of Citizenship and Immigration)*, 2004 FC 998.

171 See, for example, *Esmaeili-Tarki v Canada (Public Safety and Emergency Preparedness)*, 2010 FC 697; *Douze v Canada (Minister of Citizenship and Immigration)*, 2010 FC 1337; and *Aghdam v Canada (Minister of Public Safety and Emergency Preparedness)*, 2011 FC 131.

citizenship applications,[172] among others. In most cases, delay in making a decision is the primary reason to seek a *mandamus*. The court, in looking at the *Apotex* factors listed above, also considers the following factors when evaluating whether delay is unreasonable and, therefore, meriting a writ of *mandamus*:

(1) the delay in question has been longer than the nature of the process required, *prima facie*.

(2) the applicant and his counsel are not responsible for the delay.

(3) the authority responsible for the delay has not provided a satisfactory justification.[173]

Further, where there has been a delay in making a decision, an applicant may seek the remedy of *mandamus* to compel the government to disclose documents related to an application for the purposes of seeking *mandamus* for a final decision.[174] In addition, where the court finds the actions or lack of action of the government especially egregious, it may direct the decision maker not only to make a decision within a particular process, but to also grant a particular decision.[175]

In some cases, the court may view a *mandamus* as an extreme remedy and in the face of a delay in decision making, it may grant a different form of relief. For example, in a number of cases, the court has retained jurisdiction and has invited the parties to make further submissions in two or three months if the relevant minister has not taken action within that time frame.[176]

The government's recent zeal in pursuing cessation and vacation applications has prompted applicants to seek a *mandamus* to obtain a decision regarding pending citizenship applications to prevent

---

172 See, for example, *Stanizai v Canada (Minister of Citizenship and Immigration)*, 2014 FC 74; *Gondara v Canada (Minister of Citizenship and Immigration)*, 2006 FC 204; and *Murad v Canada (Minister of Citizenship and Immigration)*, 2013 FC 1089 [*Murad*].

173 *Conille v Canada (Minister of Citizenship and Immigration)*, [1999] 2 FC 33 (TD); *Subaharan v Canada (Minister of Citizenship and Immigration)*, 2008 FC 1228 at para 13.

174 See, for example, *Douze v Canada (Minister of Citizenship and Immigration)*, 2010 FC 1086.

175 See, for example, *Murad*, above note 172: Here, a delay of four years precipitated directions in the order; *Bageerathan v Canada (Minister of Citizenship and Immigration)*, 2009 FC 513 [*Bageerathan*]: the court directed a particular outcome of the decision and costs because of the excessive delay of seven years.

176 See, for example, *Zaib v Canada (Minister of Citizenship and Immigration)*, 2008 FC 687 at paras 23–24; and *Rousseau v Canada (Minister of Citizenship and Immigration)*, 2004 FC 602 at para 8.

the continued pursuit of the cessation or vacation application.[177] For example, in the case of *Stanizai v Canada (Minister of Citizenship and Immigration)*,[178] the applicant was a citizen of Afghanistan who came to Canada in 1995 and obtained Convention refugee status in 1996. In 2007, he applied for Canadian citizenship. During the relevant period for the calculation of residence he reported 264 days of absence during which he returned to Afghanistan, four years after the fall of the Taliban.[179] In Afghanistan, he was married, had children, and maintained a business, all of which was disclosed.[180] He passed his citizenship exam in November 2009, and his application was sent to a citizenship judge for review in February 2011.[181] He appeared before a citizenship judge in May 2011 and was asked to provide additional supporting documentation.[182] A citizenship judge approved the application in February 2012, some 740 days after the application had first been referred to the judge for consideration.[183] The court noted, "Throughout the lengthy application process, Mr. Stanizai had been required to obtain multiple immigration, security and RCMP clearances."[184] Following the approval, the Canada Border Services Agency (CBSA) continued to ask the applicant for his fingerprints to redo his criminal check, and in July 2012, the CBSA flagged him for a possible cessation proceeding resulting in an application for cessation in April 2013.[185] The citizenship application processing was suspended while cessation proceedings were ongoing.[186] The court discussed the implications of the cessation application:

> The cessation proceedings were postponed at the request of Mr. Stanizai pending the outcome of this application for judicial review. Under recent amendments to the [IRPA], if the Refugee Protection Division were to find that Mr. Stanizai had ceased to be a Convention refugee or a protected person, he would become inadmissible to

---

177 Daniel Proussalidis, "Border Services Set Quota for Stripping Refugee Status" *Ottawa Sun* (16 January 2014), online: www.ottawasun.com/2014/01/16/border-services-set-quota-for-stripping-refugee-status. The CBSA has committed to referring a minimum of 875 vacation or cessation cases per year, for the duration of the initiative to the Refugee Protection Division (RPD) of the IRB.
178 Above note 172 at para 4.
179 *Ibid* at para 5.
180 *Ibid* at para 7.
181 *Ibid* at paras 10–11.
182 *Ibid* at para 12.
183 *Ibid* at para 14.
184 *Ibid* at para 15.
185 *Ibid* at paras 17–19 and 21.
186 *Ibid* at para 24.

Canada, he would lose his permanent resident status and a departure order could be made against him.[187]

Ultimately, the court held that it was not reasonable for Citizenship and Immigration Canada to hold off on granting citizenship to an applicant whose application had been approved by a citizenship judge pending a cessation application.[188] The court was satisfied that this was a case where *mandamus* was appropriate given the inordinate and unexplained delays in the matter. It ordered the respondent to grant citizenship to Stanizai.[189]

d) Quo Warranto

Quo warranto is a rarely used remedy to compel an administrative actor to justify the powers it has used or claimed or to challenge a person to prove that he holds the public office he claims he does. As there are many other means to obtain such justification and because the remedy has such a narrow focus, it is rarely requested and awarded.

2) Ordinary Remedies

a) Declarations

A declaration is a remedy the Federal Court uses to make a pronouncement on the state of the law. It can be used to declare an administrative actor's decision or action *ultra vires*, to clarify the law, or to declare a party's rights under a particular statute.[190] For the parties involved in a judicial review, the remedy of declaration is not enforceable. For example, in *Canada (Prime Minister) v Khadr*, the remedy of declaration did not compel a response by the government to ask for Khadr's repatriation to Canada after being detained in Guantanamo Bay for a lengthy time, resulting in Khadr taking further legal action.[191] Despite

---

187 *Ibid* at para 22.
188 *Ibid* at para 31: "The jurisprudence of this Court is clear: 'unless there is an appeal, the approval or refusal by a citizenship judge, is a final matter as to the applicant's Canadian citizenship. The Minister has no further function to perform or other remedy other than an appeal.'" At para 48, the court also notes that there is no statutory authority for the obtaining of immigration clearances prior to granting citizenship.
189 *Ibid* at para 63.
190 Ford, above note 149 at 118.
191 2010 SCC 3: In this case, the Supreme Court of Canada held that Khadr (who was detained in Guantanamo Bay) was deprived of his section 7 *Charter* rights by denying Khadr's request for repatriation to Canada. The Court fell short of ordering the government to ask for Khadr to be repatriated and, instead, provided the remedy of a declaration that Khadr's s 7 rights were violated. Despite this

this limitation, the fact that the remedy has no enforcement mechanism has not often proved to be a problem because court declarations against government bodies in particular tend to be respected.[192]

Declarations can be useful remedies in non-*Charter* cases as well. For example, in *Singh v Canada (Minister of Citizenship and Immigration)*, the Federal Court used the remedy of declaration to hold that "the requirement to hold a valid passport found in s. 14(1) of the *Regulations* . . . did not require an Applicant to actually have in his or her possession a hard copy of his or her passport, when it can be established by other means that the Applicant holds a valid passport."[193]

b) Damages

While damages are rarely awarded in immigration and refugee-related matters, claims for damages may be made at the Federal Court. Although applications for judicial review in the Federal Court are commenced by way of application under section 18.1 of the *Federal Courts Act*,[194] claims for damages against the Crown and federal statutory authorities are commenced by way of *action* under section 17 of the *Federal Courts Act*.[195] Despite the distinct proceedings, section 18.4(2) of the *Federal Courts Act* provides that the Federal Court "may, if it considers it appropriate, direct that an application for judicial review be treated and proceeded with as an action."[196] There is immigration law jurisprudence from the Federal Court that contemplates the use of section 18.4(2) for this purpose.[197]

The remedial implications of the distinction between an action and an application for judicial review have been analyzed by Binnie J in *Canada (AG) v TeleZone* as follows:

> As recently affirmed in *Khosa*, the grant of relief on judicial review is in its nature discretionary and may be denied even if the applicant establishes valid grounds for the court's intervention:

---

ruling, the government did not seek Khadr's repatriation, and Khadr was forced to engage in further litigation.

192 *Ibid*; see, for example, *Lount Corp v Canada (AG)*, [1984] 1 FC 332 at 365 (TD): "[B]y long tradition, the executive abides by declarations of the Court even though not formally or specifically directed to do so." See also Peter Hogg, *Constitutional Law of Canada* (Toronto: Thomson Reuters Canada, 2011) at 40–45.

193 2010 FC 757.

194 *IRPA*, above note 5, s 18.1.

195 *Ibid*, s 17.

196 *Ibid*, s 18.4(2).

197 *Hinton v Canada (Minister of Citizenship and Immigration)*, 2008 FCA 215 at para 49.

. . . the language of s. 18.1 generally sets out threshold grounds which permit but do not require the court to grant relief. Whether or not the court should exercise its discretion in favour of the application will depend on the court's appreciation of the respective roles of the courts and the administration as well as the "circumstances of each case". [para. 36]

. . . Such an approach does not align well with the paradigm of a common law action for damages where, if the elements of the claim are established, compensation ought generally to follow as a matter of course. In judicial review, "the discretionary nature of the courts' supervisory jurisdiction reflects the fact that unlike private law, its orientation is not, and never has been, directed exclusively to vindicating the rights of individuals" . . . .[198]

Where there are breaches of *Charter* rights or negligence on the part of the minister and ministerial delegates, an applicant may commence an action by filing a statement of claim requesting damages.[199] Section 24(1) of the *Charter* provides an avenue for persons who may want to seek damages for a *Charter* breach.

The Federal Court of Appeal has held that an award of damages may be made only if it has first been shown that the decision maker has done something improper.[200] The grant of damages need not relate to the substance of a decision but may be awarded for losses flowing from the manner in which it was made.[201] Where there is an under-

---

198 2010 SCC 62 at para 56.

199 See, for example, *Samimifar v Canada (Minister of Citizenship and Immigration)*, 2006 FC 1301, [*Samimifar*]. Samimifar based his claim on unreasonable delay and abuse of process caused by the minister and claimed that the minister was negligent. He claimed damages in the amount of $5 million due to breaches of ss 7 and 24(1) of the *Charter*, as a result of loss of business and employment opportunities, loss of education opportunities, out-of-pocket expenses, such as medical expenses for his family, and emotional distress and suffering. The delay referred to in this case was seven to nine years long.

200 *R v Tremblay*, 2004 FCA 172 at para 14:

> Obviously the applicant cannot obtain reinstatement in the Canadian Forces as well as damages for loss of salary unless he first attacks the decision bearing on his retirement on the basis that the legislation underlying the retirement is inoperative under the *Charter*. The invalidity of this decision is at the heart of his claim and the relief sought depends on this alleged invalidity. The respondent will only be entitled to reinstatement once the decision is declared invalid. Damages can only be claimed once the reinstatement is ordered.

201 *Samimifar*, above note 199 at para 20: "Mr. Samimifar is not attacking the PR decision; rather, he is attacking the delay and seeking damages for the consequences that flowed from that delay."

lying decision that gives rise to the alleged harm, an application may be filed for leave for judicial review, but in the case of a decision that is no longer subject to judicial review (as time limits may have expired), an action may be commenced to claim for damages.[202] Even where an applicant may have a viable claim for damages, however, they may be denied where the court views the pursuit of damages by way of action as a "collateral attack" on a decision that can or could be pursued by way of judicial review.[203]

Recently, the court awarded damages in a case where the applicants, five orphans of Hutu ethnicity, originally from Burundi, lived alone in Rwanda until they could be accepted as refugees in Canada seven years later.[204] The applicants' uncle, a Canadian citizen, filed a sponsorship application, which was refused twice between 2001 and 2008.[205] The applicants filed an action against the federal government for damages stemming from delays in processing the children's application for permanent residence and the mistakes made in refusing multiple applications (and appeals) over the years.[206] In awarding costs, the court noted that the applicants lived in fear as Hutu refugees in Rwanda, that they had only enough food for one meal per day, that they were not able to go to school, and that the UNHCR visited them and were shocked by their living conditions.[207] In particular, the court highlighted one of the children's testimony:

> Bellancille delivered a dignified and very moving testimony. She told how she, who was not the eldest of the family, assumed leadership of the group, and how she had to fight to obtain the bare necessities of life for her sisters and brother and for herself. The applicants lived in a way that no child should have to live, even less so young minor orphans whose guardian is a Canadian citizen who showed in a sustained manner his desire to help them and see them all reunited in Canada.
>
> During these years, the applicants missed many opportunities, if only the possibility of experiencing a normal childhood/adolescence and being educated. Although it is difficult, even impossible, to quantify such damage, nevertheless they are damages that must be compensated.[208]

---

202 *Grenier v Canada*, 2005 FCA 348 at para 15.
203 *Samimifar*, above note 199 at para 28.
204 *Nkunzimana v Canada (Minister of Citizenship and Immigration)*, 2014 FC 736 at para 1.
205 *Ibid* at para 2.
206 *Ibid* at para 3.
207 *Ibid* at para 42.
208 *Ibid* at paras 47–48.

c) Injunctions

The injunction is, historically, a private law remedy that has been imported into public law. It has been used to prevent unlawful interference with a person's rights. Its effect is similar to the remedy of prohibition in the sense that it is requested and used to prevent or stop something from happening, but it can also be used to compel positive actions. In immigration matters the most common form of injunction is the stay of removal, an interlocutory or temporary measure used to delay the removal of an applicant from Canada until the substance of a dispute before the court is resolved. This type of remedy helps to ensure that the underlying issue before the court is not rendered moot before the court has considered the matter.

The established test for awarding an injunction is found in *RJR-MacDonald Inc v Canada (AG)* where the court held that there were three prerequisites that needed to be met before an injunction should be awarded:

1) The applicant must demonstrate a serious question to be tried (i.e., the underlying claim is not a frivolous one).
2) The applicant would suffer irreparable harm if the application is refused (i.e., the harm cannot be compensated with damages).
3) In considering the situation of all parties, does the balance of convenience favour granting the remedy?[209]

This test has been adopted by the Federal Court when deciding whether a stay of removal should be granted to preserve an applicant's underlying application, such as a judicial review of a permanent residence application on humanitarian and compassionate grounds or a pre-removal risk assessment.[210]

The Federal Court's jurisdiction to grant a stay is established in section 18.2 of the *Federal Courts Act*.[211] The IRPA precludes any right of appeal on an interlocutory injunction, and therefore decisions made are final.[212]

---

209 [1994] 1 SCR 311.
210 See *Toth v Canada (Minister of Employment and Immigration)* (1988), 86 NR 302 (FCA). For more information on stays of removal, see Chapter 15.
211 See *Federal Courts Act*, above note 3, s 50(1); however, in *Marshall v Canada*, 2002 FCT 1099: The court dismissed a stay application as there was no underlying application for judicial review.
212 *IRPA*, above note 5, s 72(2)(e); *Mabrouki v Canada (Minister of Citizenship and Immigration)*, 2003 FC 1104; *Canada (Solicitor General) v Subhaschandran*, 2005 FCA 27: The exception to this rule is if the judge at the Federal Court refuses to exercise his jurisdiction and deal with the case.

3) Costs

Rule 22 in the *Federal Courts Immigration and Refugee Protection Rules* states:

> No costs shall be awarded to or payable by any party in respect of an application for leave, and application for judicial review or an appeal under these Rules unless the Court, for special reasons, so orders.[213]

Rule 22, however, leaves the door open for the award of costs to be granted in exceptional circumstances. Indeed, the Federal Court has acknowledged this:

> Both parties acknowledge that pursuant to Rule 22 of the *Federal Court[s] Immigration and Refugee Protection Rules*, SOR/2002-232, special reasons must exist for the Court to award costs on application for judicial review. Special reasons may be found if one party has unnecessarily or unreasonably prolonged proceedings, or where one party has acted in a manner that may be characterized as unfair, oppressive, improper or actuated by bad faith.[214]

In cases where there has been a delay in obtaining a decision on an application or a matter or where the government did not perform its duty within a reasonable time, the court may view an application for judicial review as meriting an award of costs on the ground that "had the respondent performed its duty in a reasonable amount of time, the applicants would not have been forced to incur the costs of bringing this application for judicial review"[215] Where the applicant has in some way been complicit in the delay or failure, then costs may be denied.[216]

---

213 *Federal Courts Immigration Rules*, above note 33, s 22.

214 *Johnson v Canada (Minister of Citizenship and Immigration)*, 2005 FC 1262 at para 26; see also *Ndererehe v Canada (Minister of Citizenship and Immigration)*, 2007 FC 880.

215 See *Sellathurai v Canada (Minister of Citizenship and Immigration)*, 2008 FC 604; *Ben-Musa v Canada (Minister of Citizenship and Immigration)*, 2005 FC 764; *Bageerathan*, above note 175; and *John Doe v Canada (Minister of Public Safety and Emergency Preparedness)*, 2006 FC 535.

216 See, for example, *Tang v Canada (Minister of Citizenship and Immigration)*, 2009 FC 292.

G. APPEALING TO THE FEDERAL COURT OF APPEAL

Under the *IRPA*, a party does not have an automatic right to appeal a decision from the Federal Court. Only where the deciding judge has certified a serious question of general importance can an appeal be made to the Federal Court of Appeal.[217] The threshold for certifying a question is whether there is a serious question of general importance that would be dispositive of an appeal.[218] The corollary of the fact that a question must be dispositive of an appeal is that it must be a question that has been raised and dealt with in the decision below.[219]

It is important to note that while a certified question opens the door to an appeal to the Federal Court of Appeal, the Court of Appeal is not confined to examining the issues raised in the certified question.[220] Thus, the Court of Appeal can consider all issues that have been raised in the course of the judicial review.

H. APPEALING TO THE SUPREME COURT OF CANADA

Should a party wish to appeal a decision from the Federal Court of Appeal, she may serve on all other parties and file with the Registrar of the Supreme Court of Canada an application for leave to appeal[221] within sixty days of the date of the Court of Appeal's judgment.[222] The respondent may serve and file a response within thirty days after the

---

217 *IRPA*, above note 5, ss 74(d) and 79; *Ismail v Canada (Minister of Citizenship and Immigration)*, 2006 FCA 396 at para 4: A party cannot circumvent the statutory prohibition on appeals in immigration matters without a certified question by filing a motion under rule 397 or 399 under the *Federal Courts Rules*; *Lazareva v Canada (Minister of Citizenship and Immigration)*, 2005 FCA 181.

218 *Zazai v Canada (Minister of Citizenship and Immigration)*, 2004 FCA 89.

219 *Ibid.*

220 *Ibid.*

221 *Supreme Court Act*, RSC 1985, c S-26, s 40.

222 *Ibid*, s 58(1)(a). The Supreme Court requires that the original and five copies of the application for leave to appeal must be filed. This application includes a notice of application for leave to appeal the decision, order, and reasons for judgment from the Court of Appeal or an indication that there were no reasons, and a memorandum of argument. If the appellant wants to file an application outside the sixty-day deadline, a motion for an extension of time and an affidavit explaining the reasons for the delay must be served and filed (see *Rules of the Supreme Court of Canada*, SOR/2002-156, s 26 [*SCC Rules*]; Supreme Court of

day on which a file was opened following the submission of the application for leave to appeal.[223] The appellant can file a reply within ten days of receiving the respondent's response.[224] A panel of three judges of the court reviews the application for leave to appeal and decides whether to grant leave, and if leave is denied, reasons are not usually issued with the decision.[225] The decision granting leave is final.[226] While a party may ask the court to reconsider the decision, a decision may be overturned only in rare circumstances such as where a change in the law occurred at the same time that the application was made.[227] If leave is granted, a hearing will be scheduled before the Supreme Court of Canada and the Registry will advise on the procedure to be followed.[228]

The Supreme Court of Canada has wide discretion to grant or deny leave.[229] The existence of grounds for appeal, in itself, may not be sufficient to obtain leave. Section 40(1) of the *Supreme Court Act* sets out the standard by which the Court decides which cases obtain leave:

> . . . where, with respect to the particular case sought to be appealed, the Supreme Court is of the opinion that any question involved therein is, by reason of its public importance or the importance of any law or any issue of mixed law and fact involved in that question, one that ought to be decided by the Supreme Court or is, for any other reason, of such a nature or significance as to warrant decision by it . . . .[230]

The Court may also look "not only at the impugned legislation" but also "to the larger social, political and legal context."[231] Thus, the kinds of issues that may entice the Court to hear a case include the presence of a constitutional issue in the form of a challenge to statutory law,

---

Canada, "Guide" (31 December 2013), online: www.scc-csc.gc.ca/res/unrep-nonrep/app-dem/guide-eng.aspx [SCC "Guide"]).

223 *SCC Rules*, above note 222, s 27: The respondent will be advised of the opening of the file in writing. The original and five copies must be filed. The response may be prepared in the form of correspondence of no longer than two pages.

224 *Ibid*: The original and five copies of the reply must be filed. The memorandum of argument in reply must not exceed five pages. As well, a reply in the form of correspondence must not be longer than two pages.

225 *Ibid*, s 32: No party can serve or file additional material for the application for leave unless permission is granted by the Registrar, which follows a filing of a motion with the Registrar on the reasons for adding such material.

226 *Ibid*, s 74.

227 *Ibid*, s 73.

228 SCC "Guide," above note 222.

229 *R v Hinse*, [1995] 4 SCR 597 at para 8.

230 *Supreme Court Act*, above note 221, s 40(1).

231 *R v Turpin*, [1989] 1 SCR 1296 at para 45.

common law, or a governmental practice; a conflict of jurisdiction; a novel point of law; or interpretation of a significant piece of legislation.

I. CONCLUSION: TOWARDS A LESS DEFERENTIAL APPROACH UNDER THE NEW SYSTEM

With courts at all levels taking an increasingly deferential approach to the decisions of lower tribunals and administrative decision makers, immigration applicants, refugee claimants, and others will have a more difficult time challenging the decisions that deny them status in Canada. In light of substantial recent changes to the immigration system, the ways of the past may not be appropriate for the cases of tomorrow. For example, the deferential approach may not be appropriate in situations where applicants no longer have access to "alternative" procedures or remedies such as applications for permanent residence on humanitarian and compassionate grounds, pre-removal risk assessments, statutory stays of removal, and temporary resident permits, among others. Advocates, counsel, and applicants alike will have to press the courts to evaluate the consequences of a decision when judging whether a decision is reasonable or even correct. The lack of alternative remedies may inform what is procedurally fair or whether *Charter* rights may be violated. Applicants would be wise to communicate to the courts that, given the lack of access to other processes and remedies, the deferential approaches of the past should not continue; they should also encourage the courts to scrutinize decisions carefully to determine whether the administrative decision making has been adequate in the circumstances of the case.

CHAPTER 17

CONSTITUTIONAL CHALLENGES

A. THE *CHARTER* RIGHTS OF NON-CITIZENS

Throughout this text, reference has been made to the probability of future constitutional challenges aimed at recently introduced amendments that have rendered the status of both non-citizens and citizens more insecure and have restricted their substantive rights and access to legal forums in which full consideration could be given to their concerns and interests. In this final chapter a foundation for such challenges is laid by considering the application of the *Canadian Charter of Rights and Freedoms*[1] to the immigration process.

B. THE AMBIT OF THE *CHARTER*

The text of the *Charter* reveals that some rights are vested in citizens, others in permanent residents, and still others in "everyone" or "every individual." It also states that it has a limited application — section 32 provides:

32. (1) This *Charter* applies

---

1   Part I of the *Constitution Act, 1982*, being Schedule B to the *Canada Act 1982* (UK), 1982, c 11.

a) to the Parliament and government of Canada in respect of all
    matters within the authority of Parliament including all matters
    relating to the Yukon Territory and Northwest Territories; and
b) to the legislature and government of each province in respect of
    all matters within the authority of the legislature of each province.

The implication of this provision, rendered explicit in caselaw, is
that the *Charter* does not place constraints on private individuals who
are not agents of government. A person's constitutional rights are held
against the government. Although the text identifies both the benefici-
aries of the *Charter* and those subject to its constraints, it is silent on
the question of its geographical application. In early decisions, some
judges inferred that the *Charter* has a limited geographical application
protecting only individuals who are within Canada from government
action.

A foundation for such an inference was laid in *Singh v Canada (Minister of Employment and Immigration)*,[2] which was the first case in which
the *Charter* was held to be applicable to non-citizens. Although all six
judges who heard the case in the Supreme Court of Canada concurred
in the result, two quite different sets of reasons were given, each adopted by three judges. While Wilson J relied upon the *Charter*, Beetz J
chose, instead, to base his decision on the *Canadian Bill of Rights*.[3]

Justice Wilson held that section 7 of the *Charter* granted rights to
"every human being who is *physically present in Canada and by virtue
of such presence amenable to Canadian law*."[4] Since the appellants were
found to be physically present in Canada, there was no need for Wilson J to elaborate any further, neither to elucidate what she meant by
"amenability" nor to specify whether it is the amenability to Canadian
law or the physical presence that is the dominant consideration. These
important questions were left open. She did, however, clarify one important point. When defining those in whom *Charter* rights are vested,
she did not distinguish between those who are at a port of entry and
those who have been admitted into Canada. Such a fictional distinction
has been recognized in the United States, with constitutional protection being afforded only to those who have been admitted.[5]

In two lower court decisions subsequent to *Singh*, it was held that
the *Charter* does not protect individuals who are outside the country
and who are seeking to immigrate. In *Canadian Council of Churches v*

2   [1985] 1 SCR 177 [*Singh*].
3   SC 1960, c 44, reprinted in RSC 1985, App III (*Bill of Rights*). See Section E,
     below in this chapter.
4   *Singh*, above note 2 at 202 [emphasis added].
5   *Ibid* at 210–12.

Canada (Minister of Employment and Immigration),⁶ MacGuigan JA, offering no argument by way of justification, denied that a case founded on a *Charter* argument constituted a reasonable cause of action, "since the claimants affected would all be non-citizens outside Canada with no claim to admission, and therefore beyond the scope of the *Charter*."⁷

In *Ruparel v Canada (Minister of Employment and Immigration)*,⁸ the applicant argued that a section of the *Immigration Act, 1976*⁹ (the legislation then in force), which placed greater restrictions on immigrants over the age of twenty-one than on those under that age, discriminated against him contrary to section 15(1) of the *Charter*. In the Trial Division of the Federal Court, Muldoon J stated that the applicant could not "have the remedies which he so justly seeks" because he was not physically present in Canada. Justice Muldoon considered but rejected the argument that since the applicant was in the Canadian High Commission in London, England, when he made his application, he was *de jure* in Canada. He concluded that the use of such a legal fiction could not be countenanced in the face of the clear statement from Wilson J in *Singh* and the statement of MacGuigan JA in *Canadian Council of Churches*.

These interpretations of *Singh* are not well grounded. As noted above, not only does Wilson J not specify whether it is amenability to Canadian law or physical presence in Canada that is determinative, but, also, neither judgment offers a reason for not applying the *Charter* to visa applicants or others who are subject to negative decisions by officials within the immigration system. Furthermore, a strong theoretical case for applying the *Charter* to visa applicants can be constructed.¹⁰

The issue also surfaced in a case dealing with citizenship. In *Crease v Canada (Minister of Multiculturism & Citizenship)*,¹¹ a *Charter* challenge to a provision of the *Citizenship Act* was mounted by a non-citizen who was also a non-resident. In a thorough judgment, Wetston J accepted the proposition that such an individual may be protected by the *Charter* on the basis of an interpretation of Wilson J's holding that stresses the factor of amenability to Canadian law rather than physical presence in Canada. Nevertheless, Wetston J rejected the applicant's claim that the *Citizenship Act* had violated the applicant's equality rights.

---

6   [1990] 2 FC 534 (CA), rev'd on other grounds [1992] 1 SCR 236 [Canadian Council of Churches].

7   *Ibid* at 563 (CA).

8   [1990] 3 FC 615 (TD).

9   SC 1976-77, c 52.

10   See Donald Galloway, "The Extraterritorial Application of the *Charter* to Visa Applicants" (1991) 23 *Ottawa Law Review* 335.

11   [1994] 3 FC 480 (TD) [*Crease*].

One problem that faced Wetston J was that, in *Kindler v Canada (Minister of Justice)*,[12] an extradition case decided by the Supreme Court of Canada, the decision was grounded on the categorical holding that the *Charter* does not have an extraterritorial application. Justice Cory held that "[a]lthough the *Charter* has no extraterritorial application, persons in Canada who are subject to extradition proceedings must be accorded all the rights which flow from the *Charter*."[13] Justice McLachlin endorsed this view, stating:

> [T]his Court has emphasized that we must avoid extraterritorial application of the guarantees in our *Charter* under the guise of ruling extradition procedures unconstitutional. As La Forest J put it . . . , 'the *Charter* cannot be given extraterritorial effect to govern how criminal proceedings in a foreign country are to be conducted.'[14]

Despite the categorical nature of these claims about extraterritoriality, Wetston J, in *Crease*, recognized that they carry with them implied qualifications and that the question of the ambit of the *Charter* should be sensitive to context. He stated:

> If Mr. Crease was granted standing, would this, in the words of McLachlin J . . . improperly "cast the net of the *Charter* broadly in extraterritorial waters"? Caution against imposing our constitutional guarantees on other states was advocated by the Supreme Court . . . . The extraterritorial application of Canadian law can give rise to friction between nation states . . . . The application of the *Citizenship Act*, while having both domestic and international implications, does not involve the application of the *Charter* to the actions of a foreign government or to foreign nationals appearing before foreign courts. Thus, the primary concerns regarding the extraterritorial application of the *Charter* in extradition cases are not present in the citizenship context. As such, I do not view this line of authority dealing with extradition as a bar to the application of the *Charter* in this case.[15]

Thus, Wetston J explained the Supreme Court's reluctance to apply the *Charter* extraterritorially as being founded on its more general reluctance to be seen to be interfering with the criminal process of a foreign country, a concern that is valid where a person is being extradited but not where a person outside Canada is seeking benefits from the Canadian government. Justice Wetston further justified this interpretation

---

12   [1991] 2 SCR 779.
13   *Ibid* at 819.
14   *Ibid* at 845.
15   *Crease*, above note 11 at 491–92.

by noting that in another case, *R v A*,[16] the Supreme Court of Canada had not precluded the application of the *Charter* to Canadian citizens outside Canada.

The idea that it would be improper for Canada to interfere with the sovereignty of foreign countries was later adopted by a majority of the Supreme Court in *R v Hape*,[17] where the issue of extraterritorial application of the *Charter* resurfaced once again. Here too, the context was criminal in nature, focusing on an investigation conducted by the RCMP in another country and on whether evidence obtained should be excluded from a later trial in Canada. Justice LeBel, for the majority, allowed for a limited extraterritorial application of the *Charter*, holding that any legal activity by Canadian officials overseas must respect the principle of comity among states and the sovereignty of the other country. Recognizing that transnational criminal investigations involve high levels of co-operation, he noted,

> In order to foster such cooperation, and in the spirit of comity, Canada cannot either insist that the *Charter* be applied in other countries or refuse to participate. When Canadian authorities are guests of another state whose assistance they seek in a criminal investigation, the rules of that state govern.[18]

As a consequence of this, he held,

> When individuals choose to engage in criminal activities that cross Canada's territorial limits, they can have no guarantee that they carry *Charter* rights with them out of the country.[19]

Justice LeBel seems to be expressing the view that only those who have engaged in crime have to worry about Canadian authorities using methods of investigation that would not be condoned in Canada. To be accurate, he should have noted that, in a world where different approaches to criminal investigation are tolerated, no Canadian has a guarantee of carrying *Charter* rights out of the country even when dealing with Canadian officials.

More important, LeBel J does recognize an exception that places significant limits on his approach. In the later case of *Canada (Justice)*

---

16 [1990] 1 SCR 992.
17 2007 SCC 26 [*Hape*].
18 *Ibid* at para 99.
19 *Ibid*.

v *Khadr*[20] the Supreme Court articulates this exception clearly as follows:

> The government argues that . . . the *Charter* does not apply to the conduct of Canadian agents operating outside Canada. It relies on *R v Hape*, . . . where a majority of this Court held that Canadian agents participating in an investigation into money laundering in the Caribbean were not bound by *Charter* constraints in the manner in which the investigation was conducted. This conclusion was based on international law principles against extraterritorial enforcement of domestic laws and the principle of comity which implies acceptance of foreign laws and procedures when Canadian officials are operating abroad.
>
> In *Hape*, however, the Court stated an important exception to the principle of comity. While not unanimous on all the principles governing extraterritorial application of the *Charter*, the Court was united on the principle that comity cannot be used to justify Canadian participation in activities of a foreign state or its agents that are contrary to Canada's international obligations. It was held that the deference required by the principle of comity "ends where clear violations of international law and fundamental human rights begin" . . . . The Court further held that in interpreting the scope and application of the *Charter*, the courts should seek to ensure compliance with Canada's binding obligations under international law . . . .
>
> If the Guantanamo Bay process under which Mr. Khadr was being held was in conformity with Canada's international obligations, the *Charter* has no application and Mr. Khadr's application for disclosure cannot succeed: *Hape*. However, if Canada was participating in a process that was violative of Canada's binding obligations under international law, the *Charter* applies to the extent of that participation.
>
> At this point, the question becomes whether the process at Guantanamo Bay at the time that CSIS [Canadian Security Intelligence Service] handed the products of its interviews over to U.S. officials was a process that violated Canada's binding obligations under international law.[21]

---

20 2008 SCC 28 [*Khadr*]. Omar Khadr faced prosecution for murder before a US Military Commission in Guantanamo Bay, Cuba. He sought an order under s 7 of the *Charter* that the appellants be required to disclose to him all documents relevant to these charges in the possession of the Canadian Crown, including interviews conducted by Canadian officials with him in 2003 at Guantanamo Bay. The minister of Justice opposed the request, arguing that the *Charter* does not apply outside Canada and, hence, did not govern the actions of Canadian officials at Guantanamo Bay.

21 *Ibid* at paras 17–20.

Hape and *Khadr* make important points. The Court adopts the position that the question whether the Canadian Constitution constrains the actions of decision makers overseas will depend on whether the application of Canadian law should be regarded as an interference with the sovereignty of a foreign country or as an indication of disrespect for its equal status as a nation-state. If it is not so regarded, then it should be applied. However, even if it is so regarded, the *Charter* may also apply where the state in question and the Canadian authorities are engaged in activities that are inconsistent with Canada's international obligations. Within the immigration context, this could mean that the *Charter* does operate to control immigration decisions made overseas since immigration decision-making does not usually have an impact on another country's sovereignty. In addition, where enforcement officers working overseas take actions to prevent the departure of an individual from another country, or where they make decisions about the inadmissibility of an individual based on information provided by another country, the legality of the action or of the methods of obtaining the information according to the rules of international law will determine whether the *Charter* constrains the officers. In the past, Canadian officials have travelled overseas to convince foreign governments that they should prevent the departure of boats carrying undocumented migrants bound for Canada. Where the methods urged are contrary to international law, such complicity could be regarded as unconstitutional.

Since the decision in *Khadr*, the Federal Court of Appeal has twice had occasion to address the question of the extraterritorial application of the *Charter*, and on both occasions it has declined to recognize its application.[22] In *Slahi*, the appellants, like Khadr, sought disclosure of evidence obtained during interviews by Canadian officers at Guantanamo Bay. It was held that the *Charter* did not apply. Justice Evans distinguished *Khadr* on the ground that Khadr was a Canadian citizen and added that since there were no legal proceedings against the appellants in Canada, there was no nexus to sufficiently connect the appellants to Canada. Justice Evans also made mention of the fact that the Supreme Court in *Hape* had not made mention of a nexus requirement. He stated: "Since Mr Hape was a Canadian citizen, it was obvious that he had a nexus with Canada and it was unnecessary for the Court to address the question."[23]

In addition, Evans JA drew a controversial conclusion:

---

22   See *Amnesty International Canada v Canada (Canadian Forces)*, 2008 FCA 401; and *Slahi v Canada (Minister of Justice)*, 2009 FCA 259 [*Slahi*].

23   *Slahi, ibid* at para 7.

We would only add this. The fact that the rights contained in some sections of the *Charter* are limited to Canadian citizens, while others, including section 7, are not, is not of much significance in a case where it is argued that the *Charter* applies extraterritorially. The *Charter* normally applies to governmental action within Canada and was drafted with that in mind.[24]

In the face of such categorical claims, it is likely that the question of extraterritorial application of the *Charter* will return to the Supreme Court for clarification.

C. STANDING TO MAKE A *CHARTER* CHALLENGE

Another preliminary matter relating to *Charter* rights is the problem of identifying who has standing to raise issues relating to the constitutionality of immigration laws and procedures. Section 24(1) of the *Charter* provides that "[a]nyone whose rights or freedoms, as guaranteed by this *Charter*, have been infringed or denied may apply to a court of competent jurisdiction to obtain such remedy as the court considers appropriate and just in the circumstances." This section allows for individuals to take active steps to bring a *Charter* issue to the courts, but only those whose rights have been affected are able to seek a remedy under this section. Thus, in *Langner v Canada (Minister of Employment and Immigration)*,[25] individuals, who sought an exemption from the rules that required their deportation, failed when they tried to bring an action for a declaration based on the claim that their deportation would infringe the *Charter* rights of their children who were Canadian citizens.

However, one of the more important developments in constitutional law for non-citizens has been the adoption by the Supreme Court of liberal principles for granting public interest standing. These principles have been outlined lucidly by Mactavish J in *Canadian Doctors for Refugee Care v Canada (AG)*[26] in a passage worth quoting at length. She writes:

---

24   *Ibid* at para 5.
25   (1994), 98 FTR 188 (TD), aff'd (1995), 29 CRR (2d) 184 (Fed CA), leave to appeal to SCC refused, [1995] SCCA No 241.
26   2014 FC 651 [*Canadian Doctors*].

Those whose individual rights are at stake or who have been directly affected by government action are generally entitled to pursue legal action to enforce those rights or interests. Indeed, the respondents do not dispute the entitlement of Mr. Ayubi and Mr. Garcia Rodrigues to pursue their challenges to the 2012 OICs [orders in council] before this Court.

Standing may also be granted to individuals and organizations to advance a case before the Courts where it is in the public interest to do so. CDRC [Canadian Doctors for Refugee Care], CARL [Canadian Association of Refugee Lawyers], and JFCY [Justice for Children and Youth] seek public interest standing in this case.

The parties agree that the test for public interest standing is that articulated by the Supreme Court of Canada in *Canada (Attorney General) v. Downtown Eastside Sex Workers United Against Violence Society*, [2012] 2 S.C.R. 524 and considered again in *Manitoba Métis Federation Inc. v. Canada (Attorney General)*, 2013 SCC 14, 355 D.L.R. (4th) 57.

In these cases, the Supreme Court recognized that in public law cases such as the one before me, Courts "have taken a flexible, discretionary approach to public interest standing, guided by the purposes which underlie the traditional limitations [on standing]": *Downtown Eastside*, above at para.1.

The Supreme Court also noted in *Downtown Eastside* that "[a]t the root of the law of standing is the need to strike a balance 'between ensuring access to the courts and preserving judicial resources'" . . . .

There are three factors that a Court must weigh in deciding whether or not to exercise its discretion in favour of granting public interest standing. These are:

1.   Whether the case raises a serious justiciable issue;
2.   Whether the party bringing the action has a real stake or a genuine interest in its outcome; and
3.   Whether, having regard to a number of factors, the proposed action is a reasonable and effective means to bring the case to court.

In exercising the Court's discretion with respect to a question of public interest standing, these factors are not, however, to be treated as "technical requirements". Instead, "the factors should be seen as interrelated considerations to be weighed cumulatively, not individually, and in light of their purposes" . . . . The principles governing the exercise of this discretion should, moreover, "be interpreted in a liberal and generous manner": *Downtown Eastside* at paras. 2 and 35 . . . .[27]

---

27   *Ibid* at paras 305–11.

The development of these flexible rules of standing has rendered the task of challenging the constitutionality of immigration laws much easier. Previously, the rules had been more stringent. For example, in *Canadian Council for Refugees v Canada*,[28] the Federal Court of Appeal had dismissed a challenge to the constitutionality of the regulations establishing the Safe Third Country Agreement with the United States, on the ground that the case should properly have been brought by an affected individual.

Justice Evans expressed the following account of standing:

> Relying on their public interest standing, the respondent organizations successfully challenged the validity of the Regulations on *Charter* grounds, based on evidence . . . that a class of refugees would be subject to a real risk of refoulement as a result of the *Safe Third Country Agreement* and that therefore, their section 7 and section 15 *Charter* rights were violated. To this end, they maintained, and the applications Judge agreed, that their challenge . . . concerns a class of refugees, which they say would be treated in a certain way if they were to present themselves at a Canadian land border port of entry (idem).
>
> In my respectful view, this hypothetical approach, which the applications Judge entertained, goes against the well established principle that a *Charter* challenge cannot be mounted in the abstract.[29]

It is clear that this approach to standing by public interest groups has now been rejected and that the possibility of an individual bringing a challenge need not impede a public interest group seeking a declaration from a court that a law is unconstitutional as long as the group can persuade the court that "the proposed action is a reasonable and effective means to bring the case to court."

D. *CHARTER* RIGHTS

The *Charter* rights that are relevant to immigration law are listed under five headings: Fundamental Freedoms, Democratic Rights, Mobility Rights, Legal Rights, and Equality Rights. The rights included under these headings are not absolute. Each is subject to section 1 of the *Charter*, which provides that "the guaranteed rights and freedoms are

---

28   2008 FCA 229.
29   *Ibid* at paras 99 & 100.

subject only to such reasonable limits prescribed by law as can be demonstrably justified in a free and democratic society."

Section 1 allows governments to defend interferences with rights. In *R v Oakes*, the Supreme Court imposed heavy demands on a government attempting to justify an interference: not only must the government's objectives be pressing and substantial, but the measures must be rationally connected and proportional to the objectives sought, and must be tailored to have minimal impairment on individual rights.[30] In some cases, however, it offered a relaxed interpretation of the standards to be used.[31]

In *Doré v Barreau du Quebec*[32] the Court addressed the question whether section 1 can be raised only in response to a challenge that legislation is unconstitutional, or whether it can also be raised against a challenge to a particular exercise of discretion. In *Doré*, the appellant had not challenged the constitutionality of the law that had been applied to him; he had merely challenged the constitutionality of its application to his circumstances. The Court framed the issue as follows:

> Normally, if a discretionary administrative decision is made by an adjudicator within his or her mandate, that decision is judicially reviewed for its reasonableness. The question is whether the presence of a *Charter* issue calls for the replacement of this administrative law framework with the *Oakes* test, the test traditionally used to determine whether the state has justified a law's violation of the *Charter* as a "reasonable limit" under s. 1.[33]

The Court concluded that an administrative decision maker is not required to correctly weigh whether an infringement of a *Charter* right is justified under section 1. The following passage outlines the approach that should be taken:

> How then does an administrative decision-maker apply *Charter* values in the exercise of statutory discretion? He or she balances the *Charter* values with the statutory objectives. In effecting this balancing, the decision-maker should first consider the statutory objectives . . . .
>
> Then the decision-maker should ask how the *Charter* value at issue will best be protected in view of the statutory objectives. This is

---

30 *R v Oakes*, [1986] 1 SCR 103.
31 See, for example, *Committee for the Commonwealth of Canada v Canada*, [1991] 1 SCR 139; *RJR-MacDonald Inc v Canada (AG)*, [1995] 3 SCR 199.
32 2012 SCC 12.
33 *Ibid* at para 3.

at the core of the proportionality exercise, and requires the decision-maker to balance the severity of the interference of the *Charter* protection with the statutory objectives. This is where the role of judicial review for reasonableness aligns with the one applied in the *Oakes* context. As this Court recognized in *RJR-MacDonald Inc. v. Canada (Attorney General)*, 1995 CanLII 64 (SCC), [1995] 3 S.C.R. 199, at para. 160, "courts must accord some leeway to the legislator" in the *Charter* balancing exercise, and the proportionality test will be satisfied if the measure "falls within a range of reasonable alternatives". The same is true in the context of a review of an administrative decision for reasonableness, where decision-makers are entitled to a measure of deference so long as the decision, in the words of *Dunsmuir*, "falls within a range of possible, acceptable outcomes."[34]

1) Fundamental Freedoms

Section 2 of the *Charter* identifies a list of fundamental freedoms that everyone possesses: these include freedom of conscience and religion, freedom of expression, freedom of assembly, and freedom of association. A number of challenges to immigration laws and decisions have been based on this section, most prominently on the ground that they impede freedom of association. For example, in an early case, *Gittens v Canada*,[35] the applicant argued that a deportation order would violate a person's freedom of association, since it would sever the links between him and his family and friends. Justice Mahoney dismissed the application, holding that a deportation order made against an alien criminal would be covered by the qualification in section 1 that *Charter* rights are subject only to such reasonable limits prescribed by law as can be demonstrably justified in a free and democratic society.

In *Al Yamani v Canada (Solicitor General)*,[36] it was held that part of the section of the *Immigration Act* [which was the law then in force] was unconstitutional, on the ground that, by rendering inadmissible those who were merely members of organizations likely to engage in acts of violence, it violated the applicant's freedom of association.[37]

Justice Mackay reasoned:

[B]y providing ultimately for deportation of permanent residents who are members of an organization loosely defined, the statute does

---

34 *Ibid* at paras 55–56.
35 [1983] 1 FC 152 (TD).
36 [1996] 1 FC 174 (TD) [*Al Yamani*].
37 *Ibid* at paras 90–91.

infringe on the freedom of permanent residents to associate together in organizations. Often such persons, at least those comparatively new to this country, may maintain association or membership with organizations, associated with their homelands, many of which may have had some historic record of violence but which serve a variety of purposes, as the PFLP [Popular Front for the Liberation of Palestine] was found to do in this case. To expose all permanent residents to the possibility of deportation because of their membership in such organizations, in my view clearly infringes on their freedom of association.[38]

The provision was not saved by section 1 of the *Charter* because no rational connection was seen to exist between the aim of protecting the safety of people in Canada and restricting the freedom of individuals who are merely members of an organization. Further, it was held that the restriction was not proportional to the objective.

In *Suresh v Canada (Minister of Citizenship and Immigration)*,[39] however, the Supreme Court of Canada later rejected this approach. It stipulated unequivocally:

[S]. 2 of the *Charter* does not protect expressive or associational activities that constitute violence.

. . .

The Minister's discretion to deport under s. 53 of the *Immigration Act* is confined, on any interpretation of the section, to persons who have been engaged in terrorism or are members of terrorist organizations, and who also pose a threat to the security of Canada. Persons associated with terrorism or terrorist organizations — the focus of this argument — are, on the approach to terrorism suggested above, persons who are or have been associated with things directed at violence, if not violence itself.[40]

Nevertheless, the Court also adopted a narrow conception of "membership," holding that "[w]e believe that it was not the intention of Parliament to include in the . . . class of suspect persons those who innocently contribute to or become members of terrorist organizations."[41]

---

38   *Ibid* at para 91.
39   2002 SCC 1 [*Suresh*].
40   *Ibid* at paras 107–8.
41   *Ibid* at para 110.

Then, in *Najafi v Canada (Public Safety and Emergency Preparedness)*,[42] Gleason J observed that *Al Yamani* had been "overtaken"[43] by *Suresh* but made no comment on the Court's willingness in the latter case to define the membership requirements for inadmissibility very narrowly.

2) Democratic Rights

Section 3 of the *Charter* recognizes the right of every citizen to vote in federal and provincial elections, and to be qualified for membership in the House of Commons and in a legislative assembly. It is arguable that the section should not be read as excluding non-citizens from voting and membership, since such rights can be vested in non-citizens by federal and provincial legislation. Instead, it should be read as giving a constitutional guarantee only to citizens.

3) Mobility Rights

Section 6 of the *Charter* recognizes the mobility rights of citizens and permanent residents. Citizens have the constitutional right to enter, remain in, and leave Canada. Both citizens and permanent residents have the right to take up residence in any province and to pursue the gaining of livelihood in any province. Thus, any effort by the federal government to impose provincial residency requirements on newly admitted permanent residents would likely be met by a *Charter* challenge.

In *Machado v Canada (Minister of Citizenship and Immigration)*,[44] it was held that deportation of a permanent resident did not violate his mobility rights. The applicant had argued that the conception of citizenship found in this section was broader than that found in the *Citizenship Act* and included long-term residents. The IAD concluded that this argument was incoherent in that it failed to take account of the fact that, in section 6, citizens are distinguished from permanent residents. It seems that the IAD did not appreciate the subtlety of the applicant's arguments. His point was that the concepts of permanent resident and citizen found in the *Charter* do not mirror those found in legislation. In order to determine who is a citizen and a permanent resident within the meaning of the *Charter*, one must ask who should have the rights of mobility granted to these two groups. His conclusion was that a long-term resident who had been immersed in the social life

---

42   2013 FC 876.
43   *Ibid* at para 41.
44   (1996), 33 Imm LR (2d) 121 (IRB (App Div)).

of Canada should be accepted as a citizen, as that term is understood within the *Charter*.

Mobility rights under the *Charter* have been raised in cases where Canadian citizens have been denied a passport, which has restricted their ability to travel and enter Canada. The case of *Abdelrazik v Canada (Minister of Foreign Affairs)*[45] is illustrative. It concerned a Canadian citizen who had travelled to Sudan where he was detained and tortured by Sudanese authorities. While he was detained, Abdelrazik's Canadian passport expired, and numerous attempts to obtain a passport were met with no response from Canadian officials, forcing Abdelrazik to live at the Canadian embassy after his release.[46] Abdelrazik brought a judicial review to the Federal Court, arguing that the government's refusal to issue him a passport violated his section 6 rights under the *Charter*. The court agreed, and the government was directed to issue him an emergency passport to facilitate his return to Canada.[47] In doing so, however, the court did note that a government may justify a refusal to issue a passport pursuant to section 1 of the *Charter*. In this case, the court noted that there was no evidence before the court that Abdelrazik supported or followed Al-Qaida, as had been alleged, and thus no reason to justify the refusal under section 1.[48] A more in-depth look at other cases and the *Canadian Passport Order*,[49] which authorizes the issuance of passports, can be found in Chapter 13 on citizenship.

4) Legal Rights

a) Section 7 Rights

Section 7 of the *Charter* has been the object of more judicial analysis in immigration cases than any other section. It is also the most complex section. It states:

> 7. Everyone has the right to life, liberty and security of the person and the right not to be deprived thereof except in accordance with the principles of fundamental justice.

A number of different issues are raised by this provision and are considered below.

---

45   2009 FC 580 at para 4 [*Abdelrazik*]. See also Chapter 13 which discusses the case.
46   *Ibid* at para 14.
47   *Ibid* at para 152.
48   *Ibid* at para 25.
49   *Canadian Passport Order*, SI/81-86.

i) Procedural Aspects of Fundamental Justice

The issue that has attracted most judicial attention to this section is that of identifying the procedural requirements of the principles of fundamental justice. Where this issue has been the focus, *Charter* analysis has overlapped significantly with analysis of the administrative law principles of procedural fairness, discussed in more detail elsewhere. Two important differences should be noted: First, the *Charter* allows for challenges to primary legislation that sets out defective procedures, whereas administrative law merely identifies fair procedures that are implied by a statutory scheme, in the absence of clear contrary demands. Second, the *Charter* concern with the principles of fundamental justice arises only where the rights to life, liberty, and security of the person are in jeopardy.

The principal concern raised under this heading is whether the procedures established to resolve an issue are adequate to allow a full presentation of the case and a proper determination; where a hearing has been granted, this will involve asking whether adequate notice of , its nature has been given, whether there has been sufficient disclosure of evidence, whether adequate opportunity to respond to negative evidence has been granted, whether adequate legal representation and interpretation are available, and whether there have been unjustifiable delays in proceeding.

In *Singh*[50] the Court was asked to decide whether the procedures for determining refugee claims, that were in effect at that time, unjustifiably infringed the appellants' rights under section 7 of the *Charter*. Justice Wilson observed that the appellants, not being citizens or permanent residents, had no right to enter and remain in Canada, but she held that this lack of status did not bar their challenge to the process by which their claim to be Convention refugees was to be determined. This challenge was based on the fact that no oral hearing had been made available to them. In holding that the determination of their claims must be in accordance with principles of fundamental justice, Wilson J stated:

> [I]f the appellants had been found to be Convention refugees as defined in s. 2(1) of the *Immigration Act, 1976* they would have been entitled as a matter of law to the incidents of that status provided for in the Act. Given the potential consequences for the appellants of a denial of the status if they are in fact persons with a "well-founded fear of persecution", it seems to me unthinkable that the *Charter* would

---

50 *Singh*, above note 2.

not apply to entitle them to fundamental justice in the adjudication of their status.[51]

Although the decision to send the claimants back to their country of origin would jeopardize their right to security only if they were, in fact, genuine refugees, Wilson J concluded that principles of fundamental justice must be respected when the issue of genuineness is being determined. She insisted that, where issues of credibility were likely to arise, as they are when the genuineness of a refugee claim is being determined, the principles of fundamental justice require that an oral hearing take place. Any other type of process, where, for example, the applicant was restricted to making written submissions, would be insufficient.

The impact of *Singh* has been diluted by legislation and by some subsequent cases. The *Immigration Act* was amended to include eligibility criteria that a claimant must meet before being allowed to make a refugee claim before the Immigration and Refugee Board (IRB), and these were later incorporated into the *IRPA*. In *Nguyen v Canada (Minister of Employment and Immigration)*,[52] the applicant sought judicial review of a decision by an adjudicator that he was not eligible to have his claim considered by the Refugee Division. The ground of ineligibility was that he had committed a serious offence, and the minister had certified that he was a danger to the public. The challenge was based partly on the fact that the procedure by which the minister issued a certificate did not allow for an oral hearing. The application was denied. Justice Marceau distinguished *Singh* on the ground that under the law at the time, Singh had a right to make a refugee claim, while the applicant in this case had not been granted a right to seek refugee status. He also concluded without analysis that when eligibility to make a claim is being determined, there is no need to have an oral hearing. The attempt to distinguish *Singh* seems misplaced. First, Wilson J states clearly that whether one has a right or merely a privilege at stake should not be a determinative factor.[53] But, second, Nguyen had a right to have his eligibility assessed and made the claim that this assessment should be done fairly.

In *Dehghani v Canada (Minister of Employment and Immigration)*,[54] the Supreme Court held that principles of fundamental justice did not

---

51   *Ibid* at 210.
52   [1993] 1 FC 696 (CA) [*Nguyen*]. *Nguyen* was decided before the *IRPA* came into force.
53   See *Singh*, above note 2 at 210.
54   [1993] 1 SCR 1053 [*Dehghani*].

require that a person be provided with counsel at a port-of-entry interview during which notes are taken by an officer. These notes could later be used as evidence during an inquiry into whether there was a credible basis to the applicant's refugee claim. In a remarkably brief treatment of the issue, Iacobucci J concluded that the grant of counsel at this early stage would change the nature of the interview. He stated:

> The purpose of the port of entry interview was . . . to aid in the processing of the appellant's application for entry and to determine the appropriate procedures which should be invoked in order to deal with his application for Convention refugee status. The principles of fundamental justice do not include a right to counsel in these circumstances of routine information gathering.[55]

The introduction of counsel, Iacobucci J averred, would change the interview into a "'mini-inquiry' . . . just as complex and prolonged as the inquiry provided for under the Act and Regulations."[56] Such a change, he observed, would constitute "unnecessary repetition." However, if the purpose of the hearing were as identified by Iacobucci J, one would not expect the immigration officer to take notes that could be relied upon at a later hearing to challenge credibility. Since the decision in *Dehghani*, immigration officers have been granted broader powers, including the power to determine the eligibility of refugee claimants to have their claim heard by the Refugee Division. Arguably, the decision in *Dehghani* has been rendered obsolete by these changes.

In the post-*Singh* era, the most important and influential *Charter* case has been *Canada (Minister of Employment and Immigration) v Chiarelli*,[57] where the Supreme Court of Canada considered the constitutionality of a deportation order against a permanent resident who had resided in Canada for eleven years, since the age of fifteen. The order had been issued on the ground that he had committed a serious criminal offence. In the Federal Court of Appeal, the deportation procedures to which Chiarelli had been subjected, which involved the issuance of a security certificate,[58] had been found to be unconstitutional on the ground that they violated section 7 of the *Charter*. This decision was reversed by the Supreme Court of Canada. Justice Sopinka held that it was not necessary to focus on the question whether the appellant had been deprived of his right to life or his right to security of the person, since

---

55   *Ibid* at 1078.
56   *Ibid.*
57   [1992] 1 SCR 711 [*Chiarelli*].
58   For an examination of security certificates, see text accompanying notes 61–62, below in this chapter.

there had been no breach of fundamental justice. One of the arguments he rejected was procedural, claiming that reliance on a report of the Security Intelligence Review Committee, on which the certificate had been based, infringed section 7 rights because of defects in the process followed by the review committee.

Justice Sopinka concluded that the procedures followed by the review committee were consistent with the principles of fundamental justice. Although a part of the hearing had been conducted *in camera*, Chiarelli had been provided with a summary of the evidence sufficient to allow a response. Justice Sopinka notes that,

> [while] an individual has an interest in a fair procedure . . . the state also has a considerable interest in effectively conducting national security and criminal intelligences investigations and in protecting police sources . . . . The *CSIS Act* and Review Committee Rules recognize the competing individual and state interests and attempt to find a reasonable balance between them.[59]

It should be noted that this is not section 1 analysis. Justice Sopinka was balancing fundamental justice against state interests when determining the content of the right to fundamental justice. Had he determined that the right was infringed and then turned to the issue of whether the infringement was justifiable under section 1, he would have been constrained to apply the rigorous test of justifiability, which must be met under that section. Instead, he has determined that there is a two-step process in establishing whether the principles of fundamental justice have been breached. This was a significant change of direction.

In *Charkaoui v Canada (Citizenship and Immigration)*[60] the Supreme Court of Canada returned to the issue of balancing the interests of the state when determining the content of the principles of fundamental justice. The Court held that a process which allowed a judge to determine the reasonableness of a security certificate without allowing the person named in the certificate to have access to the information on which the certificate was based was unconstitutional in that it violated principles of fundamental justice. The Supreme Court analyzed the principle thus:

> This basic principle has a number of facets. It comprises the right to a *hearing*. It requires that the hearing be *before an independent and impartial magistrate*. It demands a *decision by the magistrate on the facts*

---

59   *Chiarelli*, above note 57 at 744–45.
60   2007 SCC 9 [*Charkaoui*].

and the law. And it entails the *right to know the case put against one,* and the *right to answer that case.* Precisely how these requirements are met will vary with the context. But for s. 7 to be satisfied, each of them must be met in substance.[61]

The Court concluded that where the individual named in a certificate did not have access to the information on which it was based, the judge would have to make a decision based on incomplete evidence. Because the judge did not have the power to independently investigate relevant facts, while at the same time the named person was not given a full picture of the case to meet and was not able to make a full legal argument, the process was deficient.

Nevertheless, the Court also concluded that considerations of national security had a role to play in the determination of whether a process is fundamentally just. In what looks like an effort to have what it wants both ways, the Supreme Court identified that security concerns may be taken into account when determining whether a process is fair but also that security concerns cannot justify reliance on an unfair process. Its argument is as follows:

> The procedures required to conform to the principles of fundamental justice must reflect the exigencies of the security context. Yet they cannot be permitted to erode the essence of s. 7. The principles of fundamental justice cannot be reduced to the point where they cease to provide the protection of due process that lies at the heart of s. 7 of the *Charter.* The protection may not be as complete as in a case where national security constraints do not operate. But to satisfy s. 7, meaningful and substantial protection there must be.[62]

ii)   The Rights to Life, Liberty, and Security of the Person

By deciding *Chiarelli* on the ground that there was no breach of fundamental justice, Sopinka J did not need to decide whether the appellant's rights to life or security of the person had been jeopardized by deportation. This issue has been addressed in later cases. Interestingly, however, the Supreme Court, in *Medovarski v Canada (Minister of Citizenship and Immigration); Esteban v Canada (Minister of Citizenship and Immigration),*[63] has cited the decision in *Chiarelli* as a ground for concluding that the rights to liberty and security of the person are not infringed by mere deportation. The Chief Justice states:

---

61   *Ibid* at para 29 [emphasis in original].
62   *Ibid* at para 27.
63   2005 SCC 51.

The most fundamental principle of immigration law is that non-citizens do not have an unqualified right to enter or remain in Canada: *Chiarelli v Canada (Minister of Employment and Immigration)*, [1992] 1 S.C.R. 711, at p. 733. Thus the deportation of a non-citizen in itself cannot implicate the liberty and security interests protected by s. 7 of the *Canadian Charter of Rights and Freedoms*.[64]

In this passage, one sees a remarkable extrapolation that is based on the failure to distinguish between, on the one hand, not interfering with a right to liberty and security, and, on the other hand, interfering with the right but doing so in a manner that accords with the principles of fundamental justice. Justice Sopinka was careful to draw this distinction, but the Court has now, it seems, decided to gloss over it.

Nevertheless, the Court has included an important qualification in the same passage. By stating that deportation *in itself* cannot implicate section 7 rights, the Court has indicated that deportation may engage the *Charter* when coupled with other factors.

Thus, in *Charkaoui*, the Court stated,

Medovarski . . . does not stand for the proposition that proceedings related to deportation in the immigration context are immune from s. 7 scrutiny. While the deportation of a non-citizen in the immigration context may not *in itself* engage s. 7 of the *Charter*, some features associated with deportation, such as detention in the course of the certificate process or the prospect of deportation to torture, may do so.[65]

The door has been left open for advocates to persuade the courts that various forms of hardship that may accompany deportation — such as separation from family, physical danger, inaccessibility of medical or psychological care, or inadequate access to education — may engage section 7 rights.

The Supreme Court has recognized that security of the person is jeopardized by measures that impose serious, state-imposed, psychological stress on the individual. The Court has specifically adverted to interference with the integrity of the parent–child relationship as a cause of serious psychological stress and, therefore, a deprivation of security of the person.

In *Blencoe v British Columbia (Human Rights Commission)*,[66] Bastarache J states:

---

64 *Ibid* at para 46.
65 *Charkaoui*, above note 61 at para 17 [emphasis in original].
66 2000 SCC 44.

The principle that the right to security of the person encompasses serious state-imposed psychological stress has recently been reiterated by this Court in *G.(J.)* . . . . State removal of a child from parental custody thus constitutes direct state interference with the psychological integrity of the parent, amounting to a "gross intrusion" into the private and intimate sphere of the parent-child relationship (at para. 61) . . . .

Not all state interference with an individual's psychological integrity will engage s. 7. Where the psychological integrity of a person is at issue, security of the person is restricted to "serious state-imposed psychological stress" (Dickson C.J. in *Morgentaler*, . . .). I think Lamer C.J. was correct in his assertion that Dickson C.J. was seeking to convey something qualitative about the type of state interference that would rise to the level of infringing s. 7 (*G.(J.)*, at para. 59).[67]

The right to liberty will be engaged where an individual has been detained. Given the impact of detention on vulnerable people, including children and traumatized refugees, detention implicates security of the person.

In *Charkaoui*, McLachlin CJ also explained that unreviewable detention will breach the principles of fundamental justice. She stated:

The overarching principle of fundamental justice that applies here is this: before the state can detain people for significant periods of time, it must accord them a fair judicial process . . . . "It is an ancient and venerable principle that no person shall lose his or her liberty without due process according to the law, which must involve a meaningful judicial process": *Ferras*, at para. 19. This principle emerged in the era of feudal monarchy, in the form of the right to be brought before a judge on a motion of *habeas corpus*. It remains as fundamental to our modern conception of liberty as it was in the days of King John.[68]

She continued by explaining that the basic principles are as applicable in the immigration context as elsewhere:

The principles underlying *Lyons* [which involved criminal detention] must be adapted in the case at bar to the immigration context . . . . Drawing on them, I conclude that the s. 7 principles of fundamental justice . . . require that, where a person is detained or is subject to onerous conditions of release for an extended period under immigration law, *the detention or the conditions must be accompanied by a meaningful process of ongoing review that takes into account the con-*

---

67   *Ibid* at paras 56 & 57.
68   *Charkaoui*, above note 60 at para 28.

text and circumstances of the individual case. Such persons must have meaningful opportunities to challenge their continued detention or the conditions of their release.[69]

iii) Fundamental Justice and Individualized Assessment

A further argument relating to section 7 of the *Charter* was raised in *Chiarelli*. It was contended that the sections of the *Immigration Act* which automatically required that a person be deported after it is determined that he has committed an offence of the type described infringe section 7 rights by not permitting consideration of all the circumstances of the offence. In effect, the claim was that the applicant had been denied an individualized assessment.[70]

In response to this argument, Sopinka J held that the condition imposed by Parliament on the permanent resident's right to stay in Canada, that she not commit a serious offence, was "a legitimate, non-arbitrary choice by Parliament of a situation in which it is not in the public interest to allow a non-citizen to remain in the country."[71] He continued:

> It is true that the personal circumstances of individuals who breach this condition may vary widely. The offences which are referred to . . . also vary in gravity, as may the factual circumstances surrounding the commission of a particular offence. However, there is one element common to all persons who fall within the class of permanent residents described . . . . They have all deliberately violated an

---

69   *Ibid* at para 107 [emphasis added].

70   The relevant sections of the *Immigration Act* provided:

> 27. (1) Where an immigration officer or peace officer has in his possession information indicating that a permanent resident is a person who
> (d) has been convicted of an offence under any Act of Parliament for which a term of imprisonment of (i) more than six months has been imposed, or (ii) five years or more may be imposed, he shall forward a written report to the Deputy Minister setting out the details of such information.
>
> . . .
>
> (3) Subject to any order or direction of the Minister, the Deputy Minister shall, on receiving a report pursuant to subsection (1) or (2), and where he considers that an inquiry is warranted, forward a copy of that report and a direction that an inquiry
>
> . . .
>
> 32. . . .
> (2) Where an adjudicator decides that a person who is the subject of an inquiry is a permanent resident described in subsection 27(1), he shall, subject to subsections 45(1) and 47(3) [Convention refugee], make a deportation order against that person.

71   *Chiarelli*, above note 57 at 734.

essential condition under which they were permitted to remain in Canada. In such a situation, there is no breach of fundamental justice in giving practical effect to the termination of their right to remain in Canada. In the case of a permanent resident, deportation is the only way in which to accomplish this. There is nothing inherently unjust about a mandatory order.[72]

Missing from this analysis is a full explanation why in this area of law it is inappropriate to expect decision makers to tailor solutions to match individual circumstances where these circumstances reveal morally salient differences. His suggestion that the grounds for deportation are "legitimate" and "non-arbitrary" ignores the arbitrariness of applying a one-size-fits-all resolution to every case. As noted in an earlier chapter, Joseph Carens has made a strong case that a person's connection with a community increases with the length of time that she is a resident.[73]

In addition, the decision seems to return immigration law to a pre-*Singh* position. Justice Wilson in that case recognized that the appellants, as non-citizens, did not have an unqualified right to remain in the country, but were entitled to fair proceedings to determine their status. The level of procedural protection accorded was based on the degree of importance of the issue to the claimants if they were refugees. But Sopinka J concludes that because a permanent resident does not have an unqualified right to remain in the country, she has no right to a process of decision making which is sensitive to the particular facts of the case. The importance of the matter to the individual is assumed to be irrelevant. This position seems inconsistent with Wilson J's holding in *Singh* that the content of the principles of fundamental justice is dependent on what might be at stake.

Moreover, Sopinka J's claim that all persons under a removal order have one thing in common — they have deliberately violated an essential condition under which they were permitted to remain in Canada — is patently false. Not only is the mental state of "deliberateness" not required for the criminal offences that lead to removal, but many individuals who are removed do not realize that they are not citizens, particularly those who arrived in Canada as children. A personalized inquiry is needed to determine whether the breach of the condition was deliberate or not. Justice Sopinka's claim that we can assume a deliberate violation without conducting a hearing in which this matter can

---

72   *Ibid.*
73   See Chapter 3.

be shown reveals a dismal appreciation of the values that underlie the principles of fundamental justice.[74]

iv) The Form of Law: Overbreadth, Vagueness, and Gross Disproportionality

When constitutional lawyers talk of a law being "overbroad," they are referring to the fact that it may go further than is needed to achieve its ends. The Supreme Court has developed the doctrine of overbreadth to express the constitutional requirement that a law be tailored to its purposes. If a net is cast too wide, the inclusion of some individuals who are caught within the net will be an unjust restriction on the right to liberty and security of the person. The determination of overbreadth then becomes an inquiry into the ambit of the law, an inquiry into its purposes, and a determination whether the scope is broader than necessary to achieve the ends. The added scope adds a quality of arbitrariness to the rule, which renders it inconsistent with principles of fundamental justice.

In *R v Heywood*,[75] Cory J outlined the basic tenets of the overbreadth doctrine:

> Overbreadth analysis looks at the means chosen by the state in relation to its purpose. In considering whether a legislative provision is overbroad, a court must ask the question: are those means necessary to achieve the State objective? If the State, in pursuing a legitimate objective, uses means which are broader than is necessary to accomplish that objective, the principles of fundamental justice will be violated because the individual's rights will have been limited for no reason. The effect of overbreadth is that in some applications the law is arbitrary or disproportionate . . . . However, before it can be found that an enactment is so broad that it infringes s. 7 of the *Charter*, it must be clear that the legislation infringes life, liberty or security of the person in a manner that is unnecessarily broad, going beyond what is needed to accomplish the governmental objective.[76]

In *R v Appulonappa*,[77] Silverman J determined that section 117 of the *IRPA*, which creates the offence of human smuggling, was unconstitutionally overbroad since it embraced within its ambit individuals

---

74   Justice Sopinka's arguments have been effectively critiqued by Russell P Cohen in "Fundamental (In)justice: The Deportation of Long-Term Residents from Canada" (1994) 32 *Osgoode Hall Law Journal* 457.

75   [1994] 3 SCR 761.

76   *Ibid* at 792–93 and 794.

77   *R v Appulonappa*, 2013 BCSC 31.

who were engaged in humanitarian efforts to assist refugees. His decision was overturned by the BC Court of Appeal. The Supreme Court of Canada heard an appeal in this case on 17 February 2015, and has reserved its decision.[78]

In addition, in *R v Nova Scotia Pharmaceutical Society*,[79] the Supreme Court held that it was a principle of fundamental justice that laws not be too vague. It identified that the "'doctrine of vagueness' is founded on the rule of law, particularly on the principles of fair notice."[80] It also outlined the following as the proper test to apply when determining whether a law is deficient on grounds of vagueness:

> A vague provision does not provide an adequate basis for legal debate, that is for reaching a conclusion as to its meaning by reasoned analysis applying legal criteria. It does not sufficiently delineate any area of risk, and thus can provide neither fair notice to the citizen nor a limitation of enforcement discretion. Such a provision is not intelligible, to use the terminology of previous decisions of this Court, and therefore it fails to give sufficient indications that could fuel a legal debate. It offers no grasp to the judiciary.[81]

The Supreme Court has also determined that grossly disproportionate restrictions on the rights to life, liberty, and security of the person will contravene the principles of fundamental justice. As explained by the Court in *Canada (AG) v PHS Community Services Society*:[82]

> Gross disproportionality describes state actions or legislative responses to a problem that are so extreme as to be disproportionate to any legitimate government interest.[83]

In *Suresh*, the Court offered additional comments on the importance of this doctrine:

> The notion of proportionality is fundamental to our constitutional system. Thus we must ask whether the government's proposed response is reasonable in relation to the threat. In the past, we have held that *some responses are so extreme that they are per se disproportionate to any legitimate government interest* . . . .[84]

---

78   2014 SCCA No 283.
79   [1992] 2 SCR 606.
80   *Ibid* at 627.
81   *Ibid* at 639–40.
82   2011 SCC 44 [*PHS*].
83   *Ibid* at para 133.
84   *Suresh*, above note 39 at para 47 [emphasis added].

The doctrine of gross disproportionality is a powerful one. It focuses on both the form and the substance of the law being challenged since it allows the Court to adjudge the unreasonableness of the methods chosen by the legislature to achieve an end. This is broader than the notion of insufficient tailoring that underlies the doctrine of overbreadth. Nevertheless, the Court relied on the doctrine sparingly in *Suresh*. On the one hand, it made the following comments about torture:

> Torture is an instrument of terror and not of justice. As Lamer J stated in *Smith*, *supra*, at pp. 1073-74, "some punishments or treatments will always be grossly disproportionate and will always outrage our standards of decency: for example, the infliction of corporal punishment". As such, torture is seen in Canada as fundamentally unjust.

When determining the constitutionality of a law that permitted the removal of a person to a country where there is risk of torture, however, the Court was unprepared to hold that such a law was invalid. Instead, it allowed the law to stand and stated the constitutionality of each decision to deport must be considered on its merits. It argued:

> Canadian jurisprudence does not suggest that Canada may never deport a person to face treatment elsewhere that would be unconstitutional if imposed by Canada directly, on Canadian soil. To repeat, the appropriate approach is essentially one of balancing. The outcome will depend not only on considerations inherent in the general context but also on considerations related to the circumstances and condition of the particular person whom the government seeks to expel. On the one hand stands the state's genuine interest in combatting terrorism, preventing Canada from becoming a safe haven for terrorists, and protecting public security. On the other hand stands Canada's constitutional commitment to liberty and fair process. This said, Canadian jurisprudence suggests that this balance will usually come down against expelling a person to face torture elsewhere.[85]

b) Rights Accompanying Detention

Section 9 of the *Charter* guarantees that "everyone has the right not to be arbitrarily detained or imprisoned." Section 10(c) of the *Charter* provides that everyone who is arrested or detained has the right "to have the validity of the detention determined by way of *habeas corpus* and to be released if the detention is not lawful."

In *Charkaoui*, McLachlin CJ expanded on the principle that underlies section 10(c):

---

85   *Ibid* at paras 51 and 58.

Whether through *habeas corpus* or statutory mechanisms, foreign nationals, like others, have a right to prompt review to ensure that their detention complies with the law. This principle is affirmed in s. 10(c) of the *Charter*. It is also recognized internationally: see *Rasul v. Bush*, 542 U.S. 466 (2004); *Zadvydas v. Davis*, 533 U.S. 678 (2001); art. 5 of the *Convention for the Protection of Human Rights and Fundamental Freedoms*, 213 U.N.T.S. 221 ("European Convention on Human Rights"); *Slivenko v. Latvia* (2004), 39 E.H.R.R. 24 (ct.).[86]

She also noted that detention is arbitrary in the absence of "standards that are rationally related to the purpose of the power of detention."[87] In addition, she drew a connection between sections 9 and 10(c) of the *Charter* by illustrating when the lack of review would render a detention arbitrary. She stated:

> The lack of review for foreign nationals until 120 days [the period imposed in relation to the security certificate process] after the reasonableness of the certificate has been judicially determined violates the guarantee against arbitrary detention in s. 9 of the *Charter*, a guarantee which encompasses the right to prompt review of detention under s. 10(c) of the *Charter*.[88]

It should be noted that McLachlin CJ has acknowledged that the law relating to arbitrariness is somewhat unsettled. In *PHS*, she observed:

> The jurisprudence on arbitrariness is not entirely settled. In *Chaoulli*, three justices (per McLachlin C.J. and Major J.) preferred an approach that asked whether a limit was "necessary" to further the state objective: paras. 131-32. Conversely, three other justices (per Binnie and LeBel JJ.), preferred to avoid the language of necessity and instead approved of the prior articulation of arbitrariness as where "[a] deprivation of a right . . . bears no relation to, or is inconsistent with, the state interest that lies behind the legislation": para. 232. It is unnecessary to determine which approach should prevail, because the government action at issue in this case qualifies as arbitrary under both definitions.[89]

Section 10 of the *Charter* also grants those who have been arrested or detained the right to be informed of the reasons for the arrest or

---

86 *Charkaoui*, above note 60 at para 90.
87 *Ibid* at para 89.
88 *Ibid* at para 91.
89 *PHS*, above note 82 at para 132.

detention, the right to retain counsel without delay, and the right to be informed of that right.

The right to counsel under section 10(b) of the *Charter* arises "from the moment [a person is] ordered to be detained" or is arrested.[90] While arrest and detention can trigger the duty under section 10(b), mere questioning by immigration officials at a port of entry is generally not considered to amount to detention.[91] In *Dehghani*,[92] it was held that a person who was being interviewed at a secondary examination in an airport was not in detention within the meaning of the *Charter* and therefore was not entitled to legal counsel. Nevertheless, the Federal Court has found that where the liberty of a person at a port of entry has been severely constrained, she may be entitled to the rights set out in section 10(b). In *Huang v Canada (Minister of Citizenship and Immigration)*, a refugee claimant had been kept in custody under close supervision for three days and had been interviewed four times without access to counsel.[93] In *Chen*, a refugee claimant had been held for two days and interviewed without counsel.[94] In both cases, statements made during the interviews were used by the Refugee Protection Division to reach their findings. On judicial review, it was held in *Chen* that the statements should have been excluded due to the violation of section 10(b), and a new hearing was ordered. However, in *Huang*, it was found that the statements did not form a significant basis for the negative decision. In *Chevez*,[95] where the claimant had been denied access to counsel before the issuance of an exclusion order which had rendered him ineligible to make a refugee claim, the exclusion order was set aside.

c) Cruel and Unusual Treatment

Section 12 of the *Charter* provides that everyone has the right not to be subjected to cruel and unusual treatment or punishment. In *Chiarelli*, Sopinka J deliberately sidestepped the question whether deportation counted as "treatment" under section 12 of the *Charter* by holding, without analysis, that it was not cruel and unusual. In *Barrera v Canada*

---

90 *Chevez v Canada (Minister of Citizenship and Immigration)*, 2007 FC 709 at para 28 [*Chevez*]; *Dragosin v Canada (Minister of Citizenship and Immigration)*, 2003 FCT 81 at para 16.
91 *Chen v Canada (Minister of Citizenship and Immigration)*, 2006 FC 910 at para 9 [*Chen*]; *Dehghani*, above note 54.
92 *Dehghani*, *ibid*.
93 2002 FCT 149.
94 *Chen*, above note 91.
95 Above note 90.

(Minister of Employment and Immigration),[96] MacGuigan JA held that Sopinka J had had permanent residents in mind rather than Convention refugees when he made this holding. He went on to conclude that the issue whether the deportation of a Convention refugee can constitute cruel and unusual treatment is still open for determination, but that it ought not to be dealt with in the case at bar. In *Canada v Sadiq,*[97] it was held that revocation of citizenship did not constitute cruel and unusual treatment.

More recently, Mactavish J, in *Canadian Doctors*, has held that the government's denial of health care to refugee claimants amounted to cruel and unusual treatment. She explained the doctrine as follows:

> In determining whether treatment or punishment is "cruel and unusual", Canadian courts have looked at a number of factors as part of a kind of 'cost/benefit' analysis. These factors include whether the treatment goes beyond what is necessary to achieve a legitimate aim, whether there are adequate alternatives, whether the treatment is arbitrary and whether it has a value or social purpose. Other considerations include whether the treatment in question is unacceptable to a large segment of the population, whether it accords with public standards of decency or propriety, whether it shocks the general conscience, and whether it is unusually severe and hence degrading to human dignity and worth . . . .[98]

She considered each of these factors and concluded:

> With the 2012 changes to the IFHP [Interim Federal Health Program], the executive branch of the Canadian government has set out to make the lives of disadvantaged individuals even more difficult than they already are in an effort to force those who have sought the protection of this country to leave Canada more quickly, and to deter others from coming here. In light of the unusual circumstances of this case, I am satisfied that the affected individuals are being subjected to "treatment" as contemplated by section 12 of the *Charter.*
>
> I am also satisfied that this treatment is "cruel and unusual", particularly, but not exclusively, as it affects children who have been brought to this country by their parents. The cuts to health insurance coverage effected through the 2012 modifications to the IFHP potentially jeopardize the health, and indeed the very lives, of these innocent and vulnerable children in a manner that shocks the con-

---

96 [1993] 2 FC 3 (CA).
97 [1991] 1 FC 757 (TD).
98 *Canadian Doctors*, above note 26 at para 614.

science and outrages our standards of decency. They violate section 12 of the *Charter*.[99]

d) Right to an Interpreter

Section 14 of the *Charter* provides:

> 14. A party or witness in any proceedings who does not understand or speak the language in which the proceedings are conducted or who is deaf has the right to the assistance of an interpreter.

The right to an interpreter is also regarded as a fundamental principle of procedural fairness.[100]

e) Equality Rights

In Chapter 3, it was noted that according to the dominant judicial view, distinctions based on immigration status are not discriminatory and do not run afoul of section 15 of the *Charter*. Canadian courts have also dismissed attempts to challenge provisions in the *IRPA* for discriminating on other grounds. Thus, in *Guzman v Canada (Minister of Citizenship and Immigration)*,[101] where an application to sponsor a husband as a member of the family class was rejected because the applicant was receiving social assistance, it was held that the law was not unconstitutional since receipt of social assistance was not a ground analogous to those enumerated in section 15.

In *Chesters v Canada (Minister of Citizenship and Immigration)*,[102] where a person with multiple sclerosis was denied permanent resident status on grounds of medical inadmissibility, she challenged the constitutionality of the decision. In an opaque question-begging decision, Heneghan J rejected the challenge, concluding:

> In my opinion, the argument of discrimination on the basis of an analogous ground must fail. The section in question focuses on excessive demands, not on disease, disorder or disability. Contrary to the stance taken by the plaintiff, this case is not about disability but the medical assessment of potential immigrants to Canada within the context of Canadian immigration law. By its nature, legislation governing immigration must be selective.[103]

---

99 *Ibid* at paras 690–91.
100 See Chapter 16.
101 2006 FC 1134.
102 2002 FCT 727.
103 *Ibid* at para 125.

Arguably, this case should have recognized that the basis for the decision was indeed the individual's disability — that the decision was discriminatory — and then should have focused on whether the discrimination in question could be justified under section 1 of the *Charter* on grounds of the excessive demand that disability places on health services.

E. THE *BILL OF RIGHTS*

The *Canadian Bill of Rights* (*Bill of Rights*)[104] is a federal statute that has the effect of rendering inoperative[105] any inconsistent federal statute or "any order, rule or regulation thereunder" unless Parliament has expressly declared otherwise. Its continuing relevance to immigration decision-making was emphasized by three judges of the Supreme Court of Canada in *Singh*. While the opinion of Wilson J relied on the *Charter*, Beetz J chose to base his reasons on the *Bill of Rights* and made no comment on the applicability of the *Charter*. He explained this decision by noting, first, that section 26 of the *Charter* provides that the guarantee of rights therein "shall not be construed as denying the existence of any other rights or freedoms that exist in Canada."[106] Since the *Bill of Rights* was enacted in 1960, the effect of this section is that the rights recognized in the *Bill of Rights* persist. Justice Beetz also asserted that he was unwilling to allow the *Bill of Rights* to fall into neglect, particularly in cases where it was "almost tailor-made for certain factual situations such as those in the cases at bar."[107] According to Beetz J, the best strategy for the protection of rights is through the cumulative effect of many legal tools, rather than reliance on the *Charter* alone.

The *Bill of Rights* recognizes rights that are not recognized in the *Charter*, and even when identifying what is arguably the same right, it uses words and phrases that differ significantly. Thus, section 1(a) of the *Bill of Rights* states:

> 1. It is hereby recognized and declared that in Canada there have existed and shall continue to exist without discrimination by reason of race, national origin, colour, religion or sex, the following human rights and fundamental freedoms, namely, (*a*) the right of the individual to life, liberty, security of the person and enjoyment of property,

---

104 Above note 3.
105 See *R v Drybones*, [1970] SCR 282.
106 *Singh*, above note 2 at 224.
107 *Ibid.*

and the right not to be deprived thereof except by due process of law[.]

Not only does this clause recognize a right not protected by the *Charter* — the right to enjoyment of property — but it also raises the question whether principles of due process are identical to the principles of fundamental justice recognized in section 7 of the *Charter*.

In *Singh*, Beetz J relied specifically on section 2(e) of the *Bill of Rights*, which reads as follows: "[N]o law of Canada shall be construed or applied so as to (e) deprive a person of the right to a fair hearing in accordance with the principles of fundamental justice for the determination of his rights and obligations."

Reliance was also placed on this clause in *Rajpaul v Canada (Minister of Employment and Immigration)*,[108] where it was held that the decision not to grant the appellant's spouse a temporary visa to enter Canada to give evidence at the hearing of an appeal against a holding that the marriage between the appellant and his spouse was a marriage of convenience deprived the appellant of his right to a fair hearing.

In *Williams v Canada (Minister of Citizenship and Immigration)*,[109] Reed J notes that "[i]n order to obtain the protection of section 7 of the *Charter*, a person must show that the consequences of the decision to which it is sought to apply that section would potentially deprive the individual of 'the right to life, liberty' or 'security of the person' . . . . [Section 2 of the *Canadian Bill of Rights* is] not so constrained."[110]

F. INTERNATIONAL LAW REMEDIES

Those who have been unable to obtain a remedy through appeals, judicial review, or by invoking the Constitution, may turn to international bodies created to monitor state compliance to international agreements. As discussed in Chapter 2, Canada is party to various international agreements that decision makers must take into account when dealing with immigration and refugee applications. An overview of the most significant international instruments related to immigration and refugee law is provided in that chapter.

There are nine international human rights treaties that have established a "treaty body" or "Committee" of experts to monitor implementation of treaty provisions by their state parties and that will, under

---

108 [1988] 3 FC 157 (CA).
109 [1997] 1 FC 457 (TD), rev'd on other grounds [1997] FCJ No 393 (CA).
110 *Ibid* at 438.

certain circumstances, consider individual complaints.[111] The most notable bodies to which immigrants and refugees have turned include the Committee Against Torture (CAT), which monitors state member implementation of the *Convention against Torture and Cruel, Inhuman or Degrading Treatment or Punishment*,[112] and the Human Rights Committee, which monitors state member implementation of the *International Covenant on Civil and Political Rights* (ICCPR) and its *Optional Protocol*.[113] These bodies provide a powerful mechanism for individuals to participate in the monitoring of state compliance by allowing complaints to be brought as individual communications.[114]

To date, Canada has been the subject of approximately seventy complaints, mostly made in reference to alleged violation of the *Convention against Torture* and the *ICCPR*.[115] Some complaints have resulted in the treaty body finding violations. For example, in monitoring the *ICCPR*, the case of *Thuraisamy v Canada* involved an ethnic Tamil from Sri Lanka who had been detained and tortured by the Sri Lankan army on several occasions.[116] Thuraisamy's refugee claim and pre-removal risk assessment were rejected on the grounds that he lacked credibility. The Human Rights Committee found, in this case, "that insufficient weight was given to the author's allegations of a real risk of being tortured if deported to this country of origin, given the high prevalence of torture in Sri Lanka" and that "inconsistencies highlighted by the State party were not directly related to his claim of having been tortured and cannot in themselves vitiate the whole credibility." The Committee

---

111 Treaty bodies have been created pursuant to, for example, the *Convention on the Rights of the Child*, 20 November 1989, 28 ILM 1448, and the *Convention on the Elimination of All Forms of Discrimination against Women*, 18 December 1979, 1249 UNTS 13. For more information on other human rights bodies and their complaints procedures, see United Nations Human Rights, Human Rights Bodies – Complaints Procedures, online: Office of the High Commissioner for Human Rights www.ohchr.org/EN/HRBodies/TBPetitions/Pages/HRTBPetitions. aspx.

112 10 December 1984, Can TS 1987 No 36, 23 ILM 1027 [*Convention against Torture*].

113 19 December 1966, 999 UNTS 171 [*ICCPR*]; *Optional Protocol to the International Covenant on Civil and Political Rights*, 19 December 1966, 999 UNTS 302 [*ICCPR Protocol*].

114 Of course, states may bring complaints forward, and these bodies may also investigate if inquiries are made regarding state compliance.

115 United Nations Human Rights, Jurisprudence, online: Office of the High Commissioner for Human Rights http://juris.ohchr.org/.

116 Committee, Communication No 1912/2009: Views adopted by the Committee at its 106th session (15 October–2 November 2012) CCPR, 106th Sess, UN Doc CCPR/C/106/D/1912/2009, online: www.ccprcentre.org/wp-content/uploads/2013/03/1912-2009-Thuraisamy-v-Canada-en.pdf.

held that the removal to Sri Lanka would violate Thuraisamy's rights under article 7 of the *ICCPR*. The Committee gave Canada 180 days to provide information about measures taken to remedy the violation identified in the case.

Similarly, at the CAT, the case of *Kalonzo v Canada* involved an individual who had been previously deported by the United States to the Democratic Republic of Congo (DRC) where he was imprisoned, beaten, tortured, and sexually assaulted due to his criminal background and his father's membership in a political party.[117] Kalonzo's refugee claim was rejected as he was found inadmissible due to his past criminal activity. Kalonzo's pre-removal risk assessment was rejected because he was not credible, was not a member of the political party his father was part of, and failed to show that his father was still a member of the political party and experienced problems as a result of his membership; what is more, it was deemed that Kalonzo could relocate to a different part of the DRC. The Committee noted Canada's moratorium on the removal of rejected asylum seekers to the DRC, did not think it was reasonable for Kalonzo to simply relocate in the country, and acknowledged the evidence provided showing that Kalonzo suffered torture when he was in his country of origin. Ultimately, the Committee found Canada in violation of article 3 of the *Convention against Torture* and gave Canada ninety days to inform the Committee of steps taken to remedy this breach of the *Convention*.

Although these two decisions point to an international venue for persons to challenge decisions regarding their immigration or refugee applications in Canada, the remedies obtained in these international bodies have limited scope. As demonstrated by the two decisions discussed, the bodies are limited to asking for information regarding steps Canada is taking to remedy the breach identified. They have no power to force Canada into halting or taking particular action or making certain decisions, leaving adherence to the recommendations in the decision voluntary. Thus, while a positive decision from these committees may be helpful jurisprudence on which to build future arguments, on a practical level, individuals seeking recourse may still fail to obtain meaningful relief.

---

117 Decision, Committee Against Torture, Communication No 343/2008: Decision adopted by the Committee at its forty-eighth session (7 May to 1 June 2012) CAT, 48th Sess, UN Doc CAT/C/48/D/343/2008, online: www.ohchr.org/Documents/HRBodies/CAT/Jurisprudence/CAT-C-48-D-343-2008_en.pdf.

G. CONCLUSION

In a number of recent cases, the judiciary has developed legal doctrines that will permit it to quash laws that impose unduly onerous consequences on individuals no matter what their status or that are formulated so poorly that their meaning is unclear or their ambit excessively over-inclusive. It has taken on the role of determining whether political programs are disproportionate. Judges have not hesitated to label legal provisions that ignore consequent human suffering as "cruel and unusual." Moreover, the Supreme Court has recognized that committed advocates should be permitted to bring these matters before it and has removed hurdles that previously prevented them from doing so. It has provided imaginative lawyers with both opportunity and incentive to question the legitimacy of measures that significantly diminish the well-being of human beings. The Supreme Court, while recognizing that immigration law is now shaped primarily by the value of public security, has nevertheless emphasized that it exists within a legal system that, at its heart, respects human worth and aims to protect the vulnerable from callous or oppressive laws and governmental conduct. It is expected that immigration law will provide an important context in which the Court will elucidate in greater depth the fundamental values that should inform and shape the legal response to the challenges that modernity has created.

APPENDIX

The following is a chart of the current Federal-Provincial/Territorial Agreements in place:[1]

Agreement	Dates Signed	Expiry	Website for PNP Program
Canada-Newfoundland and Labrador Agreement on Provincial Nominees	22 November 2006 (originally signed in September 1999)	Indefinite	www.nlpnp.ca
Agreement for Canada-Prince Edward Island Co-operation on Immigration	13 June 2008 (originally signed in March 2001)	Indefinite	www.gov.pe.ca/immigration/
Canada-Nova Scotia Co-operation on Immigration	19 September 2007	Indefinite	http://novascotia immigration.com/immigrate/

---

1   Citizenship and Immigration Canada, *Annual Report to Parliament on Immigration 2013*, online: www.cic.gc.ca/english/pdf/pub/annual-report-2013.pdf at 26.

Agreement	Dates Signed	Expiry	Website for PNP Program
Canada-New Brunswick Agreement on Provincial Nominees	28 January 2005 Amended: 29 March 2005 (originally signed in February 1999)	Indefinite	www.welcomenb.ca/content/wel-bien/en/immigrating_and_settling/how_to_immigrate/new_brunswick_provincialnominee program.html
Canada-Quebec Accord relating to Immigration and Temporary Admission of Aliens	5 February 1991	Indefinite	www.immigration-quebec.gouv.qc.ca/EN/IMMIGRATE-SETTLE/PERMANENT-WORKERS/index.html
Canada-Ontario Immigration Agreement	21 November 2005	31 March 2011 but extended to 31 May 2015; Temporary Foreign Worker Annex continues indefinitely	www.ontario immigration.ca/en/pnp/OI_PNP WORKERS.html
Canada-Manitoba Immigration Agreement	6 June 2003 (originally signed in October 1996)	Indefinite	www.immigrate manitoba.com
Canada-Saskatchewan Immigration Agreement	7 May 2005 (originally signed in March 1998)	Indefinite	www.sask immigration canada.ca/sinp
Agreement for Canada-Alberta Cooperation on Immigration	11 May 2007	Indefinite	www.alberta canada.com/opportunity/immigrating/ainp.aspx
Canada-British Columbia Immigration Agreement	9 April 2010 (originally signed in May 1998)	8 April 2015	www.welcomebc.ca/Immigrate/About-the-BC-PNP.aspx

Agreement	Dates Signed	Expiry	Website for PNP Program
Agreement for Canada-Yukon Co-operation on Immigration	12 February 2008 (originally signed in April 2001)	Indefinite	www.education. gov.yk.ca/ employers/ynp. html
Canada-Northwest Territories Agreement on Provincial Nominees	26 September 2013	26 September 2018	www.immigrate nwt.ca/en/nwt-nominee-program

TABLE OF CASES

Ababio v Canada (Minister of Employment and Immigration) (1988),
    90 NR 28, 5 Imm LR (2d) 174, [1988] FCJ No 250 (CA)............................ 320
Abawaji v Canada (Minister of Citizenship and Immigration),
    2006 FC 1065... 282
Abbott v Canada (Citizenship and Immigration), 2011 FC 344........................ 406
Abdelrazik v Canada (Minister of Foreign Affairs), 2009 FC 580 458,
    459–60, 621, 650
Abdolkhaleghi v Canada (Minister of Citizenship and Immigration),
    2005 FC 729.. 624
Adjani v Canada (Minister of Citizenship and Immigration), 2008 FC 32........ 211
Adjei v Canada (Minister of Employment and Immigration),
    [1989] 2 FC 680, 57 DLR (4th) 153, [1989] FCJ No 67 (CA 302, 346
Adroh v Canada (Minister of Citizenship and Immigration),
    2012 FC 393.. 107
Afanasyev v Canada (Minister of Citizenship and Immigration),
    2010 FC 737 477
Afanasyev v Canada (Minister of Citizenship and Immigration),
    2012 FC 1270 477
Agama v Canada (Minister of Citizenship and Immigration),
    2013 FC 135 153
Aghdam v Canada (Minister of Public Safety and Emergency
    Preparedness), 2011 FC 131 624
Aguilar v Canada (Minister of Public Safety and Emergency
    Preparedness), IMM-478-12 (21 January 2013) 391
Aguinaldo v Canada (Minister of Citizenship and Immigration),
    2010 FC 682 .... 521, 523

Ahmad v Canada (Minister of Citizenship and Immigration),
2005 FC 279...288
Ahmad v Canada (Minister of Citizenship and Immigration),
2012 FC 508.. 624
Airapetyan v Canada (Minister of Citizenship and Immigration),
2007 FC 42... 520, 522
Akinbowale v Canada (Minister of Citizenship and Immigration),
2007 FC 1221.. 394
Aksenova v Canada (Minister of Public Safety and Emergency
Preparedness), 2006 FC 557.. 507
Al Yamani v Canada (Minister of Citizenship and Immigration) (No 3),
[2000] 3 FC 433, 5 Imm LR (3d) 235, [2000] FCJ No 317 (TD)................ 479
Al Yamani v Canada (Solicitor General) (1995), [1996] 1 FC 174,
129 DLR (4th) 226; [1995] FCJ No 1453 ....647–48, 649
Alberta (Information and Privacy Commissioner) v Alberta
Teachers' Association, 2011 SCC 61.. 142, 617–18, 619
Al-Busaidy v Canada (Minister of Employment and Immigration)
(1992), 139 NR 208, [1992] FCJ No 26 (CA) 321
Alemu v Canada (Minister of Citizenship and Immigration),
2004 FC 997 482
Alexander v Canada (Solicitor General), 2005 FC 1147 565
Ali v Canada (Minister of Citizenship and Immigration) (1999),
235 NR 316, [1999] FCJ No 63 (CA) 309
Ali v Canada (Minister of Citizenship and Immigration), 2004 FC 1174 481
Ali v Canada (Minister of Citizenship and Immigration), 2008 FC 166..........526
Ali v Canada (Minister of Citizenship and Immigration), 2008 FC 448 321
Ali v Canada (Minister of Citizenship and Immigration), 2008 FC 784............ 96
Alie v Canada (Minister of Citizenship and Immigration), 2008 FC 925......... 422
Al-Kassous v Canada (Minister of Citizenship and Immigration),
2007 FC 541... 144
Al-Maari v Canada (Minister of Citizenship and Immigration),
2013 FC 1037 287
Almrei (Re), 2009 FC 1263.....................................474, 483, 577, 583
Almrei v Canada (Minister of Citizenship and Immigration),
2007 FC 1025... 558
Alvarez v Canada (Minister of Citizenship and Immigration),
2011 FC 667 96
Alvarez v Canada (Minister of Citizenship and Immigration),
2014 FC 702 295
Amin v Canada (Minister of Citizenship and Immigration),
2008 FC 168..188–89
Ammar v Canada (Minister or Citizenship and Immigration),
2006 FC 1041... 387
Amnesty International Canada v Canada (Canadian Forces),
2008 FCA 401 642

AMRI v KER, 2011 ONCA 417.. 70
Andreoli v Canada (Minister of Citizenship and Immigration),
    2004 FC 1111 278
Andrews v Law Society of British Columbia. See Law Society of
    British Columbia v Andrews
Anjum v Canada (Minister of Citizenship and Immigration),
    2004 FC 496 278
Aramouni v Canada (Minister of Citizenship and Immigration),
    2011 FC 430 144
Arguello-Garcia v Canada (Minister of Employment and
    Immigration) (1993), 64 FTR 307, 21 Imm LR (2d) 285,
    [1993] FCJ No 635 (TD) 280–81
Arora v Canada (Minister of Citizenship and Immigration),
    2011 FC 241 119
Arteaga v Canada (Minister of Citizenship and Immigration),
    2013 FC 778... 616
Arulraj v Canada (Minister of Citizenship and Immigration),
    2006 FC 529... 425
Asghar v Canada (Minister of Citizenship and Immigration),
    2005 FC 768.. 315, 321
Ashraf v Canada (Minister of Citizenship and Immigration),
    2013 FC 1160 410
Asl v Canada (Minister of Citizenship and Immigration), 2007 FC 459 240
Aslam v Canada (Minister of Citizenship and Immigration),
    2004 FC 514... 278
Ates v Canada (Minister of Citizenship and Immigration),
    2004 FC 1316, aff'd 2005 FCA 322 317
Avila v Canada (Minister of Citizenship and Immigration), 2009 FC 13 430
Aviles v Canada (Minister of Citizenship and Immigration),
    2005 FC 1369 504
Awolope v Canada (Minister of Citizenship and Immigration),
    2010 FC 540... 424
Ayach v Canada (Minister of Citizenship and Immigration),
    2010 FC 1023 .... 381, 383

B010 v Canada (Minister of Citizenship and Immigration), 2013
    FCA 87, leave to appeal to SCC granted, [2013] SCCA No 220 508,
    510, 511, 589, 616
B306 v Canada (Minister of Public Safety and Emergency Preparedness).
    See also Canada (Minister of Public Safety and Emergency Preparedness) v JP
B306 v Canada (Minister of Public Safety and Emergency
    Preparedness), 2012 FC 1282, rev'd 2013 FCA 262,
    leave to appeal to SCC granted, [2014] SCCA No 22 .... 510, 589
Ba v Canada (Minister of Citizenship and Immigration),
    2009 FC 287 412

Baffoe v Canada (Minister of Citizenship and Immigration) (1994),
    85 FTR 68, [1994] FCJ No 1429 (TD) 311
Bageerathan v Canada (Minister of Citizenship and Immigration),
    2009 FC 513.. 625, 632
Bagwandeen v Canada (Minister of Citizenship and Immigration),
    2005 FC 661 410
Bahr v Canada (Minister of Citizenship and Immigration), 2012 FC 527 100
Bains v Canada (Minister of Employment and Immigration) (1990),
    109 NR 239, 47 Admin LR 317, [1990] FCJ No 457 (CA) 602
Baker v Canada (Minister of Citizenship and Immigration),
    [1999] 2 SCR 817, 1 Imm LR (3d) 1, 1999 CanLII 699 .... 58, 69, 402,
    408, 417, 420–21, 603, 610, 612
Bakhsh v Canada (Minister of Citizenship and Immigration),
    2004 FC 1060 624
Balachandran v Canada (Minister of Citizenship and Immigration),
    2014 FC 800 346
Balogh v Canada (Minister of Citizenship and Immigration),
    2014 FC 771 329
Bank of Montreal v Marcotte, 2014 SCC 55 33
Bankole v Canada (Minister of Citizenship and Immigration),
    2011 FC 373 501
Bano v Canada (Minister of Citizenship and Immigration),
    2011 FC 401 143
Bansal v Canada (Minister of Citizenship and Immigration),
    2006 FC 226 .... 410, 419
Barnett v Canada (Minister of Citizenship and Immigration) (1996),
    109 FTR 154, 33 Imm LR (2d) 1, [1996] FCJ No 363 (TD) 503
Baro v Canada (Minister of Citizenship and Immigration),
    2007 FC 1299.. 526
Baron v Canada (Minister of Public Safety and Emergency
    Preparedness), 2009 FCA 81 372
Barrak v Canada (Minister of Citizenship and Immigration),
    2008 FC 962.. 414
Barrera v Canada (Minister of Employment and Immigration)
    (1992), [1993] 2 FC 3, 18 Imm LR (2d) 81, [1992] FCJ No 1127 (CA) 529,
    664–65
Barua v Canada (Minister of Citizenship and Immigration),
    2012 FC 59.. 283
Baylon v Canada (Minister of Citizenship and Immigration),
    2009 FC 938 100
Bazaid v Canada (Minister of Citizenship and Immigration),
    2013 FC 17 154
Begum v Canada (Minister of Citizenship and Immigration),
    2011 FC 10 615

Begum v Canada (Minister of Citizenship and Immigration),
2013 FC 265 409
Beharry v Canada (Minister of Citizenship and Immigration),
2011 FC 110 425
Belle v Canada (Minister of Citizenship and Immigration),
2012 FC 1181 348
Bellido v Canada (Minister of Citizenship and Immigration),
2005 FC 452 148
Benhmuda v Canada (Minister of Citizenship and Immigration),
2012 FC 1222 573
Ben-Musa v Canada (Minister of Citizenship and Immigration),
2005 FC 764 632
Benoit v Canada (Minister of Citizenship and Immigration),
2013 FC 185 .... 139, 618
Benyk v Canada (Minister of Citizenship and Immigration),
2009 FC 950 423
Bhuiya v Canada (Minister of Citizenship and Immigration),
2008 FC 878 142
Bichari v Canada (Minister of Citizenship and Immigration),
2010 FC 127 .... 520, 521, 523
BL v Canada (Minister of Citizenship and Immigration),
2012 FC 538 430
Blake v Canada (Minister of Public Safety and Emergency
Preparedness), 2008 FC 572 .... 565, 566
Blencoe v British Columbia (Human Rights Commission),
2000 SCC 44 .... 284, 656
Bobrik v Canada (Minister of Citizenship and Immigration)
(1994), 85 FTR 13, [1994] FCJ No 1364 (TD) 308, 334, 336
Bodine v Canada (Minister of Citizenship and Immigration),
2008 FC 848 527
Boni v Canada (Minister of citizenship and Immigration), 2005 FC 31 101
Bonilla v Canada (Minister of Citizenship and Immigration),
2007 FC 20 .... 98, 102
Boniowski v Canada (Minister of Citizenship and Immigration),
2004 FC 1161 379
Boroumand v Canada (Minister of Citizenship and Immigration),
2007 FC 1219 .... 382, 387
Bortey v Canada (Minister of Citizenship and Immigration),
2006 FC 190 285
Brannson v Canada (Minister of Employment and Immigration)
(1980), [1981] 2 FC 141, [1980] FCJ No 247 (CA) 500
Brar v Canada (Minister of Citizenship and Immigration),
2006 FC 1502 105
Brovina v Canada (Minister of Citizenship and Immigration),
2004 FC 635 280

Brown v Canada (Minister of Citizenship and Immigration),
2011 FC 585 325
Budlakoti v Canada (Citizenship and Immigration), 2014 FC 855 440
Burgon v Canada (Minister of Employment and Immigration) (1991),
78 DLR (4th) 103, 13 Imm LR (2d) 102, [1991] FCJ No 149 (CA) 503
Burton v Canada (Minister of Citizenship and Immigration),
2013 FC 549 364

Cadena v Canada (Minister of Public Safety and Emergency
Preparedness), 2012 FC 67 281
Calaunan v Canada (Minister of Citizenship and Immigration),
2011 FC 1494 .... 100, 101
Calero v Canada (Minister of Employment and Immigration),
[1994] FCJ No 1159 (TD) 230
Caliskan v Canada (Minister of Citizenship and Immigration),
2012 FC 1190 414
Calixto v Canada (Minister of Citizenship and Immigration),
2005 FC 1037 .... 285, 525
Calma v Canada (Minister of Citizenship and Immigration),
2009 FC 742 99
Campos v Canada (Minister of Citizenship and Immigration),
2008 FC 556 387–88
Canada (AG) v Bedford, 2013 SCC 72 588–89
Canada (AG) v Cain, [1906] AC 542, 95 LT 314 (PC) 10
Canada (AG) v Canada (Commission of Inquiry on the
Blood System in Canada - Krever Commission),
[1997] 2 FC 36, 142 DLR (4th) 237, [1997] FCJ No 17 (CA) 622
Canada (AG) v Hennelly (1999), 244 NR 399, 167 FTR 158,
[1999] FCJ No 846 (CA) 599
Canada (AG) v Jolly, [1975] FC 216, 54 DLR (3d) 277,
[1975] FCJ No 40 (CA) 508
Canada (AG) v Mavi, 2011 SCC 30 217
Canada (AG) v PHS Community Services Society, 2011 SCC 44 .... 661, 663
Canada (AG) v TeleZone, 2010 SCC 62 628–29
Canada (AG) v Ward, [1993] 2 SCR 689, 103 DLR (4th) 1,
1993 CanLII 105 .... 299, 308, 309,
314, 316, 319, 320, 325, 327–29, 330, 333, 336, 338, 346, 349, 350
Canada (Canadian Human Rights Commission) v Canada (AG),
2011 SCC 53 .... 73, 475
Canada (Citizenship and Immigration) v Harkat, 2014 SCC 37 .... 573, 582,
583–86, 611
Canada (Citizenship and Immigration) v X, 2010 FC 112,
abated 2011 FCA 27 554
Canada (Citizenship and Immigration) v Zhou, 2008 FC 939 73
Canada (Justice) v Khadr, 2008 SCC 28 .... 458, 627,
640–41, 642

Canada (Minister of Citizenship and Immigration) v B236,
    2010 FC 1339 558
Canada (Minister of Citizenship and Immigration) v B344,
    2013 FC 447 358
Canada (Minister of Citizenship and Immigration) v B380,
    2012 FC 1334 358
Canada (Minister of Citizenship and Immigration) v B420,
    2013 FC 321 358
Canada (Minister of Citizenship and Immigration) v B456,
    2011 FC 439 558
Canada (Minister of Citizenship and Immigration) v B472,
    2013 FC 151 .... 358, 615
Canada (Minister of Citizenship and Immigration) v Bogutin (1998),
    144 FTR 1, 42 Imm LR (2d) 248, [1998] FCJ No 211 (TD) 462
Canada (Minister of Citizenship and Immigration) v Dhillon,
    2012 FC 726 .... 475, 509
Canada (Minister of Citizenship and Immigration) v Dinaburgsky,
    2006 FC 1161 462
Canada (Minister of Citizenship and Immigration) v Dragan,
    2003 FCA 139 612
Canada (Minister of Citizenship and Immigration) v Ekuban,
    2001 FCT 65 286
Canada (Minister of Citizenship and Immigration) v Fast,
    2003 FC 1139 462
Canada (Minister of Citizenship and Immigration) v Grdan,
    2014 FC 187 618
Canada (Minister of Citizenship and Immigration) v Harkat,
    2014 SCC 37 .... 573, 582,
    583–86, 611
Canada (Minister of Citizenship and Immigration) v Hazimeh,
    2009 FC 380 189
Canada (Minister of Citizenship and Immigration) v Kandola,
    2014 FCA 85 441–42
Canada (Minister of Citizenship and Immigration) v Katriuk,
    [1999] 3 FC 143, [1999] FCJ No 216 (TD) 462
Canada (Minister of Citizenship and Immigration) v Khosa,
    2009 SCC 12 607–8,
    616, 622, 628
Canada (Minister of Citizenship and Immigration) v Kimbatsa,
    2010 FC 346 ....192, 210, 212
Canada (Minister of Citizenship and Immigration) v Kurukkal,
    2010 FCA 230 433
Canada (Minister of Citizenship and Immigration) v Li, 2010 FCA 75 615
Canada (Minister of Citizenship and Immigration) v Mahjoub,
    2001 FCT 1095 .... 482, 573

Canada (Minister of Citizenship and Immigration) v Odynsky,
2001 FCT 138 462

Canada (Minister of Citizenship and Immigration) v Rogan,
2011 FC 1007 462

Canada (Minister of Citizenship and Immigration) v Saini,
2001 FCA 311 .... 185, 505–6

Canada (Minister of Citizenship and Immigration) v Skomatchuk,
2006 FC 994 462

Canada (Minister of Citizenship and Immigration) v Stephenson,
2008 FC 82 72

Canada (Minister of Citizenship and Immigration) v USA, 2014 FC 416 478

Canada (Minister of Citizenship and Immigration) v Wahab,
2006 FC 1554 285–86

Canada (Minister of Emergency Preparedness) v Gunasingam,
2008 FC 181 286

Canada (Minister of Employment and Immigration) v Chiarelli,
[1992] 1 SCR 711, 16 Imm LR (2d) 1, 1992 CanLII 87 .... 8, 9, 472,
566, 653, 654, 655, 658, 664

Canada (Minister of Employment and Immigration) v Obstoj,
[1992] 2 FC 739, 93 DLR (4th) 144, [1992] FCJ No 422 (CA) 280

Canada (Minister of Employment and Immigration) v Satiacum
(1989), 99 NR 171, [1989] FCJ No 505 (CA) 320

Canada (Minister of Employment and Immigration) v Taggar,
[1989] 3 FC 576 (CA) 185

Canada (Minister of Employment and Immigration) v Villafranca
(1992), 99 DLR (4th) 334, 18 Imm LR (2d) 130,
[1992] FCJ No 1189 (CA) 334, 335

Canada (Minister of Manpower and Immigration) v Tsiafakis,
[1977] 2 FC 216, 73 DLR (3d) 139, [1977] FCJ No 26 (CA) 623

Canada (Minister of Public Safety and Emergency Preparedness)
v JP, 2013 FCA 262, leave to appeal to SCC granted,
[2014] SCCA No 22 .... 510–11, 589

Canada (Prime Minister) v Khadr, 2010 SCC 3 627–28

Canada (Public Safety and Emergency Preparedness) v Barci,
2010 CanLII 85379 (CA IRB) 536

Canada (Solicitor General) v Subhaschandran, 2005 FCA 27 631

Canada v Sadiq (1990), [1991] 1 FC 757, 12 Imm LR (2d) 231,
[1990] FCJ No 1102 (TD) 462, 665

Canadian Council for Refugees v Canada, 2006 FC 1046 .... 367, 602

Canadian Council for Refugees v Canada, 2007 FC 1262,
rev'd 2008 FCA 229 .... 252, 645

Canadian Council of Churches v Canada (Minister of Employment
and Immigration), [1990] 2 FC 534, 10 Imm LR (2d) 81,
[1990] FCJ No 224 (CA), rev'd [1992] 1 SCR 236, 88 DLR
(4th) 193, 1992 CanLII 116 637–38

Canadian Doctors for Refugee Care v Canada (AG), 2014 FC 651 ....31, 87, 643,
  665–66
Canadian Pacific Ltd v Matsqui Indian Band, [1995] 1 SCR 3,
  122 DLR (4th) 129, 1995 CanLII 145 620
Canadian Society of Immigration Consultants v Canada
  (Citizenship and Immigration), 2011 FC 1435 47
Cao v Canada (Minister of Citizenship and Immigration), 2010 FC 941 101
Cao v Canada (Minister of Citizenship and Immigration), 2013 FC 173 323
Cardinal v Kent Institution, [1985] 2 SCR 643, 24 DLR (4th) 44,
  1985 CanLII 23 .... 542, 543
Casseus v Canada (Minister of Citizenship and Immigration),
  2003 FCT 472 380
Castelly v Canada (Minister of Citizenship and Immigration),
  2008 FC 788 508–9
Cece v Holder, No 11-1989 (7th Cir August 9, 2013) 251
Celgene Corp v Canada (AG), 2011 SCC 1..617
Cha v Canada (Minister of Citizenship and Immigration), 2006 FCA 126 611
Chabira v Canada (Minister of Citizenship and Immigration)
  (1994), 27 Imm LR (2d) 75, [1994] FCJ No 127 (TD).........................307, 313
Chan v Canada (Minister of Employment and Immigration),
  [1995] 3 SCR 593, 128 DLR (4th) 213, 1995 CanLII 71 ....299, 302, 319
Chandrakumar v Canada (Minister of Employment and
  Immigration), 1997 CanLII 16770 (FCTD)... 281
Charkaoui v Canada (Citizenship and Immigration),
  2007 SCC 9 ....84, 553,
  561, 573, 578, 581, 585, 654, 656, 657, 662, 663
Charles v Canada (Citizenship and Immigration), 2014 FC 772 425
Charles v Canada (Minister of Citizenship and Immigration),
  2011 FC 852 271
Chaudhry v Canada (Minister of Citizenship and Immigration),
  2011 FC 22..522
Chavez v Canada (Minister of Citizenship and Immigration),
  [2005] IADD No 353.. 195
Cheddesingh v Canada (Minister of Citizenship and Immigration),
  2006 FC 124...501
Chekroun v Canada (Minister of Citizenship and Immigration),
  2013 FC 737 ....405, 408, 417
Chen v Canada (Minister of Citizenship and Immigration),
  2005 FC 678... 209
Chen v Canada (Minister of Citizenship and Immigration),
  2006 FC 910... 664
Chen v Canada (Minister of Citizenship and Immigration),
  2014 FC 749 358–59
Chen v Canada (Minister of Employment and Immigration) (1993),
  70 FTR 241, 22 Imm LR (2d) 160, [1993] FCJ No 1188 (TD)....................316

Chesters v Canada (Minister of Citizenship and Immigration),
2002 FCT 727 666

Cheung v Canada (Minister of Employment and Immigration),
[1981] 2 FC 764, 122 DLR (3d) 41, [1981] FCJ No 43 (CA) 545

Cheung v Canada (Minister of Employment and Immigration),
[1993] 2 FC 314, 19 Imm LR (2d) 81, [1993] FCJ No 309 (CA) 305, 319

Chevez v Canada (Minister of Citizenship and Immigration),
2007 FC 709 664

Chiarelli v Canada (Minister of Employment and Immigration. See Canada (Minister of Employment and Immigration) v Chiarelli

Chiau v Canada (Minister of Citizenship and Immigration (2000),
[2001] 2 FC 297, 195 DLR (4th) 422, [2000] FCJ No 2043 (CA) 352, 508

Chieu v Canada (Minister of Citizenship and Immigration),
2002 SCC 3 .... 379, 546

Chiu v Canada (Minister of Citizenship and Immigration) (1997),
140 FTR 254, 41 Imm LR (2d) 1, [1997] FCJ No 1670 (TD) 452

Cho v Canada (Minister of Citizenship and Immigration),
2010 FC 1299 385

Choi v Canada (Minister of Citizenship and Immigration),
2008 FC 577 154

Chowdhury v Canada (Minister of Citizenship and Immigration),
2008 FC 290 283

Chowdhury v Canada (Minister of Citizenship and Immigration),
2003 FC 1050 380

Chu v Canada (Minister of Citizenship and Immigration),
2001 FCA 113 611–12

Chudal v Canada (Minister of Citizenship and Immigration),
2005 FC 1073 389

Clarke v Canada (Minister of Citizenship and Immigration),
2012 FC 1225 323

Cohen v Canada (Minister of Citizenship and Immigration),
2006 FC 804 517

Colaco v Canada (Minister of Citizenship and Immigration),
2007 FCA 282 521

Committee for the Commonwealth of Canada v Canada,
[1991] 1 SCR 139, 77 DLR (4th) 385, [1991] SCJ No 3 646

Companioni v Canada (Minister of Citizenship and Immigration),
2009 FC 1315 519–20

Conille v Canada (Minister of Citizenship and Immigration) (1998),
[1999] 2 FC 33, 159 FTR 215, [1998] FCJ No 1553 (TD) 453, 625

Construction and Specialized Workers' Union, Local 1611 v Canada
(Minister of Citizenship and Immigration), 2013 FC 512 115

Coomaraswamy v Canada (Minister of Citizenship and Immigration),
2002 FCA 153 286

Cooper v Board of Works for Wandsworth District (1863),
14 CBNS 180, 143 ER 414 (CP) 608

Co-operative Committee on Japanese Canadians v Attorney
General of Canada, [1946] UKPC 48 24

Corbière v Canada (Minister of Indian and Northern Affairs),
[1999] 2 SCR 203, 173 DLR (4th) 1, 1999 CanLII 687 85

Cordeiro v Canada (Minister of Citizenship and Immigration),
2004 FC 1231.. 425

Cornejo v Canada (Minister of Citizenship and Immigration),
2010 FC 261 323

Correa v Canada (Minister of Citizenship and Immigration),
2014 FC 252 346

Cosgun v Canada (Minister of Citizenship and Immigration),
2010 FC 400.. 335–36, 338

Cramer v Canada (Minister of Citizenship and Immigration),
2011 FC 854 521

Crease v Canada (Minister of Multiculturism & Citizenship),
[1994] 3 FC 480, 78 FTR 192, [1994] FCJ No 711 (TD) 638, 639

Cuarte v Canada (Minister of Citizenship and Immigration),
2012 FC 261 520

Cunningham v Homma, [1903] AC 151 (PC) 34, 35

Cyriaque v Canada (Minister of Citizenship and Immigration),
2010 FC 1077 347

Czesak v Canada (Minister of Citizenship and Immigration),
2013 FC 1149 264–65

da Silva v Canada (Minister of Citizenship and Immigration),
2007 FC 1138... 98

Da Silva v Canada (Minister of Citizenship and Immigration),
2011 FC 347 416

Dan v Canada (Minister of Citizenship and Immigration) (2000),
189 FTR 301, 6 Imm LR (3d) 84, [2000] FCJ No 638 (TD).........................601

Danelia v Canada (Minister of Citizenship and Immigration),
2014 FC 707 324

Dang v Canada (Minister of Citizenship and Immigration),
2007 FC 15.. 102

Dash v Canada (Minister of Citizenship and Immigration),
2010 FC 1255 139

Daud v Canada (Minister of Citizenship and Immigration),
2008 FC 701... 482

De Brito v Canada (Minister of Citizenship and Immigration),
2003 FC 1379... 97

De Guzman v Canada (Minister of Citizenship and Immigration),
[1995] IADD No 1248...204–5

de Guzman v Canada (Minister of Citizenship and Immigration),
2005 FCA 436 ....42, 427

De Guzman v Canada (Minister of Citizenship and Immigration),
2004 FC 1276 209–10
De Parada v Canada (Minister of Citizenship and Immigration),
2009 FC 845 348
de Torres v Canada (Minister of Citizenship and Immigration),
2009 FC 208 382
Dehghani v Canada (Minister of Employment and Immigration),
[1993] 1 SCR 1053, 18 Imm LR (2d) 245, [1993] SCJ No 38 612,
652–53, 664
Del Cid v Canada (Minister of Citizenship and Immigration),
2006 FC 326 422
Delisa v Canada (Minister of Citizenship and Immigration),
2010 FC 88 524
Desalegn v Canada (Minister of Citizenship and Immigration),
2011 FC 268 211
Desire v Canada (Minister of Citizenship and Immigration),
2013 FC 167 .... 323, 346
Dezameau v Canada (Minister of Citizenship and Immigration),
2010 FC 559 .... 324, 347
Dhandal v Canada (Minister of Citizenship and Immigration),
2009 FC 865 97
Dhanoa v Canada (Minister of Citizenship and Immigration),
2009 FC 729 102
Dharamraj v Canada (Minister of Citizenship and Immigration),
2006 FC 674 412
Dhillon v Canada (Minister of Citizenship and Immigration),
2003 FC 1446 102
Dhillon v Canada (Minister of Citizenship and Immigration),
2009 FC 614 101
Dhondup v Canada (Minister of Citizenship and Immigration),
2011 FC 108 624
Diabate v Canada (Minister of Citizenship and Immigration),
2013 FC 129 410
Diaz v Canada (Minister of Citizenship and Immigration),
2008 FC 1243 .... 326, 343
Diaz v Canada (Minister of Citizenship and Immigration),
2011 FC 705 316
Dickenson v Law Society (Alberta) (1978), 10 AR 120,
84 DLR (3d) 189, [1978] AJ No 613 (SCTD) 34, 35
Dieujuste-Phanor v Canada (Minister of Citizenship and Immigration),
2011 FC 186 348
Divakaran v Canada (Minister of Citizenship and Immigration),
2011 FC 633 413
Djerroud v Canada (Minister of Citizenship and Immigration),
2007 FC 981 394

Djubok v Canada (Minister of Citizenship and Immigration),
2014 FC 497 324
Doré v Barreau du Quebec, 2012 SCC 12 .... 614, 646
Doumbouya v Canada (Minister of Citizenship and Immigration),
2007 FC 1186 .... 394, 409, 410
Douze v Canada (Minister of Citizenship and Immigration),
2010 FC 1337 624
Douze v Canada (Minister of Citizenship and Immigration),
2010 FC 1086 625
Dragan v Canada (Minister of Citizenship and Immigration),
2003 FCT 211 .... 623, 624
Dragosin v Canada (Minister of Citizenship and Immigration),
2003 FCT 81 .... 612, 664
Du v Canada (Minister of Citizenship and Immigration),
2012 FC 1094 .... 209, 210
Duale v Canada (Minister of Citizenship and Immigration),
2004 FC 150 269
Duda v Canada (Minister of Citizenship and Immigration),
2010 FC 512 383
Duka v Canada (Minister of Citizenship and Immigration),
2010 FC 1071 402
Dunsmuir v New Brunswick, 2008 SCC 9 .... 607, 613,
614, 616, 617, 619, 647
Duque v Canada (Minister of Citizenship and Immigration),
2007 FC 1367 422
Duraisami v Canada (Minister of Citizenship and Immigration),
2005 FC 1008 113
Duroseau v Canada (Minister of Citizenship and Immigration),
2008 FC 72 112
Dydyuk v Canada (Minister of Citizenship and Immigration),
2003 FCT 717 605

Ebonka v Canada (Minister of Citizenship and Immigration),
2009 FC 80 417
Eid v Canada (Minister of Citizenship and Immigration), 2010 FC 639 380
Ejtehadian v Canada (Minister of Citizenship and Immigration),
2007 FC 158 358
Ek v Canada (Minister of Citizenship and Immigration), 2003 FCT 526 409
El Idrissi v Canada (Minister of Citizenship and Immigration),
2005 FC 1105 528
El Kaissi v Canada (Minister of Citizenship and Immigration),
2011 FC 1234 282
El Naem v Canada (Minister of Citizenship and Immigration) (1997),
126 FTR 15, 37 Imm LR (2d) 304, [1997] FCJ No 185 (TD) 301
El Thaher v Canada (Minister of Citizenship and Immigration),
2012 FC 1439 418

Elcock v Canada (Minister of Citizenship and Immigration),
    1999 CanLII 8680 (FCTD) 337
Elemah v Canada (Minister of Citizenship and Immigration),
    2001 FCT 779 (TD) 280
Elezi v Canada (Minister of Citizenship and Immigration),
    2007 FC 240 380
Emani v Canada (Minister of Citizenship and Immigration),
    2009 FC 520 288
Eng v Canada (Minister of Citizenship and Immigration), 2014 FC 711 295
Esguerra v Canada (Minister of Citizenship and Immigration),
    2008 FC 413 154
Eslamieh v Canada (Minister of Citizenship and Immigration),
    2008 FC 722 154
Esmaeili-Tarki v Canada (Public Safety and Emergency Preparedness),
    2010 FC 697 624
Espino v Canada (Minister of Citizenship and Immigration),
    2006 FC 1255 .... 417, 418, 419
Espino v Canada (Minister of Citizenship and Immigration),
    2007 FC 74 405
*Estaban v Canada (Minister of Citizenship and Immigration). See Medovarski
    v Canada (Minister of Citizenship and Immigration)*
Evans v Canada (Minister of Citizenship and Immigration),
    2011 FC 444 55–56
Eyakwe v Canada (Minister of Citizenship and Immigration),
    2011 FC 409 478
Ezokola v Canada (Minister of Citizenship and Immigration),
    2013 SCC 40 .... 351, 353, 354–55

Faizy v Canada (Minister of Citizenship and Immigration),
    2012 FC 961 240
FAM v Canada (Minister of Citizenship and Immigration),
    2013 FC 574 267
Fan v Canada (Minister of Citizenship and Immigration),
    2004 FC 1692 364
Farenas v Canada (Minister of Citizenship and Immigration),
    2011 FC 660 501
Farhat v Canada (Minister of Citizenship and Immigration),
    2006 FC 1275 96
Fathi-Rad v Canada (Secretary of State) (1994), 77 FTR 41,
    [1994] FCJ No 506 (TD) 305
Febles v Canada (Minister of Citizenship and Immigration),
    2012 FCA 324, aff'd 2014 SCC 68 .... 351, 356, 357, 615
Feleke v Canada, 2007 FC 539 264
Felipa v Canada (Minister of Citizenship and Immigration),
    2011 FCA 272 596

Fernandez v Canada (Minister of Citizenship and Immigration),
2008 FC 243.. 154

Fernandopulle v Canada (Minister of Citizenship and Immigration),
2005 FCA 91 302

Ferraro v Canada (Minister of Citizenship and Immigration),
2011 FC 801 ....96, 404

Ferrer v Canada (Minister of Citizenship and Immigration),
2009 FC 356.. 426

Firouz-Abadi v Canada (Minister of Citizenship and Immigration),
2011 FC 835 521

Firsova v Canada (Minister of Citizenship and Immigration),
2003 FC 933..398

Fordyce v Canada (Minister of Citizenship and Immigration),
2009 FC 556..364

Fosu v Canada (Minister of Employment and Immigration) (1994),
90 FTR 182, [1994] FCJ No 1813 (TD) 312, 313

Frank v Canada (Minister of Citizenship and Immigration),
2010 FC 270 415

Frederic v Canada (Minister of Citizenship and Immigration),
2010 FC 1100 347

Fuentes v Canada (Minister of Citizenship and Immigration),
2003 FCT 379 .... 481, 482

G(DJD) v Canada (Minister of Public Safety and Emergency
Preparedness), 2010 FC 765 385

Gabriel v Canada (Minister of Citizenship and Immigration),
2009 FC 1170.. 348

Gallardo v Canada (Minister of Citizenship and Immigration),
2003 FCT 45 403

Galvan v Canada (Minister of Citizenship and Immigration) (2000),
193 FTR 161, [2000] FCJ No 442 (TD) 319, 320

Gapchenko v Canada (Minister of Citizenship and Immigration),
2004 FC 427..277, 278

Garcia v Canada (Minister of Citizenship and Immigration),
2005 FC 807.. 325

Garcia v Canada (Minister of Citizenship and Immigration),
2007 FC 79.. 337, 340

Garro v Canada (Minister of Citizenship and Immigration),
2007 FC 670.. 119

Gay v Canada (Minister of Citizenship and Immigration),
2007 FC 1280 152

Gebreab v Canada (Minister of Public Safety and Emergency
Preparedness), 2009 FC 1213 485

Gecaj v Canada (Minister of Citizenship and Immigration),
2012 FC 1369... 323

Gelaw v Canada (Minister of Citizenship and Immigration),
2010 FC 1120 422
George v Canada (Minister of Citizenship and Immigration),
2007 FC 1315 410
Ghirmatsion v Canada (Minister of Citizenship and Immigration),
2011 FC 519 239
Gil v Canada (Minister of Citizenship and Immigration) (1994),
[1995] 1 FC 508, 119 DLR (4th) 497, [1994] FCJ No 1559 (CA) 356
Gill v Canada (Minister of Citizenship and Immigration), 2008 FC 613 423
Gill v Canada (Minister of Citizenship and Immigration), 2010 FC 466 151
Gill v Canada (Minister of Employment and Immigration),
[1987] 2 FC 425 (CA) 622
Gittens v Canada (1982), [1983] 1 FC 152, 137 DLR (3d) 687,
[1982] FCJ No 86 (TD) 647
Golestaney v Canada (Minister of Citizenship and Immigration),
2005 FC 1736 453
Gomez v Canada (Minister of Citizenship and Immigration),
2010 FC 1301 409
Gondara v Canada (Minister of Citizenship and Immigration),
2006 FC 204 625
Gonzales v Canada (Minister of Citizenship and Immigration),
2002 FCT 345 320
Gonzales v Canada (Minister of Citizenship and Immigration),
2011 FC 1059 615
Gordon v Goertz, [1996] 2 SCR 27, 134 DLR (4th) 321,
1996 CanLII 191 ....67, 423
Gorzsas v Canada (Minister of Public Safety and Emergency
Preparedness), 2008 FC 1060 364
Grenier v Canada, 2005 FCA 348 630
Grewal v Canada (Minister of Citizenship and Immigration),
2011 FC 167 144
Groohi v Canada (Minister of Citizenship and Immigration),
2009 FC 837 98
Guadeloupe v Canada (Minister of Citizenship and Immigration),
2008 FC 1190 424
Guerrero v Canada (Minister of Citizenship and Immigration),
2011 FC 1210 346
Guifarro v Canada (Minister of Citizenship and Immigration),
2011 FC 182 616
Gulati v Canada (Minister of Citizenship and Immigration),
2010 FC 451 139
Gutierrez v Canada (Minister of Citizenship and Immigration),
2011 FC 1055 348
Guzman v Canada (Minister of Citizenship and Immigration),
2006 FC 1134 666

Habeeb v Canada (Minister of Citizenship and Immigration),
2011 FC 253 496
Habtenkiel v Canada (Minister of Citizenship and Immigration),
2014 FCA 180 .... 219–20, 616
Hadad v Canada (Minister of Citizenship and Immigration),
2011 FC 1503 504
Haddad v Canada (Minister of Citizenship and Immigration),
2003 FCT 405 613
Hadwani v Canada (Minister of Citizenship and Immigration),
2011 FC 888 151
Hafeez v Canada (Minister of Citizenship and Immigration),
2012 FC 747 323
Hak v Canada (Minister of Citizenship and Immigration),
2005 FC 1488 272
Hall (Litigation guardian of) v Canada (Minister of Citizenship and
Immigration), 2008 FC 865 364
Hamadi v Canada (Minister of Citizenship and Immigration),
2011 FC 317 385
Hameed v Canada (Minister of Citizenship and Immigration),
2009 FC 527 141
Hamidi v Canada (Minister of Citizenship and Immigration),
2006 FC 333 496
Hanano v Canada (Minister of Citizenship and Immigration),
2004 FC 998 624
Hanukashvili v Canada (Minister of Citizenship and Immigration)
(1997), 129 FTR 216, [1997] FCJ No 356 (TD) 310
Harinarain v Canada (Minister of Citizenship and Immigration),
2012 FC 1519 323
Hasan v Canada (Minister of Citizenship and Immigration),
2008 FC 1069 279
Hassaballa v Canada (Minister of Citizenship and Immigration),
2007 FC 489 379
Hassan v Canada (Minister of Employment and Immigration) (1994),
77 FTR 309, [1994] FCJ No 630 (TD) 280
Hausleitner v Canada (Minister of Citizenship and Immigration),
2005 FC 641 .... 380, 386
Hawthorne v Canada (Minister of Citizenship and
Immigration), 2002 FCA 475 .... 410, 422, 424, 425
He v Canada (Minister of Employment and Immigration)
(1994), 78 FTR 313, 25 Imm LR (2d) 128, [1994] FCJ No 1243 (TD) 307
Healey v Canada (Minister of Citizenship and Immigration),
2009 FC 355 142
Henguva v Canada (Minister of Citizenship and Immigration),
2013 FC 483 323

Hernandez v Canada (Minister of Citizenship and Immigration),
2004 FC 1398 152
Hernandez v Canada (Minister of Citizenship and Immigration),
2007 FC 1297 326
Hernandez v Canada (Minister of Citizenship and Immigration),
2005 FC 429 .... 537, 539–40
Hernandez v Canada (Minister of Public Safety and Emergency
Preparedness), 2012 FC 1417 364
Hilewitz v Canada (Minister of Citizenship and Immigration),
2005 SCC 57 .... 518–19, 520, 523
Hill v Canada (Minister of Employment and Immigration) (1987),
73 NR 315, 1 Imm LR (2d) 1, [1987] FCJ No 47 (CA) 499
Hillary v Canada (Minister of Citizenship and Immigration),
2011 FCA 51 269
Hinton v Canada (Minister of Citizenship and Immigration),
2008 FC 1007 601
Hinton v Canada (Minister of Citizenship and Immigration),
2008 FCA 215 628
Hinzman v Canada (Minister of Citizenship and Immigration),
2007 FCA 171, aff'g 2006 FC 420 .... 318–19, 338, 352
Hinzman v Canada (Minister of Citizenship and Immigration),
2010 FCA 177 409
Hiramen v Canada (Minister of Employment and Immigration)
(1986), 65 NR 67, [1986] FCJ No 74 (CA) 513
Ho v Canada (Minister of Employment and Immigration) (1989),
27 FTR 241, 8 Imm LR (2d) 38, [1989] FCJ No 245 (TD) 44–45
Holway v Canada (Minister of Citizenship and Immigration),
2006 FC 309 496
Hossain v Canada (Minister of Citizenship and Immigration),
2006 FC 475 519
Hu v Canada (Minister of Citizenship and Immigration),
2012 FC 544 358–59
Huang v Canada (Minister of Citizenship and Immigration),
2002 FCT 149 664
Huerta v Canada (Minister of Employment and Immigration) (1993),
157 NR 225, [1993] FCJ No 271 (CA) 300–1
Huruglica v Canada (Minister of Citizenship and
Immigration), 2014 FC 799 .... 30, 294, 295–96
Hussain v Canada (Minister of Citizenship and Immigration),
2009 FC 209 154–55
Hussain v Canada (Minister of Citizenship and Immigration),
2013 FC 636 139
Hussenu v Canada (Minister of Citizenship and Immigration),
2004 FC 283 485

Ibrahim v Canada (Minister of Citizenship and Immigration),
    2014 FC 837 379–90

Idehen v Canada (Minister of Citizenship and Immigration),
    2012 FC 1148 424
Igbinigie v Canada (Minister of Citizenship and Immigration),
    [2009] IADD No 2800 183
Ikechi v Canada (Minister of Citizenship and Immigration),
    2013 FC 361 363–64
Ikhuiwu v Canada (Minister of Citizenship and Immigration),
    2008 FC 35.. 528
Ilie v Canada (Minister of Citizenship and Immigration) (1994),
    88 FTR 220, [1994] FCJ No 1758 (TD) 300–1
Iliev v Canada (Minister of Citizenship and Immigration),
    2005 FC 395.. 285
Immeubles Port Louis Ltée v Lafontaine (Village), [1991] 1 SCR 326,
    78 DLR (4th) 175, 1991 CanLII 82 620–21
Immigration and Refugee Board of Canada, Persuasive Decision
    TA6-07453 (26 November 2007), online: IRB www.irb-cisr.gc.ca/
    Eng/BoaCom/references/pol/persuas/Pages/TA607453.aspx 333–34
Innocent v Canada (Minister of Citizenship and Immigration),
    2009 FC 1019 615
Islam v Canada (Minister of Citizenship and Immigration),
    2006 FC 424.. 144
Ismail v Canada (Minister of Citizenship and Immigration),
    2006 FC 987 496
Ismail v Canada (Minister of Citizenship and Immigration),
    2006 FCA 396.. 633
Itua v Canada (Minister of Citizenship and Immigration),
    2012 FC 631 323
Ivakhnenko v Canada (Solicitor General), 2004 FC 1249 379–80
Iyamuremye v Canada (Minister of Citizenship and Immigration),
    2014 FC 494.. 294–95

Jaballah (Re), 2010 FC 79 474
Jaballah v Canada (Minister of Citizenship and Immigration),
    2004 FCA 257.. 378
Jaber v Canada (Minister of Citizenship and Immigration),
    2013 FC 1185 .... 284, 624
Jacob v Canada (Minister of Citizenship and Immigration),
    2012 FC 1382.. 432
Jafarian v Canada (Minister of Citizenship and Immigration),
    2010 FC 40.. 519, 520
Jalil v Canada (Minister of Citizenship and Immigration),
    2007 FC 568.. 482, 487

Jalloh v Canada (Minister of Public Safety and Emergency
Preparedness), 2012 FC 317 478
Jamshedji v Canada (Minister of Citizenship and Immigration),
[2011] IADD No 2985 (CA IRB) 408
Jankovic v Canada (Minister of Citizenship and Immigration),
2003 FC 1482 209
Javed v Canada (Minister of Citizenship and Immigration),
2004 FC 1458 288
Jayasekara v Canada (Minister of Citizenship and Immigration),
2008 FCA 404 356
Jessamy v Canada (Minister of Citizenship and Immigration),
2009 FC 20 380
Jessamy v Canada (Minister of Citizenship and Immigration),
2010 FC 489 382
Jiminez v Canada (Minister of Citizenship and Immigration) (1999),
162 FTR 177, [1999] FCJ No 87 (TD) 280–81
John Doe et al v Canada, Report No 78/11, 21 July 2011 251–52
John Doe v Canada (Minister of Public Safety and Emergency
Preparedness), 2006 FC 535 632
John Doe v Canada, Case P-554-04, Report No 121/06 Inter-Am
CHR OEA/Ser.L/V/II.127 Doc 4 rev 1 (2007) 68
John v Canada (Minister of Citizenship and Immigration),
2006 FC 1422 417–18
John v Canada (Minister of Citizenship and Immigration),
2010 FC 85 415–16
John v Rees, [1970] Ch 345 543
Johnson v Canada (Minister of Citizenship and Immigration),
2005 FC 1262 632
Johnson v Canada (Minister of Citizenship and Immigration),
2008 FC 2 .... 428, 430, 507
Josile v Canada (Minister of Citizenship and Immigration),
2011 FC 39 347–48
Judnarine v Canada (Minister of Citizenship and Immigration),
2013 FC 82 410

Kaba v Canada (Minister of Citizenship and Immigration),
2007 FC 647 380
Kaberuka v Canada (Minister of Citizenship and Immigration),
[1995] 3 FC 252, 32 Imm LR (2d) 38, [1995] FCJ No 1093 (TD) 385
Kabeya v Canada (Minister of Citizenship and Immigration),
2012 FC 697 363–64
Kablawi v Canada (Minister of Citizenship and Immigration),
2010 FC 888 480
Kadenko v Canada (Minister of Citizenship and Immigration)
(1996), 143 DLR (4th) 532, 206 NR 272, [1996] FCJ
No 1376 (CA) 337, 340

Kadjo v Canada (Minister of Citizenship and Immigration),
2010 FC 1050 386
Kakonyi v Canada (Minister of Public Safety and Emergency
Preparedness), 2008 FC 1410 388
Kalachnikov v Canada (Minister of Citizenship and Immigration),
2003 FCT 777 624
Kalicharan v Canada (Minister of Manpower and Immigration),
[1976] 2 FC 123, 67 DLR (3d) 555, [1976] FCJ No 21 (TD) 622
Kalonzo v Canada, Decision, Committee Against Torture,
Communication No 343/2008: Decision adopted by the
Committee at its forty-eighth session (7 May to 1 June 2012)
CAT, 48th Sess, UN Doc CAT/C/48/D/343/2008, online:
www.ohchr.org/Documents/HRBodies/CAT/Jurisprudence/
CAT-C-48-D-343-2008_en.pdf 670
Kamana v Canada (Minister of Citizenship and Immigration),
[1999] FCJ No 1695 (TD) 300
Kambo v Canada (Minister of Citizenship and Immigration),
2012 FC 872 .... 431, 609
Kamel v Canada (AG), 2009 FCA 21, rev'g 2008 FC 338 .... 458, 459
Kamel v Canada (AG), 2011 FC 1061 .... 459, 460
Kanapathy v Canada (Minister of Public Safety and Emergency
Preparedness), 2012 FC 459 .... 485, 489
Kandasamy v Canada (Minister of Citizenship and Immigration),
2011 FC 716 366
Kanendra v Canada (Minister of Citizenship and Immigration),
2005 FC 923 485
Kaniz v Canada (Minister of Citizenship and Immigration),
2013 FC 63 323
Kanthasamy v Canada (Minister of Citizenship and
Immigration), 2013 FC 802, aff'd 2014 FCA 113 .... 57, 410, 397, 411, 412
Katkova v Canada (Minister of Citizenship and
Immigration) (1997), 130 FTR 192, 40 Imm LR (2d) 216,
[1997] FCJ No 549 (TD) 330, 331
Katwaru v Canada (Minister of Citizenship and Immigration),
2007 FC 612 .... 310, 339, 340
Kaur v Canada (Minister of Citizenship and Immigration),
2010 FC 442 146
Kaur v Canada (Minister of Citizenship and Immigration),
2011 FC 219 .... 105, 106
Kaur v Canada (Minister of Citizenship and Immigration),
2012 FC 964 416
Kawtharani v Canada (Minister of Citizenship and Immigration),
2006 FC 162 418
Kaybaki v Canada (Solicitor General of Canada), 2004 FC 32 373

Kazkan v Canada (Minister of Citizenship and Immigration),
      [1997] FCJ No 321 (TD) 313
Key v Canada (Minister of Citizenship and Immigration),
      2008 FC 838 318
Key v Canada (Minister of Citizenship and Immigration),
      2011 FC 92 601
Kha v Canada (Minister of Employment and Immigration) (1986),
      5 FTR 150, [1986] FCJ No 501 (TD) 43
Khadr v Canada (AG), 2006 FC 727 458
Khan v Canada (Minister of Citizenship and Immigration),
      2005 FC 833 278
Khan v Canada (Minister of Citizenship and Immigration),
      2005 FC 1053 481
Khan v Canada (Minister of Citizenship and Immigration),
      2008 FC 512 527
Khan v Canada (Minister of Citizenship and Immigration),
      2011 FCA 339 ....142, 615
Kharchi v Canada (Minister of Citizenship and Immigration),
      2006 FC 1160 ....499, 500
Kharrat v Canada (Minister of Citizenship and Immigration),
      2007 FC 842 429
Khatoon v Canada (Minister of Citizenship and Immigration),
      2008 FC 276 102
Kidane v Canada (Minister of Citizenship and Immigration),
      2011 FC 520 239
Kikeshian v Canada (Minister of Citizenship and Immigration),
      2011 FC 658 157
Kim v Canada (Minister of Citizenship and Immigration),
      2005 FC 1357 432
Kim v Canada (Minister of Citizenship and Immigration),
      2005 FC 437 388
Kim v Canada (Minister of Citizenship and Immigration),
      2010 FC 720 332
Kimotho v Canada (Minister of Citizenship and Immigration),
      2005 FC 1004 424
Kindie v Canada (Minister of Citizenship and Immigration),
      2011 FC 850 ....101, 102
Kindler v Canada (Minister of Justice), [1991] 2 SCR 779,
      84 DLR (4th) 438, [1991] SCJ No 63 639
Kirec v Canada (Minister of Citizenship and Immigration),
      2006 FC 800 517
Kisana v Canada (Minister of Citizenship and Immigration),
      2009 FCA 189 ....422, 423, 428
Klinko v Canada (Minister of Citizenship and Immigration),
      [2000] 3 FC 327, 184 DLR (4th) 14, [2000] FCJ No 228 (CA) 314

Kniazeva v Canada (Minister of Citizenship and Immigration),
2006 FC 268 146
Kobita v Canada (Minister of Citizenship and Immigration),
2012 FC 1479 425
Kok v Canada (Minister of Citizenship and Immigration),
2005 FC 77 504
Kolosovs v Canada (Minister of Citizenship and Immigration),
2008 FC 165 .... 422, 424
Komahe v Canada (Minister of Citizenship and Immigration),
2006 FC 1521 382
Komolafe v Canada (Minister of Citizenship and Immigration),
2013 FC 431 618
Koo v 5220459 Manitoba Inc, 2010 MBQB 132 116
Koo v Canada (Minister of Citizenship and Immigration),
2008 FC 931 .... 526, 527
Koromila v Canada (Minister of Citizenship and Immigration),
2009 FC 393 416
Kotai v Canada (Minister of Citizenship and Immigration),
2013 FC 412 256
Kotorri v Canada (Minister of Citizenship and Immigration),
2005 FC 1195 281
Kouka v Canada (Minister of Citizenship and Immigration),
2006 FC 1236 330
Kovacs v Canada (Minister of Citizenship and Immigration),
2010 FC 1003 283
Krishnamoorthy v Canada (Minister of Citizenship and Immigration),
2005 FC 237 288
Krishnamoorthy v Canada (Minister of Citizenship and Immigration),
2011 FC 1342 485
Krishnapillai v Canada (Minister of Citizenship and Immigration),
2001 FCA 378 603
Krotov v Canada (Minister of Citizenship and Immigration),
2005 FC 438 404
Kuewor v Canada (Minister of Citizenship and Immigration),
2010 FC 707 98
Kuhathasan v Canada (Minister of Citizenship and Immigration),
2008 FC 457 402
Kulla v Canada (Minister of Citizenship and Immigration),
2000 CanLII 16014 (FC) 280
Kumar v Canada (Minister of Citizenship and Immigration),
2011 FC 770 155
Kumarasamy v Canada (Minister of Citizenship and Immigration),
2008 FC 597 .... 383, 384
Kwon v Canada (Minister of Citizenship and Immigration),
2012 FC 50 .... 421, 424

Lai v Canada (Minister of Citizenship and Immigration),
    2007 FC 361 378
Lak v Canada (Minister of Citizenship and Immigration),
    2007 FC 350 142
Lalane v Canada (Minister of Citizenship and Immigration),
    2009 FC 6 419
Lamme v Canada (Minister of Citizenship and Immigration),
    2005 FC 1336 268–69
Langner v Canada (Minister of Employment and Immigration)
    (1994), 98 FTR 188, [1994] FCJ No 1287 (TD), aff'd (1995),
    184 NR 230, 29 CRR (2d) 184, [1995] FCJ No 469 (CA),
    leave to appeal to SCC refused, [1995] SCCA No 241 643
Latif v Canada (Minister of Citizenship and Immigration), 2009 FC 63 323
Latifi v Canada (Minister of Citizenship and Immigration),
    2007 FC 338 417
Latrache v Canada (Minister of Citizenship and Immigration) (2001),
    201 FTR 234, [2001] FCJ No 154 (TD) 453
Lavoie v Canada, 2002 SCC 23 85
Law Society of British Columbia v Andrews, [1989] 1 SCR 143,
    56 DLR (4th) 1, 1989 CanLII 2 .... 413, 457
Law Society of British Columbia v Mangat, 2001 SCC 67 .... 36, 37
Lawrence v Canada (Minister of Citizenship and Immigration),
    2012 FC 1523 521
Lazareva v Canada (Minister of Citizenship and Immigration),
    2005 FCA 181 633
Lee v Canada (Minister of Citizenship and Immigration),
    2006 FC 1461 .... 96, 519
Lee v Canada (Minister of Citizenship and Immigration),
    2008 FC 614 84
Legault v Canada (Minister of Citizenship and Immigration),
    2002 FCA 125 .... 420, 422
Legnin v Canada (Minister of Citizenship and Immigration),
    2013 FC 869 570
Lemus v Canada (Minister of Citizenship and Immigration),
    2014 FCA 114 .... 612, 619
Lennikov v Canada (Minister of Citizenship and Immigration),
    2007 FC 43 477
Leobrera v Canada (Minister of Citizenship and Immigration),
    2010 FC 587 .... 410, 423
Leroux v Canada (Citizenship and Immigration), 2007 FC 403 194
Level v Canada (Minister of Citizenship and Immigration),
    2010 FC 251 602
Li v Canada (Minister of Citizenship and Immigration) (1996),
    [1997] 1 FC 235, 34 Imm LR (2d) 109, [1996] FCJ No 1060 (CA) 500

Li v Canada (Minister of Citizenship and Immigration),
2004 FCA 267 598
Li v Canada (Minister of Citizenship and Immigration), 2005 FCA 1 346
Li v Canada (Minister of Citizenship and Immigration),
2008 FC 1284 99
Li v Canada (Minister of Citizenship and Immigration),
2009 FC 623, rev'd 2010 FCA 75, leave to appeal to SCC refused,
[2010] SCCA No 183 387
Li v Canada (Minister of Citizenship and Immigration), 2012 FC 484 101
Li v Canada (Minister of Citizenship and Immigration), 2012 FC 998 358
Li v Canada (Minister of Citizenship and Immigration), 2014 FC 811 343
Liang v Canada (Minister of Citizenship and Immigration),
2013 FC 765 323
Liban v Canada (Minister of Citizenship and Immigration),
2008 FC 1252 385
Lim v Canada (Minister of Citizenship and Immigration), 2005 FC 657 106
Lin v Canada (Minister of Citizenship and Immigration), 2014 FC 746 305
Lin v Canada (Minister of Public Safety and Emergency Preparedness),
2011 FC 771 379
Lindao v Canada (Minister of Citizenship and Immigration),
[2008] IADD No 1108 192–93
Lopez Espinoza v Canada (Citizenship and Immigration),
2012 FC 502 73
Lount Corp v Canada (AG) (1983), [1984] 1 FC 332, 2 DLR (4th) 723,
[1983] FCJ No 137 (TD) 628
Loveridge v Canada (Minister of Citizenship and Immigration),
2011 FC 694 103
Lovo v Canada (Minister of Citizenship and Immigration) (1995),
102 FTR 211, 30 Imm LR (2d) 308, [1995] FCJ No 1237 (TD) 415
Luc v Canada (Minister of Citizenship and Immigration), 2010 FC 826 347
Lutfi v Canada (Minister of Citizenship and Immigration),
2005 FC 1391 496

M v H, [1999] 2 SCR 3, 171 DLR (4th) 577, [1999] SCJ No 23 191
Ma v Canada (Minister of Citizenship and Immigration),
2009 FC 1042 522
Mabrouki v Canada (Minister of Citizenship and Immigration),
2003 FC 1104 631
Machado v Canada (Minister of Citizenship and Immigration) (1996),
33 Imm LR (2d) 121, [1996] IADD No 166 649
Mafwala v Canada (Minister of Citizenship and Immigration),
2009 CanLII 77783 (CA IRB) 209
Magtibay v Canada (Minister of Citizenship and Immigration),
2005 FC 397 .... 185, 501
Mai v Canada (Minister of Citizenship and Immigration),
2010 FC 192 349

Majoros v Canada (Minister of Citizenship and Immigration),
2013 FC 421 .... 335–36, 338, 339

Maleki v Canada (Minister of Citizenship and Immigration),
2012 FC 131 478

Malette v Canada (Minister of Citizenship and Immigration),
2005 FC 1400 271

Mancia v Canada (Minister of Citizenship and Immigration),
[1998] 3 FC 461, 45 Imm LR (2d) 131, 1998 CanLII 9066 (CA) 383–84

Mand v Canada (Minister of Citizenship and Immigration),
2005 FC 1637 528

Mangru v Canada (Minister of Citizenship and Immigration),
2011 FC 779 425

Mannan v Canada (Minister of Employment & Immigration) (1991),
48 FTR 259, 16 Imm LR (2d) 73, [1991] FCJ No 1009 (TD) 9

Marr v Canada (Minister of Citizenship and Immigration),
2011 FC 367 142

Marshall v Canada, 2002 FCT 1099 631

Martinez v Canada (Public Safety and Emergency Preparedness),
2013 FC 1256 570

Maruquin v Canada (Minister of Citizenship and Immigration),
2007 FC 1349 527

Mason v Canada (Secretary of State), [1995] FCJ No 815 (TD) 320

Matondo v Canada (Minister of Citizenship and Immigration),
2005 FC 416 288

Matthias v Canada (Minister of Citizenship and Immigration),
2014 FC 1053 410

Mazhari v Canada (Minister of Citizenship and Immigration),
2010 FC 467 521

McAteer v Canada (AG), 2013 ONSC 5895 454

McHugh v Canada (Minister of Citizenship and Immigration),
2006 FC 1181 145

McLachlan v Canada (Minister of Citizenship and Immigration),
2009 FC 975 .... 142, 150

Medovarski v Canada (Minister of Citizenship and Immigration);
Esteban v Canada (Minister of Citizenship and Immigration),
2005 SCC 51 .... 3, 27,
43–44, 472, 484, 655, 656

Mekonen v Canada (Minister of Citizenship and Immigration),
2007 FC 1133 481

Melchor v Canada (Minister of Citizenship and Immigration),
2004 FC 1327 412

Melendez v Canada (Minister of Citizenship and Immigration),
2014 FC 700 .... 316, 348

Melius v Canada (Minister of Citizenship and Immigration),
2013 FC 537 323

Mendivil v Canada (Secretary of State) (1994), 167 NR 91,
    23 Imm LR (2d) 225, [1994] FCJ No 2021 (CA) 337
Mervilus v Canada (Minister of Citizenship and Immigration),
    2004 FC 1206 271
Mezbani v Canada (Minister of Citizenship and Immigration),
    2012 FC 1115 240
Michel v Canada (Minister of Citizenship and Immigration),
    2010 FC 159 .... 347, 348
Mileva v Canada (Minister of Employment and Immigration),
    [1991] 3 FC 398, 81 DLR (4th) 244, [1991] FCJ No 79 (CA) 279
Miller v Canada (AG), 2002 FCA 370 73
Mina v Canada (Minister of Citizenship and Immigration),
    2010 FC 1182 602
Minhas v Canada (Minister of Citizenship and Immigration),
    2009 FC 696 101
Moghaddam v Canada (Minister of Citizenship and Immigration),
    2004 FC 680 103
Mohamed v Canada (Minister of Employment and Immigration),
    [1986] 3 FC 90, 68 NR 220, [1986] FCJ No 1054 (CA) 524
Mohammadian v Canada (Minister of Citizenship and Immigration),
    [2000] 3 FC 371, 185 FTR 144, [2000] FCJ No 309 (TD),
    aff'd 2001 FCA 191 269
Mohiuddin v Canada (Minister of Citizenship and Immigration),
    2010 FC 51 482
Molnar v Canada (Minister of Citizenship and Immigration),
    2002 FCT 1081 337
Molnar v Canada (Minister of Citizenship and Immigration),
    2012 FC 577 364
Momcilovic v Canada (Minister of Citizenship and Immigration),
    2005 FC 79 421
Momi v Canada (Minister of Citizenship and Immigration),
    2013 FC 162 101
Monemi v Canada (Solicitor General), 2004 FC 1648 612–13
Monge Monge v Canada (Minister of Public Safety and Emergency
    Preparedness), 2009 FC 809 540–41
Montchak v Canada (Minister of Citizenship and Immigration),
    [1999] FCJ No 1111 (TD) 320
Montoya v Canada (Minister of Citizenship and Immigration),
    2014 FC 808 329
Moreno v Canada (Minister of Employment and Immigration) (1993),
    [1994] 1 FC 298, 107 DLR (4th) 424, [1993] FCJ No 912 (CA) 352
Morgan v Prince Edward Island (AG), [1976] 2 SCR 349,
    55 DLR (3d) 527, [1975] SCJ No 82 .... 34, 35
Moumaev v Canada (Minister of Citizenship and Immigration),
    2007 FC 718 378

Moya v Canada (Minister of Citizenship and Immigration),
    2012 FC 971 421
Mugasera v Canada (Minister of Citizenship and Immigration),
    2005 SCC 40 .... 352, 353
Muhazi v Canada (Minister of Citizenship and Immigration),
    2004 FC 1392..239–40
Mukamutara v Canada (Minister of Citizenship and Immigration),
    2008 FC 451... 526
Mumuni v Canada (Minister of Citizenship and Immigration),
    2006 FC 1407..321
Munganza v Canada (Minister of Citizenship and Immigration),
    2008 FC 1250 209
Munoz v Canada (Minister of Citizenship and Immigration),
    2010 FC 238..348
Murad v Canada (Minister of Citizenship and Immigration),
    2013 FC 1089.. 625
Murai v Canada (Minister of Citizenship and Immigration),
    2006 FC 186 .... 100, 102
Murillo v Canada (Minister of Citizenship and Immigration),
    2008 FC 966 351
Mushimiyimana v Canada (Minister of Citizenship and Immigration),
    2010 FC 1124 240
Musleameen v Canada (Minister of Citizenship and Immigration),
    2010 FC 232... 323

Naeem v Canada (Minister of Citizenship and Immigration),
    2007 FC 123..482
Naeem v Canada (Minister of Citizenship and Immigration),
    2010 FC 1069 480
Nagalingam v Canada (Minister of Public Safety and Emergency
    Preparedness), 2012 FC 362.. 622
Nagalingam v Canada (Public Safety and Emergency Preparedness),
    2012 FC 1411 541
Najafi v Canada (Minister of Public Safety and Emergency Preparedness).
    See Najafi v Canada (Public Safety and Emergency Preparedness)
Najafi v Canada (Public Safety and Emergency Preparedness),
    2013 FC 876 .... 478, 649
Nakane, Re (1908), 13 BCR 370, [1908] BCJ No 15 (CA) 32–33
Nalliah v Canada (Solicitor General), 2004 FC 1649 ....362, 391
Narain Singh, Re (1908), 13 BCR 477, [1908] BCJ No 33 (CA) 16, 33
Narvaez v Canada (Minister of Citizenship and Immigration),
    [1995] 2 FC 55, 28 Imm LR (2d) 170, [1995] FCJ No 219 (TD) 324
Nathoo v Canada (Minister of Citizenship and Immigration),
    2007 FC 818.. 154–55
Nayyar v Canada (Minister of Citizenship and Immigration),
    2007 FC 199... 154

Ndererehe v Canada (Minister of Citizenship and Immigration),
2007 FC 880 632
Nel v Canada (Minister of Citizenship and Immigration),
2014 FC 842 301
Németh v Canada, 2010 SCC 56 511
Newfoundland and Labrador Nurses Union v Newfoundland and
Labrador (Treasury Board), 2011 SCC 62 .... 142, 617
Newton-Juliard v Canada (Minister of Citizenship and Immigration),
2006 FC 177 522
Nezam v Canada (Minister of Citizenship and Immigration),
2005 FC 446 496
Nguyen v Canada (Minister of Citizenship and Immigration),
2010 FC 30 501
Nguyen v Canada (Minister of Employment and Immigration),
[1993] 1 FC 696, 18 Imm LR (2d) 165, [1993] FCJ No 47 (CA) 652
Ning v Canada (Minister of Citizenship and Immigration) (2000),
194 FTR 63, 8 Imm LR (3d) 44, [2000] FCJ No 1545 (TD) 621–22
Nintawat v Canada (Minister of Citizenship and Immigration),
2012 FC 66 619
Njeukam v Canada (Citizenship and Immigration), 2014 FC 859 296
Nkunzimana v Canada (Minister of Citizenship and Immigration),
2014 FC 736 630
Noh v Canada (Minister of Citizenship and Immigration), 2012 FC 529 417
Norman v Canada (Minister of Citizenship and Immigration)
2002 FCT 1169 145
Nsende v Canada (Minister of Citizenship and Immigration),
2008 FC 531 281
Nyathi v Canada (Minister of Citizenship and Immigration),
2003 FC 1119 346

Obeng v Canada (Minister of Citizenship and Immigration),
2008 FC 754 97–98
Oberlander v Canada (AG) (2004), 69 OR (3d) 187, [2004] OTC 16,
[2004] OJ No 34 (SCJ) 462
Obot v Canada (Minister of Citizenship and Immigration),
2012 FC 208 100
Odewole v Canada (Minister of Citizenship and Immigration),
2008 FC 697 103
Odia v Canada (Minister of Citizenship and Immigration),
2014 FC 663 324
Odicho v Canada (Minister of Citizenship and Immigration),
2008 FC 1039 427
Ogbonnaya v Canada (Minister of Citizenship and Immigration),
2008 FC 317 100
Ogunfowora v Canada (Minister of Citizenship and Immigration),
2007 FC 471 102–3

Okoli v Canada (Minister of Citizenship and Immigration),
2009 FC 332.. 325, 343
Okoye v Canada (Minister of Citizenship and Immigration),
2008 FC 1133..424, 425
Omer v Canada (Minister of Citizenship and Immigration),
2007 FC 478...480
Onyeka v Canada (Minister of Citizenship and Immigration),
2009 FC 336.. 101, 102
Ore v Canada (Minister of Citizenship and Immigration),
2014 FC 642...348
Oremade v Canada (Minister of Citizenship and Immigration),
2005 FC 1077... 479
Ormankaya v Canada (Minister of Citizenship and Immigration),
2010 FC 1089 379
Orozco v Canada (Minister of Citizenship and Immigration),
2006 FC 1426...380
Osagie v Canada (Minister of Citizenship and Immigration),
2004 FC 1368 288
Oshurova v Canada (Minister of Citizenship and Immigration),
2006 FCA 301 404
Osorio v Canada (Minister of Citizenship and Immigration),
2005 FC 1459..348
Osorio v Canada (Minister of Citizenship and Immigration),
2012 FC 882 148
Ousmer v Canada (Minister of Citizenship and Immigration),
2012 FC 222..323
Owusu v Canada (Minister of Citizenship and Immigration),
2003 FCT 94, aff'd 2004 FCA 38.. 403, 422

Pacia v Canada (Minister of Citizenship and Immigration),
2008 FC 804 412
Padda v Canada (Minister of Citizenship and Immigration),
2006 FC 995 601
Paramasivam v Canada (Minister of Citizenship and Immigration),
2010 FC 811 100
Parmar v Canada (Minister of Citizenship and Immigration),
2010 FC 723 519
Patel v Canada (Minister of Citizenship and Immigration),
2006 FC 224.. 102–3
Patel v Canada (Minister of Citizenship and Immigration),
2009 FC 602 105
Patel v Canada (Minister of Citizenship and Immigration),
2011 FCA 187 615
Paul v Canada (Minister of Citizenship and Immigration),
2013 FC 1081 409

Pearce v Canada (Minister of Citizenship and Immigration),
2006 FC 492 287

Peer v Canada (Minister of Citizenship and Immigration),
2010 FC 752 477

Persaud v Canada (Minister of Citizenship and Immigration),
2011 FC 31 543

Peter v Canada (Minister of Public Safety and Emergency
Preparedness), 2014 FC 1073 .... 372, 392

Philbean v Canada (Minister of Citizenship and Immigration),
2011 FC 487 154

Phillip v Canada (Minister of Citizenship and Immigration),
2008 FC 19 403

Pineda v Canada (Minister of Citizenship and Immigration),
2011 FC 81 326

Pinter v Canada (Minister of Citizenship and Immigration),
2005 FC 296 412

Pizarro v Canada (Minister of Employment and Immigration) (1994),
75 FTR 120, [1994] FCJ No 320 (TD) 326

Pokhan v Canada (Minister of Citizenship and Immigration),
2012 FC 1453 424

Ponniah v Canada (Minister of Employment and Immigration) (1991),
132 NR 32, 13 Imm LR (2d) 241, [1991] FCJ No 359 (CA) 302

Porteous v Canada (Minister of Citizenship and Immigration),
[2004] IADD No 560 194

Portillo v Canada (Minister of Citizenship and Immigration),
2012 FC 678 .... 347, 615

Poshteh v Canada (Minister of Citizenship and Immigration),
2005 FCA 85 .... 484, 486,
489, 490, 511, 529, 530

Pramauntanyath v Canada (Minister of Citizenship and Immigration),
2005 FC 604 417

Prata v Canada (Minister of Manpower & Immigration) (1975),
[1976] 1 SCR 376, 52 DLR (3d) 383, [1975] SCJ No 38 8

Prieto v Canada (Minister of Citizenship and Immigration),
2010 FC 253 .... 364, 385

Profirio v Canada (Minister of Citizenship and Immigration),
2011 FC 794 148

Prophète v Canada (Minister of Citizenship and Immigration),
2009 FCA 31 .... 347, 348

Psychologist "Y" v Nova Scotia Board of Examiners in Psychology,
2005 NSCA 116 622

Puerta v Canada (Minister of Citizenship and Immigration),
2010 FC 464 385

Pushpanathan v Canada (Minister of Citizenship and
    Immigration), [1998] 1 SCR 982, 43 Imm LR (2d) 117,
    1998 CanLII 778 .... 351, 355, 357

Qin v Canada (Minister of Citizenship and Immigration),
    2013 FCA 263 616
Qu v Canada (Minister of Citizenship and Immigration),
    [2000] 4 FC 71, 5 Imm LR (3d) 129, [2000] FCJ No 518 (TD),
    rev'd 2001 FCA 399 477
Quiroa v Canada (Minister of Citizenship and Immigration),
    2007 FC 495 394
Quiroga v Canada (Minister of Citizenship and Immigration),
    2006 FC 1306 380

R v A, [1990] 1 SCR 992, 55 CCC (3d) 570, 1990 CanLII 101 640
R v Appulonappa, 2013 BCSC 31, rev'd 2014 BCCA 163,
    leave to appeal to SCC granted, [2014] SCCA No 283 .... 588, 589, 660
R v Drybones (1969), [1970] SCR 282, 9 DLR (3d) 473,
    [1969] SCJ No 83 667
R v Governor of Pentonville Prison, [1973] 2 All ER 741,
    [1973] 2 WLR 949 (CA) 8, 473
R v Hape, 2007 SCC 26 .... 69, 640, 641, 642
R v Heywood, [1994] 3 SCR 761, 120 DLR (4th) 348,
    [1994] SCJ No 101 660
R v Hinse, [1995] 4 SCR 597, 130 DLR (4th) 54, [1995] SCJ No 97 634
R v Khawaja, 2010 ONCA 862 481
R v Nova Scotia Pharmaceutical Society, [1992] 2 SCR 606,
    93 DLR (4th) 36, 1992 CanLII 72 661
R v Oakes, [1986] 1 SCR 103, 26 DLR (4th) 200, 1986 CanLII 46 .... 646, 647
R v Tremblay, 2004 FCA 172 629
R v Turpin, [1989] 1 SCR 1296, 48 CCC (3d) 8, [1989] SCJ No 47 634
Rabeya v Canada (Minister of Citizenship and Immigration),
    2011 FC 370 142
Rabiee v Canada (Minister of Citizenship and Immigration),
    2011 FC 824 141
Radics v Canada (Minister of Citizenship and Immigration),
    2004 FC 1590 .... 100, 106
Rafieyan v Canada (Minister of Citizenship and Immigration),
    2007 FC 727 402
Rahman v Canada (Minister of Citizenship and Immigration),
    2006 FC 1321 183
Rai v Canada (Minister of Citizenship and Immigration),
    2007 FC 12 612–13
Rajpaul v Canada (Minister of Employment and Immigration),
    [1988] 3 FC 157, 5 Imm LR (2d) 97, [1988] FCJ No 455 (CA) 668
Raju v Canada (Minister of Citizenship and Immigration),
    2013 FC 848 323

Rajudeen v Canada (Minister of Employment and Immigration)
(1984), 55 NR 129, [1984] FCJ No 601 (CA) 309
Ramadan v Canada (Minister of Citizenship and Immigration),
2010 FC 1093 350
Ramanathan v Canada (Minister of Citizenship and Immigration),
2008 FC 843 383
Ramirez v Canada (Minister of Citizenship and Immigration),
2006 FC 1404 412
Ramirez v Canada (Minister of Employment and
Immigration), [1992] 2 FC 306, 89 DLR (4th) 173,
[1992] FCJ No 109 (CA) 353–54, 355
Ramsawak v Canada (Minister of Citizenship and Immigration),
2009 FC 636 414
Randhawa v Canada (Minister of Citizenship and Immigration),
2006 FC 1294 114
Ranganathan v Canada (Minister of Citizenship and Immigration)
(2000), [2001] 2 FC 164, [2000] FCJ No 2118 (CA) 343
Ranji v Canada (Minister of Public Safety and Emergency Preparedness),
2008 FC 521 425
Rasaratnam v Canada (Minister of Employment and Immigration)
(1991), [1992] 1 FC 706, 140 NR 138, [1991] FCJ No 1256 (CA) 342, 611
Rashid v Canada (Minister of Citizenship and Immigration),
2010 FC 157 520
Rathinasigngam v Canada (Minister of Citizenship and Immigration),
2006 FC 988 357
Raza v Canada (Minister of Citizenship and Immigration),
2007 FCA 385 291–92,
293, 373, 380, 386
Re Almrei, 2009 FC 1263 .... 474, 483, 577, 583
Re Drinnan, [1982] FCJ No 709 (TD) 460
Re Hokayem (1990), 37 FTR 49, [1990] FCJ No 828 (TD) 452
Re Jaballah, 2006 FC 1230 375
Re Koo (1992), [1993] 1 FC 286, 19 Imm LR (2d) 1,
1992 CanLII 2417 (TD) 446
Re Petti, [1994] FCJ No 558 (TD) 450
Re Pourghasemi (1993), 62 FTR 122, 19 Imm LR (2d) 259,
[1993] FCJ No 232 (TD) 446
Re R(UW), [1991] CRDD No 501 (IRB) 326
Re Weiss, [1998] FCJ No 123 (TD) 452
Re Zündel, 2005 FC 295 .... 483, 485
Re: Sound v Fitness Industry Council of Canada, 2014 FCA 48 609
Rebmann v Canada (Solicitor General), 2005 FC 310 103
Redlin v University of Alberta (1980), 23 AR 31, 110 DLR (3d) 146,
[1980] AJ No 867 (CA) 34, 35
Revich v Canada (Minister of Citizenship and Immigration),
2004 FC 1064 277–78

Revolorio v Canada (Minister of Citizenship and Immigration),
2008 FC 1404 282
Ribic v Canada (Minister of Employment and Immigration),
[1985] IABD No 4 (CA IRB) 379, 564
RJR-MacDonald Inc v Canada (AG), [1994] 1 SCR 311,
111 DLR (4th) 385, 1994 CanLII 117 631
RJR-MacDonald Inc v Canada (AG), [1995] 3 SCR 199,
127 DLR (4th) 1, 1995 CanLII 64 .... 646, 647
Roach v Canada (Minister of State for Multiculturalism and
Culture) (1992), 53 FTR 241, 88 DLR (4th) 225, [1992] FCJ
No. 32 (TD), aff'd [1994] 2 FC 406, 23 Imm LR (2d) 1,
[1994] FCJ No 33 (CA) 453–54
Roach v Ontario (AG), 2012 ONSC 3521 454
Roberto v Canada (Minister of Citizenship and Immigration),
2009 FC 180 380
Robertson v Canada (Minister of Citizenship and Immigration),
2002 FCT 763 403
Robles v Canada (Minister of Citizenship and Immigration),
2003 FCT 374 272
Rodgers v Canada (Minister of Citizenship and Immigration),
2006 FC 1093 96
Rodrigues v Canada (Minister of Citizenship and Immigration),
2009 FC 111 145
Romero v Canada (Minister of Citizenship and Immigration),
2014 FC 671 279
Roncarelli v Duplessis, [1959] SCR 121, 16 DLR (2d) 689,
1959 CanLII 50 25
Rosenberry v Canada (Minister of Citizenship and Immigration),
2012 FC 521 431
Rousseau v Canada (Minister of Citizenship and Immigration),
2004 FC 602 625
RPD File No MB3-01312, [2013] RPDD No 11 281
RSM v Canada, Communication No 392/2009 CAT/C/50/D/392/2009 66
Rudder v Canada (Minister of Citizenship and Immigration),
2009 FC 689 98
Rudi v Canada (Minister of Citizenship and Immigration), 2003 FC 957 240
Ruparel v Canada (Minister of Employment and Immigration),
[1990] 3 FC 615, 11 Imm LR (2d) 190, [1990] FCJ No 701 (TD) 638

Sabour v Canada (Minister of Citizenship and Immigration) (2000),
195 FTR 69, 9 Imm LR (3d) 61, [2000] FCJ No 1615 (TD) 352
Sahakyan v Canada (Minister of Citizenship and Immigration),
2004 FC 1542 534–35
Sahin v Canada (Minister of Citizenship and Immigration) (1994),
[1995] 1 FC 214, 30 Imm LR (2d) 33, [1994] FCJ No 1534 (TD) 553–54

Sahota v Canada (Citizenship and Immigration),
2008 CanLII 45193 (CA IRB) 185
Sahota v Canada (Minister of Citizenship and Immigration),
2007 FC 651 412
Saifee v Canada (Minister of Citizenship and Immigration),
2010 FC 589 240
Salahaldin v Canada (Minister of Citizenship and Immigration),
2014 FC 51 496
Salcedo v Canada (Minister of Citizenship and Immigration),
2014 FC 822 306
Saleh v Canada (Minister of Citizenship and Immigration),
2005 FC 1074 266
Saleh v Canada (Minister of Citizenship and Immigration),
2010 FC 303 485
Saleh v Canada (Minister of Employment and Immigration),
[1989] FCJ No 825 (TD) 602
Saliaj v Canada (Minister of Citizenship and Immigration),
2004 FC 499 425
Salibian v Canada (Minister of Employment and Immigration),
[1990] 3 FC 250, 73 DLR (4th) 551, [1990] FCJ No 454 (CA).....301, 308, 347
Salvagno v Canada (Minister of Citizenship and Immigration),
2011 FC 595 616
Samimifar v Canada (Minister of Citizenship and Immigration),
2006 FC 1301 .... 629, 630
Sanchez v Canada (Minister of Citizenship and Immigration),
2007 FCA 99 346
Sanchez v Canada (Minister of Citizenship and Immigration),
2009 FC 101 ....382, 391
Sandhu v Canada (Minister of Citizenship and Immigration),
2010 FC 759 .... 139, 152
Sandramoorthy v Canada (Minister of Citizenship and Immigration),
2011 FC 358 432
Sandy Bay Ojibway First Nation v Canada (Minister of Citizenship and
Immigration), 2006 FC 903 78
Sapru v Canada (Minister of Citizenship and Immigration),
2011 FCA 35 .... 519, 521
Saravia v Canada (Minister of Citizenship and Immigration),
2005 FC 1296 269
Sarkar v Canada (Minister of Citizenship and Immigration),
2006 FC 1556 519
Sarmis v Canada (Minister of Citizenship and Immigration),
2004 FC 110 600
Savunthararasa v Canada (Minister of Public Safety and
Emergency Preparedness), 2014 FC 1074 .... 372, 386, 392

Sebbe v Canada (Minister of Citizenship and Immigration),
2012 FC 813 418–19
Segasayo v Canada (Minister of Citizenship and Immigration),
2010 FC 173 495
Selduz v Canada (Minister of Citizenship and Immigration),
2009 FC 361..382–83
Sellathurai v Canada (Minister of Citizenship and Immigration),
2008 FC 604 632
Selliah v Canada (Minister of Citizenship and Immigration),
2004 FC 872 379–80
Selvarajah v Canada (Minister of Citizenship and Immigration),
2014 FC 769 346
Selvarasa v Canada (Minister of Citizenship and Immigration),
2008 FC 1169.. 364
Sempertegui v Canada (Minister of Citizenship and Immigration),
2009 FC 1176.. 101
Sen v Canada (Minister of Citizenship and Immigration), 2005 FC 2 364
Seyoboka v Canada (Minister of Citizenship and Immigration),
2009 FC 104.. 286, 390
Sha'er v Canada (Minister of Citizenship and Immigration),
2007 FC 231.. 412
Shafi v Canada (Minister of Citizenship and Immigration),
2005 FC 714.. 385
Shah v Canada (Minister of Citizenship and Immigration),
2003 FC 1121... 346
Shah v Canada (Minister of Citizenship and Immigration),
2011 FC 1269...96, 404
Shahid v Canada (Minister of Citizenship and Immigration) (1995),
89 FTR 106, 28 Imm LR (2d) 130, [1995] FCJ No 251 (TD)...................... 280
Shahid v Canada (Minister of Citizenship and Immigration),
2004 FC 1607... 288
Shahid v Canada (Minister of Citizenship and Immigration),
2010 FC 405 624
Shahid v Canada (Minister of Citizenship and Immigration),
2011 FCA 40 143
Shandi (Re) (1991), 51 FTR 252, 17 Imm LR (2d) 54,
[1991] FCJ No 1319 (TD)..477, 478
Shangguan v Canada (Minister of Citizenship and Immigration),
2007 FC 75..138, 139, 152
Shanmugarajah v Canada (Minister of Employment and
Immigration), [1992] FCJ No 583 (CA) 281
Sharma v Canada (Minister of Citizenship and Immigration),
2006 FC 95 277
Sharma v Canada (Minister of Citizenship and Immigration),
2010 FC 398..521

Sharma v Canada (Minister of Citizenship and Immigration),
    2011 FC 337 154
Sharpe v Canada (Minister of Citizenship and Immigration),
    2011 FC 21 522
Sheikh v Canada (Minister of Citizenship and Immigration),
    [1990] 3 FC 238, 11 Imm LR (2d) 81, [1990] FCJ No 604 (CA) 612
Shepherd v Canada (Minister of Citizenship and Immigration),
    2005 FC 1033 501
Shirvan v Canada (Minister of Citizenship and Immigration),
    2005 FC 1509 .... 271, 272
Shpati v Canada (Minister of Public Safety and Emergency
    Preparedness), 2010 FC 367 379
Simoes v Canada (Minister of Citizenship and Immigration) (2000),
    187 FTR 219, 7 Imm LR (3d) 141, 2000 CanLII 15668 (TD) 372
Sing v Maguire (1878), 1 BCR (Pt 1) 101 (SC) 15
Singh v Canada (Citizenship and Immigration), 2007 FC 267 269
Singh v Canada (Minister of Citizenship and Immigration),
    2005 FC 718 422
Singh v Canada (Minister of Citizenship and Immigration),
    2008 FC 15 102
Singh v Canada (Minister of Citizenship and Immigration),
    2009 FC 621 102
Singh v Canada (Minister of Citizenship and Immigration),
    2009 FC 11 .... 394, 410, 616
Singh v Canada (Minister of Citizenship and Immigration),
    2010 FC 1306 114
Singh v Canada (Minister of Citizenship and Immigration),
    2010 FC 757 628
Singh v Canada (Minister of Citizenship and Immigration),
    2013 FC 295 418
Singh v Canada (Minister of Citizenship and Immigration),
    2013 FC 201 612–13
Singh v Canada (Minister of Citizenship and Immigration),
    2014 FC 1022 .... 292, 293
Singh v Canada (Minister of Employment and Immigration),
    [1985] 1 SCR 177, 17 DLR (4th) 422, 1985 CanLII 65 .... 8, 27, 38,
    243, 275, 293, 385, 457, 610, 612, 637, 638, 651, 652, 653, 659, 667, 668
Sinniah v Canada (Minister of Citizenship and Immigration),
    2011 FC 1285 .... 364, 425
Sittampalam v Canada (Minister of Citizenship and Immigration),
    2006 FCA 326 .... 475, 484,
    485, 489, 509
Sivakumar v Canada (Minister of Employment and Immigration)
    (1993), [1994] 1 FC 433, 163 NR 197, [1993] FCJ No 1145 (CA) 351,
    352, 354

Sivapatham v Canada (Minister of Citizenship and Immigration),
2010 FC 314 367
Slahi v Canada (Minister of Justice), 2009 FCA 259 642–43
Smirnov v Canada (Secretary of State) (1994), [1995] 1 FC 780,
89 FTR 269, [1994] FCJ No 1922 (TD) 334
Smith v Canada (Minister of Citizenship and Immigration),
2009 FC 1194 .... 256, 318, 321, 326
SMT (Eastern) Ltd v Winner, [1951] SCR 887,
[1951] 4 DLR 529, [1951] SCJ No 31 35
Soe v Canada (Minister of Citizenship and Immigration),
2007 FC 671 481
Sogi v Canada (Minister of Citizenship and Immigration),
2004 FC 853 375
Sohanpal v Canada (Minister of Citizenship and Immigration),
2013 FC 454 386
Soimin v Canada (Minister of Citizenship and Immigration),
2009 FC 218 347
Sökmen v Canada (Minister of Citizenship and Immigration),
2011 FC 47 522
Solis v Canada (Minister of Citizenship and Immigration),
2000 CanLII 15121 (FCA) 83
Somodi v Canada (Minister of Citizenship and Immigration),
2009 FCA 288 .... 219, 220, 598
Sow v Canada (Minister of Citizenship and Immigration),
2011 FC 1313 323
Spasoja v Canada (Minister of Citizenship and Immigration),
2014 FC 913 .... 294, 296
Spencer v Canada (Minister of Citizenship and Immigration),
2011 FC 397 347–48
Sran v Canada (Minister of Citizenship and Immigration),
2012 FC 791 157
Srignanavel v Canada (Minister of Public Safety and Emergency
Preparedness), IMM-13055-12 (28 December 2012) 391
Stables v Canada (Minister of Citizenship and Immigration),
2011 FC 1319 489–90
Stanislavsky v Canada (Minister of Citizenship and Immigration),
2003 FC 835 100
Stanizai v Canada (Minister of Citizenship and Immigration),
2014 FC 74 .... 284, 625, 626–27
Starovic v Canada (Minister of Citizenship and Immigration),
2012 FC 827 282
Stephenson v Canada (Minister of Citizenship and Immigration),
2011 FC 932 413
Su v Canada (Minister of Citizenship and Immigration), 2013 FC 518 359

Subaharan v Canada (Minister of Citizenship and Immigration),
2008 FC 1228 625
Subramaniyathas v Canada (Minister of Citizenship and Immigration),
2014 FC 583 300
Sufaj v Canada (Minister of Citizenship and Immigration),
2014 FC 373 379–80
Suleiman v Canada (Minister of Citizenship and Immigration),
2004 FC 1125 .... 280, 281
Suleyman v Canada (Minister of Citizenship and Immigration),
2008 FC 780 478
Sultana v Canada (Minister of Citizenship and Immigration),
2009 FC 533 427
Sun v Canada (Minister of Citizenship and Immigration),
2011 FC 708 505
Sunarti v Canada (Minister of Citizenship and Immigration),
2011 FC 191 602
Surajnarain v Canada (Minister of Citizenship and Immigration),
2008 FC 1165 348
Suresh v Canada (Minister of Citizenship and Immigration),
[2000] 2 FC 592 (CA), rev'd 2002 SCC 1 .... 70, 362,
365, 366, 375, 480, 481, 482, 483, 571–72, 573, 648, 649, 661–62
Swartz v Canada (Minister of Citizenship and Immigration),
2002 FCT 268 410
Sylvester v Canada (Minister of Citizenship and Immigration),
2012 FC 17 424

Tai v Canada (Minister of Citizenship and Immigration), 2011 FC 248 616
Tajadodi v Canada (Minister of Citizenship and Immigration),
2005 FC 1096 278
Takeda Canada v Canada (Minister of Health), 2013 FCA 13 615
Tan v Canada (Minister of Citizenship and Immigration),
2012 FC 1079 154–55
Tang v Canada (Minister of Citizenship and Immigration),
2009 FC 292 .... 512–13, 632
Tar v Canada (Minister of Citizenship and Immigration),
2014 FC 767 .... 275, 339
Tathgur v Canada (Minister of Citizenship and Immigration),
2007 FC 1293 154
Taylor v Canada (Minister of Citizenship and Immigration),
2007 FCA 349 438
Tekie v Canada (Minister of Citizenship and Immigration), 2005 FC 27 385
Tenzin v Canada (Minister of Citizenship and Immigration),
2009 FC 1010 364
Terenteva v Canada (Minister of Citizenship and Immigration),
2012 FC 1431 364

Terigho v Canada (Minister of Citizenship and Immigration),
2006 FC 835...403
Tessma v Canada (Minister of Citizenship and Immigration),
2003 FC 1126...506
Thalang v Canada (Minister of Citizenship and Immigration),
2008 FC 340 411
Thambiturai v Canada (Solicitor General), 2006 FC 750................................267
Thamotharem v Canada (Minister of Citizenship and
Immigration), 2007 FCA 198...54–55, 273, 274, 408
Thanabalasingham v Canada (Minister of Citizenship and
Immigration) (2003), 34 Imm LR (3d) 132, [2003] IADD No 603 546
Thanaratnam v Canada (Minister of Citizenship and Immigration),
2004 FC 349, rev'd 2005 FCA 122..485, 509
Thandal v Canada (Minister of Citizenship and Immigration),
2008 FC 489 403
Thang v Canada (Solicitor General), 2004 FC 457..364
Tharmaseelan v Canada (Minister of Citizenship and Immigration),
2003 FCT 694...402
Thirunavukkarasu v Canada (Minister of Citizenship and
Immigration), 2003 FC 1075...398
Thirunavukkarasu v Canada (Minister of Employment and
Immigration) (1993), [1994] 1 FC 589, 22 Imm LR (2d) 241,
[1993] FCJ No 1172 ....341, 342
Thiyagarajah v Canada (Minister of Citizenship and Immigration),
2010 FC 1015 364
Thomas v Canada (Minister of Citizenship and Immigration),
2009 FC 1038...98
Thuraisamy v Canada, Committee, Communication
No 1912/2009: Views adopted by the Committee at its
106th session (15 October–2 November 2012) CCPR,
106th Sess, UN Doc CCPR/C/106/D/1912/2009, online:
www.ccprcentre.org/wp-content/uploads/2013/03/1912-
2009-Thuraisamy-v-Canada-en.pdf...669–70
Tian v Canada (Minister of Citizenship and Immigration),
2011 FC 1148 616
Tikaprasad v Canada (Minister of Citizenship and Immigration),
2005 FC 843...403
Tiwana v Canada (Minister of Citizenship and Immigration),
2008 FC 100 141
TK v Canada (Minister of Public Safety and Emergency
Preparedness), 2013 FC 327...485–86, 489
Tokar v Canada (Minister of Citizenship and Immigration),
2003 FCT 77 612
Toor v Canada (Minister of Citizenship and Immigration), 2006 FC 573..........98

Toronto Coalition to Stop the War v Canada (Minister of Public Safety
    and Emergency Preparedness), 2009 FC 326 473
Toronto Coalition to Stop the War v Canada (Minister of Public Safety
    and Emergency Preparedness), 2010 FC 957 486
Toth v Canada (Minister of Employment and Immigration) (1988),
    86 NR 302, 6 Imm LR (2d) 123, [1988] FCJ No 587 (CA) 557, 631
Toussaint v Canada (AG), 2011 FCA 213 85
Toussaint v Canada (Minister of Citizenship and Immigration),
    2011 FCA 146 401
Tran v Canada (Minister of Citizenship and Immigration),
    2006 FC 1377 102
Tran v Canada (Minister of Public Safety and Emergency
    Preparedness), 2014 FC 1040 502
Traore v Canada (Minister of Citizenship and Immigration),
    2003 FC 1256 321
Trokhanovskyy v Canada (Minister of Citizenship and Immigration),
    2007 CanLII 68155 (CA IRB) 209
Tshimanga v Canada (Minister of Citizenship and Immigration),
    2014 FC 137 478
Turizo v Canada (Minister of Citizenship and Immigration),
    2013 FC 721 154
Turton v Canada (Minister of Citizenship and Immigration),
    2011 FC 1244 347

Union Colliery Co of British Columbia Ltd v Bryden,
    [1899] AC 580 (PC) 34
Uriol v Canada (Minister of Citizenship and Immigration),
    [2009] IADD No 210 187
Ustaoglu v Canada (Minister of Citizenship and Immigration,
    2003 FC 1009 346

Vairea v Canada (Minister of Citizenship and Immigration),
    2006 FC 1238 101
Vakulenko v Canada (Minister of Citizenship and Immigration),
    2014 FC 667 269
Valentin v Canada (Minister of Employment and Immigration),
    [1991] 3 FC 390, 167 NR 1, [1991] FCJ No 554 (CA) 306
Vandy v Canada (Minister of Citizenship and Immigration),
    2011 CanLII 89877 (CA IRB) 209
Varadi v Canada (Minister of Citizenship and Immigration),
    2013 FC 407 364
Varela v Canada (Minister of Citizenship and Immigration),
    2008 FC 436, aff'd 2009 FCA 145 .... 335, 494
Varga v Canada (Minister of Citizenship and Immigration),
    2006 FCA 394 .... 387, 570

Varga v Canada (Minister of Citizenship and Immigration),
2013 FC 494..323
Vashishat v Canada (Minister of Citizenship and Immigration),
2008 FC 1346 ....519, 522
Vasquez v Canada (Minister of Citizenship and Immigration),
2011 FC 477 316
Vazirizadeh v Canada (Minister of Citizenship and Immigration),
2009 FC 807 524
Veeravagu v Canada (Minister of Employment and Immigration),
[1992] FCJ No 468 (CA)...310
Victoria v Canada (Minister of Citizenship and Immigration),
2006 FC 857..453
Vifansi v Canada (Minister of Citizenship and Immigration),
2003 FCT 284..350
Villagonzalo v Canada (Minister of Citizenship and Immigration),
2008 FC 1127...98
Villegas v Canada (Minister of Citizenship and Immigration),
2011 FC 105 ....480, 521, 522
Voloshina v Canada (Minister of Citizenship and Immigration),
2008 FC 1202...380
Vukic v Canada (Minister of Public Safety and Emergency
Preparedness), 2012 FC 370 478

Wai v Canada (Minister of Citizenship and Immigration), 2009 FC 780......... 157
Walcott v Canada (Minister of Citizenship and Immigration),
2011 FC 415 ....318, 414
Walia v Canada (Minister of Citizenship and Immigration),
2008 FC 486 528
Wanchuk v Canada (Minister of Citizenship and Immigration),
2014 FC 885 331
Wang v Canada (Minister of Citizenship and Immigration),
2001 FCT 148 ....372, 378
Wang v Canada (Minister of Citizenship and Immigration),
2007 FC 1188...501
Wang v Canada (Minister of Citizenship and Immigration),
2008 FC 798 ....151, 152
Wang v Canada (Minister of Citizenship and Immigration),
2011 FC 1510 500
Weldesillassie v Canada (Minister of Citizenship and Immigration),
2011 FC 521 239
White v Canada (Minister of Citizenship and Immigration),
2011 FC 1043 410
Williams v Canada (Minister of Citizenship and Immigration) (1996),
[1997] 1 FC 457, 35 Imm LR (2d) 286, [1996] FCJ No 1410 (TD),
rev'd on other grounds, [1997] 2 FC 646, 147 DLR (4th) 93,
[1997] FCJ No 393 (CA) 668

Williams v Canada (Minister of Citizenship and Immigration),
2005 FCA 126 .... 330, 331
Williams v Canada (Minister of Citizenship and Immigration),
2006 FC 1474 .... 411, 425
Winifred v Canada (Minister of Citizenship and Immigration),
2011 FC 827 282–83
Wodajio v Canada (Minister of Citizenship and Immigration),
2004 FC 429 460
Woldeselassie v Canada (Minister of Citizenship and Immigration),
2006 FC 1540 211–12
Woldeselassie v Canada (Minister of Citizenship and Immigration),
[2007] IADD No 1187 212
Wong v Canada (Minister of Citizenship and Immigration),
2006 FC 1410 429
Worthington v Canada (Minister of Citizenship and Immigration),
2008 FC 409 443
Wu v Canada (Minister of Immigration), [1989] 2 FC 175,
7 Imm LR (2d) 81, [1989] FCJ No 29 (TD) 602
Wynne v Canada (Minister of Citizenship and Immigration),
2010 FC 440 398

X (Re), 2007 CanLII 47398 (CA IRB) 326
X (Re), 2012 CanLII 95544 (CA IRB) 357
X (Re), 2012 CanLII 99423 (CA IRB) 357
X (Re), 2013 CanLII 76469 (CA IRB) 332
X (Re), 2013 CanLII 92933 (CA IRB) 326
X (Re), 2014 CanLII 20447 (CA IRB) 292
X (Re), 2014 CanLII 24188 (CA IRB) 292
X (Re), 2014 CanLII 24199 (CA IRB) 292
X (Re), 2014 CanLII 33085 (CA IRB) 292
X (Re), 2014 CanLII 55520 (CA IRB) 292
X (Re), 2014 CanLII 60386 (CA IRB) 292
X (Re), 2014 CanLII 60409 (CA IRB) 292
X (Re), 2014 CanLII 60411 (CA IRB) 292
X (Re), 2014 CanLII 64251 (CA IRB) 296
X (Re), 2014 CanLII 66650 (CA IRB) 296
Xiao v Canada (Minister of Citizenship and Immigration), 2009 FC 195 501
Xuan v Canada (Minister of Citizenship and Immigration), 2013 FC 673 613

Y Sotomayor v Canada (Minister of Citizenship and Immigration),
2013 FC 962 .... 415, 431
Yakut v Canada (Minister of Citizenship and Immigration),
2009 FC 1190 .... 365, 379
Yamba v Canada (Minister of Citizenship and Immigration),
2000 CanLII 15191 (FCA) 280

Yang v Canada (Minister of Citizenship and Immigration),
    2001 FCT 1052 .... 310, 312, 313
Yansane v Canada (Minister of Citizenship and Immigration),
    2008 FC 1213 380
Yansane v Canada (Minister of Citizenship and Immigration),
    2009 FC 1242 380
Yetna v Canada (Minister of Citizenship and Immigration), 2014 FC 858 296
YLH (Re), [2006] RPDD No 238 (CA IRB) 357
Yohalingam v Canada (Minister of Citizenship and Immigration),
    2003 FCT 540 600
Younis v Canada (Citizenship and Immigration), 2008 FC 944 506
Younis v Canada (Minister of Citizenship and Immigration),
    2010 FC 1157 496
Yu v Canada (Minister of Citizenship and Immigration), 2005 FC 1323 528
Yu v Canada (Minister of Citizenship and Immigration), 2006 FC 956 416
Yusuf v Canada (Minister of Employment and Immigration) (1995),
    179 NR 11, [1995] FCJ No 35 (CA) 281
Yusufzai v Canada (Minister of Citizenship and Immigration),
    2005 FC 113 431

Zacarias v Canada (Minister of Citizenship and Immigration),
    2011 FC 62 315–16
Zaib v Canada (Minister of Citizenship and Immigration),
    2008 FC 687 625
Zalzali v Canada (Minister of Employment and Immigration),
    [1991] 3 FC 605, 14 Imm LR (2d) 81, [1991] FCJ No 341 (CA) 329
Zambrano v Canada (Minister of Citizenship and Immigration),
    2008 FC 481 431
Zamora v Canada (Minister of Citizenship and Immigration),
    2004 FC 1414 384
Zazai v Canada (Minister of Citizenship and Immigration),
    2004 FCA 89 633
Zazai v Canada (Minister of Citizenship and Immigration),
    2005 FCA 303 492
Zazai v Canada (Minister of Citizenship and Immigration),
    2012 FC 162 .... 422, 425
Zemo v Canada (Minister of Citizenship and Immigration),
    2010 FC 800 .... 382, 385
Zeng v Canada (Minister of Citizenship and Immigration),
    2010 FCA 118 .... 349, 350
Zeon v Canada (Minister of Citizenship and Immigration),
    2005 FC 1338 501
Zhang v Canada (Minister of Citizenship and Immigration),
    2005 FC 1313 526
Zhang v Canada (Minister of Citizenship and Immigration),
    2006 FC 1381 106

Zhang v Canada (Minister of Citizenship and Immigration),
    2012 FC 1093 525
Zhang v Lin, 2010 ABQB 420 189–90
Zheng v Canada (Minister of Citizenship and Immigration),
    2008 FC 430 155
Zheng v Canada (Minister of Citizenship and Immigration),
    2012 FC 608 323
Zhong v Canada (Minister of Citizenship and Immigration),
    2011 FC 980 148
Zhou v Canada (Minister of Citizenship and Immigration),
    2012 FC 1252 308
Zolfagharkhani v Canada (Minister of Employment and
    Immigration), [1993] 3 FC 540, 20 Imm LR (2d) 1,
    [1993] FCJ No 584 (CA) 304–5, 317
Zrig v Canada (Minister of Citizenship and Immigration),
    2003 FCA 178 ....350, 351
Zuo v Canada (Minister of Citizenship and Immigration),
    2007 FC 88 102

INDEX

Administrative law principles, 72. *See also* Judicial review
  prerogative writs. *See* Prerogative writs
  procedural fairness. *See* Procedural fairness
Admissibility hearings, 543–47. *See also* Inadmissible persons
  burden of proof, 547
  decision from Immigration Division, 547
  evidence, 545–47
  parties, 544–45
  public and private hearings, 543–44
Admission into Canada. *See* Entry into Canada
Adopted children
  Canadian citizenship, 443–44
  family class sponsorship, 181, 202–5, 207
Affirmation of citizenship, 453–54
Agricultural workers, 121–22
Aliens. *See* Foreign nationals
American Declaration of the Rights and Duties of Man, 68
Appeals. *See also* Judicial review
  family class, sponsorship decisions, 217–19

Federal Court of Appeal, 633
  refugee claims, 288–97. *See also* Refugee Appeal Division
  refugee resettlement, visa officer's decision, 239–40
  removal orders, 562–64
  Supreme Court of Canada, 633–35

Baker case, 420–21
Best interests of the child
  humanitarian and compassionate applications, 420–26
    alert, alive, and sensitive to child, 421–23
    Baker decision, 420–21
    balancing factors, 423–24
    children outside Canada, 425–26
    children within Canada, 425
    hardship test, 424–25
  pre-removal risk assessments, 387–88
Bill of Rights, 667–68
Border. *See* Canadian border
Business immigrants, 165–71
  Business Skills Program, 171
  Entrepreneur Program, 168, 171
  Immigrant Investor Program, 168, 171

Immigrant Investor Venture Capital
Fund, 171
provincial nominee programs, 171
self-employed person class, 165–68
selection criteria, 165–67
start-up business class, 168–71
Business Skills Program, 171
Business travel, 70–71

Canada Border Services Agency. *See
also* Minister of Public Safety and
Emergency Preparedness
division of functions, 29–30
establishment, 29
Most Wanted list, 573–74
Canada-Québec Accord, 60–62
Canadian Bill of Rights, 667–68
Canadian border
open borders, 78–87
securitization, 530–31
*Canadian Charter of Rights and Freedoms.
See Charter of Rights and Freedoms*
Canadian citizenship, 436–67
emergence, historical overview,
436–39
losing citizenship, 460–65
renunciation, 460–61
resumption of citizenship, 465
revocation, 361, 461–65
current law, 461–63
humanitarian and compassionate applications, 399
new amendments, 463–65
obtaining citizenship, 439–56
birth in Canada, 439–40
birth to Canadian parent outside
Canada, 440–45
adopted children, 443–44
lost Canadians, 444–45
naturalization, 445–56. *See also*
Naturalization
adequate knowledge of an
official language, 448–49,
451–52
adequate knowledge of Canada, 449–50, 451–52
adequate knowledge of citizenship responsibilities,
450–51
barriers to, 455–56

citizenship test, 449–51
current residency requirements, 445–47
new income tax filing requirement, 447–48
new intention to reside requirement, 448
new physical presence test, 447
oath or affirmation of citizenship, 453–54
process, 452–53
waiving of language and knowledge requirements, 451–52
recent reforms, criticisms, 466–67
rights and responsibilities, 456–60
Charter rights, 636–43
generally, 456–57
passports, 457–60
Canadian Citizenship Act, 1947, 23–24
Caregivers, 123–28
abuse, 125–26
child-care providers, 173
high medical need-care providers,
173–74
humanitarian and compassionate applications, 432
permanent residence status, 172–74
Certiorari, 621–22
Chairperson's Guidelines, 41–42, 54–56.
See also Immigration and Refugee
Board
Charter of Rights and Freedoms, 37–38,
636–67
ambit, 636–43
challenges under. *See* Constitutional
challenges
gross disproportionality doctrine,
661–62
inadmissibility determinations, application, 529–30
influence on immigration law, 27, 38
non-citizens, application, 636–43
overbreadth doctrine, 660–61
rights under. *See Charter* rights
vagueness doctrine, 661
Charter rights, 645–67. *See also Charter
of Rights and Freedoms*
democratic rights, 649
fundamental freedoms, 647–49

legal rights, 650–67
  cruel and unusual punishment, re,
    664–65
  detention, accompanying, 662–64
  equality rights, 666–67
  interpreter, 666
  section 7, 650–62
    form of law, 660–62
    fundamental justice, 651–55,
      658–60, 661
    life, liberty and security of the
      person, 655–658
  mobility rights, 649–60
Children. *See also* Adopted children;
    Dependent child; Family members
  best interests. *See* Best interests of
    the child
  detention, 559
    designated foreign nationals, 560
  international convention, 67–68
CIC. *See* Citizenship and Immigration
    Canada
Citizenship
  Canadian. *See* Canadian citizenship
  foreign. *See* Foreign nationals
Citizenship Act, 4, 45–46
Citizenship and Immigration Canada.
    See also Minister of Citizenship
    and Immigration
  division of functions, 29–30
  establishment, 46
  operational manuals and bulletins,
    57–58
  Program Delivery Instructions, 57–58
Classes of permanent residents. *See also*
    Permanent resident status
  economic classes. *See* Economic
    classes
  family class. *See* Family class
  refugees. *See* Refugee protection
Colonization, 5–6
Common law partners. *See also* Family
    members
  family class sponsorship, 190–93
    conditional status, 197–99
      abuse or neglect, exception,
        198–99
      genuineness of relationship,
        194–95

pre-existing undertaking of spon-
    sor, effect, 196
  relationship entered for purpose
    of acquiring, 195–96
  sponsored partners in Canada,
    196–97
humanitarian and compassionate ap-
    plications, 400
Common law principles, 72
Common law rights, 7–9
Compassionate grounds. *See* Humanitar-
    ian and compassionate grounds
Comprehensive Ranking System, 162–64
Conjugal partners
  defined, 193–94
  family class sponsorship, 193–94
    conditional status, 197–99
      abuse or neglect, exception,
        198–99
      genuineness of relationship,
        194–95
    pre-existing undertaking of spon-
      sor, effect, 196
    relationship entered for purpose
      of acquiring, 195–96
Constitution Act, 1867, 13, 14, 32–38
  concurrent powers over immigration,
    32–33
  naturalization and aliens, 33–37
Constitutional challenges, 636–71. *See
    also Charter of Rights and Freedoms*
  Charter rights, violations. *See Charter*
    rights
  form of law, 660–62
    gross disproportionality, 661–62
    overbreadth, 660–61
    vagueness, 661
  notice requirements, 267
  removal to torture, 571–72
  security certificates, 582–86
  standing, 643–45
*Convention against Torture and Other
    Cruel, Inhuman or Degrading Treat-
    ment or Punishment*, 66, 345, 669
Convention on the Rights of the Child,
    67–68
Convention refugees, 298–43. *See also*
    Refugee protection
  abroad, resettlement, 231. *See also*
    Refugee resettlement

definition, 299
determination difficulty, 359
determination process. *See* Refugee
    determination process
economic migrants distinguished,
    307
exclusions, 348–57
    availability of state protection in
        another country, 349–50
    recourse after finding of, 357
    serious criminals, 350–57
        contrary to purposes of United
            Nations, 356–57
        crimes against peace or human-
            ity, 352–55
        non-political crimes, 355–56
        war crimes, 352–55
internal flight alternative, 341–43
international convention. *See* Con-
    vention Relating to the Status of
    Refugees
membership in particular social
    group, 319–26
    gender, 322–24
    sexual origin, 325–26
nationality, 310–11
persecution, 302–9. *See also* Persecu-
    tion
    agents of persecution, 307–8
    cumulative grounds, 308
    discrimination and harassment,
        303–4
    economic, 307
    enumerated grounds, 309–26
    individual versus group, 308–9
    prospective risk, 303, 358
    punishment or prosecution,
        304–6
political opinion, 314–19
pre-removal risk assessment, eligibil-
    ity, 365–66
race, 310
religion, 311–13
state protection, 326–41
    adequacy of, 333–37
    Canadian conception, 326–30
    multiple nationalities, 330–33
    obligation to seek, 337–41
sur place claims, 358
well-founded fear, 299–302

*Convention Relating to the Status of
    Refugees*, 23. *See also* Convention
    refugees
exclusion provisions, 348–57
    Article 1E, 349–50
    Article 1F, 350–57
implementation, 298
Crimes against humanity, 491–94. *See
    also* Human or international
    rights violations
Criminality. *See also* Inadmissible
    persons
citizenship barrier, 455–56
criminality not classified as serious,
    498–507
    discharges, 502
    equivalency between inside and
        outside Canada, 501
    equivalency of foreign offences,
        499–501
    having been convicted, 503
    pending appeals, no automatic
        deferment, 507
    permissible entries after convic-
        tion irrelevant, 506–7
    record suspensions, 502, 505–6
    rehabilitation, 502, 504–5
    term of imprisonment, 501–2, 505
    young offenders, 506
entry barrier, 104, 497–513. *See also*
    Inadmissible persons
organized criminality, 507–13
    convictions, relying on, 512–13
    international convention, 587
    member of an organization, 508–9
    people smuggling, 510–11, 587–90
        designated foreign nationals,
            511–12
    transnational crimes, 509–10
pre-removal risk assessments, 373–75
refugee barrier, 350–57
serious criminality, 350–57, 497–98
    commission not conviction, 501
    contrary to purposes of United
        Nations, 356–57
    crimes against peace or humanity,
        352–55
    non-political crimes, 355–56

Cruel and unusual punishment
  Charter rights, 664–66
  international convention, 66
  person in need of protection, 345. *See
    also* Refugee protection
  removal to, 571
    non-refoulement principle, 360
    pre-removal risk assessments. *See*
      Pre-removal risk assessments

Damages remedy, 628–30
Declarations
  Federal Court, 627–28
  ministerial declarations, 89–90
Department of Citizenship and Immigration Act, 46
Department of Public Safety and Emergency Preparedness Act, 47
Dependants. *See* Family members
Dependent child. *See also* Children;
    Family members
  defined, 200–2
  family class sponsorship, 199–205
    adoption requirements, 202–5
    dependence, 199–202
Deportation. *See* Removal from Canada
Designated country of origin, 252–57,
    368
  what is, 252–55
Designated foreign nationals, 257–61,
    511–12
  detention, 560–61
  humanitarian and compassionate applications, 398–99
  what is, 257–59
Detention, 548–61. *See also* Inadmissible
    persons
  Charter rights, 662–64
  children, 559
  criticisms surrounding, 548–50
  decisions to detain or release, standard used, 550–51
  designated foreign nationals, 560–61
  review of detention. *See* Detention
    reviews
  security certificates, 577–81
Detention reviews, 551–61. *See also*
    Detention
  designated foreign nationals, 561
  IRB guidelines, 553–54

overview, 551–54
release may not be immediate,
    557–59
security certificates, 578–81
statutory grounds to detain, 552–53
  children, 559
  identity in question, 556–57
  interpretation, 554–56
Discretion
  humanitarian and compassionate
    grounds, 393–94, 434–35
  inadmissibility, section 44 report,
    537–41
Discrimination and harassment
  humanitarian and compassionate
    grounds, 412–13
  persecution as, 303–4
Divorce, validity, recognition, 187–90

Economic classes, 132–76. *See also*
    Permanent resident status
  business immigrants, 165–71
    Business Skills Program, 171
    Entrepreneur Program, 168, 171
    Immigrant Investor Program, 168,
      171
    Immigrant Investor Venture Capital Fund, 171
    provincial nominee programs, 171
    self-employed person class,
      165–68
      selection criteria, 165–67
    start-up business class, 168–71
  caregivers, 172–74. *See also* Caregivers
  objectives, 133
  skilled workers, 133–65. *See also*
    Skilled workers
    Canadian experience class,
      158–59
    Express Entry program, 160–65
    federal skilled trades class,
      159–60
    federal skilled worker class,
      134–55
      application process, 152–55
      eligibility requirements,
        135–39
      points system, 139–51

self-supporting upon arrival,
151–52
objectives, 133–34
provincial nominee class, 155–58
Québec skilled worker class, 155
uninspiring approach, 174–76
Economic migrants, 307
Educational Credential Assessment, 138
Electronic travel authorization (eTA),
90, 103–4. *See also* Temporary
resident status
Employment
arranged employment, 147–48
labour market impact assessments.
See Labour market impact assessments
work permits. *See* Work permits
Employment and Social Development
Canada. *See also* Minister of Employment and Social Development
International Mobility Programs,
119–20
IRPA compliance investigations, 116
job bank, 162, 164
labour market impact assessments.
See Labour market impact assessments
Enforcement mechanisms, 532–91
detention. *See* Detention
removal from Canada. *See* Removal
from Canada
Entrepreneur Program, 168, 171
Entry into Canada
grant of status, 104
inadmissible persons. *See* Inadmissible persons
ministerial prohibition, 89–90
permanent basis. *See* Permanent
resident status
port of entry. *See* Port of entry
privilege not right, 471–73
temporary basis. *See* Temporary
resident status
Espionage, 476–78. *See also* Security
threats
Expert medical evidence, 264–67
Express Entry program, 135, 140,
160–65
Extradition proceedings, persons subject
to, 368–69

Family class
distinguished from family members,
178–80
membership, 181–208
dependent children, 199–205
adoption requirements, 202–5
dependence, defined, 199–202
eligibility, 181–82
ineligibility, 179, 208–12
judicial review, 219–20
other relationships, 207–8
parents and grandparents, 205–7
partner of sponsor, 182–99
abuse or neglect, 198–99
common law partners, 190–93
conditional status, 197–99
conjugal partners, 193–94
genuineness of relationship,
194–95
pre-existing undertakings, 196
relationship entered for purpose of acquiring, 195–96
sponsored partners in Canada,
196–97
spouses, 182–90
sponsors
appeal rights, 217–19
eligibility, 212–15
undertaking, 215–17
Family members
children. *See* Dependent child
common law partners. *See* Common
law partners
conjugal partners. *See* Conjugal
partners
family class members distinguished,
178–80
inadmissibility, 529, 536–37
non-accompanying, failure to identify, 179, 208–12
humanitarian and compassionate
applications, 426–28
parents and grandparents. *See* Parents and grandparents
refugees
protected persons, 297
resettlement, 232–33
siblings. *See* Siblings
spouses. *See* Spouses

Family reunification, immigration objective, 177, 180, 220–22
Federal Court, 596–97
  hearings, 604–5
Federal Court of Appeal, 633
Federal-provincial/territorial agreements, 58–60
  Canada-Québec Accord, 60–62
  provincial nominee programs, 155–58
    chart of current agreements, 673–75
Foreign divorces, 187–90
Foreign nationals
  Charter, application, 636–43
  detention in Canada. *See* Detention
  family class membership. *See* Family class
  federal jurisdiction, 33–37
  humanitarian and compassionate applications, 395
  in need of protection. *See* Refugee protection
  inadmissibility. *See* Inadmissible persons
  removal from Canada. *See* Removal from Canada
  status in Canada. *See* Status in Canada
  students. *See* Study permits
  visitors. *See* Temporary resident status
  workers. *See* Work permits

General Agreement on Trade in Services, 70–71
Government-assisted refugees, 234–35
Grandparents. *See* Parents and grandparents

Health inadmissibility, 513–24. *See also* Inadmissible persons
  danger to public health, 515
  danger to public safety, 516
  excessive demand on health or social services, 516–24
    change in circumstances, 524
    exceeding total cost of average Canadian, 517

    health and social services distinguished, 518–20
    overcoming inadmissibility, 520–22
  humanitarian and compassionate applications, 431, 523–24
  medical examinations. *See* Medical examination requirement
Human or international rights violations, 491–97. *See also* International law
  crimes against humanity, 491–94
  remedies, 668–71
  restricted by sanctions, 496–97
  senior official of government engaging in, 494–96
  war crimes, 491–94
Human smuggling and trafficking, 510–11, 587–90
  designated foreign nationals, 257–59, 511–12
  smuggling, 587–89
  trafficking, 589–90
Humanitarian and compassionate grounds, 393–435
  best interests of the child, 420–26
    alert, alive, and sensitive to child, 421–23
    Baker decision, 420–21
    balancing factors, 423–24
    children outside Canada, 425–26
    children within Canada, 425
    hardship test, 424–25
  designated foreign nationals, 398–99
  discretionary nature, 393–94, 434–35
  eligibility, 395–400
    Canadian citizens, 399
    foreign nationals not meeting requirements, 395
    inadmissible persons, 395
    permanent residents, 399
    refugee claimants, 257, 260, 262, 395–97
    spouses or common law partners, 400
  evaluating application, 407–32
    criteria, 409–32
    flexibility and consistency, balancing, 407–8
    standard of proof, 408

hardship, 409–20
  caused by application outside
    Canada, 416–20
    establishment in Canada,
      417–20
  caused by denial of entry or re-
    moval from Canada, 415–16
    de facto family member, 415–16
  country of origin, 411–15
    discrimination not amounting
      to persecution, 412–13
    excluding persecution or tor-
      ture, 411–12
    generalized risk, 413–14
    lack of critical medical care,
      414–15
    other adverse conditions, 414
inadmissible persons, 428–32
  criminal charges outstanding,
    429–30
  family member, 431–32
  health inadmissibility, 431,
    523–24
  rehabilitation or pardon eligibil-
    ity, 430
  ministerial instructions and, 399
negative decisions, 433–34
  judicial review, 434
  request for reconsideration,
    433–34
pre-removal risk assessments of applicants, 388
procedural requirement exemptions,
  432
process, 401–7
  assessing officer, 404
  fees, 401
  final examination, 407
  onus on applicant, 403
  paper application, 401–3
  temporary resident permit in
    conjunction, 404
  two-step assessment process,
    404–7
    approval in principle, 405–6
    assessing permanent residence
      eligibility, 406–7
undeclared family members, 426–28
waiving of other criteria, 432

Immigrant Investor Program, 168, 171
Immigrant Investor Venture Capital
  Fund, 171
Immigration Act, 1976, 23, 26
Immigration and Refugee Board
  chairperson's powers and duties, 41
  guidelines. *See* Chairperson's
    Guidelines
  divisions, 41
    Immigration Appeal Division. *See*
      Immigration Appeal Division
    Immigration Division. *See* Immi-
      gration Division
    Refugee Appeal Division. *See*
      Refugee Appeal Division
    Refugee Protection Division. *See*
      Refugee Protection Division
  establishment, 26–27, 41
  jurisprudential guides, 56
  legislative changes to, 30
  rules. *See* Immigration and Refugee
    Board rules
Immigration and Refugee Board rules,
  41, 51
  refugee hearings, 272
  regulatory status, 50
Immigration and Refugee Protection Act,
  38–45
  broad principles, 28
  enforcement authority, 533
  enforcement mechanisms. *See* En-
    forcement mechanisms
  inland refugee protection regime,
    298–359
    section 96, 298–343
    section 97, 344–48
    section 98, 348–57
  legislative history, 3–4, 26, 27–31
  non-compliance
    inadmissibility based on, 528–29
    investigations, 116
  non-refoulement principle, 360
  objectives, 42–45, 177, 471
  regulations under. *See Immigration
    and Refugee Protection Regulations*
  structure, 38–42
*Immigration and Refugee Protection Regu-
  lations*, 47–51
  flexibility, 28, 48

IRB rules, status, 50
structure, 47–48
Immigration Appeal Division. *See also*
Immigration and Refugee Board
jurisdiction, 41
removal order appeals, 562–64
Immigration Division. *See also* Immigration and Refugee Board
admissibility hearings. *See* Admissibility hearings
detention reviews. *See* Detention reviews
jurisdiction, 41
Immigration law
constitutional challenges. *See* Constitutional challenges
evolution, 3–31
current situation, 27–31
early origins, 6–11
modernization, 21–27
racialization, 15–21
restrictive legislation, 11–14
sources, 32–74
administrative law principles, 72
Canada-Québec Accord, 60–62
CIC. *See* Citizenship and Immigration Canada
Citizenship Act. See Citizenship Act
Constitution Act, 1867. See Constitution Act, 1867
Department of Citizenship and Immigration Act, 46
Department of Public Safety and Emergency Preparedness Act, 47
federal-provincial/territorial agreements, 58–60
international law. *See* International law
IRB. *See* Immigration and Refugee Board
IRPA. See Immigration and Refugee Protection Act
IRPR. See Immigration and Refugee Protection Regulations
ministerial instructions, 51–53
ministerial orders, 53–54
stare decisis, 72–74

Inadmissible persons, 471–531
Charter rights, 529–30
criminality, 497–513. *See also* Criminality
detention. *See* Detention
family members, 529, 536–37
financial reasons, 524–25
grounds of inadmissibility, 473–529
facts constituting, 474
statutory interpretation and judicial review, 474–75
health reasons, 513–24. *See also* Health inadmissibility
hearings re. *See* Admissibility hearings
human or international rights violations, 491–97
crimes against humanity, 491–94
restricted by sanctions, 496–97
senior official of government engaging in, 494–96
war crimes, 491–94
humanitarian and compassionate applications, 395, 428–32
criminal charges outstanding, 429–30
family member, 431–32
health inadmissibility, 431, 523–24
rehabilitation or pardon eligibility, 430
IRPA non-compliance, based on, 528–29
misrepresentation, based on, 525–28
directly or indirectly misrepresenting, 526–28
withholding material facts, 526–28
Most Wanted list, 573–74
pre-removal risk assessments, 373–75
removal from Canada. *See* Removal from Canada
removal, precarious distinction, 511–12
security threats, 104, 472, 476–90. *See also* Security threats
alternative remedies, 489–90
endangerment to Canada, 483
espionage, 476–78

member of an organization,
483–87
subversion, 478–80
terrorism, 480–82
listed terrorist entities, 487–89
Injunctions, 631
Internal flight alternative, 341–43. See
also Convention refugees
International Covenant on Civil and Polit-
ical Rights, 64–65
International law, 9–10, 63–71
American Declaration of the Rights and
Duties of Man, 68
Convention against Torture and Other
Cruel, Inhuman or Degrading Treat-
ment or Punishment, 66
Convention on the Rights of the Child,
67–68
Convention Relating to the Status of
Refugees, 23
domestic significance of international
agreements, 68–70
International Covenant on Civil and
Political Rights, 64–65
remedies, 668–71
Safe Third Country Agreement, 71,
249–50, 251–52, 366–67
trade agreements, 70–71
International Mobility Programs, 119–20
International remedies, 668–71. See also
International law
Interpreter, right to, 666
IRB. See Immigration and Refugee Board
IRPA. See Immigration and Refugee Protec-
tion Act
IRPR. See Immigration and Refugee Protec-
tion Regulations
Irregular arrivals. See Designated for-
eign nationals

Judicial review, 595–635. See also Ap-
peals
appeals from, 633–35
Federal Court of Appeal, 633
Supreme Court of Canada, 633–35
Convention refugee exclusion, 357
costs, 632
DCO claims, denial, 255
family class sponsorship, 219–220
Federal Court, 596–97

hearings, 604–5
grounds for relief, 606–7
humanitarian and compassionate
decisions, 434
inadmissibility findings, 474–75
pre-removal risk assessments, 391
process of judicial review, 597–605
commencing application, 597–99
hearing, 604–5
notice of application, serving and
filing, 599–600
obtaining leave, 601–4
perfecting application, 600
Refugee Appeal Division decisions,
297
refugee resettlement, visa officer's
decision, 239–40
remedies, 620–32
ordinary remedies, 627–31
damages, 628–30
declarations, 627–28
injunctions, 631
prerogative writs, 621–27
certiorari, 621–22
mandamus, 623–27
prohibition, 622
quo warranto, 627
removal orders, 564–65
statutory stays, 605
standards of review, 607–19
deferential approach, 616–19, 635
procedural fairness, 608–13
substantive aspects of decision,
613–16
visa exemptions, 97
Jurisprudential guides, 56

Labour market impact assessments,
114–16
arranged employment, 147, 148
exemptions, 117–20
Legislative history of immigration law,
3–31
Lost Canadians, 444–45

Magna Carta, 6–8
Mandamus, 623–27
Marriage. See also Spouses
arranged marriages, 195–96
defined, 183

foreign divorces, 187–90
genuineness of relationship, 194–95
purpose of acquiring benefit, 195–96
validity, 183–87
Medical care
excessive demands, 516–24. *See also*
Health inadmissibility
change in circumstances, 524
exceeding total cost of average
Canadian over five years, 517
humanitarian and compassionate
applications, 431, 523–24
overcoming inadmissibility,
520–22
social services, distinction,
518–20
inadequate in country of origin
children, best interests, 424
humanitarian and compassionate
grounds, 414–15
Medical evidence, 264–67
Medical examination requirement,
513–15. *See also* Health inadmissibility
certificate expiry, 514
circumstances, 513–14
designated examiners, 514
evidence, obtaining, 515
expenses, 514
refugee assistance, 234, 235
permanent resident status, 48, 513
refugees, 231
super visas, 92, 206
work permits, 117
Member of an organization. *See also*
Inadmissible persons
criminal organizations, 508–9
security threats, 483–87
Minister of Citizenship and Immigration. *See also* Citizenship and
Immigration Canada
administrative authority, 38
delegation of powers, 39
designated country of origin, 252–54
designated foreign national, 257–59
instructions, 30, 51–53
humanitarian and compassionate
exemptions, 399
orders, 53–54

powers and duties
domestic or international agreements, 46
IRPA, under, 38–39
refugee claims, determinations,
30–31
temporary resident prohibition,
89–90
Minister of Employment and Social Development. *See also* Employment
and Social Development Canada
IRPA, powers, 39
Minister of Public Safety and Emergency
Preparedness. *See also* Canada
Border Services Agency
IRPA, enforcement authority, 38–39
Ministerial declarations, temporary
resident prohibition, 89–90
Ministerial instructions, 30, 51–53
humanitarian and compassionate
exemptions, 399
Ministerial orders, 53–54
designated country of origin, 252–54
designated foreign national, 257–59
Misrepresentation
dependent family members, 208–12
inadmissibility based on, 525–28
directly or indirectly misrepresenting, 526–28
withholding material facts,
526–28
refugee claimants, 285–87
Most Wanted list, 573–74

National Occupation Classification,
136–37
Naturalization, 445–56. *See also* Canadian citizenship
adequate knowledge requirements
Canada, of, 449–50
citizenship responsibilities,
450–51
official language, 448–49
testing, 449–51
failing test, 451
waiver of requirements, 451–52
barriers to, 455–56
current residency requirements,
445–47
federal jurisdiction, 33–37

new income tax filing requirement, 447–48

new intention to reside requirement, 448

new physical presence test, 447

oath or affirmation of citizenship, 453–54

process, 452–53

Non-refoulement principle, 360–63
erosion of principle, 391–92
exceptions, 361–62
pre-removal risk assessments. *See* Pre-removal risk assessments

North American Free Trade Agreement, 70–71

Oath of citizenship, 453–54

Open borders, 78–87

Organized criminality, 507–13. *See also* Criminality
convictions, relying on for inadmissibility, 512–13
human smuggling and trafficking, 510–11, 587–90
designated foreign nationals, 511–12
international convention, 587
member of an organization, 508–9
transnational crimes, 509–10, 587–90

Pardons. *See* Record suspensions

Parents and grandparents
family class sponsorship, 205–7
super visas, 92–93, 206

Passports, 457–60

People smuggling. *See* Human smuggling and trafficking

Permanent resident status
application from abroad, 395
available routes, 132
Charter rights, 636–43
economic classes. *See* Economic classes
family class. *See* Family class
humanitarian and compassionate basis. *See* Humanitarian and compassionate grounds
loss of, 361, 399
medical examinations, 48, 513

non-accompanying family members, undeclared, 179, 208–12, 426–28

refugees
designated foreign nationals, 260, 297
family members, 297
pre-removal risk assessments, after, 389
protection determinations, after, 297
resettled persons, 228–29. *See also* Refugee resettlement

Persecution, 302–9. *See also* Convention refugees
agents of persecution, 307–8
cumulative grounds, 308
discrimination and harassment as, 303–4
economic persecution, 307
enumerated grounds of persecution, 309–26
membership in particular social group, 319–26
gender, 322–24
sexual origin, 325–26
nationality, 310–11
political opinion, 314–19
race, 310
religion, 311–13
humanitarian and compassionate grounds, exclusion, 411–12
individual versus group, 308–9
prospective risk, 303, 358
punishment or prosecution as, 304–6
sur place claims, 358
well-founded fear, 299–302

Persons in need of protection, 344–48. *See also* Refugee protection
definition, 345
determination
difficulty determining, 359
process. *See* Refugee determination process
exclusion, 348–57
generalized risk, 346–48
pre-removal risk assessment, eligibility, 365–66

Points systems. *See also* Economic classes
self-employed persons, 166–67

skilled workers, 139–51
  adaptability, 149–51
  age, 146–47
  arranged employment, 147–48
  education, 141–43
  language skills, 143–44
  work experience, 144–46
Port of entry. *See also* Entry into Canada
  pre-removal risk assessments, 371
  refugee claims, 245
  Safe Third Country Agreement, 249
Pre-removal risk assessments, 360–92.
  See also Non-refoulement principle
  applying for, 369–70
  assessment, 385–88
    issues and considerations, 386–88
      best interest of children,
        387–88
      country of removal, 388
      humanitarian and compassion-
        ate grounds, 388
      section 97 only evaluations,
        387
      section 98 exclusion evalua-
        tions, 387
      sections 96 and 97 evaluations,
        386–87
    oral hearing, 385–86
  concerns regarding, 362–63
  decision final when delivered, 389
  eligibility, 363–64
    notification as prerequisite,
      369–70, 371
  evidence and submissions, 379–84
    applicant's burden, 379–83
    officer's duty to disclose, 383–84
  ineligibility, 365–69
    designated country of origin ar-
      rivals, 255, 257, 368
    extradition proceedings, persons
      subject to, 368–69
    previously rejected applicants,
      367–68
    protected persons, 365–66
    refused refugee claimants, 255,
      257, 260, 262, 367–68
    safe third country arrivals,
      366–67
  ineligible refugee claimants, 373–76

inadmissible persons, 373–75
  security certificates, persons sub-
    ject to, 375–76
non-refoulement assessments, 376
port of entry arrivals, 371
positive decisions, 389
purpose, 361
refused refugee claimants and repeat
  applicants, 371–73
  new evidence rule, 373
  time bar, 371–72
regulatory stay of removal, 376–79
rejected decisions
  deemed rejected, 390–91
    abandoned applications,
      390–91
    vacated decisions, 390
    withdrawn applications, 391
  judicial review, 391
Prerogative writs, 621–27
  certiorari, 621–22
  mandamus, 623–27
  prohibition, 622
  quo warranto, 627
Procedural fairness, 541–43, 608–13
  interpreter, right to, 666
Program Delivery Instructions, 57–58.
  See also Citizenship and Immigration Canada
Prohibition, writ of, 622
Provincial nominee programs. *See also*
  Economic classes
  business immigrants, 171
  current agreements, chart, 673–75
  skilled workers, 155–58
Public health danger, 515
Public Safety and Emergency Preparedness. *See* Minister of Public Safety
  and Emergency Preparedness
Public safety danger, 516

Québec Accord. *See* Canada-Québec
  Accord
Québec skilled worker class, 155
Quo warranto, 627

Racialization of immigration law, 15–21
RAD. *See* Refugee Appeal Division
Record suspensions, 502, 505–6

Refoulement. *See* Non-refoulement principle

Refugee Appeal Division, 288–97. *See also* Immigration and Refugee Board
eligibility to appeal, 289
establishment, 30, 288–89
judicial review of decisions, 297
jurisdiction, 41
new evidence, submitting, 291–93
oral hearings, 293
paper-based hearings, 293–94
powers, 294, 296
precedential value of decisions, 73–74
process for appealing, 290–91
standard of review or intervention, 294–96

Refugee Assistance Program, 234

Refugee claims. *See also* Refugee protection
humanitarian and compassionate applications and, 395–97
inland process. *See* Refugee determination process
persons abroad. *See* Refugee resettlement

Refugee determination process, 243–88. *See also* Convention refugees; Persons in need of protection
appeals. *See* Refugee Appeal Division
cessation, 279–85
change of circumstances, 282–83
implications, 283–85
increases in applications for, 287
reavailing oneself of protection of country of nationality, 281–82
designated country of origin claimants, 252–57
designation of safer countries, 252–54
implications for claimants, 252, 255–57
process, 255
designated foreign nationals, 257–61
designation of foreign national, 257–59
implications, 260, 261, 297
process, 260–61
eligibility assessment, 247

following finding of eligibility, 247–48
hearings. *See* Refugee hearings
interviewing client, 245–47
making claim, 245
inland, 245
port of entry, 245
ministerial intervention, 30–31
other claimants, 261–62
overview chart, 244
rejected claims
consequences, 262, 367–68
pre-removal risk assessments. *See* Pre-removal risk assessments
reforming process, 30, 244
reopening claims, 287–88
safe third country claimants, 71, 248–52
designation of safe countries, 248–50
implications for claimants, 249, 250–52
process, 250
Singh decision, 243
two-tier process, 30–31
vacating decision, 285–87
increases in applications for, 287
withdrawal of claim, 277–79
deemed abandonment, 277–79

Refugee hearings, 262–77. *See also* Refugee determination process
appeals from. *See* Refugee Appeal Division
cessation hearings, 279–85
credibility assessment, 275–77
failure to appear, 277–79
participation, 267–72
board member, 267
claimants, 270–71
designated representatives, 269–70
interpreters, 268–69
minister or representative, 268
observers, 268
right to counsel, 271–72
witnesses, 272
preliminaries, 262–67
constitutional questions, notice, 267
dates and times, 262–63

documentary evidence, submitting, 263–64
medical evidence, obtaining, 264–67
vulnerable persons applications, 267, 274
right to, 243
rules and procedures, 272–74
reverse order questioning, 273–74
specialized knowledge by board member, 274
withdrawal of claim after commencement, 277
Refugee protection
Canada's diminishing role overseas, 240–42
cessation, ministerial application, 279–285
increases in applications, 287
claims for. See Refugee claims
inland refugees
Convention refugees. See Convention refugees
persons in need of protection. See Persons in need of protection
pre-removal risk assessments, after, 389
overview, 223
permanent resident status, 228–29, 297, 389
persons abroad. See Refugee resettlement
underlying principles, 224–26
discretionary-humanitarian approach, 224–26
rights-based approach, 226
vacating decision for, 285–87
increases in applications, 287
Refugee Protection Division. See also Immigration and Refugee Board
appeals from. See Refugee Appeal Division
hearings. See Refugee hearings
jurisdiction, 41, 244
rules, 272
Refugee resettlement, 227–42. See also Refugee protection
Canada's diminishing role, 240–42
Canada's resettlement program, 228–40

criteria for application, 229–31
emergency cases, 232
exceptional cases, 231–32
family members, 232–33
overview, 228–29
process, 239–40
settlement assistance, 234–36
government assistance, 234
private sponsorship, 235–36. See also Refugee sponsorship
visa officer's decision, 239–40
durable solution, 227–28
Refugee sponsorship, 235–39
eligibility to sponsor, 236–37
overview, 235–36
sponsors, 237–39
blended visa office-referred program, 239
community sponsors, 238
groups of five, 238
joint assistance sponsorship, 238–39
sponsorship agreement holders, 237
Relatives. See also Family members
family class sponsorship, 207–8
Remedies. See Appeals; International remedies; Judicial review
Removal from Canada, 533–47
appeals, 562–64
criticisms of process, 591
enforcement of removal order, 569–90
as soon as possible, 569–71
sanctuary, 574–76
torture, removal to, 571–73
grounds, 361
humanitarian and compassionate applications, 397–98
inadmissibility finding, precarious distinction, 511–12
judicial review, 564–65. See also Judicial review
non-refoulement principle. See Non-refoulement principle
order for removal, 533–35
pre-removal risk assessments. See Pre-removal risk assessments
process of removal, 535–47

admissibility hearing, 543–47
  burden of proof, 547
  decision of Immigration Division, 547
  evidence, 545–57
  parties, 544–45
  public and private hearings, 543–44
  section 44 report, 535–43
    family members, against, 536–37
    issuance, 535–36
    officer's discretion, 537–41
    procedural fairness, 541–43
  regulatory stays, 376–79, 391, 564–65
  security certificates, 576–86
  statutory stay, 565–69, 605
Residency
  permanent status. *See* Permanent resident status
  temporary status. *See* Temporary resident status
RPD. *See* Refugee Protection Division

Safe Third-Country Agreement, 71
  criticisms, 250–52, 367
  overview, 249–50
  pre-removal risk assessments and, 366–67
  process for refugee claimants, 250
  what is a safe third country, 248–50
Sanctuary, 574–76
Section 22.1 declarations, 89–90
Security certificates, 576–86. *See also* Security threats
  constitutional challenges, 582–86
  detention under, 577–81
  pre-removal risk assessments, 375–76
  reasonableness, 577–78, 581
Security threats
  citizenship barrier, 455–56
  entry barrier, 104, 472, 476–90. *See also* Inadmissible persons
  alternative remedies, 489–90
  endangerment to Canada, 483
  espionage, 476–78
  member of an organization, 483–87
  subversion, 478–80
  terrorism, 480–82

listed terrorist entities, 487–89
pre-removal risk assessments
  inadmissible persons, 373–75
  security certificates, persons subject to, 375–76
security certificates. *See* Security certificates
Self-employed persons, 165–68. *See also* Economic classes
  selection criteria, 165–67
  points system, 166–67
Siblings. *See also* Family members
  family class sponsorship, 179, 207
Singh case, 243
Skilled trades, 159–60. *See also* Economic classes
  Express Entry program, 160–65
Skilled workers, 133–65. *See also* Economic classes
  Canadian experience class, 158–59
  Express Entry program, 160–65
    Comprehensive Ranking System, 162–64
  federal skilled trades class. *See* Skilled trades
  federal skilled worker class, 134–55
    application process, 152–55
    eligibility requirements, 135–39
      burden of showing, 138–39
      education credential, 138
      language evaluation, 137–38
      National Occupation Classification, 136–37
    points system, 139–51
      adaptability, 149–51
      age, 146–47
      arranged employment, 147–48
      education, 141–43
      Express Entry program, 162–64
      language proficiency, 143–44
      work experience, 144–46
    self-supporting upon arrival, 151–52
  objectives, 133–34
  provincial nominee class, 155–65
  Québec skilled worker class, 155
Smuggling of people. *See* Human smuggling and trafficking
Social assistance, persons needing, 524

Social services, excessive demand, 516–24. *See also* Health inadmissibility
  change in circumstances, 524
  exceeding total cost of average Canadian over five years, 517
  health services, distinction, 518–20
  humanitarian and compassionate applications, 431, 523–24
  overcoming inadmissibility, 520–22
Sponsorship
  family members. *See* Family class
  refugees. *See* Refugee sponsorship
Spouses. *See also* Family members; Marriage
  family class sponsorship, 182–90
    conditional status, 197–99
      abuse or neglect, exception, 198–99
    genuineness of relationship, 194–95
    pre-existing undertaking of sponsor, effect, 196
    relationship entered for purpose of acquiring, 195–96
    sponsored spouses in Canada, 196–97
  humanitarian and compassionate applications, 400
Stare decisis, 72–74
State protection, 326–41. *See also* Convention refugees
  adequacy of, 333–37
  Canadian conception, 326–30
  multiple nationalities, 330–33
  obligation to seek, 337–41
Status in Canada, 77–467
  citizenship. *See* Canadian citizenship
  open borders, 78–87
  permanent status. *See* Permanent resident status
  relevancy, 77–78
  temporary status. *See* Temporary resident status
Stay of removal. *See also* Removal from Canada
  Immigration Appeal Division, 563
  regulatory stay, 376–79, 391, 564–65
  statutory stay, 565–69, 605
Students. *See* Study permits

Study permits, 107–11. *See also* Temporary resident status
Super visas, 92–93, 206
Supreme Court of Canada, appeals to, 633–35

Temporary resident permits (TRPs), 95–97. *See also* Temporary Resident Status
  expiry or cancellation, 97
  humanitarian and compassionate applications, in conjunction, 404
  issuance, criteria, 96–97
  visa exemption, 95–97
Temporary resident status, 88–131. *See also* Status in Canada
  conditions of residency
    amendment of conditions, 105–6
    failure to comply, 106
    permit requirements, 107–29
  eTAs. *See* Electronic travel authorization (eTA)
  extensions, 105
  grant of status, 104
  implied status, 105
  ministerial prohibition, 89–90
  overview, 90–91
  permits
    study permits. *See* Study permits
    TRPs. *See* Temporary resident permits (TRPs)
    work permits. *See* Work permits
  recent immigration reforms, consequences, 130–31, 134–35
  restoration of status, 106–7
  section 22.1 declarations, 89–90
  visa requirement. *See* Temporary resident visas (TRVs)
Temporary resident visas (TRVs), 91–102. *See also* Temporary Resident Status
  exemptions, 93–97
    citizens of listed countries, 94–95
    judicial review, 97
    particular limited purpose, 95
    re-entry, 95
    TRP holders, 95–97
  parent or grandparent super visa, 92–93
  requirements for acquiring, 97–102
  types of visa, 91–92

Terrorism, 480–82. *See also* Security threats
  listed terrorist entities, 487–89
Torture
  humanitarian and compassionate grounds, exclusion, 411–12
  international convention, 66
  person in need of protection, 345
  removal to, 571–73
    non-refoulement principle, 360
    pre-removal risk assessments. *See* Pre-removal risk assessments
  resettlement to escape, 231–32
Trade agreements, 70–71
Trafficking in people. *See* Human smuggling and trafficking
Travel authorizations. *See* Electronic travel authorization (eTA)
Treaties. *See* International law

Vacated decisions
  pre-removal risk assessments, 390
  refugee protection, 285–87
    increase in vacation applications, 287
Visas
  permanent residents. *See* Permanent resident status

temporary residents. *See* Temporary resident visas (TRVs)
Visitors to Canada. *See* Temporary resident status
  visas. *See* Temporary resident visas (TRVs)

War crimes, 491–94. *See also* Human or international rights violations
Work permits, 111–29. *See also* Temporary resident status
  International Mobility Programs, 119–20
  labour market impact assessments, 114–16
    exemptions, 117–20
  legal framework, 112–29
    criteria and eligibility, 114–28
      agricultural workers, 121–22
      caregivers, 123–28
      higher-skilled occupations, 122–23
      lower-skilled occupations, 122
    reforming program, 128–29
    what is work, 112–13
      defined, 112
      prohibited work, 112–13
    who needs a permit, 113–14

ABOUT THE AUTHORS

A daughter of a stateless immigrant to Canada, **Jamie Chai Yun Liew** is an immigration and refugee lawyer who has appeared at the Immigration and Refugee Board, Federal Court, Federal Court of Appeal, and the Supreme Court of Canada. She is also an assistant professor at the Faculty of Law, University of Ottawa, where she teaches, among other courses, Immigration and Refugee Law, Advanced Refugee Law, and Administrative Law. Professor Liew is the holder of degrees in political science and commerce from the University of Calgary, international affairs from Carleton University, and law from the University of Ottawa and Columbia University. She is a member of litigation committees for the Canadian Council for Refugees and the Canadian Association of Refugee Lawyers, and her research focuses on the performative and consequential aspects of how Canadian law is affecting refugees and immigrants. Having clerked with Justice Douglas Campbell at the Federal Court of Canada, Professor Liew was also a member of the Sesay defence team at the Special Court in Sierra Leone and the Commission counsel team at the Cornwall Public Inquiry.

Donald Galloway is a professor of law at the University of Victoria, where he teaches Immigration and Citizenship Law, Refugee Law, and Torts. Professor Galloway has degrees in law and philosophy from the University of Edinburgh and Harvard University. He has served as a member of the Refugee Division of the Immigration and Refugee Board and as a member of the executive of the Canadian Association of Refugee Lawyers.

Professor Galloway has appeared as an expert before House of Commons and Senate committees, and is the recipient of the Bora Laskin National Fellowship in Human Rights Research.